History of the Violoncello, the Viol da Gamba, their Precursors and Collateral Instruments

2 VOLUMES BOUND IN ONE BOOK.

TRAVIS & EMERY.

Edmund van der Straeten:

History of the violoncello, the Viol da Gamba, their Precursors and Collateral Instruments with Biographies of all the most eminent players in every country.

First published in two volumes by William Reeves 1915.

Republished in one book Travis & Emery 2008.

Published by
Travis & Emery Music Bookshop
17 Cecil Court, London, WC2N 4EZ, United Kingdom.
(+44) 20 7240 2129
neworders@travis-and-emery.com

Hardback: ISBN10: 1-904331-67-X   ISBN13: 978-1904331-67-4
Paperback: ISBN10: 1-904331-68-8   ISBN13: 978-1904331-68-1

Frontispiece.

C. F. ABEL

History of the Violoncello,
The Viol da Gamba, their Precursors and Collateral Instruments

VOLUME 1

History of the Violoncello, the Viol da Gamba, their Precursors and Collateral Instruments

WITH

BIOGRAPHIES OF ALL THE MOST EMINENT PLAYERS
OF EVERY COUNTRY

BY

EDMUND S. J. VAN DER STRAETEN

Author of " Technics of Violoncello Playing," " The Revival of the Viols," " Hints to
Violoncellists," " The Viola," " The Romance of the Fiddle," etc.

———

THE RESULT OF THIRTY YEARS RESEARCH

———

ILLUSTRATED WITH PORTRAITS, MUSICAL EXAMPLES, FACSIMILE LETTERS,
REPRODUCTIONS FROM RARE AND CURIOUS PAINTINGS AND ENGRAVINGS

VOL. I.

LONDON: WILLIAM REEVES, 83 CHARING CROSS ROAD, W.C.
MCMXV

PREFACE.

TO every thinking person occupied with or interested in any branch of art, it has a great fascination to know how that art originated and developed, and the manner in which it was practised in past ages. It is not mere curiosity that underlies this desire, but the knowledge that widens and broadens our views, that brings the past nearer and shows it in its relation to the present and the probable or possible future. Apart from this, we love to hear all we can about the masters of our art that are past and gone, whose works we love and admire, and who gain in interest and significance by a closer acquaintance with their personality. It is true that a Beethoven symphony proclaims its own grandeur like a pyramid in the desert, yet we feel a desire to know all about the man who was the creator of so grand a monument, and when we have gained that knowledge the man recalls his work as the work recalls the man. Both seem to be inseparably connected.

Thus an early desire to become acquainted with the past history of my favourite instrument, caused me to collect what information I could, and to do as Captain Cuttle in "Dombey and Son": "When found make a note of." In my student's days I began to collect many valuable notes, not too methodically arranged maybe, partly from published works, historical works, essays, memoirs, etc., partly from personal communications by older friends or artists with whom I came into contact, as, for instance, the versatile Ferdinand Hiller, with whom I was a favourite in my youth. After I had settled in London in the early eighties of last century, I became an ardent reader at the British Museum, and my historical researches were henceforth undertaken in a more systematic manner. With some enthusiasm I greeted the small volume of Wasielewski on the history of the violoncello in 1889, and placed myself into communication with him with a view to translating the work for an English edition. On further consideration I came to the conclusion that, although it had the merit of being a pioneer work, yet I already possessed so much additional information and matter that the idea of a translation was abandoned, and I commenced a more serious study of the subject myself, the outcome of which is now placed before the public. Every available biographical dictionary was examined, memoirs, periodicals, monographs, letters, essays and the title pages of original editions of violoncello pieces, as well as manuscript music, which frequently gave information about the position a violoncellist held at the time, or his relation to other artists or patrons as expressed in a dedication. Space will not permit of a detailed account of these sources, which are often referred to in the text of the book. With regard to modern artists, my difficulties were of the greatest. Some had died within recent years and dates of death were not always ascertainable, others had retired from the public eye and were with difficulty traced. To many living violoncellists of various nationalities forms were recently sent out asking for particulars of their careers. From the returns received I have been able to compile many biographies and tabulate much valuable information which appears here for the first time. In the case of other living violoncellists I had to be satisfied with indirect information, not, of course, always too reliable. The work, in fact, was of an almost overwhelming nature, and if in spite of the most strenuous efforts covered over a period of more than thirty years there is still room for improvement and completion I must ask the indulgence of those in particular who use this book as a source of reference. I hand it over herewith to all who are interested in the subject with the assurance that I have seriously endeavoured to examine all statements found in other works, as far as that was in my power. I am also happy to say that I have succeeded in elucidating many uncertainties, and to add a considerable number of hitherto unknown facts especially with regard to the older history of both the viol da gamba and of the violoncello. Several important illustrations have never been published before, as, for instance, the magnificent Gainsborough pictures, which the kindness of the late Mr. Charles Wertheimer and Mr. W. Cummings enabled me to add, likewise a number of illustrations of equal interest added by the kind permission of Messrs. Wm. E. Hill and Sons, from whom I also received much other valuable information, then the interesting autographs from Mr. Wm. Reeves's collection. If I cannot thank individually all who have rendered their kind assistance they must forgive me as their names would fill many pages, and I should still run the risk of leaving out some of them. I hope they will accept my sincerest thanks herewith. I cannot, however, omit to express my particular gratitude and indebtedness to the following, who have rendered me such vital assistance as Mr. Barclay Squire and Mr. Hughes-Hughes, of the British Museum, Dr. Georg Kinsky, of the Heyer Museum; Messrs. A. Wotquenne and V. Mahillon, of the Brussels Conservatoire library and museum; M. Julien Tiersot, of the Paris Conservatoire library; Dr. Eusebius Mandicewsky, of Vienna; the director of the "Germanische Museum" in Nürnberg; Messrs. J. E. Matthew and E. Heron-Allen, who placed their unique libraries at my disposal; Dr. Koester, of the Royal Library, Berlin; Baron von Marschalk, of Bamberg; Dr. Alfred Einstein, of Munich; Mr. Paul Pannier, of Lille; Mr. John Shedlock. Also let me do homage to the memory of those trusty and devoted collaborators, who are—alas—no longer with us: Count Luigi Francesco Valdrighi, of Modena; Mr. Johannes Klingenberg, of Brunswick; and Messrs. Laurent Grillet and L. van Waefelghem, of Paris.

LONDON, *April 29, 1914.*

CARICATURE OF FIRST MULLER QUARTET. BY CHR. REIMERS.

N.B. A Special Edition of this work is issued bound in two volumes with some Additional Plates, and limited to One Hundred Sets, Signed and Numbered.

Edmund S. J. van der Straeten

Photograph by Walter Benington.

CONTENTS.

PART I.

THE VIOLONCELLO FROM ITS ORIGIN TO 1800.

CHAPTER I.
The Precursors of the Violoncello 1

CHAPTER II.
The Viol da Gamba 9

CHAPTER III.
The Viol da Gamba in Italy 29
The Viol da Gamba in Germany 54

CHAPTER IV.
The Viol da Gamba in Germany *(continued)* 74

CHAPTER V.
The Viol da Gamba in Austria 92

CHAPTER VI.
The Viol da Gamba in the Netherlands 94

CHAPTER VII.
The Viol da Gamba in France 96

CHAPTER VIII.
The Viola Bastarda and the Baryton 111

CHAPTER IX.
The Violoncello 121

CHAPTER X.
The Violoncello in Italy **132**

CONTENTS.

CHAPTER XI.
The Violoncello in Italy during the Eighteenth Century ... 157

CHAPTER XII.
The Violoncello in Germany from the Seventeenth to the Beginning of the Nineteenth Century 177
List of Violoncellists in the Imperial Chapel, Vienna 206

CHAPTER XIII.
German Violoncellists of the Second Half of the Eighteenth Century 210

CHAPTER XIV.
Position of the Violoncello in Germany at the End of the Eighteenth Century 254

CHAPTER XV.
The Violoncello in France 258

CHAPTER XVI.
Transition to the Modern French School 289

CHAPTER XVII.
The Violoncello in England 307

CHAPTER XVIII.
The Violoncello in Bohemia 333

CHAPTER XIX.
Summary of the Development of the Violoncello up to 1800 ... 350

CHAPTER XX.
The Progress of the Violoncello (continued) 369

PART II.

THE VIOLONCELLO FROM 1800-1900.

CHAPTER XXI.
The Violoncello in Germany during the Nineteenth Century ... 383

CHAPTER XXII.
German Violoncellists from 1820-40 417

CHAPTER XXIII.
German Violoncellists from 1840-50 440

CHAPTER XXIV.
German Violoncellists from 1850-60 455

CONTENTS.

CHAPTER XXV.
German Violoncellists from 1860-70 ... 476

CHAPTER XXVI.
The Violoncello in England from 1800-1900 ... 504

CHAPTER XXVII.
France ... 524

CHAPTER XXVIII.
The Violoncello in Belgium from the End of the Seventeenth Century to 1900 ... 540

CHAPTER XXIX.
The Violoncello in Holland from the End of the Eighteenth Century to 1900 ... 560

CHAPTER XXX.
The Violoncello in Switzerland during the Nineteenth Century 576

CHAPTER XXXI.
The Violoncello in Italy from the Eighteenth Century to 1900 579

CHAPTER XXXII.
The Violoncello in Spain and Portugal ... 597

CHAPTER XXXIII.
Czechian Violoncellists from 1800-1900 ... 601

CHAPTER XXXIV.
The Violoncello in Hungary from 1800-1900 ... 606

CHAPTER XXXV.
Polish Violoncellists of the Nineteenth Century ... 611

CHAPTER XXXVI.
The Violoncello in Russia from 1700-1900 ... 614

CHAPTER XXXVII.
American and New Zealand Violoncellists ... 629

CHAPTER XXXVIII.
The Violoncello in Scandinavia from 1800-1900 ... 632

CHAPTER XXXIX.
Various Forms of the Violoncello ... 637

CHAPTER XL.
Conclusion ... 641
Appendix and Errata ... 647
Index ... 661

LIST OF ILLUSTRATIONS.

FULL PAGE PLATES.

C. F. ABEL. FROM THE PAINTING BY GAINSBOROUGH. REPRODUCED BY PERMISSION OF THE LATE MR. CHARLES WERTHEIMER ... *Frontispiece*

	To face page
EDMUND S. J. VAN DER STRAETEN	ix
PLATE I. GASPARO DUIFFOPRUGCAR (KASPER TIEFFENBRUCKER). FROM THE ENGRAVING BY WOERIOT	1
PLATE II. CHRISTOPHER SIMPSON. FROM THE ENGRAVING IN "THE DIVISION-VIOL"	8
PLATE III. THOMAS MACE. FROM THE FRONTISPIECE TO "MUSICK'S MONUMENT," 1676, ENGRAVED BY W. FAITHORNE	16
PLATE IV. SIR ROGER L'ESTRANGE. FROM AN ENGRAVING BY R. WHITE OF THE PORTRAIT BY G. KNELLER	24
PLATE V. MRS. THICKNESSE (NÉE ANN FORD). FROM THE PAINTING BY GAINSBOROUGH IN THE POSSESSION OF THE LATE MR. CHARLES WERTHEIMER	32
PLATE VI. GEORGE NEUMARK. FROM AN ENGRAVING IN THE COLLECTION OF THE LATE JOHANNES KLINGENBERG (APPARENTLY A FRONTISPIECE TO ONE OF HIS WORKS)	40
PLATE VII. REPRODUCTIONS OF THE TITLE PAGE AND THE FIRST PAGE OF THE MUSIC OF KÜHNEL'S SONATAS FOR THE VIOL DA GAMBA. THE FIGURES OF THE PLAYERS ON THE TITLE PAGE REPRESENT A. KÜHNEL AND TWO MEMBERS OF HIS FAMILY	48
PLATE VIII. JOHANN SCHENCK. FROM AN ENGRAVING IN THE POSSESSION OF MESSRS. W. E. HILL AND SONS	56
PLATE IX. PORTRAIT OF CONRAD HÖFFLER FROM "PRIMITIÆ CHELICÆ"	64
PLATE X. TITLE PAGE OF HÖFFLER'S "PRIMITIÆ CHELICÆ" ...	64
PLATE Xa. CONSTANTIN BELLERMANN	72
PLATE XI. JOHANNES DANIEL HARD	80
PLATE XII. CARL FRIEDRICH ABEL. FROM THE PAINTING BY GAINSBOROUGH IN THE POSSESSION OF SIR W. H. CUMMINGS	88

LIST OF ILLUSTRATIONS.

To face page

PLATE XIIa. REDUCED FACSIMILE OF ORIGINAL MANUSCRIPT OF THE VIOL DA GAMBA OBBLIGATO TO THE ARIA, "ES IST VOLLBRACHT," FROM THE "ST. JOHN'S PASSION," BY J. S. BACH 96

PLATE XIII. HOTMAN. FROM AN ENGRAVING BY VAN MERLE ... 72

PLATE XIV. MARIN MARAIS. FROM A MEZZOTINT 104

PLATE XV. MARAIS, LULLY AND THE BROTHERS HOTTETERRE. FROM THE PAINTING BY HYACINTHE RIGAUD IN THE NATIONAL GALLERY 112

PLATE XVI. FACSIMILE OF THE FINELY ENGRAVED TITLE OF "PIÈCES A UNE ET A DEUX VIOLES" BY MARAIS 120

PLATE XVII. MADAME HENRIETTE DE FRANCE, 1727-52. ON MANY PRINTS HER NAME APPEARS AS MADAME ADÉLAIDE DE FRANCE. FROM A PAINTING BY NATTIER IN THE MUSEUM AT VERSAILLES 128

PLATE XVIII. BACK OF VIOLONCELLO BY DOMENICO GALLI, SHOWING THE EXQUISITE CARVING 136

PLATE XIX. ATTILIO ARIOSTI. FROM A MEZZOTINT 144

PLATE XX. GIOVANNI BATTISTA BUONONCINI 152

PLATE XXI. CERVETTO, THE ELDER 160

PLATE XXII. FRANCISCHELLO 168

PLATE XXIII. GIOVANNI BATTISTA CIRRI 176

PLATE XXIV. C. J. LIDARTI. FROM A PAINTING IN THE POSSESSION OF MESSRS. W. E. HILL AND SONS 184

PLATE XXV. MAX BOHRER. FROM A CRAYON DRAWING BY KRIEHUBER, 1842 232

PLATE XXVI. F. A. KUMMER 256

PLATE XXVII. MARTIN BERTEAU. FROM THE ETCHING BY HILLEMACHER 264

PLATE XXVIII. J. L. DUPORT 280

PLATE XXIX. BARTHOLOMEW JOHNSON 304

PLATE XXX. JOHN HEBDEN 312

PLATE XXXI. BENJAMIN HALLET 320

PLATE XXXII. JOHN CROSDILL. FROM A CRAYON PORTRAIT BY GEO. DANCE 328

PLATE XXXIII. JAMES CERVETTO (THE YOUNGER). FROM A PAINTING IN THE POSSESSION OF MESSRS. W. E. HILL AND SONS ... 336

PLATE XXXIV. A MUSIC PARTY IN THE GARDENS OF KEW PALACE. FREDERIC LEWIS, PRINCE OF WALES, PLAYING THE VIOLONCELLO. FROM A PAINTING BY PHILIP MERCIER, 1733 344

PLATE XXXV. ROBERT LINDLEY. FROM A MEZZOTINT 352

PLATE XXXVI. SEBASTIAN LEE (AGED FORTY-FIVE). FROM A PRINT KINDLY LENT BY MR. CHARLES VOLKERT 368

PLATE XXXVII. BERNHARD COSSMANN 417

PLATE XXXVIII. DAVID POPPER 448

PLATE XXXIX. R. HAUSMANN IN THE BERLIN JOACHIM QUARTET ... 456

PLATE XL. AUGUSTE FRANCHOMME. PENCIL DRAWING FROM AN ORIGINAL PORTRAIT BY LUDWIG VAN DER STRAETEN 520

PLATE XLI. LISA B. CHRISTIANI 536

LIST OF ILLUSTRATIONS. XV

To face page

PLATE XLII. WILLIAM DEFESCH 544
PLATE XLIII. FRANÇOIS DE MUNCK. FROM A PORTRAIT IN THE POSSESSION OF HENRY FRANCIS BROWN, ESQ. 552
PLATE XLIV. ALFREDO PIATTI 584

ILLUSTRATIONS APPEARING IN THE TEXT.

page

CARICATURE OF FIRST MULLER QUARTET, BY CHR. REIMERS viii
FIG. 1. THE RAVANASTRON 1
FIG. 2. THE CRWTH 2
FIG. 3. THE GROSSE GEIGE FROM VIRDUNG (THE BIG FIEDEL) ... 6
FIG. 4. THE GROSSE GEIGEN FROM JUDENKÜNIG'S "AIN SCHONE KUNSTLICHE UNTERWEISUNG" 7
FIG. 5. THE TUNING OF THE GROSSE GEIGEN 8
FIG. 6. THE TUNING OF A DUIFFOPRUGCAR BASS VIOLA DA GAMBA ... 15
FIG. 7. THE TUNING OF A GERLE'S GEYGEN 18
FIG. 8. A GEIGE BY HANS GERLE 19
FIG. 9. THE TUNING OF A SIX-STRINGED VIOL DA GAMBA 19
FIG. 10 (1), FIG. 11 (2), FIG. 12 (3), VIOLN DA GAMBA. FIG. 13 (4), VIOL BASTARDA. FIG. 14 (5), ITALIANISCHE LYRA DE BRACIO. FROM PLATE XX OF PRÄTORIUS'S "SYNTAGMATIS MUSICI TOMUS SECUNDUS DE ORGANOGRAPHIA" 21
FIG. 15. THE TUNING OF A SEVEN-STRINGED BARYTON 24
FIG. 16. THE TUNING OF THE ARPEGGIONE, ALSO CALLED THE GUITAR-VIOLONCELLO 26
FIG. 17. THE TUNING OF THE VIOLA POMPOSA 27
FIG. 18. AUTOGRAPH SIGNATURE OF LEONARDO DA VINCI, A FAMOUS MUSICIAN AND COMPOSER OF OPERAS 32
FIG. 19. INSTRUMENTAL COMPOSITION KNOWN AS THE "IN NOMINE." 37
FIG. 20. THE TUNING OF THE LYRA VIOL 38
FIG. 21. GAMBA PLAYER FROM SIMPSON'S "DIVISION-VIOL" ... 48
FIG. 22. THEMATIC RELATIONSHIP IN SCHENCK'S SIXTH SUITE ... 70
FIG. 23. ABEL. FROM AN ETCHED CARICATURE BY F. N., DATED 1787, ENTITLED "A SOLO ON THE VIOLA DI GAMBA" 87
FIG. 24. BARYTON BY JACQUES SAINPRAE IN THE SOUTH KENSINGTON MUSEUM 112
FIG. 25. THE TUNING OF THE ARPEGGIONE 115
FIG. 26. THE TUNING OF THE VIOLA POMPOSA 115
FIG. 27. THE TUNING OF THE FIVE-STRINGED VIOLONCELLO 122
FIG. 28. A FIVE-STRINGED VIOLONCELLO IN THE COLLECTION OF THE REV. F. W. GALPIN. THE LABEL RUNS: "MARCUS BROCHÉ A BRUXELLES AU ROY DAVID: L'AN 1720." BROCHÉ IS A FRENCH FORM OF "SNOECK," A WELL-KNOWN FLEMISH MAKER 123
FIG. 29. THE BAS GEIG DA BRACIO. FROM PRÄTORIUS'S "SYNTAGMA MUSICUM" 125
FIG. 30. RICECARE FOR TWO VIOLONCELLOS BY DOMENICO GABRIELI 136

LIST OF ILLUSTRATIONS.

		page
Fig. 31.	Aria of the Fifth Sonata by Domenico Galli	140
Fig. 32.	Giga by Domenico Galli	141
Fig. 33.	Tonelli. From an Engraving by Antonio Montanari	146
Fig. 34.	Cervetto, the Elder. From a Contemporary Caricature	152
Fig. 35.	Antonio Vandini	162
Fig. 36.	Facsimile Signature of Abaco	165
Fig. 37.	Luigi Boccherini	175
Fig. 38.	Joseph Weigl	189
Fig. 39.	Bernhard Romberg	222
Fig. 40.	J. J. F. Dotzauer	241
Fig. 41.	Facsimile of a "Canon" from an Album Leaf by J. J. F. Dotzauer	242
Fig. 42.	F. A. Kummer	249
Fig. 43.	Jean Baptiste Breval	296
Fig. 44.	Louis Pierre Norblin. From the Etching by Hillemacher	304
Fig. 45.	A. Theodor Müller	391
Fig. 46.	Reproduction of the First Page of an Adagio and Rondoletto for Violoncello by C. L. Boehm. Original in the Possession of the Author	396
Fig. 47.	Charles Schuberth	406
Fig. 48.	Karl Schlesinger	410
Fig. 49.	Georg Goltermann	423
Fig. 50.	Facsimile Letter, Julius Goltermann	426
Fig. 51.	F. Grützmacher	429
Fig. 52.	Facsimile of an Album Leaf for Mr. Willy von Mumm in Grützmacher's Handwriting	431
Fig. 53.	Wilhelm Müller	434
Fig. 54.	Autograph of Robert Hausmann	457
Fig. 55.	Johannes Klingenberg	459
Fig. 56.	Victor Herbert	473
Fig. 57.	Facsimile of an Album Leaf by Lisa B. Christiani, giving the Opening Bars of Offenbach's Musette	532
Fig. 58.	A. F. Servais	543
Fig. 59.	William Paque	550
Fig. 60.	Charles Davidoff	620
Fig. 61.	The St. Petersburg Quartet	622
Fig. 62.	Christian Laurentz Kellerman	633
Fig. 63.	Showing the Model Invented by Dr. Stelzner for his Group of Stringed Instruments. The Dotted Lines show the Outline of the Orthodox Violin Model	640
Seventeenth Century Serenaders, from a Dutch Woodcut		660

LIST OF ILLUSTRATIONS.   xvii

ADDITIONAL ILLUSTRATIONS.

Appearing in the Special Edition only.

To face page

LIRONE DA BRACCIO (BACK), BY VENTURA LINAROLO, VENICE, 1577. ORIGINAL IN THE WM. HEYER MUSEUM, COLOGNE 192

VIOL DA GAMBA BY JOACHIM TIELKE, CIRCA 1700, IN THE WM. HEYER MUSEUM, COLOGNE. THE INSTRUMENT, WHICH HAD BEEN ENLARGED TO BE USED AS VIOLONCELLO, AS SHOWN BY ORNAMENTED PART ON UPPER BOUTS, BELONGED AT ONE TIME TO MR. PAUL DE WIT IN LEIPZIG, WHO ON ACCOUNT OF ITS LUMPY AND LUMINOUS VARNISH, BELIEVED IT TO BE BY CARLO BERGONZI 208

FACSIMILE (REDUCED) OF AN ALBUM LEAF BY BERNHARD ROMBERG ... 224

REDUCED FACSIMILE OF A LETTER BY JEAN PIERRE DUPORT REFERRING TO A REQUEST BY HIS BROTHER, JEAN LOUIS, TO SEND THE LATTER'S SON TO PARIS 272

JOSEPH LIDEL. FROM AN ENGRAVING IN THE POSSESSION OF MESSRS. W. E. HILL AND SONS 488

ARNAUD DANCLA. FROM AN ENGRAVING IN THE POSSESSION OF MESSRS. W. E. HILL AND SONS 512

FACSIMILE AUTOGRAPH (MUCH REDUCED) BY A. BATTA, OF AN ALBUM LEAF FOR THE WIFE OF AD. HENSELT. IT IS TAKEN FROM HIS "ETUDES CHARACTERISTIQUES" 560

VIOL DA GAMBA BY BARAK NORMAN (1688-1740), WITH ORIGINAL INLAID FINGERBOARD AND TAIL-PIECE, BELONGING TO MR. HENRY SAINT-GEORGE, LONDON 592

POCHETTE OR DANCING MASTER'S FIDDLE. FROM MERSENNE'S "HARMONIE UNIVERSELLE" 608

NICOLAUS ZYGMANTOWSKI. FROM AN ENGRAVED PORTRAIT BY C. SATZEN 616

PART I.
THE VIOLONCELLO FROM ITS ORIGIN TO 1800.

PLATE I.

GASPARO DUIFFOPRUGCAR (KASPER TIEFFENBRUCKER). FROM THE ENGRAVING BY WOERIOT.

THE HISTORY OF THE VIOLONCELLO.

CHAPTER I.

THE PRECURSORS OF THE VIOLONCELLO.

THE violin family, to which the violoncello belongs, has been traced back by historians to the ravanastron, a stringed instrument ascribed to Ravana (Ravanon), a king of Ceylon (the ancient Leuka) who lived about 5,000 B.C. He was so great a musician, so the legend goes, that even Siva, the God of Darkness, was moved by his art. The

Fig. 1. THE RAVANASTRON.

ravanastron *(see Fig. 1)* still survives in the hands of wandering Buddhist monks in India who play it with a bow. We possess no proof that it was thus played in its earliest stages.

Paul Stoeving, in "The Story of the Violin," tells us that "the tone of this ravanastron is by no means so bad as the miserable outward appearance of the instrument would lead one to suppose. It is soft, thin (a little muffled, as if muted), ethereal, suggestive, if you will, of thought rather than emotion."

Besides the ravanastron the Hindoos possessed the "omerti," an instrument with a circular body not unlike a banjo, and the sarinda which bears a remote resemblance to the violin. These, the Arabian rebab and the mediæval rebec which was the forerunner of the "gigue" or German "geige" are fully described in Grove's "Dictionary of Music," and many similar works easy of access; it is, therefore, unnecessary to deal with them more fully in this place.

The latter instruments cannot be regarded as ancestors of the violin for reasons stated hereafter. Although they have been described as such by many historians. A greater claim to that honour appertains to the crwth, a Celtic instrument of great antiquity *(see Fig. 2)*.

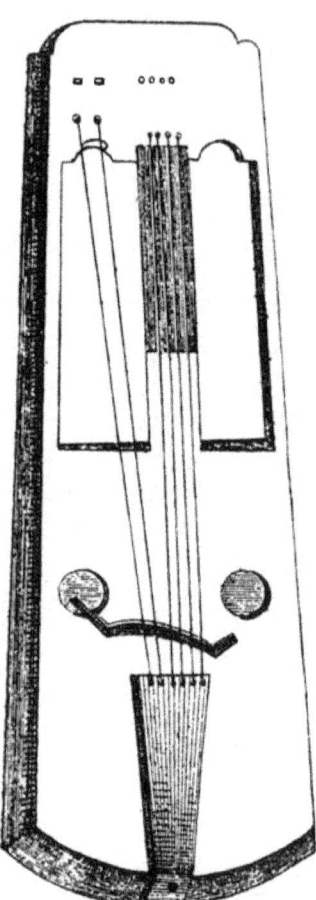

FIG. 2. THE CRWTH.

In its earliest stages it was played in the same way as the lyre and the kythara, the strings being plucked with the fingers of the right hand.

When, where, and to what instrument the bow was first applied is a matter of conjecture. There is nothing to prove that it was known to the ancient Greeks or Romans, nor is there any proof to the contrary. The earliest known illustration of a bow with a fixed nut is to be found in an Arabian MS. of the seventh century. (See Fétis, "Antoine Stradivarius," page 113), and the earliest illustration of a bowed instrument in Europe is to be found in a translation of the psalms by Labeo Notker, the MS. of which belonging to the tenth century is preserved in the famous library of St. Gall in Switzerland. The illustration shows King David playing a seven-stringed lyre with a plectrum, surrounded by four musicians, playing a harp, a cithara, a dulcimer and rebec. The latter is played with a bow which has a handle. The first crwth played with a bow is depicted in a MS. of St. Martial of Limoges in the Royal Library, Paris. The crwth possesses the essential three parts of the violin: a back and a belly held together by the ribs, which form a separate part. In the upper part of the crwth we find two openings to enable the fingers of the left hand to touch the strings. These openings thus formed a short neck, and it is easy to see how by cutting away part of the frame surrounding these openings that neck was freed and a primitive shape of the fiddle was reached. This was in all probability the fiddle of the northern races, who during the first centuries of our era had extremely little knowledge of southern Europe, and for that reason it appears more likely that one of their national instruments should be the obvious development and transition from the crwth, than that they should have received it from peoples with whom they would only come into contact on the farthest and rarest of their depredatory expeditions. Unfortunately, we possess no documentary evidence regarding their instruments as their oldest lore was handed down by tradition only, and the first of the northern epics mentioning the "fiedel" (vedel) is the "Niebelungen-Lied" which originated towards the middle of the twelfth century.

The rebec and gigue or geige were instruments with a pear-shaped body, like the mandolin, covered by a flat sound-board. They had, therefore, no separate ribs like the crwth, the fiedel and its descendants, and cannot be enumerated among the ancestors of the violin. Their last degenerate survival was the kit, pochette or dancing master's fiddle, which did not survive the eighteenth century.

The latest and most logically substantiated theory with regard to the origin of the violin is that propounded by Miss Kathleen Schlesinger in her "Instruments of the Orchestra, and Precursors of the Violin Family." (London: William Reeves.)

She traces the latter back to the Egyptian kithara as an instrument possessing the three constituents of the violin: "belly and back joined by separate ribs." Her etymological deduction is clear and convincing, viz.:

> Egyptian: kithara.
> Assyrian: chetarah or ketharah.
> Greek: kithara.
> Roman: cithara, also called fidicula, from the Roman cithara is derived the Spanish guitar and guitar fiddle, from the Roman fidicula the
> Spanish: vihuela de Arco
> French: vielle or viole.
> Italian: viola, violino.
> German: fidula, fidel, figella, fythele.
> English: fiddle.

For the deduction of the formal development from the cithara to the guitar fiddle Miss Schlesinger relies chiefly on the "Utrecht Psalter," a MS. of the ninth century, emanating from the famous school of Rheims. The illustrations of this MS. appear to be the work of Greek artists of the Smyrna school dating still further back. In these illustrations we find the cithara proper with a bar across from arm to arm, then the cithara in transition with rounded-off corners, and openings for the fingers to pluck the strings from both sides. Next we find a fretted neck which eventually appears considerably prolonged above the sound body; the ribs have a decided inward curve. One illustration shows the instrument held across the chest from left to right resting against the right shoulder in the same manner as some of the large viols "da braccio."

Taking into consideration the derivation of the name, as shown above, together with the fact that the forms of the kithara-fiddle in the Utrecht Psalter had their origin in the Greek parts of Asia Minor, we may take it for granted, as Miss Schlesinger points out in her book, that the guitar-fiddle of the Provençale troubadours was derived from those strange kithara forms which were introduced probably from the eastern countries during the Middle Ages.

An important step in the development of the guitar fiedel was the stronger indentation of the ribs which was absent in the earliest forms, which either had a flat bridge or none at all, as in the case of Virdung's "grosse geige." The next step was the introduction of the corner blocks. They appeared at first in the viol forms of the fidel, and originated in Germany. In a picture by Hans Burgkmair, of the procession of the Emperor Maximilian (1517) a viol-fiedel shows only an upper corner block whereas Raphael in a sketch for his Apollo statue (fifteenth century) shows a viol with only a lower corner block. About the same period other instruments appeared with two corner blocks. The position and shape of the soundholes varied as much as the outlines of the instrument in the old "fidels," they were sometimes four in number. These soundholes were of a crescent shape, two in the upper and two in the lower part of the table. Sometimes there was a centre rosette like in a guitar, at other times there was a small rosette in the centre of the upper table and two crescent or "C" shaped soundholes near the centre bouts. The bridge was likewise fixed in different places, sometimes in the upper part and sometimes in the lower part of the table, and not before the position of the soundholes was finally fixed between the centre bouts, did the bridge receive its proper position. Sebastien Virdung's "Musica getuscht und ausgezogen" (music illustrated and described), published 1511 in Basle, contains an illustration of the "grosse geige" (the big fiedel), *(see Fig. 3)*, which will illustrate the above. The treble, alto and tenor geigen had five strings, all except the first or "discant" being in pairs. The bass geige had six strings. It had a centre rosette and two "Cs" in the upper table, no bridge at all, and the strings were fixed to a bar glued to the lower table as on the lute and guitar.

FIG. 3. THE GROSSE GEIGE FROM VIRDUNG (THE BIG FIEDEL).

Towards the end of the fourteenth century the name viol was generally applied to this instrument. It was first used by the troubadours who called it viùl from the Latin form "fidula." The French altered the word to "viole." Towards the end of the fifteenth century the viol appeared in its perfect form which it retained with but slight alterations during the following centuries. Those who wish to acquaint them-

Fig. 4. The Grosse Geigen from Judenkünig's "Ain Schone Kunstliche Unterweisung."

selves more closely with the history of the earlier forms will find a more detailed account in "The Revival of the Viols" by E. van der Straeten" (The Strad Library).

The grosse geigen (as well as the kleine geigen with four strings) were built in sets of four representing the four voices: discantus, altus, tenor and bassus. Their tuning is given in the "Musica Getuscht" as:

FIG. 5. THE TUNING OF THE GROSSE GEIGEN.

As there was no fixed pitch in those days the way to tune these instruments—according to Agricola's instructions in his "Musica Instrumentalis" (1529)—was to pull up the first string of the discantus as high as it was possible without fear of its breaking. The note which the open string would then produce represented the treble C and from this the other strings on all four instruments were tuned. The grosse geigen were suspended from the left shoulder as described in Hans Judenkünig's "Ain schone kunstliche Unterweisung" (nice and scientific instructions), published in Vienna, 1523 *(see Fig. 4)*.

PLATE II.

CHRISTOPHER SIMPSON. FROM THE ENGRAVING IN "THE DIVISION-VIOL."
(Kindly Lent by Joseph A. Chanot, London.)

CHAPTER II.

THE VIOL DA GAMBA.

TOWARDS the end of the fifteenth century the lute had become the principal instrument for the accompaniment of the voice as well as for the playing of airs and dance tunes. In Gentile Bellini's picture of the procession in the Place of St. Marc's, Venice, in 1491, a body of lutenists and violists accompanies the singing of the clergy. Instrumental music as a higher art had not yet come into existence except for the improvisations of a few great organists and the achievements of the Italian, and more particularly, Venetian lutenists among whom Marco d'Aquila, about 1500, acquired European fame. The lute was considered the best instrument suited for the use of a gentleman, and more attention was paid to its technical development than to any other instrument. It cannot surprise us, therefore, to find that when the viol began to assume a more perfect shape bringing forward its higher qualities in sustained notes of sweetness and power, musicians turned their attention more and more to that instrument. Being for the greater part lutenists, they naturally conceived the idea to arrange the neck of the viol in the same manner as that of the lute providing it with six strings like the latter instrument, and the neck with seven "frets" of gut string marking the position of the semitones. Martin Agricola in his "Musica instrumentalis teutsch" (1532), advocates the use of these frets in the following rhyme:

> Idoch sag ich dir zu dissen Stunden das es ohn bünd ist schwer zu fassen darumb soltu das nicht farn lassen.
> (I tell you now that without frets it is difficult to play upon (literally "to grip"), therefore thou shalt not let them go (leave them off).)

In 1495 the Countess Isabella of Mantua sent her lutenist, Gio. Angelo Testagrossa, to Brescia to examine some viols which she had ordered from the famous Giovanni Kerlino (Hans Gerle or Kerl? apparently of German origin). Another lutenist, Hans Gerle, of Nuremberg, published the first book of pieces for the viols which was then still a new instrument. The title was:

Musica Teusch
Auf die Instrument Der grossen und kleinen Geygen/
Auch Lautten/

Welcher massen die mit grundt und art jrer Composicion aus dem gesang in die Tablatur zu ordnen und zu setzen ist (sampt verborgener applicacion und kunst).

Darynen ein liebhaber un anfenger berürter Instrument so dar zu lust und neygung tregt/ on ein sonderliche Meister mensürlich Durch tegliche übung leichtlich begreiffen und lernen mag/ vormals im Truck nye und ytzo durch Hans Gerle Lutinist zu Nurenberg ausgangen.

1532.

(Musica German—for the instruments of the big and small geigen *(see Figs. 3, 5 and 8)*, also lutes, in which way it has to be arranged on the manner and basis of their composition from the vocal music (the cantus) into the tablature (together with the hidden application and art). wherein any amateur and beginner of those instruments, if he feels thus inclined, may learn and understand easily, without a special master, by daily practice. Never published in print before and now issued by Hans Gerle, lutenist at Nuremberg, 1532.)

A second edition appeared in 1537 and a third in 1546. Dr. Alfred Einstein gives a list of the contents in his essay, "Zur deutschen Literatur für Viola da Gamba im 16. und 17. Jahrhundert" (Leipzig: Breitkopf and Härtel), and points out that Gerle has in this work already covered the whole ground of elementary forms which went to the building up of instrumental music, showing a remarkably keen sense in his transcriptions for that which is suited to the nature of the instruments. There is a dance tune, "Die Gugel," of the jig kind, a canon representing the polyphone form corresponding to the motet and ricercar, and twenty-eight transcriptions of songs by various German and French composers. In the selection of these songs Gerle again shows his natural feeling for that which is essentially vocal and that which is essentially instrumental; the symmetrical construction of periods, contraction of notes repeated in the vocal form only on account of the words, figuration of cadences, etc.

THE FIRST VIOL MAKERS.

The first viol maker whose name has been handed down to posterity was Henry aux Vièles, who lived in Paris about 1292. There was also a trumpet maker in Paris whose name appears in 1297 as Henry L'Escot. It seems not improbable that they were one and the same person, and if that were the case we should come to the conclusion that the first viol maker whose name has been preserved to this day was a Scotchman (l'Escot). Another viol maker of that period was Ludwig Vanvaelbeck, 1294-1312, who lived at Vaelbeck in Flanders, from which place he took his name. He made rebecs and fidels like the above, for the viol forms did not appear before about the middle of the fourteenth century. Vanvaelbeck is also credited with the invention of the organ pedal.

Giovanni Kerlino was the first instrument maker who is known to have made real "viols." According to the latest researches he was of German origin, born in the Italian Tyrol in 1391. From 1410 till 1437 he is said to have lived in Brescia, whence he migrated to lower Brittany. There he remained until 1446 when he returned to Brescia. In 1450 he set out once more for Brittany where he died in the following year, 1451 (according to the memoirs of an old instrument maker communicated by Count Luigi Francesco Valdrighi).

De Laborde in his "Essay sur la Musique" (1780), describes a violin labelled "Joan Kerlino, 1449."

Fétis relates that he saw that instrument in 1804 when it was in the possession of Koliker, a Paris luthier. It proved to be an instrument of the older viol form which had been provided with a new neck and strung as a violin.

The greatest viol maker of the fifteenth century after Kerlino was Pietro Dardelli, a monk of the Franciscan order who lived in a monastery at Mantua in 1497. He was one of the first to make viols of ebony and ivory inlaid with gold and silver and ornamented with the most beautiful miniatures. Some of the instruments which he produced simply for the love of art, form the most precious gems in Italian museums and private collections.

Following upon Dardelli, almost all the great Italian "liutarii" of the sixteenth and seventeenth century made viols to wit, Gasparo da Salo, Ciciliano, Grancino, Corna, Busseto, Cattenaro, Storioni, etc. Fétis speaks of a gamba which he had seen, and tells us that it was made in 1693 by Acero, of Saluzzo, a pupil of Gioffredo Cappa, and that at one time it belonged to Marin Marais, the famous French bass viol player.

The most remarkable viol maker of thé early sixteenth century was Gasparo Duiffoprugcar, whose biography was steeped in mystery until Dr. Henry Coutagne, of Lyons, produced documentary evidence which places many essential points beyond doubt. He discredits all the stories which appear in earlier biographical dictionaries, etc., that "Duiffoprugcar came from the Italian Tyrols, settled in Brescia, thence removed to Bologna, and was in 1515 induced to follow Francis I to Paris, afterwards settling in Lyons where he died."

Coutagne points out that the beautiful portrait designed and engraved by the celebrated Pierre Woeriot, of Lyons, in 1562 *(see Plate I)*, gives the age of Duiffoprugcar as forty-eight. He also tells us that in a letter of naturalisation made out in January, 1559, he is described as "Caspar Dieffenbruger, alleman, faiseur de lutz, natif de Fressin, Ville impériale en Allmaigne." The natural deduction from these facts is, therefore, that Duiffoprugcar (Duiffopruckar) or rather Tieffenbrucker, as the name would appear in its original German form, was born in Freising, a small but important Bavarian town (seat of a bishop), about twenty miles from Munich, in 1514, and settled in Lyons, somewhere about the middle of the century.

Coutagne's reasons for refuting the theory of Duiffoprugcar's sojourn in Italy are: (1) That his workmanship, especially as regards his marquetry shows no influence of the Italian art of his time. (2) That the merchants of Nuremberg, Augsburg, and other trade centres of Southern Germany were strongly represented at the Lyons Fair, and the name "Tieffenbrucker," a relative of Duiffoprugcar (whose real name was Kaspar Tieffenbrucker), appears among them. Coutagne holds, therefore, that he went from Freising straight to Lyons, which appears a most natural solution of all the mysterious stories concerning him. From the finely-engraven portrait by Woeriot, we learn not only the date of Duiffoprugcar's birth, but also that he was an instrument maker of exceptional ability. There is hardly a stringed instrument of the time that is not represented among those surrounding the master's portrait, including one (between two lutes on the extreme left) which has a very strong resemblance to the modern violin, an instrument which about this time had *notably* made its appearance in Brescia.

The viols of Duiffoprugcar were distinguished by their perfect proportions, symmetry of outline, and the inventive genius in their decorative treatment. The world-wide reputation which he acquired even during his lifetime called into existence many imitators; the most notable being Vuillaume, of Paris, who made violins which he painted and decorated in the style of Duiffoprugcar's instruments (see Coutagne), and which passed until recently as proofs that Duiffoprugcar was the first maker of the violin proper.

That fact has been refuted by later experts and historians. The author has, however, been assured by the late August Wilhelmj that an instrument discovered in a garret of his father's old mansion in Geisenheim on the Rhine (which in the olden times belonged to the Elector of Mayence) proved to be a genuine Tieffenbrucker violin. He described it as a battered old instrument dated 1505. When restored it was found to be a very beautiful instrument with a tone as sweet as it was powerful. The date speaks against its genuineness. Before Coutagne's discoveries, published in 1893, the date of Duiffoprugcar's birth was fixed by Rochefort and others at 1469, hence the early dates of the forgeries by Vuillaume and others. Although there is no proof of any violin in the strict sense of the word having been made before the middle of the sixteenth century, there is as little proof to show that Duiffoprugcar never made a violin even though he may not have been the first, for he worked to the year of his death, and by that time violins were being made by both Andreas Amati and Gasparo da Salo, and it is hardly

DUIFFOPRUGCAR'S VIOLS.

credible that Duiffoprugcar, one of the greatest masters of his time should not have been acquainted with this instrument, in spite of the fact that merchants from all parts of northern Italy visited annually the fair at Lyons; moreover the instrument (above mentioned) between the lutes on Woeriot's picture appears to possess all the essential characteristics of the violin. Might it not be possible that the date on the label of the Wilhelmj specimen was either 1565, the six being faded, and thus wrongly deciphered, or else that it was faked to make it appear older?

The greatest strength of Duiffoprugcar lay no doubt in his lutes and viols, and of the latter we can fortunately judge by several specimens which are still in existence, the most celebrated being the bass viol da gamba with the bird's-eye view of Paris inlaid in various coloured woods on the back of the instrument.* The design corresponds with a still existing print in the National Library at Paris dated 1564, thus fixing the date of the instrument. Above the "Plan de Paris" is a copy of the vision of Ezekiel after Raphael, inlaid in a similar manner. Tailpiece and fingerboard are also elaborately inlaid with beautiful designs and the pegbox is surmounted by a horse's head carved in ivory. The instrument has seven strings which were tuned:

FIG. 6. THE TUNING OF A DUIFFOPRUGCAR BASS VIOLA DA GAMBA.

Coutagne gives the tuning an octave higher, but that would make it a discant viol da gamba which is incompatible with its dimensions. The presence of seven strings in this instrument

---

* An illustration of this instrument is given in E. van der Straeten's "The Revival of the Viols."

disposes for once and all of statements crediting either Marin Marais or Sainte-Colombe with the introduction of the seventh (bass) string which have found their way into almost every musical dictionary.* Jean Rousseau in his "Traité de la Viole" (Paris, 1687), says that Sainte-Colombe introduced the seventh string about 1675 at the same time that he introduced the use of strings spun with silver wire for the three lower strings. The latter statement deserves more credence than the former, which we have seen from the above facts to be distinctly incorrect. It appears certain that during the first half of the sixteenth century no spun strings were used on either viols or lutes. Laurent Grillet in his "Ancêtres du Violon" reproduces a print dated "1675," showing a gentleman playing a viol da gamba which, judging from the manner in which the strings are fixed to the tailpiece, had three spun strings. This inference is drawn from the fact that gut strings were fixed with a loop (as on the lute) while the spun strings were simply knotted at the back of the tailpiece.

Another authentic viol da gamba by Duiffoprugcar is preserved in the Donaldson collection at the Royal College of Music. It is a six-stringed instrument of small dimensions, the length of body being only sixty-five millimetres, which circumstance led Laurent Grillet to the supposition that it was either a lady's instrument or a *tenor* viol da gamba. The length of the neck which makes the stops identical with that of a *bass* viol speaks against that theory, although the neck may have been lengthened at a later period. The instrument which is of elegant proportions has only the upper corner, and lozenge-shaped soundholes. The back is covered with most beautiful designs in marquetry surrounding the figures of an

---

* Even the learned and critical Rühlmann has fallen into the trap, mentioning Marin Marais as the author of the seventh string.—"Geschichte der Bogeninstr," page 228.

PLATE III.

THOMAS MACE. FROM THE FRONTISPIECE, ENGRAVED BY W. FAITHORNE, TO "MUSICK'S MONUMENT," 1676.

evangelist and an angel. The pegbox is surmounted by the characteristic horse's head which recurs in several viols by this master as does also his device:

> Viva fui in sylvis; fui dura occisa securi.
> Dum vixi, tacui; mortua dulce cano.
> While living my home was in the forest; the cruel axe felled me.
> Alive I was mute, dead I sing sweetly.

This as well as the figure of a salamander, appearing on the neck of some of his instruments have served to deceive the unwary in the numerous forgeries mentioned before.

The salamander was pointed out as proving Duiffoprugcar's connection with the court of Francis I—who was supposed to have brought him to Paris from Bologna—the salamander, however, was an emblem of the house of Valois, and did not belong exclusively to Francis I. Vidal in his "Les Instruments a Archet," gives an illustration of another authentic viol da gamba by Duiffoprugcar with a design attributed to Baccio Dardinelli, and known as the "old man in a baby's chair." It was engraved by Agostino Veneziano and published between 1520-30. This instrument, which is a very fine specimen of Duiffoprugcar's art belonged in 1876 to Mr. Louis de Waziers. The "violin" preserved in the Paris Museum, which has a flower design with the picture of a cock inlaid in the back, is really a small viol which has been cut down and altered. There are other instruments mentioned by the same master, but some are not authentic, while the present whereabouts of others is entirely unknown.

During the fifteenth and sixteenth centuries German viol makers enjoyed a world-wide reputation, particularly those of the town of Nuremberg. One of the first whose names have been handed down to us was Hans Frey, the father-in-law of Albrecht Dürer, who worked about 1440. From his family descended another Hans Frei who was a noted maker of lutes and viols at Bologna about 1597. This Frei is mentioned in

Evelyn's "Diary" in 1645, where, after eulogising the cheese and sausages of Bologna, he refers to the famous old lute makers of that city, and the extraordinary prices paid for their instruments. Mentioning Hans Frei, he says that the workmen were chiefly Germans. A viol by Conrad Müller, of Nuremberg, dated 1520, is, according to Rühlmann, preserved in the Royal Museum at Copenhagen. Hans Gerle has been mentioned as the author of "Musica teutsch auf die Instrumente der grossen und kleinen Geigen" (music in German for the big and small fiddles—meaning instructions for these instruments in the German language). The first edition of this book appeared in 1532, the second in 1537, and a third edition in 1546. In the book we find the first elements of a tutor for viols. His "geygen" still retained the number of five strings as we found them in Virdung, Agricola and Luscinius, with this difference, that whereas the older instruments were suspended from the shoulder as we have seen in Fig. 5, Hans Gerle gives precise instructions to hold the "geygen" between the knees.* They were, therefore, viol da *gambas* in the strict sense of the word, "gamba" being the Italian for leg. Their compass and tuning corresponded with that of the later viols, with the exception of the arrangement of the intervals (the third appearing nearer the bass), and the additional higher fourth which was added by increasing the number of strings from five to six. The lower compass was preferred in the olden times, though the difficulty of producing strings that would stand the strain of a higher tuning may have been an additional reason. Gerle's tuning was:

Fig. 7. The Tuning of a Gerle's Geygen.

---

* Hence the German name "Kniegeige."

Hans Gerle's instruments remind one in their outward shape still of the old "guitar-fiedel" as may be seen from the accompanying illustration. They had only five strings, although six-stringed viols existed already in Italy. They are mentioned in Lanfranco's "Scintille," published in 1533, and their tuning was already the standard viol da gamba tuning, viz.: bass—D, G, C, E, A, D'; tenor and alto—A, D, G, B, E', A'; treble—D, G, C', E', A', D"

These six-stringed viols were, however, not in general use at that time, for Ganassi del Fontego's "Fontegara," 1536, shows on the title page only five-stringed viols, and such appear also on the same author's "Regola Rubertina," published in 1542, at Venice. Both title-pages are reproduced in E. van der Straeten's "The Revival of the Viols" (Strad Library). The second edition of the "Regola Rubertina" appeared in 1543, and may be looked upon as the first instruction book for the six-stringed viol da gamba in four sizes, tuned as already described by Lanfranco:

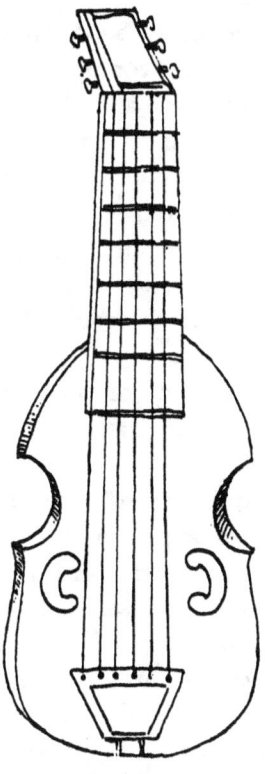

FIG. 8. A GEIGE BY HANS GERLE.

FIG. 9. THE TUNING OF A SIX-STRINGED VIOL DA GAMBA.

The book contains a number of exercises which are printed

in ordinary staff notation but without bar-lines; some of these exercises were intended for the study of pure intonation. The German compositions for viols were exclusively written in tablature, and the study of intonation is not touched upon in the earliest German instruction books. From about the middle of the sixteenth century the viol in its perfect form was made by the instrument makers of Italy, Germany, France and England, which acquired great fame for its viols as we shall see anon.

Prätorius in his "Organographia," 1620, gives an illustration of the four sizes of the viol da gamba, Figs. 10, 11, 12 and 13.

The art of playing on the viol da gamba consisted chiefly in improvisation which left its traces in the published music down to the end of the seventeenth century. The art of "diminution" (splitting up larger values of notes into smaller ones, say semibreves first into minims, then into crotchets, etc.) was practised in Italy about this time, and was introduced into England towards the middle of the sixteenth century by Alfonso Ferrabosco. The viol itself, however, was not introduced by Ferrabosco as has been often stated. It existed already in Henry VIII's band, where we find several Italian viol players. In England the art of viol da gamba or "bass viol" playing attained such heights that English players became the masters of French and German gambists. The viol da gamba, apart from becoming the principal solo instrument, gradually superseded the lute as instrument for accompanying the voice, especially the recitative where the player had to complete the harmonies of the figured basses by arpeggios or sustained chords according to individual taste and ability.

The tablature, this "simplified" system of notation, which indicated frets on six lines representing the strings of the instrument instead of marking actual notes on a five-line stave, had already been held up to ridicule by Martin Agricola in his "Musica Instrumentalis deutsch" in 1528. It disappeared on

Fig. 10 (1), Fig. 11 (2), Fig. 12 (3), Violn da Gamba. Fig. 13 (4), Viol Bastarda. Fig. 14 (5), Italianische Lyra de Bracio. From Plate XX of Prätorius's "Syntagmatis Musici Tomus Secundus de Organographia."

the Continent early in the seventeenth century, but in England the tablature was used for the lyra (leero) viol as long as that instrument was used, viz.: the end of the seventeenth century. The most important work dealing with divisions or diminutions was Christopher Simpson's "Division-Viol,' published in 1659, which is described on page 47; it contains all the elements of the more elaborate passage-work of the later composers.

In France De Caix d'Hervelois and Marin Marais chiefly employed the dance forms with terse rhythms and graceful, and very often charming, melodies. Now and again they bring a ciacconna, but De Caix never launches out into larger forms as Marais sometimes does; without, however, approaching the breadth and grandeur which we find in August Kühnel's sonatas, or even in some movements by Joh. Schenck in his "Scherzi Musicali," as well as in "L'Echo du Danube."

Forquerai shows a formal advance upon his earlier compatriots, but although his music is full of life and spirit, and not without some of the graceful charm of the older masters it does not attain the mastery of form as well as instrumental technique which is apparent in the above-named German masters, not to mention J. S. Bach who stands so mountain high above all. When the orchestra began to develop, and instruments were harmoniously contrasted according to their technical qualities as well as tone colour, it was found that the tone of the viol da gamba was not sufficiently powerful to serve as bass to a body of violins, flutes, oboes and sometimes clarinets. In chamber music likewise a new era had begun and the style of the composers of the eighteenth century was no longer favourable to the character and capabilities of the viol da gamba; with the result that it had to cede its place to the violoncello which took over the heritage of its relative as we shall see in the next chapter.

In Italy the viol da gamba began to be neglected as soon as the violin made its appearance, about the middle of the sixteenth century, and about the same time its chief cultivation was—mainly through Ferrabosco—transplanted to England, where it soon became a favourite and found its foremost representative makers and players. From here it went over to France and in the two countries it remained in favour to a later period than in most other countries.

About 1600 the acoustic principle of sympathetic strings was investigated by English scientists (see Bacon's "Natural History," 1620) with the result that Farrant, a musician in King Charles I's band, applied them to the viol. A Duke of Somerset is mentioned by Kircher ("Musurgia") as the inventor of a stringed instrument with sympathetic strings. The "bass viol d'amore" and "lyra viol d'amore," as these instruments were called, were, however, not long lived on account of the complicated mechanism, and the difficulty to keep so many strings in tune. One instrument, however, of the bass viol kind retained them in a modified way, and that was

"THE BARYTON."

It had six or seven gut strings running over the fingerboard, while from eight to twenty, and more, sympathetic strings resting on a lower bridge—by the side of the ordinary but rather high bridge. These strings, which were of steel or brass, were placed side by side in the hollow back of a very wide neck, and they were plucked by the thumb of the left hand, thus supplying a bass to the melody played by the fingers of the left hand on the gut strings, which were sounded with the bow. The seven-stringed instrument was tuned:

FIG. 15. THE TUNING OF A SEVEN-STRINGED BARYTON.

and the lowest sympathetic string was [notation]. A beautiful specimen by Joachim Tielke, of Hamburg, 1686, and richly inlaid with ivory, is in the South Kensington Museum.

The baryton never had many votaries except in Germany, especially in Austria, where it was cultivated from the latter part of the seventeenth to the latter part of the eighteenth century. It was essentially a chamber instrument of a soft and pleasing tone which offered the advantage of being able to play melody and accompaniment on one instrument, but would not permit of technical display. The Austrian Emperor Francis and Prince Esterhazy were both executants on the baryton, and at their request Haydn wrote one hundred and sixty-three pieces for the instrument, which partly perished in a fire which destroyed the Schloss Eisen containing the Prince's library, in 1774. The library of the "Gesellschaft der Musikfreunde" is in the possession of some of these pieces which escaped destruction, and (Mr. Victor Mahillon, in his catalogue of the museum of the Brussels Conservatoire, tells us on the authority of Mr. Mandycewski, the librarian of the above society) were to be published shortly (this was in 1893, the author is unaware if they have appeared). He gives the following list thereof:

1 Duo, in G, for two barytons.
7 Divertissements, in C major, for baryton, alto and bass.
36 ,, D ,, ,, ,, ,,
1 ,, D minor ,, ,, ,,
2 ,, F major ,, ,, ,,

PLATE IV.

SIR ROGER L'ESTRANGE. FROM AN ENGRAVING BY R. WHITE OF THE PORTRAIT BY G. KNELLER.

24 Divertissements, in G major, for baryton, alto and bass.
17   ,,   A ,,   ,,   ,,   ,,
2   ,,   D minor   ,,   ,,   ,,
1   ,,   A ,,   ,,   ,,   ,,

Haydn wrote also a cantata on the death of Frederic the Great commencing with the words:

> Er ist nicht mehr,
> Tön' trauernd Baryton!
> (He is no more, sound mournful baryton!)

The "Lyra Tedescha" mentioned as the favourite instrument of the King of Naples, who, on his visit to Vienna in 1790, ordered Haydn to write him some pieces for the instrument, is the same as the baryton, the former being the Italian name.

The principal virtuosos were: August Kühnel, Marc Antonio Berti, Anton Lidl, Sebastian Ludwig Friedel and Karl Franz (biographical notices under "German Viol Players").

The viola bastarda was a viol da gamba slightly smaller than the bass viol, and sometimes provided with sympathetic strings *(see Fig. 13)*.

THE LYRA.

There were three kinds of lyras: the lyra da braccio, played in the manner of the shoulder viol *(see Fig. 14)* and the bass lyra (Lirone perfetto, arce Violyra), corresponding to the bass viol only that the body and neck are considerably larger on account of the great number of strings. "For," as Prätorius says, "some have twelve strings, some fourteen; some also an additional two running beside the neck, which makes sixteen strings." They were used for the playing of madrigals, etc., as well as in dramatic (operatic) and church music. The third kind stood between the two and had nine strings running over the fingerboard and two bourdons. They were chiefly used during the early part of the seventeenth century, but the very facility they offered for playing chords was detrimental in the playing of single parts. They never seem to have called forth any particular literature, nor do we possess the name of any great virtuosos on the lyra. (For further details see "The Revival of the Viols," by E. van der Straeten.)

THE ARPEGGIONE

May be regarded as the latest instrument of the viol type. It was also called guitar-violoncello, and was constructed by G. Staufer, of Vienna, in 1823. It had six strings tuned:

Fig. 16. The Tuning of the Arpeggione, also called the Guitar-Violoncello.

Schubert composed a sonata (posthumous) for this instrument, and Vincent Schuster wrote a tutor. The instrument has since completely disappeared.

THE VIOLA POMPOSA.

The nature of this instrument has been shrouded in mystery hitherto. Rühlmann has but imperfect knowledge of it and even the painstaking Laurent Grillet has but hazy notions about it, and deliberately tells us that Bach, "in his numerous works has not left us anything for the viola pomposa." To M. Paul de Wit, of Leipzig, belongs the credit of bringing light into the history of this instrument, of which he succeeded in securing no less than three specimens, which are now in the museum of the Cologne Conservatoire.

According to tradition, J. S. Bach is credited with the idea of constructing this instrument to facilitate the playing of quick passages on the violoncello which went beyond the neck positions, and consequently beyond the technique of his average orchestral players. To obviate this he added another string a fifth above the A string, at the same time he reduced the size to about seventy-eight to eighty centimetres.

Several historians assert that the instrument was tuned like the violoncello with the addition of the higher fifth, and that it was also held in the same manner as the latter, viz., between the knees, although the size was reduced to that of a large viol d'amore (one by Partl, 1764, in the Brussels Conservatoire Museum is 78.5 centimetres long), and the one and only artist who treated the instrument in virtuoso fashion was Johann Georg Pisendel, a famous violinist in Dresden. Whichever way it may have been held the instrument was not tuned like the violoncello but like the viola, viz. :

FIG. 17. THE TUNING OF THE VIOLA POMPOSA.

The "Zeitschrift für Instrumentenbau," October 11, 1906, which contains an illustration of a viola pomposa by Johann Christian Hoffmann, in Leipzig, gives the total length as seventy-eight centimetres. In a letter to the author Mr. Paul de Wit gives the dimensions as follows:

Total length—800 mm.
Largest width—270 mm.
Height of ribs—75 mm.

The additional two centimetres in the length of the instrument constitutes, of course, a distinct increase in the difficulty of handling it.

The dimensions tally exactly with those given by Mr. Mahillon for an instrument formerly in the collection V. and J. Mahillon, but now in the Museum of the Brussels Conservatoire. The label of that instrument runs:

Joh. Christian Hoffmann, Königl, Poln, und Chürf, Sächs Hoff Instrument und Lautenmacher in Leipzig, 1720.

An inventory taken in 1773 of the instruments in the orchestra of the Prince of Anhalt Cöthen, of which Bach was conductor from 1717 to 1723, enumerates under No. 20: "Ein Violon Cello Piculo mit 5 Seiten von J. C. Hoffmann, 1731," and No. 21: "Ein Violon Cello Piculo mit 4 Seiten von J. H. Ruppert, 1724." The latter was evidently nothing else but a large viola used to reinforce the violoncellos in florid passages. That it was not intended for viola work is evident from the name and the fact that three violas form the Nos. 17, 18, 19. The Hoffmanns were a family of instrument makers which for several generations enjoyed a high reputation.

Bach's compositions for the viola pomposa comprise a Solo Suite in D, better known as No. 6 of the solo suites for violoncello, the *obbligato* to "My Faithful Heart," as well as a number of *obbligato* and other parts in his cantatas, etc.

CHAPTER III.

THE VIOL DA GAMBA IN ITALY.

AS we have mentioned already the reign of the viols was but of short duration in Italy, and ceased altogether about the beginning of the seventeenth century, although here and there it might still be found down to the beginning of the eighteenth century. During the sixteenth century things were different. Italy produced some of the finest instruments in the world. Girolamo Brensio (Hieronymus Brensius) worked in Bologna towards the end of the fifteenth century, and a viol of his make was in the possession of the late Mr. George Hart, in London. Pietro Dardelli made his wonderful instruments inlaid with ebony, ivory, gold, silver and precious stones, about 1500. Giovanni Busseto worked in Cremona between 1540 and 1580. Count Valdrighi mentions eight viols by Autentico del Fontico which were sent to Germany in 1541. Giovanni Cellini, the father of Benvenuto Cellini, one of the greatest artists that Italy proudly claims, lived in Florence at the commencement of the sixteenth century, and Benvenuto tells us many amusing little anecdotes concerning him in his autobiography, which, by reason of its contents as well as its style, forms one of the most fascinating books; in fact, Goethe thought it worth his while to translate it into the German language. He (Benvenuto) tells us how his father taught him to sing and to play the flute, but that he did not succeed in imbuing him with any love for his art. The father was a remarkably clever artist, who made all sorts of "wonderfully conceived organs with wooden pipes," *clavicembles* as good and as beautifully executed as any to be seen at that time. He also made harps, lutes and viols. When he first fell in love with the girl who afterwards became his wife, and Benvenuto's mother, he began to express his emotions by means of his flute. And, gaining thereby the admiration of the pipers of Lorenzo di Medici, he was induced by them to join their band. The duke and his son Pietro, who knew his talents, and were favourably inclined towards him, saw that he neglected his higher vocation, and dismissed him. Although Giovanni regarded this as an act of great injustice, it had the desired effect, as it again restored him to his art. In 1528 he, and several members of his family, fell victims to the plague. About the following viol makers very little is known, except that here and there a specimen of their workmanship may be met with. They are Lancilotto, of Modena, 1507-51; Pietro Zamuri, Brescia, 1509; Sebastian Scotto, 1511, whose name seems to indicate that he was of Scottish extraction. This is all the more probable as the French court maintained a Scotch bodyguard, which drew a great many of their countrymen to France to seek their fortune. Ventura Linarolo worked in Venice about 1514-20; one of his gambas formed part of the collection of Count Valdrighi at Modena. Peregrino Zanetto, Brescia, about 1530; Morglato Morella, Venice, about 1550; Johannes Marcus, 1540-80; Mariani, 1570; Monti Chiaro, 1533; and Testator il Vecchio, a contemporary of Gasparo da Salo. He was one of the first to reduce the size and alter the shape of viols, calling them violini. Andreas Amati, head of the Amati dynasty, 1510-80, was a maker of rebecs, viols and violins, as was also his great contemporary, Bertolloti, called Gasparo da Salo, who worked between 1550 and 1610. Several fine gambas by the latter maker are in the South Kensington Museum. Accro, 1650-95, a pupil of Cappa, is said to have made a gamba for Marin Marais in 1693. Ciciliáno Grancino, Corna Frei, Cattanaro, Ruger detto il per, Storioni and Bergonzi made viols, some elaborately ornamented. Many of these are preserved in various collections and museums. (Description in "Revival of the Viols.")

The French gambist, Maugars, in his "Response fait à un Curieux sur le Sentiment de la Musique d'Italie" (dated Rome, October 1, 1639), confirms our statement that viol playing in Italy began to decline as soon as the violin made its appearance. This is a passage from his letter. "As regards the viol, there is nobody at the present time in Italy who excels on it, and in Rome it is very little played at all. This astonishes me all the more, seeing that in former times they had a Horatio of Parma who did wonders on it and who left very good pieces for it to posterity, and also that the father of the great Italian, Farabosco (Ferrabosco) was the first to teach the English the use of it, who have since then surpassed all other nations."

"Horatio of Parma," mentioned above by Maugars, lived about the end of the sixteenth century. His fame as a composer spread all over Europe, and his pieces for the viol were arranged for sundry instruments and had become very popular. Horatio was personally known to Maugars. He was then at a very advanced age. The real name of this famous musician was Horatio Bassani, also called Horatio del Violono. Scipio Cerreto mentions him in his list of Neapolitan musicians which was printed in 1601 as a player of the "viola d'arco" (viol played with a bow) who was then dead. It appears that some time before his decease he left Parma and settled in Naples. Some of his vocal compositions are preserved in the library at Bologna.

The first virtuoso on the viol da gamba of whom we have any knowledge is no less a person than Leonardo da Vinci, the famous painter, who lived 1452-1520. He was, in his early youth, gambist to the Duke Ludovico Sforza at Milan, at a salary of seventy-five pounds per annum. Unfortunately we have no clue to judge of his powers as an executant, as no pieces

Fig. 18. Autograph Signature of Leonardo da Vinci's Father, a Famous Musician and Composer of Operas.

for the gamba exist dating back to that period, and it is doubtful whether any solos for that instrument existed beyond the playing of a vocal part of some canzonetta, or perhaps a dance tune, since the instrument was chiefly used to accompany the voice.

The next viol da gambist whose name has been handed down to posterity is Vincenzo Galilei, born 1533 at Florence, where he died after 1602. He was the father of Galileo Galilei and an excellent lutenist, gambist, composer and a very learned master of musical theory. He was a pupil of the famous Zarlino, with whom he entered into a controversy about the old contrapuntal form of vocal music, advocating a freer style of melody, and thus paving the way for the musical drama which emanated from the house of Count Bardi, to whom he was greatly attached. His great son, Galileo, 1564-1642, was also an executant on the lute and viol da gamba, as was also another member of that family, Michael Angelo Galilei, who lived as lutenist and viol da gambist in Florence at the beginning of the seventeenth century.

PLATE V.

MRS. THICKNESSE (NÉE ANN FORD). FROM THE PAINTING BY GAINSBOROUGH IN THE POSSESSION OF THE LATE MR. CHARLES WERTHEIMER.

ORIGIN OF ENGLISH SCHOOL OF BASS VIOLISTS.

Alfonso Ferrabosco was born in 1515 and settled about 1540 in London, where he was retained a "gentiluomo" (gentleman) in the service of the Duke of Savoy. Apparently he took up his abode in Greenwich, where his son, Alfonso, was born. The latter was the head and founder of the English school of gambists, or bass viol players as they were called, of whom Maugars says that they surpassed all others in the world. We shall speak of him later on.

Alessandro Romano was born about 1530 in Rome, and entered the papal chapel in 1560 as a singer. He entered the Chapel of Paul III in 1549, and was surnamed "della viola," Marco Fratinelli (Grillet, page 254). He entered the monastery of "Monte Oliveto" as Frater Giulio Cesare, but his quarrelsome disposition placed him in an unpleasant position with some of the monks of his order. He published "Canzone alla Napolitana" and a book of motets in five parts between 1572-9.

Teobaldo Gatti, born 1650, at Florence, was an excellent gambist and opera composer. He followed the school of Lully, who appointed him member of the orchestra of the Grand Opera at Paris, which position he held for nearly fifty years. In 1696 he published twelve "Airs Italiens." He died in 1727. Schilling and Gerber speak of him as a violoncellist, which seems to point to the fact that he played also the latter instrument. In his time no violoncellists were engaged at the Opera.

Leonora Baroni lived about the early part of the seventeenth century and was celebrated for her beauty, virtue and musical talent. She played the lute and the gamba, and belonged to a very musical family. In 1644 she visited Florence at the request of Cardinal Mazarin, and returned to Italy before 1660.

Giorgio Antoniotti, born at Milan in 1692 and died there in 1776, is to all appearances the last Italian composer who wrote for the viol da gamba. His Op. 1 consists of twelve sonatas for violoncello *or* viol da gamba. They were published in Holland, where he lived for some time, afterwards residing in London for about twenty years, when he returned to Italy. Some of the above sonatas have been republished for violoncello and pianoforte.

This closes the list of Italian gambists of repute, as the violin began to assert its supremacy, and the violoncello soon took the place of the gamba altogether. At the beginning of the eighteenth century the Italians appear to have tried to effect a compromise between the gamba and the violoncello by abandoning the flat back of the viol for the modelled back of the violin tribe, whereby the tone approaches that of the violoncello, at the same time retaining the softness of the former instrument. A magnificent specimen of this kind by "Vincenzo Ruger, detto il per," made at Cremona in the year 1702, may be seen at the Royal Museum at Berlin. It exhibits the most finished workmanship, has excellent varnish, and its tone is said to be of a beautiful quality. It was bought by the Prussian Government from the collection of M. Paul de Wit, of Leipzig. This gentleman gave a description of it in the "Zeitschrift für Instrumentenbau," Vol. VI, No. 21.

The author has seen a similar instrument by Gagliano. It is a peculiarly deep model and has a rosewood fingerboard fretted with inlaid brass frets.

THE VIOL DA GAMBA IN ENGLAND.

The viols had been cultivated in England from an early period, and we find rebec and viol players in the bands of our mediæval kings. The former instrument survived in England longer than in any other European country, as we find that rebec players were included in the band of Charles I. Henry

VIII, who was the first king who held complete sway over the conflicting parties of England, and therefore had leisure to turn his attention to the cultivation of the fine arts, attracted many Italian musicians to his court, and among them several viol players. In 1559 the "violetts" in Queen Mary's band were: Albert de Venice, Ambrose Lupo (of Milan), Paul de Galliardo, Frances de Venice, Mark Anthony Galliardo, George de Comyn and Innocence de Comyn (their real name was Conti, and they were, in all probability, relatives of the celebrated Italian composer of that name). Ambrose Lupo was the head of a long line of excellent players and composers, of whom we shall hear more by and by. In 1581 we find, also, mention of the name of Alfonso Ferrabosco as a musician-in-ordinary to Queen Elizabeth, at a salary of £26 13s. 4d. In 1599 Thomas Lupo, son of Pietro Lupo, was appointed violinist, and in 1602 we find, besides these two members of the Lupo family, two more, viz., Joseph Lupo, and Thomas, his son. The latter was also a composer. He died in 1628 and was followed by his son Theophil, who was apparently the father of Thomas Lupo, the bass viol player and composer. There was besides a Horatio Lupo, who was violinist to the king in 1612.

Alfonso Ferrabosco, the musician-in-ordinary to Queen Elizabeth, whose biography appears among the Italian gambists, became the founder of the English school of bass viol* players, and a few of his compositions for that instrument are preserved in the British Museum. More important as executant and composer was his son:

Alfonso Ferrabosco, mentioned in Maugars's letter, was born at Greenwich about 1580. He was the greatest master of the bass viol of his time, and composed a

---

* Bass viol was the English name for the viol da gamba; French, basse de viole.

number of pieces for his instrument. Some "Lessons for One and Two Lyra Viols" by him are preserved in the British Museum. He was a collaborator of Leighton's "Tears," published in 1614, and wrote also a number of "Fancies" for viols. Riemann says that he died in 1652. Certain it is that he was a musician-in-ordinary to Charles I in 1641, and that he was dead in 1661, when his place was filled by William Childe. He was one of the music masters of Prince Henry, to whom he dedicated a book of "Ayres" in 1605. The "Fancye" (fantasia) was one of the earliest forms of purely instrumental composition. It followed upon the madrigal and was largely practised and developed by the English bass viol players. Hawkins says that the early fantasias "abounded in fugues and little responsive passages, and all those other elegances observable in the structure and contrivance of the madrigal." They were written for various numbers of viols with and without organ or harpsichord. Thomas Mace, in "Musick's Monument" (1676) says: "We had for our Grave Musick Fancies of 3, 4, 5 and 6 Parts to the Organ; Interpos'd (now and then) with some Pavins, Allmaines, Solemn and Sweet Delightful Ayres; all which were (as it were) so many Pathetical stories, Rhetorical and Sublime Discourses . . . . they have been to myself (and many others) as Divine Raptures, Powerfully captivating all our unruly Faculties and Affections . . . . making us capable of Heavenly and Divine Influences." Another form of instrumental composition which originated about 1600 was known as the "In Nomine."

The "In Nomine" was originally a kind of motet or antiphon based upon the Gregorian setting of these words in the Church Liturgy *(see illustration)*.

During the seventeenth century it was also applied to instrumental music, introducing the Gregorian plainsong as a cantus fermus for one of the instruments (usually tenor or bass), while another embellished it with divisions. These "In

"IN NOMINE" AND "FANCYE."

Fig. 19. Instrumental Composition known as the "In Nomine."

Nomines" remained in favour for a considerable period. Dr. Burney tells us that he possessed a large collection of Fancies, particularly one book of Fancies in 6 parts, folio size, composed by John Jenkins for the L'Estrange family in Norfolk. It was corrected by the composer and six or eight eminent masters of the time. "These pieces," he says, "consist more of motets, madrigals and 'In Nomines' than Fantasie expressly made for instruments and were the product of Wm. Bird, A. Ferrabosco, senior and junior; Wm. White; John Ward; Thomas Ravenscroft; Wm. Crawforde; Thos. Lupo; Giov. Coperario and others. They appear now very dry and fanciless and it would be difficult to find *one* only that would afford any amusement, except to see how ingenious and well disposed lovers of music then were. Infinite pains were taken in collecting and correcting these books, which proves that however insipid and despicable we may think their contents, our forefathers were of a different opinion. Contemptible as they now seem they were the best which the first musicians could then produce." Burney is somewhat severe in his judgment, for some of the old Fancies will still exercise the fascination of their solemn gravity, but when we consider the achievements of the German and Italian schools in Burney's time, we can understand that he was so dazzled by their brilliancy that he could not recognise the quiet and massive though somewhat sober beauties of the old English masters. With the introduction of the airs and dance tunes, which in France were almost the only form of instrumental composition known, the polyphonic "consorts" for a greater number of viols (four to eight) became rarer and rarer, and the "chest of viols" of Mace and Jenkins's time, consisting generally of two trebles, two means (two tenors, or one alto and one tenor) and two basses, gradually gave place to the division viol and the lyra viol (see later on). The violone or double bass viol was never used in "consort" playing. The viols used in "consort" were *all viols da gamba* or knee viols. Thomas Mace tells us with regard to the sizes of the consort viols:

> Let your Bass be large, then your Treble must be just as short again in the String, as they stand eight notes higher. The Tenor just so long as from the Bridge to "F" Fret because they stand a fourth higher than your Basses. (This makes the tenor about two-thirds the size of a bass.—THE EDITOR.)

Christopher Simpson says:

> I would have a Division Viol to be of something a shorter size than a Consort-Basse, so that the hand may better command it.

With regard to the lyra viol, which was tuned in a chord, for instance:

FIG 20. THE TUNING OF THE LYRA VIOL.

or in the chord of G major or minor (called harpway sharp

and harpway flat) he says that the strings should be a little thinner than those of the division viol.

At the end of the sixteenth and beginning of the seventeenth centuries it was a common practice for composers to write "Ayres" *to sing and play for lute or viol.* This practice was followed in all countries about that time.

As florid passages for instruments had not yet made their appearance, and as the compass of the instruments were restricted to the first position only of the respective instruments, the parts being contrived in the same contrapuntal style, it became a simple matter to fit them with words and use them either as vocal or instrumental pieces or both together. There are a great number of such compositions still in existence. William Corkine wrote "Ayres to sing and play for the Lute and Bass Viol, with Pavins, Galliards, Almaines and Corantes for the Lyra Violl." London, fol., 1610. A second part was published in 1612.

Almost all of the famous lute players and madrigal composers of that period contributed to the literature of the bass viol. John Dowland wrote in 1600 an "Adew for Master Oliver Cromwell, a Lesson for Lute and Bass Viol." Others were William Byrde, Thomas Ravenscroft, Dr. Wilson, Mico, Dr. Charles Coleman, William White, William Crawforde, John Ward, Nathaniel Giles, Orlando Gibbons.

One of the greatest English bass viol players of that era was TOBIAS HUME, known by the name of Captain Hume. He published in 1605 the first part of "Ayres, French, Polish, and other together, some in Tabliture, and some in Pricke. With Pavines, Galliardes, and Almaines for the Viole de Gambo alone, and other musicale conceites for two Bass Viols, expressing Five Partes, with pleasant Reportes, one from the other, and for two Leero-Viols, or two with one Treble. Lastly, for the Leero-Viol to play alone, and some songes to be sung to the Viole with the Lute, or better, with the Viole alone. Also an invention for two to play upon one Viole." This shows that he practised the art of writing duets which could also be played on one single instrument, and also that he could lead various distinct parts by means of passages, arpeggios, and chords on the same instrument. In 1607 he published another book entitled "Captain Hume's Poeticall Musike, principally made for two Bass Viols, yet so construed that it may be played eight waies, upon sundrie instruments with much facilitie." London. He died in the Charterhouse in 1645.

J. DANYEL or DANIEL, a Bachelor of Music, Oxon, 1604, is supposed to have been a brother of Daniel the Poet. His songs for the lute, viol and voice were printed by Thomas Este for Thomas Adams, London, 1606, fol.

THOMAS FORD, born about 1580, was another of Prince Henry's musicians, at a salary of £40 a year. In 1625, on the accession of Charles I, he was appointed to the Royal band at £80 per annum, and in the following year he received £120 as singer and lutenist, but when the King's financial troubles began this was reduced again, and in 1640 he received £80. Ford died in 1648 and was buried November 17. He was the author of "Musicke of sundre kindes set forth in two bookes, the first whereof are ayres for four voices to the Lute Orpherion, or Basse Viol, with a dialogue for two voices, and two Basse Viols in parts, tunde the lute-way. The second are Pavens, Galiards, Almaines, Jiggs, Thumpes, and such likes for two Basse Viols, the liera-way, so made as the greatest number may serve to play alone, very easy to be performed." London, by John Browne, 1607, fol. Burney republished two of his vocal canons in his "History of Music."

JOHN EST, a barber, lived about this time, and was famous for his skill on the lyra viol. He was a brother of the famous Michael Est (Este or East) who was a master of the cathedral choir at Lichfield, and a celebrated composer of his day, who wrote between about 1600 and 1638 seven "sets of books" with

PLATE VI.

GEORGE NEUMARK. FROM AN ENGRAVING IN THE COLLECTION OF THE LATE JOHANNES KLINGENBERG (APPARENTLY A FRONTISPIECE TO ONE OF HIS WORKS).

compositions in various parts *apt for viols and voices*; the seventh containing duets for two bass viols. John and Michael were apparently the sons of Thomas Est, who first published the Psalms in parts.

THOMAS BREWER, educated at Christ's Hospital, London, and bred to the practice of the viol, composed seven excellent fantasias for that instrument. He lived between 1610-80, but the dates of his birth and death are not known.

DANIEL NORCOME (Norcum), born at Windsor in 1576, was bass viol player, organist and composer. He was the son of a lay clerk at Windsor, and probably singer in the Chapel Royal. Religious troubles caused him to leave England, and he became a member of the Archducal Chapel at Brussels, where he was in 1647. He contributed a madrigal to the "Triumphs of Oriana," 1601.

JOHN MAYNARD, a lute player and composer (16—-17—?), published: "The XII Wonders of the World, set and composed for the Violl de Gambo, the lute, and the voyce, to sing the verse, all three jointly and non severall; also Lessons for the Lute and Basse Violl to play alone; with some Lessons to play lyra-wayes alone, or if you will, fill up the parts with another violl set lute-way." London, 1611. These songs describe twelve different characters, of such perfection that they would be wonders of the world. They are full of quaint humour. A delightful melody is "The Mayde," which the author produced recently very successfully, with accompaniment of two bass viols.

SIMON IVES, born 1600, was a lute and viol player, and lay vicar of St. Paul's. He wrote a considerable number of fancies, lessons, etc., for bass viols. A very pretty little piece for lyra viol, "La Cloche," is to be found in Playford's "Musick's Recreation." He died in London in 1662. Together with H. and W. Lawes he composed Shirley's masque, "The Triumph of Peace" (1633).

HENRY BUTLER and the two Rowes are mentioned by Dr. Alfred Einstein ("Zur Deutschen Literatur für Viola da Gamba") as English bass viol players who went to the Continent about this period on account of the religious persecutions. A manuscript collection of pieces, composed between 1653-69, for theorbo and viola baryton contains some "baryton" (see page 23) pieces in tablature signed W. R. Dr. Einstein thinks that they were probably by Walter Rowe. He gives the translation of a pretty saraband with "double" by this master, which he considers the best piece in the collection.

THOMAS ROBINSON, born after the middle of the sixteenth century, published "The School of Musicke: the perfect method of true fingering the Lute, Pandora, Orphorion, and Viol da Gamba"; London, printed by Thomas Este (see John Est) for Simon Waterson, dwelling at the sign of the Crowne in St. Paul's Church Yard, 1603. As an instruction book it deals chiefly with the lute and the voice. The instructions for the viol are of the most meagre description, merely pointing out that the neck (tuning and fretting) of the lute and the viol are the same and that the lessons, in tablature, at the end of the book, may serve for both instruments. They form an interesting collection. About Thomas Robinson's life no particulars are obtainable.

WILLIAM BRADE, an Englishman born during the second half of the sixteenth century, was at the commencement of the seventeenth century "bass viol player to the town of Hamburg," as he styles himself in 1609, and following years. He published: "Paduanen," "Galliarden," "Canzonetten," etc., 1900; "Neue Paduanen und Gagliarden mit stimmen," 1614; "Neue Lustige Volten Couranten, Balletten," etc., 1621, in five and six parts. He died in Frankfort in 1647.

JOHN JENKINS, born 1592 at Maidstone, in Kent, may be regarded as the patriarch of English bass viol players, and composed numerous works for bass viols. His amiable temperament secured him many friends, and after the Commonwealth had deprived him of his royal patron, he spent the rest of his life as the guest of his many friends among the English nobility, staying first with one and then with another at their country houses. He died October 29, 1678, at the advanced age of eighty-six, at the residence of the L'Estrange family in Kimberley (Norfolk). The assertion of Wasielewski that he was in the direct service of Charles I seems to be unfounded, as he does not appear among the King's musicians. Roger North gives a lengthy account of John Jenkins in his "Memoirs," in which he relates many anecdotes about him. He says that of his compositions there were "cartloads," which were dispersed about, and very few collected by any one amateur. He supplied in a great measure all the chamber music for the England of his time, and it stood in high favour with amateurs as his style was new, and his technical resources in the treatment of his instrument were greater than those of his predecessors and contemporaries. Roger North says: "He could hardly forbear divisions and some of his consorts were too full of them." He was often in a merry humour, and would compose catches, and some strains called Rants. The Mitter Rant in Playford's "Musik's Handmaid" (1678), as also the Fleece Tavern Rant and the Peterborough Rant were favourite airs of the time. He wrote a piece called the "Cryers of Newgate," which was all humour and very bizarre. But his most popular piece was "The Bells," composed at the request of Lady Katherine Audley, who had resided in the Netherlands and acquired a love for carillons. The piece was called "The Lady Katherine Audley's Bells, or the Five Bell Consort," and it was played everywhere. Burney gives the piece in his history of music. He has also written a three-part fancy, "The Bells." Others of Jenkins's pieces may be found in Playford's "Musick's Recreation on the Lyra Violl" (London, 1652). It was the lyra viol which we have described above, which was particularly cultivated by Jenkins. The "lyra viol" was a bass viol with a different tuning from the one described at the beginning of this chapter, and will be explained later on. The British Museum contains also a considerable number of his compositions for the bass viol in manuscript. In 1666 he published "Twelve Sonatas for two Violins and a Bass," with a thorough bass for the organ, and some vocal compositions.

The reason which Roger North gives for the early and total disappearance of Jenkins's compositions is "that his style was thought to be slow, heavy, moving from concord to concord, and consequently dull." He says, moreover, that it was a general weakness of English composers to move too much by step "without much saltation or battering, as the Italians use." The loss of Jenkins's early compositions is mourned by North, as he thinks they were better in that respect, and more lively. He says that he possessed "true musicall ayre" in his passages. Ward says of him that he was "a little man but a great soul." The later compositions were adapted to the capacity of his friends in diverse country-families with whom he spent the latter part of his life. Some of his more elaborate pieces of that period were sent by him to:

THEODORUS STEFKINS (Steiffkin, Stepkin, Steffken—the last was probably the correct spelling of the name), who lived during the latter half of the seventeenth century. His brother Dietrich was in 1636 appointed by Charles as musician for the consort in place of Maurice Webster, lutenist; and his sons FREDERIK and CHRISTIAN were both famous performers on the viol. They were members of the Royal band of William III in 1694.

A contemporary of Jenkins, who excelled as bass viol player, and still more as a composer, was:

JOHN COOPER, called Coperario, born about 1570. He studied music in Italy and it was during that time that he

Italianised his name. After his return to England he was appointed by James I teacher of the Royal children, and he found a talented pupil in Henry, Prince of Wales, a highly gifted and promising prince, who died in early youth. At his death Coperario wrote his "Songs of Mourning for the Voice, Lute and Bass Viol," which rank among his most inspired compositions. The author frequently produces two of these beautiful songs with accompaniment of two bass viols (instead of lute and viol) and harpsichord. Prince Henry's brother, afterwards Charles I, who was likewise Coperario's pupil, was an excellent performer on the bass viol; it is said that he even played the organ fantasias of his master on the viol. During this time Ben Jonson, John Daniel and Dr. Campion wrote the "Masques for the Court," which were composed by the last-named poet, Ferrabosco the younger, Nicholas Laniére, Thomas Lupo, Nathaniel Giles and Coperario.

The "Masque of Flowers" presented by the gentlemen of Graies-Inne, at the Court of Whitehall in 1613, was composed by Coperario. It was one of the most brilliant of its kind in the production of which fabulous sums were expended on scenery and dress. Coperario was also the master of WILLIAM and HENRY LAWES, destined to play a prominent part in the history of English music. They received their musical training at the expense of the Earl of Hertford, and though essentially composers and organists, they were also bass viol players and contributed both to the literature of the gamba. Charles I was an ardent admirer of William Lawes, and when the latter fell at Chester the King wore particular mourning for him. William Lawes was also an excellent lute player and was in 1625 appointed musician-in-ordinary for the lute and voice. He died in 1626, when Alfonso Ferrabosco was nominated in his place, and Henry Ferrabosco (son of the former?) was appointed as "composer of the King's Musicke" at a salary of forty pounds.

DANIEL FARRANT appears as a viol player in Charles I's private music. Playford, who calls him Farunt, tells us that he was the inventor of two musical instruments, the polyphant and the stump, two instruments strung with wire, and that he also introduced sympathetic strings for the lyra viol. Playford says: "Of this sort of viols I have seen many, but time and disuse has set them aside." Bass viols with sympathetic strings are scientifically discussed in Bacon's "Natural History" (1620-5); they were called gamba or lyra d'amore. The latter expression refers to the *sympathetic vibrations*, and has nothing to do with love, as has commonly, but erroneously, been supposed.

THOMAS SIMPSON, who lived at the beginning of the seventeenth century, was in the service of the Prince of Holstein-Schaumburg. He published "Opusculum neuer Pavanen Galliarden, Couranten und Volten" (Frankfort, 1610); "Pavanen, Volten, and Galliarden" (Frankfort, 1611); "Tafel-Consort, allerhand lustige Lieder von 4 Instrumenten und Generalbass" (Hamburg, 1621), (Table consort, all kind of merry songs for four instruments with a thorough bass). He published also some books on theoretical subjects in England. It would be interesting to know whether or not he was related, as appears very probable, to the following:

CHRISTOPHER SIMPSON, born about 1610, died at "Turnstile," Holborn, London, about 1677 *(see Plate II)*. He appears to have been by far the greatest English bass viol player. A staunch Royalist, he fought for the King under the Duke of Newcastle. After the fatal day of Marston Moor, Robert Bolles, a Royalist and Roman Catholic like Simpson, took him to his house in Leicestershire, where he instructed his son, John Bolles, on the bass viol. The latter was a talented amateur who died at Rome in 1676 and was buried in the Pantheon. The work which established Simpson's lasting fame was "The Division-Viol, or an introduction to the playing upon a Ground," divided in two parts, the first directing the hand, with other preparative instructions; the second laying open the method and manner of playing, or composing divisions to a ground. London, 1659. The second edition appeared as "Chelys Minuritionum artificio exornata, sive Minuritiones ad Basin, etiam extempore Modulandi ratio . . . . or the Division-Viol, etc.," London, 1667. The third edition with a fine portrait by Faithorne appeared in 1712. The work is preceded by eulogistic poems addressed to the author, as was the custom in those days. They are by John Carwarden, Edward Gelsthorp, Matthew Locke and John Jenkins, and all show that Simpson enjoyed the reputation of a great master on his instrument. We add the end of John Jenkins's poem as a specimen:

> Pack hence ye Pedants then, such as do bragg
> Of *Knowledge, Hand* or *Notes;* yet not one Ragg
> Of *Musick* have, more than what got by *Theft*
> Nor know true *Posture* of Right *Hand* or Left:
> False finger'd Crew, who seem to understand,
> Pretend to Make, when you but marre the *Hand.*
> You may desist; you'l find your trade decay:
> Simpson's great work will teach the world to Play.

A fuller account of the work is contained in the author's "The Revival of the Viols."

Of his compositions for the bass viol the library of the British Museum contains a book of twenty-one pieces (pavans, galliards, sarabands, courantes and gigs) for three viols which rank among the finest compositions of their time. Also four suites for two viols and bass entitled "The Seasons," which demand for their execution the powers of a virtuoso. The passage work is of the most florid style, employing very rapid figures. The examples given in "The Division-Viol" are of such excellence that Piatti considered it worth while to republish some in an arrangement for violoncello with pianoforte accompaniment (Schott and Co.). Other published works by Simpson are of a theoretical nature including his edition

Fig. 21. Gamba Player from Simpson's "Division-Viol."

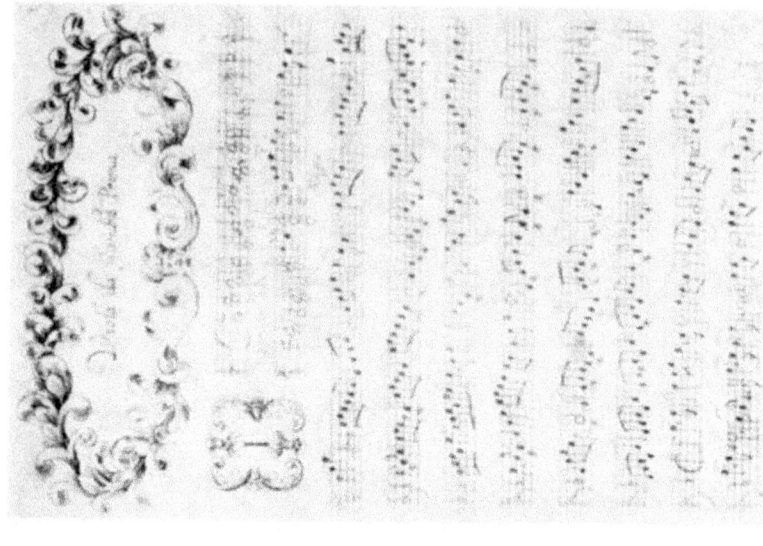

PLATE VII.

REPRODUCTIONS OF THE TITLE PAGE AND THE FIRST PAGE OF THE MUSIC OF KÜHNEL'S SONATAS FOR THE VIOL DA GAMBA. THE FIGURES OF THE PLAYERS ON THE TITLE PAGE REPRESENT A. KÜHNEL AND TWO MEMBERS OF HIS FAMILY

of Thomas Campion's "Art of Descant" which appeared in John Playford's introduction to the "Skill of Musick."

JOHN HINGSTON, a pupil of Orlando Gibbons, was a musician in Charles I's private band, but when the organ of Magdalen College was removed from Oxford to Hampton Court, about 1654 Cromwell appointed him as his organist, and music master of his daughters, with a salary of one hundred pounds per annum. He trained two boys to sing with him Deering's Latin songs for which Cromwell had a great liking, and often had them performed before him at the cockpit at Whitehall. He lived in St. James's Park where he gave concerts at which Cromwell was often present. Sir Roger L'Estrange in his pamphlet, "Truth and Loyalty Vindicated," London, 1662, in which he tries to clear himself of certain accusations, relates an instance of the Protector's visits, which procured for him the name of "Cromwell's fiddler":

"Concerning the story of the fiddle this might be the rise of it. Being in St. James's Park, I heard an organ touched in a little low room of one, Mr. Hinckson's; I went in, and found a private company of five or six persons; they desired me to take up a viol and bear a part, I did so, and that a part too, not much to advance the reputation of my coming. By and by, without the least colour of a design or expectation, in comes Cromwell. He found us playing, and as I remember so he left us." Hingston, according to Hawkins, was the first master of Dr. Blow, and a nephew of his, Peter, studied under Purcell and became organist at Ipswich. John Hingston was buried at St. Margaret's, Westminster, December 17, 1683. A portrait of his is in the music school at Oxford. The British Museum is in the possession of a number of his pieces for viols.

DR. JOHN ALCOCK, organist and composer, born in London, April 11, 1715, who died as lay vicar at Lichfield, was an executant on the bass viol for which he wrote a solo. (Mendel-Reissmann.)

THOMAS MACE, 1619-1709, a clerk of Trinity College, Cambridge, was a composer, writer on musical subjects and executant on the organ, lute and bass viol *(see Plate III)*. He wrote a most delightful book, "Musick's Monument; or a Remembrancer of the Best Practical Musick, both Divine and Civil, that has ever been known to have been in the World," London, 1676. It is divided into three parts which on account of the quaintness of the style, and the many interesting allusions to the customs and happenings of his times are most entertaining.

The first part deals with church music. The second book is: "The Noble Lute made Easie." The third book treats of the viol, the *generous viol* as he calls it sometime. In his introductory remarks he says: "I . . . . Love the Viol in a *very* High Degree; yea close unto the Lute: and I have done much more, and made very many more *Good* and *Able* Proficients upon It, than I ever have done upon the Lute.—And this I shall presume to say, That if I Excel in Either, it is most certainly upon the *Viol*."

We have already quoted his description of the "consorts" at which they played fancies in various parts to the organ. (See page 36.)

He gives also the plan of a "Musick-Roome, with conveniency for severall Sorts of Auditors" with the illustration of a table organ, as used with the viols, in the centre of the room. The esteem in which Mace was held by the university is shown by the many illustrious names from among its members, appearing in the list of subscribers to his book including Drs. Barrow, Cudworth and Isaac Newton. Sir Robert Bolles, a great amateur viol player and patron of Christopher Simpson, appears likewise among their number.

From the end of the sixteenth to the beginning of the eighteenth century the bass viol was the favourite instrument of an accomplished Englishman. In fact his education would hardly be considered as complete unless he could take up his part in consort. At Oxford musical meetings among the students and fellows of the colleges were a regular institution.

FRANCIS NORTH, LORD GUILDFORD, Keeper of the Grand Seal, 1637-85, and brother of Sir Roger North, the author of the well-known musical memoirs, was a performer on the bass viol, who often took his part in *consorts* as did also Dr. Nathaniel, afterwards Lord Crewe, Bishop of Durham. We have mentioned already that Charles I was an excellent performer on the bass viol in the playing of which he had been instructed by Coperario. It is said that although very fond of music he had a great aversion to the "fantasia."

SIR ROGER L'ESTRANGE (latter part of seventeenth century), the licenser of books in Charles II's times *(see Plate IV)*, has already been mentioned in connection with an incident at John Hingston's house, which procured for him the nickname of Cromwell's fiddler.

Evelyn speaks of him in his "Diary":

1656, March 4: "This night I was invited by Mr. Roger L'Estrange to hear the incomparable Lubicer on the violin."

This refers to Baltzar of Lübeck. Samuel Pepys has even more to say about him. Under date December 17, 1664, we find the following entry:

At noon I to change, and there had my first meeting with Mr. L'Estrange (Licensor of the Press and Pamphleteer) who has endeavoured several times to speak with me. It is to get, now and then some newes of me, which I shall, as I see cause, give him. He is a man of fine conversation, I think, but I am sure most courtly and full of compliments.

It is curious that he does not mention his musical talents as Pepys was himself an ardent musical amateur.

He was connected with various city concerts as, for instance, that of the two Youngs held at the Castle Tavern. The most notable of these concerts was that of:

THOMAS BRITTON, the famous musical small coalman, born at Higham Ferrers in Yorkshire in 1651. Britton came to

London and settled in Jerusalem Passage, where eventually he took over his master's business as a small coalman, spending his leisure hours in the study of science and art. Over a kind of stable serving for his warehouse he constructed a music-room, the only access to which was by means of a little wooden staircase fixed on the outer wall. In this room he founded a music club which was patronised by the highest aristocracy. His deep learning and great modesty endeared him to people of fashion and fame. Handel sometimes played the organ at his concerts and many famous artists came to his humble abode. Matthew Dubourg, the celebrated violinist, made his debut there at the age of nine. Britton was a good executant on the bass viol and possessed three fine instruments, one by Jay, described as "the finest he ever made," one by Baker, of Oxford, and one by Barak Norman all being enumerated in the catalogue of his instruments which were sold after his death which took place in 1714. It was accelerated by a practical joke. A member of his club brought with him to one of the meetings a ventriloquist, named Honeyman, from Bear Street, Leicester Square. This man announced in sepulchral tones that sounded as from afar, that Britton would die within a few hours unless he fell on his knees immediately and said the Lord's Prayer. The poor man did so without hesitation, but the shock was so great that he went home, took to his bed and died within a few days on September 27, 1714, at the age of sixty-three. He was buried on the first of October in the churchyard of St. James, Clerkenwell.

Throughout the seventeenth century England was considered the "high school" for viol da gamba playing, and many eminent musicians came to London to perfect themselves in that art. Maugars, among others, came from France; Paul Kress, David Adams, W. L. Vogelsang, August Kühnel, etc., from Germany. Mersenne, in his "Harmonie Universelle," gives a fragment of an English six-part "Fancye" to show the use and technique of the viol da gamba.

English bass viol players, in fact (as Dr. Einstein justly remarks), advanced the technique of their instrument to a higher standard than that of the violin *in any country* during the seventeenth century.

Charles II did not share his father's love for the bass viol, who, as well as his brother, Prince Henry, was a fair executant thereon, and pupil of Coperario.

Charles II loved the violin and lively tunes to which he could beat time with his foot in an audible manner. Henry Purcell, the great master of his chapel, had also an aversion to the viol, while his friend, the Sub-Dean Gosling, was an ardent lover of that instrument. Purcell induced a friend of his to write him the following mock eulogium which he set in the form of a round for three voices, to tease his friend the dean. The round appeared in "The Pleasant Musical Companion," published by John Playford in 1701. The words are:

> Of all the instruments that are,
> None with the viol can compare:
> Mark how the strings their order keep,
> With a whet, whet, whet, and a sweep, sweep, sweep.
> But above all this still abounds,
> With a zingle, zingle, zing, and a zit, zan, zounds.

ANN FORD, born in London, February 22, 1737, and died there January 20, 1824, may be looked upon as the last English bass viol player. She was considered a rival of the famous C. F. Abel. Miss Ford married the Hon. P. Thicknesse. Her portrait was painted by Gainsborough *(see Plate V)*. She was also a noted executant on the musical glasses for which she published an instruction book.

THE VIOL DA GAMBA IN GERMANY.

We have seen already that the art of viol making had been communicated by the German makers to the Italians during the fifteenth century. That does not imply that it should have drifted out of the former country.

The town of Nuremberg, in particular, was always noted for its artistic atmosphere, and the prominent part it took in music and musical instrument making. It was here that Hans Frey (see page 18), was born, as well as his son John, a celebrated wood carver and clever musician, who died there in 1523; Conrad Müller (see page 18); Conrad Gerle, a famous lute maker, about 1462. He died in 1521 on the eve of St. Barbara, and is buried in the church of St. Rochus. His eldest son Hans, already mentioned as the author of "Musica Teusch," 1532, died in Nuremberg in 1570, with the reputation of a great musician, composer, executant and instrument maker. In the latter capacity he was rivalled by his younger brother, whose name was also Hans Gerle.

LAUXMIN POSSEN, whose name as a lute maker was famous all over Europe, worked at Schongau about 1550, but removed to Munich in 1564 on his appointment as instrument maker to the Chapel Royal. Johann Kohl succeeded him in 1599. Above all these there shone two great stars in the history of bass viol making: KASPAR TIEFFENBRUCKER, known as Duiffoprugcar, of Freising, and JOACHIM TIELKE, of Hamburg. The former has been mentioned in Chapter II, page 13; the name of the latter appears from 1539, till about 1702, on instruments which are miracles of workmanship in ebony, ivory, gold, silver and precious stones. Needless to say, the name applied to several generations of that family. Vidal gives the date of

Tielke as 1539-1686. Gerber says Tielke lived from 1660-1730. Lutgendorff says October, 1641, to September 19, 1719.

George Hart gives the date of the first Joachim Tielke as about 1539-92. There is a chiterna of his bearing the former date in the Kensington Museum. The body is ornamented with tortoiseshell, with mythological figures of Italian draughtsmanship in ivory and precious stones. A guitar of a similar kind is in the Donaldson Collection. It is dated 1592, and considered the finest known work by that master. So far we do not know of any viols by the first Joachim Tielke who was a contemporary of Duiffoprugcar. The great viol (and violin) maker of that name lived about 1660-86. One of his most beautiful instruments is a bass viol made for William, the Elector Palatine (1690-1716) to whom Corelli dedicated his "Concerti Grossi" (published 1712). It is now in the National Museum at Munich. The back, ribs, tailpiece, neck and fingerboard are decorated with the most exquisite designs of allegorical and mythological figures, arabesques and flower designs inlaid in ivory, silver and mother-of-pearl on a background of ebony and tortoiseshell. In the upper part of the back is a figure (the Prince Palatine?) in the centre of a medallion. The pegbox and carved head are cut out of one solid piece of ivory.* Two other fine bass viols by the same maker exhibited by M. Wilmotte, of Antwerp, at the Paris Exhibition in 1878 are dated 1669 and 1701. The former which is also richly inlaid is now in the museum of the Brussels Conservatoire. It is a six-stringed instrument, total length, 1.31 metre; largest width, .410 metre; height of ribs, .135 metre. The latter instrument, of 1701, which at one time belonged to François Servais, the great violoncellist, is described in Hipkins's "Musical Instruments, Historical, Rare and Unique" (Edinburgh, 1887-8). The bass viol was an

---

* An illustration of this gamba may be found in E. van der Straeten's "The Revival of the Viols."

important component of the German orchestra of the seventeenth century, where it was in great demand for the accompaniment of voices. An instance of this will be found in HEINRICH SCHÜTZ'S preface to his "Fröhliche Auferstehung, etc." (Resurrection), 1623. He says with regard to the part of the evangelist: "If one can have four *viole da gamba* it is better to let the organ and other instruments be silent, the viols alone accompanying the voice." He goes on to explain the necessity of practising the parts well together, as the evangelist should recite his part as he would speak it in ordinary life, while the viols play the "falso bordone"; "one among their number breaking up the chords in arpeggios as is customary and of good effect." This manner of playing the accompaniment in recitative was afterwards allotted to the violoncello as we shall see anon.

FRANCK MELCHIOR, born about 1580, at Zittau (Lausitz), lived about 1600 in Nuremberg. In 1603 he became master of the ducal chapel at Coburg where he died in June, 1639 (Gerber says June 1; Mendel, June 6). He was chiefly a church and song composer and some of his sacred songs are still used in parts of Germany. Like all prominent musicians of his time he was no doubt a gambist and lutenist as well as an organist, and among the list of his compositions contained in Gerber's lexicon there are a great number of instrumental pieces:

5. Opusculum etlicher neuer and alter Reuter Liedlein (cavalier's songs) to be executed (musiciret) in all manner of ways in four parts. Nuremberg, 1603; 6. New Quodlibet in four parts. Magdeburg (also Nuremberg and Francfort), 1604; No. 10. German Songs and Dances in four parts (four Stimmen means "voices" as well as parts). Coburg, 1605; No. 12. New Musical Intradas to be used for all kinds of instruments especially Viols, in six parts, printed at Nuremberg by Balthasar Scherff. Published by David Kaufmanns, 1608. A

PLATE VIII.

JOHANN SCHENCK. FROM AN ENGRAVING IN THE POSSESSION OF MESSRS.
W. E. HILL AND SONS.

complete copy exists at Danzig and an incomplete copy at Wolfenbüttel. They have been republished in "Denkmaeler Deutscher Tonkunst" (Breitkopf and Härtel). 13. Flores musicales, new and graceful musical flowers in four, five, six and seven parts. Nuremberg, 1610. 14. Musicalische Fröhlichkeit (Mus. Jollity), songs and dances, galliards and concerts, etc. Leipzig, 1610. 17. VI Teutsche Concerte (German concerts) in eight parts, 1611. 28. Lilia musicalia, nice new little songs with merry words, together with pavans, galliards and courantes. Nuremberg, 1616. There are altogether forty-four numbers and in some cases it is not clear whether the works are for instruments or voices, in some cases as the "Newes liebliches musicalisches Lustgärtlein" (of all manner of German love (amorischen) songs), he directs "at honest (ehrlichen) convivials to be used for *voice* and *instrument.*" The "XXXX Teutsche lustige musicalische Tänze" (forty merry German dances) in four parts. Jena, 1624. Were no doubt for instruments only.

ZACHARIAS FUELLSACK and CHRISTIAN HILDEBRAND, musicians to the town of Hamburg, published a book of bass viol pieces at that town in 1607 and 1609, containing also pieces by William Brade, Joh. Sommer, Holborn (?, evidently an Englishman), Melchior, Borchgreving, B. Grep, Thos. Mons, Jac. Schulz, etc.

DIETRICH BUXTEHUDE (1637-1707), composed seven sonatas for violin, viol da gamba and harpsichord. This work is in so far of the greatest interest as being one of the first, if not *the* first instance of a combination of instruments which gradually lead up to the pianoforte trio. One of these sonatas has been recently republished by Messrs. Breitkopf and Härtel, unfortunately only in score.

Although Germany could boast of some of the greatest viol players during the early part of the sixteenth century, we do not hear of any prominent viol da gamba player until about the middle of the seventeenth century. One of the first German gambists concerning whom we possess any information was:

GEORG NEUMARK, born at Mühlhausen in Thuringia, May 16, old style (28, new style), 1621, died July 8, 1681, at Weimar *(see Plate VI).* He visited the "Gymnasium" (grammar school) at Schleusingen and Gotha. In 1640 he intended to *tramp* to Königsberg in Prussia to enter the university as a law student, but on the road he fell into the hands of robbers who took away all the money intended to pay for his studies and maintenance. Being an excellent viol da gamba player he walked from place to place earning his livelihood by his musical talent. In 1641 he arrived at Kiel where he obtained the position of a "paedagogus" (school teacher). There he composed the song, "Wer nur den lieben Gott lässt walten" (who only will place his trust in the Lord) which is a household song to this day. In 1643 he went via Lubeck to Königsberg. In 1646 he lost once more everything he possessed in a fire. He left Königsberg for Danzig, where he remained some time, but in 1649 we find him in Thorn, where he published a book of songs, "Keuscher Liebesspiegel."

1650 he was in Hamburg and 1651 in Weimar where he obtained a government position as librarian to the prince. In 1653 he became a member of the "Fruchtbringende Gesellschaft" under the pseudo name, "Der Sprossende" (the budding—sprouting. See inscription on portrait.) In the same year he became "archivar" (head librarian). He filled the post of poet laureate to the court, writing all manner of occasional poetry for the prince and his household. In 1653 he was admitted to the Order of the Pegnitz Sheppards (a society of arcadian lyricists) by the name of Thyrsis II. His songs of which there are many still known, are of the simple folk-song character. Of Neumark's compositions for the gamba none appear to have been preserved. In his "Fortgepflanzten Musikalisch-poetischen Lustwald" he employs two gambas in the accompaniment to a wedding song, one playing the bass the other a florid accompaniment, and adds that it was really intended for two gambas tuned in the chord of F minor.

HOTMANN or HOTTEMANN, a gambist of German origin, lived in Paris during the early part of the seventeenth century. As he is closely bound up with the history of gamba playing in France we shall speak of him when treating of the French gambists.

DAVID FUNK, born at Reichenbach in Saxony about 1630. The biographical notice contained in Gerber's "Dictionary" was supplied by the chief cantor, John Martin Steindorf, of Zwickau, who was personally acquainted with Funk. That notice describes him as "an excellent musician and master on the violin, viol da gamba, angelique (a lute species), the clavichord (klavier) and the guitar." "In fact," he says, "Funk was in the true sense of the word a genius. His principal study, in which he acquired no mean perfection, was that of the law. Moreover he was a *bel esprit* and a poet, and he was classed among the good German poets of his time. As musician (tonkünstler) he was not only a virtuoso on all the above enumerated instruments, but also a composer and he gained the approbation of his public in various styles, for the church as well as the house (cammer-chamber). In his "Drama Passionale" he wrote a Jew's chorus imitating the vocal manner of that nation with a degree of truth sufficient to persuade the auditors that they are in the middle of a synagogue.

He was appointed "cantor" of his native town, and in 1660 he received the post of private secretary to the Duchess of East Frisia, whom he followed to Italy in 1682. After the decease of the duchess in 1689 he returned to Germany and led an unsettled and dissipated life until necessity compelled him, being then nearly sixty years old, to accept the humble post of organist and master of a girl's school at Wunsiedel (Wohnsiedel), which afterwards became known to the world as the birthplace of Jean Paul. Misconduct drew upon him the wrath of the people in the town, and he was compelled to seek safety in flight. After many wanderings he arrived one day in an abject condition at the castle of Count Schleitz, and asked at the gate for permission to play before the count on the "klavier" (either harpsichord or clavichord is meant here). The audition took place in the presence of the court and the master of the prince's music and court organist, and Funk acquitted himself to the admiration of all.

The count gave him an appointment, but a warrant for his arrest had been issued at Wunsiedel, and he had to leave Schleitz before three months had elapsed. The count provided him with means and he set out for Arnstadt, hoping to find safety at the little court of Schwarzburg. He never reached his destination, for a few weeks later he was found dead under a hedge. His compositions, especially those written for the church, were highly praised, and a "Drama Passionale" to which he wrote also the words, was looked upon as one of the greatest masterpieces. A chorus of the Jews contained in it was known and admired all over Germany. Unfortunately it has never been printed. His only published compositions were: "Davidi Funccii/ Bohemi/ Stricturæ/ Viola di Gambicae/ ex/ Sonatis, Ariis, Intradis/ Allemandis, etc./ Quatuor/ Violis da gamba/ concinendis/ promicantes/ Lipsiae, Jenae and Rudolstadii/ apud Johannem Theodorum Christopf/ and David Fleischern/ Anno MDCLXXXVII" (a collection of pieces for four gambas), advertised in the German periodical, "Walther," of 1670, and his "Compendium Musices." A copy of the former work is preserved in the National Library in Paris.

AUGUST KÜHNEL, born August 3, 1645, at Delmenhorst in Oldenburg, was not only a great virtuoso on the viol da gamba and the baryton, but he also ranks with the best composers of his time. It has been stated that he was a pupil of the famous Agostine Steffani in composition, but there appears nothing to substantiate this theory. At the early age of sixteen he entered the court chapel of Duke Maurice of Saxe-Zeitz, and remained a member of this orchestra from 1661 until the duke's death in 1681. In 1665 he visited France in order to acquaint himself with the art of the famous French gambists. The state papers of the Saxon court mention him in 1670 as court viol da gambist at Zeitz. In 1678 he visited the court at Dresden, where, according to Eitner, he received forty thaler (six pounds) a year. Eitner does not state the source of this information.* The sum mentioned may refer to a present from the court, as Kühnel did not leave the service of Duke Maurice. In 1680 he played at the court of the Elector Max Emmanuel, who was himself an executant on the viol da gamba, and admired Kühnel so greatly that he offered to appoint him at his court whenever he should consider himself at liberty. As a further inducement he told him that his conversion to the Roman Catholic faith would not be insisted upon, although it was a strict rule that none but Roman Catholics should be employed at the Bavarian court.

After the death of Duke Maurice, Kühnel wrote to the private secretary, Prielmair, at Munich on September 6, 1682, referring to the Elector's offer, and asking if it would be safe for him to undertake the journey to Munich in view of "the contagion" (the plague). Baron von Rechberg, on the elector's behalf, instructed Prielmair to answer that Kühnel might come if he would first embrace the Roman Catholic religion. His wife and child need not do so for the present as "by the grace of God and the father's example" that would no doubt come to pass in due course. Kühnel, who was a staunch Protestant, refused, in a letter dated October 15 (25?), 1682, to accept under those conditions, and told Prielmair that he

---

* Fürstenau, "Gesch. d. Musik in Sachsen," 1861, I, 9.

would start within a few days on a journey to England, "to find out what viol players there were in that country from which the viol da gamba had come." He hopes to pass through Holland without going into quarantine, and promises to write again on his return in the following spring. (Letters published in "Denkmäler der Tonkunst," in Bayern, 1901.) Of this visit there appears no record in England, neither is it known what became of Kühnel until we come across the following advertisement in "The London Gazette," Thursday, November 19, to Monday, November 23, 1685:

> Several Sonatas composed after the Italian way, for one and two Bass Viols with a Thorough-Basse, being upon the request of several Lovers of Musick (who have already subscribed) to be Engraven upon copper Plates are to be perform'd on Thursday next, and every Thursday following at six of the clock in the Evening, at the Dancing School in Walbrook, next door to the Bell Inn, and on Saturday next and every Saturday after at the Dancing School in York Buildings, at which places will be also some performance on the Barritone, by Mr. August Keenell, the Author of this Musick. Such who do not subscribe, are to pay their Half Crown, towards the discharge of performing it.

In 1686 he was back in Cassel, according to an entry in the state papers of that court:

> 1686. To the Violdagambist, Aug. Kühnel, for fiddle strings ("Geigenseiten"). 6 g. 15 alb.

In 1687 the Landgrave appointed him violdagambist and director of the instrumental music at a salary of three hundred florins per annum; the appointment to become operative from April 1, 1686. Some time after this he went to Weimar as "vicekapellmeister" to the Duke Wilhelm Ernst. There we find him in 1695. In that year the Landgrave of Cassel, with the hereditary Prince Frederic (afterwards King of Sweden) and some princesses, paid a visit to the court of Weimar, and in July of the same year Kühnel was appointed kapellmeister to the Landgrave of Hesse, and took up his residence at Cassel. His sonatas were not published before 1698. They testify not only to his absolute mastery of style and form, but also to his inventive genius. As an executant on his instrument he must likewise have been in the front rank for none but a virtuoso could attempt to play some of his partitas. Two of these called "Serenata" and "Echo" respectively, are evidently written for the use of amateurs, as they are easy from a technical point, while containing melodies of the greatest charm. Both have been provided with additional pianoforte accompaniments by the author, and figure frequently in his concerts of ancient music. An interesting analysis of Kühnel's compositions may be found in Dr. Alfred Einstein's "Zur Deutschen Literatur für Viola da Gamba im 16$^{\text{ten.}}$ and 17$^{\text{ten.}}$ Jahrhundert" (Breitkopf and Härtel), with extracts from his sonatas.

The tenth sonata is based upon the chorale, "Herr Jesu Christ du höchstes Gut," slightly modified to suit his requirements. If we remember the attempt on the part of the Elector of Bavaria to convert him to the Roman Catholic religion, the use of this Protestant chorale gains a special signficance, as it appears as a simple-hearted protestation of his unalterable faith. The use of church tunes and even secular melodies as subject matter for compositions of various kinds was of common occurrence among seventeenth and early eighteenth century composers, so much so, in fact, that a list of instances would contain the name of almost every composer of note of that period. The date of Kühnel's death is unknown; it occurred according to Mendel about 1700. The title page of his sonatas *(see Plate VII)* shows Kühnel with two members of his family. His instrument appears to be of an early type as it has a large centre rosette between the upper part of the soundholes. The line of the upper bouts is broken by an angle near the neck, and the peg-box ends in a faint attempt at a scroll. A reproduction of the title page, as well as a page from the book itself, are given *(see Plate VII)*.

AUGUST KÜHNEL (II), about whom very little is known, was "Hofkapellmeister" (master of the music) at the court of Zeitz about the same period that the former A. Kühnel was there as solo gambist (Konzertmeister). On September 26, 1682, he was appointed organist at the Church of St. Thomas at Leipzig, and died 1684.

JOHANN MICHAEL KÜHNEL was a virtuoso on the lute and on the bass viol during the latter part of the seventeenth century. He was for some years attached to the court of Berlin, whence he went to Weimar in 1717, and afterwards joined the orchestra of the famous Marshal Flemming at Dresden. The remainder of his life he appears to have spent at Hamburg. He published through Roger in Amsterdam "Sonates à 1 et 2 violes de gambe" in 1730.

JOHANN SCHENCK, born after the middle of the seventeenth century, probably at or near Düsseldorf on the Rhine, where the name is not infrequent, and where he began his career at the court of the Prince Palatine towards the end of that century. He was one of the greatest viol da gambists of his time, and a composer of distinct merit. He wrote six important works for his instrument:

1. Konst oeffeningen, quinzes Sonates à une Basse de viole et Basse continue opera 2. Amsterdam, 1688.
2. Il Giardino armonico consistente in diverse Sonate a due violini, viola di gamba e basso continuo, Op. 3. Amsterdam, 1692.
3. Scherzi Musicali per la viola di gamba con Basso continuo ad libitum Da Giovanni Schenck, opera Sesta, *ibid.*, in oblong folio.
4. La Ninfa del Rheno, contenant douze Sonates pour basse de viole composés de Preludes, Allemandes, Sarabandes, etc., Op. 8.
5. L'Echo de la Danube, contenant six Sonates, dont les

PLATE IX.

PORTRAIT OF CONRAD HÖFFLER FROM "PRIMITIÆ CHELICÆ."

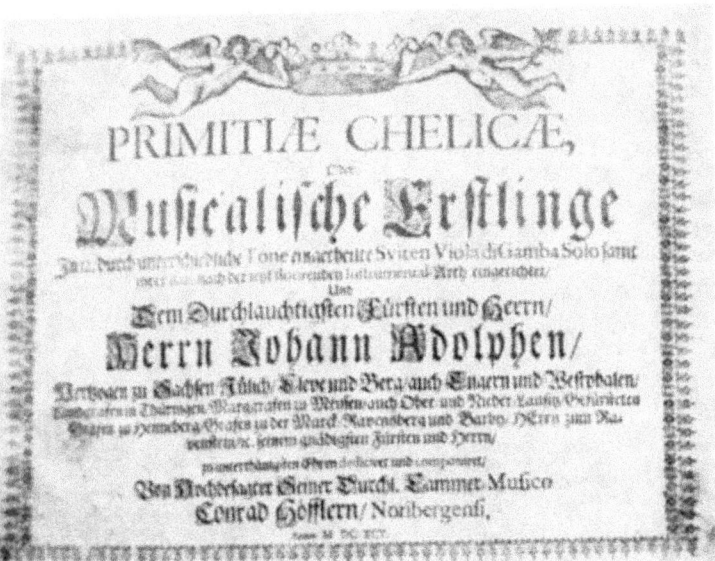

PLATE X.

TITLE PAGE OF HÖFFLER'S "PRIMITIÆ CHELICÆ."

To face page 64.

deux premières sont à une viole de gambe et une Basse continue, les deux suivantes à une Viole de gambe et une Basse continue ad libitum et les deux dernières à une Viole de Gambe seule. Dédié à son Excellence Monsieur le Baron de Diamanstein, Conseiller intime, Grand Chambellan, Grand Fauconnier et Surintendant de la Musique de son Altesse Electoralle Palatine, etc., par Jean Schenck, Commissaire, homme de chambre et Musicien de la chambre de S. A. Electoralle Palatine—Œuvre IX—Prix 9lb—Gravée par Joseph Renon—à Paris chez: Mr. Le Clerc le Cadet, rue St. Honoré vis-à-vis de l'Oratoire; Le Sieur le Clerc, rue du Roule à la Croix d'Or; Mme. Boivin, rue St. Honoré, à la Regle d'Or. Avec Privilège du Roy.

6. Les Fantaisies Bisarres de la Goutte/ contenant XII Sonates pour une Viole de Gambe Seule avec la Basse continue,/ ou avec une autre Viole de Gambe ou Theorbe .... Par .... Jean Schenck, Conseiller de la Chambre des/ Finances, Commissaire Receveur de la licence, Homme de Chambre and Musicien de la/ Chambre de Son Altesse Serenissime Monseigneur l'Electeur Palatin./ Dixième Ouvrage/ A Amsterdam aux depens d'Estienne Roger and le Cene Libraire.

Of this work, unfortunately, the basso continuo only has been preserved in the Royal Library in Berlin.

Only two of these works appear to be still in existence: "Scherzi Musicali" and "L'Echo de la Danube." A copy of the former is in the library at Sondershausen, while Mr. Paul Pannier, of Lille, was fortunate enough to secure a MS. copy of the latter work, of which he had the kindness to present the author with a copy. Both works testify to Schenck's virtuosity. They abound with difficult passages, runs, double stopping and chords. They are in the form of sonatas or suites. Although they lack the terseness and symmetry of form of the Italian masters of that time yet they show more unity and coherence, and are a much nearer approach to the Italian "suite" or chamber sonata than the works of the contemporary French composers who, after the customary prelude and allemande string together an indefinite number of dances and airs having no internal connection, and only the outward sign of unity of key to hold them together.

As Schenck has been rather sharply criticised by some historians, it appears but just that we should give a short analysis of his extant works, as they certainly rank among the most important monuments of viol da gamba literature (see also Dr. Alfred Einstein's very able analysis in "Zur deutschen Litteratur für Viola da Gamba").

The hundred and one pieces of the "Scherzi Musicali" group themselves into thirteen suites, although the composer has not formally indicated this by headings, yet the arrangement clearly proves it, as may be seen from the following list of contents in which we have indicated the division:

Suite No. 1, in G minor. (1), Preludium; (2), Allemande; (3), Courante; (4), Tempo di Sarabande; (5), Gigue; (6), Tempo di Gavotte.

No. 2, F. (7), Fantasia; (8), Praeludium; (9), Allemande; (10), Allemande; (11), Courant; (12), Courant; (13), Sarabande; (14), Variatio; (15), Tempo di Gavotte; (16), Tempo di Sarabande; (17), Ciaccone; (18), Gigue; (19), Tempo di Passagato; (20), Gigue.

No. 3, B minor. (21), Preludium; (22), Allemande; (23), Courante; (24), Sarabande; (25), Variatio; (26), Gigue.

No. 4, A minor. (27), Sonata; (28), Adagio, Vivace,

SCHENCK'S "SCHERZI MUSICALI."

Allegro, Adagio, Canzona, Adagio, Alla Breve, Adagio, Allemande; (29), Courant; (30), Sarabande; (31), Gigue.

No. 5, A minor. (32), Fantasia; (33), Allemande; (34), Courant; (35), Sarabande; (36), Variatio; (37), Gigue.

No. 6, A minor. (38), Praeludium; (39), Allemande; (40), Courante; (41), Sarabande; (42), Gigue; (43), Gigue; (44), Gavotte; (45), Rondeau; (46), Boure; (47, 48, 49), Three Menuets; (50), Tempo di Passagallo.

No. 7, A major. (51), Praeludium; (52), Allemande; (53), Courant; (54), Sarabande; (55), Gigue; (56), Gigue; (57), Gigue; (58), Rondeau; (59), Menuet.

No. 8, E minor. (60), Preludium; (61), Allemande; (62), Courant; (63), Sarabande; (64), Gigue; (65), Menuet.

No. 9, G major. (66), Overture; (67), Adagio, Allegro, Adagio, Allabreve, Adagio, Aria; (68), Menuet; (69), Tempo di Gavotto; (70), Boure; (71), Aria; (72), Capriccio.

No. 10, G major. (73), Preludium; (74), Allemande; (75), Courant; (76), Chacone.

No. 11, D major. (77), Capriccio; (78), Fuga; (79), Allemande; (80), Courant; (81), Sarabande; (82), Gigue; (83), Menuet.

No. 12, D minor. (84), Preludium; (85), Allemande; (86), Courant; (87), Tempo di Sarabande; (88), Gigue; (89), Tempo di Gavotta.

No. 13, D minor. (90), Preludium; (91), Ouverture; (92), Adagio, Allegro, Adagio, Tempo di Gavotta; (93), Tempo di Sarabande; (94), Gigue; (95), Fuga; (96), Caprice; (97), Allemande; (98), Courant; (99), Courant; (100), Sarabande; (101), Gigue.

As we know the Italian "sonata di camera" or "suite" consisted of an introduction (generally though not invariably a prelude), and four dance movements: allemande, courante, sarabande and gigue. At the end of the seventeenth century another dance movement was generally interpolated between the sarabande and gigue, and this consisted as a rule of either two minuets, gavottes, bourrés, braules, passepieds or similar movements, of which the second served as "alternativo" to the first. If we examine Schenck's suites from this standpoint we find that he has kept fairly close to the accepted form.

The first suite brings the gavotte *after* the gigue. There is no reason why it should not be played before to satisfy the most punctilious mind, and the suite would be quite correct. The second is really a combination of two suites in which all movements appear twice: fantasia, praeludium (two introductions), two allemandes, two courantes, one sarabande with variations and one tempo di sarabande, two gigues. If we take the tempo di gavotte as fifth dance movement for one, and the ciaconne or passagato for the other, we find only one movement more than the strict rule would allow, although the jumble of movements and contraction of two suites into one would not be defensible if Schenck intended them to appear by that name. No. 3 is a suite in the strict sense of the word. No. 4 brings a complete "sonata da chiesa" as introduction to the suite. This is not a solitary example, as we find A. Kühnel doing exactly the same in his delightful serenata for two gambas and continuo, but Schenck was apparently the first to apply this form to viol da gamba music. The following movements in Schenck's suite keep strictly to the orthodox four. No. 5 again makes no exception, only bringing a fantasia instead of prelude, which was a favourite way with the French composers, of whom Schenck had a thorough knowledge as all eminent German gambists, many of whom went to study in Paris.

Let it be stated that we do not insinuate any slavish imitation.

CONSTRUCTION OF SCHENCK'S SUITES. 69

Schenck was essentially German in his musical conception, and if he lacked the elegant grace and sweetness of a Marais, he rose sometimes to heights where the latter could not follow him. It is true that he takes liberties with his fugues, especially in the episodes where the desire to display the possibilities of his instrument induces him to overstep the limit, to introduce irregular entries of the subject and similar incongruities, to which the desire for technical display are answerable. On the whole, however, his fugues for the gamba keep much nearer to the strict form than those of the French gambists, which are merely pieces in fugal style or rather in imitative counterpoint introducing extraneous matter at any given moment without the slightest compunction. The subjects of Schenck's fugues, moreover, are of great strength, as, for instance, that of the fugue in D minor, in the thirteenth suite, which is identical with that used by Mozart in the second finale of the "Magic Flute."

The sixth suite commences with the usual order of movements, followed by an extra gigue, a gavotte, etc. *(see list)*. These movements, on closer examination, show more relationship than would appear at first glance.

This becomes patent from the rondeau onwards especially, see the following:

TEMPO DI PASSAGALLO 50

FIG. 22. THEMATIC RELATIONSHIP IN SCHENCK'S SIXTH SUITE.

It seems as if the possibilities of this motive had enticed him to see what he could do with it, without troubling whether it belonged organically to a suite or not, and as we pointed out before, he never mentions the word in connection with these pieces. No. 7 again has the usual movements, with the addition of two extra gigues, a rondeau and a minuet; No. 8 exceeds neither number nor order of pieces, except that the minuet follows the gigue instead of preceding it, and this is a notable feature with Schenck, that the fifth dance movement (minuet, gavotte, bourrée, etc.) is always placed in the same way.

No. 9 opens with an overture in the Italian style, finishing with a spirited "alla breve," followed by sundry movements *(see list)* which remind us distinctly of the French suite. Several of their number are particularly attractive and melodious. In No. 10 the courant is followed by a long chaconne which is only partly interesting. No. 11 opens with a fugue introduced by a capriccio, followed by the usual dance movements, and No. 12 keeps still more strictly to the rule, while No. 13 breaks entirely away from it.

While rising to a considerable height at times in his longer and worked-out movements, Schenck is unable to keep on that level. The desire to show off his instrument and his scholastic ability cause him to lose the thread of his inspiration to the detriment of his work. Among the dance movements, on the other hand, we find some perfect gems which are essentially gamba music.

In his later work, "L'Echo du Danube," he becomes more ambitious in employing the abstract forms of the "sonata di chiesa." The first of the two sonatas with continuo, in D major, is entirely in that style, although Schenck's evident striving after big proportions without the power of thematic development, caused him to destroy the beautiful symmetry we admire in the works of the Italian masters by adding extra movements. He begins with a strong and virile subject vivace in 3-4 time, followed by a kind of short moto perpetuo vivace in 4-4 time, with an "adagio e tremulo" of ten bars as a sort of coda. Next comes an expressive aria followed by an allegro in fugal style ending in a prestissimo (alla breve); then a noble adagio in 3-4 time, and an allegro 12-8, which partakes of the character of a gigue. The thematic invention is fine and lofty, and but for the lack of proportion, the work would compare well with the best contemporary work.

The second sonata opens with an adagio followed by a gigue and a corrente, then follows an adagio and vivace in the style of the church sonata. No. 3 is a suite finishing with a gavotte in place of the gigue.

No. 4 has a complete sonata da chiesa: adagio, allegro, adagio, prestissimo, followed by a complete suite: allemanda, corrente, sarabanda, giga, minuetto. We have seen this combination of church and chamber sonata once before in "Scherzi Musicali," and Kühnel's "Serenata," also Schenck's method of placing the minuet (or gavotte, etc.) after the gigue. The fifth sonata in E minor for gamba solo (unaccompanied) is of the nature of a suite: adagio, aria, gavotta, adagio, giga, aria; and the sixth sonata, also unaccompanied, is again a combination of both styles: adagio, a few bars of allegro as a kind of episode returning to the adagio followed by a presto. Another adagio, in the nature of an improvisation (see Christopher Simpson, "The Division Viol"), introduces an aria with several episodes, viz.: aria largo (I), vivace, largo (I), allegro, largo (new subject), largo

(I). The (I) indicates the subject of the "aria." Another aria follows and a giga ends the whole work.

If we have dwelt at great length upon Schenck's work it is not that he was so much greater than other gambist composers but that his work is typical and highly interesting with regard to form, invention and technique. If Kühnel was his superior in point of form, and Marais in pleasing grace, Schenck surpassed the former in the charm and wealth of his melodic invention and the latter in depth and power of his greater moments, especially in "L'Echo du Danube," while for the variety and freedom of his passage work, double stopping, chords, etc., he stands at the head of all. Höffler rivals him in successions of full chords, but he is, unfortunately, musically very uninteresting.

It is evident from the title pages of his works that they were all written while he lived at Düsseldorf, where he held various appointments at the court. According to Wasielewski the "Scherzi Musicali" were dedicated to the Elector Palatine Johann Wilhelm, to whom Corelli dedicated his "Concerti Grossi," and for whom Joachim Tielke made that exquisite gamba, a reproduction of which appears in "Revival of the Viols."

Schenck had risen to the position of chamberlain and chamber musician to the Prince Palatine, yet early in the eighteenth century he left the court and settled in Amsterdam. Mattheson tells us that he was made "bailiff of the fish market" in that town on account of his fine gamba playing. No doubt this was a sinecure which was offered as a compliment on account of the emoluments. It was during this time that the excellent portrait by Pet. Schenck (his brother?) was made, of which we give a reproduction on Plate VIII from a print kindly lent by Messrs. W. E. Hill and Sons. It is mentioned in Eitner, who apparently did not see a copy of it. On this print he is described as "the most famous musician

PLATE XIa.

CONSTANTIN BELLERMANN. See page 81.

PLATE XIII.

HOTMAN. FROM AN ENGRAVING BY VAN MERLE.

To face page 72.

among Amsterdamers." It proves that Schenck played on an instrument with seven strings. The year of his death is unknown.

PAUL KRESS, second "Kapellmeister" of the Royal Chapel at Stuttgart during the latter part of the seventeenth century, asked for leave, in 1662, to visit England in order to perfect himself on the viol da gamba "which is flourishing in that country."

DAVID ADAMS, gambist in the Royal Chapel in Berlin, received permission to visit England in 1672 for renewed studies of his instrument.

W. L. VOGELSANG, after studying the viol da gamba in England and other countries, is appointed member of the Royal Chapel in Berlin in 1677.

CHAPTER IV.

THE VIOL DA GAMBA IN GERMANY *(continued)*.

CONRAD HÖFFLER, born about 1647 at Nüremberg, was gambist and chamber musician to the Duke of Saxe Weissenfels, as stated on the portrait which appears to the frontispiece of his "Primitiæ Chelicæ oder Musicalische Erstlinge" (musical firstlings), in twelve suites, divided by various tones (modes) for viol da gamba solo, with their basses arranged in the now flourishing instrumental manner, and dedicated to the Prince Johann Adolph, Duke of Saxe, Jülich, Cleve, Berg, etc. Nuremberg, 1695. On the portrait his age is given as forty-eight.

Although he speaks of "modes" in which the suites are divided, they are in reality in the modern major and minor keys, viz.: F major, B minor, D major, A major, D minor, G major, A minor, C minor, B major, G minor, C major and E minor.

Höffler explains in his preface that he has sometimes written the "regular fugues irregularly and the irregular vice versa, and not kept to the rule of those who were frightened to sin against conscience, when they jump the musical convent walls and change keys." As a matter of fact, his fugues are only fugatos and imitative counterpoints. The suites are all in the orthodox form: prelude, allemand, courant, saraband, gigue, with the exception of a fugue preceding the allemand in Nos. I and II. The thematic invention, on the whole, is very poor, although Höffler is at pains to point out that he has not been "steeling other people's work." On the other hand, there are instances of a boldness of style and figuration which reminds one, though slightly, of Bach's solo sonatas, as, for instance, the prelude to the sixth suite, which is treated quite in virtuoso style. The technical part in all the suites is highly developed, especially with regard to double stopping and chord playing. The demands upon the player exceed those in Schenck's "Scherzi Musicali" by a long way.

The portrait and title page are taken from a copy made by the late Johannes Klingenberg for the author. *(Plates IX and X.)*

A description of the work, with reproduction of several movements, is to be found in "Monatshefte für Musikwissenschaft," Berlin, Vol. XXVII.

JOHANN FRIEDRICH HELWIG received his musical education by command and at the expense of Frederic William the Great, Elector of Brandenburg, and was appointed as gambist in the Court Chapel at Berlin, on January 2, 1654. Nothing is known of his subsequent career, but it appears possible that he is identical with a chapel master of the same name, who died while in the service of the Duke of Saxony at Eisenach in 1729.

JOHANN GLETTINGER, born August 20, 1661, at Breslau, was *Rathsmusicus* (musician of the town council) at Breslau. He was a virtuoso on the viol da gamba and bariton, violin, harp, harpsichord, sundry wind instruments, and a celebrated organist. In 1684 he made a successful tour through Lithuania, Prussia and Pomerania, which secured for him the appointment as musician to the Senate of Danzig *(Rathsmusicus)*. In 1690 he was appointed first organist at the Church of St.

Elisabeth, in Breslau, and died in 1739 with the reputation of one of the finest organists in Silesia.

JAC. SCHEIFFELHUT, musician at St. Anne's, Augsburg, about 1682. He died in 1714 according to the catalogue of the "Musikfreunde in Wien" ("Friends of Music in Vienna") He published "Musicalischer Gemüths Ergötzungen Erstes Werk" ("First Work of Musical Delights of the Soul"), consisting of sonatas, allemands, courants, ballets, sarabands and gigues, for two violins, basso viola (? bass viol) and continuo. Augsburg, 1684. The Church Institute, Berlin, has the violin and continuo parts (the gamba probably largely contained in latter). The following is an amusing instance of the extravagantly florid style of titles during the latter part of the seventeenth century:

"Lieblicher Frühlings-Anfang oder Musikalischer Seyten-Klang, welcher unter dess Auges anmuthiger Blumen-Schau, dess Geruchs empfindender Balsam Duft, auch dem Gehör in Præludien, Allemanden, Couranten, Ballo, Sarabanden, Arien und Giguen annehmlicher fället mit 2 Violinen, Viola di braccio, Basso Viola and Continuo. Augsburg, 1685." (Copy said to be in Leipzig.)

ERNST CHRISTIAN HESSE, born April 14, 1676, at Gross Goltern, Hannover (not Gross-Gottern, Thuringia, as in Gerber, Wasielewski and others). He made his preliminary studies at Langensalza and Eisenach. On leaving the college he was appointed as a clerk in the chancellery of Hesse Darmstadt. In 1694 he followed the court to Giessen, where he entered the university for the study of law. In 1698 the prince sent him to Paris to perfect himself in the study of the viol da gamba.

He became the pupil of Marin Marais and Forqueray at the same time, and, as the two masters were rivals, he covered his identity by passing with one under his own name, giving the name of Sachs to the other. Both were so proud and boastful of their pupil's extraordinary talents that they eventually challenged each other to produce the wonderful youth.

They arranged to meet at the house of Forqueray. Hesse was already there when Marais entered at nine a.m., according to appointment. Both masters saluted their pupil by the name by which they knew him. Their astonishment was great when they found out the mystification, and that they had both praised one and the same man under different names. Hesse excused the ruse which he employed in order to benefit by the instruction of two such great masters, and, fearing their displeasure, he was about to leave, when Forqueray held him back, and told him that as he had done justice to both his masters, he was quite willing to continue giving him the benefit of his instruction. Marais would not appear less generous than his rival, and the incident was the reason of cementing a close friendship between the two famous masters, who did their best to communicate all their art to the delighted Hesse.

On his return to Darmstadt in 1702 he received an appointment as secretary to the foreign department and the war office. In 1703 he married his first wife. Two years later, in 1705, he gave a series of concerts in Holland and England, gaining laurels for his gamba playing wherever he went.

In 1707 he visited Italy to enlarge his knowledge of composition. On his return he played at the Viennese court with Pantaleon Hebenstreit, the inventor of the "Pantaleon," a kind of improved dulcimer. The Emperor was so delighted with his playing that he presented him with his portrait on a golden chain. There is a statement to the effect that he was engaged as capellmeister at the Austrian Court in Vienna until 1719, yet that does not appear reconciliable with the fact that in 1713 (shortly after the death of his first wife) he was provisorially appointed capellmeister at Darmstadt, where he settled finally. More authentic is a notice in Eitner (quoting Fürstenau as his authority) that in 1709, after visiting

Vienna, he went to Dresden, where he was offered an engagement at the Court at a salary of 1,200 thaler (£180) a year—a large sum in those days—which he refused. Not long after the death of his first wife he married the celebrated singer, Johanna Elisabeth Doebbrecht (Doebricht). In 1715 he was raised to a higher position in the war office. In 1719 he started on his last professional journey, when he visited Dresden in company of his wife, to attend the nuptials of the Elector of Saxony. Several operas by Lotti and Heinichen were given in honour of the occasion, in the performance of which both Hesse and his wife took part. Both gained fresh laurels as well as ample pecuniary reward. In 1726 Hesse was nominated Councillor of War to the court of Hesse-Darmstadt, after which he lived a retired life and died May 16, 1762, at the age of eighty-six, after a prosperous and happy career. He had twenty children, of whom only eight survived him, and died surrounded by forty-nine grandchildren.

The library at Rostock contains two duos for viol da gamba and bass.*

CHRISTIAN LUDWIG HESSE, eldest son of Ernst Christian Hesse, was born at Darmstadt. He studied the viol da gamba under his father, and was appointed as chamber musician in the Royal Chapel at Berlin in 1754. In 1766 the Crown Prince of Prussia, afterwards Frederic William II, engaged him as gambist for his private band. Christian L. Hesse was not only one of the greatest bass viol players of his time but also one of the last virtuosi of that instrument.

JOHN CHRISTIAN HERTEL, the only son of the capellmeister of the Prince, was born 1699 at Oettingen in Suabia. His father was soon after appointed in the same capacity to the

---

* No. 1, "Paysan en Rondeau"; No. II, Minuet 1 and 2. They are graceful and melodious pieces in the French style of the seventeenth century.

court at Merseburg. As his father had destined him for the church, he gave him some instructions in singing and on the bass viol, as secondary subjects. The boy, who was filled with the love for music, went to the court organist, Kaufmann, who clandestinely instructed him on the violin, the harpsichord, and in theory. At the court concerts he was already much admired for his solos on the bass viol as well as his fine vocal delivery of arias, etc. The father, who dreaded his becoming a musician, sent him, in 1716, to the University of Halle to enter upon a theological career. This suited our young hero admirably, as he felt himself now free to follow his beloved musical studies without hindrance. He paid frequent visits to the famous Kuhnau at Leipzig, by whose advice he profited to a great extent.

When he returned for his holidays, his father heard him play a violin sonata by Corelli, and was so struck with his evident talent that he no longer objected to his choice of music as a profession.

The Duke likewise came to his assistance and sent him, in 1717, to the famous Ernst Christian Hesse at Darmstadt. There he studied also under the capellmeister Graupner, Grünewald and Simonetti, for theory and composition. Hesse, who never before nor after accepted a pupil, took the boy Hertel into his own house, and, in reply to a letter from his father, wrote that once he thought he was working hard when, in France, he practised eight hours a day, but that Hertel practised day and night, and that it would be better to recall him, and prevent his overworking himself. In 1718 he returned to Merseburg, and the Duke sent him to the courts of Weissenfels, Côthen, Zerbst and Dresden. In Eisenach he was, in 1719, engaged as second leader of the violins in the court orchestra, and began to compose instrumental works of all kinds, which he always submitted to Stölzl at Gotha for the latter's approval. Pantaleon Hebenstreit and Telemann were at that time at the head of the ducal chapel, and it was in conjunction with them that he often played at the court concerts, where his bass viol solos were highly appreciated. In 1723 he left Eisenach for Anspach, and thence he went to Cassel (1725), and Weimar (1726); meeting everywhere with enthusiastic receptions on account of his superb playing. At the end of this journey he visited his father at Merseburg, and thence went to Leipzig, where he met J. S. Bach. In the same year he met Graun, with whom he formed a lasting friendship. In 1727 he paid a visit to the Netherlands. Returned to Eisenach he received, through Graun, an invitation from the Crown Prince of Prussia, afterwards Frederic the Great, to come to Ruppin, where he played before the court in 1732. On that occasion he gained the friendship of Benda, who was a great admirer of his talent. On his return he played before Prince Günther of Sondershausen, who encouraged him to send his compositions as often as possible and to come at least once a year himself.

After the decease of the celebrated violinist and capellmeister Birkenstock, in 1732, Hertel was installed in his place at the court of Eisenach. In 1739 he played at the court of the Prince of Orange at Dillenburg (the home of William the Silent), when the Princess asked him to improvise a fugue, on the bass viol, on a theme which she gave him. He accomplished the task to the great admiration of all who were present. On the decease of the Duke of Eisenach in 1742, the court orchestra was dissolved, and Hertel, as well as his friends Hebenstreit, Telemann and Benda, travelled again, visiting several courts. On Benda's recommendation he was appointed concertmeister (leader) at the court of Strelitz. As his duties occupied only a small part of his time, he devoted the greater part to composition and the study of the newest works by contemporary masters. John Adam Hiller says that he composed innumerable symphonies, trios, overtures, and

PLATE XI.
JOHANNES DANIEL HARD.

To face page 80.

six quatuors for violin, flute and viol da gamba (the continuo which he does not mention probably completed the "quartet"). In 1748 he lost his sight through cataract, which prevented him from attending to his musical duties. During this period he devoted most of his time to his beloved bass viol, and to improvisations on that instrument, wherein he proved to be perhaps the greatest master of his time. Through a successful operation he regained his sight, but being of fragile build and delicate constitution, his health began to fail. In 1753 the court orchestra at Strelitz was dissolved, and Hertel retired on a pension, but the necessity of parting with his children, who had to seek employment abroad, accelerated his end. He died in October, 1754.

GABRIEL SCHÜTZE, a noted gambist towards the end of the seventeenth century, took up the study of theology in 1696, and after visiting the universities of Jena, Giessen and Altorf, he became a preacher at St. Margaret's in Nürnburg. His pupil:

MICHAEL DIETELMAIER, was born at Nüremberg, August 16, 1677. He distinguished himself as virtuoso on the bass viol, and composed at an early age. No further particulars about his life are known.

CONSTANTIN BELLERMANN, imperial poet laureate, was born at Erfurt in 1696. He studied law at the university of his native town, and devoted a great deal of his time to the study of musical compositions as well as to the playing of the lute, viol da gamba, violin and flute. In 1719 he was appointed "Cantor" at Münden, and 1741 rector of the school at that town. When he died is not known. He left a great number of unpublished compositions for various instruments, choral works, and even an opera. Six suites for flute, viol da gamba and clavecimbel appear to have possessed real merit.

JOHANN DANIEL HARDT was born at Frankfort-on-the-Main, May 8, 1696. About 1716 he was gambist and chamberlain to Stanislaus, King of Poland, at the court of Zweibrücken, and about 1721, Kammermusikus (chamber-musician) to Philip Franz von Schönborn, Bishop of Würzburg and Duke of Franconia. Four years later, in 1725, he exchanged that post for the position of Kammermusiker at the court of Würtemberg. He rose gradually to the position of director of the chapel (capellmeister) to which he was nominated by the Duke Karl Eugen, and which he held down to 1757, if not later. The date of his death is unknown. Six Sonatas "a une sitte (?) Viole e Basse continuo," Op. 1, dedicated to the King of Poland, and a "Solo per la Viola da Gamba" are in the library at Rostock. They are not particularly interesting. The portrait by Val. Dan. Preisler is dated Nüremberg, 1750. *(See Plate XI.)*

During the second half of the seventeenth century we come across some compositions for the bass viol which must evidently be attributed to virtuosi of that instrument, although nothing is known of the composers beyond their names and the titles of their works, which are: J. E. KINDERMANN: "Neu Verstimmte Violen Lust, mit drei Violen nebst dem Generalbass," Frankfurt, 1652. PETER ZACHAEUS (ZACHOV), "Erster Theil verstimmter Viol' d'Gamb. Lustspielen Solo," consisting of allemands, courants, ballo, sarabands and "chiqven" (jigs), preceded by a sonata. Engraved on forty-eight copper plates, folio, Lübeck at the author's, and Danzig, Bruno Laurentio Tanken (1683). JOHANN CHRISTOPH ZIEGLER, "Intavolatura per Viol da Gamba," consisting of entratas, allemands, courants, etc. Oblong octavo. (This and the former are lost—see Einstein.) NICOLAS HASSE: "Deliciæ Musicæ," allemands, courants and sarabands for two or three viols, violone, harpsichord and theorbo, Rostock, 1656, Richel. One copy in the "Germanisches Museum," Nüremberg. Bass only in British Museum. MATTHIAS KELZ: "Exercitationum Musicæ" (for violin and bass viol), Vienna, 1669. Einstein mentions "Epidigma harmoniae," Novae, 1669. DIETRICH BECKER, violinist and Rathsmusikus (musician to the Senate), Hamburg, 1644-78: Sonatas for violin, viol da gamba and continuo, based on hymn tunes (über Chorallieder), Hamburg, 1668, and "Musikalische Frühlings früchte," three to five-part instrumental pieces with continuo. One of the sonatas has been republished from an edition dated 1674 in Einstein's "Zur deutschen Litteratur für Viola da Gamba." JOHANN PHILIPP BECK: Allemands, Gigues, Courants, Sarabands, to be played on the bass viol with continuo "Auf der Viola da Gamba zu Streichen und mit einigen Accorden," third part, Frankfurt, 1677, folio. A. SCHOLL: "Den Spelende Kunst Hemel," Delft, 1669. CLAMOR HEINRICH ABEL, "3 Theil Musikalischer Blumen" (dance tunes), partly with a violin, partly with a "verstimbte gamba" (tuned in a chord, see Lyra Viol, page 38) and violin, w. B. for harpsichord, Frankfort, 1677. Matthias Kelz, of Schongau, Bavaria, copy in Paris N.L. JACOB KREMBERG: "Musikalische Gemüth's Ergötzung," 1689. J. M. NICOLAI: Twelve Sonatas for two violins, some with a bass viol and some with a bassoon, and four with gamba or *trombone!* Augsburg, 1675. JOHANN GEORG AHLE: "Unstrutische Thalia," Mühlhausen, 1679; "Anmuthiges Zehn vierstimmiger Gambenspiele," Mühlhausen, 1681, 4to (ten graceful pieces for four gambe). There were also published in Amsterdam, 1683, in a folio volume: Speelstukken, "12 Sonaten mit 1 Viool en Basso continuo," to which can be added a theorbo or viol da gamba, composed by Petersen, a Dutchman. J. SCHEIFFELHUT: "Lieblicher Frühlings Anfang" ("Early Spring"), Augsburg, 1685. GOTTFRIED FINGER, a German violinist and composer, living in London during the latter part of the seventeenth century, published three sonatas for two violins and viol da gamba in 1688 (copy in British Museum). KRIEGER: Twelve Sonatas for the viol da gamba, Nürnberg, 1693. PHILIPP HEINRICH ERLEBACH: Six Sonatas for the viol da gamba, Nürnberg, 1694; "Sonata II à 2, etc." (copy in Upsala). One of these appears in Alfred Einstein's "Zur deutschen Litteratur," etc., see also above: Dietrich Becker, Sonata à 2, violin, viol da gamba and continuo.

Dr. Einstein, in his above-mentioned book, gives also the fifth sonata for violin, viol da gamba and continuo from PH. FR. BUCHNER'S "Plectrum Musicum," 1662; and one of DIETRICH BUXTEHUDE'S "VII Sonate a 2 violini and viola da gamba," 1694-6, which have also been republished in "Denkmäler Deutscher Tonkunst XI." Apart from these, Dr. Einstein mentions and describes: NUB (Georg (?) member of Imperial Chapel, Vienna, latter part of seventeenth century), sonata, two violins and gamba. EBNER: Sonatina for two violins and gamba. I. K. KERLL: Three Sonatas for two violins, viol da gamba and bass continuo (republished "Denkmäler Deutscher Tonkunst in Bayern II," 2. s. LXVII f.). J. J. LÖWE: Canzon and two capriccios for violin and gamba. KASPAR FÖRSTER: Two violins and gamba, MS. at Upsala. J. H. SCHMELZER: One sonata, violin, gamba and continuo, and one sonata for two violins, gamba and continuo, 1672, MS. Upsala. SEB. A. SCHERER: Sonatas for two violins and gamba or bassoon, Op. 3, Ulm, 1680 (gamba part missing). J. ADAM STRUNCK: Sonata, two violins and gamba, MS. Upsala. NICOLAUS ADAM STRUNCK: "Uebung auf der (lesson on the) violin and viol da gamba," 1691.

CHRISTOPH SCHAFRATH, born 1709 at Hohenstein, near Dresden. In 1755 he was chamber musician to the Princess Amalia of Prussia (sister of the King).

He was a highly esteemed composer of his time, which, as far as the general musical taste is concerned, was shallow and commonplace. A sonata for viol da gamba and harpsichord is preserved in the "Amalienbibliothek" at Berlin, and a copy at the British Museum. Duets for two viol da gambas and six soli for harpsichord, gamba and oboe, are in the "Joachimsthal" Library, Berlin, and two sonatas for viol da gamba, violin, violoncello and harpsichord, in Darmstadt.

JOHN GOTTLIEB GRAUN, 1698-1771 (brother of Carl Heinrich, the famous composer of the Passion music, "Der Tod Jesu"), was highly esteemed as instrumental composer. He wrote a Concertante in A minor for viol da gamba. MS. in "Amalienbibliothek" of the Joachimthal Gymnasium, Berlin. Copy in author's library.

CHRISTIAN FERDINAND ABEL, a gambist, who lived about the end of the seventeenth and the beginning of the eighteenth century, was member of the court chapel at Coethen. He followed Charles XII in his campaigns in Germany, afterwards exchanging the sword for the bow, and lived still in Coethen in 1737, after retiring into private life, devoting the rest of his days to music.

CARL FRIEDRICH ABEL, his son, born at Coethen 1725, was one of the greatest and also one of the last virtuosi on the viol da gamba. He received his musical education from J. S. Bach, and became, in 1748, a member of the Polish Court Chapel at Dresden, where he found ample opportunity to continue his musical studies under Hasse. The unsettled times of war absorbing all the resources of the king, allowed but a scant existence to the members of the Royal Chapel, and this induced Abel to seek his fortune abroad. After visiting several minor courts, where he was always well received, he came eventually to London with the Princess Charlotte Sophia, afterwards Queen of George III, whose teacher he was, in 1759, when he obtained the patronage of the Duke of York. Soon afterwards, on the foundation of the queen's band, he was appointed chamber musician to her majesty with a salary of £200. This income he increased considerably by giving lessons to members of the nobility, and by his compositions, which enjoyed a great popularity. In spite of all this he appears to have been troubled over money matters, for Cramer in his "Musical Magazine" tells us that in April, 1783, the London public was deprived of the pleasure of hearing their favourite Abel as well as Sacchini through their getting into debt, and he adds that neither of them understood how to regulate his affairs. The former found refuge in the house of a friend of his in Paris, who was known to have a well stocked wine cellar, which proved an additional attraction for Abel. The first master of the queen's band was J. C. Bach, youngest son of the great Sebastian Bach, with whom Abel lived on terms of the closest friendship. They instituted the Bach-Abel concerts, which became the most fashionable entertainments of their kind. In 1766 they were engaged by the notorious Mrs. Cornelis to give their concerts in Carlisle House, in Soho Square. On the site of the grand hall of that mansion now stands St. Patrick's Church. From about 1775, they gave concerts at Hanover Rooms. According to Dr. Burney, they first started their concerts about 1763, and they lasted for fully twenty years with uninterrupted prosperity, and were afterwards continued as the "professional concerts," with the advantage of a greater variety of compositions, while Bach and Abel performed almost exclusively their own. When the latter artists opened their grand concert room in Hanover Square, part of the decoration consisted of transparent figures painted by Cipriani, representing Apollo and the Muses. They were finely executed and the effect was brilliant, but unfortunately they had a desire to leave Olympus and mix with the mortals in the hall by dropping down in particles, so that it was found necessary to assist their ardent desire by taking them down altogether. When the room was opened again a lady asked Abel what had become of Apollo and the Muses. "They have quitted their late station," was his answer, "but when the performance begins, I hope your ladyship will hear them all." Both Bach and Abel were well versed in other arts besides music, especially in drawing. They lived together in King's

Square (now Soho Square) Court next to Carlisle House. Rimbault thinks it was the house which in 1782 was described as No. 1 Carlisle Street, then known as Mr. Angelo's Riding School. Mr. Angelo bought Carlisle Mansion, and his son told Mr. Rimbault that he could well remember the delightful evenings under his paternal roof, when the two above-named artists, with Bartolozzi and Cipriani, formed a little friendly party and amused themselves with drawing, music and conversation, till long after midnight. Abel accumulated a great number of drawings from his friend Gainsborough, mostly in exchange for notes on the viol da gamba. The walls of his apartments were covered with them, slightly pinned to the paperhangings. After his

FIG. 23. ABEL. FROM AN ETCHED CARICATURE BY F. N., DATED 1787, ENTITLED "A SOLO ON THE VIOLA DI GAMBA."

death they were sold at Longford's rooms (afterwards the famous George Robins's) under the Piazza, Covent Garden. A beautiful portrait of Abel, painted by Gainsborough, formed part of the famous collection of the late Mr. Charles Wertheimer, who kindly gave permission for its reproduction *(see Frontispiece)*. Another portrait attributed to Gainsborough, belongs to Sir W. H. Cummings, who has also kindly consented to its reproduction *(see Plate XII)*.

There is also a curious etching by W. Gardiner, from a caricature by F. N., dated 1787 *(see Fig. 23)*. As a teacher, Abel produced many excellent pupils, the most prominent of whom was Baptist Cramer, the famous pianist, whom he instructed in the art of composition. He also gave lessons to Giorgi (the daughter of a Venetian gondolier) who possessed a magnificent voice, but who was absolutely untrained, and disheartened most of her teachers by her superficiality and indolence. Abel took her in hand and instructed her out of pure love for art, at his country house in Fulham. James Cervetto, Crosdil and Barthelemon, all adopted his style of playing and phrasing. He had a hand which no difficulties could embarrass. His taste was most refined and delicate, and his judgment so correct and certain as never to let a single note escape him without meaning. His manner of playing an adagio was most pathetic, and served as a model for all, while his way of simply breathing a few notes here and there was absolutely inimitable. He was a master in improvising on his instrument, and his modulations in different keys were done with so great a mastery of all the available harmonic resources that it astounded the greatest masters of his time. In 1782, he revisited Germany to see his brother Leopold August, born 1785, who was an excellent violinist and pupil of Benda. On that occasion he played before the Crown Prince of Prussia, who was so deeply impressed by his performance that he presented him with a valuable box and one hundred louis d'or. He died in London on June 21 or 22, 1787, after three days' sleep, from which he never woke up. His obituary appeared in the "Morning Post" on the latter date. His beloved gamba was placed in the grave with him. His numerous compositions, which were once so generally admired, are now entirely forgotten. Some of his gamba sonatas, dedicated to the Countess of Pembroke, who was his pupil, are preserved in manuscript in the British

PLATE XII.

CARL FRIEDRICH ABEL. FROM THE PAINTING BY GAINSBOROUGH IN THE POSSESSION OF SIR W. H. CUMMINGS.

Museum. An amusing story of his ready wit is the following: one evening, when taking a walk with Lord Kelly in a suburb of London, they heard sounds of music issuing from a tavern, and on approaching the place, recognised it as a gamba concerto by Abel, which was being murdered by the tavern musician. "I wonder who that is," said Lord Kelly. "Who else could it be but Cain?" was Abel's reply.

JACOB RHIEMANN or RIEMANN, a gambist, who was in the service of the Elector of Hesse-Cassel about the commencement of the eighteenth century, wrote pieces for "bass viola und bass continuo, Op. 1," and a trio in sonata form for violin, bass viola and bass continuo, Op. 3.

Among German gamba virtuosi we have also to mention the name of a lady, DOROTHEA VON RIED, who appears to have taken a high rank among contemporary players. Her father, Fortunatus Ried, was an Austrian musician, living in the early part of the eighteenth century, who had four highly-gifted daughters and several sons. Two of the latter and two of the former appeared as prodigies with phenomenal success at Vienna, Prague, Leipzig, Wittenberg and other German towns, when Dorothea was only eight years old.

Among the reigning princes the viol da gamba counted several votaries: FREDERIC THE GREAT and FREDERIC WILLIAM II of Prussia, his successor (1786-97); the Markgraf FREDERIC OF BRANDENBURG CULMBACH, who died 1771; and last, but not least, the Prince Elector MAXIMILIAN JOSEPH, born March 28, 1728, died December 30, 1777. Burney, who heard him in 1772, speaks in the highest terms of his ability as an executant and a musician, ranking him second only to C. F. Abel. He was also violinist, violoncellist and composer.

FRANZ XAVER HAMMER, born at Oettingen (Bavaria?), was one of the most prominent violoncellists of the eighteenth century. Apparently he was also a good executant on the viol da gamba, as there are four gamba sonatas of his in the library at Schwerin, where he was engaged as chamber musician from 1785 to the time of his death, which occurred apparently in 1813, as his name disappears from the list of court musicians as well as the "Wiener Tonkünstler Societät," of which he was a member.

Of the four gamba sonatas, the first is in A major, signed "Da me Xavjer Hammer," the three others are all in D major, No. 3 being signed and dated 1786. They are in the well-known "Zopfstiel" of that period.

Among the most prominent German composers who wrote for the gamba, we have to mention G. F. HANDEL, who wrote a sonata for viol da gamba and cembalo in C major, the manuscript of which is in the library of the museum at Berlin. It consists of four movements, a majestic adagio, an allegro, which is less important, an andante in A minor, which is a perfect gem, resembling in character the first of the Forty-eight Preludes by Bach, republished (without alteration of the gamba part) in the author's "First Album of Music for Violoncello and Pianoforte," and a lively vivace for the last movement. Important gamba parts will be found also in the score of his "Resurrection," where he has made use of two staves, bass and tenor clefs, for the gamba part on account of its large compass. JOHANN SEBASTIAN BACH wrote the famous three sonatas for viol da gamba and cembalo, which are well-known to the musical public by Peters's edition for violoncello and pianoforte. He has also made use of the gamba in the "St. Matthew" and the "St. John" passion music,* in several of his cantatas, viz., "Gottes Zeit," "In deine Hände," "Die Himmel Erzählen," and an *obbligato* for viola d'amore and gamba in "Tritt auf die Glaubensbahn." He found some ex-

---

* The accompanying illustration is a reproduction of the original autograph of the gamba *obbligato* to the aria: "Es ist vollbracht" (It is finished).

cellent gambists at Coethen, which circumstance made him prefer the gamba to the violoncello, which in the hands of orchestral players of his time was still an unwieldy instrument, incapable of executing that which Bach's genius created, although he soon discovered its capabilities, as his solo sonatas clearly show. The way in which he treats the gamba shows how thoroughly he understood and appreciated its distinctly lyric and more intimate character, which Leopold Mozart admired, when describing the instrument as one "principally used for an upper (treble) part which has a more agreeable tone than the violoncello." Bach's contemporary, GEORG PHILIPP TELEMANN (1681-1767), has also composed for the gamba. A copy of a very pretty trio for violin, gamba and continuo, may be seen at the British Museum. His godson, PHILIPP EMANUEL BACH, has written a sonata for gamba and cembalo, containing a very fine slow movement. HAYDN has also written for the gamba, viz., "lyra viol," but apparently none of these compositions are preserved.

CHAPTER V.

THE VIOL DA GAMBA IN AUSTRIA.

AUSTRIA does not appear to have produced many gambists of renown. The instrument was represented in the Imperial Chapel for a much shorter time than in other countries, although it may have been introduced somewhat earlier than the records show. The first gambist in that chapel was, according to those documents, KARL SCHMIDBAUER, who was appointed in or about 1680, at a salary of forty-five florins per annum, and pensioned October 1, 1711. He died October 1, 1722, seventy-three years old. JOSEPH HUEFNAGEL was engaged in the same capacity from 1697 to October, 1711, at a salary of thirty florins. He also was pensioned in the latter year, and died at the age of fifty-eight, December 23, 1714. FRANZ HUEFNAGEL was also engaged as gambist, from 1707 to 1714. He received thirty florins per annum until 1712, when his salary was raised to 720 florins. He was perhaps the greatest virtuoso on the viol da gamba whom Austria has produced, and was highly praised by J. J. Fux, who probably wrote his canon for two gambas for him and Schmidbauer. Huefnagel died about 1717, apparently in absolute poverty, as Johann Joseph Fux, the famous contrapuntist, made a public appeal on behalf of his four orphans. FRANZ ANTON SCHMIDBAUER was apparently the last gambist in the Imperial Chapel at Vienna. He was appointed on January 1, 1707, at a salary of sixty florins, which was raised to 720 florins in 1712. He remained in active service until December 1, 1737, on which day he died at the age of forty-eight years. After him no more gambists were appointed, although there was still a theorbo player, Joachimo Sarao, who received one thousand florins per annum, and died in 1755. MÜLLER, a gambist in the chapel of Count Brühl at Varsovy, travelled about 1750 with Capellmeister Gebel in Germany.

Bohemia possessed a great virtuoso on the gamba in SIMON TRUSKA, born April 5, 1734, near Randnitz. He belonged, in 1758, to the lay fraternity of the "Stift Strahof" (monastery). He was a famous organ-builder and instrument maker, and also a composer of numerous quintets, quartets, trios, sonatas and dances.

CHAPTER VI.

THE VIOL DA GAMBA IN THE NETHERLANDS.

THE Netherlands have also produced a number of excellent gambists, who probably received their technical training originally from English masters, several of whom visited that country, while a few settled there altogether; as, for instance, DANIEL NORCOME, who was exiled in 1602 for religious reasons and entered the Archbishop Governor of the Netherlands' chapel, where he remained till 1647.

CAROLO HACQUART or HAKART, born 1649, at Huy, in Belgium, died 1730, in Holland. He was an excellent gambist and composer, who published through Roger in Amsterdam, "Ten Sonatas for Two Gambas and Bass," a book of preludes, allemands, courants, etc., for the viol da gamba and continuo, and motets for three, four and five voices, with instrumental accompaniments.

DEUTOKAM is mentioned as a gambist of Dutch nationality (1675-85), in the service of Charles, Landgrave of Hesse-Cassel.

JOHANN ANDREAS DAMEN or DAHMEN, as he is sometimes called, was born about the middle of the eighteenth century in Holland. He played the viol da gamba and the violoncello;

and was at Drury Lane Theatre in 1794. He travelled in Germany, 1796-7. Damen was an excellent virtuoso and composer, but none of his gamba compositions appear to have been published. In 1799 he played in a trio for viol da gamba and two French horns of his own composition at the King's Theatre (Haymarket).

His son, DAMEN, junior, was a violoncellist in Salomon's Quartet. (See later on.)

CHAPTER VII.

THE VIOL DA GAMBA IN FRANCE.

LEONARDO DA VINCI, the great painter, who followed his royal friend and patron, Francis I, to the French court, and died in 1520, was an excellent performer on the viol, which was greatly beloved by the Italian painters of that time. An instance to that effect is given in Veronese's "Marriage at Canaa," where Tintoretto and Veronese are portrayed playing small bass or tenor viols while Titian is playing the violone. There is no doubt that Leonardo's enthusiasm for his instrument would not remain without influence upon the court and its surroundings. A reproduction of his father's autograph found by the author in a manuscript collection of music in the British Museum, has already been given *(see Fig. 18)*. The elder "Leonardo Vinci" was a celebrated opera composer. We find but rare instances of French viol players of that time whose names have been preserved in history. The first is:

CLAUDE GERVAISE, chamber violist to Francis I, who published a book of viol pieces in four parts in 1556. Grillet describes them as very advanced and interesting for their time. They contain no bar lines but the repeats are marked by double bars and dots in the usual way. When Francis I,

PLATE XIIa.

REDUCED FACSIMILE OF ORIGINAL MANUSCRIPT OF THE VIOL DA GAMBA OBBLIGATO TO THE ARIA, "ES IST VOLLBRACHT," FROM THE "ST. JOHN'S PASSION," BY J. S. BACH. *See page 90.*

in 1543, created the "Musique de la Chambre" as distinct from the court orchestra, he appointed Claude Gervaise as his violist.

GRANIER is mentioned in Mersenne's "Harmonie Universelle" as an executant on the bass viol. This was really a violone, for Mersenne tells us that Granier, when playing before Queen Margaret, used to enclose a page-boy inside his viol, and that the boy sang the soprano while Granier sang tenor and played the bass on his viol. Margaret of Valois was of great personal beauty, but haughty and vindictive, and for a trivial offence she ordered another of her musicians, Choisnin, to be caned. History does not state whether Granier was treated with equal liberality. He was afterwards a second master of the King's chapel, and died about 1600.

ANDRÉ MAUGARS (MAUGARD). The date and place of his birth are unknown. His father wanted him to embrace the Protestant religion, and he was further induced to do so by his English friends, but he remained a Roman Catholic, and even took holy orders, or at least they were conferred upon him as complimentary titles. About 1620 he came to England and joined the private music of James I. During that time he perfected himself on the gamba. It is said that he studied under Ferrabosco and Coperario. As he was still unknown at that period, we should hardly have any proof of his connection with the king's private music, were it not for a story which reflects little credit upon his character, and which elicited from the "Commandeur de Jars," in speaking of it, the epithet of "mad knave" for him. The facts are as follows: Sivette, the son of a hotel keeper in Lyons, who was also in the private band, had some unknown grievance against Maugars, and got him a severe thrashing. The latter, who was of a vindictive temperament, found means to drop a slip into the envelope of a letter which was being delivered to the king, insinuating that Sivette was planning an attempt on the life of his majesty. He added that no further particulars could be given as it was a secret revealed in confession. Sivette was imprisoned in the Tower of London for two years, and the truth would never have been known had not Maugars bragged about it in later years. Returned to France, he published in 1624 a translation of Bacon's essay on the "Advancement of Learning," which he dedicated to Messire Auguste de Memoine, a privy councillor, and which, according to Tallemaut des Reaux, secured him the living of a priory. The incidents which led to this show his scheming and crafty nature. They are told thus by Tallemaut. One day he was seen in the chamber of Cardinal Richelieu with a letter in his hand. Asked by the latter what he had there, he said: "Monsigneur, my modesty forbids that I should let you hear the extravagant praise which my cousin, Ogier, the Dane, and de Richelieu, bestow upon a poor translation of mine." "Ah! Maugars, I was not aware that I had the honour to be your relative," said the cardinal. Whereupon Maugars observed: "Monseigneur, this is an advocate in parliament, an excellent man, who is no discredit to that illustrious name." "Read it then," demanded Richelieu. Maugars read praises which raised him beyond everything, and the cardinal began to doubt whether the letter actually contained all this, and seeing that Maugars began to hesitate, he signed to Bois-Robert, who took the letter from him, which simply ran thus: "I have received the translation of your cousin, which I shall read at my leisure." "Oh! M. Maugars, you play tricks of that sort?" "Monseigneur, if he did not say it he ought to have done so," answered Maugars. Soon afterwards Richelieu offered him the livings of two priories to choose from. Maugars chose that of Saint Pierre Eynac (or Esnac), which was five hundred francs per annum less than the other. Asked why he did so, he said: "This priory is called St. Julien, and I shall be known henceforth as St. Julien the Minstrel." In 1634 he published a translation of Bacon's "Political Reasons for a War with Spain." As this work was of practical interest, it was probably translated at the instigation of Richelieu, to whom the translation was also dedicated. E. Thoinan in his biography of Maugars opines that it was this latter work which brought him in the prioryship. A curious little pamphlet of Maugars in the form of a letter has also been republished in Thoinan's biography. It is called "Response faite a un Curieux sur le Sentiment de la Musique d'Italie, escrite à Rome le premier, Octobre, 1639." This pamphlet, which appeared anonymously, was the starting point of the "Guerre des Bouffons," which was waged with even more animosity than the famous war of the Gluckists and Piccinists. He tells in this how he visited the house of the Baroni, where, in the presence of ten or twelve of the most prominent artists, he played the viol da gamba, and how they induced Signora Leonora Baroni to keep his instrument there, asking him to return the next day to show his art of improvisation, which was said to be generally wanting in the French. He solved this problem to the satisfaction of all, and then appeared at the French church on the day of St. Louis and improvised on a given theme to the accompaniment of a small organ during high mass in the presence of twenty-three cardinals. He acquitted himself of his task to the admiration of all, and they asked him to play again after the Agnus Dei, when *a more lively theme* was chosen. Maugars played again in such a manner that all those present overwhelmed him with praise, and he adds that no player of an instrument deserves any particular consideration unless he can do this, which, especially on the bass viol, on account of the limited number of strings and consequent difficulty of playing chords, requires a great amount of talent. "Two innate qualities are indispensable for this," he says, "a strong and lively imagination, and the necessary skill of the hand for the immediate execution of one's ideas." Maugars tells us also that in his time there was no great gambist in Italy, and that in Rome the gamba was very little played, in spite of the fact that Horatio de Parma left a number of excellent compositions for it, which were much played in France, even on various other instruments. He also says that the father of Ferrabosco the younger first acquainted the English with the viol da gamba, and that since then they have surpassed all other nations on that instrument. Mersenne, in his "Harmonie Universelle". (1636-7), has a lengthy chapter on the viols, in which he says: "Nobody in France equals Maugars and Hottman, very clever men in their art. They excell in divisions by their incomparable art of bowing and the delicacy and sweetness of their tone. There is nothing in harmony which they cannot execute with perfection, especially when accompanied by a clavichord. The former, however, executes two, three, or more parts on the basse viol with so many ornamentations, and an agility of the fingers without any visible effort, than one has never heard the like of by those who played the instrument before him." Mersenne also speaks about the capabilities of the viols, and that they may be used for any number of parts, but that as their tone is sadder and more sombre, they require pieces of a more serious character and slower time, and are therefore better suited than violins to accompany the voice. He gives, also, a "Fantaisie à cinq par le Sieur Henry le Jeune" as a specimen, which is not above the better average pieces of that time.

HOTMANN (HOTTEMANN, HAUTMANN), whom Mersenne praises as sharing the palm of the greatest gambist in France with Maugars, was to all appearances of German extraction. The word Hotmann is on the face of it German. To this may be added the fact that in 1570 François Hotman (1524-90), a lawyer who enjoys a high reputation and fills a prominent post under the French Government, writes to a friend of his, on September 1 of that year, that he intends to leave France and to *return* to Germany, as the uncertainty between war and peace appears intolerable to him. The name is very uncommon and the time makes it quite possible that this lawyer was a relative, if not the father, of the gambist, thus proving the theory of his German descent to be correct. Grillet quotes some verses from Loret's "Muze Historique" (April 15, 1662), describing a visit of Louis XIII and his court to a convent to hear the "Musique Royale," consisting in the singing of the Psalms of David, to which Hotman, the *illustrious*, made his gamba shine forth, by introducing each chant with a prelude on his instrument. About Hotman's private life nothing is known, and in spite of his great popularity and several important references, not even his Christian name can be found. The date of his death is given in the above-mentioned "Muze Historique," consisting of rhymed letters by J. Loret to the Duchess of Nemours, giving the news of the day. The letter in question is dated Saturday, April 14, 1663, just a year less one day after the former notice. We give the passage verbatim:

Translation.

Hotman que depuis plusieurs lustres,	Hotman, who years ago, Had been added to the rank of the "Illustrious,"
On métoit au rang des Illustres,	
Et qui, sous le rond du Soleil,	And who under the round of the sun
N'avait d'égal ny de pareil,	Had neither his like nor equal
Pour bien jouer de la Viole,	In his fine Viol playing,
Est décédé, sur ma parole:	Has died, on my word,
Car j'aprens tout prézentement	For I learn just this moment
Ou'ou le met dans le Monument.	That he has been put in his monument.
Grande perte pour l'Harmonie,	
Et je crois que son beau Génie	Great loss for Music (l'Harmonie) And I believe that his genius
Qui plaizoit à sa Majesté,	Which pleased his Majesty
En sera longtemps regrété.	Will long be mourned by him.

The often repeated story that Hotman invented the theorbo about 1650, is just as ridiculous as the statements regarding Marais which we shall have occasion to mention presently.

Hotman was the master of two famous pupils, Sainte-Colombe and Marin Marais. The portrait which we add spells his name Hautman, but this misspelling is of frequent occurrence in old prints, especially in the case of *foreign* names, which Hotman's evidently was. The print is by S. Benard (*see Plate XIII*).

SAINTE-COLOMBE is mentioned by Jean Rousseau as an eminently gifted virtuoso on, and composer for, the viol da gamba. He enjoyed a considerable reputation as a remarkable artist, and with two of his daughters, one of whom played the treble viol, the other the bass viol, he gave concerts at his house. Titon du Tillet relates that their concerts for three viols were heard with pleasure, although they consisted only of ordinary (!) symphonies and a "harmonie peu fournie d'accords" (a harmony employing chords but sparsely). It does not appear quite clear whether this refers to poverty of harmonic treatment or the absence of chord playing on the viols.* After Hotman's death, Sainte-Colombe became the teacher of:

MARIN MARAIS, born March 31, 1656. He was a choir-boy of the Sainte-Chapelle. Chaperon the choirmaster, gave him his first instructions in music, and soon after, Hotman began to teach him to play the viol da gamba. After Hotman's death Sainte-Colombe took over his master's pupil, but at the end of six months—so Titon du Tillet tells us—he found that his pupil was likely to surpass him. He told him therefore that he had nothing more to teach him. Marais, who was passionately fond of his viol, was nevertheless anxious to profit by his master's knowledge, and to perfect himself on his instrument. As he had access at any time to his house, he waited till the summer came, when Sainte-Colombe studied in a little

---

* J. Rousseau, in his "Traité de la Viole," says that about 1675 Sainte-Colombe added the seventh string to the gamba and introduced spun strings. Duiffoprugcar used already seven strings, as we have seen, and Praetorius used already spun strings. Still Sainte-Colombe may have introduced their use in France. The seven strings, however, were on a Duiffoprugcar gamba *belonging to the king!*

wooden summer-house, which he had constructed between the branches of a mulberry tree, so as to enjoy absolute quietness and the pleasant position. As soon as Sainte-Colombe had locked himself in this quaint studio, Marais slipped underneath, and benefited by watching how he played certain passages and by studying certain particular bowings which the old masters liked to keep as their secrets. This ruse did, however, not succeed very long, and once discovered, Sainte-Colombe took care that his pupil should no longer overhear his studies. He was, all the same, proud of his pupil, and when Marais was playing once before a distinguished audience, and Sainte-Colombe was asked his opinion of him, he answered: "There are sometimes pupils who can surpass their master, but young Marais will never find one that will surpass him."

In 1685 he was appointed solo gambist to the king's private music, and remained in that position for forty years. He belonged to the orchestra of the opera and became its director conjointly with Colasse. He wrote several operas, one of their number, "Alcione," remaining a favourite on account of a storm which produced a marvellous effect. For his instrument he wrote five books of pieces, containing many charming numbers. The Eritish Museum has Nos. 1, 3, 4 and 5, but without the basses. Paris has a complete set. Marais was married to Catherine d'Amicourt and they had nineteen children. Nine were still living in 1732, six sons and three daughters. In 1709 he presented four of his sons to the king, three taking part with their father in the performance of some of his pieces for viols, the fourth son had to place the books on the stands and turn over the pages. The performance over, the king heard the three sons singly, and then turning to Marais, he said: "I am well satisfied with your children, but you remain still Marais and their father." One of Marais's daughters was also a clever executant on the viol da gamba.

In 1691 Marais lived in the Rue Quincampoix and in the following year in the Rue Bertin-Poirée (Grillet, "Le Livre commode").

Three or four years before his death Marais retired. He lived in a house in the Rue de Lourcine, in the suburb of Saint-Marceau, where his favourite occupation was to tend to his garden and his flowers. He did not entirely forsake his viol, and even rented a large room in the Rue du Batoir, in the 'quartier Saint André-des-Arts, where he received pupils two or three times a week. Titon du Tillet credits Marais with the addition of the seventh string and spun strings on the gamba, and his statement has been copied into most modern dictionaries, but we have pointed out its fallacy, and therefore need not refer again to the matter. Marin Marais died August 15, 1728. We give his portrait from a fine mezzotint on Plate XIV. A painting by Rigaud in the National Gallery shows Marais with Lully and the brothers Hotteterre (celebrated flautists and composers). A reproduction appears on Plate XV. The finely engraved title page of his "Pièces a une et a deux Violes" is given on Plate XVI. His son:

ROLAND MARAIS followed his father as solo gambist in the royal private music, on the retirement of the latter in 1725. Quantz heard him in 1726 and praises him as an excellent player. He published a "Nouvelle Méthode de Musique" in 1711, and two books of pieces for viol da gamba and bass in 1735 and 1738.

PIERRE DE LA BARRE and CHARLES DE LA FONTAINE were gambists in the queen's private band in 1665, and PIERRE MARTIN was gambist to "Monsieur," the king's brother.

SALOMO, born 1661, in the Provence, came to Paris and studied the bass viol under Sainte-Colombe. He was a great artist on his instrument, but only at the age of fifty-one he became a member of the king's private music in the place of

PLATE XIV.
MARIN MARAIS. FROM A MEZZOTINT.

To face page 104.

LEMOYNE, of whom we possess no particulars at all. Salomo wrote operas and motets, and died at Versailles in 1731.

The FATHER ANDRÉ, a Benedictine monk, who lived about the middle of the seventeenth century, was so excellent a player on the gamba that Jean Rousseau asserts that he would have put in the shade all his contemporaries had he made a profession of his art.

There are no particulars obtainable about this Père André, but it seems a curious coincidence that André Maugars was at the time a priest and titular prior of the Abbey of St. Pierre Esnac. On the other hand, Maugars was in reality a professional gambist.

JEAN ROUSSEAU, who lived in Paris during the latter part of the seventeenth century, as a teacher of the viol da gamba was a pupil of Sainte-Colombe, to whom he dedicated a tutor for his instrument:

"TRAITÉ DE LA VIOLE."

The "Traité de la Viole," published in Paris in 1687, besides giving some interesting information about French gambists of the seventeenth century, gives a clear insight into the technique of the instrument. The holding of the bow is explained exactly as we see it in contemporary pictures. The right hand held the bow from underneath, not unlike holding of the double-bass bow still practised by some players. "The first finger and thumb hold the bow stick about two or three fingers' breadth from the nut, the middle finger resting on the hair below the stick. In bowing the stick should slant a little towards the bridge; care must be taken not to let it slant too much so as to touch the string as that produces a bad effect." Then comes a long explanation of the position of the semitones and their respective frets on the neck of the seven-stringed gamba, and also of the neck in tablature, viz., letter *a* for the open string, *b* for the first fret (first semitone), *c* for the second fret, etc., as explained before, the letters which go beyond the highest fret *(h)* "mark the frets *which are not there*" (the higher semitones).

Rousseau published two books of pieces.

HENRI DESMAREST, who was born in Paris in 1662, made his debut as "violiste de la chambre." (chamber violist to the king). He was an excellent musician and competed in 1683 for one of the four appointments of "maître de la chapelle du roi," but Louis XIV thought him too young, and put him off with an annuity. He composed some motets, and Goupillier, chapel master at Versailles, produced them as his own. The king heard of this and, learning that Desmarest had sold them to Goupillier under these conditions, he dismissed him. In 1700 Desmarest stayed with his friend Gervais, chapel master of the cathedral at Senlis, where he made the acquaintance of a young lady of good family and married her without the knowledge and consent of her family. The parents lodged a complaint, and Desmarest was condemned to death. He fled to Spain and became chapel master of Phillipp V, but the climate did not suit his wife, and he went to Luneville as *intendant* of the music of the Duc de Lorraine. In 1722, during the Regency, he obtained his pardon and a pension from the Duke of Orleans. He died at Luneville September 7, 1741.

LOUIS DE CAIX D'HERVELOIS, born about 1670, was another prominent pupil of Sainte-Colombe. He was appointed valet de chambre to the Duke of Orleans, and published five books of pieces for viol da gamba.

It is a curious fact that his christian name does not appear on any title page of his books where he calls himself "Monsieur de Caix d'Hervelois." The title page of the first book tells us, however, that he lived in the Rue St. Sauveur in Paris where his book could be obtained at the price of eight francs. The other address given on the title page is that of Foucault, Rue St. Honoré à la Règle d'Or, which was essentially a music printers' and publishers' street. The author has only seen the first two books of De Caix's pieces. They are quite simple from a technical point, as compared with Schenck's or Höffler's pieces, or even those of his contemporary, Forqueray, but in melodic invention they surpass most of them. In fact they contain many pearls of melody which appear as beautiful and fresh as they were two hundred years ago. The "Papillon" from the second book has proved one of the most successful concert pieces in the repertoire of the late Jules Delsaert, Messrs. Jacob, Casadesus and other artists interested in the revival of the viol da gamba. He published also a book of duos for pardessus de viole and three books of sonatas for flute solo.

Grillet mentions his son and three daughters as gambists in the royal chamber music in 1749.

ANTOINE FORQUERAY (Forqueroy, Forcroix), was born 1671 in Paris, as the son of a gambist, who instructed his son in the playing of his instrument, with the result that young Anton appeared at the age of five before Louis XIV, who was so much struck with the child's playing that he called him his little wonder. On December 31, 1689, he was appointed as gambist in the royal chamber music. The Duke of Orleans chose him for his master, and rewarded him with an annuity of one hundred thousand livres (four thousand pounds), according to the "Gazette d'Amsterdam" of 1723. The "Hallische Zeitung" of the same year, attributes that princely gift to the Duc de Chartres. In 1725 the Elector of Cologne visited Paris, and on hearing Forqueray play he presented him with one hundred Louis d'ors and an annuity of five hundred livres. Quantz heard him in 1726 and greatly admired his playing. Hubert le Blanc, in his "Defense de la Viole," accuses him of having affected bizarre manners to make himself interesting and to have pursued his own interests at the expense of those of the viol. He also states that he trained no pupils (?). He retired eventually to Nantes where he died June 28, 1745.

JEAN BAPTISTE ANTOINE FORQUERAY, the son of Antoine, was born April 3, 1700, in Paris. Like his father he was a prodigy and appeared like him at the age of five before the same monarch, Louis XIV, who appointed him later on as a member of his private music. He was considered the greatest gambist of his time. He composed a number of very interesting and clever pieces which were published by his son, Jean Baptiste Forqueray, born about 1728. The latter was also a gambist, but less distinguished as an executant. Marpurg mentions him as being an organist at the Church of St. Mary's in 1750. On the title page of the pieces published by J. B. Forqueray as "Livre I," it states that they are composed by Mr. Forqueray *le père*, Ordinaire de la Musique de la Chambre du Roi. They are dedicated to the Queen Henrietta of France, and were engraved by Mme. Leclair.

In the preface Forqueray says that in giving these pieces to the public it was his intention to amuse three people at a time by forming a "concert for two viols and harpsichord." "I thought it advisable," he says, "to keep the basses very simple, to avoid the confusion which would otherwise arise with the harpsichord bass which I have ornamented as much as it was possible for me to do. The third suite not having been found complete for the number of pieces, I was obliged to add three of my own which are marked with a star." These pieces, "La Angrave," "La Du Vaucel" and "La Morangis ou La Plissay," a chaconne, do him credit as a composer. The pieces of the elder Forqueray demand a considerable amount of technical skill, especially in the polyphonic writing in two and three parts with frequent employment of bigger chords. The book contains in all five suites, consisting of six or seven pieces each, bearing as title the names of famous musicians, prominent personages from the court, mythological names or indicating realistic imitations like "La Mandoline" and "Le Carillon de Passy." According to a statement on the title page the pieces could also be played on the pardessus de viole. The price of the book was twelve livres (francs) and it was to be obtained at Forqueray's house in the "rue de la Croix des petits champs," opposite the rue Coquillière, also from the Veuve Boivin, rue St. Honoré à la Règle d'Or (a celebrated music publisher in this street noted for its publishers, see *De Caix*), a third address was that of Le Sieur Leclerc, rue du Roule a la Croix d'Or. It is interesting to note these names as reappearing on many eighteenth century musical publications.

With J. B. Forqueray closes a dynasty of gambists which through four generations covered a period of over a century. The date of his death is not known. Grillet mentions DE MACHY, GARNIER, BELLIER, MLLE. MAUGEY and DU BUISSON as gambists of the royal chamber music during the early part of the eighteenth century. Two pieces in Forqueray's book bear Du Buisson's name (La Du Buisson) as well as those of Rameau, Leclair, etc. Rameau, on the other hand, has called one of his "Pièces en Concert" La Forqueray.

A. Vidal mentions besides some of the above the names of LE MORE, LE COUVREUR, HUREL, HATOT, LÉONARD ITIER, who was also teacher of the lute and theorbo to the king's pages, and GASTON ITIER. Grillet mentions Nicolas Itier. We do not know whether this was a third Itier, or whether it is merely a mistake in the Christian name. LOUIS COUPERIN, the first of that name, played dessus de viole in the royal private music, although he was chiefly clavecinist. NICOLAS DANICAN and PIERRE DANICAN PHILIDOR belonged to it as gambists in 1736.

Among prominent female gambists was a daughter of

Sainte-Colombe, a daughter of Marin Marais, three daughters of De Caix d'Hervelois, Mlle. Maugey, Mlle. de Cury, who is described as a clever gambist and a very amiable lady, who married the famous composer, La Lande, in 1723, and Mlles. Hilaire, Sercamann and de la Barte, who were gambists in the royal private music in 1694.

MADAME ADÉLAIDE of France, daughter of Louis XV, was also an enthusiastic performer on the viol da gamba, and a charming portrait of her with her favourite instrument, painted by Nattier, is in the gallery at Versailles *(see Plate XVII)*.

PHILIPPE PIERRE DE SAINT-SEVIN and probably also his brother, PIERRE DE SAINT-SEVIN, called "the brothers Abbé," exchanged the viol da gamba for the violoncello before 1727, and so did also the famous BERTEAU, who, in his younger years, travelled in Germany as gambist. He studied the instrument under a Bohemian named Kozecz. As they were all better known as violoncellists we shall speak of them later on.

One of the last French gambists is probably ALEXANDRE SALLENTIN, who was chamber violist from about 1736 to 1749 or later. In 1755 Sallentin (Salentin) is mentioned by Marpurg as gambist in the orchestra of the Paris opera.

CHAPTER VIII.

THE VIOLA BASTARDA AND THE BARYTON.

THE viola bastarda was a viol da gamba, which in size stood between the lyra viol (a small kind of gamba) and the bass viol. From this fact it was called the bastard viol or viola bastarda. Prætorius describes it in his "Syntagma" and gives various tunings for it, the first being identical with that of the ordinary bass viol, but some going to the contra A below *(for illustration see Fig. 13, page 21)*.

In England it was fitted with sympathetic strings, and this may have gradually led to the idea of the baryton, a viol of the size of a large gamba *(see Fig. 24)*. It had, besides the ordinary gamba strings running over the finger-board, from eight to twenty-four and more metal strings running over a separate bridge and through the open neck of the instrument, where they could be plucked with the thumb of the left hand to supply a bass accompaniment to a melody played by the four fingers on the strings running over the finger-board (see the author's "The Revival of the Viols"). It was chiefly used in Germany and particularly in Austria.

Leopold Mozart gives the following description of it: "This instrument has six or seven strings like the viol da gamba.

The neck is very wide, hollow and open at the back, fitted with nine or ten metal strings, which are plucked with the thumb, so that, while the bow touches those over the finger-board, the thumb plays the bass part on the metal strings. For that reason the music to be performed on this instrument has to be specially set for it. It is, however, one of the sweetest and most pleasing instruments." The baryton had only one representative in the Imperial Chapel at Vienna, and this was:

MARC ANTONIO BERTI, who was engaged on March 1, 1721, at a salary of 540 florins, and remained there until 1740. All further particulars are wanting. The baryton was not used in the Imperial Chapel after 1740.

KARL FRANZ, born at Langenbielau, near Reichen= bach, in Silesia, was one of the few and one of the foremost virtuosi on an instrument which contemporaries describe as one of the finest and one of the most difficult. At nine years of age he entered the house of his uncle, who was a horn player and bailiff of

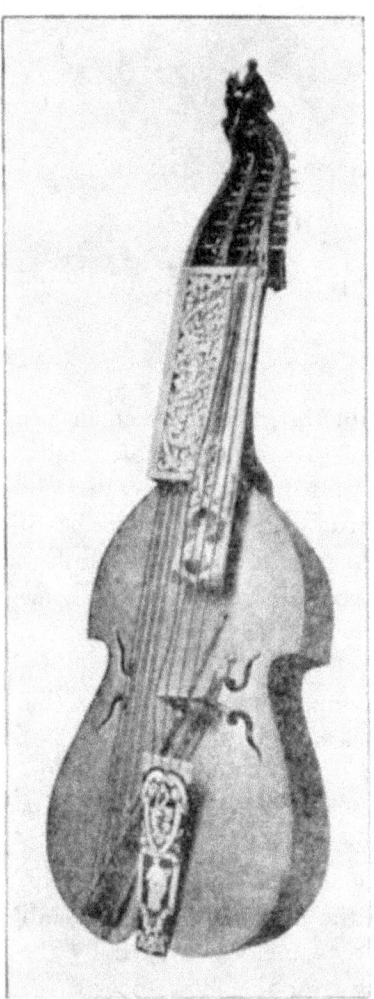

FIG. 24. BARYTON BY JAQUES SAINPRAE IN THE SOUTH KEN- SINGTON MUSEUM.

PLATE XV.

MARAIS, LULLY AND THE BROTHERS HOTTETERRE. FROM THE PAINTING BY HYACINTHE RIGAUD IN THE NATIONAL GALLERY.

To face page 112.

Count Zerotin at Falkenberg. From him he received instruction in music and in agriculture. At the age of twenty he entered the service of the bishop of Olmütz as a horn player, and by dint of study he became one of the first virtuosi of his time. His particular gift was in the playing of chromatic passages in rapid time, and with the most perfect intonation on the hand horn. After the demise of the bishop he entered the chapel of Prince Esterhazy, who induced him to take up the baryton, which was the prince's favourite instrument. He made rapid progress, and became, with Lidl, the greatest virtuoso of the eighteenth century on that instrument. As the prince would not allow him to get married while in his service, he left him and joined the chapel of Cardinal Prince Bathyani at Presburg until the accession of Joseph II, when the cardinal was obliged to dismiss his musicians. He turned to Vienna, where, during the space of two years, he gave twelve concerts on the baryton, which were very successful. From 1786 to 1788 he travelled in Germany, France, England, Holland and Russia, with a view to obtaining a new position. In the latter year he appeared at Nuremberg. His instrument resembled that of Lidl, but had only sixteen metal strings in the neck and seven on the fingerboard. Its tone was of a sweet but rather melancholy character. Franz's great piece, by which he earned most applause, was a cantata by Haydn, "Germany's Lament on the Death of Frederic the Great," which he sang with a sympathetic voice, playing the original baryton accompaniment at the same time *(see page 114)*.

ANTON LIDL, born about 1740 in Vienna, shared as baryton virtuoso the palm with Franz, whom, perhaps, he even surpassed. He increased the number of brass wire strings in the neck of the instrument to twenty-seven, including semitones. His playing was generally admired for richness of tone and delicacy of style. In 1778 he made his debut in London with great success. Dr. Burney, who heard him, gives an account of his concerts in his history of music. According to the latter authority, Lidl died before 1789. The exact date or even year of his death is unknown. We have already mentioned that August Kühnel gave concerts on the gamba and baryton in London as early as 1685. Lidl gave concerts together with the famous Giulio Regondi, who played a kind of concertina called the melophon. The novelty of this new combination took public and critics by storm.

SEBASTIAN LUDWIG FRIEDEL, born February 15, 1768, at Neuburg, was member of a numerous family of musicians. He received his musical education from the "Hofmusikus" Simon, and the famous Peter Ritter at Mannheim. He was a virtuoso on the baryton as well as on the violoncello. In the latter capacity we shall meet with him again later on. Prince Carl Theodore (Prince Palatine), a great patron of all arts, presented him with a baryton made by Tielke and repaired by Straube in Berlin, which was richly inlaid and set with precious stones. He played on this instrument before the court at Schwetzingen, earning the greatest admiration of the prince and all present. He entered afterwards the royal chapel at Berlin as violoncellist, where we shall renew acquaintance with him.

Several Austrian composers wrote for the baryton; EYBLER, WEIGL, PICHL and others, and, above all, HAYDN. He composed no less than 163 pieces for that instrument for his patron, Prince Esterhazy, who was passionately fond of the baryton, which he played himself. Haydn wrote also the cantata on the death of Frederic the Great, in which Franz used to shine, and which commenced "Er ist nicht mehr, tön trauernd baryton!" ("He is no more, sound mournful baryton!"). E. van der Straeten, in "The Revival of the Viols," gives an illustration of the baryton, on which Haydn used to play, and which has fortunately been preserved. He tells us that the instrument, which is a very perfect specimen of excellent workmanship, must be attributed either to Felden Magnus (1654) or to Jacobus Stainer. It is surmounted by a beautifully carved head of an old man. The dimensions are as follows: total length of front, 1·25 metres; total length of back, 1·23 metres; greatest width of table, 36·5 centimetres; width of ribs, 12 centimetres; length of finger-board, 45 centimetres. The instrument had no frets.

The lyra tedesca, mentioned as the favourite instrument of the King of Naples, was the same as the baryton, the former being its Italian designation. A number of Haydn's pieces for that instrument were composed by him at the request of the King of Naples, who met him on his visit to Vienna in 1790.

Another instrument somewhat similar to the gamba was the arpeggione (guitar-violoncello), constructed in 1823 by G. Staufer in Vienna. It had six strings and was tuned:

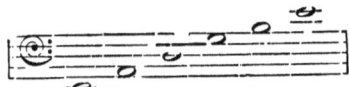

FIG. 25. THE TUNING OF THE ARPEGGIONE.

Schubert composed a sonata for this instrument, and Vincenz Schuster wrote a tutor.

There is one more instrument which remains to be mentioned as a connecting link between the old viol tribe and the violoncello, and that is the viola pomposa, which was an instrument of the violin pattern with five strings. In size it was equal to a very large viol d'amour, the total length being about 27½ inches. The tuning was:

FIG. 26. THE TUNING OF THE VIOLA POMPOSA.

The instrument was conceived by J. S. Bach to secure a

satisfactory rendering of florid bass passages to which the technique of his violoncellists was inadequate. It appears as "violoncello piccolo" in a number of Bach's scores, and was constructed according to his instructions by J. C. Hoffmann, of Leipzig, an instrument-maker of a high reputation.

The Suite in D which is now generally known as the Sixth Solo Suite for Violoncello was originally written for the viola pomposa, and so was the famous *obbligato* part to "My Faithful Heart," as well as many other *obbligato* passages in his cantatas, etc. With the technical development of the violoncello the instrument became obsolete, and, in fact, never appears to have been used after Bach.

JOHN GEORGE PISENDEL, born December 26, 1687, at Karlsburg, died November 25, 1755, at Dresden, a famous violinist of his time, pupil of Torelli and Antonio Vivaldi, appears to have been the only virtuoso on the viola pomposa.

The instrument soon became shrouded in mystery, and in many dictionaries we find the most confused statements about it.

Mr. Paul de Wit, of Leipzig, the celebrated collector of musical instruments, was the first to bring light again into the matter. He secured several specimens of the instrument, including one originally belonging to Bach's orchestra. They are now in the instrument museum of commercienrath W. Heyer, in Cologne.

THE REVIVAL OF THE VIOL DA GAMBA.

In Hector Berlioz's book on instrumentation we find a lengthy article in which he extols the merits of the viol d'amour, and advocates the introduction of that singularly beautiful instrument into the modern orchestra. As a matter of fact it has been employed with marked success by several nineteenth century composers, one of the most notable instances being the *obbligato* part in Meyerbeer's "Huguenots." The viol da gamba might be used with equal effect and even more so on account of its greater capabilities, but, unfortunately, the rapid development of the violoncello, which commenced only during the second half of the eighteenth century, caused the absolute neglect of the former instrument. Those who still knew the gamba in the hands of its last votaries compared it with the violoncello, and condemned it as lacking in power, brilliancy of tone and possibilities of technical display. Those who came after them and never heard the instrument at all, accepted their verdict, and talked about the bass viol as a poor old primitive sort of instrument which in the days of the violin family was utterly useless and deservedly forgotten. These people made, and still make, the same mistake that was made with regard to the viol d'amour, which was abandoned in favour of the violin and the viola.

Would anybody be bold enough to assert that the clarinet is a useless instrument because we have the trumpet, which is much more powerful and brilliant, and can also execute rapid passages? The obvious answer would be that they have nothing to do with each other, that they serve totally different purposes, and have a totally different quality of tone. Everybody will agree to that, yet they cannot see that it is exactly the same in the case of viol da gamba and violoncello. The tone of the former is of a peculiar silvery quality, slightly veiled, refined and of great sweetness. Although not loud as the violoncello, its tone has great carrying power. Double notes can be played very easily and produce a fine effect. As a solo instrument in such parts as the *obbligatos* in Bach's oratorios, his exquisite three sonatas with harpsichord, or some of those delightful little rococo pieces of the French and German schools, it can never be replaced by the violoncello as that instrument can in no way produce the effect intended by the composer. But apart from that, as an instrument in the modern orchestra it offers wonderful opportunities. A quartet of four bass viols for a sustained melody of a mystic or romantic character contrasted by the modern strings or brass instruments; again a melody part for bass viols accompanied by florid wood-wind passages, the bass strengthened by double basses or a flute accompanied by arpeggios of two or more bass viols. There are in fact limitless combinations which would give the most ravishing effects. From the early part of last century the bass viol has not been wanting for a casual champion but the tyrannical absolutism of ignorance has always defeated their efforts by ridiculous ridicule.

JEAN MARIE RAUOL, 1766-1837, a Paris lawyer and violoncellist, who was the fortunate owner of the famous Duiffoprugcar gamba with the plan of Paris (see "Revival of the Viols"), tried all he could to revive the instrument. Vuillaume supported him in his endeavour and made a fine bass viol on the old models for him, but their united efforts had no result. The late F. A. Gevaërt arranged concerts of ancient music at the Brussels Conservatoire in which the original instruments were employed, and Mr. Edward Jacobs played the bass viol, yet they only awakened a passing interest, more satisfying curiosity than engaging sympathy.

JEAN AUDRIES, born April 25, 1798, at Ghent, devoted himself to the study of the viol da gamba as well as that of the violoncello. He was director of the Conservatoire at Ghent from 1851 to 1855, and wrote several works on musical history, etc. He died January 21, 1872.

PAUL DE WIT, born 1852 at Maestricht, started the "Zeitschrift für Instrumentenbau" in Leipzig, and opened his rich collection of old instruments to the public in 1886 as a "museum" in the Thomaskirchhof. He tried to revive the bass viol by public performances, but the result was little better than in the former cases. Towards the latter part of last century the interest in the ancient music and instruments seemed to awaken a little. Mr. Arnold Dolmetsch gave some concerts at which his daughter, Miss Helène Dolmetsch, appeared first as a performer on the bass viol which she treats now with perfect mastery, as does also Miss Mabel Chaplin, one of the author's pupils.

The author has devoted himself to the study of the gamba for over twenty years, and is still giving concerts in conjunction with his son and other pupils. These concerts, at which they produce old English consorts and fancies as well as the suites by Marais, etc., for two and three gambas, solos, songs with gamba accompaniments and pieces with viol d'amour (Miss Maria Thaler), etc., are gradually gaining in popularity. Messrs. George and Henry Saint-George also took part in some of these concerts, where they produced sonatas for two gambas by Kühnel, etc., and also J. S. Bach's famous Sixth Brandenburg Concerto for two violas, two gambas, bass and continuo.

JULES DELSAERT, the late professor of the Paris Conservatoire, who died in 1900, was an eminent virtuoso on the bass viol. In conjunction with L. van Waefelghem, L. Grillet and L. Diemer, he formed the first "Société des Instruments anciens," appearing at the Salle Erard in London in 1895. Delsaert's solos on the bass viol were received with rapturous applause, especially the sonata by Handel and De Caix d'Hervelois's "Le Papillon." The latter piece is also a favourite with Edward Jacobs and Marcel Casadesus, who is the bass viol player in the *new* "Société des Instruments anciens," in which his brother plays the viol d'amour, Edward Celli the quinton, Maurice Devilliers the bass (violone) and Alfred Casella the harpsichord. Their appearance in London in 1908 met with an enthusiastic reception and has done much to awaken the interest for the old instruments, especially the viol d'amour and the bass viol, in wider circles.

ROBERT HAUSMANN, the late violoncellist in the Joachim Quartet, had also taken up the viol da gamba.

The late JOHANNES KLINGENBERG, of Brunswick *(see under German Violoncellists)*, was an excellent performer on the bass viol. He was also an enthusiastic collector of the literature for that instrument, and copied a large number of books for viol da gamba from various libraries, and many a duplicate he presented to the author. MR. PAUL PANNIER, of Lille, is another enthusiastic viol da gambist of the present day

The number of viol da gamba players has so much increased within the last few years that we cannot give the names of all its votaries for want of space.

PLATE XVI.

FACSIMILE OF THE FINELY ENGRAVED TITLE OF "PIÈCES A UNE ET A DEUX VIOLES" BY MARAIS.

CHAPTER IX.

THE VIOLONCELLO.

BIRTH AND INFANCY.

THE origin of the violoncello, like that of its twin sisters, the violin and the viola, is shrouded in mystery. Some of the stories that have been told by superficial historians, and repeated by people who believed their statements, are too ridiculous to be treated seriously. The most popularly known story was launched upon the world by Laborde in his "Essay sur la Musique," which appeared in Paris in 1780. He tells us that the Abbé Tardieu, of Tarrascon, in the Provence, "invented the violoncello" about the beginning of the eighteenth century. This Abbé Tardieu was the brother of a well-known "maître de chapelle." He has also been credited with reducing the number of strings on the violoncello from five to four. Gerber's "Tonkünstler-Lexikon" contains the same story, which has even found its way into the dictionary of Mendel-Reissmann, which generally excels for the accuracy of its articles. Corette, in his violoncello tutor (Paris, 1741), mentions Giovanni Battista Buononcini as the inventor of the violoncello. All these statements belong to the domain of fables and fairy tales.

THE FIVE-STRINGED VIOLONCELLO.

The five-stringed violoncello was, however, not a myth, and the stories about the Abbé Tardieu probably resolve themselves in the fact that he used such an instrument tuned:

FIG. 27. THE TUNING OF THE FIVE-STRINGED VIOLONCELLO.

The Rev. F. W. Galpin is in the possession of a fine specimen of a five-stringed violoncello which forms part of his famous collection of old instruments. The reproduction, Fig. 28, is from a photograph kindly supplied by him.

Mr. Galpin acquired this instrument at Brussels. It is in its original condition and the printed label runs as follows:

Marcus Broché à Bruxelles au Roy David, l'an 1720.

The last two figures are in faded ink.

It is covered with a good and bright oil varnish which has suffered at the back from wear and neglect.

The tone is excellent and the first string, which Mr. Galpin tunes to E, he declares to be charming, but adds that, owing to the thin string he has to use, it does not stand changes of temperature and breaks frequently. This is not surprising considering the length of string. The original tuning as mentioned above, was a full tone lower, which would render it less liable to break. The name of Broché does not appear in any of the known books on musical instrument makers.

The tuning was by no means fixed. In fact, it was custom-

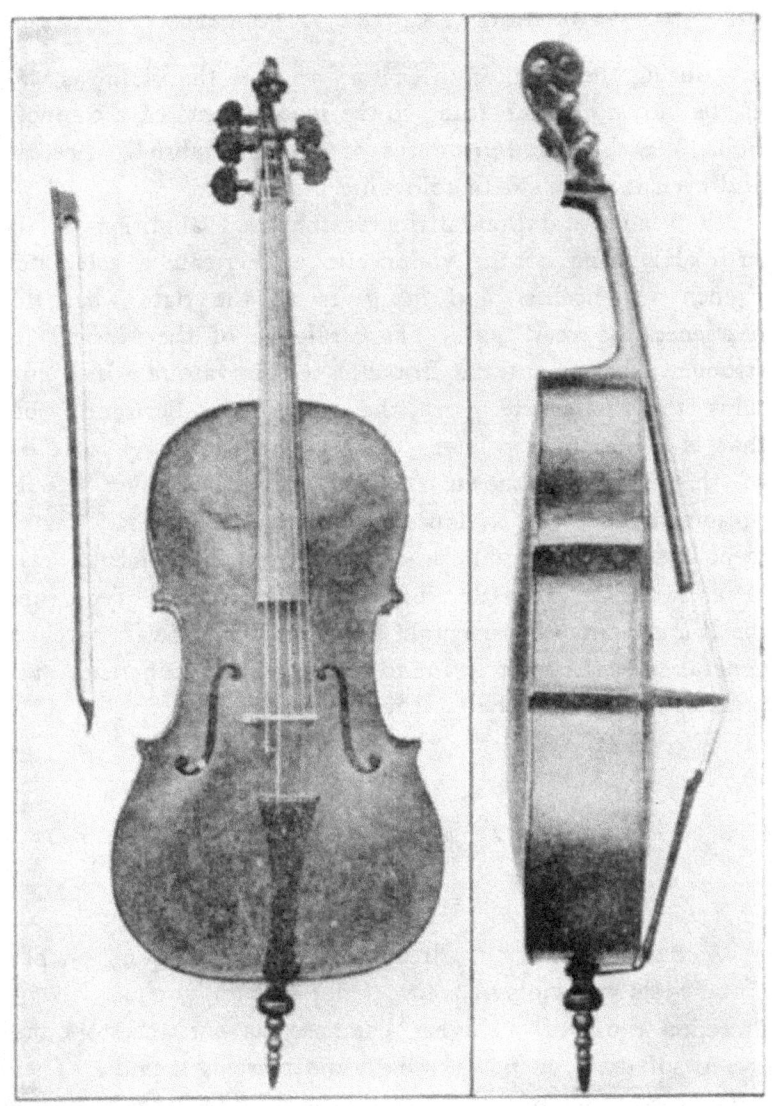

Fig. 28. A Five-Stringed Violoncello in the Collection of the Rev. F. W. Galpin. The Label runs: "Marcus Broché a Bruxelles au Roy David: l'an 1720." Broché is a French Form of "Snoeck," a Well Known Flemish Maker.

ary during the seventeenth century to tune the violin as well as the violoncello according to the requirements of a composition. We shall find instances of this in Gabrieli's ricercari and even in Bach's fifth solo suite.

Mr. Victor Mahillon attributes the final abolition of the fifth (E) string of the violoncello to Berteau, a celebrated French violoncellist, and he gives as the date when this happened the year 1725. The catalogue of the Musical Instrument Museum of the Bruxelles Conservatoire which contains this statement gives the name as "Bertrand," but that is evidently a printer's error as no French violoncellist of that name is known at that period. It must not be presumed that the violoncello was a five-stringed instrument before it became a four-stringed instrument. The latter was, as a matter of fact, the original type, and the former an experimental variation, which was never in general use, although it found a few casual adherents until practice had proved the fallacy of the system.

FIRST APPEARANCE OF THE VIOLONCELLO.

We have pointed out already in our introductory chapter that fiedels and viols of a low (tenor or bass) compass always preceded those of a higher compass, as our ancestors preferred soft and low notes to high and piercing sounds. There is no reason to suppose that the order of development should have been suddenly reversed with regard to the violin family, and the violone and violoncello ("violon-cello," diminutive of violone) appeared no doubt before the viola and the violin. Galilei, in his "Il Fronimo," dialogue on the art of writing in tablature and correct playing of music (1583), mentions the Neapolitans as rightful claimants to the honour of having constructed the first violoncello. Vidal in "Les instruments à archet," opines that this took place about 1520. Valdrighi states that the *violin* is mentioned among the instruments used at a convent in Modena about 1536.

These dates, however, remain open to controversy, especially if we take into account that the names of instruments were by no means fixed as they are now, and that the word viol*ino* might stand for a small viol (*viol* with diminutive ending *ino*) as well as for the instrument known to us by that name.

GASPARO DA SALO (Gasparo Bertolotti), 1542-1609, who took his name from his native town of Salò on the Lake Garda, is the first to whom we can point with absolute certainty as a maker of violoncellos, as well as violins and violas. Some of his instruments have been preserved. Their tone is powerful

FIG. 29. THE BAS GEIG DA BRACIO. FROM PRÆTORIUS'S "SYNTAGMA MUSICUM."

and of the finest quality, they are bold in design and testify to the high artistic qualities of the master.

ANDREAS AMATI (1535-1611), who worked at Cremona, is said to have made among others, twenty-four violins (twelve large and twelve small pattern), six tenors and eight basses for Charles IX of France. They were kept in the Chapel Royal at Versailles until 1790 when they disappeared. On the backs of these instruments were painted the arms of France and other devices with the motto, "Pietate and Justitia."

Several modern authorities regard this statement as apocryphal, yet in "The Violin Times" of October 15, 1894, Mr. Edward Heron Allen informs us that:

> In the sale of the late Sir William Curtis on May 3, 1827, lot nine was a violoncello by Andreas Amati, Cremonensis faciebat, 1572. A document was given to the proprietor when he purchased this instrument, stating that it was presented by Pope Pius V to Charles IX, King of France, for his chapel. It has been richly painted, the arms of France being on the back, and the motto, "Pietate et Justitia," on the sides. The tone of this violoncello is of extraordinary power and richness. This was evidently one of the instruments made for Charles IX. Mr. Hollander sold it to Sir William Curtis. It was put up at five hundred guineas and bought in at two hundred and eighty.

In a note to the above, Mr. Heron Allen says:

> In 1872 this violoncello belonged to the Rev. A. H. Bridges, who lent it to the Loan Exhibition. It was numbered 183 in the catalogue. I do not know whence the amateur who sold the instrument to Sir William Curtis got his information to the effect that the instrument reached King Charles through Pope Pius V. I cannot find any sort of authority for the statement. Pius V was sovereign pontiff from 1566-72, and 1566 has been the date generally ascribed to these illuminated fiddles.

There is no doubt, therefore, about the instrument having formed part of the famous loan collection at South Kensington.

Michael Prætorius in his "Syntagma Musicum," published in 1618, gives the picture of an instrument which he describes as

"Bas geig da Bracio" *(see Fig. 29)*. The total length of the instrument according to the scale given at the foot of the page is about three feet, it has four strings and is fitted with a tailpin. It has in every detail the appearance of the violoncello which no doubt it really does represent, the name bas (bass) geig da bracio (braccio) signifying that it is the bass of the *armgeigen* (violins).

It appears certain that the whole violin family was in use about 1550, as the Marshal de Brissac, governor of Piedmont, sent about that time the famous Baltazarini with a band of violins to Paris as private musicians to the Queen Katherine of Medici. Baltazarini, besides being an excellent violinist, was the inventor of the ballet, and that merry art procured him the nickname of Beaujoyeux.

In conjunction with Charles de Beaulieu and Jacques Salomon, who composed the music, he wrote the "Ballet comique de la Reine," which was produced at the Louvre on October 15, 1581. It contained an air called "La Clochette" (the bell) which marked the appearance of Circe. This air is written in five parts, and was executed by *twenty violins*, proving clearly that tenor and bass violins were included in their number. The air created quite a sensation, and is still very popular under the name of "Air de Louis XIII," republished by Ghys. As it is one of the oldest monuments of music written for instruments of the violin family, we add the piece in its original form.

LA CLOCHETTE.

From the "Balet comique de la Royne, faict aux nopces de Monsieur le Duc de Joyeuse et Mademoyselle de Vaudemont, sa soeur. Par Baltasar de Beaujoyeulx, valet de chambre du Roy, et de la Royne, sa mère. A Paris par Adrian le Roy, Robert Ballard, et Mamert. Pattison, Imprimeurs du Roy, 1582. Avec Privilège."

"Le son de la Clochette, auquel Circé sortit de son jardin."

The above is printed in the original on five staves for Dessus, Quinte, Haute Contre, Taille and Basse, without bar lines and even without indication of time and rhythm. It is evidently a gavotte, and began on the third beat of the bar, but printed as it was—without bar lines—it appeared to necessitate the insertion of half a bar before the final chord.* In the above illustration we have placed the bar lines so that the air commences with the third crotchet, conforming with the general rule, thereby dividing it into eight bars. The last bar, which thus becomes superfluous, appears in parenthesis.

At a grand reception given by the authorities of the town of Rouen to Henry II and Catherine of Medici, violins were played by "The Nine Muses," who danced and sang to the accompaniment of their instruments. Flanders, which at that time was in close contact with Italy in everything respecting music, was one of the first countries to introduce the new in-

---

* In the sixteenth and seventeenth century gavottes often started on the first beat of the bar. In this case the accent is so evidently on the third crotchet that it could not be arranged in any but the above way.

PLATE XVII.

MADAME HENRIETTE DE FRANCE, 1727-52. ON MANY PRINTS HER NAME APPEARS AS MADAME ADÉLAIDE DE FRANCE. FROM A PAINTING BY NATTIER IN THE MUSEUM AT VERSAILLES.

struments. We find, for instance, in 1559, a Pietro Lupo,* of Antwerp, who sells to a musician, sent by the magistrate of Utrecht a *chest of five violins* for sixty-two livres, i.e., francs. They were played before a committee by a professional player, and the wine consumed at the trial came to six livres! In England the violin was introduced about 1561, in which year violins were appointed in Queen Elizabeth's private band. In 1571 they were increased to the number of seven. The following lines, taken from Edmund Spenser's "Shepherd's Calendar," 1579, seems to prove that the violin was then known in England:

> I see Calliope speed her to the place
> Where my godesse shines,
> And after her the other muses trace
> With their violines.

We must remind the reader, however, of the fact that the naming of instruments at that time was very arbitrary and that we cannot be absolutely certain that Spenser did not mean small viols.

The word "violoncello," which is now generally adopted as the name of the instrument which forms the object of this history, is of comparatively recent date. The oldest designation appears to have been "bass violin" (French: "basse de violon"), which word was still frequently used during the eighteenth century. In Italy it was sometimes described as "violone," although that name was generally applied to the double bass.

---

* This Lupo was probably the forefather of the musicians of that name which appear in the "Private Musick" of the English court, as also the celebrated violin and bow makers of that name. We find that he sold the instruments in sets or "chests," like the viols, which proves that the name "violin" designates here the whole family. Ben Jonson expresses this fact still clearer in "St. Bartholomew Fair," published in 1600. The passage runs thus: "A set of these violins I would buy too, for a delicate young niece I have in the country; they are everyone a size less than another, just like your fiddles." By the latter he probably means the old viols.

In some of the earlier editions of Corelli's sonatas, for instance, that of Op. 3, printed at Bologna in 1690, the bass part, which is not for the organ, is entitled "violone," whereas in the later edition printed at Amsterdam by Estienne Roger, the same part is entitled "violoncello." In a work of Freschi, which was published in 1660, it is called the "violoncino," also in the sonatas by Giovanni Battista Fontana. Both the endings "ello" and "ino" are diminutive, signifying that the instrument is a "small violone" or bass. Besides these two names, the word "viulunzel" was also used in Italy about 1640, as we shall see later on that the violoncellist and composer, Domenico Gabrieli, was called "Mingheein del Viulunzel." In Germany we find the word "Violuntzen" (see Prætorius, "Syntagma"), which seems to point to the same origin. In chamber music works of the eighteenth and the first part of the nineteenth century, we find as a rule simply the word "basso" or "basse," instead of violoncello, and Löhlein, as well as Johann Adam Hiller, calls it: "Kleine Bassgeig, auch Bassetel." During the first century of its existence the violoncello was used only as a bass instrument to support the voices in church music, and with the appearance of the violin sonata, at the middle of the seventeenth century, the place of accompanying instrument was filled almost exclusively by the violoncello. Great violinists, like Corelli and Tartini, had each a violoncellist attached to their person who accompanied them in all their travels. Yet, although at the end of the seventeenth century, the finest instruments had already emerged from the hands of masters like the Amati, Maggini, Grancino, Ruggeri, Stradivari and others, nobody suspected what the instrument was capable of, nor the rôle it was to play in times to come.

The viol da gamba held its sway and asserted, at least in England and France, its supremacy, even over the violin, throughout the seventeenth century, and retained many admirers throughout the eighteenth century, one of its last votaries being the famous C. F. Abel.

Yet all the enthusiasm of Mr. Hubert le Blanc and many kindred spirits could not arrest the progress of the violoncello. Although it took a much longer time than the violin to develop a technique of its own, and to free itself from the bondage of a mere bass, yet we find already, during the latter part of the seventeenth century, that it was breaking the fetters, and that some of the foremost composers of the day began to recognise its higher claims. We have mentioned already that Prætorius has given an illustration of an instrument which must have been a violoncello with five strings from its proportions and the peg or tail-pin. The next illustration which has been preserved is that in Marin Mersenne's "Harmonie Universelle," which was published in Paris, 1636-7. His description of the instrument runs as follows: "As to the bass, the four pegs of which are marked by numbers, it is done so well that it is not necessary to describe it at length. The length of its neck is one-third of the length of the table, and equals the width between the sound-holes or at the bridge. .... I leave all the other parts of which I have spoken previously" (when speaking of the violin generically). He says later on: "I come now to the concert which one can compose of five hundred divers violins, although twenty-four suffice, viz., six trebles (Dessus), six basses, four altos, four tenors and four 'quintes.'" The latter took the place of the "cinquième" among the viols, and was one of the odd size patterns which were afterwards abolished.

CHAPTER X.

THE VIOLONCELLO IN ITALY.

THE art of the ancients had been literally stamped out after the fall of Rome, yet it was in Rome again, or rather in Italy, that art rose like a phœnix from its ashes under the auspices of young Christianity. Tenderly nursed by wealthy, powerful and intelligent princes, it soon developed to such a flourishing state that the whole world looked up in wonderment when it beheld the wealth and beauty of its forms. We have already seen that Italy was the birthplace of the violoncello (Naples, according to Galilei), and we naturally look to that country for its first virtuosi. By reason of its subordinate condition as a mere bass instrument during the first century of its existence, prominent executants on the violoncello appeared at a much later time than on the violin. When they did appear, and composers as well as virtuosi began to write for the instrument, the same process of evolution which had begun during the early part of the seventeenth century with regard to the technique of the violin repeated itself in the case of the violoncello. Both executant and composer were experimenting and trying to develop the resources of the instrument, which was done at the expense of musical ideas and expression.

The first whose name has been handed down to posterity as executant and composer for the violoncello was DOMENICO GABRIELI, surnamed Mingheein del Viulunzel. He was born at Bologna in 1640, and died about 1690. In 1688 he received six doubloons (doble) for playing at the memorial service of the late Duchess of Modena. Buononcini played on the same occasion. For some time he held the post of *maestro di capella* at the church of St. Petronio, at Bologna, and afterwards entered the service of Cardinal Panfili at Rome. At one time he was apparently in the service of the Duke of Parma, at Modena, where the manuscript of some solos of his composition for the violoncello has been preserved. An exact copy of this interesting, and perhaps oldest, monument of violoncello literature was presented to the author by the well-known music historian, the late Count Luigi Francesco Valdrighi, of Modena, who had access to the Museo Estense containing the original autograph, among countless musical and historical treasures. The existence of this work was unknown until the appearance of Count Valdrighi's "Musurgiana" (No. IV), which led Wasielewski to the belief that Gabrieli had composed nothing for his instrument. The title is "Ricercari e Sonate per Violoncello di Gabrieli Domenico chiamato Mingheein del Viulunzel (Secolo XVII), 15 gennaro, 1689." The name *ricercari* really applies to pieces of imitative counterpoint. Ricercare: French, *rechercher*—meaning to search and research for the subject. During the seventeenth century it was applied to all sorts of compositions which might with the same amount of reason have been called fantasia or sonata.

There are ten ricercari and one canon; none of the pieces bear the superscription sonata, although that name occurs in the title of the book, and several of the ricercari show distinctly the form of the sonata in Corelli's time.

The compass used in these pieces is:

but the A occurs only once and even the G and the F are very sparingly used. The construction of the pieces seem to prove that they were written for a *five-stringed* instrument. The neck of the violoncello at that time was very short, as it was also on the violin, and as on the latter instrument, shifting was still of rare occurrence, only the neck positions being used, it is not likely that the violoncello, whose technique was even more primitive, should in this particular have been in advance over the violin. An almost absolute proof of this theory is the frequent occurrence of chords like these: which are, to say the least, very awkward, and passages like the following:

which necessitate shifts of a quite unusual kind for the time at which the pieces were written, while on a five-stringed instrument with this tuning:  they can be played quite easily. Moreover, the "A," highest note of the compass given above, would only form the highest note of the second position on the upper D string. In all likelihood the neck of the instrument was still fretted with gut string frets. It may interest the reader to obtain an idea of the nature of Gabrieli's work, for which purpose a short description is here added.

The first ricercare is a short movement in G minor and in 3-4 time. The second number in A minor begins with a movement in C time, evidently an allegro, to judge from its character. The second movement in 3-2 time, might be a "grave" or "largo," which is just as free from any attempt at melody or any trace of the emotional element as most compositions of the experimental stage, and might just as well stand for a quick movement, were it not for the 3-2 time which usually marked the slow movement or saraband. It is comparatively a long movement (some 120 bars) followed by another in C time, which looks more like an allegro, and is followed by a finale in 12-8 time in the character of a gigue. Number three is a single movement in D major, with a lot of semiquaver figures and a good deal of skipping from high to low strings and vice versa, which forms an essential feature in viol da gamba music. In number four, a single movement in E flat major, as well as in number five, in C major, that kind of bowing is still more freely employed, and testifies to a great agility of the wrist. The ricercare 5 is followed by a "Canone a 2 Violoncelli" in D major, the second violoncello entering at the beginning of the second bar. Ricercare 6, in G major, begins with a kind of short, primitive moto perpetuo, followed by another short movement in 3-4 time, which introduces the first double stopping and chords of the above description. Ricercare 7, in D minor, shows a boldness of conception, which comes as a surprise after the previous numbers, which are absolutely barren as regards melodic or thematic invention. Of course, one must not expect too much all of a sudden. After a fairly long movement of various semiquaver figures in C time, follows a very short movement in 3-4 time, with specimens of two-part writing, finishing with three bars in C time. So far, all the pieces are for violoncello solo, although they seem to imply an accompaniment in several instances. The remaining three ricercari are for two violoncellos. Number eight, in G major and in C time, begins with twelve bars for which no *tempo* is given, followed by two bars marked "adagio," and finishing with three bars marked "presto," with a few chords. Number nine contains only eight bars in G major; as they are a fair average specimen of these pieces, with regard to technique as well as contents, we give them here in full:

Fig. 30. Specimen of a Ricecare for Two Violoncellos.

PLATE XVIII.

BACK OF VIOLONCELLO BY DOMENICO GALLI SHOWING THE EXQUISITE CARVING.

The tenth and last, although called ricercare 10 is really a full-blown sonata in G major of the familiar Corelli type, consisting of three movements: allegro (not marked as such), largo and presto. The two latter movements are thus headed. The first movement introduces a new feature in the shape of a short passage in the *tenor clef!* The largo in the Phrygian mode, with a plagal ending, is a fair specimen of its kind, followed by a spirited presto of the gigue character. It was played with great success by Mr. Boris Hambourg at the first of his historical recitals at the Æolian Hall, London, in 1906, with a pianoforte accompaniment by E. van der Straeten.

In the passage work of these ricercari the influence of the gamba technique is unmistakable, especially in the frequent employment of the skipping bow, which formed an essential feature in gamba pieces of the seventeenth century. Again, there are many points showing the germs of the genuine violoncello technique. Gabrieli was a composer of great repute. Fétis enumerates eight operas of his which were written for Bologna and Venice. Besides these he wrote church music and "Balletti, gighe, correnti e Sarabande a due Violini e violoncello con Basso continuo," Op. 1.

The latter work was republished in 1703.

A contemporary of Gabrieli was DOMENICO GALLI, of Modena, where he lived during the latter part of the seventeenth century. Unfortunately no particulars concerning the life of this artist appear to have been preserved, beyond such information as may be gathered from his own works consisting of a violin and a violoncello, a harp and a book of sonatas for the latter instrument. He was a man of universal talent, and it is difficult to say whether he shone more as a sculptor, painter, composer or violoncellist, proving himself to be an accomplished master in all those arts. The discovery of his sonatas is due to the researches of the well-known musical historian, Count Luigi Francesco Valdrighi in Modena. The title of the autograph manuscript runs as follows: "Trattenimento Musicale Sopra il Violoncello a Solo, Consecrato all' Altezza Ser ma di Francesco II duca di Modona, Reggio, etc." (Musical entertainment on the violoncello solo dedicated to His Serene Highness Francis II, Duke of Modena, Reggio, etc.), consisting of twelve sonatas adorned with elegant vignettes in clare-obscure, painted by Galli himself. In the ribbon round the ducal coat of arms is written: "Domenicus Gallus Scripsit atque Pinxit." The above dedication, as well as that of the violin and the violoncello are dated September 8, 1691.

The two instruments are perfect miracles of wood-carving, the whole of the back even, being carved in the most elaborate designs of the Baroque style. Curiously enough the carving is done in open work, the back being absolutely perforated in many places. It is, of course, quite impossible that the instruments are anything else but show pieces, as they cannot give a satisfactory result as regards tone. Count Valdrighi gives a full description of the instruments in his "Nomocheliurgografia," from which the following is an extract: "The violoncello, phantastically ornamented with political and religious subjects, represents as 'Hercules slaying the Hydra'; Hercules representing the son of the duke's sister, Beatrice, Duchess of York, who herself figures as 'Pallas.' The Prince of Wales, James Stuart, is symbolised by the lion trampling down English perfidy under the patronage of the 'Roy Soleil.' The whole was to indicate his (Galli's) fervent wish that the noble house of Este might be instrumental, through the medium of the Duchess of York, in bringing back the English nation into the fold of the Church of Rome in conformity with the ardent desire of Pope Clemens X." The Princess "Beatrice" is known in English history as "Mary," and the "Prince of Wales" above mentioned is "James II," who in 1691 had fled to France, where he found the protection of Louis XIV, known as the "Roy Soleil."

In defence of the style of the instruments, which is somewhat overladen, yet very rich and artistic of its kind, Count Valdrighi quotes some interesting remarks by the French art critic, Sancet. They form a splendid refutation of that narrow-mindedness which worships one certain style as the one and only ideal, before which everything else must vanish, and we cannot resist quoting them on that account. Sancet says: "The beautiful is not absorbed in one style. Neither does the monopoly thereof belong to one school, nor is it right to compare a work of art of one epoch with that of another time. As different seasons bring forth different fruits, so do the different epochs in art produce works of different style and taste. The arts serve as a commentary to social life as manifest in the works of artists, who express the ruling spirit of their time." An illustration of the violoncello will serve to acquaint our readers with the wonderful instrument above described *(see Plate XVIII)*.

The twelve sonatas of Galli forming the "Trattenimento" are of a very primitive character, and for the greater part very uninteresting. They are composed of three or four short movements mostly in primary form, without any indication of *tempo* or other heading except in the case of a few gigas (in the second, third, fifth, sixth, seventh, ninth, tenth and twelve sonata) and one "aria" in the fifth sonata. This last piece is one of the best. It is characteristic, and has a distinct flavour of the folk-melody about it; moreover it is one of the few specimens in binary form, and being short, may be given in this place:

140 THE HISTORY OF THE VIOLONCELLO.

No. II. Aria.

Fig. 31. The Aria of the Fifth Sonata by Domenico Galli.

The gigas are mostly in 12-8 time, except the one which concludes the seventh sonata, which is in 9-8 time, while the tenth sonata finishes with one in 3-4, and the twelfth has one in 6-8 time. They are all in binary form but not always at the end of the sonatas, being followed by short movements in primary form and 4-4 time in the second, fifth, ninth and twelfth sonata. The gigas are generally a little more interesting than the other movements, for instance, that which follows the above aria in the fifth sonata, followed in its turn by a twelve-bar movement, being very uninteresting but for the chromatic writing, a very curious feature at that period. A curious little movement occurs at the end of the eleventh sonata. It is in 6-8 time, and consists of four sentences, each marked with a repeat and with a full cadence in a minor (aeolic) mode. It is so curious and characteristic that the author of these lines cannot forbear to give the first sentence in condensed form :

No. III, p. 11.

Fig. 32. Extract from a Giga by Domenico Galli.

In the original the repeats of the two-bar phrases are written out, the first being marked *forte*, the second *piano*. To save space we give them above with repeat signs.

Galli employed also a different tuning as he makes frequent use of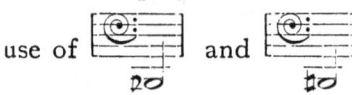

Antonio De'Pietri, called Antonio Tonelli—a name by which his family was generally known—was born at Carpi, August 19, 1686. His father was a cavalry officer, and his mother a lady of great musical accomplishments. She instilled her son with her love for music, teaching him the rudiments of that art, but after a short period D. Nicolo Pace, choirmaster of the cathedral of Carpi, undertook the musical education of young Antonio. Showing early signs of musical talent he was sent to Bologna, where he received a thorough liberal education. He distinguished himself, not only in the study of science and literature, but also in all chivalrous accomplishments, as fencing and dancing, devoting his principal energies to the study of music. He played the organ, viol d'amour and the violoncello. The last instrument was at that period beginning to attract the attention of the musical world, and to make its way into the orchestra and the concert-room. Tonelli's remarkable talent soon brought him into prominence. After finishing his studies in 1707, he was elected as music and singing master at the college of the nobility at Parma. In that capacity, he attracted the attention of Farnese, Duke of Parma, who was so much impressed with his talent, that he invited him to live in Colorno (one of his palaces). The duke delighted in testing Tonelli's capacity as a musician in all manner of ways. After finding out that he could play at sight the most difficult compositions of his time, he placed before him a sonata upside down. Tonelli, without the slightest hesitation, played the piece forthwith to the greatest admiration of the whole court. After the death of his mother, in 1706, his father married Anna Olivari, a lady of distinction, who presented him with a son, "Giuseppe." Antonio acted as godfather to his new-born brother. Holding the baby at the christening he turned with a smile to the spectators, and, showing it to them, said: "Do you see this *salame* (sausage)? He will have to take yonder cantor's place, and become a great master." Curiously enough, this prophecy was fulfilled afterwards. In 1726, a great church festival was held in honour of the sanctification of Luigi Gonzaga, by Benedict XIII. Tonelli was asked to play a solo on the violoncello on that occasion, and the famous violinist, D'AMBREVILLE, was also to appear. Each tried to outshine the other in improvised passages and cadenzas until the whole congregation broke out in rapturous applause, and brought the virtuoso duel to an end.

This mode of applauding favourite artists in a church and during divine service was quite a common occurrence in Italy during the seventeenth and early eighteenth centuries.

His biographers (Tiraboschi and Cabbasi), differ in their statements with regard to the time of Tonelli's sojourn at the court of Parma. He was a most eccentric man, a kind of stoic philosopher. He despised money, and he could never stay long in one place. "The denarius" (penny)—he used to say—"is the enemy of man, but as long as there is an organ in the town, Tonelli will not be without bread." One day he left Parma, dressed in black cloth (like Stracciapane, the minstrel) which he declared to be the best protection against the heat as well as the cold. With an unkempt wig, and his violoncello on his back, he set out on his wanderings which eventually brought him to Denmark. There he was well received at court, and remained in the service of the king for three years. After that time his stepmother died, and he returned to Italy to claim his patrimony. The means and ways by which he travelled remained known only to him. In the same mysterious way he appeared one day at Genoa. Finding himself absolutely penniless, he sat himself down on a stone in the market-place. Placing his cap on the floor in front of him, as is the custom of beggars, he took his violoncello and began to play. A large crowd soon collected and testified its delight in so liberal a fashion, that he was able to return to Carpi with a nice little sum of money, but always travelling "per pedes Apostolorum." His fame as a musician did not allow him to remain inactive, and we find him soon after this happened at Modena, in the capacity of first violoncellist at the opera. The name of the *prima-donna* was Agata Elmi, and he composed a sonnet on her name (Agat-Helmet), which came to the knowledge of the duke, as well as his remark that "though Agata Elmi cannot enter the papal chapel (being a woman), it would be well if the members of that body would enter her school that they might learn." The Duke Francesco, who had a quick eye in discovering talent and wit, attached him to his court. Tonelli was given to practical joking, and, at the theatre of Sassuolo, he put some rosin on the leader's chair, and when the poor unsuspecting victim rose quickly at the end of an act, his nether garments stuck to the chair, which provoked even the unqualified mirth of Duke Rinaldo, whom they called "the never laughing." The next evening, the violinist took his revenge by ordering someone to pull off Tonelli's wig during the performance by means of fishing tackle, which was managed from the stage. The audience roared with laughter, Tonelli never lost his composure, but played on without flinching. Gaining popularity as an organist, violoncellist and poet, he proved one day that he had not forgotten the art of acting. The first comic singer at Sassuolo had fallen ill during a performance, and Tonelli, hearing of this while playing in the orchestra, put down his violoncello, and jumping on the stage in his ordinary dress (which was very shabby at the best of times) continued the part, singing with a miserable voice, but with as much ease and accuracy as if he had been on the stage all his life and the piece had belonged to his repertory. In 1730 he was principal "maestro" and singing master in Modena, and wrote his opera, "Lucio Vero." Like many men of great talent, he had an ambition to shine in that part of his art which, on account of natural shortcomings—viz., an indifferent voice—was his weakest point.

In his private life he was a kind of Diogenes, or stoic philosopher, who did many a wise thing in a foolish garb, and many foolish things with a semblance of wisdom. He cared neither for money nor for fame, and he was the kindest of men. To his pupils he was a friend and a father, directing their studies, and watching their progress with the keenest interest. At Carpi he founded a free school of music for poor children whom he taught on a system entirely his own, and proved himself as great a teacher as he was an executant. This new occupation led him to discover the extraordinary talents of a little girl, Rosina Parteggioti, who at the tender age of six years, astounded the musical world by singing ariettas with a sweet voice and pure intonation, playing her own accompaniments on the spinet. At the age of fifteen, she was entrusted with the direction of the choir and post of organist of the nunnery of St. Clare at Carpi, and declared her intention of renouncing the world and joining the order.

PLATE XIX.
ATTILIO ARIOSTI. FROM A MEZZOTINT.

To face page 144.

Tonelli had become so attached to his talented pupil, that he moved heaven and earth to prevent her from taking that step. He even asked her to become his wife, and promised to settle his whole fortune upon her, when he was already seventy-six years of age. But Rosina remained obdurate, and in 1763, took the vow, entering the order as "Sister Illuminata," making a great name for herself as a musician in all branches of the art. Tonelli gave vent to his feelings by writing a series of "Canzone" against the nuns, and dedicating it to the abbess of the nunnery. Count L. F. Valdrighi, in his biography of Tonelli, tells many more interesting anecdotes about this remarkable man, which, however, we cannot include here as not bearing directly on the subject. Some of these are told in a charming sketch of Tonelli's life by Miss Olga Racster in "The Cremona," Volume II, No. 21. He was prolific as a composer, but apparently left no compositions for the violoncello. An extensive treatise on music which he wrote remained in manuscript. He continued his erratic wanderings until the end of his life. One day he was staying at a villa of Count Carraci. A number of noble guests were expected to dinner. At the time when they were expected to arrive, the count found Tonelli in the garden lying on the ground in dirty clothes. He told him that distinguished guests were expected, and asked him to go and change his clothes, and to appear clean and neat at the dinner. When the hour arrived, Tonelli was nowhere to be seen. They searched all over the house, and asking the servants if they had seen anybody answering to his description, they came across one who said that such a man had passed with a violoncello on his back, and a bundle under his arm, who walked away on the road to Novellara. His robust health held out to the very end, which came suddenly. He caught a chill in December, 1763, and fever supervening, he died on the 25th of that month, and was buried on the 28th, in the church of St. Nicholas at Carpi. The portrait, Fig. 33, given below, is taken from an engraving by Antonio Montanari, in the Town Hall at Carpi.

ATTILIO ARIOSTI, a Dominican friar, born at Bologna about 1660, was, according to Gerber, one of the best violoncellists

FIG. 33. TONELLI. FROM AN ENGRAVING BY ANTONIO MONTANARI.

of his time. He excelled also as executant on the viol d'amour, the bass viol and the harpsichord. Among the composers of that period he held a prominent position and received a dispensation from the strict rules of his order by the Pope to enable him to follow his inclinations as an opera composer.

in which capacity he earned fame, and was sought after by the principal courts of Europe. At first he followed the school of Lully, but afterwards he adopted Scarlatti's style, as did his rival Buononcini. About 1698 he went to Berlin as master of the chapel of the Elector of Brandenburg. In 1700 he played at Lützenburg on the anniversary of the nuptials of Frederic, the hereditary Prince of Hesse-Cassel, with Louisa Dorothea Sophia, Princess of Brandenburg. In 1716 he came to London, where he was connected with the Italian opera and produced some successful works, but Handel's genius proved too powerful and all-absorbing for him as well as for Buononcini. He collaborated with his two rivals in the opera, "Mucio Scaevola," of which he wrote one act, but after some unfruitful attempts to outshine them, he left the field and returned to Bologna. In London he published six very fine sonatas for the viol d'amour, of which Signor Piatti has adapted some movements for the violoncello. No original compositions of his for the latter instrument are known.

His portrait, from a fine mezzotint by E. Seeman, in the British Museum, appears on Plate XIX.

CATTANEO (born about 1666 at Lodi, in Italy) was teacher of the violoncello and psaltery at the Jesuit College for sons of Italian noblemen at Brescia. He wrote "Trattenimenti armonici da Camera a tre stromenti" (due violini, violoncello e basso) con due brevi cantate a Soprano Solo ed una Sonata per Violoncello (Modena, 1700).

GIOVANNI BUONONCINI (BONONCINI) was a member of a remarkable family of musicians. The date of his birth has been given by various authors as 1660, 1667 or 1668 and 1672.

According to the preface to his Op. 1, it is either the end of 1671 or the beginning of 1672, as the work was published in 1685, and his age therein is stated to be *a little over thirteen.*

In musical dictionaries he figures as Giovanni Battista, yet there is nothing to prove the correctness of that second christian name. Valdrighi, from documentary evidence, calls him simply *Giovanny*, and that is also the only name appearing in official documents and on title pages of his works. Had he been christened Giovanni Battista, which was used in the contracted form of Giambattista, it would certainly have been used by him in one or the other form.

Giovanni was one of three sons, the others being Antonio and Angelo Maria. His father, Giovanni Maria Buononcini, was *maestro di cappella* at St. Giovanni in Monte at Modena (where Giovanni was born), and also a composer, but was accused of plagiarism by his compatriots. He conducted the first musical training of his son. He published three works of his own composition: Op. 1, Trattenimenti for two violins and violone, dedicated to Francesco II, Duke of Modena (to whom Galli dedicated his Trattenimento); Op. 2, Concerti da Camera, for two violins and violone; and Op. 3, Sinfonie for various instruments, dedicated to his master, Colonna; and in the following year, he entered the Philharmonic Academy of Modena, and studied composition under Colonna. In 1687, he was appointed violoncellist at the Church of St. Petronio, rivalling the famous Gabrielli in his mastery of the instrument. In a treasury account of a memorial service for the Duchess of Modena in 1688, both Menghino (Gabrielli) and Buononcini are mentioned as having received six gold doubloons each for playing the violoncello on that occasion. In 1688-9 he was appointed *maestro di cappella* at St. Giovanni, in Monte. During this time he composed mostly instrumental music, his Op. 4, which appeared in 1686, consisting of "Sinfonie a tre Istrumenti," with bass for the organ; Op. 5, "Sinfonie da chiesa," for two violins, viola and violoncello *obbligato*. This work, which is one of the first for that combination which still constitutes our string quartet, was written for the Church of St. Petronio in 1687, and in the same year appeared his Op. 6, consisting of "Sinfonie" for violin and violoncello, with a bass for the organ, and also his first oratorio, "David and Goliath." In 1689 he was in Venice, where the ruling taste for music was little in accordance with his own. He said that the composers of that town produced nothing but ditties and dance tunes. About 1692 he went to Vienna, but was called back to Rome in 1694, where he produced two operas, returning to Vienna in 1699. The statement frequently to be met with, that he was engaged as violoncellist by the emperor, appears doubtful, as he does not appear in that capacity in the list of members of the private band. Certain it is that he held the post of conductor and composer to the imperial court from July 1, 1700, to September 11, 1711, after which date he received a pension. During this time, the opera "Camilla," which made the round of all the principal opera houses, was produced at the King's Theatre, Haymarket. (This opera was really the work of his far more gifted elder brother, Antonio.) Its success was so great that no subsequent opera could be given without containing some piece or other from "Camilla." In 1703 he went to Berlin, where he was appointed as conductor and composer for the Royal Opera. After some time, however, he was considered overrated, and returned in 1705, living alternately in Vienna and in Italy. In Vienna he appears to have been the hero of numberless amorous adventures. Twice he was on the point of being married, and to one lady he gave a written undertaking to marry her on his return from a journey to Italy. It appears that he returned without the least intention of fulfilling his promise, and added insult to injury by writing an opera, "Dido Abandoned in Vienna." Unscrupulous as he was in this, so he appears to have been in other matters, which by right-minded people are regarded as points of honour, and this caused eventually his downfall in London. He arrived here in 1720, and was appointed composer and conductor of the King's Theatre. Sarah Duchess of Marlborough, the wife of the great Duke, became a staunch supporter of Buononcini, who posed as a rival of Handel, and as the latter was supported by the Royal family and the Tory aristocracy, the Whigs embraced the cause of the former, and the war raged as fiercely between the two parties as did that of the Gluckists and Piccinists in Paris. Ariosti also entered the ranks on his own behalf, and the three rivals collaborated in an opera, "Mucio Scaevola," the first act of which was written by Ariosti, the overture and second act by Buononcini, and the third act by Handel. Buononcini's work was weakest, appearing but a feeble imitation of Scarlatti. He continued, however, in the good graces of his patroness, who settled a pension of £500 a year upon him, and received him into her house in the Stable Yard, St. James's. The Duchess had concerts twice a week, in which no other music was performed than the works of her favourite master, and all her friends had to subscribe for a certain number of copies of his works, of which a collection was then published. His sonatas for two violins and bass appeared in 1732, and about the same time appeared also a sonata for two violoncellos, published in a collection of six solos for that instrument by J. Simpson, "in the Strand." Wasielewski, who deals with it rather severely, thinks that it belongs to the beginning of the century. It consists of an andante, allegro, grazioso and minuet, after which the grazioso is repeated. The latter is a really graceful and melodious movement, and the whole sonata, which has been republished by De Swert ("Collection de Morceaux Choisies," in eight suites —Schott and Co.), is distinctly in advance of the compositions of Gabrielli and Galli, although it was written only about twenty years later, and does not exceed their compass (octave above open A). His overbearing and haughty character had militated against his making friends, and his lack of principle completed his downfall. He had sent in a madrigal to the Academy of Ancient Music for competition against Handel. This madrigal, which he declared to be his own composition, was discovered to be the work of Antonio Lotti, of Venice. Shortly after this, in 1733, he left London for Paris, in the company of a so-called Count Ughi, an adventurer. This worthy, who pretended to have discovered the Philosopher's Stone, managed to swindle the vain and ambitious Buononcini out of his considerable fortune. He was thus compelled to resort again to his violoncello, and in 1740 he composed a cantata, with violoncello *obbligato*, for the Royal chapel, playing the *obbligato* himself in the presence of the King. After the peace of Aix-la-Chapelle, in 1748, he returned to Vienna, where he conducted the music he had composed for the peace festivities. Soon after this he went to Venice in the company of Monticelli, the famous singer, who had concluded his engagement with the London Opera. In Venice, at the advanced age of eighty years, Buononcini composed several more operas. According to Count L. F. Valdrighi, he returned again to Vienna, where he died in 1755. In 1735 he paid a prolonged visit to Portugal, and instructed the King in the art of violoncello playing. While in London he became acquainted with Sir Richard Steel, who wrote several libretti for him. A portrait of Buononcini is given on Plate XX. Dean Swift wrote the following lines with regard to the war between the adherents of Handel and those of Buononcini, which show more wit than judgment. They supplied, however, a proverbial saying in the "tweedle-dum and tweedle-dee":

> Some say that Signor Buononcini
> Compared with Handel's a mere ninny;
> While others say, that to him Handel
> Is hardly fit to hold a candle.
> Strange that such difference should be
> 'Twixt tweedle-dum and tweedle-dee!

GIACOBO BASEVI (or BASSEVI), called CERVETTO, was born in 1682, in Italy, of Jewish parents. The name of his birthplace is unknown. He died June 14, 1783, in London. His

Fig. 34. Cervetto, the Elder. From a Contemporary Caricature.

PLATE XX.
BUONONCINI.

portrait appears on Plate XXI, and the reproduction of a contemporary caricature, Fig. 34. Nothing is known about his earlier life until 1737 (the year of the first presentation of Dr. Arne's "Comus"), although he came to London in 1728 as a dealer in Italian instruments, and a violoncellist. Finding the former occupation little remunerative, he devoted himself entirely to his instrument, and was one of the first to promote its cultivation in this country. Burney, speaking of him, says: "The elder Cervetto is now (1739) first mentioned as just arrived, and this worthy professor, who remained in England till the time of his death, at above a hundred, with Abaco, Lanzetti, Pasqualini and Caporale (about the four last-named violoncellists, see later on), about this time brought the violoncello into favour, and made us nice judges of that instrument." In 1744, Cervetto is mentioned as playing at the subscription concerts at Hickford's rooms, in Brewer Street, together with Pasqualini and Caporale, and Burney states that, while the two former virtuosi had infinitely more hand and knowledge of the finger-board, as well as of music in general, their tone was raw and crude, and their style of delivery uninteresting, while Caporale was their superior with respect to these latter qualities. During a considerable number of years he was solo violoncellist at Drury Lane Theatre, where Garrick was then scoring his triumphs. Eventually he became the manager of that theatre, thereby laying the foundation of his considerable fortune. He was one of the most popular figures in London, of whom numerous anecdotes were told. The following are given as authentic: Being gifted with a very marked protuberance of his proboscis, the gallery at Drury Lane used to hail him with the call: "Play up, Nosey!" which remained, according to Pohl, *en vogue* down to 1737. One day an individual from among the gods threw a potato at him which hit his nose. As soon as the piece had finished, Cervetto ran up, and the man being pointed out to him, he gave him a severe beating in the passage. Some time after this, he met, on riding to Paddington, a cavalcade leading a culprit to Tyburn. The convict, on seeing him, called out: "Nosey! Nosey!" Riding up to the cart, Cervetto found that it was the man who threw the potato at him, and who now, in a penitent voice, told him that he wanted to die in peace with all mankind, and therefore heartily forgave him the drubbing which he received from him. Then taking leave, he added: "Now, Nosey, I shall die in peace." Another well-known anecdote is the following: "One day Garrick was playing Sir John Brute, and the audience observed the most profound silence, fixing their eyes on the incomparable actor. At such a critical moment, poor Cervetto from the orchestra uttered a loud yawn, which, by its suddenness and oddity, excited violent laughter through the house. Garrick, offended, sent for the musician, who assuaged the rage of the hero by saying, with a shrug: 'I beg ten thousand pardons, but I alway do so ven I am ver much please.'"—(Universal Biographies: J. Lempriere, D.D., London, 1808). Cervetto formed many pupils, one of the most talented being his son James, to whom he left the considerable fortune of £20,000. Being born and educated in London, where he spent all his life, we shall speak of the latter when discussing "English Violoncellists."

The elder Cervetto composed solos and duets for his instrument which are entirely antiquated (see the author's "History of Violoncello Literature").

FRANCISCHELLO (FRANCISCHIELLO, FRANCISCELLO or FRANCISELLO). Undoubtedly the greatest violoncellist of his time, was born about the end of the seventeenth century, but the year and place of his birth are unknown. Geminiani relates that in 1713 he was present at a concert where Nicolini sang a cantata by Alessandro Scarlatti. He was accompanied by Francischello, who played a violoncello *obbligato* part, and the composer, who played the harpsichord. Francischello charmed his listeners to such an extent that Scarlatti exclaimed: "Only angels in human shape can play like that." Francischello did, to some extent, for the violoncello what Corelli did for the violin, and his astounding technique, as well as the beauty of his tone and delivery, caused the early disappearance of the viol da gamba in Italy, where it was relegated from the orchestra about 1730. In 1725, Francischello was in Naples, where Quantz, the great flautist, heard him, and was deeply impressed by his playing at a concert given in honour of Prince Lichtenstein. Geminiani likewise heard him there when he accompanied Nicolini in a cantata by Scarlatti, who played the additional accompaniment on the harpsichord. In 1730 he received an appointment as chamber virtuoso to Count Uhlenfeld in Vienna, where Franz Benda, the celebrated violinist and head of a family of very distinguished musicians, heard him, and even played trios with him and the Count. J. A. Hiller says that Count Ostein recommended Benda to Count Uhlenfeld, who was then taking lessons from the "imperial violoncellist" Francischello. Benda's admiration for Francischello's playing was so great that he imitated and entirely adopted his style. Quantz's assertion (contained in Marpurg's "Beiträge") that Francischello was a member of the Imperial Chamber Music, is evidently based upon the fact that he *was in Vienna*, but as chamber musician to Count Uhlenfeld, for he does not appear in the registers of the court musicians. The statement of the "Musikalische Almanach für Deutschland' ("Musical Almanac for Germany") of 1782, that he was still a member of the Imperial Chamber Music in 1766, is of course equally groundless, as he was at that time in Genoa, having left Vienna about 1740. The elder Duport (who was born in 1741), when quite a young man, travelled to Genoa for the express purpose of hearing Francischello. The interview, as related by Marpurg, will be found under Jean Pierre

Duport. One of the greatest achievements in the technique of violoncello playing—the use of the thumb in fingering (thumb position)—has been attributed to Francischello, who also composed for his instrument, as the acquaintance with a solo of his is given by Fétis as one of the reasons why the French artist, Berteau, exchanged the gamba for the violoncello. Unfortunately his compositions appear to have disappeared entirely. He died at Genoa about 1770.

The portrait *(Plate XXII)* is taken from an engraving by Jacob Haid, after a painting by Martin Meiten in Vienna. A copy of which was presented to the author for this reproduction by the late Count Luigi Francesco Valdrighi.

CHAPTER XI.

THE VIOLONCELLO IN ITALY DURING THE EIGHTEENTH CENTURY.

JOHANN BAPTIST STRUCK was born at Florence in 1680. He was the son of German parents. At the beginning of the eighteenth century he went to Paris, and was appointed member of the private band of the Duc d'Orleans. It is said that he was the first to introduce the violoncello into France. In 1709 (Torino says 1727) he was appointed first violoncellist in the orchestra of the grand opera, which before only knew the bass viol and violone as bass instruments. He held that position for many years, and was still a member of that body when the brothers Abbé caused the downfall of the bass viol, which through their influence was replaced by the violoncello. Either on account of his small stature or as a mark of distinction from the "great Baptiste" (Lully), he was called Baptistin (Battistin—the little Baptist, Louis XIV granted him an annuity to retain him in Paris with an additional five hundred francs for theatrical compositions. He wrote operas, cantatas and ballets, but no compositions of his for the violoncello are known to exist. He died on December 9, 1755, in Paris. As the use of the thumb position was already known in

Italy when Baptistin came to France, it is probable that he was the first to introduce it in that country.

GIOVANNI BOSTONI is mentioned by Mendel-Reissmann as a musician from Florence, who introduced the violoncello into France during the reign of Louis XIV. As no other information exists regarding such a name, and the credit of introducing the violoncello into France (during the first years of the eighteenth century) devolves upon Baptistin, according to good authority, it appears more than probable that the above mentioned virtuoso owes his existence only to the misspelling of the name of Giovanni Battista Struck, called Baptistin, mentioned above.

LEONARDO LEO, one of the greatest Italian composers of his time, whose powerful genius imprinted his stamp upon the musical creations of his time. He was well versed in all branches of composition, and was also an excellent violoncellist. Born at San Vito degli Schiavi in the province of Lucca, in 1694, he died in 1746, at Naples. Besides his famous operas and numerous works of sacred music, he wrote concertos for the violoncello with string accompaniment.

The MSS. of six concertos are preserved in the Milan Conservatoire and five are preserved in Naples, they all date from the years 1737-8. The author has not been able to obtain access to the MSS. in order to ascertain if any of them are duplicates. Even Count Valdrighi tried in vain to see or obtain copies of the MSS. at Naples.

LORENZO BALBI, the descendant of an ancient Italian family of title, earned great applause as a violoncellist about the commencement of the eighteenth century. He played solo pieces of his own composition with great success at various Italian towns. They remained apparently, however, unpublished, while some sonatas for violin, violoncello and continuo, which were printed, were highly praised. Six sonatas for violin, violoncello and cembalo, Op. 1, in the Wagner Library;

sonata for violin, violoncello *obbligato* e cembalo, Berlin Library. He died about 1740 (see R. Eitner, "Quellen Lexicon").

ANGELO MARIA FIORE was violoncellist in the Royal Chapel at Turin in 1699, with a salary of fifteen hundred lire (G. Roberti, "La Capella regia di Torino"). He is also mentioned by Hawkins.

RUBINI is mentioned as violoncellist in the court orchestra, Stuttgart, in 1701, when the celebrated Cousser was the conductor.

THEOBALDE, an Italian by birth, was an excellent violoncellist and composer, who lived about the beginning of the eighteenth century. He was member of the orchestra at the opera in Paris, for which institution he wrote the opera, "Scilla," famous for the beauty of its symphonies.

GAETANO AGAZZI published six sonatas, Op. 1, for violoncello and bass at Amsterdam (British Museum); ten sonatas for violoncello and bass in MS. (Milan Conservatoire). These sonatas written entirely in the treble and tenor clefs contain a great deal of double stopping and use of thumb in high and difficult positions. They testify not only to Agazzi's technical ability but prove him also to have been a composer of distinct talent.

BENEDETTO MARCELLO, the great Venice musician and composer, who lived 1686-1739, although not known as executant on the violoncello, has left twelve sonatas for violoncello and continuo, in two books, Op. 1 and Op. 2, of six sonatas each. Although Vidal speaks lightly of them they are now appreciated according to their real merit, and may be found in the repertoire of every prominent violoncellist of the present day.

GIORGIO ANTONIOTTI was born in 1692 in or near Milan, and died there in 1776. He was composer and violoncellist, and lived for many years in Holland. In 1736, he published twelve sonatas for violoncello or viol da gamba with bass, Op.

1, at Amsterdam. Copies in Paris National and Wagner Libraries. They show a decided progress in the technique of the instrument as well as in their musical construction, and are not without interest. After his sojourn in the Netherlands he came to London, where he remained for about twenty years. He occupied himself a good deal with the theory of music.

ANDREA CAPORALE, one of the most popular and highly esteemed violoncellists of his time, came to London in 1735. The year and place of his birth are unknown. Burney says about him that, "though no deep musician, nor gifted with a powerful hand, he was always heard with great partiality, from the almost single merit of a full, sweet and vocal tone." Together with Cervetto, Pasqualini and Abaco, he was instrumental in introducing the violoncello as a solo instrument in England. Handel appointed him as his principal violoncello, and the solo part in the third act of his "Deidamia" ("Come all unto," etc., composed in 1740) was originally designed for his violoncello. He was also one of the soloists at Handel's benefit concert for the musical fund in 1741, when his cantata, "Parnasso in Festa," was performed (the others being: Clegg, violin; San Martini, oboe; Wiedmann, flute; Miller, bassoon) and again in 1743. The admission to these concerts was fixed at ten shillings and sixpence, and five shillings for the gallery! In March, 1743, and November, 1744, he appeared as soloist at concerts of vocal and instrumental music at the Castle Tavern, Paternoster Row. A sonata of his composition was published in the collection by J. Simpson, mentioned before *(see Buononcini)*. It consists of an adagio, allegro and a theme with variations, and bears out Dr. Burney's statement with regard to his musicianship. Some solos of his for the violoncello were published by W. Randall and J. Abell, late Mr. Walsh's, in Catherine Street, Strand. Although his tone was sweet and singing, while that of Cervetto and Pasqualini is described as crude, yet both the latter possessed a

PLATE XXI.
CERVETTO, THE ELDER.

far greater technique of the left hand. Their success mortified Caporale to such an extent that it accelerated his death, which took place in 1746 in London (see note in Appendix).

PASQUALINI appeared at Hickford's Rooms and the Swan and Castle concerts in 1744 and in 1750, and in the latter year at the concerts instituted at Drury Lane by Rophino Lacey, and he appeared also at the professional concerts under the direction of Lord Abingdon. A violoncello sonata of his which appeared in the afore-mentioned book by J. Simpson *(see Buononcini)* has been republished by J. de Swert (Schott and Co.). He possessed a good technique of the left hand, but his tone is characterised by Burney as crude and raw, and his style as uninteresting.

PASQUALI THE YOUNGER was another violoncellist about whom no particulars are to hand, except that he appeared at the professional concerts in 1752, the same year as Pasqualini made his debut there.

ANTONIO PIETRO AVANDONNO, born at the commencement of the eighteenth century, died in 1786. He was an excellent violoncellist and prolific composer of operas, oratorios, pianoforte pieces and duets for violin and violoncello. Some of his compositions are preserved in the Berlin Library.

GIUSEPPE DALL' OGLIO, born at Padua about 1700. He was the younger brother of the famous violinist, Domenico dall' Oglio. In 1735 he went to St. Petersburg, where both brothers were engaged as members of the imperial chamber music. The Leipzig "Musikalische Nachrichten" of 1770, give us some information about the latter part of their career: "In the summer of this year, 1764, the imperial chamber music (St. Petersburg) lost two excellent virtuosi, the pillars of the orchestra, to wit, the great violoncellist, Dall' Oglio, and his brother, Domenico, the violinist and composer of most beautiful symphonies. Both had been in the imperial service here for twenty-nine years, and asked for permission to return to their native country, Venice or Padua.

The noticeable gap left by the departure of the violoncellist was filled to some extent by another Italian, CICIO POLLIARI, and a young Russian, Tchorchewski (Chorchewski), who is almost his equal. Domenico was attacked by apoplexy near Narva and died. Giuseppe, who has but few equals on the violoncello in Europe, returned to Vienna."

FIG. 35. VANDINI.

On his journey home, Giuseppe visited Warsaw, where Augustus, King of Poland, made him his political agent to the republic of Venice. According to Schilling he died at the latter town in 1771. He composed duos for two violoncellos published in Vienna.

CICIO POLLIARI in the imperial chamber music, about 1764 (see Dall' Oglio). No further particulars are obtainable.

ALESSANDRO CANAVASSO was in 1735 violoncellist in the chapel of Louis XV. In 1773 he published sonatas for violoncello, Op. 2, in Paris, which prove his genuine artistic talent, and an advanced technique with frequent introduction of thumb position (Paris Library).

ANTONIO VANDINI was first violoncellist at the Church of St. Antonio at Padua. The Italians said of him that he could make his instrument speak *(faceva parlare il suo instrumento)*. He was an intimate friend of Tartini, who was engaged as first violin at the same church, and followed him as his accompanist when Tartini was engaged by Count Kinsky in Prague in 1723, where they remained for three years. Tartini had a long illness in Prague, where he never felt happy. At the end of the three years they returned together to Padua where Vandini was still living in 1770. He died there in 1773, according to Schilling, who unfortunately is not very reliable. Vandini wrote twelve sonatas for his instrument which, according to Torino, are of distinct merit. Three sonatas for violoncello and bass are in the Königl. Hausbibliothek, Berlin. The portrait, Fig. 35, was supplied by the late Count Valdrighi.

CARLO FERRARI, brother of the great violinist, Domenico Ferrari, was born at Piacenza about 1700. From a lameness in one foot he was called "il zoppo di Piacenza" (the hobbler of Piacenza). He studied in Cremona. In 1756, he was a chamber musician of Don Philippe, in Paris, and in 1758 he made his debut at the "concert spirituel" with his own compositions for violoncello solo, which pleased greatly, and were afterwards published. In 1765 he was appointed to the court orchestra at Parma, where Dr. Burney heard him in 1770, and where he died in 1789. He has been credited with the introduction of the thumb position in France, but as has been stated already, this goes in all probability to the credit of Baptist Struck. In any case it was known there before Ferrari's arrival. He published a book of sonatas, Op. 1, at Paris.

ANTON FERRARI is mentioned as violoncellist of the court orchestra in Salzburg, in Mozart's time, until 1785 or 1786, when he was succeeded by Fuetsch. (See Jahn and Schilling.)

PARASISTI, whom Gerber calls an artist of more than ordinary merit, was violoncellist of the Italian Opera in Breslau (Silesia) in 1727.

GIUSEPPE CLEMENS FERDINAND, BARONE D'ALL ABACO was to all appearances the son of Evariste Felice d'all Abaco, master of the chapel of the Elector of Bavaria at Munich, who was born at Verona in 1662 and died at Munich in 1726. Verona has been mentioned also as the native town of Giuseppe ("Allgemeine Musik Zeitung," 1799-1800). The date of his birth is unknown, but it may be assumed with safety to fall within the first years of the eighteenth century. On March 29, 1729, he was appointed titular valet de chambre to the Elector of Cologne at Bonn, at a salary of four hundred guilders. On September 26, 1738, he advanced to the post of director of the electoral chamber music, with a salary of one thousand rhenish guilders (florins-Thayer). Pohl tells us that he appeared with great success in Vienna in a concert piece for five violoncellos of his own composition.

About 1740 he was in London where Burney heard him, and said that together with Cervetto, Caporale and Pasqualini he was making the English "nice judges" of his instrument. About this time he was the teacher of Nochez, who acquired a great reputation in Paris. Abaco was a great virtuoso on his instrument, for which he wrote a considerable number of sonatas, some for two violoncellos, and some for violoncellos and bass. They are written in a good musicianly style and testify to their author's technical skill, as he makes frequent use of double stopping and even of the thumb position. Thirty of these sonatas, mostly in the original handwriting and composed probably before and during his sojourn in London, are preserved in a volume of the Julian Marshall Collection at the British Museum.

One sonata contains a short movement, "a modo di viola da gamba," followed by another, "arpegiato a modo arciliuto" (in the style of the gamba and arpeggio, in the style of the archlute). Another contains a movement, "in modo d'un organo" (in the style of an organ), with a lot of clever suspensions in double stopping, and another movement, "la zampogna" (the bagpipe), a brilliant piece in the character of a gigue which requires the technique of a modern virtuoso, and proved a brilliant success when played by Mr. Boris Hambourg at his historical recitals, with an accompaniment

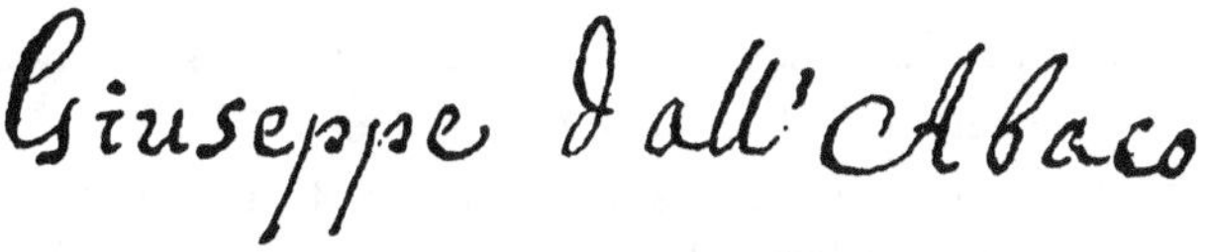

Giuseppe d'all'Abaco

FIG. 36. SIGNATURE OF ABACO.

by the author. Girolamo Ortiz, in the above-quoted article of the "Allgemeine Musik Zeitung" of 1800, speaks of Giuseppe d'all Abaco as one of the great Veronese artists shining abroad *at the present time*. There is no mention of him anywhere during the latter part of the eighteenth century, and Ortiz's statement must be based upon a misconception. It is hardly likely that he was then still living as he would have been about ninety-five years old. The year of his death is unknown, as, in fact, anything concerning his latter years. A reproduction of his signature from one of his sonatas given here for the first time *(see Fig. 36 above)*.

MORIA, an Italian violoncellist, played at the Concert Spirituel in Paris in 1755. No further details are obtainable.

DOMENICO DELLA BELLA, an admirable violoncellist, wrote twelve sonatas for two violins and violoncellos, published at Venice 1704, and in 1705 appeared also at Venice his concerto for violoncello, to all appearances the first of its kind, which proves him to have been a great virtuoso of his time.

GIUSEPPE JACCHINI was a violoncellist of great fame, appointed to the church of San Petronio at Bologna, where he stood in such high esteem that in 1701 he received the rare distinction of membership of the Bologna Philharmonic Society. He wrote "concerti" per camera a 3 e 4 stromenti, con violoncello obligato, Op. 4, Bologna, 1701.

QUIRINO GASPARINO, an excellent violoncellist and musician, master of the chapel of the King of Sardinia, and conductor at the Court of Turin from 1749 to 1770, composed church music and also string trios which were published in London.

PIPPO AMADIO played a concerto on the "bass violin" at Signor Carbonelli's concert in London, May 4, 1722, according to an advertisement in the "London Gazette."

Gerber says that his art surpassed anything that could be achieved on the violoncello in his time. Romberg used to play one of his adagios which he describes as "der schönste tief empfundene morgentraum" (the most beautiful deeply-emotional dream of dawn). Unfortunately it appears to be lost.

SALVATORE LANZETTI, born about 1710 at Naples, died about 1780 at Turin. He received his musical education at the Conservatoire of Santa Maria di Loreto at Naples, the oldest and most illustrious institution of its kind, which produced some of the greatest Italian composers, and accorded at the expense of the State free tuition in all branches of music. As we have seen from Burney's statement *(see Pasqualini)*, Lanzetti was one of those who brought the violoncello into favour in England as a solo instrument. The exact period of his residence in London is not known. He arrived probably between 1745 and 1750, and he was living there still in 1754, according to C. F. Pohl ("Mozart und Haydn in London"). It is told of him that he was very strong in the "staccato," which he executed with equal facility in up and down bow. A considerable part of his later life he passed in the service of the King of Sardinia, where he remained up to his death. Besides a tutor, which appeared in Paris under the title "Principes ou l'applicatur de Violoncel par tous les tons" (Gerber), he published for his instrument two books of sonatas in Amsterdam, 1736; six solos in London, 1740, and six sonatas for two violoncellos with a thorough bass for the harpsichord, London (?). Vidal, in speaking of Lanzetti's sonatas, says: The difficulties are not very great, but show a clever artist, and the sixth sonata of his Op. 1 contains on page 28 a gavotte with variations which is well set. The eighth sonata is an excellent bowing exercise. The adagio of the tenth sonata goes up to indicating the thumb position and thus enlarging the compass of the instrument. Some of his sonatas have been republished by Signor Piatti, C. Schroeder and others.

TOMMASO GIORDANI, born at Naples 1740, who settled as singer and composer in England about 1762, wrote a book of violoncello duets, published by Bailleux, Rue St. Honoré in Paris (at six livres).

GIOVANNI BATTISTA CIRRI, born 1740, at Forli, was an excellent violoncellist and composer. He made his debut in London at a concert of the violinist Marella, on May 16, 1764. His father, Ignazio, was choirmaster at Forli Cathedral. Giovanni left a considerable number of vocal and instrumental compositions, and in 1776 he composed a prize canon, "Nos autem gloria," for the Catch Club. On May 10, 1765, he played a solo at a benefit for "Miss and Master Mozart." He published twenty-six works of chamber music. His portrait appears on Plate XXIII.

STEFANO GALEOTTI, born at Velletri in 1745, lived for some time as violoncellist in Holland, but returned to Italy on account of his health after a short sojourn in Paris, where he published six sonatas for violoncello and bass, Op. 4, in 1785, six violin trios, Op. 3, in Berlin in 1790. One of his sonatas in C minor, with accompaniment by Alfred Moffat, has been republished by Simrock, Berlin.

FRANCESCO ALIANI, born about 1745 at Piacenza, was a pupil of Guido Rovelli at Parma. After five years of study he was appointed first violoncello to the Duke of Parma, afterwards returning to Piacenza in the same capacity at the church and theatre. He passed for one of the greatest virtuosi of his time. He composed three books of duets, and died in 1812.

BERNARDO ALIPANDRI was the son of a Tuscan opera composer, who was afterwards conductor at the Bavarian court in Munich about the middle of the last century, where Bernardo, his son, was appointed as violoncellist in the court orchestra. He retained that position from 1780 to 1786, rising to the post of conductor at a salary of 353 gulden. He wrote a number of compositions for violoncello as well as for viol' da gamba, which show artistic feeling and musicianly workmanship.

GERHARD ALIPANDRI was violoncellist in the Court Chapel, Munich, in 1785 (Eitner).

GRAZIANI, an excellent violoncellist and composer for his instrument, resided for some time in London, where he announced a concert to be given on May 17, 1764, at Hickford's Rooms in Brewer Street. The young Mozart was to appear on that occasion. On account of rehearsals for Giardini's opera, "Enea and Lavinia," the concert was postponed to May 22, when Giardini paid him the compliment of playing for him, although he had given up playing in public. Mozart, however, did not appear on account of indisposition. After the decease of E. C. Hesse, the famous gambist, he came to Berlin and was appointed as teacher of the Crown Prince (afterwards Frederic William II). When the elder Duport came to Berlin he had to resign his appointment in favour of the former, and retired to Potsdam, where he died in 1787. He published six

PLATE XXII.
FRANCISCHELLO.

solos for the violoncello, Op. 1, in Berlin, and six solos, Op. 2, in Paris, both in 1780.

GIUSEPPE ROVELLI, born at Bergamo in 1753, studied at Milan, where he remained in the service of the Duke of Parma until 1806, the year of his death. He wrote a few compositions for violoncello.

PIARELLI, a virtuoso on the violoncello, published six solos for his instrument in Paris in 1784.

CAMILLO BARNI, born January 18, 1762, in Como, was instructed in the rudiments of violoncello playing by his grandfather, David Ronchetti, and afterwards received the instructions from Giuseppe Gadgi, a canon of the cathedral at Como. He entered the orchestra of the Milan opera at the age of twenty, where, in 1791, he was appointed as principal violoncello. In 1802 he went to Paris, where he appeared as soloist, and was also appointed to the orchestra of the Italian Opera. Here he wrote an opera, "Edouard," which was produced at the "Theatre Feydeau" in 1811. Between 1804 and 1809 he wrote duos for violin and violoncello, and also left a concerto for his instrument. He died in 1840.

BERTOJA. Two brothers of that name lived in Venice about 1800, and were considered the greatest Italian violoncellists of their time. Forkel mentions Bertoja as member of the Prince Esterhazy's band in 1782.

JOANNINI DEL VIOLONCELLO, a great virtuoso, who in 1779 was appointed as conductor at St. Peter's in Rome. He composed church music, piano pieces and solos for the violoncello.

FRANCESCA ZAPPA travelled about 1781 in Germany, where he charmed his audiences by his beautiful tone and delivery.

FILIPPO LOLLI, son of the great violinist, Antonio Lolli, was born in Stuttgart in 1773, according to Fétis. Gerber states that he was eight years old in 1792 when he appeared in Berlin and Copenhagen. Fétis turns the eight into eighteen, and says: "At the age of eighteen he started on his first concert tour, which brought him to Berlin, where he pleased the king so much that he made him a present of one hundred Frederico d'or." He then went to Copenhagen and thence returned via Holland and France to Italy. In 1794 he visited Vienna (according to Wasielewski in 1804), where he met with great success, and also published variations for violoncello as well as a book of solos with viola and one with bass through Artaria. According to Schilling he lived down to 1836 in Naples.

SANDONATI was born in Verona, and came, about 1785, to Salzburg to undertake the training of Joachim Fuetsch, who was destined as the successor of Antonio Ferrari. He visited France, Germany and England, and was universally admired for his fine playing. About 1800 he returned to Verona, where he appears to have spent the rest of his life.

SCEVIONI is mentioned by Gerber as a great violoncellist living in Verona about 1800.

GAETANO CHIANDELLI, virtuoso on the violoncello and the violin, on which latter instrument he was a pupil of Paganini. He lived as a teacher of these instruments at Naples during the first part of this century.

JEAN AUGUSTIN PERROTTI, born 1774, at Vercelli, composed operas, church and chamber music. Two sonatas for violoncello in MSS. in the library of the British Museum under the name of Porretti are apparently by him. In 1798 he was accompanist at the Italian Opera in London.

NICOLA TACCHINARDI, born September 10, 1776, at Livorno, destined for the church in which he had taken orders, left the latter, and became a painter. Then he took up the violoncello and became a member of the chapel of the Duke of Tuscany, but afterwards he turned out a great singer at that court. He was the father and teacher of the celebrated singer, Mme. Tacchinardi-Persiani.

ANTONIO BARETTI, born about 1720 at Turin, was the son of the architect, Luca Baretti. He published six sonatas for violoncello in Paris about 1770 and a Divertimento for violoncello, published by Longman, Clementi and Co., about 1800. His elder brother, Giuseppe B., born at Turin, March 22, 1716, was secretary of the Society of Fine Arts in London in 1772, and wrote about music in diaries of his travels.

AGOSTINO SPOTORNO appears as member of the Royal chapel at Turin in 1771 (together with Chiabrano), receiving a salary of 450 lire.

SALVATORE TINTI, born about 1740 at Florence, died in 1800, is described as one of the first virtuosi in Italy. He composed six string quartets and two quintets.

GAETANO CHIABRANO, or CHABRAN as he is usually called, was either a younger brother or perhaps even a son of François Chiabrano or Chabran, as he was called in Paris, where he settled in 1751. The latter, a great violinist, was born 1723, in Piedmont, and was a nephew and pupil of the famous "Somis," the master of Paganini. Two solos for violoncello and bass of his are in the British Museum. The date of Gaetano Chiabrano's birth seems unknown, but Marpurg mentions "Capperan" as a violoncellist in the orchestra of the Concert Spirituel, and the opera in 1755 (together with Edouard, Torcade, Habram, Saubley, Dun, senior and junior, Labbe (L'abbé), elder and younger (two brothers), Davesne and Salentin). Considering the phonetic similarity of Chiabran and Capperan, and taking into account the carelessness in spelling which is evident in the case of Labbe for L'abbé, it can be safely surmised that this artist was none other than Gaetano Chiabrano, who was in the royal chapel at Turin at a salary of 850 lire in 1771. In 1784 he was playing, together with Cervetto and Crosdil, at the concerts under Lord Abingdon, under the name of Chabran. He wrote a considerable number of solos and sonatas, which seem to have been very popular in his time, as Longman, Clementi and Co. advertise that they are among others also publishers of the works of Chabran; six solos with thorough bass were published by R. Bremner. There are a number of sonatas for violoncello solo at the British Museum on which he calls himself by his proper name. According to Ricordi's "Gazetta Milano" of 1891, he was violoncellist in the Royal chapel at Turin from 1752 to 1755 (Eitner). The date of his death is unknown.

FRANCESCO DE PIANTANIDA composed three solos for violoncello and bass, published with Chiabrano's sonatas in 1780 (British Museum).

ALESSANDRO DELFINO and ALESSANDRO BERTUZZI are mentioned as members of the orchestra of La Scala in Milan in 1779.

LUIGI BOCCHERINI was born February 19, 1743, at Lucca (other dates given by Vidal and in various dictionaries are incorrect) as the son of a double-bass player. He received his first musical education from the Abbate Vanucci, *maestro di cappella* of the Archbishop. His progress determined his father to send him to Rome, where his talents soon developed into maturity under the guidance of eminent masters. Returned to Lucca, he met Tartini's pupil, Filippo Manfredini, an excellent violinist. Boccherini had devoted himself assiduously to the study of the violoncello, which he played with the mastery of a virtuoso, and a close friendship soon sprang up between the two young artists, who determined upon a concert tour through Spain, Piedmont, Lombardy and the South of France. The success which followed them everywhere encouraged them to visit Paris in 1768. Boccherini's compositions were received there with enthusiasm, and the publishers, La Chevardière and Venier, undertook the publication of some of his string quartets and trios. The price which they paid for the copyright was extremely low, and poor Boccherini never received an adequate remuneration for his work. Encouraged by the Spanish ambassador in Paris, the two artist friends visited Spain in 1769, where Boccherini gained special favour with the Infante Don

Luiz, who engaged him as his chamber virtuoso and composer (compositore e virtuoso di camera). Don Luiz died in 1785, and Boccherini was appointed *maestro di cappella* to Charles III of Spain and his successor, Charles IV. In 1787 Frederic William II of Prussia nominated him his chamber composer, in recognition of a work dedicated to him, accompanying the honour with a princely reward. Boccherini resolved henceforth to dedicate all his compositions to this liberal patron, who allowed him an annuity. With the death of the King in 1797 that allowance ceased, and Boccherini lost his position as master of the Royal chapel at Madrid somewhere about the same period. His circumstances became more and more straitened, and as he received next to nothing from his publishers, he and his family lived in great want until death released him May 28, 1805.

Boccherini was one of the greatest virtuosi of his time, and a highly gifted composer, whose compositions were looked upon by his French contemporaries as absolutely ideal, and even German writers of eminence speak enthusiastically of their beauty of form, and truth and delicacy of expression. This was of course at a time when graceful form passed for genius. He followed the lines of Haydn, whom he often rivals, when the latter is in his lighter moods, but in his more powerful moments Haydn towers high above Boccherini.

His was a simple gaiety of heart, ever-flowing melody, elegance of form and a humour which often bordered on frivolity. He was distinctly original in thought, yet it was here where he lacked that deeper undercurrent and power which are requisite to place a work beyond the influence of fashion, and enable it to defy the crushing tooth of time. Boccherini always wears the powdered wig, the spotless frills and knee-breeches of the times of minuets, of scrapes and bows and artificial woes and sentimentality. Yet for all that, his genius breaks through these fetters every now and then, producing works of such delightful freshness that they fully deserve to become more generally known. Had it not been for the mighty giants who crushed and overshadowed the lighter muse of Boccherini during the early part of last century, he would never have fallen into such utter neglect. His published compositions consist of ninety-one string quartets, one hundred and twenty-five string quintets, one hundred and thirteen of their number with two violoncellos, forty-two trios for two violins and violoncello, twelve trios for violin, viola and violoncello, forty-two pianoforte trios, twelve pianoforte quintets, eighteen quintets with flute or oboe, sixteen sextets, two octets, violin duets, violin sonatas, violoncello sonatas, violoncello concertos, twenty symphonies, an opera, and numerous vocal works for the church. Apart from these, there are a great number of manuscript compositions in the Royal Library at Berlin and other places.

For the development of the violoncello technique Boccherini did more than any of his predecessors. He developed the passage work with the daring of a great virtuoso, freeing it from all the cramped writing and stiff conventionalities of his predecessors, which arose, of course, chiefly from their limited technique.

The six violoncello sonatas which have since been re-edited by Piatti, Grützmacher and others are standard pieces in the repertoire of all virtuosi. Five of his violoncello concertos have also been republished, one by Breitkopf and Härtel and four by Leduc in Paris, there are many instances of his amiable grace and elegance of style which should commend them to the notice of violoncellists. The first violoncello parts of the quintets with two violoncellos are often quite as florid and difficult as the solo part of a concerto, and therefore well worth studying. In many cases the first part is headed alto violoncello, and written in the alto clef so that it could also be played on the viola. This part is in reality a concertante part, the

Fig. 37. Boccherini.

other parts serving more or less as an accompaniment. Some of Boccherini's string quintets have been republished by Peters in Leipzig, and C. F. Schmidt in Heilbronn, the latter edited by Fritz Vollbach, who also prepared an edition of some of the quartets for Schott in Mayence. A portrait of Boccherini, Fig. 37, is a reproduction from an early print.

Boccherini's absence from Italy was a great loss to his native country which thereby lost the educational and artistic influence of its greatest virtuoso on the violoncello before Piatti. Had he remained in Italy he would no doubt have become the founder of a school of violoncello playing of equal importance to that of Corelli and Tartini for the art of violin playing. As it was his art was transferred to France and Germany, as we shall see later on.

FATHER FILIPPO-MARIA DA LUGO, a Franciscan monk, living in the convent of Mirandola, was violoncellist in the chapel of the Duke of Este in Modena until the conquest by Napoleon, and his suppression of the dukedom. After that time he lived as theologist with Monsignor Bellono, Bishop of Carpi, where he seems to have died. He was also an excellent singer.

CRISTIANO GIUSEPPE LIDARTI lived at Pisa about 1770 (according to Eitner, who quotes "Burney I, 294," which reference the author has been unable to discover). He lived for some time in Vienna according to the title page of a sonata in the library of the "Gesellschaft der Musikfreunde," which runs as follows: "Sonata a Solo / Per la Pomposa (Viola Pomposa, E. v. D. S.) col Basso / del Sig$^{re.}$ Cristian Giuseppe Lidarti / Di Vienna / Academico Filarmonico / Di Bologna e Modena." The sonata (in E flat, 4-4) is mentioned in G. Kinsky's catalogue of the Wm. Heyer Museum. Although his numerous chamber music compositions contain no works for the violoncello, he appears as violoncellist on a fine portrait in oils in the possession of Messrs. W. E. Hill and Sons, which we give on Plate XXIV.

PLATE XXIII.
CIRRI.

To face page 176.

CHAPTER XII.

THE VIOLONCELLO IN GERMANY FROM THE SEVENTEENTH TO THE BEGINNING OF THE NINETEENTH CENTURY.

ALTHOUGH nothing is known about the introduction of the violoncello in Germany, it is certain that it must have been shortly after its appearance in Italy, as we find at least the name of one German violoncellist before 1700. This was GREGOR CHRISTOPH EYLENSTEIN, born October 28, 1682, at Gelmroda, near Weimar. In 1696 he was apprenticed to the "stadtpfeifer" (town musician; waits), and in 1706 he was appointed chamber-musician to the Duke of Saxe-Weimar. He was, no doubt, a bass viol player as well as violoncellist, the profession of the "stadtpfeifer," to which he was originally brought up, requiring a practical knowledge of all the principal instruments as well as of thorough bass and composition. About Eylenstein's career we possess no further detail. His son was a good instrument maker, and his grandson an esteemed song composer.

GOTTLOB HAYNE (HEINE), born 1684, was violoncellist in the court chapel at Berlin. In 1720 he was appointed conductor of a Berlin choir, and died about 1760.

JOHANN PHILIPP EYSEL, born 1698, at Erfurt, died 1763.

He was originally a barrister, but changing the calling of a lawyer for that of a musician, he perfected himself on the violoncello, which he had previously chosen as his principal instrument. He was also a composer of vocal and instrumental pieces, which were published in Nürnberg between 1738 and 1746. In the latter town appeared anonymously his "Musicus autodidactus," which book is interesting on account of its illustrations and descriptions of twenty-four kinds of musical instruments. He left apparently no compositions for the violoncello.

JOHANN SEBALD TRIEMER, born towards the end of the seventeenth or at the beginning of the eighteenth century, at Weimar, was the first German violoncello virtuoso, whose art carried him beyond the limits of his native country. His first instruction in the playing of several instruments he received from the ducal chamber lackey, and chamber musician, Eylenstein. It is a curious fact, that at the small courts of Germany the court musicians usually were at the same time court lackeys, and bondsmen of their respective sovereigns, who sometimes freed them if they showed exceptional talents. It was from the court lackeys that the members of the private bands were recruited. If the son of a lackey, member of the band or otherwise, showed signs of musical talent, he was apprenticed to one or several good masters, and sometimes even sent abroad to perfect himself, at the expense of his sovereign. After finishing his musical education, he was enrolled as a member of the court orchestra. Such was Triemer's career, and also that of a good many of the greatest German virtuosi of the seventeenth and early eighteenth centuries. Triemer received his first instructions in the theory of music from Ehrbach, at Weimar. After the completion of his studies he started on a concert tour, which brought him eventually to Hamburg, where he joined the orchestra of the theatre. He left that position in 1727, and went to Paris to pursue his studies in composition under Boismortier. Two years later, in 1729, he went to Alkmaar in Holland, and thence to Amsterdam, where, after having retired into privacy, he died in 1761. In 1739, he published, in the Dutch language, a work on the rudiments of music, and the art of violin and violoncello playing. In Amsterdam appeared also the "VI Sonate a Violoncelle solo e Continuo," of his compositions.

RIEDEL, another excellent German violoncellist at the beginning of last century, was born at Silesia. About 1727 he went to St. Petersburg, where he was appointed master of fencing at the academy for noblemen, the Czar, Peter II, appointed him a teacher of violoncello playing and fencing to the court, and member of the court orchestra, to which he belonged down to 1740.

JOHANN WOLFGANG WOLFF, born 1704 at Anspach, where he received his first musical training as a choir boy. He was then sent to the "Gymnasium" (Latin college) at Heilbronn, where an Italian instructed him in the art of violoncello playing. In 1734, he was appointed chamber musician to Prince Günther of Sondershausen. On the decease of this prince in 1740 the court chapel was disbanded, and Wolff went to Strelitz, where he died in 1778. He composed several concertos for his instrument.

JOHANN GEORG ROELLIG, born 1710 at Berggieshuebel in Saxony, was in 1757 court violoncellist and organist to the Prince of Anhalt Zerbst.

JOHANN CHRISTIAN SCHWEDLER, born 1710 at Zielenzig, was in 1754 violoncellist in the chapel of the Prince and Markgrave Charles.

As violoncellists in the orchestra of Frederic II at Berlin, in the year 1754, besides Ignatius Mara, a Bohemian, will be found among the violoncellists, CHRISTIAN FRIEDRICH SCHALE, from Brandenburg, ANTONINO HOCK, a Bohemian, and GEORG SPEER, from Zerbst. Particulars relative to the two last-named artists are wanting. The conductor of the court orchestra was at that time Carl Philipp Emmanuel Bach, the son of the great Johann Sebastian.

CHRISTIAN FRIEDRICH SCHALE, born 1713 in Brandenburg as the son of a vicar of the cathedral (Domvicar). At the age of sixteen he visited the Stadtschule at Magdeburg, and gained his musical education at the hands of the excellent organist, Christian Ernst Rolle, at Altstadt. He then visited the University of Halle as a student of law. He was an excellent violoncellist, pianist and organist. In 1735, he received an appointment as violoncellist to the Markgrave Henry. On the foundation of the royal opera in 1742 he was appointed violoncellist in the orchestra, and in 1782 as chamber musician in the court orchestra at Berlin. In 1760 he received as addition to this, the post of organist at the cathedral. He died March 2, 1800, after several years of retirement. Among his compositions, there appears to be nothing for the violoncello. Schale, together with Concialini, was the founder of the amateur concerts in Berlin in 1782.

JOHANN GEORG ROELLIG, born 1710 at Burghausen in Saxony. His first instructions in music he received from the Rector Balthasar Grellmann at Burghausen. Between the years of 1727-35 he visited the Kreuzschule at Dresden where the Cantor Theodor Christlieb Reinhold conducted his general musical studies, while Charles Hartwich instructed him in harpsichord playing and composition. His friendly intercourse with some of the most prominent members of the royal chapel, especially with Zelenka, did much to advance his musical knowledge. After absolving his studies at the Kreuzschule he visited the university at Leipzig where he pursued his literary and scientific as well as musical education for several years, at the end of which he entered the court chapel of Anhalt Zerbst as violoncellist and court organist. That position he filled still in 1757. The date of his death is unknown

He left twenty-four concertos and concert pieces and fifteen trios for various instruments, also fourteen symphonies for orchestra.

JOHANN BAPTIST BAUMGARTNER, born in 1723, at Augsburg, died May 15, 1784, was chamber virtuoso to the Prince Bishop at Eichstädt. He received his musical training at Munich. The name of his master on the violoncello is unknown. In 1774 he began his concert tours, which brought him successively to the principal towns of Germany, Holland, England, Norway and Sweden. In 1774 he settled in Amsterdam, and in 1777 he published at the Hague his "Instruction de musique théoretique et pratique à l'usage de Violoncelle," a book which for its clearness and thoroughness was translated into English and German. In 1778 he went to Stockholm, but being in delicate health he soon returned, and went to Hamburg, where he was greatly admired for his rendering of duets by Boccherini. From Hamburg he went to Vienna, where he was equally successful, and towards the end of 1781 he was appointed chamber virtuoso to the court at Eichstädt, where he died in the following year from consumption, much lamented as artist and as man, as is shown by the necrologue in Cramer's magazine of that year. He left behind him a number of concertos and solos for his instrument which in his necrologue are recommended for the use of amateurs as melodious, and not too exacting.

CASPAR CRISTELLI, born about 1730 at Vienna, was in 1757 at the court of the Prince Bishop of Salzburg, together with Leopold Mozart. He was the solo violoncellist and court composer. In the former capacity the power and mellowness of his tone together with a broad and expressive style of delivery are much praised. He was also a masterly accompanist. Besides works for chamber music, he wrote duets and solos for the violoncello.

JOHANN ANTON MARSCHALL, a pupil of Cristelli, was also a

member of the Prince Bishop's chapel in 1757. He is also mentioned as a good accompanist and violinist. Besides Marschall and Cristelli there were at the same time the following violoncellists in the court orchestra at Salzburg, concerning whom no particulars are available: JOSEPH SCHORN, of Salisburg; ANDREAS SCHACHTNER, a Bavarian, and IGNATIUS FINCK, an Austrian, all of whom played also the violin, and the two latter were in addition "court trumpeters."

JOHANN PHILIPP DEGEN, born 1728 at Wolfenbüttel. His first appointment as violoncellist was in the orchestra of Nicolini's theatre in Brunswick. On the dissolution of that establishment he travelled as virtuoso, visiting the principal towns of Germany, Sweden and Denmark. In 1758 he came to Copenhagen, where he was well received, and in 1760 was appointed chamber musician to the royal court, and first violoncellist in the court orchestra. He died there in January, 1789. Among his compositions are a number of solos for violoncello, and a cantata which was very successful and popular ("Zur Hohen Johannisfeier," composed 1779).

JOSEPH RIEPEL was a violoncellist and chamber musician at the court of the Prince of Thurn and Taxis at Regensburg and Augsburg about the middle of the eighteenth century.

WENZEL HIMMELBAUER, born about 1725 in Bohemia. In 1764 he was in Prague, and later on he went to Vienna, where he was held in high esteem on account of his powerful tone, pure intonation and excellent sight reading. He was still active as violoncellist in 1782. C. F. Daniel Schubart (many of whose songs were set to music by Schubert), speaking about Himmelbauer in his "Æsthetics of Music," says: "He was a solid, and very agreeable violoncellist, quite without conceit. An open-hearted and most amiable man. Nobody has such a steady and unconstrained bow as this master. He plays the most difficult passages with the greatest ease, and he puts all his heart into the *cantabile* His sweet expression, the charm of his graceful rendering, and especially his powerful middle shades, are admired by all hearers and connoisseurs. He has composed but little for his instrument, but that little has all the more intrinsic value." His Op. 1, consisting of duets for flute or violin and violoncello appeared at Lyons in 1776. Some duets for two violoncellos remained in manuscript, and were in the possession of the violoncellist, Emeric Peterzik, and afterwards of Dlabacz, the author of a biographical dictionary. Himmelbauer was also a famous singing master.

JOHANN JOACHIM CHRISTIAN BODE, born 1730, started life as a shepherd boy. He showed early signs of musical talent, and was apprenticed with a town musician, where he studied the violoncello. In later years he became the intimate friend of Lessing, and died a court councillor in 1763.

IGNAZ MALZAT, born about 1730, at Vienna, was a virtuoso chiefly on the French horn. He wrote a concerto for the violoncello which remains in manuscript, and is probably still at Salzburg.

JOHANN GEORG BISCHOFF, born 1735, was the second of five musical brothers, the sons of a town trumpeter and clever mechanician at Nürnberg. He published six solos for the violoncello as Op. 1 in 1780, and also an "Air Varié" in Amsterdam.

JOHANN CARL BISCHOFF, the fourth brother of the above family, was also a clever violoncellist and mechanician. He was appointed chamber-musician at the court of Dessau, and was the inventor of the "Harmonicello," an instrument of the violoncello type with five gut strings and ten metal strings, which were placed underneath on a separate finger-board, so that they could be played separately.* He produced this instrument in various towns, and was received with great enthusiasm. Glowing stanzas in his praise appeared in the contem-

---

* Apparently a kind of baryton with violoncello model.

porary newspapers. He studied in 1773 under the famous F. W. Rust. In 1797 he produced the harmonicello at Hamburg. His youngest brother, Johann Friedrich, was a virtuoso on the kettledrum: he played pieces on *seventeen* kettledrums!

CARL AUGUST WESTENHOLZ, master of the court music of Mecklenburg-Schwerin at Ludwigslust. He was born 1736 at Lauenburg. He studied singing and composition under J. A. Kunzen, and the violoncello under the famous Franz Xaver Voczitka. He composed a great quantity of church music as well as pieces for the violoncello. His first wife was the excellent singer, Affabili, and his second wife, whom he married in 1779, was Eleonore Sophie Maria Fritscher, excellent pianist and harmonika virtuoso, who accompanied at the court concerts. Westenholz died at Ludwigslust January 1, 1789.

A remarkable family of musicians which in the course of several generations produced no less than nine excellent musicians, of whom three were violoncellists of note, was that of the HEMMERLEINS, of Bamberg. Their history has been cleared up by Baron von Marschalk, of Bamberg, who very kindly furnished the author with the following detail contained in his pamphlet on the "Bamberger Hof Musik" (court music at Bamberg). The first known representative of the Hemmerlein family was FRANZ ANTON, a court musician about the middle of the eighteenth century. With him begins a chapter of confusion which has been perpetuated with more zeal than discrimination, even down to the latest biographers of violoncellists, where Franz Anton appears among their number, although there is nothing to prove that he ever played that instrument. Another member of the family, JOHANN NICOLAUS, published in 1748, five masses for four voices with accompaniment, by the celebrated Italian composer, Caldara. The third of these masses was Hemmerlein's composition. His daughter, EVA URSULA, was for about fifty years solo soprano

PLATE XXIV.

C. J. LIDARTI. FROM A PAINTING IN THE POSSESSION OF MESSRS. WM. E. HILL AND SONS.

To face page 184.

singer in the chapel of the Prince Bishop. June 9, 1762, she married her cousin:

ANTON HEMMERLEIN, who was by several years her junior. Anton was born 1730 at Bamberg, the son of the schoolmaster, John Hemmerlein, of Bischberg, and was attached to the court as lackey on May 15, 1762, at an annual salary of eighty florins (about six pounds, sixteen shillings), apart from his livery, with a Christmas box (New Year's money) "by special favour' of six shillings and one florin, thirty-six kreutzer (a little over two shillings) a week for his board! For this he had to serve as lackey to the court, and play any instrument he had learned as required, at church, court-concert or dinner. The Prince Bishop sent him to Regensburg to study the violoncello under Joseph Riepel, violoncellist and chamber-musician to the Prince Thurn and Taxis. Hemmerlein proved an adept pupil and appeared as soloist at the court of the prince in Regensburg and Augsburg. On November 19, 1766, the Prince Bishop, to award his studious zeal, sent him to Munich for four months (with an increased salary of seventeen shillings a month and about three pounds travelling expenses) to finish his studies under the celebrated violoncellist, Francis Woczitka. After eighteen years of "noviceship" Hemmerlein was at last installed as a "court kettledrummer" to fill a vacancy caused by the death of Goeser. This position he held besides that of a violoncellist until the secularisation of the episcopal principality, August 30, 1781, the newly-appointed kettledrummer, Anton Hemmerlein, was sent to Würzburg, to take some lessons in the higher art of kettledrumming from the court drummer, Michael Schlegel, and for that time he received an additional payment of *sixpence* a day. On July 21, 1783, he received his freedom as a court kettledrummer, "after drumming certain given test pieces in the presence of his Excellency the Court Marshal, to the satisfaction and approbation of all the court trumpeters. His Excellency, therefore, did not hesitate to declare him free under the usual ceremony of giving him a box on the ear, handing him the sword and holding an admonitory lecture." After this the "herren" trumpeters and kettledrummer were regaled by "special grace" with twelve quarts of officers wine and a number of loaves of bread. Hemmerlein composed a good deal of the music required for court festivals and dances, as appears from various trifling payments made to him for sundry compositions, as, for instance, on February 26, 1779, when he received eight florins (thirteen shillings and sixpence) for twelve minuets for the court balls. He had to instruct the pages (Hofedelknaben) in the art of violoncello playing, and he was allowed to instruct private pupils. On February 6, 1763, Hemmerlein and his wife received permission to accompany the commissary of the provisioning department, von Ernst, whose daughter they were instructing in various branches of music, to Nuremberg. They were, however, enjoined not to appear at that town at a theatre "or other public, *and not over respectable place*" for money. The only exception was to be made in favour of a request to play for the commanding general of the imperial army, Prince Charles Christian of Stollberg.

Hemmerlein was pensioned at an advanced age on account of failing sight and stiffness of the arm, and died September, 1811, at Bamberg at the age of eighty-one years.

If we have dwelled at some length on the history of Anton Hemmerlein's life it is not so much on account of his importance in the history of the violoncello, as on account of the graphic picture which it affords of the social position of prominent musicians who were the subjects of continental princes during the seventeenth and eighteenth centuries.

They were little better than serfs, about whose person the prince had absolute power to dispose. It has been argued that at least they were placed beyond the cares for the ordinary necessaries of life, but those dreams are rudely dispelled by the frequent memorials presented by well-known artists to their princes for increase of their salaries to save them from urgent want.

There is much which reminds one of the status of the ancient "jongleurs," which, by the English law, were declared to be "vagabonds and sturdy beggars."

KARL IGNAZ HEMMERLEIN, the son of Anton, was born at Bamberg in 1773. He studied the violoncello in 1789 under J. K. Schlick at Gotha, and composition under Uhlmann at Bamberg. He was a virtuoso on his instrument and published a concerto for violoncello and orchestra, Op. 1, in 1801. For one period of his life he was director of the court orchestra at Fulda where the position of treasurer of the salt mines was bestowed upon him as producing an increase of his salary. After his return to Bamberg he conducted for a number of years the opera at that town, and an amusing story is related in connection with that period of his musical career. Dr. John Daniel Elner, a humorous account of whose life appears in Bechstein's "Fahrten eines Musikanten" (wanderings of a musician), competed with Hemmerlein for the conductorship at Bamberg. On November 19, 1837, he made the daring innovation to conduct the opera "Zampa" with a black lacquered baton instead of the customary fiddle bow, and to assist the singers here and there by softly singing the notes of their entries. This upset the conservative Bamberg audience, and cut short the rule of the baton. Before long Hemmerlein found himself installed again in his comfortable arm-chair, the four legs of which were securely screwed down to the platform. He died in 1840 at the age of sixty-seven.

THOMAS HEMMERLEIN, the youngest son of Anton, and brother of Charles Ignatius, was also a talented violoncellist, who from the year 1784 was often heard at the court concerts, but he found no favour in the eyes of the prince. On his application in 1786 for a permanent engagement at the court of Bamberg he was told that "if he were the most perfect violoncellist he would not be able to render to me and the 'Hochstift' (episcopal abbey) the services which it is hoped we shall receive from the 'Regierungsadvocat' (barrister) Pfister, whom I have sent to Göttingen for one year. He does not receive more than five hundred taler (seventy-five pounds) for the whole of that year, out of which he has to pay his travelling expenses, university fees and all expenses for his maintenance during that period." A month later (December 17), when he repeated his application to be appointed at Bamberg or to be allowed to go to Salzburg he was told he might go to Salzburg *unmolested* or seek service at any other court. What became of him eventually is unknown.

ANTON KRAUS was born at Winterberg in Bohemia about 1745, and was still living in 1795 at his native place as conductor and organist, as well as an excellent violoncellist and violinist.

FRANZ JOSEPH WEIGL, born March 19, 1740, was the father of the well-known opera composer, and an intimate friend of Haydn, who was the godfather of his talented son. He was born at an obscure village in Bavaria, and, on Haydn's recommendation, was appointed to the celebrated private band of Prince Esterhazy on June 1, 1761. He exchanged that position for an engagement in the orchestra of the opera at Vienna in 1769, where he remained for twenty-three years. In 1792 he became a member of the emperor's private band, with the title of a court and chamber musician. In 1818 he celebrated his fifty years' golden jubilee, and was decorated with the gold medal for special merit. He died January 25, 1820. He composed little, and apparently nothing of importance. An opera, "La Cafetiera Bizzarra," has been attributed to him. His portrait is given here, Fig. 38.

ANTON FILZ was, in 1763, a violoncellist and composer of great talent. He died in early manhood, in 1768, a member of the famous Mannheim orchestra. Schilling relates that, according to tradition, he died of eating spiders, which, he said, tasted like strawberries. Von Bury in his sketch of Schetky's life (see below), confirms this statement. His untimely death cut short a career full of promise. He had great

FIG. 38. JOSEPH WEIGL.

melodic invention, and six symphonies in eight parts, Op. 1; six pianoforte trios, Op. 2; six string trios, Op. 3; as well as a MS. concerto and solos, testify to his eminent talent and mastery of form in composition.

ERNST LUDWIG GERBER, born September 29, 1746, at Sondershausen, where he died, as court secretary, June 30, 1819.

He published the famous "Dictionary of Musicians." While studying at the University of Leipzig in 1765, he was appointed violoncellist in the town orchestra. During that period he composed ballets for the theatre, some orchestral works and three concertos for violoncello, which met with distinct success. He was appointed teacher of the Princes of Sondershausen, and devoted himself henceforward to musical literature.

CHRISTOPH SCHETKY, born 1740, at Darmstadt, generally known as Johann Georg S. from the fact that the initials J. G. appear sometimes added to his christian name, received his first musical training from his father, a singer in the court church choir. The capellmeister Endeler, a mediocre musician, instructed him in musical theory, while he commenced to study the violoncello as autodydact. For one month only he received some instructions from Anton Filz, of Mannheim. These, as well as the following details, are taken from a biographical notice in the "Allgemeine Musikzeitung" of 1799, based upon communications from his brother-in-law, "Oberstwachtmeister von Buri," a poet and musician.

In 1761 the Schetky family started on a concert tour to Hamburg, viz., the father, two sisters, one a high soprano, the second, Ludomilla (later on Frau von Buri), a contralto of exceptional compass and quality of voice—who was from all accounts also endowed with great personal beauty—and young J. Georg Schetky, the violoncellist. They travelled at the expense of the Hamburg merchants and passed right through the lines of the hostile French and German armies.

This was young Schetky's first debut outside his native town, and his success was unqualified, as the following incident amply proves. Schetky's violoncello, an indifferent instrument, was accidentally knocked over the platform of the concert room by an attendant, and seriously injured. The Hamburg amateurs, full of sympathy for the young artist, joined together and presented him with a fine Cremonese violoncello by "Hieronymo Straduary" (the name, of course, is misquoted by the author of the article). Schetky remained in Hamburg for six months, where he had the opportunity of hearing many eminent artists, whereby he was encouraged to further study and improvement of his style and technique.

On their return journey the Schetky family gave successful concerts at Osnabrück and Göttingen. Arrived at Darmstadt young Schetky was for some time engaged in the court orchestra, but after the death of his parents in 1768, he left Darmstadt for good. He went to Hamburg, where he appeared six times on the concert platform between June 11, 1768, and October, 1769, and thence, in 1870, to London, where he made the acquaintance, and obtained the patronage of Johann Christian Bach. Here he published six trios for two violins and violoncello, Op. 1, six duos for violin and violoncello, Op. 2, and six sonatas for violoncello and bass, Op. 3; also his six sonatas for violoncello and bass, Op. 4; six string quartets, Op. 6, with an introductory essay on the performance of concerted music by Bremner, published by R. Bremner, London, and twelve duos, Op. 7, appeared in London, but he was then living in Edinburgh, where he married a widow possessed of a considerable income, and retired into private life, devoting his time to composition. The twelve duets, Op. 7, were published "With some Observations and Rules for Playing that Instrument." He published also six easy duos for two violoncellos through Sieber in Paris. Von Buri tells us also of three trios for violoncello *obbligato*, viola and bass, composed on his suggestion. Schetky's compositions testify to his great ability as an executant, and also to his musical knowledge, while they are less remarkable for their contents. A complete list of his compositions may be found in Eitner's "Quellen-Lexikon." Schetky was regarded as a virtuoso of the first order, who astounded people by playing the first violin part of a string quartet from sight, and who could play staccato passages in the down bow as well as in the up bow. This is all the more surprising as he still held the bow gamba fashion, that is with the thumb on the top of the nut and the fingers underneath. His biographer, von Buri (Schetky's brother-in-law) tries to justify this holding of the bow from scientific reasons! It appears, however, from all accounts, that his tone was round and full like that of an oboe up to the highest registers, and in the adagio "like sweet oil dropping from the ripe olive." He was also praised for his accompaniment of the "recitative" from the figured bass, "a legacy which has been left to the violoncello by the late gamba." It is curious to note how many points there were still at that time connecting the gamba with the violoncello, for Schetky was by no means the only violoncellist holding the bow in gamba fashion (see TONELLI, HEBDEN, GRAUL, etc.).

Schetky is described as a very handsome man, and a great favourite with the fair sex. He was blind in his left eye, but to those who did not know him well this was scarcely noticeable. "When playing he used to hide the left eye behind the neck of his instrument while reading the smallest notes with the right eye at an incredible distance" (!!).

This statement discloses a very curious holding of the instrument for which we can find no parallel.

Schetky was extremely temperate, he had apparently no vice except that in his youth he was fond of gambling, and although he earned a great deal of money during his concert tours, his favourite sister was often appealed to and always came to his rescue when he had brought himself into difficulties. Sandys and Forster's "History of the Violin" contains an extensive sketch of his life. He died at Edinburgh in 1824.

MARCUS HEINRICH GRAUL, born at Eisenach, was a chamber musician at the Prussian court at Berlin from 1742 till 1798. He was an excellent virtuoso, and according to some accounts, also a good composer, although Dr. Burney makes the fol-

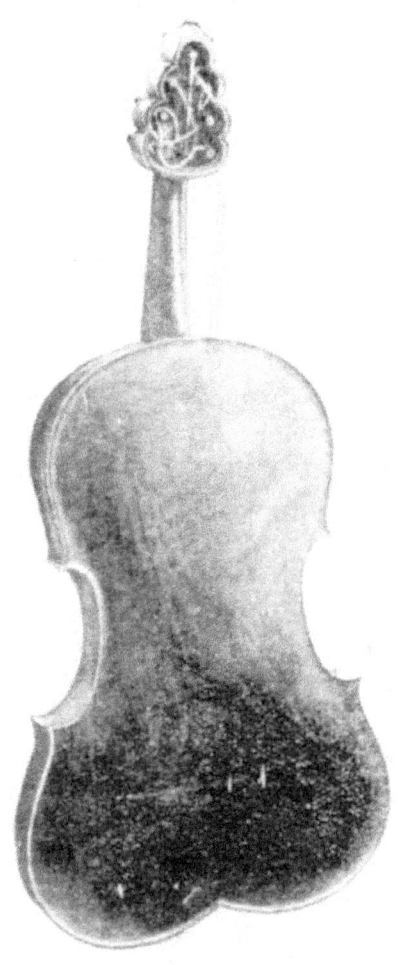

LIRONE DA BRACCIO (BACK) BY VENTURA LINAROLO, VENICE, 1577.
ORIGINAL IN THE WM. HEYER MUSEUM, COLOGNE. *See pages 25-6.*

lowing remark: "M. Graul, a violoncello performer in the king's band, played a concerto; it was but ordinary music, however it was well executed, though in the old manner with the hand under the bow." This proves that this way of holding the bow, as shown in the picture of Tonelli, was still extensively practised about the middle of the last century. Very few of Graul's compositions have been preserved.

ALEXANDER ALBERTI, a clever violoncellist, was musical director of the chapel of the Bishop of Breslau in 1754.

JOHANN HEINRICH VIKTOR ROSE, born December 7, 1743, at Quedlinburg. He received his first musical education from his father, who was one of the town musicians and organist at the cathedral. The Princess Amalia, who was then Abbess of the Frauenstift (lay-nunnery for ladies of rank) recognised young Rose's talent, and took him in 1756 to Berlin, where she placed him under Graul and Mara. In 1763 he entered the service of the Prince of Anhalt Bernburg as court organist in his native town, and in 1767 he started on a concert tour. The year 1768 found him in the service of the Prince of Anhalt Dessau, and in 1772 he returned to Quedlinburg in the capacity of organist. He published three sonatas with bass through Hummel in Amsterdam, and in Berlin 1793.

JOHANNES JÄGER, born August 31, 1748, at Schlitz (a Hessian town belonging to Count Gorz), was looked upon by his contemporaries as one of the greatest virtuosi of the century. Schubart, the poet-critic, speaks of him in the most enthusiastic terms. "Jäger," he says, "is quite original, his style of bowing new, unconstrained and fiery to the verge of impetuosity. All masters begin with the thumb on the D string, and thus produce the passages in higher positions. Jäger deviates entirely from that system—to prove that his genius has more than one way to obtain his ends. He runs up on the D and A strings with lightning speed to the highest notes, and plays the most delicate movements with the most perfect grace and tenderness. . . .

Jäger is, at the same time, a splendid sight-reader. .... He composes, not according to rules, but follows the judgment of his ear. His concertos and sonatas consist principally of self-invented movements, which are great and noble in character, suited to the instrument, and full of difficulties. Jäger had his pieces revised by some excellent composers, whereby they have received the proper form. At the same time, one must admit that the exuberant shoots of an often unbridled fantasy still require pruning." Schubart also states that Jäger was the only violoncellist who could surmount the difficulties of Duport's compositions. As none of his compositions have been left, it is impossible to say how far Schubart's remarks are justified. Anyhow, it is evident that he was entirely an automath in composition, and it is more than probable that he was the same as a violoncellist. At all events, nothing is known as to his studies, and, apparently, he never did receive a regular training at the hands of a master. In his early youth he was in Dutch service as oboist, and cultivated the horn as his favourite instrument. Thence he came about 1775-7 to the court of Württemberg at Stuttgart, and improved greatly by the surroundings of artists like Jomelli, Deller and Seeman, who stood on the pinnacle of their time. Gerber says that under their influence he became "the great artist whom the century admired." During this period he appeared with great success at Frankfort-on-Main. In 1776 he was appointed chamber-virtuoso (Eitner says "Musikdirector") at the court of Anspach-Bayreuth. This position left him ample time for concert tours, which in 1781 brought him to London. His leisure hours were devoted to the education of his sons. The elder son, JOHANN ZACHARIAS LEONHARDT, born 1777, at Anspach, showed early signs of musical talent, and was able to execute solos on the violoncello with perfect accuracy at the age of nine. In 1787 he played before the court in Berlin, and was so much admired by the Queen that she offered to

THE JÄGER FAMILY AND THEIR CONTEMPORARIES. 195

appoint him a member of the Royal chapel. The father, however, declined this offer on account of the youthful age of his son. The Queen then settled upon him a life pension of one hundred thaler (a large sum in those days). He relinquished his position at the court of Anspach in 1798, and followed his father to Breslau, where the latter retired into private life. At Breslau, ERNST JÄGER, the younger of the two brothers, first saw the light in 1800. He possessed even more talent than his elder brother. Scarcely ten years old, he went on a concert tour with his father, visiting all the principal towns of Germany and Hungary, where both father and son created quite a sensation, especially by their wonderful ensemble playing. He made the acquaintance of Bernhard Romberg, who accepted him as a pupil, and, under the care of this great master, he developed into a virtuoso of the *very* first order. In 1825 he left Breslau, and was appointed solo violoncellist to the court of Bavaria, where his father followed him in 1826. The two brothers do not appear to have contributed anything of importance to the literature of their instrument.

JOH. DAVID SCHEIDLER was born in the same year as Joh. Jäger, viz., 1748, and died October 20, 1802. He married the famous singer, Sophie Elizabeth Susanne Preysing. He was a member of the ducal private band at Gotha, together with Joh. K. Schlick (of whom we shall speak later on). A guitarrist of exactly the same name as Scheidler lived in Vienna in 1820.

MARTIN CALMUS, born at Zweibrücken 1749, was appointed violoncellist in the Royal chapel at Dresden in 1800, after holding a similar position in the "National Orchestra" at Altona for three years. He enjoyed the reputation of an excellent virtuoso and died at Dresden 1809.

KARAUSCHECK, or KARASECK, was a member of the private band of the Prince of Thurn and Taxis at Regensburg from 1750-60 at a salary of 260 florins. He was an excellent composer, who combined melodious invention with mastery of form. The greater part of his works, including three concertos and eight solos, remained in manuscript. He became a religious enthusiast, entered a Carmelite monastery, and died in 1789.

GRETSCH was also a member of the Thurn and Taxis band at Regensburg, where he probably followed Karauscheck, and remained until his death in 1784. He came twice to Holland with the above orchestra, and was so pleased with the country and the people that he accepted an engagement as *first violinist* at the opera at Amsterdam in 1773, but apparently only temporarily. According to Gerber, he composed three concertos and eight solos for his instrument. Of these Eitner accounts for three sonatas and one concerto in C in various libraries.

PHILIP SCHINDLÖCKER, born of German parents at Mons, in Belgium, October 25, 1753, came to Vienna at an early age, and studied the violoncello under Himmelbauer. In 1795 he was appointed solo violoncellist at the Opera, and three years later in the same capacity at the Cathedral of St. Stephen at Vienna. In 1806 he received the title of an Imperial Chamber Virtuoso, but retired in 1811, and died April 16, 1857. Most of his compositions remained in manuscript, including a concerto and sonatas with bass, and only a serenade for violoncello and guitar was published. His nephew:

WOLFGANG SCHINDLÖCKER, born in 1789, in Vienna, appeared as a prodigy at the age of fourteen. He studied first the violin, and exchanged it for the violoncello. His first appointment was at the Court Theatre in Vienna. In 1807 he became a chamber musician at the court of Würzburg. He published a Grand Duo, Op. 5, and three duets for two violoncellos. He travelled a great deal, and visited even North America, returning again to Würzburg.

An accomplished votary of the violoncello was also the PRINCE WITTGENSTEIN BERLEBERG, born December 12, 1753.

He studied the piano and singing at an early age, and afterwards the violoncello. He appeared at Wetzlar, then an important town on the Lahn, in a public concert under a pseudonym. He had an excellent little orchestra at his Chateau Berleberg in Westphalia, and died October 4, 1800.

GREGOR HAUER, a Benedictine monk of the Monastery of Seitenstetten and Ernstbrunn, born February 3, 1753, played the violoncello with great mastery. He was a friend of Michael Haydn (Joseph's brother). Besides variations for his instrument Hauer composed a mass and an operetta!

About the middle of last century there appear a number of violoncellists in the private bands of various German princes of whom nothing but the names have come down to us. As some particulars concerning their lives may be supplied at some time or other, they are recorded here as given by Marpurg: N. HOFMANN, JOH. GEORG KNECHTEL, ANTONIO PINCINETTI, junior, and INNOCENZ DANZI (father of Franz Danzi) appeared together with JOS. ZYKA and A. FILZ, as members of the private band of the Prince Palatine at Mannheim in 1756.

JAHN BOTHOF, junior, and RADAUER, were in the Stuttgart orchestra under Jomelli in 1757, together with VAN MALDERE, a Belgian violoncellist. The latter was brother of the director of the private chapel of Prince Charles at Brussels, whom he succeeded. He went to Venice to study composition under Martinelli in 1754, and in the same year he entered the private band of the King of Württemberg at Stuttgart. Eberhard Malterre is mentioned in Schwickert's "Almanach" as a chamber musician in the Stuttgart orchestra in 1782, but his instrument is not mentioned. He is no doubt a son or relative of Van Maldere. L. Maltere is mentioned in notices of that time, the L. probably being the initial of Van Maldere's christian name.

In the famous Salzburg Orchestra, together with Leopold

Mozart, were, in the year 1757, JOH. ANTON MARSCHALL, a pupil of Cristelli, JOSEPH SCHORN, a native of Salzburg, ANDREAS SCHACHTNER, a Bavarian, and IGNATIUS FINK, an Austrian. The two latter were also trumpeters.

KARL KASPAR EDER, born 1751 in Bavaria, studied composition under Lang and Koehler, and was appointed solo violoncellist to the Elector of Bavaria at Trèves when he was quite young. He visited all the courts of Germany, and was greatly admired in concertos and solos of his own composition. He wrote two symphonies, one quintet, fourteen concertos, twenty solos, three duos and two trios for the violoncello.

CARL HEINRICH GRAUN, 1701-59, the famous composer, was also a skilful executant on the violoncello. Fux wrote an opera, "La Constanza e la Fortezza," for the coronation in 1723 of Charles VI of Germany. On that occasion Graun was principal violoncello, Quantz, flute, and Conti, the composer, principal theorbo.

The court at Vienna always attracted all the musical talent that came within its sphere, and the Austrian nobility took a very active part in musical matters, and produced a considerable number of good executants. In 1724, on May 16, Caldara's "Euristes" was performed by members of the highest nobility. The Archduchesses Maria Theresia (afterwards the famous empress) and Maria Anna led the dances, and JOH. BAPTIST COUNT VON PERGEN, SIGMUND COUNT HERBERSTEIN, and JOH. KARL COUNT VON HARDECK figured as violoncellists in the orchestra. The Emperor conducted the performance at the pianoforte.

FRIEDRICH BERGER, died in 1786 as violoncellist of the Opera at Leipzig. He was closely allied to Karl Gottlieb Berger, a violinist, but whether as relative, or only as friend, is unknown. They lived together as inseparable friends for more than thirty years.

HEINRICH GRIESBACH, born at Koppenbrügge. He came to

London, where he studied under Crosdill, and joined the Queen's private band. He played at Abel's concerts in 1783, and was still a member of the Concerts of Antient Music in 1793. His brother George was first violin in the Queen's band. Three duets of his for violin and violoncello, Op. 1, are in the British Museum library.

FRIEDRICH LUDWIG SCHROEDEL, born February 4, 1754, at Baruth, died January 19, 1800, at Ballenstedt. He studied the violoncello under Rose, and was appointed chamber musician at the age of twenty-five. Gerber says that he was one of the greatest virtuosos of his time, and many people thought that he surpassed even the famous Mara in delicacy of rendering and precision. The Prince of Ballenstedt, after appointing him about 1770 as "lackey," sent him once a week to Rose to pursue his studies. He visited all the principal towns of Germany with great success. Six duos with bass were published by Breitkopf and Härtel. A few days before his death, in January, 1800, Schroedel, who was then chamber musician of the Prince of Anhalt Dessau, played at a concert at Leipzig with great success.

CARL GOTTFRIED WILHELM WACH, born September 16, 1756, at Loebau (Ober Lausitz), excellent violoncellist and virtuoso on the double bass. He was a student of law at Leipzig in 1777, where he joined the orchestra as violinist, which he exchanged in 1783 for the contrabass. March 9, 1788, he became secretary of the "grand concerts" and contrabass player in the town orchestra. In 1805 he received from the town council an annuity for life and a free residence. He died January 25, 1833. He arranged about thirty operas for quintet and sextet, with and without voice parts. This form of playing operas among amateurs was much in vogue down to the middle of this century. Wach was also a collector of biographical notes, which Gerber used for his dictionary.

PAUL ANTON WINNEBERGER, born 1758, at Mergentheim on

the Tauber (Württemberg). He received his first musical instruction from Magister Heilig, an excellent musician, who had formerly been a Jesuit, and who produced many talented pupils. At the age of nine, Winneberger was appointed alto singer to the court, with a salary of one hundred thalers (£15), four malter (bushels) corn, and two eimer (about fifteen gallons) wine. At the age of fourteen he became assistant organist. When he was seventeen years old he lost his voice, and in consequence took up the study of theology at Würzburg and Heidelberg. Three years later, then only twenty years old, he was, at the recommendation of Heilig, appointed teacher and organist at the musical seminary at Mannheim. There he continued his theoretical studies under Abt. Vogler and Holzbauer. At the same time he studied the violin under Fraenzl, who induced him to take up the violoncello. When Danzi left Mannheim temporarily to go on tour, Winneberger became attached to the court orchestra. In 1780 he was appointed director of the "Jagd und Tafel musick" (hunting and table music) of Prince Wallerstein. On the dissolution of that orchestra during the French War in 1800, Winneberger went to Hamburg as violoncellist of the "French Theatre" and teacher of music, and died there on February 8, 1821. He published three string quartets (André in 1800), two concertos (Schott), three sonatas for piano, flute and violoncello, Op. 7 (Böhme, Hamburg). A cantata remained unpublished.

JOSEPH ANTONY, born January 12, 1758, at Rengersbrunnen, County Rheineck. He was an excellent violoncellist, organist and church composer. He died in 1832 at Münster. At the latter town his son, Franz Joseph, was born in 1790. He was a well-known musical author and church composer.

ANTON THADDAEUS STAMITZ, brother of the famous violinist, was born 1721 at Deutschbrod, in Bohemia. He was an excellent violoncellist who entered the Church at Prague, and after becoming a dean at Deutschbrod in 1750, he was raised to the position of a canon at Alt Bunzlan, where he died, August 23, 1768.

JOHANN KAUFMANN, born 1760, at Stuttgart, received his musical and general education at the famous "Karlsschule," which afterwards received Schiller among a number of distinguished pupils. He was an excellent violoncellist, who shone more as ripieni player than as soloist. He married Julia, the daughter of Daniel Schubart, the poet critic. She was an excellent singer and actress, who died in 1802, at the early age of thirty-three. Kaufmann was appointed teacher at the seminary, at Maulbronn, where he died in 1834.

FRIEDRICH HUGO BARON VON KERPEN, capitular of the Würzburg Cathedral in 1780, 1790 in Mayence, afterwards in Heilbroun. An excellent violoncellist, conductor and prolific composer of operas, quartets, trios, sonatas of a good flowing and melodious style. For his instrument he wrote apparently nothing.

KARL LOCHNER, born about 1760 at Pforzheim, in Baden, was violoncellist in the court orchestra at Mannheim, where he died from hæmorrhage in 1795. Between 1793-5 he published a collection of songs and a melodrama, "Orpheus," but apparently nothing for the violoncello.

PETER RITTER. About this remarkable composer and virtuoso very little has been heard so far, and it will, therefore, be an opportunity to give some generally interesting details concerning his life, which are taken from an excellent little biography recently published by William Schulze in Berlin, who is in possession of a great number of Ritter's manuscripts. Peter Ritter was born July 2, 1763, at Mannheim, where his father, Georg Ritter, was engaged as violinist. The time in which he received his first musical impressions was the most remarkable period in the annals of that court as far as its musical life is concerned. The worthy old Holzbauer was at the head of the opera, which counted among its artists some of the greatest virtuosos which the world possessed at that time. There were the inimitable Dorothea Wendling, Raaff (the famous tenor), Aloysia Weber, who won the early affection of young Mozart (who was present in Mannheim in 1777, and full of admiration for the bevy of musical talent by which he was surrounded); as violins: Cannabich, Toeschi, Cramer, Stamitz, Fraenzl; Wendling as flautist, Le Brun and Ramm as oboists, Wenzel Ritter (the greatest bassoon player of his century, and Peter's cousin), and Lang (the great horn virtuoso). Anton Filz and Innocenz Danzi were the principal violoncellos, and both charged themselves with the technical training of young Peter, who had already studied the violin and the rudiments of thorough-bass at an age when children generally begin to read and write. In the autumn of 1776 he appeared at the "Rothe Haus" (the Municipal Palace) at Frankfurt, together with a sister, aged fourteen, who sang, and a brother, aged eighteen, who played the violin. Soon after this he went with his father to Berlin, and played before the Crown Prince (afterwards Frederic William II), who was an enthusiastic amateur of the violoncello. Peter was greeted with unbounded admiration, especially when he played a concerto by Duport at sight from a copy which was placed upside-down on his desk. He had to appear again and again at the court, and the Princess Royal was so delighted with a violoncello concerto of his own composition that she handed him a poem and asked him to compose it for her. When she came to Mannheim, about twenty years later, she sent for Ritter and told him that she still sang his aria with great pleasure. The King presented him with a violoncello of the value of one hundred dukaten (which would correspond to an instrument of at least £500 in our time). The great Abbé Volger heard him play one day when he was only nine years of age, and was so struck with the boy's talent that he offered to undertake his theoretical education. When Ritter was seventeen, Volger published a string quartet of his gifted pupil in his monthly musical paper. At the age of sixteen he had already composed a symphony which evoked general admiration. His quartets are said to be truly masterly. He wrote a number of violoncello concertos, of which ten are still in existence, as well as a number of sonatas. But Ritter cared nothing for fame, and kept all his compositions, with very few exceptions, in manuscript. Among the concertos there is one in D which is absolutely a masterpiece. It opens with an Adagio in D minor, which in pathos and breadth of style reminds one of Tartini. This is followed by an Allegro in D major, which is quite modern in character and of a most buoyant spirit. A short, slow movement (no *tempo* is indicated) in A major follows, and the finale is a delightful Andante grazioso with variations, in D major. Its publication would form a very acceptable addition to the literature of the violoncello. In 1784 he took Franz Danzi's place in the Mannheim Court Orchestra with a salary of 150 florins (about £15) per annum! His extraordinary mastery of the violoncello, combined with his musical genius, gave him quite an exceptional position in the orchestra, of which he soon became the actual leader. He combined a powerful and singing tone with great facility of the left hand. A curious fact is stated in the "Leipziger Musikalische Zeitung" of 1804. He played a concerto of his own composition, and after praising the facility with which he executed his passages, the writer says: "In the adagio he muted his instrument by a heavy sordino, which he is said to do generally. A connoisseur might have thought that one heard a different tone and a different player." It seems strange to hear this related from an artist who in his compositions displayed such refined taste! In 1806 he was ordered by the Prince Palatine to play at a concert which was given in honour of Napoleon's presence in Karlsruhe. About 1787 he married Katherina Baumann, the first actress of the

Mannheim Theatre, who was greatly admired and praised by Schiller. In 1788 he produced his first opera, "The Eremit of Formentera" (words by Kotzebue), which made the round of all the principal German opera houses. In 1792 he produced a choral piece, "Die Weihe," to celebrate the reappearance of the princess after a long illness, and this shows his mastery of the treatment of choral masses, as well as the melodious and typical folk character of his musical conceptions. Shortly afterwards he composed the sacred song, "Grosser Gott wir loben Dich" ("Lord of Glory"), which to this day remains the common property of the whole German nation. In England it is likewise a well-known hymn which has lately come into prominence by the impressive use Humperdinck has made of it in his music to "The Miracle." He was so careless about his own merit that this fine composition, which became rapidly popular, passed for some time as Haydn's work, as Ritter had not taken the trouble even to sign it. In 1800, on Christmas Day, he produced Haydn's "Creation," for the first time in Mannheim, with enormous success. Soon afterwards Ritter was formally engaged as leader, and in 1803 as conductor, of the orchestra, in which position he continued until 1823. He died August 1, 1845, admired and loved by all who knew him. Weber was on terms of closest friendship with him, and admired his talent greatly. Curious is the fact that a melody from Ritter's "Mandarin" so grew upon Weber that he used it intentionally, or unintentionally, as the subject for the andante of his famous terzetto in the "Freischütz." Besides the Concertos in D, there are in Mr. Schulz's possession two Concertos in A, and one each in E, B flat, G and A minor. String quartets with violoncello *obbligato* in C, G, D and F minor. The latter being marked No. V, bears the date 1781. A Sonata with cembalo accompaniment in F; a Concertante for horn and violoncello, in F;

Two Duets (Nos. 4 and 6 of the set), in B flat and G, and fragments of a concertino with a fine slow movement.

In the court orchestra at Copenhagen there were as violoncellists in 1785 (according to Cramer) PHILIPP DEGEN, who came from Brunswick, and wrote about 1779 the much admired "St. John's Cantata," with pianoforte accompaniment. He died in 1789. He was first violoncellist, the others being MOREL and SCHALL, junior, about whom we possess no further information.

WINKIS and THORWART represented, in 1782, the violoncello at the court of Hesse-Cassel. The former was a Belgian by birth and will be dealt with later on; of the latter details are missing. In the following year Thorwart appears no longer at Cassel, but we find BUSCH, from Thuringia, in his place. (No particulars.)

At the court of Bentheim Steinfurt we find A. BOLANDER and J. C. SIEGMANN as violoncellists, but no further details about their career are obtainable.

THE MARKGRAVE OF BAYREUTH, heir to Frederic Christian, who died 1769, played the violoncello at his private evening concerts.

Koechl has given a complete list of the violoncellists in the Imperial Chapel at Vienna which we include here in full. The first is the date of entry into the chapel, the second is the date of leaving or death. The salaries are given in florins (Austrian florin nominally about two shillings).

LIST OF VIOLONCELLISTS IN THE IMPERIAL CHAPEL, VIENNA.

Name.	Date of Entry.	Date of Leaving.	Notes.	Salary before 1712.	Salary from 1712.
Fred. Leopold Pückl.	May 1, 1686.	Died June, 1711.		fl. 30.	
Jos. Malagotti.	July 1, 1702.	Died February 28, 1719.	Age forty-five.	fl. 45.	
Joh. Cramner (Cramer?).	1705.	June 30, 1740.	Pensioned.	fl. 40 up to 50.	fl. 360.
Ant. Schnautz.	1710.	June 30, 1740.	From 1721 violin.	fl. 40.	fl. 480.
Franz Peter Schnautz.	January 1, 1719.	1722.	From 1722 violin.	fl. 45.	fl. 540.
Pietro Adó.	1720.	June 30, 1740.	Died August 7, 1762, aged seventy-five, as pensioned lay priest.	fl. 75.	fl. 900.
Ant. Rajola.	1721.	June 30, 1740.		fl. 60 up to 83.20.	fl. 720 up to 1,000.
Franz Alborea.	1721.	Died June 20, 1739		fl. 105.	fl. 1,260.
Giov. Perroni.	April 1, 1721.	June 30, 1740.	Died March 10, 1748, aged sixty.		fl. 150.
Karl Fr. Drenger	December 28, 1725.	June 30, 1740.	Died June 15, 1745, aged forty-three.		fl. 500
Christ. Röttig.	March 7, 1740.	June 30, 1740.	Died April 7, 1764, aged fifty-five.		fl. 450.
In 1741 Perroni appears with a salary of fl. 1,000 and Adó with fl. 800, Drenger with fl. 600 and Röttig with fl. 450. In 1756 only two violoncellists were in the chapel, viz., Adó and Röttig.					
		From 1772 to 1792.			
Joh. Nic. Hofmann.	1772.	1791.	Schwickert, in his "Almanack," 1782, gives the names as Joh. Victor Hoffmann and Jos. Oessler.		
Jos. Orsler.	1772.	1792.			

From 1793 to 1823.			
Jos. Orsler.	April, 1792.	Died June 2, 1806.	Age seventy-nine.	fl. 300.
Jos. Weigl.	April, 1792.	Died January, 1820.		fl. 300.
Phil. Schindlöcker.	July 1, 1806.	1823.		
Caj. Gottlieb.	1819.	1823.		
From 1824 to 1846.			
Phil. Schindlöcker.	1824.	Died April 16, 1827.	Age seventy-four.	
Caj. Gottlieb.	1824.	Died September 16, 1837.	Age sixty-nine.	
Jos. Merk.	1827.	1846.		
Aegid Borzaga.	1837.	1846.		
From 1847 to 1867.			
Jos. Merk.	1847.	Died June 16, 1852.	Age fifty-eight.	
Aegid Borzaga.	1847.	Died November 15, 1858.	Age fifty-seven.	
Jos. Hartinger.	June 21, 1852.	1867.		
Karl Schlesinger.	November 18, 1858.	1867.		

Giovanni Buononcini, July 1, 1700, to September 11, 1711, does not appear as violoncellist. He was only engaged as composer.

The name of Pückl belongs to a family of musicians which appear back as far as 1544, when Georg Pueckl is mentioned as Cantor of the Imperial Chapel. Virgil Pickhl, a bass, was a singer in the chapel from 1637 to 1645, Paul Pückl (also Bickl) violinist, 1650, died 1688, and Wm. Christ. Bickl (Pückl) 1670-5.

Giovanni Perroni, of whom only the dates given in the table, page 206, are known, married the famous opera singer, Ambreville. He composed, besides oratorios, etc., a concerto for violoncello with orchestra.

Carlo Perroni appears on the MSS. of a concerto with orchestra and a solo with bass in the University Library at Rostock. Eitner questions the correctness of the christian name.

Franz Alborea must have been a very extraordinary player, as he received by far the highest salary paid to any violoncellist in the Imperial Chapel at Vienna down to modern times.

Heinrich Balthasar Preysing, born about 1718, died October 6, 1802, at Gotha. In 1783, together with Johann David Scheidler, he represented the violoncello in the Ducal Chapel of Saxe-Gotha, and was considered one of the first virtuosos in Germany. In his youth he toured a great deal, and composed solos for his instrument, which remained in manuscript. His sons, Frederic and Charles, he trained to the musical profession, and both were members of the Gotha Orchestra. Preysing died October 6, 1802, at the age of eighty-four.

Riga possessed one violoncellist in 1783, in the person of Adams, about whom nothing more is known.

Stockholm, in the same year, had one native violoncellist,

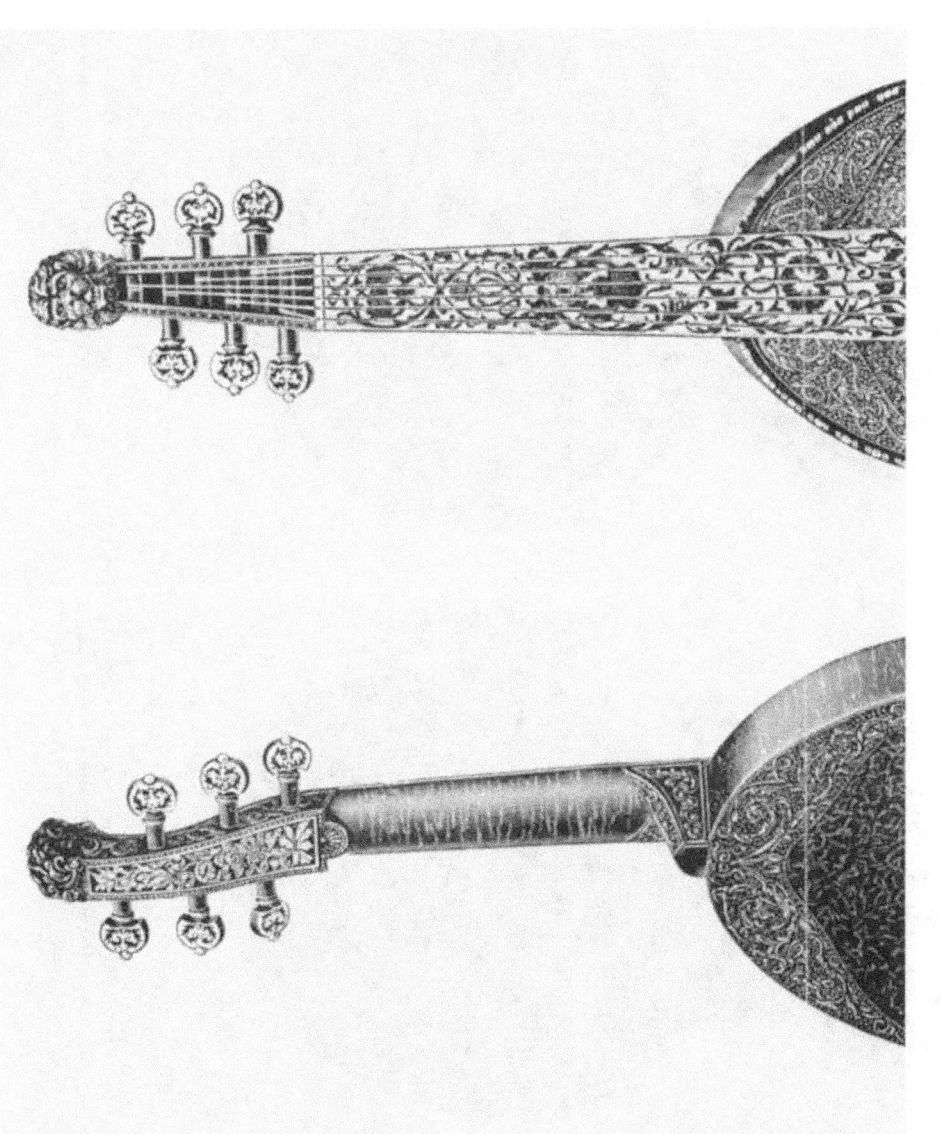

VIOL DA GAMBA BY JOACHIM TIELKE, CIRCA 1700, IN THE WM. HEYER MUSEUM, COLOGNE. THE INSTRUMENT WHICH HAD BEEN ENLARGED TO BE USED AS VIOLONCELLO AS SHOWN BY ORNAMENTED PART ON UPPER BOUTS, BELONGED AT ONE TIME TO MR. PAUL DE WIT IN LEIPZIG, WHO, ON ACCOUNT OF ITS LUMPY AND LUMINOUS VARNISH, BELIEVED IT TO BE BY CARLO BERGONZI.

viz., CLOOS, and three foreigners: URIOT, BAPTISTE and SAEGER.

Dresden had four violoncellists in the Court Chapel of 1783,. viz.: HEINRICH MEGLIN, KARL WILHELM HOECKNER, excellent violoncellist and noted medal engraver, who died 1806, MICHAEL RASCH and JEAN TRICKLIR. About Hoeckner and Rasch no further details are available.

CHAPTER XIII.

GERMAN VIOLONCELLISTS OF THE SECOND HALF OF THE EIGHTEENTH CENTURY.

JEAN TRICKLIR, or TRICKLER, was born at Dijon in 1750 (about 1745—Eitner). He was of German descent, and his parents intended him to enter the Church. His love for music, and his great talent for the violoncello ripened in him the decision to devote himself altogether to musical art, and at the age of fifteen he went to Mannheim (in 1765), where he perfected himself under distinguished masters, and thence went to Italy. After repeated visits to the latter country he was appointed chamber musician to the ducal court at Dresden in March, 1783. A few years before his death he was pensioned, and died November 29, 1813. He was distinguished as virtuoso as well as composer. In the latter capacity he produced seven concertos and twelve sonatas. The latter appeared in two sets under the title: "Six Sonates pour le violoncelle dédiées aux vrais amateurs du chant et de l'harmonie par Tricklir, premier Violoncelle à la cour électorale de Dresde": Paris, Imbault; also six solos, Op. 3: London, W. Forster. They are interesting and well set, and several have recently been republished. He played with the violinist, E. Schick, at Leipzig on May 12, 1782. On the programme both are described as chamber virtuosos to the Elector of Mayence. On November 9 and 16, 1782, he played some double concertos of his own composition at the Hamburg Theatre with E. Schick, the famous violinist. In a report, given by Cramer, it says: "Since Lolli's time the house has never been so crammed as on these occasions." Two of his Concertos in B flat and G appeared in the same year. His Op. 1 consists of three concertos. In 1785 he startled the musical world with an invention to keep stringed instruments always in perfect tune. He called it the "Microcosme Musical," but it proved to be the result of self-deception.

HEINRICH MEGLIN or MEGELIN was, according to Gerber, "one of the strongest in his art." He belonged to the Dresden Orchestra since 1774, and died in 1806, leaving a number of concertos and other compositions in manuscript.

JOHANN KONRAD SCHLICK, born about 1759, at Münster in Westphalia (the home of the Romberg family and a great many distinguished musicians), was one of the greatest virtuosos of the latter part of last century. In 1776 he was appointed violoncellist by the Bishop of Münster. In 1777 he was attached to the court of Gotha as secretary to the court of Charles Augustus. In 1785 he visited Italy and married the violin virtuoso, Regina Strinasacchi. In the company of his wife he visited all the principal towns of Europe, appearing at Leipzig on sundry occasions between 1793-1800. His daughter developed into an excellent pianist, and they travelled as a trio, appearing in 1799 in Leipzig, where Schlick was engaged as soloist for the "Gewandhaus" concerts during the winter 1799-1800. In 1809 he played in Rome. He died at Gotha about 1825. He published concertos for violoncello, double concertos for violin and violoncello, duets, solos (one with variations on "God Save the King," evidently written for England), also quartets with violoncello *obbligato*, a symphony concertante for violin, violoncello and orchestra and three sonatas with bass (Paris, Sieber). One of J. K. Schlick's Concertos, Op. 5, in E minor, has been republished by Carl Schroeder.

His son, JOH. FRED. W. SCHLICK, born 1801, joined the Dresden Chapel as violinist. He was also a clever fiddle-maker, who, in 1840, at the Saxon Industrial Exhibition, received the gold medal for violins and violoncellos. He died at Dresden, April, 1874.

A contemporary of Schlick and Tricklir was J. J. KRIEGK, born June 25, 1750, at Bibra, in the district of Merseburg. He started his career as a violinist, and was engaged as violinist at the court of Meiningen at the early age of twelve. When nineteen years old he joined the Prince of Hesse Philippsthal, who, in 1773, took him to Amsterdam. There he became leader of the Flemish Opera. In 1774 he accompanied the Marquis de Taillefer to Paris, where he made the acquaintance of Jean Louis Duport, who induced him to exchange the violin for the violoncello. He studied for one year under that eminent master, and was, at the recommendation of Jarnovich, engaged by Prince Laval-Montmorency, in whose service he remained for four years. At the end of that time he returned to Meiningen, where he was engaged as chamber musician, advancing, in 1798, to the post of concertmeister. He died at Meiningen in 1813. His compositions consist of three concertos and four sonatas with bass, which rank among the better productions of that period. His violoncello he bequeathed to his son-in-law, the violoncellist Knoop.

RÖMISCH is mentioned by Schwickert as violoncellist in the Court Chapel at Dresden in 1782, and GOEDECKE as chamber musician for the same instrument, in Brunswick, in 1812.

SCHWACHHÖFER, of Mayence, and GANSS, of Cleve, are mentioned by Schilling as good violoncellists, but he gives no date or particulars.

OTTOMAR VON RODA, born 1813, at Rudolstadt, studied the violin at a very early age under the chamber musician Brömmel, and the little virtuoso was appointed to the ducal chapel. At the age of twelve he commenced the study of the violoncello under Knoop. Making rapid progress, he was soon after engaged as violoncellist in the Bethmann orchestra (Bethmann'sche Gesellschaft at Magdeburg). He exchanged that position for a similar one at the German Theatre, Copenhagen, and returned to Rudolstadt as court musician in 1836. In 1837 he went on a concert tour with the violinist Walter Brandum, whose death ended the tour prematurely. The duet playing of the two artists was highly praised. The time of his death is apparently not known. He left several compositions for the violoncello.

ALEXANDER VON RODA, brother of the above, lived about 1840 in Switzerland, as virtuoso on, and teacher of the violoncello.

ANTON KRAFT, born December 30, 1752, at Rokitzau, in Bohemia, the son of a brewer and musical amateur. He studied the violoncello already at an early age, but his father intended him for the study of the law, and for that purpose he visited the University of Vienna. During a sojourn at Prague he had received instruction from Werner, a violoncellist of note in his time, and with his decided natural talent he soon acquired such command of his instrument that he succeeded in obtaining an engagement in the Court Chapel in Vienna. Haydn induced him in 1778 to join the chapel of Prince Nicolaus Esterhazy, of which Haydn was the director. On the death of the Prince in 1790 the chapel was dissolved, and Kraft joined in 1791 the chapel of Prince Grassalkowitz in Vienna. In 1793 he founded in connection with Schuppanzigh the famous string quartet which brought him in contact with Beethoven, who had a high opinion of his ability and jocularly called him "Die alte Kraft" (the ancient power).

The Schuppanzigh Quartet played every Friday morning at the house of Prince Lichnowsky, where they performed, besides those of Haydn and Mozart, the quartets of Beethoven in the presence and under the direction of the composer. Between 1775 and 1790 Kraft visited Berlin, Dresden and several other German towns, where his playing was greatly admired. He died in Vienna, August 28, 1820. Kraft studied composition under Haydn, who always continued to take an interest in him and his work. This led to the absurd statement that the violoncello Concerto in D major, by Haydn, was really a composition by Kraft, the MS. of which had been found among Haydn's papers after his death. Apart from internal evidence, which is strong enough, the fact that it is enumerated in the original catalogue of Haydn's works made during the master's lifetime is sufficient refutation.

The published compositions of Kraft consist of six Sonatas with bass, Op. 1 and 2, three Duos Concertants for violin and violoncello, Op. 3, a violoncello Concerto, Op. 4, two Duets for two violoncellos, Op. 5 and 6, a Divertimento with bass, and several trios for two barytons and violoncello, which he wrote for Prince Esterhazy, who had a great partiality for the baryton, on which Kraft was likewise an executant.

IMMLER was born about the middle of the eighteenth century at Weitramsdorf, near Coburg. He lived mostly at Goettingen, and had the reputation of possessing a good tone and a good style. He is said to have been also a good violinist. Towards the end of the century he was appointed cantor at Coburg, and composed chiefly church music.

KARL SIEGMUND SCHOENEBECK, born October 26, 1758, at Lauben in the "Niederlausitz," was originally destined for the medical career, but his love for music was so great that it overcame all obstacles. At the age of fourteen he was apprenticed with the town musician (Stadt-Musicus) of his native town. During the five years of his apprenticeship he studied various instruments, mostly without a master. After that time he became assistant to the town musician of Gruneberg in Silesia. There he heard for the first time a virtuoso on the violoncello who visited the town, and was so struck with the instrument that he began immediately to study it without the assistance of a master. After two years' practice he was, in 1778, appointed violoncellist in the private band of Count Dohna, where he remained until 1780, when he accepted the post of town musician at Sorau. During a visit to Berlin he heard Duport, who inspired him with renewed zeal for the violoncello, and shortly afterwards he heard Trickler at Dresden, from whom he also benefited by close observation. Then he started on a nomadic career, occupying, among others, positions at the courts of the Duke of Kurland at Sagan, Count Truchsess at Waldenburg, at Königsberg and various other places. Tired of an unsettled life, he returned to his native town and took to farming. But that occupation did not satisfy him and he returned again to his musical career. In 1800 he settled at Leipzig, where his pleasing compositions as well as his beautiful tone and great technique were generally admired. His compositions are: Concerto, Op. 1 (Offenbach, André, 1797); Concerto, Op. 3 (Berlin, Hummel); Concerto, Op. 6 (Berlin, Hummel, 1802); Three Duos for alto and violoncello (*ibid.*); Three Duos for violin and violoncello, Op. 8 (Leipzig, Kühnel); Three Duos Faciles, Op. 12 (Leipzig, Kühnel)—the latter have been republished by F. Grützmacher, Leipzig, Peters, and are excellent pieces for beginners; Schönebeck composed also two operas which were performed at Königsberg.

PHILIPP PETER EIFFERT was in London as violoncellist in 1770. Here he published six solos with bass. They are of an elementary character and without the use of the thumb.

LUBBE entered the orchestra of the Royal Opera in London in 1758, and is said to have contributed much by his performance on the violoncello towards the abolition of the bass viol.

His father was a "base" player in the same orchestra as early as 1720 (probably also violoncellist).

JOHANN RUDOLF ZUMSTEEG, born January 10, 1760, at Sachsenflur in the "Odenwald," died January 27, 1802, at Stuttgart, from an apopletic stroke, which attacked him after conducting a concert. He received his education at the celebrated "Karlsschule" together with Schiller. To the latter he was allied by closest friendship and by composing Schiller's famous ballads he revived successfully a long-forgotten form of composition. His musical education he received from Agostino Poli, master of the court orchestra. At the age of seventeen he took up the violoncello as his principal instrument, for which he wrote a concerto, sonatas, a duet and a trio. Gerber says he played the violoncello with deep feeling, great precision and power. He was appointed violoncellist in the court orchestra at Stuttgart, and on Poli's retirement he was, in 1793, appointed conductor in the place of his late master.

ERNST HÄUSLER, born 1761, at Stuttgart, was also a pupil at the Karlsschule. He was a man of extraordinary talent, but of a most restless disposition. In 1788 (1785—Schilling) he began touring as a violoncellist, making successful debuts in Berlin and Vienna. Soon afterwards he accepted an engagement by the Prince of Donau Eschingen. That position he relinquished in 1791, when he accepted the post of director of music at Zurich, where he created a sensation by his exquisite playing and singing, and also as a singing master of exceptional gifts. He appeared mostly as a soprano singer with a voice reaching, when he sang falsetto, to E flat in alt., while his natural voice went down bass E flat. He wrote a cantata for the tercentenary to the festival of Swiss independence, at the performance of which he was greeted with flourishes of trumpets and drums and the acclamations of the people. In 1796 he revisited his native town, where his playing and singing were highly appreciated by the court. About 1800 he appeared at Augsburg, and in 1802 he played at Vienna. Some time after he was appointed director of the choir of the Protestant Church at Augsburg, where he earned great praise for his revival of classical music. On the cession of Augsburg to Bavaria, Häusler received the title of royal director of music, and an offer to take Danzi's place at the court, but this offer he declined. He was a prolific composer, who wrote among other compositions for his instrument: one concerto, two concertinos and one divertimento; also a sextet for two violins, two horns, viola and violoncello. His songs to words by Goethe, Matthison, Salis and others were great favourites with the musical public of his time. Most of his compositions were printed by André, and Gombart in Augsburg.

CASPAR GOTTLIEB SCHOLZ, born December 25, 1761, at Nürnberg, by trade a music seller, was an excellent violoncellist, who, after a few primary lessons by Capellmeister Meinberger, studied without the aid of a master. He composed several concertos, quartets and solos for violoncello.

JOHANN GEORG RAUPPE, born July 7, 1762, at Stettin, began to study the violoncello at an early age, and perfected himself under Duport at Berlin. After finishing his studies he travelled in the North of Germany, Denmark and Sweden. In 1782 he went to Amsterdam as principal violoncello of the German Opera and the concert orchestra. He remained until 1784, when he visited England and France, returning to Amsterdam in 1786. He was elected a member of the Society for Art and Science. As he had to support his parents and sisters and brothers he was always very poor. In 1813 he lost his wife, and this blow so affected his mind and constitution that he died in 1814, leaving a son and daughter entirely unprovided for. He was a great master of his instrument, whose tone and technique were highly praised; especially were his clearness and purity of intonation in the highest positions, and the brilliancy of his harmonics commented upon. His younger brother was also a violoncellist, but no further particulars concerning him are available.

The following year witnessed the birth of one of the most lovable figures in the musical world of his time in the person of FRANZ DANZI, son of Innocenz Danzi, the principal violoncellist at Mannheim, whom we have mentioned before. Franz was born May 15, 1763. He developed signs of musical talent as a child, and composed several pieces when only nine years of age. His father instructed him on the violoncello and the famous Abbé Vogler undertook his theoretical education. His progress was rapid, and in 1778 he entered the celebrated Mannheim Orchestra, which was one of the finest in Europe. He had an excellent general education, and wrote some good verses. At the age of twelve he composed some pieces for the violoncello. About this time the Palatinate and Bavaria were amalgamated, and the famous orchestra followed the Prince to Munich. Here he composed his first operas, and in 1790 he married the excellent singer, Margarethe Marchand, daughter of the director of the opera. In 1791 the young couple were in Leipzig and Prague, where Danzi conducted the performances of Guardassoni's Italian Opera Company, in which the wife was engaged as a singer. 1794-5 they visited Italy, but the unsatisfactory state of his wife's health caused their return to Munich, where Danzi was made "Vice Kapellmeister" (assistant conductor of the court orchestra). His wife died June 11, 1800, and this preyed so upon his mind that he was unable for some years to attend to his professional duties, and he felt that he could not remain in a place which contained the tomb of all his happiness. This caused him in 1807 to accept the post of conductor at the court of Württemberg. He remained only one year at Stuttgart when he went in the same capacity to Karlsruhe, where he died on

April 13, 1826. Danzi's instrumental compositions are antiquated, but some of his fine songs and other vocal compositions remain. A pure and noble style of vocalisation, which was the strength of the Mannheim school, influenced also the phrasing and delivery of the instrumentalists, and the style of vocal composition. Danzi was himself an excellent singing master. He published for the violoncello two concertos (Hug, Zurich; Nadermann, Richault, Paris); one concertino (Peters) and duets for viola and violoncello, and two violoncellos.

IGNAZ DANZI was a violoncellist in the court chapel at Mannheim, and from 1778 at Munich, with a salary of 333 florins, 20x. His death was reported to the Elector Palatine, April 26, 1798.

About that time (towards the end of the eighteenth century) there was in the court orchestra at Munich a violoncellist, VIRGILI, who was the master of Philipp Moralt, of whom we shall hear later on. Gerber mentions a violoncellist belonging to that orchestra in 1788 whom he calls Virgil Michael (Michael being the christian name which according to southern custom follows the family name). This is apparently the same as Virgili (mentioned by Fétis).

Another violoncellist who conducted Moralt's later studies was ANTON SCHWARZ, who, with JOHANNES FÜRST and LUDWIG SIMON, represented the violoncello in the Mannheim orchestra about that period.

FERDINAND HANSMANN, born August 1, 1764, was a pupil of Jean Pierre Duport (the elder). He made rapid progress in his studies, and was in 1784 made a member of the private band of the Crown Prince of Prussia, and at the prince's accession to the throne he joined the royal private band as a chamber musician to the king. He was pensioned in 1828 and died December 26, 1843, at Berlin. The "Berliner Musikzeitung" of 1793 contains a very eulogistic article by Spazier on Hansmann. "The O. F. G. Hansmann," mentioned by Wasielewski, owes his existence to a mistake by that worthy professor. He was a younger brother of Ferdinand H. who never played the violoncello.

HERBIG, a pupil of the younger Mara, was also a member of the Prussian court chapel of that time.

G. J. FOURNES, born at Leipzig in 1764, was the son of a merchant, who showed distinct and early talents, for arts as well as for science. His favourite and principal instrument was the violoncello, which he cultivated with great perseverance and so much success that his friend, Johann Adam Hiller, the celebrated cantor of St. Thomas, recommended him to the Duke of Kurland, who engaged him for his private chapel at Mitau. On his journey thither he received the news of the cession of that principality to Russia, and the dissolution of the chapel. Thereupon he formed a string quartet with Kleeberg, Reuter and Wagner, visiting the principal towns of Germany. He was also an excellent singer, and appeared at Gera in the rôle of Papageno, winning the favour of the prince, who rewarded him with a government appointment, which he retained until he died, after 1840. In 1790 he published some piano pieces with Kleeberg and afterwards some songs, but apparently nothing for the violoncello.

BERNHARD HEINRICH ROMBERG, generally known as Bernhard Romberg, belonged to a large family of musicians, every member of which gained more or less distinction in the musical world, as the following genealogical sketch will show:

I.—ANTON ROMBERG, bassoon player, born 1745. (Riemann gives the date of his birth as March 6, 1742, and Mendel and Reissmann mentions one Anton R. as brother of Gerh. Heinrich, speaking of Bernhard's father as another Anton R.). Certain it is that the above was the father of Bernhard and a brother of Gerh. Heinrich.

THE ROMBERG FAMILY.

His children were:

1. BERNHARD HEINRICH, the great violoncellist, born at Dinklage, November 11, 1767, according to the baptismal certificate in the possession of his daughter who lived in Hamburg. His son:

KARL, born at St. Petersburg, January 17, 1811, was a talented violoncellist in the Russian court band from 1832-42, and afterwards in the imperial private band at Vienna.

2. ANTON, bassoon player, born 1777, with whom the father played concertos for two bassoons at Hamburg in 1812 (Mendel Reissmann).

3. ANGELIKA, singer and pianist.

II.—GERHARD HEINRICH ROMBERG, director of music and famous clarinet player, born at Münster, in Westphalia, August 8, 1748.

His children were:

1. ANDREAS, violinist and composer, born April 27, 1767, at Vechta, near Münster, and died November 10, 1821. His sons:

CYPRIAN, violoncellist, born at Hamburg, 1807. (See later.)

HEINRICH, violinist, born 1802 in Paris; 1827 leader, afterwards conductor at the opera in St. Petersburg, died 1859 at Hamburg.

2. BALTHASAR, a promising violoncellist, born 1775, died at the age of seventeen years in 1793.

3. THERESA, singer and pianist of talent.

The name of Bernhard Romberg's teacher is unknown, but in all probability he was one of the orchestral musicians of the prince elector at Münster, where his uncle was engaged as conductor, and his father as clarinettist. These two brothers kept house together, travelled together, and even dressed alike. Young Bernhard's genius supplied probably much which his teacher could not give, and he sprang upon the world as a full blown virtuoso. The brotherly devotion that existed between

FIG. 39. BERNHARD ROMBERG.

Anton and Gerh. Heinrich Romberg was transmitted to their two most gifted sons, Bernhard and Andreas, who undertook their first concert tour at the age of only seventeen. The two Romberg families visited Holland and Belgium and thence went to Paris, playing at the house of the celebrated Baron Bagge. Their success was immense, and Bernhard was engaged to appear at the "concert spirituel," on March 18, 1784.

On March 24, 1784, the two Romberg families performed a symphony concertante at the "concert spirituel," and on the 29th, Andreas R. played a violin concerto of his own composition. On April 1 the two families played again a symphony concertante at a final concert. The success was not so great as it might have been under more favourable circumstances. There was at that time a great influx of talent from all sides and Bernhard R., then only a boy, was not yet able to contest the success of Louis Duport, who appeared several times at the "concert spirituel" about that time, and who then ruled supreme on the violoncello over the whole of Europe. Returning to Münster, Bernhard resumed his studies with redoubled zeal. On April 27, 1784, the elector, Maximilian Franz, succeeded to the archiepiscopal throne of Cologne, and hearing the Rombergs, at Münster (which belonged to his principality), he engaged them for his chapel at Bonn. The document containing their appointment bearing the date of December 19, 1790.

In 1791 the prince elector was at Mergentheim, the seat of the order of German Knights (Deutsch Herren) where he commanded some twenty members of his court chapel in Bonn to follow him. The court chaplain of Prince Hohenlohe, Karl Ludwig Junker, reports the concerts, which were given in the apartments of the prince elector, in Bossler's "Musical Correspondence," of 1791. He says: "Mr Romberg, the younger, combines in his playing of the violoncello extraordinary agility with a charming delivery; his execution (Vortrag) is more precise and clearer than one is accustomed to hear from the majority of violoncellists. His tone is, moreover, especially in the darker passages (Schattenparthien—probably he means the medium and lower register of the instrument) firmer and more incisive. Taking into consideration the difficulty of the instrument, one might feel inclined to praise above all the absolute purity of his intonation in the rapid execution of the allegro. But, after all, that is only a mechanical achievement; the connoisseur has another standard whereby to measure the importance of a virtuoso. That is the style of playing, the perfection of expression or the sensitive reproduction. And here the connoisseur will declare in favour of the speaking expression of the adagio. It is impossible to express more deeply all the delicate shades of feeling, impossible to give more variety of colour, especially by delicate shading, impossible to find the quite unique tone, which goes straight to the heart, and which Mr. Romberg succeeds in producing in his adagio. . . . . How he knows all the beauties of detail which lie in the nature and the given sentiment of the piece, and for which the printer has no mark of expression! What effects he produces by swelling his tone to the most powerful fortissimo, followed by the diminuendo which dies out in a scarcely audible pianissimo!" Enthusiastic as this may sound, it echoes the popular impression of Romberg's playing. The author's father, who heard him in his later years at the house of his uncle, Ignaz van Houtem, a well known art patron of Aix la Chapelle, spoke in similar terms of his rendering of some of the divertimentos on national airs. Romberg's position in Bonn was rendered precarious by the outbreak of the French Revolution, and his salary of six hundred florins offered little inducement for his remaining there. In 1794 the celebrated director, Schroeder, of the theatre at Hamburg, offered an engagement to both Bernhard and Andreas Romberg, which they accepted, entering their new sphere of activity at Easter, in the same year. Three years later they started on a fresh concert tour, visiting Italy, and returning by way of Vienna, where they made their debut with the assistance of Beethoven. The two young artists visited "Father" Haydn, whom they worshipped with all the ardour of youthful enthusiasm, and who received them with all that kindness which endeared him to everybody. He was very much struck with their eminent

FACSIMILE (REDUCED) OF AN ALBUM LEAF BY BERNHARD ROMBERG.

talent, and, after hearing a string quartet, composed by Andreas, always called him his "son." About 1798, Romberg visited London, and some absurd stories were afterwards invented to darken his fame in order to raise Lindley's. Such attempts, needless to say, could never have the effect which was intended, and are discreditable to those who tried to smudge the image of a great and brilliant artist, who stood immeasurably above Lindley, although the latter was a very excellent player, and may have even possessed more tone, but all who heard both artists impartially, endorsed the judgment expressed by Antoine Vidal, that Lindley's technique and style remained far behind Romberg's, to say nothing about their respective compositions. After leaving England he went to Spain and Portugal. At a soirée at the court in Lisbon, King Ferdinand VII played in person the accompaniments on the violin to Romberg's solos. In 1800 he visited Vienna (according to Hanslick), and returning to Hamburg, married in the same year Katharina Ramcke (Magdalena Rancke, according to Meyer). He also made his reappearance in Paris about this time, playing at the "Concerts de la rue de Cléry," and the "Théâtre des Victoires," with such immense success that he was offered, and accepted, the professorship at the Conservatoire. This position he held only for two years, from 1801 till 1803, when he returned to his beloved Hamburg. The year 1805 found him solo violoncellist at the court of Prussia, but the troubles of war drove him away again in the following year, when he revisited Vienna (1806), and thence went on to Russia, via Königsberg. In 1807 he visited the Ukraine and the Russian provinces in the company of Ries. On that tour he collected the Slavonic airs, which are embodied in one of his divertimentos. The two artists were on their way to Moscow when the great fire consumed the greater part of the town and compelled Napoleon to retreat. Thus, forced to abandon their original plan, they visited Stockholm, and returned to Hamburg via Copenhagen. In 1813 Romberg visited, according to Wasielewski, Holland and Belgium, returning to Russia. He remained nearly two years in Moscow. Mendel and Reissmann say that he went via Sweden to England, but the former appears more correct. In 1815 he was appointed conductor of the Royal Orchestra at Berlin, where he remained until 1819. In 1822 he revisited Vienna, giving four concerts at the "Landständische Saal," which brought him in a net profit of one thousand pounds, at that time almost a record sum. At these concerts he was assisted by his son, Charles, who was then only in his twelfth year.

At the same time Max Bohrer appeared with his brother Anton and gave concerts at the same hall and at the Kärntnerthor Theatre. The public flocked in crowds to hear both artists, some declaring in favour of Romberg, others of Bohrer. As a matter of fact, each of these two admirable virtuosos had but one rival and that was—the other. Romberg openly declared himself a great admirer of Bohrer *(see the latter, page 244)*. The "Wiener Zeitschrift" says that "Romberg's playing was more classical, grander and more correct (finished), though somewhat too sober, while Bohrer showed more grace and feeling, combined with a more modern technique." The report sums up in the following words: "Romberg plays for eternity, Bohrer for the drawing-room." In 1825 he paid another visit to Petersburg and Moscow. After that time he retired into private life at Hamburg. There he wrote his tutor for the violoncello, and this work, probably coupled with the ambition to taste once more the sweetness of public applause and favour, induced him to pay again a visit to London and Paris to introduce his work at the conservatoire of the latter city. He was then in his seventy-third year, and although he only appeared in private circles, he could no longer exercise the spell of former years. He felt the want of that success which had marked his whole career so far, and it preyed upon his mind, undermining his health, which rapidly declined. He died soon after his return to Hamburg, August 18, 1841 (according to the "Neue Zeitschrift für Musik" of September 7, 1841; Wasielewski and Mendel and Reissmann give the date as August 13).

Romberg's compositions are very numerous, including all branches of music, even the opera in which, however, both Bernhard and Andreas were least successful. Bernhard wrote his first opera in 1790, while in the service of the prince elector at Bonn, where it was performed, as well as his second opera in 1791. Another opera, "Don Mendoza," he wrote together with his cousin, Andreas, for the Theatre Feydeau in Paris. He wrote also a number of string quartets. The only composition of his that can interest us still are his concertos and duets for the violoncello, as also his divertimentos which are instructive as well as melodious, and the exercises from his tutor. The latter, as such, is not a successful work. It contains much that is superfluous, and omits much that is desirable in the text. There are, moreover, many things, as for instance, his instructions for the holding of the left hand, which are not in accordance with the more modern style. He makes an extraordinary statement with regard to the best instruments: "The best violoncellos, both in tone and form, after those of Stradivarius, are those of Nicolas Amati; and then those of Joseph Guarnerius. The latter are so wide across that they cannot be conveniently held in playing thumb passages, and, therefore, require to be cut!" This is curious, as contradicting the assertion of some good connoisseurs that Joseph Guarnerius never made violoncellos. Another interesting remark is this: "If the whole length of the string be divided into eighteen parts, the first part will mark the first semitone, i.e., upon the A string B flat. Reckoning from this B flat divide the *remaining length* again into eighteen parts, and the first part will give B natural. Continuing in this way, all the further semitones can be found."

Later on he says: "To chamber music belong nonets, octets, septets, etc., and trios; *sonatas and duets are not adapted for public performance.*" The "staccato" was apparently not his strong point, and is, in fact, about the only kind of bowing which he never employed in his concertos or solos. In his tutor, he says, with regard to the staccato: "It must either be made with a stiff arm, or the bow must be screwed up so tightly as to spring on the strings by its own tension, and even then the player cannot be sure of success. Indeed, as the violoncellist is so seldom called upon to employ the staccato, it would be a great pity that he should spoil his bow hand by practising it to any extent, and I would rather abstain from it wholly and entirely." He recommends to play staccato passages simply with a short, detached bow. This absurd notion had an unfortunate result by inducing a great many German violoncellists to tell their pupils that *staccato* and *spiccato* are *idle tricks*, which have nothing to do with legitimate playing!

In a chapter on *tempo*, Romberg makes the following very interesting observation: "The allegro is played faster in Paris than in Vienna, and in Vienna, again, faster than in the north of Germany. . . . . I can by no means undertake to give the exact time in which any particular movement should be taken, since there is scarcely a single composer who would play all the movements of his own compositions, marked with the same *tempo* signature, in exactly the same time."

Whatever his little weaknesses and peculiarities may have been, BERNHARD HEINRICH ROMBERG was one of the most brilliant figures in the whole history of the violoncello. Romberg, virtuoso, composer, untiring in his studies, saturated with the love of his art, was for the violoncello what Viotti and Spohr were for the violin. He may even be more justly compared to the latter, as he created the German school of violoncello playing, while Spohr was the father of the German school of violin playing, with one notable difference, however, that the latter outshone him by a long way as a composer. Although it must not be overlooked that Spohr had *all* our great classics before him, while the giant Beethoven was born three years after Romberg, who never grasped the full importance of that supreme genius. In fact, it is related on good authority, that when asked to play the violoncello in the Rasoumoffsky Quartet, Romberg, after struggling with it for some time without being able to grasp its meaning, threw down his part, trampled on it, and said : "That is a 'cello part ? No —— can play that music!" Spohr, in his Autobiography, relates how Romberg once asked him how he could play such *absurd stuff* as Beethoven's Quartet, Op. 18! Spohr knew better, and proves it in his own works, which take a much higher flight than the graceful and elegant, but conventional, bel canto style of Romberg's compositions. Yet, though the majority of his compositions are no longer suitable for the concert-room, they are incomparable as studies, as requiring a most perfect technique, combined with the highest degree of refinement in phrasing and expression, and in offering the best means to acquire both. Although excellent players had already made their appearance before and with Romberg, yet it was reserved for him to revolutionise the technique of the instrument, and, by developing all its capabilities, fit it for the important part which it was to take in the music of the nineteenth century. His importance in that direction will be more clearly illustrated by the description which has been given above of his playing, and even more by his compositions, which we still possess.

The most important of these for actual use are his Concertos Nos. 2, 5, 8 and 9 and the Concerto in D minor, Op. 51. His duets belong to the best productions of their kind, and his divertimentos on national airs are instructive as well as effective for the use of amateurs and for concert purposes. For a complete list of Romberg's compositions see the author's "History of Violoncello Literature."

JOACHIM JOSEPH FUETSCH, chamber musician to the Prince Bishop of Salzburg, where he was born, August 12, 1766. He received his first musical instruction from the pastor of Salzburg and choirmaster, Freistädtler. In 1775 he became a choirboy at the cathedral, remaining there for eight years. During that time he studied the violin under Jos. Hafeneder and Leopold Mozart. With the loss of his beautiful alto voice, 1784, he lost also his position in the chapel. Thereupon, he began to study the violoncello as autodidact, and was so successful that he was nominated as the successor of Anton Ferrari, in the court orchestra, finishing his studies under Luigi Zandonati, or Sandonati *(see Italian violoncellists)*. He studied theory under the master of the chapel, Abbé Luigi Gatti making great progress. He composed concertos, solos, studies and sonatas with bass. The latter are mentioned by Schilling as particularly praiseworthy, on account of their purity of style. They were, however, not published, and it appears unknown whether they still exist. Continuing his studies in composition under Michael Haydn, he produced three and four part songs for male voices, being one of the first to cultivate that particular branch of music.

HEINRICH GROSS (wrongly called "Grosse" by Wasielewski), born August 1, 1764, studied the violoncello under Duport, and appeared in public with great success as a prodigy. In 1783 he received an engagement as member of the private band of the Swedish Count de Geer. In 1793 he was a member of the king's band in Berlin, and died in 1806. Of his compositions only a few were published. A sonata, Op. 1, with bass, dedicated to Prince Ant. Radziwill, was published at "Orangebourg chez Werkmeister."

A. W. F. MATERN, chamber musician to the Duke of Brunswick, where he died in 1789. He enjoyed a high reputation as a soloist, but refrained from appearing in public at the age of seventy on account of his advancing years. He remained, however, a "ripieno" player in the ducal private band up to 1784. Both his sons became violoncellists under their father's guidance. Several concertos and solos of his remained in manuscript.

FRIEDRICH ERNST BENEKE, and his brother, PHILIPP FRIEDRICH, were both violoncellists in the Hanoverian Orchestra about the latter part of the eighteenth century.

A violoncellist, BENECKE, is mentioned by Pohl as appearing in London in 1752, and some pieces in a MS. volume of 1776, in the Lübeck Library, are by Beneke. Apparently both refer to the above.

CHRISTIAN FRIEDRICH BAUERSACHS, born June 4, 1767 (Schilling gives 1770), at Pegnitz in the principality of Anspach, was a virtuoso on the violoncello as well as on the corno di bassetto. He introduced the bent corno di bassetto from England into Germany. An appointment which he held at one of the minor Rhenish courts he lost in 1790 through the outbreak of war. In 1796 he visited the principal towns of Austria, Hungary, Italy and Germany with great success as a soloist, but the unsettled times prevented him from obtaining a permanent engagement. He joined a military regiment as oboist, and afterwards retired from the musical profession, and followed that of a mining engineer. Bauersachs died at Sommerda, near Erfurt, December 14, 1845. He composed with good taste, but his compositions seem to be forgotten.

JOHANN DANIEL BRAUN, born July 24, 1767, in Cassel, where his father held an appointment as violinist in the service of the Landgrave. His three brothers and sisters were all remarkable virtuosos on the violin, oboe, bassoon, mandolin and piano respectively. In 1787 Daniel became a pupil of Jean Pierre Duport in Potsdam. There he won the favour of Frederic William II who was himself at the time studying the violoncello under Duport. The king appointed him as chamber musician, and he thought so much of Braun that he had to accompany him in 1793 throughout the Rhenish campaign, and in the following year to Poland to play at the concerts at headquarters. During these expeditions he contracted gout and retired in 1824 on a pension. He died in Berlin, June 16, 1832. In 1798 he married the celebrated singer, Catharina Brouwer, who had the remarkable compass of three and a half octaves from [musical notation] to [musical notation]. She died at the Hague in 1855.

JOHANN CHRISTIAN THEOPHIL SCHINDLER, violoncellist and lutenist during the latter part of the eighteenth century at the court of Mayence. He composed concertos, sonatas and duets for the violoncello, also other compositions, the first appearing in 1768. Apparently still in Mayence about 1782 (Eitner).

SEBASTIN LUDWIG FRIEDEL, born February 15, 1768, as member of a numerous family of musicians at Neuburg (Palatinate). He studied the violoncello under Peter Ritter at Mannheim, and later on under Duport, and cultivated also the baryton, the favourite instrument of the Emperor Francis II. Prince Carl Theodore, the great art patron, presented him with a magnificent instrument by Tielke in recognition of his performance at the court at Schwetzingen. The instrument was one of the finest specimens by that master, richly inlaid and set with jewels. It was repaired by Straube in Berlin. What has become of that instrument? It certainly would be very interesting to know. In 1798, he published three sonatas for the violoncello and bass, Op. 1, dedicated to his master Duport. They were published by André in Offenbach, the capellmeister Anton André, being his best friend. Frederic William II was so pleased with Friedel's playing that he engaged him for his court orchestra in Berlin where he remained for some time. In 1826 he was pensioned and died about 1857-8. Until 1857 he appears in the Address Calender

PLATE XXV.
MAX BOHRER. FROM A CRAYON DRAWING BY KRIEHUBER, 1842.

To face page 232.

of Berlin, but it is stated by some that he returned to Frankfort-on-Main.

MAXIMILIAN WILLMANN, born about 1761, at Forchtenberg, near Würzburg. He made his debut in Vienna, but went to Bonn (chapel) towards the end of the century. Here he was engaged, together with Reicha and Bernhard Romberg. Thence he went to the court of Count Thurn and Taxis at Regensburg. He returned afterwards to Vienna as violoncellist of the "Theater an der Wien," where he ended a life full of cares and trouble in 1812. He had two daughters, the elder, Marie (Willmann-Huber), being a pupil of Mozart; the younger, an excellent singer (Willmann-Galvani), was greatly admired by Beethoven, who proposed to her, but with the same result that marked all his love episodes.

IGNAZ FRANZ, EDLER (Knight) VON MOSEL, born at Vienna, April 2, 1772. He played the violoncello and the violin, and studied composition and æsthetics. Entering the service of the court, he became director of the concerts at the Imperial Riding School, was raised to the rank of nobility in 1818, court councillor in 1821, director of the opera and court librarian, and died April 8, 1844. A fertile composer, but wrote apparently nothing for violoncello.

JOHANN GOTTFRIED ARNOLD, born February 15, 1773, at Niedernhall, in Württemberg (near Forchtenberg, where Willmann was born), as the son of a schoolmaster, who gave him his first instruction in music. The violoncello was his favourite instrument, and at the age of eight his performances began to attract the attention of a larger circle of musical amateurs. In 1785 his father apprenticed him with the town musician at Künzelsau, where he studied for five years. After this time he received an engagement by his uncle, who was a town musician in Wertheim on the Tauber, following up his studies with great zeal. After a few futile attempts to appear as a soloist, he went to Regensburg, where he took lessons from Willmann, the first legitimate teaching he ever received on the violoncello. In 1796 he heard Romberg at Hamburg, and benefited by his instruction. In 1797 he was appointed at the opera in Frankfurt at Romberg's recommendation. He was looked upon as a great virtuoso, who combined a most enchanting tone with great technical ability. Arnold wrote a considerable number of compositions for various instruments, among which a concerto for two flutes is mentioned as a classical piece of distinction. He wrote a number of solos, duets and terzets for his instrument which were greatly praised. The third of five concertos, in F, has been republished by C. Schroeder.

JOHANNES EISERT, born 1775, at Georgenthal, near Rumburg, was chamber musician in the court chapel at Dresden. His son, Johannes E. Eisert, was composer and court organist in that town.

AUGUST DANIEL MANGOLD, born July 25, 1775, at Darmstadt, as the second of five brothers who all became excellent musicians, as was also their father. Aug. Daniel was already a good clarinet player when he took up the violoncello. In 1798 he joined the private band of Bernhard, a merchant at Offenbach, who soon afterwards appointed him as his conductor. At the beginning of this century he was engaged as violoncellist at the Frankfurt opera, but relinquished that position soon after to go on an extended concert tour with his cousin, Wilhelm Mangold, an excellent violinist. They visited Holland and northern Germany. In 1814 he became a member of the Grand Ducal Orchestra in Darmstadt, with the title of "concertmeister." He died in 1842. His playing was finished, intellectual and full of temperament. His cousin, Carl Amand Mangold, was a popular composer of operas and choral works, notably for male voices.

SAMUEL BENJAMIN SANTO, born June 30, 1776, at Dresden, was the son of a court musician. He received his first musical instruction from chamber musician, Meissner, and theory lessons from the famous cantor, Weinlig. At the age of twelve, he was a member of the opera orchestra and accompanist of the recitatives. At the age of nineteen he came to Count Platen at Adelsbach, in Silesia. Afterwards he was appointed by Count Schweinitz, where he began to devote himself to composition. Eight years later he became the teacher of the twelve children of the elder brother of that Count von Schweinitz. In 1824 he went to Breslau, where he was still in 1842 highly esteemed as composer and solo violoncellist. He wrote concertos, solos, duets and sonatas, with piano for his instrument, as well as a number of chamber music compositions.

CHRISTIAN FRANZ AMBROS, BARON VON LEYKAM, born 1777, in Vienna, an excellent amateur violoncellist and violinist, with a good knowledge of counterpoint. He lived at the beginning of this century at the court of Naples, where he was a great favourite on account of his many accomplishments; not the least of which was his art of miniature painting. He composed very popular pieces for voice and piano, but nothing, apparently, for the violoncello.

JOHANN BAPTIST GÄNSBACHER, born May 8, 1778, at Sterzing, in Tyrol. The friend of Weber and Meyerbeer, with whom he formed the celebrated "triumvirate of friendship," about which Weber wrote some interesting letters published in the "Caecilia." He was a pupil on the violoncello of the famous "Father Fendt," lieutenant colonel of the "Fenner Jäger" (chasseurs), and Tyrolese hero during the war with France. Gänsbacher was afterwards "Domcapellmeister" at the Cathedral of St. Stephen's at Vienna.

CHRISTIAN URBAN is mentioned by Schilling as a clever violoncellist. He was born at Elbing, October 16, 1778. 1812-6 he was musical director at that town; 1827 he was in Berlin where he lectured on musical theory. Afterwards he was musical director at Dantzig. He composed an opera, incidental music to Schiller's "Bride of Messina" and wrote several theoretical works. The author has not been able to verify Schilling's statement.

NICOLAUS KRAFT, the son and pupil of Anton Kraft, was born at Esterhazy in Hungaria, December 14, 1778. At the age of four he made his debut before Prince Esterhazy, playing on a large viola which he treated violoncello fashion. Two years later he played before the prince a concert piece which his father had specially written for him. At the age of eight he went on a concert tour with his father, appearing with great success at Vienna, Pressburg, Dresden and Berlin. On the dissolution of Prince Esterhazy's chapel in 1791, his father resolved that Nicolaus should devote himself to the study of science, and this he did for the next five years, during which time violoncello playing was only resorted to as a relaxation from his studies.

At the end of that period Prince Lobkowitz persuaded his father to let Nicolaus return to the musical career, and in 1796 he appointed both father and son as members of his chapel. The prince took a great interest in the promising young artist, and sent him to Berlin at his expense to perfect himself still further under the guidance of the famous Jean Louis Duport. At the end of his studies under that master in 1801 he gave a farewell concert in Berlin with remarkable success.

After leaving Berlin he went to Holland with the intention of giving concerts in the principal towns, but the prince demanded his return to Vienna, and he was obliged to restrict his public appearances to Leipzig, Dresden, Prague and such towns as he passed on his journey. Everywhere he met with the most enthusiastic reception.

In 1809 he was engaged as solo violoncellist at the opera, remaining all the same in the service of Prince Lobkowitz, who offered him an annuity for life if he would bind himself not to play without his permission anywhere, except at his palace. This arrangement fell to the ground as the prince became more and more involved in pecuniary difficulties which, in 1811, deprived him altogether of the absolute disposition over his fortune and estates. In 1814 Nicolaus Kraft played, together with Mayseder and Anton Romberg, at the congress of princes in Vienna, when the King of Württemberg was so favourably impressed with his playing that he engaged him as his chamber virtuoso. Consequently he removed to Stuttgart, whence he started on a concert tour in 1818, in company of Johann Nepomuk Hummel. They travelled down the Rhine and eventually reached Hamburg where Kraft met Bernhard Romberg, who formed a high opinion of his talents, and accorded proof of it by playing a double concerto for two violoncellos with him at a concert in 1820 at Stuttgart.

In 1821 he undertook a second concert tour in order to bring out his son and pupil, Frederic Kraft (see below) when they visited the principal towns of Germany, gaining laurels for both.

In 1824 Nicolaus Kraft had the misfortune to hurt the forefinger of his right hand in tuning his instrument. In spite of many attempts to cure the injury he had to abandon his public career and retire on a pension on December 11, 1834. Wurzbacher states that he removed to Chemnitz in 1838. If he did so at all it can only have been temporarily, as he died at Stuttgart, May 18, 1853. The same biographer mentions Wielhorsky, Jos. Merk, the sons of Wranitzky (violinist and composer) and Birnbach as pupils of Nicolaus Kraft, whereas we have only been able to find sufficient evidence to prove that statement with regard to Birnbach. Nicolaus Kraft combined the technique of a virtuoso with his father's beauty of tone. As a composer he contributed largely to the literature of the violoncello, his most important works being: Five concertos (the second is the best), a concertino for two violoncellos, six duets, eight divertimentos, two rondos, a bolero, scene pastorale, polonaise, fantasias and potpourris.

FRIEDRICH KRAFT, son of Nicolaus, mentioned above, was born in Vienna, February 12, 1807. He toured with his father in 1821. In 1824 he was appointed as chamber musician in the court orchestra at Stuttgart, which position he held for a number of years. No further particulars are obtainable.

JOHANN GOTTFRIED KUNSTMANN, born 1780, at Kastell, in Franconia, was an excellent violoncellist, although he exercised art only as an amateur, following a commercial career as his principal calling. He came to Gotha in 1794, and to Chemnitz in 1798. In the latter town he founded a choral society. He was also a good pianist and composer.

HEINRICH AUGUST BIRNBACH, born 1782, at Breslau. His father, a peasant's son, was a virtuoso on the violin. In 1792 (or 1795 according to Schilling) Heinrich Birnbach came to Berlin, and studied the pianoforte and the violoncello as autodidact, as he had no means to pay for his tuition.

In 1802 he went to Vienna and obtained an engagement at the "Theater an der Wien," and this enabled him to study under Nicolaus Kraft. Probably on the latter's recommendation, Prince Lubomirski appointed him in 1804, as violoncellist of his private band in Galicia, but he returned to Vienna in 1806 or 1807, and became a solo violoncellist of the opera in Budapest, in 1812. He was also the first and only virtuoso on the "chitarra col'arco," or guitar d'amour, a bow instrument which was also known as arpeggione (see page 26). It was invented by Stauffer, in Vienna, in 1823, and had six strings tuned:

 Birnbach had returned to Vienna in 1822, and evinced great enthusiasm for this new instrument, for which he wrote a concerto, and produced it at public concerts. This same instru-

ment induced Schubert to write a very fine sonata with pianoforte for it, which has been published by Breitkopf and Härtel. Apparently this is all that is left of the arpeggione literature. A rare specimen of the arpeggione, dated 1824, is preserved in the Wilhelm Heyer Museum at Cologne. The above sonata has been arranged for the violoncello, but it is more suitable for the viol da gamba, which has lately been revived by several violoncellists, on account of its similar tuning. Vincenz Schuster in Vienna, wrote a tutor for the arpeggione. In 1825, Birnbach was appointed to the Royal Chapel in Berlin as violoncellist and virtuoso on the arpeggione, of which instrument he was apparently the chief exponent. Further particulars are wanting. He published variations for violoncello and guitar, and a concerto for violoncello and orchestra.

ALEXANDER UBER, born 1783, at Breslau, was the son of an enthusiastic musical amateur, who was a lawyer by profession. He composed chamber music, and every Wednesday and Saturday he had a musical meeting at his house, performing symphonies one night, and devoting the next to chamber music. These evenings were attended by the leading musicians of Breslau, and Karl Maria von Weber, who came to that town in 1804, took an active part in them. Thus Alexandra Uber grew up in a musical atmosphere, and received at an early age instructions on the violin from Janiczeck, while Schnabel introduced him to the mysteries of musical theory. He exchanged, however, the violin for the violoncello, and became a pupil of the famous Jaeger. In 1804 he started on a short concert tour. But his talent as a composer and conductor soon manifested itself and drew him more in that direction. An overture of his was performed in 1803, under Berner, musical director at the university. He filled, afterwards, several posts as conductor, being, in 1820, at Basel, where he married a singer of that town, returning to Breslau in

1821. In 1823 he was appointed master of the private band of Count Schoenaich, Prince Karolath, but died the following year. He wrote a concerto for the violoncello (Op. 12), which has been republished by Schroeder, in his "Concertstudien." Also six caprices, Op. 10; variations with quartet accompaniment, Op. 14; and variations on a German air.

JUSTUS JOHANN FRIEDRICH DOTZAUER, born January 20, 1783, at Häselrieth, near Hildburghausen. He was the son of a pastor, a talented musical amateur. Young Justus received lessons on the pianoforte from Henschkel, and violin lessons from Gleichmann, the director of music at Hildburghausen. A blacksmith of Häselrieth, who played the double bass at fairs and dances, instructed him in his gentle art, and a court trumpeter, Hessner, who had studied the violoncello under Schlick, gave him his first instruction on what was to be his principal instrument. Besides these he played also the horn and clarinet. His theoretical studies were conducted by the organist, Rüttinger, who had studied under Kittel, a pupil of J. S. Bach. He showed a decided predilection for the violoncello on which he soon surpassed his master, appearing at a court concert at Hildburghausen at the age of fifteen. On that occasion he played variations for the violoncello by Pleyel. In 1799 his father sent him to Meiningen, where he studied for two years under Kriegk. In 1801 he was appointed as violoncellist in the court orchestra at Meiningen where he remained until 1805 when he received an appointment in the Leipzig orchestra, which he held until 1811. In the latter year he joined the court orchestra at Dresden where he advanced to the position of solo violoncellist in 1821, and graced that post until 1850, when he retired into private life, and died March 6, 1860.

In 1806 Dotzauer visited Berlin where he heard and studied Romberg with great advantage. The concertos of that great artist, together with those of Arnold, formed chiefly his concert repertoire. He paid a great deal of attention to quartet playing, and was one of the founders of the famous quartet of the Leipzig professors. Spohr praises his excellent qualities as a quartet player, especially the purity of his intonation and the perfection of his technique. In 1834 he appeared

FIG. 40. J. J. F. DOTZAUER.

with great success in Vienna and visited all the principal towns of Germany and the Netherlands. Dotzauer's chief importance lay in his work as a pedagogue. In fact, he was the founder of the Dresden school of violoncellists. Among the foremost of his pupils were: Kummer, Schuberth, Voigt, Drechsler; the latest representative of that school being Friedrich Grützmacher, a pupil of Drechsler. Dotzauer was a very prolific composer who contributed to all branches of his art. His opera, "Graziosa," was performed at Dresden in 1841. He wrote also a mass, several symphonies, overtures and a considerable number of chamber works which have all been included in the long list of the things of the past, and (to use the words of Gilbert Sullivan's Mikado) "they never will be missed." Nor will his nine violoncello concertos, three concertinos, concertante for two violoncellos and orchestra,

Fig. 41. Facsimile of a "Canon" from an Album Leaf by J. J. F. Dotzauer.

or the two sonatas with bass, variations and divertimentos for the same instrument.

With his educational works the case lies different. He wrote a "Violoncello School," Op. 126 (Vienna, Haslinger), "Violoncello School," Op. 165 (Schott), "Practical Violoncello School," Op. 155 (Schuberth), and a "Flageolet-Schule" (school of harmonics), Op. 147. There are about one hundred and eighty exercises and caprices contained in Op. 35, 47, 54, 70, 107, 116, 120, 121, 155, 158, 160, 168, 175, 176 and 178.

The latter number containing preludes and fugues. Mr. Johannes Klingenberg has arranged one hundred and thirteen of the best of these exercises in progressive order, and also made a new edition of the violoncello tutors by amalgamating them, and bringing the school up to modern requirements by the addition of some exercises by Duport. Both these works have been republished by Litolff, and belong to the best teaching material extant. In his playing he combined power of tone with nobility and gracefulness of style. His son, Justus B. F., was an excellent pianist, while the younger, Karl Ludwig, was also a violoncellist of whom we shall speak later on.

JOSEPH LINCKE was born in the same year as Dotzauer, viz., June 8, 1783 (Mendel gives 1784) at Trachenberg, in Silesia. He received his first tuition from his father, continuing under the violoncellist Oswald. At the age of twelve, he became a choirboy at the Dominican friars at Breslau, where Lose and Fleming supervised his studies on the violoncello, and the excellent organist, Hanisch, was his master in musical theory. Lose was violoncellist at the opera, which was then conducted by Weber, and on the retirement of Lose, Lincke took his place. In 1808, he went to Vienna, where Schuppanzigh engaged him for the famous quartet of Count Rasoumowsky, which brought him in frequent contact with Beethoven, whom he worshipped, and who esteemed him greatly. That famous quartet party was dissolved in 1816, and Lincke followed Count Erdödy to his seat in Croatia, returning to Vienna in 1818 as solo violoncellist at the "Theater an der Wien." About 1831, he shared the same position with Merk at the Royal Opera, and died March 26, 1837, on the anniversary of the death of Beethoven, who had always been his ideal, and who wrote some of his violoncello compositions specially for him, and Lincke studied them under his supervision. Lincke composed and published some variations.

MAX BOHRER, born 1785, at Munich, was the second of four brothers, whose father was a double bass player. Max Bohrer received his first lessons on the violoncello from the excellent violoncellist, Anton Schwarz, who was also the master of Moralt. The four brothers Bohrer appeared as a prodigy string quartet at the respective ages of nine, ten, twelve and fourteen years. They gave concerts in various German towns with great success, visiting Vienna in 1805, and returning to Munich soon afterwards. Two of the brothers, Peter and Franz, died about this time, and Max undertook another concert tour in 1806 with his surviving brother, Anton, an excellent violinist, visiting Eastern Germany and Poland. In Vienna they met Romberg, whom Max Bohrer took for his model. The father died in 1809, and in the following year the two brothers started on another tour, visiting the greater part of Europe, appearing with unqualified success. In 1812 they were in Russia, but the appearance of the French before Moscow drove them from that town. At St. Petersburg they met Romberg, who had a great affection for the younger artist. He said on one occasion when he heard Bohrer play: "If I stand at the end of the hall and close my eyes, I imagine myself sitting on the platform, and it sounds to me as if I were playing myself." A contemporary writing about the two artists says: "Romberg's playing is that of the purest German school, and as such unparalleled. Max Bohrer as a virtuoso stands outside of any school. His tone is fantasy itself, the earthly echo of the innermost vibrations of his very soul. This gives his style and manner of playing the stamp of originality, and it is so interwoven with his psychical being, so characteristic, light and skilful, that it must be regarded as absolutely individual, unlike everything else, and excluding all comparison. Technically he stands on the same level as Romberg, with whose compositions he usually appears before the public, the two artists being as yet unequalled by any other player." The duets for violin and violoncello which had won so much public favour are the compositions of the brothers Bohrer. On May 12, 1828, they appeared at the Philharmonic concert in London, and on May 1, 1837, Max Bohrer played a duet for two violoncellos with Moritz Ganz at a concert of the same society. In 1830 he appeared with immense success in Paris, where he was engaged at the "Theatre Italien." During this time he wrote his first concerto, Op. 1, in D, dedicated to the King of Bavaria, and published by Nadermann in Paris. Previous to this he had been a member of the Berlin Court Orchestra. In 1838 he revisited St. Petersburg, and went afterwards to Italy; in 1842 and 1843 he toured in America. In 1847 he appeared in several towns of Northern Europe, but failed to evoke the usual enthusiasm as his executive powers began to diminish. In 1852 the King of Württemberg appointed him solo violoncellist with the title of a "concertmeister." He died in 1867. His compositions for the violoncello consist of three concertos, one in E minor being considered to be the best. Schroeder, in his concert studies, republished one in D major, Op. 8. Besides these he wrote rondos, fantasias and variations, which are antiquated. The best of his compositions are his duos for violin and violoncello which he wrote, together with his brother Anton, who was the better composer, while Max was the greater virtuoso—another point of similarity with the brothers Romberg. Bohrer's portrait from a drawing by the celebrated Kriehuber appears on Plate XXV.

SCHNYDER VON WARTENSEE, born 1786 at Lucerne, was a celebrated musician, and friend of Goethe, who founded a school for singing at Frankfort, and instituted a school for children under Froebel at his castle, Wartensee, near Sempach. He was also a teacher at the famous school of Pestalozzi, and a well-known composer. He was a good violoncellist, but his manifold talents did not admit of a proper development of this gift.

FRIEDRICH MÜLLER, born December 10, 1786, at Orlamünde in Sachsen-Altenburg. He was in the court orchestra at Rudolstadt as violoncellist in 1802, where he rose to the post of conductor. He was also a clever clarinettist and composer. In 1831 he received the title "musikdirector," and in 1835 he became "hofcapellmeister," conductor to the court, and on his jubilee in 1853 he was made a court councillor.

JOSEPH BRAUN, born 1787, at Regensburg, was the son of an organist. He received an early education as a violoncellist, but as he developed a predominant talent for conducting, he took more to the latter art. In 1826 he was appointed conductor in Philadelphia, whither his wife accompanied him as *prima donna.* The brutality of the public, which tried first by threats and then by violence to make him conform to their degraded taste for music of the lowest order, induced him to exchange this golden misery for a more honourable position in Germany, to which country he returned in 1828. He wrote two operas, and a number of vocal and instrumental compositions, including some good pieces for violoncello and piano.

JOSEPH M. MARX, born 1792 at Würzburg, where he received his musical training. He was engaged as violoncellist at Frankfurt, which city he left in order to study under Merk at Vienna. He was afterwards engaged at Stuttgart, and still later at Karlsruhe, where he rose to the post of conductor. He died in that position on November 11, 1836. His daughter, Pauline, attained high rank among dramatic singers of her time.

JOH. GEORG HERMAN VOIGT, born at Osterwick, May 14, 1769, was the son of a town musician. He received his musical education from his grandfather, the celebrated Rose of Quedlinburg, who instructed him in violoncello, violin and organ playing. Voigt continued his studies under his cousin Rose, who introduced him also to the mysteries of musical theory. In 1788 he went to Leipzig and in 1790 he was court organist (Schlossorganist) in Zeitz. In 1791 he became organist at St. Peter's, Leipzig, and first violoncellist at the "Grosse Concert" (afterwards "Gewandhaus Concerte"). In 1802 he took the great Bach's seat at the church of St. Thomas, and died from consumption in 1811. His son:

KARL LUDWIG VOIGT, born at Zeitz, November 8, 1792, received his first instructions on the violoncello from his father, and soon showed such signs of marked talent that the directors of the Gewandhaus Concerts, after his father's untimely death, sent him to Dotzauer. When Dotzauer left Leipzig, Voigt was installed in his master's place. After 1826 he retired from the concert platform. He had a great technique of the left hand, and an agreeable tone, but he lacked emotion and power. He composed a capriccio, divertimento, polonaise, potpourri, fantasia, scena and variations, all with orchestral accompaniment; also four duets for two violoncellos, four sonatas, three sets of variations and a potpourri for two violoncellos. His compositions are antiquated, but the sonatas and duets still serve for educational purposes.

JOHANN HINDLE, born February 10, 1792, in Vienna, started his musical career as violoncellist. He exchanged the violoncello afterwards for the double bass, becoming one of the greatest soloists on that instrument. He made his debut as solo player on the double bass in 1817.

JOHANN FRIEDRICH SCHWENCKE, born April 30, 1792, at Hamburg. He studied the violoncello under Prell and Bernhard Romberg. He played also the organ and the piano, and studied composition under his father. In 1829 he was appointed organist of St. Nicolas at Hamburg, where he died on September 28, 1852. He wrote a serenade for five violoncellos, double bass and tympani, which (in the "Allgemeine

Musik Zeitung" of 1835) is described as a soft and agreeable piece, but too sombre for the concert room.

EDWARD ULRICH, born at Weimar in 1792. He received lessons on the violoncello from the ducal chamber musician, Haase, and his theoretical training at Berlin, but it appears to be unknown who was his master at the latter place. In all probability, however, it was the famous Zelter, Goethe's friend, who was much sought after as a teacher of composition. He was appointed violoncellist to the ducal chamber at Weimar, in 1811, at the early age of sixteen. Apparently, he was more important as a composer than as an executant, as he wrote two operas (performed at Weimar in 1841), a concertino for horn and orchestra (Breitkopf and Härtel), and a number of solos for violoncello and bassoon.

Among the greatest German violoncellists who were born at the end of last century, and exercised considerable influence upon the more modern school, we see a remarkable figure in the person of FRIEDRICH AUGUST KUMMER, who was born at Meiningen, August 5, 1797. His father was a highly esteemed oboist in the ducal chapel, which position he afterwards exchanged for a similar one in the Dresden orchestra at the commencement of this century. Friedrich August, who had in his early years cultivated the instrument of his father, exchanged the latter for the violoncello, and became a pupil of Dotzauer. After completing his studies, Kummer was destined to enter the court orchestra. As there was no vacancy for the violoncello at that time, he was engaged as oboist. In 1813 he played the recitative accompaniments on the violoncello during rehearsals to gain experience. Karl Wilhelm Hoeckner, violoncellist and famous medal engraver, died in 1814, and Karl Maria von Weber chose Kummer to fill his place in the orchestra. He was installed on November 18, 1814, with a salary of two hundred thaler (£30 per annum!) Kummer was untiring in his endeavours to perfect himself in his art, and when his late master, Dotzauer, retired into private life in 1850, he was appointed solo violoncellist in the place of the former. He held this position until 1864, when he celebrated his golden jubilee, after fifty years' service in the same orchestra. He was made a Knight of the Order

FIG. 42. F. A. KUMMER.

of Albrecht on that occasion, and retired with a pension. He retained his position as professor of the violoncello at the Dresden Conservatoire until his death, which took place on May 22, 1879. During these latter years he devoted also part of his time to private pupils and to composition. Portraits of Kummer appear in Fig. 42 and Plate XXVI, which will be the more interesting as very few are known to exist. He wrote innumerable works, which for the greater part did not survive him. One hundred and sixty-three opus numbers appeared in print, while two hundred entr'actes, etc., for the royal court theatre, and numerous concert pieces for wind instruments remained in manuscript. For the violoncello he wrote: Concerto in F, Op. 10; Concertino in E, Op. 16; Concertino Suisse, E minor, Op. 30; Concertino in E, Op. 73; Grand Fantasia, Op. 26; Duets for Two Violoncellos, Op. 22, 103, 105, 107, 126, 156, 162, 165, "Twenty Instructive Duos" (Berlin, Fürstner), and a considerable number of solo pieces, drawing-room pieces and arrangements. All these are more or less antiquated. Some of the duets are useful for teaching purposes, as also are his concerted pieces, while his arrangements of songs by Schubert will be welcome additions to the repertoire of amateurs. Of distinct and lasting merit, however, are his "Violoncello School, with an Appendix of One Hundred and One Excellent Studies" (translated by Piatti), his "Ten Melodic Studies," Op. 57, and the eight "Grand Etudes," Op. 44, which belong to the finest studies that have ever been written for the instrument. Very useful are also his Twenty-four Caprices, Op. 71; Eight Studies, Op. 106; a book of daily exercises, and "Repertorium und Orchester Studien," extracts of difficult violoncello passages from orchestral and choral works. With Concertmeister Franz Schubert (the violinist) he used to travel and give concerts, when they played duets composed by themselves for their own use. They founded also a quartet party, in which, afterwards, Lipinsky succeeded Schubert. Kummer shone to great advantage in these as well as in the orchestra, combining truly classical dignity with a great and noble tone and technique. Unfortunately he remained a stranger to the lighter and more brilliant technique of the bow, cultivated by the French and Belgian school, upon whose members he looked down as upon so many tricksters. This view was unfortunately shared by many of his pupils, as the author found out to his cost, having received his first instructions by Johannes Hoecke, a worthy member of the Cologne orchestra, and excellent teacher for beginners. He quoted his master Kummer with nothing short of veneration, and with all his good qualities shared his master's views upon spiccato, spring bow arpeggios, and even staccato, which he declared to be idle tricks. He also told an amusing anecdote about a Strad violoncello belonging to Kummer. This instrument had a wolf. One day his children were romping about, and one, by accident, poked the point of a stick right through the table below the bridge. After the necessary chastisement had been dealt out to the culprit, Kummer proceeded to try his instrument to find out how far the damage would injure the tone, and to his surprise the wolf had gone. When the instrument was repaired the old enemy had returned again. Kummer was of an even and quiet temperament, which was also expressed in his playing, in which he was perhaps nearest akin to Piatti. In 1821 and 1835 he played with great success at Vienna, and was declared to be the nearest approach to Romberg and Bohrer. The Kummer family was essentially musical, one brother being an excellent violinist, whose son, Alexander, late professor of the Leipzig Conservatoire, is at present a successful teacher of the violin in London, who kindly supplied the originals from which Plate XXVI and Fig. 42 were taken. FERDINAND WILHELM, the youngest brother of Friedrich August, born October 15, 1802, was a good violoncellist, and as such, since 1820, member of the Dresden orchestra, where he died June 21, 1834. Two sons of Friedrich August were also violoncellists, viz., ERNST KUMMER, born November 8, 1824, who entered the court orchestra in 1844, and died August 2, 1860, and MAX KUMMER, born April 23, 1842, the youngest son, who died September 18, 1871.

FRANZ ORSLER (Schwickert in his "Almanack" calls him

Oessler (see list of violoncellists in the Imperial Chapel, Vienna, page 206), was violoncellist in the Viennese court orchestra, and died about 1798. His son:

JOSEPH ORSLER was in the same capacity in that orchestra, and wrote some compositions for the violoncello which remained in manuscript.

A few violoncellists are mentioned in various musical dictionaries, of whom nothing or little is known:

ALEXANDER ALBERTI, musical director from Austria. He was a clever violoncellist, and as such was in the band of the Bishop of Breslau in 1754 (Marpurg, "Beiträge").

AGOSTINO POLI was chamber musician at Stuttgart in 1782, according to Schwickert's "Almanack."

HELLER, from Munich, and PARAGUIN, are mentioned by Cramer ("Magazin," Vol. 1) as violoncellists in the orchestra of the Prince Elector at Bonn in 1783.

JOHANN GEORG FLEISCHMANN was violoncellist to the Duke of Kurland. He exchanged this position for that of a royal chamber musician to the King of Prussia, who was himself an amateur violoncellist, and took Fleischmann with him as an accompanist during the Rhenish campaign against the French in 1792. He died in 1810, leaving behind him a considerable number of compositions which remained in manuscript.

FRIEDRICH PAULSEN, son of Carl Friedrich Ferdinand Paulsen, organist and song-composer at Flensburg. The date of his birth is not known. He was an excellent violoncellist, and particularly strong as a quartet player. He died in 1826, a member of the Imperial court orchestra at St. Petersburg. A fine tone, purity of intonation and artistic phrasing were the characteristics of his playing.

MARIA JOSEPH ANTON HÖFFELMAYER, born at Rastadt after 1750, travelled as violoncello virtuoso between 1780-90 in Germany, England, Holland and France. During 1798-9 he lived in Hamburg, and in 1800 he went to Paris in the company of Pieltain. He enjoyed a great reputation as virtuoso.

MEDECK—? (no date of birth or death), an excellent violoncellist, who married a Russian pianist, with whom he went on tour in 1816. In 1820 both were engaged by the court at Madrid, but they were dismissed in 1824. Medeck lived still at Madrid in 1845, flourishing as favourite master of his instrument, and in very good circumstances.

The band of Prince Esterhazy had two excellent violoncellists in 1782, in the persons of KRAFT and PERTOJA (Forkel). In 1790 Kraft remained, while TAUBER had taken Pertoja's place (Gerber). AUGUST TAUBER, described as "Militär" (military musician) was a member of the Thurn and Taxis private band in 1860. In the same orchestra the violoncello was represented by the following artists at different times: KARAUSCHECK in 1755, salary, two hundred and sixty florins per annum; PRONATH, since 1769 he received three hundred and ninety-two florins, in 1783 and remained till 1806 as did the following: SCHMID, his son, SEBASTIAN S., who received only one hundred florins, while his father received eight hundred florins and sixty-four florins for his clothing. Since 1787 there was SCMITZ with four hundred florins per annum, JOSEPH WALDHAUSEN, who was also flautist in 1806, and the famous MAX WILLMANN, who after 1806, went to Vienna, where he died in 1812.

FRANZ XAVER HUBER, born at Öttingen, in Bavaria, was a highly esteemed violoncellist at the court of Mecklenburg in 1785.

AUGUST FERDINAND CUBELIUS, born in January, 1798, in Berlin, commenced his career as flutist, and made his debut as such in 1813. He exchanged that instrument for the violoncello and at the recommendation of the famous capellmeister Zelter in Berlin he was engaged as violoncellist for the royal chapel in 1816.

CHAPTER XIV.

POSITION OF THE VIOLONCELLO IN GERMANY AT THE END OF THE EIGHTEENTH CENTURY.

THE violoncello had made its way into Germany by way of Vienna during the latter part of the seventeenth century. Looking back on its gradual development in that country, we find the instrument taking a very important position among the violin family towards the end of the eighteenth century, yet it was then only emerging from its experimental stages. Although its technique had been led into more modern channels by Romberg, Bohrer, Dotzauer, Kummer and others, the confusion that existed with regard to the various clefs used in its notations caused a general outcry which found vent in several musical papers. Romberg speaks also about it in his violoncello school. Haydn in his Concerto in D, Op. 101, uses the bass clef, tenor clef, alto clef and treble clef. The last he uses an octave higher than it sounds, whether following bass or tenor clef.

Cramer, in his "Magazin," Volume II, under November 8, 1783, brings a "proposal for an alteration of the clef in violoncello musik." He says: "One has at last arrived at the necessity to inflict the tenor, alto, discant, G and F clef upon the poor, already greatly overburdened violoncellist. .... It is a very disagreeable circumstance that composers have not yet come to a general understanding as to the use of the treble clef. They compel the executant to find out by dint of experiment what is meant, and he sometimes has to leave it undecided. Carlo Graziani in his Sonata, Op. 2, uses the C clef on the second (fourth) line, which Rousseau calls 'taille' (tenor) clef, and Lulli 'basse taille.' In vocal compositions it is called baryton clef." The author of the articles recommends this clef as "contralto" clef, and says it would save the use of any other than the bass clef, which should only be used for the octave commencing with the open C string.

Boccherini makes ample use of the various C clefs, but adheres strictly to the rule, which has since generally obtained, of writing the treble clef, following the bass clef, one octave higher than it is to be played, and when following the tenor clef, in its exact position. The discanto, mezzo-soprano and alto clef have since disappeared from violoncello music, while the tenor clef holds its own, covering as it does the middle compass of the instrument without the use of ledger lines.

After finally abandoning the use of a fifth string, the outward form had been absolutely fixed, yet the size of the instrument induced the viol d'amour virtuoso, JOHANN WILDE (a Russian chamber virtuoso and Bavarian by nationality), who died in 1770, to construct the "*violoncello portatile*" (portable violoncello) which is talked about in all the musical papers of its time (Hiller's "Mus. Nachrichten," Volume IV, page 192, and "Wöchentliche Nachrichten," Volume I, page 193, also in the "Harmonicon"). It consisted of a wooden box two feet long, and about nine inches wide, which formed the body of the instrument, and which contained the neck with the finger-board and strings, bridge, tailpin and even the bow. The whole could be pulled out and screwed on in a few minutes, and it says in the "Wöchentliche Nachrichten" that the tone equalled in strength that of a violoncello three times its size. It was evidently unsuccessful, because we hear no more of it, nor of a movable finger-board mentioned in the "Harmonicon," of 1823, page 3, as an *improvement on the violoncello.*

They only go to prove that down to the beginning of this century people were not quite sure that the violoncello had actually reached its standard shape, and thus were induced to dabble here and there in eccentricities. The only real improvement, which consisted in cutting the finger-board lower under the C string, met with disapproval. The finger-board originally had the same shape as that of the violin, thus giving the C string insufficient room to vibrate, which caused it to rattle against the wood.

The "Allgemeine Musik Zeitung" of 1809, No. 38, page 593, has an article on "Virtuosittät" (virtuosity) which contains the following remarks: "Several violoncellists make use of another finger-board, to wit, one on which the C string is placed higher above the board than the three other strings. I can neither warmly recommend this invention nor oppose its use. So much is certain that without it one can do just as much as with it."

This remark has been proved fallacious by the universal adoption of the modified shape.

The same article contains another remark which fixes an episode in the annals of the violoncello. It informs us that the art of accompaniment had greatly diminished in 1809, as the violoncellists did not study sufficiently "thorough bass" (harmony) for that purpose. The fact of the matter was, that people began to find the accompaniment of a violoncello to all the recitatives rather monotonous, even if it was ever so cleverly executed, and although it was practised in some instances down to the second part of last century; the organ,

PLATE XXVI.
F. A. KUMMER.

and even the full orchestra, were more and more employed for that purpose. Although the change may be lamented by some rabid antiquarians, the musical public at large will never clamour for the reinstatement of the violoncello for that particular purpose. On the other hand, it had risen to far more important functions in the orchestra. Having emerged from the position of a mere bass instrument, simply doubling the contrabass, florid passages and even melody parts were sometimes given to the violoncello, especially by Beethoven. As a solo instrument it had already become second only to the violin.

CHAPTER XV.

THE VIOLONCELLO IN FRANCE.

CHAPTER IX (origin and early history) contains the condensed score of a little piece, "La Clochette," from Baltazarini's "Ballet comique de la Royne," which was produced at the Louvre, on October 15, 1581. It was for "violins," and is written in five parts, which indicate the use of a "bass" violin. As we know that Andreas Amati and Gasparo da Salo made already violoncellos of different sizes, the largest being called "basso di camera," it may be safely surmised that Baltazarini really introduced the violoncello into France, together with the violin, of which he was one of the first masters. The music of the above ballet was not by Baltazarini, but by Jacques Salmon (see page 127). Although it is pretty certain that the *instrument* was thus introduced into France shortly after its appearance in Italy, there were no players of any note whose names have been preserved in history until much later. The "basse de viole" (gamba) was the fashionable instrument during the seventeenth century, and its technique had been greatly developed by such excellent virtuosos as De Caix, Marais, Forqueray, and many others, while the violoncello had so far remained a simple bass to accompany other instruments or voices. The viol asserted its supremacy, and it is amusing to read the remarks of the learned Dominican father, MARIN MERSENNE, who was a most enthusiastic musician, with regard to the violins and the viols.

He gives in his "Harmonie Universelle," a description of the violin, in which he says: "Those who have heard the twenty-four violins of the king admit that they never heard anything more charming or more powerful; and on that account this instrument is the best of all for dance music, as executed in the ballets, and everything else."

In his chapter on viols he says: "Certainly if instruments are prized in proportion to their capability of imitating the voice, and if of all skill that which is most natural is esteemed most, it appears that one should not refuse the prize to the viol, which counterfeits the voice in all its modulations, and even in those accents which are most expressive of grief and joy." After comparing the bow to the breath, and carrying this clever simile into detail, he continues: "As regards the violin and the modern lyra, one might call them imitators of the viol, as they are also of the voice, but they did not equal it (the viol), for the violin is too rough, as it has to be strung with strings which are too thick to let it shine in those subjects which belong to its natural sphere; and if it were mounted like the viol there would be no difference, except that they are not fretted."—(!!!). The lyra he describes as coming nearer to the viol, except that it is impossible to play passages on it as on the former instrument, on account of the flat bridge which gives a greater facility for playing chords.

He describes the "basse," which corresponds entirely to the violoncello. The finger-board was, however, very short. Mersenne gives its length as one-third the length of the table, which would be about ten inches, or less than half its present length. The illustration which he gives shows it to be rather more than that, about fourteen to fifteen inches. Very amusing is the following passage: "One could mount the violins with five strings, which might have the effect of their superseding the ordinary instruments with four strings, as the rebec has been superseded, which had only three strings . . . . they would then have a sufficient compass for all the modes, while at present only three or four can be played right through, while the rest finishes on the *fourth*, which constitutes a plagal cadence, and has a bad effect"—at the end of the chapter he finds out he has made a mistake. That does not deter him from printing the above statement, but he adds at the end of the chapter that he has since been informed on good authority that all the modes can be played right through on four-stringed instruments.

Five-stringed violoncellos did, however, exist, as mentioned on page 122. They have also been mentioned by Matheson, and their tuning was: The ABBÉ TARDIEU, of Tarrascon, brother of the "maître de chapelle" of the church of that town, is credited with the final abolition of the top string. The absurd story contained in several musical dictionaries crediting him with the *invention* of the violoncello, does not call for any serious comment. The first to acquaint the French with the use of the violoncello as a solo instrument was JOHANN BAPTIST STRUCK, called BAPTISTIN, who (as related in Chapter XI), came to Paris at the beginning of last century, entering the private band of the Duc d'Orleans. He was the first to play the violoncello in the orchestra of the Grand Opera, of which he became a member in 1709.

The first *French* violoncellists of note were the brothers "PHILIPPE PIÈRRE" and "PIÈRRE" DE SAINT SÉVIN, commonly called "L'ABBÉ AINÉ" and L'ABBÉ CADET," as they were both musicians at the church at Agen, and consequently had to wear clerical dress, which was the same as or similar to that of an abbot (abbé). On June 11, 1727, a son of Philippe was born at Agen. He was afterwards known as "L'ABBÉ FILS." According to some he was a violoncellist, but there is a violin tutor by Jos. Barnabé de Saint Sévin, called "L'abbé fils," which makes that statement doubtful. Philippe, called "L'abbé ainé," went to Paris towards the end of 1827, where he was appointed violoncellist for the Grand Opera by the side of Baptistin, and Pièrre joined his brother in the same capacity in 1739. The richness and beauty of Pièrre's tone showed the supremacy of the violoncello over the gamba as an orchestral instrument to such an extent, that it caused the entire expulsion of the latter instrument from that famous institution. Both brothers were still members of the Grand Opera in 1761. One of them, probably Pièrre as the greater virtuoso, was also in the orchestra of the "Concerts Spirituels" in 1755, together with EDOUARD, FORCADE, HABRAM, DUN and SAUBLEY. Marpurg, who gives the foregoing list of violoncellists of the "Concerts Spirituels," tells us that the following were the violoncellists, gambists and contraviol (double bass) players at the Grand Opera in the same year: L'ABBÉ VATER (he means L'abbé ainé), HABRAM, DAVERNE (DAVESNE), GIANOTI (contraviol), CAPPERAN (perhaps Chabran, the French name for Gaetano Chiabrano, see Chapter XI), ANTHEAUME, FORCADE, L'ABBÉ CADET, DUN, senior, DUN, junior, SAUBLAY, SALENTIN. No further particulars about the majority of these are available. L'abbé (probably the younger) was brought to London with Mlle. Subligny by Betterton, who, on the decline of Lincoln's Inn Theatre, instituted a kind of miscellaneous entertainment.

JEAN BARRIÈRE was one of the first French violoncellists of note. He flourished between 1730 and 1750. The date of his birth is unknown, as is also the name of his master. In all probability he studied under one of the Saint Sevins, and in

1736 he visited Rome, where he remained for three years to study under Francischello. In 1733 he published his first set of sonatas, Op. 1. They show a decided advance on his predecessors, and contain passages which might even now be practised with advantage by violoncello students, and his subsequent works, composed after his return from Italy in 1739, are more important still. He died apparently in 1753, as the "Siècle de Louis XV" of that year contains the following notice: "The famous Barrière, who died recently, possessed everything one could wish for from a violoncellist; nobody could equal his execution." Barrière and his contemporary, Berteau, are looked upon as the founders of the French school of violoncello playing.

The use of the *thumb position* was introduced in France about this period. The idea, which originated probably with Francischello, was taken from the Trompetta Marina. That instrument had a single string of great length (about four to five feet), which was sounded by a short bow at the top of the neck (near the peg box), while the notes were stopped with the thumb between the bow and the bridge. It is possible that Struck (Baptistin) introduced the thumb position in France, as it was already known in Italy when he left that country. Barrière's compositions also seem to indicate its use, while Berteau has employed it freely in his music.

GIOVANNI BUONONCINI, who came to Paris in 1733, made no use of the thumb position in any of his compositions as far as the author has been able to ascertain, while it is mentioned and explained in a tutor for the violoncello by Michel Corette, which appeared in Paris in 1741, and was perhaps the first detailed and systematic instruction book for the instrument.

RICHER, son of André Richer, born 1714 in Paris, is mentioned by Mendel as a clever violoncellist.

There was living about the same time, at Paris, JEAN BAPtiste Masse, "Ordinaire de la Chambre du Roi," who published three sets of sonatas for the violoncello, which possess distinct merit and testify to their author's technical ability.

Martin Bertèau, born at Valencienne about the beginning of the eighteenth century, was more important even than Barrière. He began his career as a bass viol (gamba) player, which instrument he studied under Kozecz, a Czeskian virtuoso, whose acquaintance he made while travelling in Germany. When, however, he became acquainted with the violoncello, and a solo piece for that instrument, composed by Francischello, he abandoned the bass viol, devoting himself entirely to the violoncello. His studies were so successful that his compatriots hailed him as a genius, and the first "salons" of gay Paris made a feature of his presence. He was an original, and not only delighted the company by his exquisite playing, but also by his quaint humour. He usually began by saying that in order to play well he required rosin, whereupon a footman brought him, on a salver, a flagon of wine and a glass which he plied very freely. The "Siècle de Louis XV" (page 151) says: "Nobody can flatter himself at present on possessing more fire than M. Berteau." He developed very largely the use of harmonics, by the use of which he attracted the general admiration of his contemporaries. In 1739 he made his debut at the "Concert Spirituel," which institution was founded in 1725, and scored an enormous success by the performance of one of his own compositions. Beauty of tone and expression appear to have been the chief features of Berteau's playing. His death took place in 1756. Berteau composed four concertos and three books of sonatas, one being Op. 2 (Paris, Bailleux, Rue Ste. Honoré). One of these sonatas has been republished by A. Moffat. A copy of his first concerto is preserved in the library of the Brussels Conservatoire, and the twenty-one exercises, which form an appendix to Duport's "Art of Fingering," contain also a piece by Berteau. He counted among his pupils the foremost French violoncellists of the latter part of the last century, viz., Jean Pierre Duport, Cupis, Janson and Tillière, who inherited their master's power of tone, and handed it down to their pupils. An excellent portrait of Berteau, from an original etching by Hillemacher, may be seen on Plate XXVII.

CHARLES HENRI DE BLAINVILLE, born 1711, in a village near Tours, was a violoncellist and teacher of music, who enjoyed the protection of the Marquise de Villeroy, who had been his pupil. Through her influence he became a popular teacher of music in Paris. He wrote several theoretical works, including an essay, "L'Esprit de l'art musical," which was translated in Hiller's "Nachrichten" ("News") in 1754.

His theory of a third mode, keeping the middle between major and minor, and based upon the scale E, F, G, A, B, C, D, awakened some interest in him as a theorician. He composed a symphony in this mode which was performed at the "Concert Spirituel" on May 30, 1751. Serre attacked his theory, but J. J. Rousseau wrote an enthusiastic letter in his defence, which appeared in the "Mercure" of 1751. His compositions shared the fate of his many unsuccessful theoretical works, which were soon forgotten. He appeared at the "Concert Spirituel" in solos of his own composition, but neither in his capacity as executant or composer did he meet with any particular success. No compositions of his for violoncello were published, but a book of sonatas for the "dessus de viole" with bass, was published by Boivin in Paris.

ALEXANDER CANAVASSO, THE ELDER, a violoncellist of Italian origin, settled in Paris about 1735, and was a member of the royal chamber music (King's band). He published a set of sonatas, Op. 2, which appeared in 1773. They are well written, and testify to their author's executive skill, making extensive use of the thumb position. An interesting figure was:

PLATE XXVII.
MARTIN BERTEAU. FROM THE ETCHING BY HILLEMACHER.

NOCHEZ, a pupil of Cervetto and Abaco. The latter was his master in 1740. In his earlier years he visited Italy, and joined, on his return the orchestra of the Opera Comique, which position he exchanged for one in the Grand Opera in 1749. In 1763 he became a royal chamber musician. He was also the first violoncellist at the "Concert Spirituel," and an excellent solo accompanist, an art which was considered one of the first requirements of every solo violoncellist. It has been asserted (among others by Wasielewski in his "History of the Violoncello") that Nochez was the author of an article on the violoncello in De La Borde's "Essai sur la Musique Ancienne et Moderne" (Paris, 1780), but this has been refuted by Vidal, at least as far as the historical part of that article is concerned ("Les Instruments à Archet," Vol. I, page 76). Nochez retired in 1799, and died in 1800.

CUPIS L'AINÉ (the elder) was violoncellist at the Paris Opera, but exchanged that instrument for the double bass in 1769, and died 1772.

JEAN BAPTISTE CUPIS (CUPIS LE JEUNE), born 1741, in Paris, became Berteau's pupil at the age of eleven, after having received preliminary instruction from his father, who was apparently the above Cupis *l'ainé*, as on the title page of his tutor Cupis calls himself "Le Jeune." He made rapid progress, and before he had attained the age of twenty he was counted among the foremost violoncellists of his time. He was appointed solo accompanist at the Grand Opera, where he remained until 1771. In this year he visited Germany, and remained for some time at Hamburg. Thence he went via Paris to Italy, and was, in 1794, at Milan. During this tour he married a well-known singer, Gasparino. Nothing appears to be known about the later part of his life. A NEPHEW OF HIS, son of his brother François (a violinist), was violoncellist at the Brussels Opera about 1768, but apparently was not of much consequence. Cupis wrote two concertos, "Petits Airs," and some sets of variations—the second appeared only after his death. He wrote also an instruction book, which was apparently published in 1771 or 1772, as it contains on the back of the title page an advertisement of Clément's "Journal de Clavecin," giving contents of numbers from 1762 until 1771. The title runs thus: "Méthode nouvelle et raisonnée pour apprendre a jouer du violoncelle, où l'on traite de son accord, de la manière de tenir c'est instrument avec aisance, de celle de tenir, l'archet, de la position de la main sur la touche, du tact, de l'étendue du manche, de la manière du doigter dans tous les tons, majeurs et mineurs, du tirer et du pousser, avec un nombre de Leçons, Romances, Ariettes et Menuets variés, etc., par *M. Cupis Le Jeune*, Professeur de Violoncello et Elève du Celèbre *Bertaud* [*sic!*]. Prix 7l. 4s., a Paris chez Le Menu. Editeur et Marchand de Musique de Madame la Dauphine, rue du Roule à la clef d'Or, etc., etc. Sold in London by Calkin and Budd, 118 Pall Mall." He describes the holding of the instrument (without tailpin) and bow in the modern fashion. Then he gives seven major and seven minor scales in two octaves not exceeding the octave of the A string. His fingering accords with the modern system, which apparently was employed already by Berteau. He advocated the use of the tempered scale, as he says: G sharp and A flat, A sharp and B flat, etc., are stopped in exactly the same place. After explaining how to play thirds with the first and fourth finger, and how to advance into higher positions up to D (eleventh of open A) without the use of the thumb, he gives two pages of bowing exercises, without text. These are followed by thirty-five exercises, mostly with a second violoncello accompaniment, which have, at all events, some melodic interest, and make a greater demand upon the bow than upon the left hand containing staccato passages and even spring-bow arpeggios. The thumb position is not even mentioned

Wasielewski, who gives the same text of the title, mentions "Boyer" as publisher.

JEAN BAPTISTE AIMÉE JOSEPH JANSON, another of Berteau's pupils, was born at the native place of his master, i.e., Valencienne, in 1742. He made his debut as a soloist at the "Concert Spirituel" in 1766, and in the following year he accompanied the hereditary Prince of Brunswick to Italy, where he remained until 1771, when he returned to France. In 1783 he was in Hamburg, and thence visited Denmark, Sweden and Poland on his return. He met everywhere with the greatest success, and the richness and beauty of his tone were particularly praised. In 1789 he returned to Paris, where he was honoured with the first professorship of his instrument at the conservatoire on its foundation in 1795. Here he was drawn into the nortorious quarrel between Lesueur and Sorette, which ended in the reorganisation of that institute in 1802, and Janson's dismissal. Advanced in years, and no longer ahead of the younger virtuosos on the violoncello, he fell into the most necessitous circumstances.. His troubles so undermined his constitution that he broke down completely, and died in 1803, at the very moment when the government had resolved upon his reinstatement at the conservatoire. He wrote three Concertos, Op. 3, and three Concertos, Op. 7, both with a bass; six Concertos, Op. 15, with orchestra, which were published by Durien in Paris, in 1799, and six Sonatas with bass, Op. 4.

One of the most remarkable figures among French musicians of the eighteenth century was MICHEL CORRETTE. His technical knowledge of musical instruments is astounding, seeing that he wrote complete instruction books for almost every instrument then in use. He was a virtuoso on the harpsichord and the violin, and organist to the Duke of Angoulême and at the Temple Church. In recognition of his merits he was made a Knight of the Order of Christ. He was a man of frank and open mind, who expressed his opinions without fear of censure or public prejudice, and when he openly acknowledged the superiority of Italian violinists over the French virtuosos of the early eighteenth century, he created, naturally, a deal of ill-feeling among the latter. They retorted by calling his numerous pupils "les anachorètes" (les ânes à Corrette), a revenge which exhibited more French wit than fairness. In 1741 he published a violoncello tutor under this title: "Mêthode, théorique et pratique, pour apprendre en peu de tems le violoncelle dans sa perfection . . . . composée par Michel Corrette, XXIVᵉ, Ouvrage. A Paris chez l'auteur, Mme. Boivin et le Sr. Le Clerc: à Lyons chez M. de Bretonne. Avec Privilège du Roi, MDCCXLI." Fétis gives the date of publication as 1761, which is evidently an error in the reading of the above figures. This book is of great historical interest in the annals of violoncello technique, as it gives an insight into its early development. In his introduction to this work Corrette makes an addition to sundry erroneous statements about the origin of the violoncello by asserting that it was *invented* by "Bonocino" (Buononcini), at present Master of the Royal Chapel of the King of Portugal. There is no proof that that artist played the violoncello at all. Anyway, he is as little to be credited with its invention as the famous Abbé Tardieu of Tarrascon, who, at least, has the credit of abolishing the fifth or highest string. After sundry remarks about the elements of music, forming part of the introduction, he divides his book into the following chapters: (1) Manner of holding the violoncello; (2) Manner of holding the bow, and bowing; (3) The use of the bow in the up and down stroke; (4) Tuning of the violoncello; (5) Division of the fingerboard in diatonic and chromatic progression; (6) Fingering of the lowest (first) and following positions; (7) Manner of shifting from higher positions into the first; (8) Shake and appoggiatura; (9) Different bowings; (10) Double stops and arpeggios, and (11) *Thumb position*. This is followed by instructions for those who intend to exchange the bass viol for the violoncello, and for the accompaniment of solos and recitatives. He describes three different ways of holding the bow: one, as generally practised in Italy, by placing the fingers *on* the stick, and the thumb underneath—not close to the nut, however, but four or five inches nearer the middle (as shown in the picture of Francischello in an earlier part of this work). The second way was to place the fingers on the stick, and thumb on the hair of the bow (!). The third way was to place the fingers on the stick over the nut, and the thumb underneath the nut. Corrette opines that either way is good, but recommends each player to choose the manner which gives him the best grip and the most power. In one point he follows the old rules of the gambists, of playing mostly in the middle of the bow, thus reducing its length to about one-third. The manner of holding the bow gamba fashion, with the hand underneath the bow (as shown in the picture of Tonelli, Fig. 33, page 146), which was still practised in Germany and England, and even by Berteau, who retained it from the gamba, is not mentioned in his work. He says that there are sundry different schools of violoncello playing, but that he regards Buononcini as the master whose example is followed by the best European players. As Buononcini was in Paris from 1733 till 1748, Corrette had ample opportunity of acquainting himself with the methods of that famous master. Very curious is the fingering which Corrette gives in his tutor, and which was generally followed more or less closely during that time until Duport finally fixed the modern system of fingering. This old system was taken from the violin, and consisted in using the first, second and fourth fingers in the first and second positions, taking A sharp on the A string with the first finger, B natural with the second, and C with the fourth finger, thus placing only one semitone between the second and fourth fingers. The chromatic scale was fingered:

THE HISTORY OF THE VIOLONCELLO.

C	C♯	D	D♯	E	F	F♯;	G	G♯	A	A♯	B	C	C♯;
0	1	1	2	2	4	4	0	1	1	2	2	4	4

D	D♯	E	F	F♯	G	G♯;
0	1	1	2	2	4	4

A	A♯	B	C	C♯	D	D♯	E	F	F♯	G	G♯	A
0	1	1	2	2	4	1	2	3	3	4	4	3

The shifting from higher to lower positions is done in a very awkward way, as is exemplified in the following:

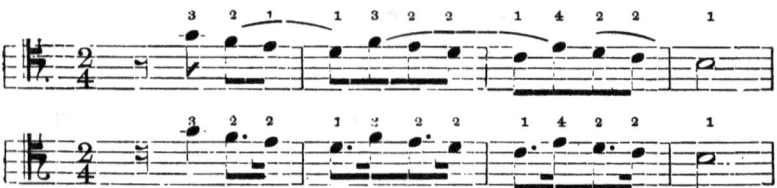

Corrette prefers the latter way.

In the instructions for changing from the gamba to the violoncello, he gives a comparative scale showing the fingering on each instrument. The ordinary fingering on the gamba commenced in the half position, viz., one semitone from the nut, and only requires one or two fingers between each two strings, as the interval is only a fourth or third (between third and fourth string). The fingering on the violoncello A string is marked here in the following manner:

The direction, "thumb position," seems to indicate that the thumb was placed behind the first finger from the beginning of the fourth position, as the neck of the instrument was very short, and the upper notes of the fourth position, consequently, almost out of reach in the ordinary way. The bowing of the violoncello differed still wider from that of the gamba than the fingering. The bridge of the latter instrument being cut very flat to facilitate the playing of chords, precluded all firmness of attack, which the violoncello required, and, moreover, the bowing was absolutely reversed. The accented beats on the gamba requiring an up bow had to be played with a down bow on the violoncello, and all others in conformity. Corrette still advocates the system of marking the position of the fingers by lines on the fingerboard to ensure purity of intonation. This system was then generally in use, but was abolished soon afterwards. Leopold Mozart, for instance, condemns it in his violin tutor published in 1756. The use of the fourth finger in the thumb position was declared impracticable on account of its shortness, which proves that the left hand was held too slanting instead of holding it in as near a right angle to the fingerboard as possible, thus bringing the little finger properly over the strings.

We shall find a proof of the general adoption, during the early eighteenth century, of the fingering as described by Corrette in a tutor for the violoncello by Robert Crome, published in London in 1765.

After this digression illustrating the state of the violoncello technique at that period, we return to the school of Berteau, encountering as a distinguished pupil of his:

JOSEPH BONAVENTURE TILLIÈRE, the years of whose birth and death are unknown. On the conclusion of his studies under Berteau he entered the private band of Prince Conti about 1760. In 1771 he was also member of the orchestra of the Grand Opera. In 1774 (Wasielewski gives 1764) his "Tutor" was published by Jolivet in Paris ("Mercure de France," July, 1774, Volume II, page 212). In this he discusses the technique of the neck positions as well as the higher positions with the raised hand (but without use of thumb positions, which he pursues into the higher registers). After a chapter on double stopping he gives some well chosen exercises. Vidal calls this book the first of its kind which can be regarded as a serious work. Another edition of this work, published by Bailleux, Rue Ste. Honoré, Paris, liv. 7.45, is preserved in the British Museum. The title is "Méthode pour le Violoncelle dédié a M. Rigaut, Physicien de la Marine, Composée par M. Tillière, Elêve du celèbre Bertau [*sic*!]." Among the advertisements on the cover are to be found: "Tillière's Recueil d'airs pour 2 violoncellos" (liv. 7.45), Sonatas, Op. 5 (liv. 7.45), another set of sonatas (same price, vice liv. 7.45). The above "Tutor" gives the various intervals up to the tenth, and after that the scales in two octaves, going up to the second B on the A string. A number of exercises follow, of which only one remains in the first position. They are excellently written for developing the technique of the bow. In dealing with the thumb position he begins on the G and D of the first position on the D and A string (*see* "Corrette," who also calls the fourth position "thumb position" in his example for fingering the A string). In that way Tillière goes up to F-C, the tenth of the open strings, taking all the intermediate thumb positions. A few examples of arpeggios follow, in which he makes use of the fourth finger in the thumb position. After giving the fingering for thirds and sixths he has four exercises for double stopping and syncopation, finishing up with a "Sounata" for two violoncellos, introducing cadenzas in the first allegro and the adagio. The last movement, "allegro moderato," requires a fair amount of technique, especially as far as the bowing is concerned. The sonata leads into very high positions, and in some instances Tillière employs the soprano "C" clef as well as the usual clefs. Six sonatas with bass appeared in Paris in 1777 (probably the Op. 5 already referred to). He wrote nine duets for two violoncellos, of which three were published as Op. 8, by Sieber in Paris, who also published an edition of his above "Méthode" as well as Im-

Monsieur

je vien de recevoir une lettre de monfrere qui me charge de lui envoyé son fils a paris, il me dit de vous ladessé monsieur. je ne doute pas de tout le soint que vous en aurès vue la mitié que vous avez pour le pere, je suis charmèn que cette occation me rapelle avôtre souvenire et me mets a porté de vous asfurés des sentiments destime et consideration avec le quelle jai lhonneur dêtre

Monsieur

votre tres humble et tres obeisant serviteur

Duport

berlin le 15 juillet 1808

REDUCED FACSIMILE OF A LETTER BY JEAN PIERRE DUPORT REFERRING TO A REQUEST BY HIS BROTHER, JEAN LOUIS, TO SEND THE LATTER'S SON TO PARIS.

bault and Frères, 23 Rue Neuve des Maturins. It was entitled: "Méthode de Violoncelle Revué et Augmentée. Illustrée de vignettes, etc., par M. Tillière." This edition forms part of a series of elementary tutors for various instruments, and contains only four of the exercises from the original edition, the rest consisting of little melodies from operas and chamber works; these do not exceed the fourth position. The thumb position is shown from the G-D up to the middle D-A on the first and second string. The title page shows a violoncellist in the costume of the early part of the nineteenth century. The bow described and illustrated is of a clumsy pattern with a perfectly straight stick and a light nut. The position of the left hand is slanting downwards, instead of standing almost at a right angle, and the fingers, consequently, are slanting sideways.

The foremost among Berteau's pupils was JEAN PIERRE DUPORT, usually called the elder Duport (Duport l'ainé) to distinguish him from his still more famous brother, Jean Louis. Their father was a dancing-master in Paris, and Jean Pierre was born on November 27, 1741. At the age of twenty he made his debut as violoncellist at the "Concert Spirituel" on Ascension Day, 1761, and scored an immense success, which immediately led to his appointment in the private band of Prince Conti. From this time he became a popular favourite, and the Parisians were quite enthusiastic in his praise. In 1762 he played a solo at every one of the "Concerts de la Quinzaine de Pâques" (fortnight round Easter), and the "Mercure de France," in the April number of that year, says: "M. Duport has produced fresh wonders every day on his violoncello, and has merited renewed admiration. Under his hand the instrument does not appear the same, it speaks, expresses, renders all, and with even more of that charm which was thought to be the exclusive property of the violin. The agility of his fingers is combined with perfect intonation in passages the difficulty of which can only be realised by those who know the instrument. It appears an accepted fact that this young man is the most singular phenomenon that has appeared in the *salons*. Choron and Lafayolle, in their "Musical Dictionary," say that: "He was stronger in the allegro than in the adagio." In 1769 he gave up his position in Prince Conti's band in order to travel. His first journey brought him to England, which he had already visited in 1758, and in the following year (1770) he went to Spain. It was probably on this journey that the memorable visit to Francischello took place, which is related by Marpurg as follows: The elder Duport was still a very (?) young man when someone praised to him the art of Francischello. He resolved to go and hear him, and instantly set out on a journey to Genoa. He presented himself before Francischello and told him how anxious he was to hear a specimen of his highly praised art. Francischello informed him that his fee for playing to anyone was never less than one hundred zechins. Duport replied that the pleasure of hearing so great an artist was undoubtedly cheaply bought at one hundred zechins, as he considered his divine gift absolutely priceless. As, however, he was a musician himself, and as such not overweighted with worldly treasure, he must leave it to princes and lords to reward him as he deserved; that, moreover, his slender means had already been severely taxed by the expense of the long journey from Marseilles to Genoa, which he undertook for the express purpose of hearing him play. Francischello was touched and flattered, and immediately took his instrument and proceeded to play his most brilliant "capriccios" (so Marpurg!). He played for quite an hour, and when he had finished the delighted Duport thanked him most profusely, and was about to take his leave when Francischello asked him to give him also a specimen of his art. Duport complied with the request, and his hearer appeared to be greatly pleased. After Francischello had complimented the young artist on his talent, they parted, and Duport went straight to the harbour and took sail to Marseilles, without seeing anything of the sights of the town and after a sojourn of only three hours. This meeting is so far interesting as it made Duport the elder a connecting link between the old Italian school and the masters of this century. Duport was a man of a most amiable and benevolent disposition, of which the following anecdote is a good illustration. Visiting a certain provincial town in France one day, Duport found, to his utter astonishment, his name placarded all over the town announcing that he would give a concert on that very same night. He resolved to attend the concert supposed to be given by himself, and found a room crowded from end to end, for his fame as a virtuoso had gone all over France, and everybody was anxious to hear him play. Presently the pseudo Duport made his appearance, and his playing being anything but what the public expected to hear, murmurs were heard among the audience. These became louder and louder as he proceeded, and finally became threatening. At this juncture Duport could restrain himself no longer, and approaching the poor humbug he disclosed his identity, took the instrument from his trembling hands, and began to play. No sooner did the first notes resound which the master's hand drew from that instrument, than perfect tranquillity was at once restored, and a spell-bound audience listened in deepest silence. When he had finished he was greeted with ringing cheers from a delighted and enthusiastic multitude.

The pseudo Duport approached him in penitent and dejected attitude, and handed him a considerable sum of money which the magic of his name had brought to the house. But Duport indignantly refused to accept it, handing it back to his impersonator with a warning never to misuse his name again.

In 1773 Duport left Spain and went to Berlin, where he met with a most favourable reception.

Frederic the Great engaged him as chamber musician for the Royal Chapel and solo violoncellist for the Royal Opera. At the same time he became the teacher of the Crown Prince, afterwards Frederic William II.

On the succession of the latter in 1786 Duport was nominated director of the royal chamber music. From that time he played only at the court concerts. He died December 31, 1818.

He composed a Concerto in A major; a Concerto for violin and violoncello (the violin part is by Vachon); six Sonatas, Op. 2, dédiés a Messire Fitzwilliam par J. P. Duport de la Musique de Mgr. le Prince de Conti chés M. de la Chevardière Md. de Musique, Rue du Roule a la Croix d'Or. Prix 7₶ 4ˢ

Six sonatas dedicated to Prince Conti, published by Chevardière (English edition by Bremner). The Royal Hausbibliothek in Berlin possess twelve sonatas and fragment of a sonata for violoncello solo and bass, also MS. 5351, one sonata with bass.

JEAN LOUIS DUPORT, born October 4, 1749, was the younger brother of Jean Pierre Duport, whose phenomenal successes induced him to exchange the violin (which was originally his instrument) for the violoncello. By the aid of his brother's instruction he made such rapid progress that he eventually even surpassed the former. On February 2, 1768, he made his debut at the "Concert Spirituel," which the "Mercure de France," 1768 (page 214), notices thus: "M. Duport, the younger, a pupil of his brother, played a sonata, which the latter accompanied. His execution is brilliant and amazing, his tone full and of great sweetness. Boldness and great certainty characterise his playing, and predict the greatest talent." This success was followed up by his almost sensational appearance at the Société Olympique (formerly the "Concert des Amateurs"), and the *salons* of the leading aristocracy. He was engaged by the Prince Guéménée for his private band, and also by the well-known Baron Bagge, while the Société Academique des Enfants d'Apollon conferred their membership upon him. In 1783 he visited London, and we read in Cramer's "Nachrichten" of that year that he surpassed Cervetto in expression and style, although his tone was less powerful. This statement refers, of course, to James, the son of Jacopo Bassevi, called Cervetto. On February 8 and March 26, 1783, both Cervetto and Duport played at the "Professional Concerts" (under Lord Abingdon's management) at the Hanover Rooms, Hanover Square. His brother, Jean Pierre, appeared at the same concerts about 1765, when he played with Lahoussaye and Signora Magdalena Sirmen, a pupil of Tartini, to whom the famous master addressed that interesting letter which afterwards appeared as a preface to his "Art of Bowing."* Jean Louis Duport had been induced by his fellow student, Crosdill (also a pupil of Jean Pierre Duport), to visit London, where he stayed for about six months. The two artists appear to have been close friends all through life. They even appeared together at the court concerts. One evening, when Viotti was to play a concertante with Crosdill at the "petits appartements" of Marie Antoinette, the former artist did not arrive in time. The Queen noticed the delay, and the situation became embarrassing, when Duport, who had just been playing a sonata, asked to see the violin part. No sooner had he read over the part than he took up his instrument and asked Crosdill to begin. He played the violin part from sight so admirably that it appeared doubtful if Viotti could have secured a finer or more pleasing rendering of the piece. He had taken Viotti

---

* This letter has recently been reprinted (1913) in English, together with original Italian text, and published by William Reeves, London. Price one shilling net.

as a model, just as Vaslin learned from Baillot (as stated in his "L'Art du Violoncelle"), as we shall see later on, and his contemporaries, who noticed the similarity of style, called him "the Viotti of the violoncello." The two artists appeared frequently together in public, and it is related of them that when they played a certain passage alternately it was impossible to decide who played it best.

When Duport and Crosdill, in playing duets or sonatas together, began to improvise their cadenzas, they seemed to stimulate each other's imagination in the production of fresh figures and embellishments, which were so much alike in character that they seemed to emanate from one and the same genius.

What Duport possessed in a prominent degree was expression. All the days of his life he spent in trying to overcome the greatest difficulties and intricacies of his instrument, in order to produce the simplest pieces in absolute perfection. Like Viotti, he strove to give dramatic emphasis to quick and brilliant movements, in order to give a full and strong relief to the simple sweetness of the cantilena.

During the eighties he visited Geneva, which was then famous for the excellence of its concerts. During his sojourn there he was introduced to Voltaire at Ferney. Voltaire knew little about musical matters, and when Duport played to him, he was surprised at the sweetness of tone emanating from so big an instrument. Never at a loss for a witty remark, he said: "Monsieur Duport, you will make me believe in miracles, when I see that you can turn an ox into a nightingale." The outbreak of the French Revolution drove him away from Paris, and he hastened to join his brother in Berlin in 1789, where he received an appointment in the royal chapel. He remained there for seventeen years, and was a great favourite, as his personal qualities were on a par with those of the artist.

The unfortunate events of 1806 (invasion of the French army) drove him from Berlin. He followed the King to Königsberg, and returned to France in 1807 after the demise of his august protector. Eitner states that he went to Munich in 1806 as member of the electoral chapel. This can only refer to a temporary visit.

His long absence from Paris had almost effaced the memory of his former triumphs, but his first reappearance sufficed to reinstate him as popular favourite. The occasion was a concert given by Mlle. Colbran (afterwards the wife of Rossini) at the Salle Chantereine in 1807. The unsettled condition of Paris, however, prevented him from obtaining a satisfactory position, and he joined the private band of the ex-King Charles IV of Spain, who was then living at Marseilles: but when the latter went to Rome in 1812, Duport returned to Paris, and then began his most successful period. He appeared at several concerts, which turned to absolute triumphs for Duport, and secured him the appointments as solo violoncellist to the Emperor, member of the chamber music of Marie Louise, and professor of the conservatoire. In 1815 the conservatoire was dissolved, and Duport's name was not included in the list of professors of the new "Ecole Royale de Musique" on its reconstruction in 1816. Between 1812 and 1815 he composed his nocturnes for violoncello and harp, which he played with the celebrated harpist, Bochsa.

In his capacity as solo violoncellist to the imperial court, Duport was frequently heard at the private concerts at the Tuilleries. One evening when he was playing at a "Réunion intime" Napoleon entered quite unexpectedly in riding boots and spurs. He listened attentively and with evident signs of pleasure. No sooner had Duport finished than the Emperor walked up to him, and taking the instrument from his hands, in his vivacious and direct manner, he asked him "how the —— do you hold that thing Mr. Duport?" and sitting down on a chair he tried to hold the violoncello between his spurred boots. Poor Duport when he saw his magnificent Strad treated like a charger, was for a moment struck dumb with terror, and then advancing towards the Emperor he called out "Sire!" in such a pitiful tone that the Emperor handed him back his bass with a smile, and left him to demonstrate his art without trying again to interfere with his instrument.

That instrument was the famous Strad which descended to Franchomme, who bought it for 25,000 francs, and then to J Servais, who left it to his son Joseph, whose widow sold it for 100,000 francs. A beautiful illustration of this instrument appears in Messrs. Hill's book on "Antonio Stradivari."

Duport's compositions consist of Easy Variations in D, Op. 1 to 4, consisting of six sonatas each, with bass, of which one in C has been republished with a piano accompaniment by Carl Schroeder (Leipzig, Kistner), three duets, eight "airs variés," three duos for harp and violoncello, in conjunction with NADERMANN (the famous harpist), and nine nocturnes with BOCHSA, Fantasia in D with RIGEL, with variations on the rondeau, "Petit Oiseaux." He wrote a number of concertos, the third of which in E minor has been republished by Grützmacher in his "Hohe Schule des Violoncell Spiels (Breitkopf and Härtel). The sixth concerto, originally published by Janet and Cotelle, has been republished by Richault. These concertos are distinct children of their time, and are only of historical interest, and for the purpose of study. Of far more importance is his essay on fingering, which, although antiquated in many ways, contains some of the most excellent studies that have ever been written for the violoncello, especially the twenty-one exercises at the end of the book, which have appeared separately in various editions, the latest being that by Johannes Klingenberg (Litolff). There is also a posthumous duo concertant for piano and violoncello, and three nocturnes published by Richault.

PLATE XXVIII.
J. L. Duport.

To face page 280.

Jean Louis Duport's personality was simple, yet dignified, modest and generous. Towards his friends he was frank and jovial. As he had seen and observed a great deal, and had an eloquent way of expressing his thoughts, his conversation was most fascinating. Plate XXVIII. gives Duport with his instrument, and is from a print in the possession of Messrs. W. E. Hill and Sons.

The following is an instance of his disinterested generosity. His friend Guerin, the violinist, died in poverty, leaving an infant daughter, whom Duport looked upon as his friend's legacy. When he went to Germany, he took the child with him, gave her a good education, and fostered her musical talents. She married a gentleman in a good position, and received a handsome dowry from her foster father.

Duport did not lose his tone or his technique to the very last, and when complimented upon the fact, he would say: "All technical skill is acquired and retained by dint of work. As for the sureness of intonation, I have to thank Nature alone for it." Then with a certain pride, he used to take up a glass filled with water to the brim, and placing it on the palm of his outstretched hand, he would carry it round the room without spilling one single drop. He was then in his seventieth year. He retained his position at court, when it changed from an Imperial to a Royal house, and died on September 6 (Wasielewski gives September 7) 1819, from a liver complaint, at his residence, Rue des Deux-Boules, No. 7, in Paris.

One of Duport's greatest merits was that he established a sound system of fingering, and Baudiot says that it was he who invented the fingering of the chromatic scale. He is very explicit about the double stopping, which had never been extensively treated, and which (he says) cannot be executed without a clear system of fingering. He says in the preface to this work: "Much will be found that is difficult, but nothing that is impossible to execute, as I have tried everything repeatedly myself, and had it tried by my brother, *who ever was and will be my master*, and also by my best pupils at Berlin and Potsdam."

An excellent English edition by John Bishop was published by Robert Cocks and Co., now Augener Limited. A new German edition of the whole work was revised by Lindner, who unfortunately did not adhere strictly to the original text.

Duport left one son, who for several years was violoncellist at Lyons, but afterwards opened a pianoforte manufactory at Paris.

CHARLES ANTOINE CHRESTIEN, or CHRÉTIEN, was evidently a violoncellist of note, for the "Siècle de Louis XV" (1753, page 152) has the following: "I am told that young Chrétien, violoncellist in ordinary of the king's music performs the most astounding feats on the violoncello, and that he knows no difficulties whatever on his instrument. In a word he is said to be a prodigy."

He composed several "divertissements" and an opera comique, "Precautions inutiles."

GILLES LOUIS CHRETIEN, born 1754, at Versailles, died March 4, 1811, in Paris, he was in all probability a son of the former. It is said of him that he played the most difficult violin sonatas on the violoncello with the greatest facility. His tone was very fine, but he was wanting in expression. At the age of twenty he was appointed a member of the royal chapel, and in 1780 he became a member of the orchestra of the Concerts Spirituel. The Revolution deprived him of the former appointment, but in 1807 he was appointed to the imperial chapel. He composed trios and divertimentos, and wrote some articles on various musical subjects. Four sonatas for violoncello with bass by Chrétien, are preserved in the Imperial Private Library at Berlin. They are in all probability by Gilles Louis. He did not devote himself solely to music, but had a considerable reputation as a clever portrait painter.

HAILLOT was violoncellist at the "Comédie Italiénne." He appears to have been a well-known teacher of his instrument, for which he wrote a number of duets on operatic airs for the use of amateurs, a divertimento and trios. His Op. 1, six duos on comic operas appeared in 1780.

In the same year NICOLAS JUTIEN appears as a violoncellist of the Italian opera in Paris. He also wrote "Ariettas" for two violoncellos.

PRARELLI published "solos" for violoncello in 1748, but apparently he was not of much importance.

LE PIN published in Paris six sonatas for violoncello, Op. 1, dedicated to the Marquise de Lestang. Op. 2, six sonatas, for the study of the higher positions. About this the "Mercure de France" (April, 1772, Volume II, page 176) says: "The author has indicated all the positions beyond the neck in an introductory chapter. He describes himself on the title pages as 'amateur.'"

DOMINIQUE BIDEAU or Bidaux, was of more importance than the foregoing. He was a pupil of Tricklir. The dates of his birth and death are unknown, but he was a member of the orchestra of the Théâtre Italien during the latter part of the last century. Schilling describes him as a virtuoso on the violin and the violoncello. Fétis states that he was violoncellist at the Dresden opera in 1809, when he dedicated his "Airs variés et dialogués" to the Elector of Saxony. Six duos for violin and violoncello of his composition appeared as Op. 1 and 2 in 1796 in Paris, and also "Trois grand divertissements concertants" for the same instruments, two easy duets for two violoncellos. His most important work is, perhaps, his "grande et nouvelle méthode raisonnée pour' le violoncelle composé par Dominique Bidaux." Paris, 1802 (Nadermann). Wasielewski mentions also among his compositions an "Air écossais varié avec quatuor," but Richault's catalogue contains a "Thème écossais avec quatuor" as Op. 2, by E. A. BIDEAU, which makes it appear that the above was by another violoncellist of that name, perhaps a son.

F. CARDON was violoncellist at the grand opera in Paris about the middle of last century. His nephew:

PIÈRRE CARDON, born 1751, became his pupil on that instrument, while Richer trained him in the art of singing. Down to 1788 he was violoncellist at the opera, but afterwards he appeared as a singer in the royal chapel in Paris and Versailles, giving violoncello lessons at the same time. In 1800 he appears again as violoncellist at the Opera Comique. He wrote a book on the elements of music, and was still alive in 1811.

PIERRE FRANCOIS LEVASSEUR, born March 11, 1753, at Abbeville, was destined for the church but his inclination for the violoncello predominated, and at the age of eighteen he decided to devote himself entirely to the study of his favourite instrument. His first master was Belleval, whom he left after the first three months trying to improve himself empirically. In 1782 he went to Paris and took some lessons from Louis Duport.

He succeeded in acquiring his master's tone and style, and proved himself worthy of the latter when he made his debut at the Concert Spirituel, playing compositions by Duport. He appeared also at the Théâtre Feydeau, and was violoncellist at the opera from 1785 until 1815 when he retired. He died in 1816. He published two books of six duets each for two violoncellos.

ESPRIT AIMON, born 1754, at Lisle (Vaucluse), was an excellent violoncellist, and for some time leader of the private band of Count Rantzau, the Danish Minister. He lived for some time at Marseilles and died in Paris in 1828. His son, PAMPHILE LEOPOLD FRANCOIS AIMON, born in 1779, was a clever composer, who wrote a concertino for violoncello, published by C. Pacini in Paris, and "recreations" for two violoncellos, horn and piano. His compositions are said to show originality.

LOUIS CHARLES JOSEPH REY, born at Lauzerte (Farnet-Garonne), October 26, 1738, brother of the opera composer and conductor of the Paris opera, Jean Baptiste Rey, received his first musical training at the abbey of St. Sernin, and joined the orchestra of the opera at Montpellier at the age of sixteen as violoncellist. In 1755 he went to Paris where he studied for two years under Berteau, and on completion of his studies went to Bordeaux as violoncellist at the theatre of that town. In 1766 he returned to Paris and received in the following year an appointment in the orchestra of the Grand Opera in Paris, where he remained for forty years, when he retired. In 1772 Rey became also a member of the Royal Chapel, and held that post until its dissolution in 1792. He committed suicide by cutting his throat during a fever, on May 12, 1811. For his instrument he wrote two books of duets (Paris, Bailleux), sonatas for violoncello and bass, which are not without merit, a minuet with variations from the sixth sonata of Op. 1, may even now be recommended to the attention of amateurs.

CLAUDE DOMERGUE, born at Beaucaire in 1734, is mentioned by Wasielewski as an original who never left his native place. His importance as a violoncellist is illustrated by the fact that on a tour through the south of France, Duport stopped at Beaucaire for the sole purpose of making the acquaintance of Domergue. He was elected president of his district in 1790, but fell a victim of the Revolution, and was beheaded with thirty of his townsfolk at Nîmes in 1794.

PIERRE-HYACINTHE AZAÏS was born 1743 at Ladern (Languedoc), died at Toulouse in 1796. He published twelve sonatas, one duo and lessons for the violoncello through Bignon, in Paris. He was chiefly known as a church musician.

JEAN BAPTIST ROCHEFORT, born June 24, 1746, distinguished himself as a composer of operas. He began his career as a double-bass player at the opera in 1775. "The Musical Magazine" states that, at the court of the Thuilleries [*sic!*] he used frequently to play the violoncello in symphony performances.

About 1780 he became conductor of the French opera at the court of Cassels, but returned to Paris as deputy conductor at the opera. He was pensioned in 1815, and died about 1819.

FRANCOIS JOSEPH GIRAUD, violoncellist and composer. He was a member of the orchestra at the opera 1752-67. Giraud was also a musician of the royal chapel and the king's chamber music, and wrote, besides operas and motets (successfully performed at the "Concert Spirituel") a book of sonatas for the violoncello. He died about 1790, in Paris.

FREDERIC ROUSSEAU, born January 11, 1755, at Versailles, studied the violoncello under Jean Louis Duport. He was a member of the orchestra at the Paris opera from 1787 until 1812, when he retired from that position and founded a school of music at Versailles. He was one of the founders of the concerts in the "rue de Clery," which became a well-known institution. At his suggestion a number of well-known artists clubbed together for the first performance of Haydn's "Creation" in Paris, and they had a special medal struck, which they presented to the composer. He was also a successful singing master, and produced several pupils who rose into eminence. His compositions for the violoncello consist of six duos concertants (Op. 3 and 4) and a potpourri for two violoncellos (Paris, Nadermann).

JEAN PIERRE SOLIÉ, born 1755, at Nîmes, was the son of a violoncellist who was engaged at the theatre of that town. He started his career as a choirboy at the cathedral. He studied the violoncello under his father, and was engaged as violoncellist in various theatre orchestras in the south of France, giving at the same time singing lessons. Eventually he became an opera singer, and from his twenty-fourth year also a composer of very successful one and two-act operas. He died August 6, 1812.

JEAN BAPTISTE REY, born 1760, at Tarrascon, received his first musical education from the master of the Chapel Royal of that city. He was a performer on the violoncello, the violin and the piano, on the two latter instruments he was autodidact. Eventually he became organist and musical director at the cathedrals of Viviers and Uzer. In 1795 he settled in Paris as a teacher of music. Napoleon appointed him as director of his private chapel and violoncellist of the Imperial Academy, later on called the Grand Opera. That post he filled to the time of his death in 1822. The Paris Conservatoire library possesses twelve violoncello sonatas, Op. 4, which appear in the catalogue under the name of Jean Rey.

It is interesting to note that the name of the opera composer Reyer was in reality also Rey!

CHARLES HENRY PLANTADE, born at Pontoise, October 19, 1764, studied the violoncello under Duport (probably the elder). He showed, however, remarkable talent as a vocal composer, and his song, "Ta bien aimer, O! ma chère Celine," met with such phenomenal success that it procured him the appointment as singing master of Hortense Beauharnais and professor of singing at the Paris Conservatoire, and conductor at the opera. When Hortense married the King of Holland, he followed her court to Amsterdam in 1808 as director of the royal orchestra, and lived still in Amsterdam in 1840. He appeared as violoncello virtuoso in Paris, in 1790.

JEAN MARIE RAOUL, born in Paris, 1766, by profession a lawyer (avocat á la cour de cassation), was a distinguished violoncellist who wrote a tutor (Op. 4), "Méthode de violoncelle, contenant une nouvelle exposition des principles de cet instrument, à ceux de l'étude de la double corde." He composed also three sonatas (Paris, Pleyel) and airs variés for his instrument. Interesting were his endeavours to reinstate the viol da gamba, which he played himself. He was in possession of the famous gamba, by Duiffoprugcar, made in 1521 for Francis I. The back of the instrument showed a bird's eye view of Paris, inlaid in coloured wood. After his death, the instrument passed into the hands of Vuillaume, and forms now one of the greatest treasures of the famous museum of the Brussels Conservatoire. Dr. Henry Coutagne, whose friends heard the instrument played by Raoul, describes its sound as one of penetrating sweetness (une douceur penetrante de ces sons). Raoul conceived the idea of having a gamba made which should come nearer the violoncello in proportion, and Vuillaume made one on a new model in 1827, exhibited in the same year as the "Heptachord" (see notice by R. in the "Revue Musicale," Volume II, page 56, also "Annales de la litterature et des arts," 335^e livre, tome 28). The popular verdict was, however, not in favour of this revival of the gamba, which had not been heard of again until quite recently, when several musicians have shown a renewed interest in historic instruments. Raoul died 1837, in Paris.

CHAPTER XVI.

TRANSITION TO THE MODERN FRENCH SCHOOL.

PIERRE FRANÇOIS OLIVIER AUBERT, born at Amiens in 1763, was autodidact (self-taught) on the violoncello. He received his general musical education at the "Maîtrise" (apparently a school of the guilds) of his native town. He was evidently successful in his study of the violoncello, as he received an engagement as violoncellist at the Opera Comique in Paris, which he held for twenty-five years. On the title pages of his later works he calls himself professor at the Paris Conservatoire. He published a "Méthode de Violoncelle," Op. 11, at Amiens; German translation published by Simrock in 1837, which Fétis describes as the first good instruction book after the elementary work of Cupis and Tillière. He published also seven books of duets, Op. 2, 3, 6, 7, 12, 13, 30. Op. 13 is called "La Marchande d'Artichaux"; etudes, Op. 8, nouvelles etudes, a history of music and various other compositions.

AUBERTI, whose real name was also Aubert, though not related to the former, was violoncellist at the Comédie Italienne. He died in 1805, according to Wasielewski. He published six sonatas, Op. 1, and six duets for two violoncellos.

JEAN HENRY LEVASSEUR, born 1765, in Paris, was the son of the inspector general and vocal instructor at the Paris Opera. He was not related to Jean Pierre Levasseur, mentioned before. He received his instruction on the violoncello from Cupis, and afterwards studied some time under Jean Louis Duport. In 1789 he was appointed principal violoncello at the Grand Opera, which position he filled until 1823—the year of his death. He was a member of the imperial private music, and continued in the royal private music after 1814. He was one of the chief contributors to the "Méthode de Violoncelle et de Basse d'Accompagnement," by Baillot, Levasseur, Catel and Baudiot. This was the official instruction book of the Imperial Conservatoire of Music which appeared also in a German translation published by C. F. Peters at Leipzig. It is curious to read some of the remarks contained in this book, as they show that the violoncello was by no means a familiar instrument, and still in an early state of development at the beginning of this century. In the introduction we find a statement to the following effect: "The bass is to be considered in a double sense. As solo instrument it is called violoncello, and as an accompanying instrument it is commonly called bass." Then there follows a long chapter on the character of the violoncello, a chapter thoroughly characteristic of the sentimental age which gave birth to the creations of Matthison, Salis, and above all, "the sufferings of Werther." In this chapter the authors set forth the superior qualities of the violoncello, describing it as "an instrument of an essentially religious character, which, though the emotional character supervenes, is one of the purest, and free from all taint of sensuality [Berlioz and Wagner would hardly have subscribed to this opinion]—but lifting the soul to higher and purer regions." After a warning of the dangers to which a great facility for technique may lead, the authors recommend the study of the works of Haydn, whose compositions are described as the first purely instrumental music of importance. The study of the works of Gluck, Mozart and Boccherini is also strongly advocated, especially the quintets of the last-named, are praised as a new departure in chamber music. The adagios in these latter works are compared to pictures by Albano and poems by Gessner. "When changing his style," it says, in this description, "he suddenly shows a dark and sombre countenance. He goes straight to the heart by means so subtle that the tears will drop without your becoming aware of it; he afflicts in order to touch the heart. He seems to take the soul's own self away in order to reconcile it with itself, to appease the tumult of passions, resolve it into a delicious calm, and transport it into a better world to taste the pleasures of the golden age." There is, perhaps, more sentimental reflection than is required for a technical instruction book, yet a little less of the technical and practical sense of our day, and a little more of the poetical reflection of our forefathers would be of immense advantage to some of our present-day artists. The elementary advice as to the holding of the instrument and the bow essentially conforms with that given in modern instruction books, except that the use of a tail-pin was unknown, and the position of the right foot which is bent sideways inward from the ankle. As to the bowing itself, the views differed widely from those that are now generally adopted. The use of the point of the bow for detached notes is condemned altogether on the score of not being strong enough to make the thick violoncello strings vibrate, and as giving a hard and dry tone. The numerous exercises which follow are useful, but the work altogether is very elementary. Of Levasseur's own compositions, only a book of sonatas, two books of duets and one book of exercises were published. His most prominent pupils were Lamarre, Baudiot and Norblin.

JACQUES MICHEL HUREL DE LAMARRE (some give his name

as Lamare, some as La Marre, but Videl gives it as above) was born in Paris, May 1, 1772, as the son of poor parents. At the age of seven he entered the Institute of the Pages of the Royal Music, where he received his first musical training, and in his fifteenth year he commenced the study of the violoncello under Jean Louis Duport. The harbingers of the French Revolution caused him to return from that Royal Pages' Institute to his parental home, and in 1794 he was appointed violoncellist at the Théâtre Feydeau, where he remained until 1801, appearing frequently as soloist at the concerts given at that institute. His fame as a virtuoso soon spread all over Europe. He became a professor at the Imperial Conservatoire, but in 1801 he left Paris for Berlin, where he gained the admiration and friendship of Prince Louis Ferdinand, with whom he played a great deal, and who presented him with his own ring as a keepsake in return for Lamarre's. Rode was then at the height of his fame, and Lamarre practised his concertos on the violoncello, and as Duport was likened to Viotti, so was the former likened to Rode. In a letter, dated April 3, 1802, Ignace Pleyel writes to Muzio Clementi, who was then in London: "I have three superb concertos for violoncello by Lamar, who is a young *Rode* on the bass." Those three concertos were not composed by Lamarre, although four concertos, and an air varié were published under his name. These compositions were entirely the work of the great AUBER, who was an intimate friend of Lamarre, and as a young beginner, was anxious to make his compositions known by the help of a well-established name. Lamarre, who possessed no creative talent, never made a secret of the fact. The best of these concertos is the one in A minor. After his departure from Berlin, Lamarre visited Russia, residing alternately in St. Petersburg and Moscow, appearing at the court as well as in public concerts of his own. In 1808 he left Russia, returning, through Poland and Austria to France, where he arrived in

April, 1809. Soon after his arrival he appeared at a concert at the Odéon, which is discussed in the "Allgemeine Musikalische Zeitung" of that year (page 605). He did not meet with the same success that was wont to greet him on former occasions, and this circumstance caused him to retire from the concert platform. He continued, however, to play in private circles where he was greatly admired. Fétis, who had frequent occasion to hear him play, says: "He had a most wonderful execution, but his main strength lay in the rendering of chamber music. He entered more deeply into the spirit of works of that class than any other violoncellist I have ever heard, and he succeeded better than any of them to bring out all the beauties of such compositions." In 1815 he married a lady of fortune, and after that cultivated his art only for his private amusement. The loss of two children grieved him so intensely that it undermined his health, and he succumbed to a disease of the larynx on March 27, 1823. Schilling, in "Das Musikalische Europa," mentions JEAN FRANÇOIS LA MARRE as a violoncellist already advanced in years (in 1841), who was celebrated as a virtuoso during the first two decades of the nineteenth century, but who, since 1818, had distinguished himself principally as a composer of numerous minor and more important works for the violoncello. He states also that he was engaged at the Grand Opera. The author has not yet been able to ascertain whether this was perhaps a relative of Jacques Michel H. Lamarre, or whether Schilling, who is frequently at fault, confounds him altogether with the former.

LOUIS AUGUSTE JOSEPH JANSON, born July 8, 1749, at Valenciennes, received his first lessons from his father, and afterwards continued to study the violoncello under his elder brother, Jean Baptiste A. Janson, whom he eventually equalled in technique, but not in tone or delivery. In 1783 he went to Paris, and was appointed to the orchestra of the Grand Opera in 1789, which position he retained until 1815, when he retired.

He died a few years later. His published compositions for the violoncello consist of six sonatas with bass. He wrote also some string trios.

PIERRE LOUIS HUS-DESFORGES was born at Toulon on March 14, 1773. His mother, an actress, was the daughter of the celebrated violin virtuoso, Jarnovick. He began his musical career as a choirboy at the cathedral of La Rochelle when he was eight years old. There he employed his leisure hours in practising the violoncello and the trumpet, and joined the fourteenth regiment of the *chasseurs à cheval* as trumpeter in 1792. Following his regiment through the various campaigns of the revolutionary army he lost a finger of his right hand through a bullet, and was invalided home. He then took up the violoncello as principal instrument, and succeeded in obtaining an appointment in the theatre orchestra at Lyons.

This position he relinquished after six months, and went to Paris, where he was admitted as pupil of the elder Janson at the conservatoire. At the same time he held an engagement as violoncellist at the Théâtre des Troubadours. On the completion of his studies the Bohemian blood of his grandfather asserted itself, and he began a restless wandering life. In 1800 he went to St. Petersburg as conductor of a French opera company, returning to France after ten years' absence. The next seven years he was touring as solo violoncellist, and in 1817, he was appointed in that capacity to the Théâtre Porte Saint Martin. In 1820 he went to Metz, where he founded a conservatoire, but after a comparatively short time we find him touring again as virtuoso. In 1828 he received the post of conductor at the Théâtre du Gymnase, but after twelve months he resigned again, and the same thing happened when in 1831 he was appointed conductor of the Théâtre du Palais Royal, and finished his eventful career as teacher of a small school of music at Pont le Voy near Blois, where he died January 20, 1838 (Eitner gives 1836). Although a clever artist he cannot be counted among the *great* violoncellists of his day. His tone was small, and the failing so common to many of his compatriots—want of emotional power, and even of brilliancy—characterised his playing. His compositions, though once very popular, are almost entirely forgotten. For violoncello he wrote: one symphony concertante for violin, violoncello and orchestra, four concertos, four books of duets for two violoncellos, nine sets of variations called "soirées musicales," two books of sonatas with bass, and a tutor published by Lanner in Paris. He published also a number of chamber works.

CHARLES JOSEPH DUMONCHEAU lived at Strassburg as violoncellist and became the teacher of his son:

CHARLES FRANCOIS DUMONCHEAU, born April 11, 1775, who afterwards gave up the violoncello for the piano, on which he became a great virtuoso. He was also a good composer. He died between December 31 to January 1, 1820-1, at Lyons.

SILVAIN DUMONCHEAU, son of Charles François, was a virtuoso on the violoncello and a good pianist, about 1842 in Strassburg, where he remained for the greater part of his life. He married the excellent harpist, Antoinette Sophie Malade, born 1789 in Paris, who died in 1833. Silvain Dumoncheau wrote several compositions for the violoncello.

JEAN BAPTISTE BRÉVAL, born in 1756 in the "Department de l'Aisne," showed early signs of an exceptional talent for the violoncello, which he studied under the supervision of the famous Cupis. On the completion of his studies he made his debut at the Concerts Spirituel with brilliant success, playing his own concertos. He joined the orchestra of the Paris Opera in 1781 (Schilling says 1786 (?) but as he also talks about him as a *violinist*, one can hardly take him seriously!) He held this position for twenty-five years, retiring from it in 1806 with a pension. In 1796 (Wasielewski gives 1781!) he was appointed professor of the second violoncello class at the conservatoire, but was pensioned on its reconstruction in 1802, as the number of pupils was insufficient to justify his reappointment.

After 1806 he lived for a few years alternately in Versailles and Paris, but eventually he retired to the village of Chamouille, near Laon, where he died towards the end of 1825.

FIG. 43. BREVAL.

Bréval was a prolific composer for his instrument. He wrote seven concertos (some say there were ten!) which belong to the best he has written. One of these in F major, Op. 20, has been republished by Carl Schroeder in his concert studies. It shows the influence of Haydn, but is not very interesting. For a list of his numerous trios, duets, solos and sonatas, see R. Eitner's "Quellenlexikon." A symphonie concertante for violin and violoncello was performed in 1787 by the brothers Guérin (who were then respectively eleven and ten years of age) with immense success at one of their concerts in Paris. One of his solos, or rather sonatas, has been republished with pianoforte accompaniment by Alfred Moffat, and makes an effective work for concert purposes.

Bréval's compositions enjoyed great popularity in their time, but they have since been almost forgotten on account of their conventionality. He wrote also a tutor: "Méthode raisonnée de Violoncelle," published in Paris in 1804. The following remarks appear at the end of the English edition of that work, under the heading, "Dictionary of Italian and other Words used in Music." "Graund (ground) a piece of music in which the original bass is continually repeated, sometimes with some variations." It is curious to see that the ancient, and very popular form of variations or divisions upon a ground was still in existence at that time. In fact Paganini's "Carnaval de Venise" variations are nothing else. During the sixteenth and early seventeenth century the "divisions upon a ground" formed a most important feature in instrumental music. "Farinelli's ground" supplied Corelli with the subject for the "Folies d'Espagne," one of his finest works, and the celebrated French opera composer and gambist, Marin Marais, wrote a set of variations on the same subject, as did a good many more of the seventeenth and early eighteenth century composers.

"Sellenger's ground" and "John come kiss me now" were the favourite *English* "grounds for divisions" during that period.

·A sonata is described in the above dictionary as "a kind of lesson or overture for the pianoforte with or without a few accompaniments."

"Tasto solo implies that the bass is to be played without

any thoroughbass" (i.e., without the addition of any notes or chords).

Violoncello is translated as the bass viol! The latter was really the name for the viol da gamba, but as this instrument was practically extinct (although it had one famous exponent left in Carl Friedrich Abel), the name seems to have been transferred to the violoncello.

Bréval was also the composer of an opera, "Ines et Léonore ou La Soeur jalouse," which was produced in 1788 (?). His technique on the violoncello is described as *perfect*, but he lacked vigour and emotion, which was a fault apparently not uncommon among French violoncellists. Fig. 43 is from a print of Bréval in the possession of Mr. F. H. Brown.

CHARLES NICOLAS BAUDIOT, born March 29, 1773, at Nancy, died in Paris, September 26, 1849. He was a pupil of the elder Janson, whom he succeeded as professor at the conservatoire in 1802. On the reconstruction of the conservatoire in 1816 he retained his appointment, to which was added that of first violoncellist in the Royal Chapel, remaining in that position until 1822, when he retired on a pension, but continued to play in public as a soloist. Soon after his appointment at the conservatoire he collaborated with Baillot, Levasseur and Catel in compiling the official instruction book for the violoncello for the Paris Conservatoire. The book has been previously discussed in the biographical notice of Levasseur. Baudiot was a born teacher. As a soloist he was uninteresting in spite of a well-developed technique and perfect intonation. He was afflicted with the failing common to many of his countrymen, viz., lack of power and emotion. The musical *nerve* was defective, and it is perhaps characteristic that during his musical career he found it possible to fulfil the duties imposed upon him as an official in the Ministry of Finance, which post he held for many years. A scurrilous incident, of which Fétis was an eyewitness, happened at one of his public appearances in 1807. In the latter year he appeared in a concert of Madame Catalani. He entered the concert room just in time for his appearance, and started a fantasia on an andante from one of Haydn's symphonies, not knowing that the whole of that symphony had just that moment been played by the orchestra. The audience, thinking that he was playing a joke, showed evident signs of amusement. Baudiot, who could not account for the reason of their merriment, grew very nervous, and played so badly that his marked embarrassment drew forth volleys of laughter from a public which was already inclined to be amused. This brought poor Baudiot's nervousness to such a crisis that he had to be led from the platform in a fainting condition.

Baudiot wrote a great number of compositions for his instrument, which for the greater part are entirely obsolete. They consisted of two concertos, two concertinos, duets, potpourris, fantasias, nocturnes, sonatas with bass, transcriptions of violin pieces by De Beriot and Lafont, a duo for violoncello and piano in F minor, Op. 10, a theme varié in A which he wrote, together with Pleyel; a number of studies, of which Schroeder has published twenty-three in two volumes (Leipzig, Kistner), and a tutor, Op. 25 (Paris, Philipp and Co.; Bonn, Simrock and Co.). In this work he received the assistance of his quondam pupil, and afterwards colleague, Louis Pierre Norblin. The work is dedicated to Cherubini, director of the conservatoire, and Baudiot is described on the title page as professor at that institute, and first violoncello (principal) of the king's private music. In the preface he says: "It is generally recognised that in science, literature and art, as well as in our social life the *first* education requires the greatest care, its neglect leaves traces which sometimes prove indelible!"

Unfortunately this very true fact is *not generally recognised* nowadays.

In the case of beginners in the study of music people generally consider terms more than the qualification of the teacher. The results are deplorable and very discouraging to the pupil, who in most cases only finds out the mischief when he is placed under a good teacher who will point out to him the bad habits contracted under his incapable predecessor. Curious are Baudiot's instructions for holding the bow, which he does in a similar way to that of the violinists, by placing all the fingers on the bow stick *in front* of the nut. He does not make use of a tail pin in holding his instrument.

The tutor contains many excellent explanations and good advice, especially with regard to overwork as injurious to the technique, and how to overcome nervousness in playing before an audience. The book is well arranged, but not very complete, like most tutors of that time, which are more for beginners than for more advanced pupils. Besides Norblin, Baudiot formed an excellent violoncellist in Scipion Rousselot, of whom we shall speak later on.

NICOLAS JOSEPH PLATEL was born at Versailles in 1777, and died at Brussels, August 25, 1835. His father, originally a musician in the French Chapel Royal, took to the stage, and after appearing as an actor for some time, he obtained an engagement as choirmaster at the Théâtre Feydeau. He succeeded in placing his son in the Institute of the Royal Pages, which was similar to that of His Majesty's Chapel Royal. There he received singing lessons by Richer. At the age of ten, however, he began to show a marked predilection for the violoncello, and his father, who was a friend of Louis Duport, entrusted him to the tuition of that famous master. Duport soon recognised the boy's talent, and spared no pains to impart to him that beauty of tone for which he and his pupils were celebrated. For about two years he continued his studies under Duport, when the latter went to Berlin in 1789, and Platel continued to study on the basis of his master's instructions. His remarkable talent, and the energy with which he pursued his studies attracted the sympathetic attention of Lamarre, who was also a pupil of Duport, and whose fame as a virtuoso was spreading fast.

In 1793 Lamarre began to supervise Platel's studies, and in 1796 the latter was appointed at the Théâtre Lyrique (afterwards Théâtre Feydeau). There he fell deeply in love with an actress, and followed her to Lyons in 1797, remaining there for two years.

In 1801 he returned to Paris and appeared with great success at the concerts in the "Rue de Cléry" and others. He held at that time the first position among French violoncellists, Duport being in Berlin and Lamarre in Russia. His Bohemian temperament did not, however, allow him to make the best of his successes and to secure a fixed position. April 1, 1803, he gave a concert at Brussels, and thence he went to England. The year 1805 found him again touring in the Bretagne. At Quimper he fell in with an amateur violoncellist who induced him to stay, and he remained for two years in that quaint little country town.

At the end of that time he played with great success at Brest and Nantes, and thence he went to Belgium with the intention to pursue his journey through Holland to Germany. The town of Ghent seems to have taken his fancy, and he stayed there for several years as teacher of singing and of the violoncello. In 1813 he went to Antwerp, and finding a very good opera company in that interesting and flourishing town, he accepted an engagement as principal violoncello in their orchestra, and stayed there for six years. In 1819 he went to Brussels where he obtained the same position at the Royal Opera. In 1826 the Prince de Chimay secured his services as teacher of the violoncello for the newly-founded Royal School of Music at a salary of five hundred francs per annum! When that institution was reorganised in 1831 as the "Conservatoire de Musique," his appointment as professor at that institute was confirmed. During that period he became the founder of the famous Belgian school of violoncellists which was continued in the first instance by his pupils, Servais, Batta and De Munck. The last-named was appointed as his successor on his decease in 1835.

The excellent qualities of Platel's character were as marked as his Bohemianism. Intrigue and jealousy, unfortunately rampant among artists, were entirely foreign to his nature, and he was ever ready to help those who stood in need of help. In money matters he was as ignorant as a new-born baby. While he was living in Antwerp the brokers came in one day to seize his furniture. While they were looking round he took up his violoncello and walked away without ever troubling himself about the rest of his belongings. At another period some money was left to him by a relative which he received in specie. He had never seen so much gold together, so he put it up in an old silk hose and carried it about with him. His friends advised him to invest it so that it might bring him interest, but he was afraid of failures, and thought it safer in his own keeping. This blissful state was of very short duration, as he began to lend money right and left without troubling himself about the repayment. The loss of his money never disturbed his equanimity, and he went on in the same happy-go-lucky style until death overtook him in his fifty-eighth year. He wrote five violoncello concertos, the first in E minor, Op. 3, was published by Janet and Cotelle in Paris; the second in G, by Imbault; the fifth was entitled "le quart d'heure." Three books of sonatas with bass, variations, caprices or preludes, six romances with pianoforte, six duets for violin and violoncello, and three trios for violin, viola and violoncello.

EMMANUEL GUÉRIN, called Guérin *aîné*, was born at Versailles in 1779. He entered the Paris Conservatoire in 1796 as pupil of Levasseur, and received three years later the first prize for violoncello playing. The "Histoire du Conservatoire," by Lassabathie, contains the following notice: "An VI (1799) Prix de violoncelle au citoyen Guérin." His younger brother studied the violin under Kreutzer. According to the "Journal de Paris," of April 12, 1787, the two brothers when respectively eleven and ten years of age, appeared in public, playing a symphony concertante by Bréval for violin and violoncello. The journal says that "their astounding talent created quite a sensation and would have earned the same applause for grown-up artists." Emmanuel Guérin was engaged as violoncellist at the Théâtre Feydeau in 1799, and was pensioned as member of the Opéra-Comique in 1824. He wrote sonatas, variations and duets for his instrument.

BERNARD BÉNAZET, born at Toulouse in 1871, was the son of a distinguished architect. He was a pupil of Bernhard Romberg at the Paris Conservatoire, and carried off the first prize for the violoncello August 22, 1804 (fourth fructidor year XII). He was solo violoncellist at the Théâtre Italien for a considerable number of years. Great virtuoso and excellent teacher he held a prominent position among the best artists of his time. He died in Paris, September 16, 1846. His daughter became a famous singer as Madame Ganeaux-Sabatier.

HENRY AGUS, born 1749, resided for some time in England, where two books of solos for violoncello were published as Op. 1 and Op. 2. He went to Paris and became professor of singing at the conservatoire. He died in 1798. Fétis speaks of him as a mediocre musician.

EUDE AGUS, a virtuoso on the violin and violoncello, was a popular artist during the latter part of the eighteenth century, and published duos and trios for various instruments in London and Paris, where he lived between 1782-6. About 1800 he was professor at the Paris Conservatoire and died in 1845.

LOUIS PIÈRRE MARTIN NORBLIN de la Gourdaine was the son of a celebrated painter and one of the finest engravers of the century, who was greatly admired and patronised by the art-loving Prince Radziwill. His brother also takes a high rank among nineteenth century painters. Louis Pièrre was born December 2, 1781, at Warsaw, where

FIG. 44. NORBLIN. FROM THE ETCHING BY HILLEMACHER.

his father had settled in 1772 and married a Polish lady. In 1798 Louis Norblin went to Paris, where he entered the conservatoire and studied the violoncello successively under Baudiot and Levasseur. In 1803 (the year XI of the French Republic) he received the first prize as solo violoncellist. In 1809 he received an appointment at the Théâtre Italien, and

PLATE XXIX.
BARTHOLOMEW JOHNSON.

two years later, in 1811, he became solo violoncellist at the Grand Opera, which position he held until 1841. On January 1, 1823, he succeeded his late master, Levasseur, as professor of the conservatoire, and he held this position until June 5, 1846, when he retired into privacy. The date of his appointment at the conservatoire is given by Hugo Riemann and by Wasielewski as January 1, 1826, but as Levasseur died in 1823 and as Norblin was his successor, Antoine Vidal is undoubtedly correct in giving 1823 as the year of Norblin's appointment at that institution. Fig. 44 is a reproduction of the etching of Norblin by Hillemacher.

Norblin was an excellent soloist as well as quartet player, in which capacity he was for many years connected with the Baillot quartet. He played also together with Habeneck, founder of the famous conservatoire concerts, celebrated for the perfection of their performances of classical works, which opened in 1828. He was not only a great violoncellist, but a gentleman of great accomplishments, whose collection of paintings, drawings, prints and coins was one of the finest in Paris. His son, Emile, also violoncellist, will be mentioned later on.

VASLIN, born 1794, professor at the Paris Conservatoire, about whose private life little or nothing is known, was the teacher of a great many of the most prominent violoncellists of our present day. On June 1, 1884, he published his "L'art du violoncelle." Advice to young violoncellists on the art of bowing (conseils aux jeunes violoncellistes sur la conduite de l'archet), Paris, Richault. In the preface to this work he relates that he was then ninety years of age, and had studied for eighty-two years. The work is one which deserves to be widely known for its lucid explanations on the holding of the right hand and the bow. He condemns, in the strongest terms, the manner of letting the wrist of the right hand sink below the level of the arm, a point which appears to be very hazy to some violoncellists who undertook to write about violoncello playing.

Vaslin entered the Paris Conservatoire in 1808 at the age of fourteen, becoming a pupil of Baudiot. In the following year he was already engaged in the orchestra of the Théâtre Variétés.

He tells us in the above-named work that he formed his style of playing by watching the excellent violinist, Baillot, for whom he had the greatest admiration. This fact brought him the nickname, "le Baillotin." He wrote for his instrument, besides the above, "L'art du violoncelle," "Le motif obstiné, petite fantaisie en La mineur"; "Mes 80 ans fantaisie originale" in A major and "Brimborion, petite fantaisie d'un nonogenaire" (Paris, Richault).

AUGUSTE PANSERON, born 1795 in Paris. A man who is of importance in the history of music as the father of the modern vocal "romance," the form of which he developed and fixed. He was also an excellent violoncellist, for which instrument he gained a prize at the conservatoire in 1811. Panseron was a pupil of Levasseur.

FRANÇOIS MARTIN was a violoncellist and composer about 1750 in Paris. He was in the chapel of the Duke of Grammont, and composed six violoncello sonatas, Op. 2, published in 1746, string trios and cantatilles, etc. He died in Paris 1773.

VICTOR CORNETTE, born 1795, at Amiens, as the son of an organist, published a "Méthode du Violoncelle." He was chiefly known as a choirmaster.

CHAPTER XVII.

THE VIOLONCELLO IN ENGLAND.

IN the early part of the seventeenth century, the education of an English gentleman was hardly complete if he could not take his part in a consort of viols, and particularly the bass viol, was then in great favour as the principal solo instrument.

It counted among its votaries the most prominent figures of that time. Even the chivalrous Charles I was no mean performer, and a long line of noblemen and gentlemen followed his example, including such names as Lord Francis North, Keeper of the Grand Seal (whose brother, Sir Roger North, wrote the famous "Memoirs"), Lord Crewe (Bishop of Durham), Sir Roger Lestrange and many more.

Although the bass viol was eventually supplanted as solo instrument by the violin, it died hard, and for a long time the violin was rejected by the higher classes as the instrument of ale-houses and fair-musicians. Anthony A. Wood tells us that the students at Oxford University preferred the gentle viol to the harsh and noisy (!) violin.

WILLIAM SAUNDERS is the first whose name has been handed down to history as an English "bass violin" and trombone player in Charles II's band in 1661. His petition is signed by Nicholas Lanier, master of the "private musicke," as well as those of George and Richard Hudson, Davis Mell and Simon Hopper, all well known musicians of their time. The term "bass violin" was applied to the violoncello in England during the early times of its existence until it came into prominence by the appearance of the Italian artists mentioned below.

ROBERT THOMPSON, music publisher and instrument maker, worked at the sign of "The Bass Violin" at the corner of St. Paul's Alley and St. Paul's churchyard, about 1750. At times the violoncello was simply spoken of as a "bass," and that term has survived to this day as a conversationism. It is no doubt in this sense that we have to take the word "bass" as applied to Claude de Granges, "Musitian in Ordinary" to the King in 1663.

What the qualifications of Saunders and de Granges as violoncellists were cannot be ascertained with certainty, but it is safe to conclude that their technique did not go much beyond the execution of the extremely simple and primitive bass parts of seventeenth century instrumental music.

It was not before 1733 that the violoncello entirely superseded the bass viol in English orchestras. The stormy times of the Commonwealth turned men's minds away from peaceful pursuits. The war trumpet took the place of principal instrument, and the bass bow was exchanged for the sword. The unsettled times which followed saw the introduction of the violoncello into England. If we take into account the very primitive state of its technique at the beginning of the eighteenth century, it cannot be wondered at if it did not awaken the same sympathies which the bass viol, its predecessor, commanded in earlier times. During the first half of that century it was almost exclusively represented by Italian artists, who were the first to distinguish themselves on the violoncello, as we have seen from Dr. Burney's remarks that

Cervetto with Abaco, Lanzetti, Pasqualini and Caporale "about this time (about 1740) brought the violoncello into favour, and made us nice judges of that instrument." Even as late as the latter part of that century, there have been very few English violoncellists of distinction. Wasielewski attributes this fact to the growing commercial spirit which, from the restoration of peace, at the end of the civil war, spent its whole energy upon colonial politics, employing foreign artists to meet all musical requirements. Granted that this was undoubtedly a point which has to be taken into account, it is certainly not the only and sole reason. The English nation is essentially a sporting nation, and sports and arts have very little in common with each other. During the early part of the eighteenth century, and even beyond the fifties, it was considered a sign of effeminacy if a young gentleman employed part of his time in learning to play a musical instrument. This has vastly changed during the last fifty years, but it accounts for a numerically poor list of virtuosos on any musical instrument during that earlier period.

The first violoncellist of English nationality whose name has been handed down to posterity was:

BARTHOLOMEW JOHNSON, born October 3, 1710. Gerber relates that on the anniversary of his hundredth birthday (in 1810), a banquet, to celebrate the occasion, was given at the Freemason's Hall, Scarborough, when Lord Mulgrave presided over a distinguished assembly of more than seventy eminent personages. A portrait of Johnson in oil, which was painted about that period, is still in existence. Plate XXIX is a reproduction of an engraving made from that portrait. During the musical "academy" (a concert) which followed in the evening, the centenarian played the violoncello in a minuet which he had composed sixty years previously, viz., about 1750. He appeared as a soloist in London about 1770.

CAPTAIN MARCELLUS LAROON, son of old Laroon, the painter,

who, according to Hawkins, played on the violoncello and composed solos for that instrument. He died at Oxford in 1772.

JOHN HEBDEN, about whose private life no details are at hand, was also born during the early part of the eighteenth century. He was not only violoncellist, but played also the bass viol and the bassoon. By his contemporaries Hebden was considered a great soloist on the violoncello. His portrait, playing the violoncello (not the viol da gamba, as stated by Wasielewski and copied by some of the later biographists) was engraved by John Faber from a painting by F. Mercier in 1741, and is a very fine mezzotint, of which a reproduction is given on Plate XXX. At a concert given by Hebden in London, in the year 1749, he produced a concert piece for five violoncellos by the famous Barone d'all Abaco.

The latter was then in London, and it appears more than probable that he took part in the performance, as it would have been difficult otherwise to find five efficient executants. The same piece had been produced by the composer in Vienna (see "Abaco"). Hebden held his bow about two inches from the nut, as shown in the portrait. The date of his death is unknown.

GORDON, who was the son of a Norfolk clergyman, is mentioned by Burney as a contemporary of Paxton, while Pohl ("Mozart and Haydn in London") tells us that he appeared in 1750, when Hebden was also playing in London.

Burney praises both Gordon and Paxton for their full and sweet tone on the violoncello, and for their judicious manner of accompanying the voice, which placed them high in public favour. He played at a concert given by Signora Frasi, on May 1, 1764, and appeared still in public concerts about 1780. On June 22, 1765, he took over the management of Covent Garden Theatre together with Crawford and Vincent. Further details are wanting.

WILLIAM PAXTON was born in 1737, in London. About his life and musical career there is hardly anything more known than about other contemporary violoncellists of English nationality. As we have seen above (see "Gordon"), Burney praises his tone and skill in accompanying the voice. The sparse details regarding his musical career are curiously mixed up with those concerning his brother Stephen (so by Wasielewski and Mendel and Reissmann, who credit him with the latter's compositions). Certain it is that he played concertos for his instrument at the concerts for the Musical Fund in 1764 and 1765, and also apparently at Yates's "Composers' Concert," in 1764.

Mendel and Reissmann reports that he went to Paris in 1780, where he published Six Duets, Op. 1. The latter work is advertised by Bailleux, publisher in Paris, on the back of Tillière's "Méthode pour le Violoncelle," as STEPHEN PAXTON'S Six Duets, Op. 1, for two violoncellos. In Stratton's "Dictionary of English Musicians," the latter appears also as the composer of Eight Duets for a violin and violoncello, Op. 2; Six Easy Solos for the violoncello or bassoon, Op. 3; Twelve Easy Lessons, in which are introduced several favourite airs, for violoncello or bass, Op. 6. There are also Two Solos, Op. 4, and Six Solos, Op. 8, both for violoncello. Eitner attributes all these compositions, as well as a MS. solo in D for violoncello and bass in the Imperial Library (Kaiserl. Hausbibliothek), unhesitatingly to William, and not to his brother Stephen, who was a glee composer. William Paxton died in 1781.

BENJAMIN HALLET, born 1743. All information that is obtainable regarding him is from a print by James McArdell, after Thomas Jenkins, where it says "A child not five Years old who under the tuition of Mr. Oswald Performed on the Flute at Drury Lane Theatre An°· 1748 for 50 Nights with extraordinary Skill & Applause, and in the following Year was able to play his part in any Concert on the Violoncello." Hallet holds the instrument double bass fashion, and the position of the violoncello, which appears supported only by the left hand, as well as the holding of the bow at about one-third of its length from the heel, seem to effectually prevent the execution of any technical difficulties. The idea of dressing the boy in woman's attire is very comical. He does not seem to have followed up the success of his early years, for nothing further is known about him. A reproduction of the print appears on Plate XXXI.

HERON was a virtuoso on the violoncello, who made his debut in London in 1753. Nothing else is known about him. Perhaps he is identical with Claudius Heron, of whom two canzonettes appeared in 1757 (Eitner).

CLAGGET was a violoncellist and bass viol player, who appeared in concerts together with C. F. Abel about 1760. As violoncello virtuoso he played in London in 1762 (Pohl).

He is probably identical with WALTER CLAGGET (Stratton and Brown, "Dictionary of British Musicians"), who composed "Six Solos and Six Scots Airs, with variations for the violin or violoncello, with a thorough bass for the harpsichord . . . . Op. 2 . . . . London, printed for the author, and sold by him at the Sedan Chair, Great Hart Street, Covent Garden, and Messrs. Thompson and Son, in St. Paul's Church Yard" (about 1759). Stratton and Brown also mention a "Discourse on Musick, to be delivered at Clagget's Attic Consort, October 31, 1793."

JOHN CROSDILL, born 1755 in London, was one of the best virtuosos of his time. He started his musical career as a choirboy of Westminster Abbey. According to Messrs. G. C. and T. A. Trowell his father was his first violoncello teacher. At the age of nine (in 1764) he appeared as a prodigy at a concert given by Siprutini, with whom he played a duet for two violoncellos. Siprutini was, in all probability, his teacher at that time. In 1775 (according to Mendel and Reissmann, Wasie-

PLATE XXX.
JOHN HEBDEN.

lewski gives 1772), Crosdill went to Paris to continue his studies under the elder Duport (not Janson, as stated by Wasielewski). Some facts and incidents relating to that episode have already been communicated in the biographical sketch of Jean Louis Duport. According to Stratton and Brown he was a *violinist* in the Chapel Royal in 1777. This is evidently a mistake, and should be "violoncellist" instead of violinist. Crosdill was a great favourite in English court circles. The Duke of Rutland was his particular patron, and Viscount Fitzwilliam, one of the directors of the "Concerts of Ancient Musick," was his intimate friend. This, no doubt, was an important factor in his very brilliant career. About 1780 he came back to London, and was made a chamber musician to Queen Charlotte in 1782. Soon afterwards he was appointed teacher of the violoncello to the Prince of Wales (afterwards George IV), whose studies he supervised for two years. He became, consequently, the most fashionable teacher of his instrument, and amassed a considerable fortune. He was also manager of the ladies' concerts which took place on Fridays alternately at the residences of the Earl of Exeter, Lord Vernon, Lady Somers, Mrs. Smith-Burges, and other houses of fashion. At the principal London concerts he appeared frequently as soloist, especially at the professional concerts at the Hanover Square Rooms, which were under the management of Lord Abingdon. At these concerts he played a duet for two violoncellos with the famous J. Mara in 1784; in the same year Crosdill and Chabran (Chiabrano) are mentioned as violoncellists in the orchestra of these concerts, and Crosdill was principal violoncellist at the Handel commemoration. From 1789-99 he was principal violoncellist at the Three Choirs Festival at Gloucester, except in one year when James Cervetto took his place. Plate XXXII is taken from the print of Crosdill by George Dance.

He appears to have been possessed of a most amiable disposition, free from all professional jealousy, for it was he who brought Jean Louis Duport, his former co-student under the elder Duport, to London, and with James Cervetto he used to play a duet in public which Abel had specially composed for the friendly rivals. In 1794 he married a lady of fortune and retired from professional life. He appeared once more in public at the coronation of George IV in 1821, with Lindley as *second* principal. His tone was considered to possess a particular grandeur, which appears quite credible, seeing that he was a pupil of J. P. Duport, whose pupils inherited for the greater part power and beauty of tone from their master. Reichardt, the composer, who heard him play, is stated to have said that Crosdill's tone was not free from a certain crudeness. Be this as it may, one thing is certain, that he earned the admiration of the whole musical world of his time. He trained a great number of pupils, and among them many of the most prominent players of the early nineteenth century. Robert Lindley and Henry Griesbach, who came from Copenhagen to London with his brother, were of their number, as well as many others whom we shall encounter in the course of this history. Crosdill died in October, 1825, at Escrik, in Yorkshire, bequeathing £1,000 to the Royal Society of Musicians, to which he belonged for over fifty years.

JAMES CERVETTO, born 1747 (Schilling gives 1741), in London, was the son of the celebrated Italian violoncellist who was instrumental in introducing the violoncello into England *(see page 151 ff.)*. His father taught him the violoncello at a very early age, and he made rapid progress, so that he was able to appear successfully at the "Little Haymarket Theatre" on April 23, 1760, at a concert given by Mlle. Gertrud Schmeling, better known to fame as Mme. Mara (she married the violoncellist, Johann Bapt. Mara), the great singer, who was then only ten years old. Associated with the former in the same concert was Master Barron, aged thirteen, a pupil of Giardini, the violinist, and Miss Burney (daughter of Dr.

Burney, author of the well-known "History of Music"), a pianist of nine years. In 1765 Cervetto played together with his father at a concert given by Parry, the harpist. He had neither the fiery temperament nor the execution of Crosdill, whose senior he was by eight years, but his tone was sweeter and he played with more expression. The latter quality he had developed under the guidance of Abel, who served as model for nearly all the English artists of his time. Interesting is Dr. Burney's opinion of the Cervettos; he says: "The younger Cervetto, when a child and hardly acquainted with the gamut, had a better tone, and played what he was able to execute, in a manner much more 'chantant' than his father. Arrived at manhood his tone and expression were equal to those of the best tenor voices." From 1780 James Cervetto played at the professional concerts, which were held at the Hanover Rooms under the direction of Lord Abingdon. In 1783 Duport and Baumgarten played at these concerts together with Cervetto. In 1784 Cervetto played a concerto by Haydn at these concerts. Unfortunately, it does not say which of the five violoncello concertos by Haydn it was.

In that year Chabran is mentioned as violoncellist at these concerts, together with Cervetto. This was Gaetano Chiabrano mentioned on page 171.

At the fourth concert of that season, on March 10 Cervetto played a concerto of his own composition "with the power of tone and nobility of style which one is accustomed to hear from this artist," as Cramer says in his magazine of 1784. At the eleventh concert in that year he played a solo of his own composition and took part in a trio for violin, viola and violoncello by Giardini. A small picture painted by Cipriani, engraved by Bartolozzi, shows a portrait of Giardini on a tombstone surrounded by mourning genii.

Between 1763 and 1770 he travelled all over Europe, playing at the principal towns. In the latter year he returned to

London, and in 1771 he was appointed violoncellist in the Queen's private band. His published compositions consist of "Twelve Solos for a Violoncello with a Thorough Bass for the Harpsichord." This work, which is dedicated to the Prince Elector of the Bavarian Palatinate, was published by himself. Six Solos for a Violoncello, with a Thorough Bass for the Harpsichord. Opera Terza, London. Twelve Sonatinas for a Violoncello and Bass, Op. 4A, London. Six Lessons or Divertimenti, London. Also six solos for the flute and six trios for two violins and violoncello. Cervetto's violoncello compositions show a decided advance in the technique over the compositions of the early Italian writers for that instrument; they are more akin to the compositions by Abaco showing a certain development of the passage work and greater variety in double stops. Two of his solos have been republished by Carl Schroeder (Augener Ltd.), and one by R. Walthew (W. E. Hill and Sons).

Cervetto died at the age of ninety on February 5, 1837. His was a life of ease and comfort, as his father secured for him a position in society as well as in his profession, and left him, moreover, a fortune of £20,000. His portrait, from a fine oil painting in the possession of Messrs. W. E. Hill and Sons, appears on Plate XXXIII.

FREDERIC LEWIS, PRINCE OF WALES, the son of George II, 1707-51, was an amateur violoncellist, whose sisters were likewise musical and received lessons from Handel, who composed for them the first book of his "Suites pour clavecin." The Prince of Wales himself patronised Handel's operatic enterprise in connection with the theatre in Lincoln's Inn Fields in 1734 or soon after.

A music party in the gardens of Kew Palace painted in 1733 by Philip Mercier, forming part of the collections in the National Portrait Gallery, shows the Prince of Wales playing the violoncello, his sister Anne, the Princess Royal, playing the harpsichord, Princess Caroline Elizabeth playing the mandolin and Princess Amelia Sophia Eleanora reading a book. Kew Palace in seen in the background. A reproduction of this interesting picture is given on Plate XXXIV.

GEORGE FREDERIC AUGUST, Prince of Wales, born August 12, 1762, who ascended the throne of England as George IV, was a great lover of music and a good amateur violoncellist. He studied for two years with Crosdill, who was a familiar figure in the musical court circles of that time. Both the Duke of Gloucester and the Duke of Cumberland, brothers of the Prince of Wales, were also musical amateurs, the former playing the violin and the latter the viola. In 1783 the Prince of Wales began to give his regular concerts at Carlton Place, which stood at the lower part of Waterloo Place, going towards Green Park. There he received all the most famous musicians of his time. He showed, however, more appreciation than generosity towards them. The most deplorable incident in this respect was his attitude towards Beethoven. The latter had dedicated his "Battle of Victoria" to him when George was Prince Regent of England. In a letter to Ries, Beethoven complains that not only had his actual expenses for the copying of the work not been refunded, nay, not even a letter of thanks did he receive! Griesbach, the oboist, and father of the violoncellist, had to send a written statement by the twopenny post to receive payment for his services.

The Prince used to have two concerts a day at his residence. One took place in the morning, when, besides himself, only his brothers and a few intimate favourites would be present. This was chiefly for the execution of chamber music. The other took place in the evening before a larger audience. On these occasions the Prince used to play the violoncello in the orchestra. The programmes comprised exclusively instrumental music. He used to play on a Forster violoncello, bearing the royal coat of arms painted on the back of the instrument. This instrument was, about 1900, for some time on view in the shop of Mr. Chanot, of Wardour Street.

About the middle of last century there appeared what is probably the first English tutor for the violoncello. It consisted of a single sheet with this heading: "The Gamut for the Violoncello, Printed by Henry Waylett, at the Black Lyon in Exeter Change. Price 6d." 1745-6.

After explaining the tuning of the instrument, it gives the fingering of the C major scale up to G in the fourth position on the A string, followed by chromatic scales, giving the enharmonic equivalents for some of the notes. After that there are two "lessons" with variations, and this finishes the whole work. The author, very wisely, has not appended his name to the work, and so he could not receive the public recognition he really deserved!

If the fingering in Corrette's work is impracticable in many instances, the fingering of "the gamut" goes against all sense and reason. The following examples are so amusing that they deserve being quoted.

And from the second lesson:

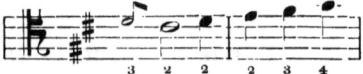

More explicit is "The Complete Tutor for the Violoncello, containing the best and easiest Instructions for Learners, by Robert Crome. To which is added a collection of favourite airs, marches, minuets, song tunes, and duetts. Price 2s. Printed for and sold by C. & S. Thompson, at No. 75, St.

Paul's Church Yard, London, where Books of Instruction for any single instrument may be had."

The above tutor appeared in 1765, and gives us a good picture of the position which the violoncello held in those days. The author (who also wrote "The Fiddle New Model'd," historically a very interesting work, see E. van der Straeten, "The Romance of the Fiddle"), says, in his preface: "As the bass violin is in great esteem I have here given some useful and plain instructions for the learner, as this instrument appears to be built on the ruins of another—I mean the six-stringed bass—which in the last century was held in great esteem, and was of general use in concerts. Viols were of three sorts, viz., bass viols, tenor viols and treble viols. The violin in those days was looked upon as a contemptible instrument; it was harsh and too loud, they could not bear to have their viols overpowered. However, as the violin became more general, it was judged necessary to use bass violins, or violoncellos (that is four-stringed basses), as being much more powerful and suitable to the fiddle, and since these last have been in such frequent use, the former have been entirely laid aside."

The compass of the exercises does not exceed F sharp on the A string (fourth position), and that note is used only on rare occasions. The fingering is the same as that shown in Corrette's work.

It was evidently the custom to mark the semitones on the fingerboard by drawing lines across it, which took the place of the frets used on viols, for Crome says, in speaking about tuning the instrument: "Measure out the seventh line from the nut (giving the fifth of the open string, or unison to the next higher string) and when you have got the exact distance tie a piece of fiddle string tight on the neck under the strings, which will make a frett, and will be standard for tuning all the strings."

The length from nut to bridge he gives as $26\frac{1}{2}$ inches, which is exactly one inch less than our present standard measure, and, in fact, we know that the original neck of an old instrument is invariably much too short and very broad and thick, which made great agility of the fingers, and particularly playing in the fourth position, a matter of extreme difficulty.

Amusing are also his remarks on time: "Time, in music," he says, "is difficult except it is begun very early, but time in itself is simply plain, such as in our ordinary walking, for though we think nothing of it when we walk, yet we keep pretty regular motion." Then he gives what he calls two "time tables." In the first he gives the subdivision of the "semibrieve" [*sic!*], which, he says, is as long as one can moderately count four, or walk four steps in. The second subdivides the minim down to demisemiquavers. Later on he says: "All musical performances must be done by the rule of time, keeping either with the hand or foot, but on an instrument with the foot."

His holding of the bow and drawing it straight across the strings at the distance of $1\frac{1}{2}$ to 2 inches from the bridge does not differ from the present manner.

He gives indications for drawing the bow "backwards" (down bow) and "forwards" (up bow) by putting "B" or "F" over the notes, and underneath he puts "D" for beating the foot down and "U" for taking it up. "The 'spring'" (spring bow), he says, "can't be explained but by demonstration."

After some more instructions which do not call for special remark, the book is brought to a close by a collection of minuets, jigs, gavottes, hornpipes, movements from cotillons, "See the Conquering Hero Comes," "Lovely Nancy" (with variations), "Come Haste to the Wedding," the famous "Belle-isle March," "Lady Coventry's Minuet," "Handel's Gavotte," "Coldstream March," "Dearest Creature," and other pieces jumbled together in the most promiscuous manner.

PLATE XXXI.
BENJAMIN HALLET.

To face page 320.

Another tutor for the violoncello was published by "Preston & Son, at their wholesale warehouse, No. 97, Strand." It contains a frontispiece showing a gentleman in the costume of the latter part of the eighteenth century, playing the violoncello. The title runs thus: "A New and Complete Tutor for Violoncello, wherein the present much improved fingering is clearly and fully explained, showing by sections of the fingerboard the various modes of fingering in different keys as used by the most eminent masters." This latter device has recently been made use of again in a tutor by Philipp Roth. The former work, which is of a very primitive nature, does not give the author's name. It winds up with the then customary collection of "airs" of various countries. The most curious part of this book is "A Drawing of the New Invented Patent Fingerboard."

This fingerboard was invented by Charles Clagget, who was born in London in 1755—probably a relative of Claget (or Clagget), mentioned previously as violoncellist, who appeared about 1760 in London. He was a violinist with an inventive turn of mind, who constructed an organ without pipes, strings, bells or glasses, which never required tuning. He also constructed a chromatic horn and chromatic trumpet. They were apparently no more successful than the "patent fingerboard." The latter contained nineteen lines, marking the position of the tones and semitones. For instance, C sharp on the C string was on the first line, D flat on the second, D natural on the third line, and so forth. It was provided with movable nuts, so as to enable the player to play in different keys without changing the position of the hand. It certainly shows a deal of ingenuity, but like all the rest of the many *simplifications* of musical technicalities, it was unsuccessful. The holding of the bow and fingering in this as well as the following work are the same as those of the present day.

The following tutor appeared also anonymously. The title

is: "New Instructions for the Violoncello, containing the best and easiest method," etc., "to which is added a favourite collection of airs." The whole selected and adapted for the instrument by a celebrated performer. Printed for Thomas Cahusac and Sons, 196 Strand. It also contains a frontispiece, showing a violoncellist in somewhat later (before 1798), costume than that of the former book. Towards the end of the eighteenth century there appeared a series of tutors for various instruments, known as "Addison and Hodson's Standard Tutors." The authors were:

JOHN ADDISON, born in London, 1765. He was violoncellist at Vauxhall Gardens, and double bass player at the Italian Opera, the Concerts of Ancient Music and the Vocal Concerts. He enjoyed also a considerable reputation as a composer of musical dramas, songs, etc.

Commercial speculations caused the loss of almost the whole of his savings, and he died in London, in very reduced circumstances, January 30, 1844.

His collaborator was George Alexander Hodson, the composer of many fine melodies, including such popular favourites as: "Tell me, Mary, how to Woo Thee," "O Give me but my Arab Steed," and others. He died in 1863.

The above tutor, which on the whole is based upon the principles of modern violoncello technique, still advises the holding of the bow *about one inch from the nut.*

As a tutor the book is very primitive; it contains the usual collection of airs, and under the first of these is a note: "In beating the time, the foot must descend at the first note of each bar." Among the airs is "See the Conquering Hero Comes" under the heading "March King Arthur."

HARDY published a "Violoncello Preceptor, with Scales for Fingering in the Various Keys," about 1800. No further particulars are known with regard to this artist.

JOSEPH REINAGLE, born 1762, at Portsmouth. He was the

son of an Austrian musician. It was intended that he should join the navy, but after his first voyage he was apprenticed to an Edinburgh jeweller. There he became Schetky's pupil on the violoncello, and Schetky married his sister. He studied also the violin under Aragoni and Pinto, and became leader at the Edinburgh Theatre, and conductor of the concerts of that town. Wasielewski states that previously to studying the violoncello, he was for some time trumpeter in an English regiment. In 1784-6 he lived in Dublin and came to London in 1791. Reinagle played in Solomon's concerts in London and Oxford. In the latter town he resided for several years, and died there in 1836. For the violoncello he composed Twelve Duets, Op. 2, and three sets of Six Duets, each Op. 3, 4 and 5, one or more concertos, and "Concise Introduction on the Art of Playing on the Violoncello." The last-named work, published in London, reached four editions.

HUGH REINAGLE, born 1766, at Portsmouth, was a younger brother of Joseph Reinagle. He studied the violoncello under Crosdill, and was from all accounts an excellent executant on that instrument. On account of ill-health he went to Lisbon, where he died at an early age. He composed six solos, Op. 1. Six Favourite Solos, Op. 2, by the late H. Reinagle. Printed and sold by J. Bland at his music warehouse, 45 Holborn. Four of these solos (studies) have been republished in the "Standard English Edition." He also wrote Six Duets, Op. 3 (London, Preston).

JOHN GUNN, born about 1765 in the Highlands of Scotland (some mention Edinburgh as his birthplace). About 1789 he came to London, exercising his profession as teacher of the violoncello there, and in Cambridge. In 1793 he published "The Theory and Practice of Fingering the Violoncello, containing Rules and Progressive Lessons for Attaining the Knowledge and Command of the whole Compass of the Instrument." This work, which appeared in two editions, contains also an essay about the origin of the violoncello, and the history of stringed instruments.

As a supplement to this tutor, he wrote: "Forty favourite Scotch Airs, adapted for Violin, German Flute or Violoncello, with the Phrases Marked." Another of his works with reference to the violoncello was: "An Essay, Theoretical and Practical, on the Application of Harmony, Thorough-bass and Modulation to the Violoncello."

In 1795 Gunn returned to Edinburgh, where he married Miss Anna Young, an excellent pianist. He died about 1824.

ROBERT LINDLEY, born March 4, 1777, at Rotherham, in Yorkshire, was by far the greatest English violoncellist of his time. He began his musical career by studying the violin under the guidance of his father. Lindley exchanged that instrument for the violoncello at an early age, and progressed so quickly that he received an engagement at the Brighton Theatre when he was only nine years old. At the age of sixteen he placed himself under James Cervetto, who was then one of the best masters of his instrument in England. In 1794 he joined the orchestra of the King's Theatre, in London, as successor to Sperati, and he retained that position as principal of the Opera until 1851. He appeared at the King's Theatre on May 15, 1794, with a "solo" for his instrument, and played as principal violoncellist at the "Ancient Concerts" and the Philharmonic Concerts. His intimate friend and constant companion was Dragonetti, with whom he used to play Corelli's sonatas in public. A marginal note in the handwriting of Rophino Lacy in an edition of Handel's Sonata V (British Museum, add. MSS. 31575) says that the second allegro "is from his Harp Lessons, 1720. It used to be frequently played at the Ancient Concerts (arranged for violin, violoncello and double bass) by Franz Cramer, Linley [sic] and Dragonetti." On May 19, 1847, he played the violoncello *obbligato* to Staudigl (the famous German oratorio singer) in "Qui tollis peccata" from Haydn's Second Service at the same concerts. The following appearances are recorded in the programmes of the Philharmonic Society (as published in the "Musical Courier" of June 25, 1896):

The first time that Lindley appeared as successor to Percivall at these concerts was Monday, February 24, 1817, when he took part with Weichsel, Reeve and Watts, in a quartet by Haydn, and in a performance of Beethoven's septet, together with Weichsel, Lyon, Anfossi, Willman, Petrides and Holmes.

On March 10 he played in a pianoforte quartet by Dussek, with Cipriani Potter, Weichsel and Watts, and in a string trio by Romberg, with the latter two. A string quintet by Romberg, and concertante for Spanish guitar, and string trio by Sor; pianoforte quartet by Griffin, string trio by Mozart; sextet by Ries, pianoforte quintet by Kalkbrenner (with the composer at the piano), string quartet and pianoforte quintet by Ries, and a string quintet by Mozart were the chamber music works performed at the seven following concerts in 1817.

It would be interesting to go through the list of chamber works performed at these concerts to see how few of these works, though excellent in their way, have proved of sufficient vitality to survive. And yet it might even now prove interesting to hear one, or part of one of these forgotten works.

On April 19, 1819, Lindley played a manuscript trio of his own composition, with Weichsel and the violoncellist, Eley. As the first violoncello part is entirely a "principale" this may be looked upon as his first debut as a soloist at these concerts. On May 8, 1820, Robert Lindley, together with his son William, and Dragonetti, played for the first time a sonata by Corelli, and again, March 11, 1822, and June 2, 1823.

R. Lindley and Dragonetti played the ninth sonata by Corelli on March 3, 1823 and April 17, 1826, and one (the same?) on March 23, 1835. Lindley and Howell (double bass) played Corelli's Sonata, Op. 5, No. 6, on April 23, 1836, June 3, 1839, and June 5, 1843.

The eleventh sonata by the same composer he played with Brooks (second violoncello) and Dragonetti, on April 11, 1831, and (probably the same) with Crouch and Dragonetti on March 26, 1832, and May 29, 1837, and again, with Lucas as second violoncello on April 11, 1836, and on May 3, 1841. Dragonetti died in 1846, and the last of Lindley's Corelli performances was on May 20, 1850, with Lucas and Howell.

With the exception of a concertante for two violoncellos, of his own composition, which he played on April 17, 1826, together with his son William, the above-mentioned trio for two violoncellos and violin, also by himself, are the only other works he produced at the Philharmonic Society. What the "solo" was which he played at the King's Theatre in 1794, and the concerto he played at the Professional Concerts (under Pleyel) on February 2, 1792, is not recorded.

With Shram he played a "duo" at the King's Theatre, in 1795, and about the same time he played a duo for violin and violoncello, by Stamitz, with Cramer (father of the great pianist, J. B. Cramer).

If one looks at this repertoire, played at a time when *so many* fine and important works for the violoncello had been written, one can understand Vidal's remark: "His playing was cold, and in technique and style he remained far behind Romberg, Lamarre, Bohrer and Servais." At all events, the ridiculous, but often repeated story that Romberg had fled from London as soon as he heard Lindley play is a malicious invention by over-zealous admirers of the English master. There was certainly no reason for a man like Romberg to avoid meeting Lindley, whom he admired all the same, frankly and openly. Lindley was much admired in Germany, although Vidal's judgment is echoed to some extent in the "Berliner Musikzeitung," which says: "Lindley plays the violoncello as beautifully, with perfect intonation and surety of technique, as Hausmann (from Berlin, who played at the first Philharmonic concert in 1838), but he has not the fire (emotion)."

He died June 13, 1855.

His compositions for the violoncello consist of: Four Concertos (Op. 6, 8, 10 and 27); "Methode de Violoncelle," Op. 4; Trio, Op. 13, for violoncello *obbligato*, with violin and violoncello; Six Solos, Op. 9; Three Duos for two violoncellos (Witzendorff, Vienna, published them as Op. 27). They are entirely antiquated, and without interest.

In 1795 Lindley appeared as soloist at Haydn's concert. What he played is not certain. His portrait taken from a mezzotint appears on Plate XXXV.

CHARLES HANBURY, English Consul in Hamburg, who died in London, November 11, 1783, was an excellent amateur violoncello player, who also played the pianoforte and the viola.

WILLIAM SUDLOW, born 1772, was violoncellist, organist and composer of vocal music. He was organist in Manchester, where he died in 1848. His brother, Edward, was a viola player in Manchester.

GEORGE COLLINS, son of the celebrated violinist, Isaak Collins, is mentioned by Trowell as a violoncellist of some distinction about the middle of last century.

CHARLES JANE ASHLEY, born 1773 in London, was an excellent violoncellist. His tone was powerful and of a refined quality. As an accompanist he was second only to Robert Lindley. In 1783 he made his debut at the age of ten (according to Pohl). In 1798 he appears already among the violoncellists of the "Antient Concerts" at Hanover Square Rooms, the others being Cervetto, Waterhouse and C. Schram. He was one of the founders of the "Glee Club" in 1793, and on the foundation of the Philharmonic Society he became one of the original members. For some time he was secretary of the Royal Society of Musicians. At the *first* Philharmonic Concert on March 8, 1813, he took part in the performance of a Boccherini quintet with Salmon, Cudmore, Sherrington and Robert Lindley at the old Argyll Rooms which were burnt down in 1830. Charles and his brother, General Ashley, a violinist, were for some time joint managers of the Oratorio Concerts at Covent Garden. Twenty years of his life were passed as a prisoner for debt in the King's Bench prison. In 1843 he became the proprietor of the Tivoli Gardens at Margate, and the anxieties connected with this enterprise hastened his death, which occurred on August 29, 1843.

Ashley was a member of a noted musical family. His father, John, was assistant conductor to Joah Bates. Two of his brothers were violinists and one an organist and teacher of singing.

MENEL, of whose private life nothing is known, appears frequently as soloist in concerts of that period. In 1789 he made his debut in London. In 1791 he played as soloist at Salomon's concert. On February 9, 1792, he played at Haydn's benefit concert at the Hanover Square Rooms, in a concertante by Gyrowetz, with Salomon and Hindmarsh. On February 24, 1791, he played in a Haydn quartet with Salomon at the New Musical Fund Concert, on March 18 in a concertante by Haydn, at the Hanover Rooms, on June 11 at Mme. Mara's benefit concert, in a quartet by Haydn, and again in a divertimento by the same master on May 3, 1792.

CHRISTOPHER SHRAM (the original spelling was no doubt Schramm), a violoncellist of either German nationality or extraction. He played at the "Concerts of Ancient Music" at the New Room, King's Theatre, Haymarket, where he made his debut in 1792, and is mentioned, together with Griesbach, Lindley and Muller in the programme book of 1797. He was also violoncellist in Barthelemon's quartet.

DAMEN, junior (son of J. A. Damen or Dahmen, a Dutch

PLATE XXXII.

JOHN CROSDILL.　FROM A CRAYON PORTRAIT BY GEO. DANCE.

To face page 328.

gambist and violoncellist) *(see page 94)* was violoncellist in Salomon's quartet in 1794. He played a solo at the fifth or sixth of the twelve Haydn concerts at the Hanover Square Rooms.

At the Professional Concerts between 1791-3, we find also a violoncellist, JOHN SMITH, who made his debut in 1784, and played, among others, in a concertante for violoncello, flute and violin, by Mazzinghi, in 1791. He was the master of F. W. Crouch.

MAHON was violoncellist at the Ranelagh Rotunda.

Violoncellists of whom apparently nothing but the names have been preserved, with the year of their first appearance as soloists in London are: BENECKE, 1752; FALCO, 1759; XIMENES, 1772; PHILLIPS, 1781; ABEL (a cousin of the great gambist), 1789; C. ATTWOOD, 1791, he died in 1807.

RICHARD CUDMORE, born 1787 at Chichester, where he received his first musical training as pianist from a local musician, James Fargett. Later on he studied the violin and made his public debut at the age of nine years, playing a violin concerto. In the following year he became Reinagle's pupil on the violoncello, and at the end of one year's study of that instrument he played a violoncello concerto of his own composition in public. After that he studied the violin under Salomon for two years, and then he returned to Chichester where he was engaged as violinist at the theatre from 1799. In 1808 he returned to London to resume his studies of the pianoforte under Woelfl. He appeared again in public as pianist, and in Liverpool he gave a concert, where he played a pianoforte solo by Kalkbrenner, a violin solo by Rode, and a violoncello solo by Cervetto. He was a member of the Philharmonic Society from its foundation in 1813, where he took part in the chamber music performances alternately as pianist, violinist and viola player, but not as violoncellist. During the latter part of his life he resided in Manchester as leader of the "Gentlemen's Concerts." He died there December 29, 1840.

CHARLES NEATE, born March 28, 1784, although a violoncellist, was chiefly known as pianist and composer, and through his personal relations to Beethoven.

In 1814, at the second Philharmonic concert on February 28, he appeared as violoncellist in the first performance of a string quartet by Griffin, Vaccari being leader and Potter viola, and at the third concert on March 14 of the same year he appeared in the same capacity, playing a string quartet by Romberg with Messrs. Beer, Watts and Sherrington.

FREDERICK WILLIAM CROUCH, son of William Crouch, a composer and organist of St. Luke's, Old Street, London, was born in Great Smith Street, Westminster, about the year 1773. He received his first instructions in music from his father, afterwards studying under John Smith *(see page 329)*, a fine player. Crouch made rapid progress, and appeared at an early age in public concerts as a soloist. On May 2, 1814, he played the violoncello in a string trio by Beethoven and a sextet by Bernhard Romberg, in which the latter made his first appearance in England. In 1817 he became second principal at the Italian Opera as well as a member of the orchestras of the Ancient Concerts and the Philharmonic Society. For many years, and up to a few months before his death, he played everywhere with Robert Lindley. He married the daughter of John Nicholls, an eminent barrister, whose family name was given as an additional name to Crouch's son. F. W. Crouch died in July, 1844. He wrote "A Complete Treatise on the Violoncello" (London, Chappell, 1826)—erroneously attributed by Trowell to his son—based on the method by Baillot, Levasseur, Catel and Baudiot used at the Paris Conservatoire; a supplement, with accompanied scales, and exercises on double stops; duets for two violoncellos; duets for pianoforte and violoncello; arrangements, etc.

JOHN PEILE, who describes himself as professor of the violoncello, made a translation of "Breval's New Instructions for the Violoncello," and arranged "Select Airs from Mozart" for the same instrument. He belonged to the latter part of the eighteenth century, but no further particulars are obtainable.

SIR CHARLES RICH, a good amateur violoncellist, received Haydn as his guest in Surrey on August 26, 1794, and conducted him over the ruins of Waverley Abbey, which deeply impressed Haydn, according to some notes in his diary.

THOMAS BINFIELD, a son of Richard Binfield, organist and music seller in Reading about 1799, settled in London in the early part of last century, and appeared as soloist at the Philharmonic Concerts.

Binfield was a member of the Royal Society of Musicians, and died in London, December 23, 1840.

Of the following violoncellists appearing at the end of the eighteenth and the early part of the nineteenth century we possess no further details:

WATERHOUSE appeared at Antient Concerts in 1789.

HANCOCK played the Concerto in A minor, Op. 5, by Kraft, at the Philharmonic Society on June 20, 1849.

PERCIVALL, of Bath, played at the Philharmonic Society on February 26, 1816, also

BROOKS is mentioned by Trowell as a violoncellist who lived in London during the early part of last century, and fulfilled engagements at most of the important concerts of that time.

BRODLET appeared at the Monday Popular Concerts in 1860.

DONALD GOW, 1727-1807, a brother of Niel Gow, the famous Scottish fiddler of Inver, is said to have been a violoncellist of merit.

MALCOLM MCDONALD, a violoncellist in Niel Gow's band, and composer of reels, strathspeys, etc., lived at Inver, in Dunkeld parish, in the latter part of the eighteenth century.

LIEUTENANT-COLONEL JOHN MCDONALD, born 1759, a son of Flora McDonald, the Scottish heroine, and McDonald of Kingsburgh, Skye. He entered the East India Company, and held various military and scientific appointments. He was a Fellow of the Royal Society in 1800, and died at Exeter, August 16, 1831. He published a treatise explanatory of the principles constituting the practice and theory of the violoncello in 1811. Also a "Treatise on the Harmonic System, etc.," in 1822, containing a table of the harmonics as they appear on the violoncello.

CHAPTER XVIII.

THE VIOLONCELLO IN BOHEMIA.

THE Czechs have always been distinctly musical people, although they have frequently proved that "harmony" is their weakest point in every other respect. The little kingdom of Bohemia has produced more prominent composers and virtuosos on all kinds of musical instruments than many a larger country. Among violoncellists it produced some of the greatest virtuosos of the eighteenth century—to wit, Mara and the brothers Stiastny.

The first Czechian violoncellist whose name has been handed down to us is JOH. CERMAK, born about 1710 in Bohemia, the name of his birthplace being unknown. He went to Warsaw, where he still lived in 1790. According to a report by Joseph Fiala, who heard him there, he was an excellent player, whose strongest point lay in the rendering of the *cantilena*. He wrote a number of concertos, which always met with the most enthusiastic reception. They have, however, entirely disappeared in the course of time. The date of his death is unknown.

JOHN GEORGE NERUDA, born 1716, according to Theo. Schulz, excelled both on the violin and the violoncello. He was for thirty years master of the court chapel and teacher of the violoncello and the violin at Dresden. He was pensioned in 1772 and died in 1780. Besides six trio sonatas which were published he left a great number of symphonies, violin concertos, violin solos and trios in MS. Two of his sons were violinists in the court chapel, and his brother, John Chrysostomus, born 1705 at Rossicz (whom Riemann has evidently mixed up with John George) was likewise a well-known violinist. It is from these that sprang the long line of excellent musicians which culminated in Lady Hallé, better known as Madame Norman Neruda, and Franz Neruda *(see later on)*.

PAUL KÖCHER, born at Tausch (Domazlicy), in Bohemia, in 1719, died at Kukus, February 21, 1783. He entered the monastery of the Brothers of Mercy (Fratres Misericordiæ) at Prague. Passing through various monasteries, he was sub-prior in Vienna, then successively prior in Gratz, Neustadt an der Mettau in Bohemia, and Teschen in Silesia. He then retired to Kukus, where he died at the age of sixty-four. He was an excellent violinist, violoncellist and viol d'amour player, for which latter instrument he wrote several concertos.

IGNAZ (HYNCK) MARA, born at Deutschbrod (Nemeky Brod), about 1721, was apparently a pupil of Petrik. In 1742 he went to Berlin, and through the influence of Franz Benda, his countryman, and leader of the Royal chapel, he was appointed to the King's private music, to which he belonged for about thirty years. He died in Berlin in 1783. Mara combined beauty of tone with great expression. His compositions, which appear to have been much appreciated, remained unpublished. Two Sonatas in D and A for violoncello and bass are in the Royal Library at Berlin.

JOS. ANT. KOMARECK enjoyed a great reputation as violoncellist about 1742. He was a native of Bohemia, and during the latter part of his career became director of music to the Archbishop of Würzburg.

JOHN BAPTIST MARA, son of Ignaz Mara, was born July 20,

1744. He was an artist of extraordinary talent and personality. His father instructed him in the art of violoncello playing, in which he made such rapid strides that he appeared as a soloist at a very early age, and attracted the notice of Prince Henry of Prussia, the famous protector of musical art, who engaged him as one of his chamber musicians. As he developed his histrionic talent, he took part also in the theatrical performances which the Prince arranged at his castle, Rheinsberg.

His handsome personality and engaging manners ingratiated him with the famous singer, Gertrud Elisabeth Schmeling, who became his wife, after many obstacles which lay in their way had been overcome.

Unfortunately, Mara was a weak character whom prosperity led on to dissolute courses. He squandered not only his own earnings, but also the very large earnings of his wife.

His intemperate and immoral life deprived him of the esteem of his Prince, and, as he began to show also want of respect towards the former, he was dismissed from the Royal private band. His domestic happiness he had himself destroyed, his debts increased, and his creditors becoming more and more pressing, he resolved to flee the country, together with his wife, who still clung to him in spite of his treatment. Their plans to escape were discovered, and Mara was imprisoned. His wife's appeal to the Prince obtained for him his liberty, and shortly after the couple made good their escape to Vienna, Paris, and thence to London, where they arrived in 1784. In that year Mara played a duet for two violoncellos, together with Crosdill, at the professional concerts, and had immense success. In 1788 he went to Italy with his wife, returning to London in 1790. They remained there but for a short period, returning to Venice. In 1792 they were again in London. From this time the downward course of Mara went on with rapid strides. In 1799 Madame Mara, tired of her husband's profligacy, separated finally from him. Mara returned to Berlin, but his brilliant achievements were a thing of the past, and meeting no longer with his former success, he sank lower and lower. He appeared once more in public, but intemperance and debauchery told their tale; the hand had lost its cunning, and the want of success to which once he was accustomed drove him away from the capital. He visited the smaller towns, and came, among others, to Sondershausen, where Gerber, the celebrated author of the musical dictionary, heard him. He reports that he was still admirable in the rendering of a slow movement, and that if here and there a note failed it was solely due to the wretched condition of his strings. The choice of his solos he criticised more severely as having been quite forty years behind the times. During his sojourn at Sondershausen he appeared to Gerber as a highly-educated gentleman, who betrayed no signs of his intemperate habits, but appeared to be in very straitened circumstances.

Madame Mara, who had been a favourite with Londoners ever since she appeared as a child, together with James Cervetto and Miss Burney (all children) at a concert in 1760 *(see page 314)*, retained the sympathy of the public, as is shown by various concerts given for her benefit, in which the leading artists of the day took part. Her noble and generous spirit is shown by the fact that she still supported her wretched husband by considerable sums of money long after they had separated. But Mara's career was drawing towards its close. He had gone to Holland, and having become an absolute dipsomaniac, he lost all self-respect, and was to be found in the lowest sailors' haunts playing for drink-money, until death released him from that wretched existence in the summer of 1808 at Schiedam. A pathetic ending to a career that commenced under such brilliant auspices!

His compositions, consisting of two concertos, twelve solos with bass, a duet with violin, and a sonata with bass, remained

PLATE XXXIII.

JAMES CERVETTO (THE YOUNGER). FROM A PAINTING IN THE POSSESSION OF MESSRS. W. E. HILL AND SONS.

To face page 556.

unpublished. The MS. of a Sonata in C is in the imperial private library, Berlin.

ANTONIUS HOCK is mentioned as a native of Bohemia, who was engaged as violoncellist in the royal chapel at Berlin, together with Mara, in 1754, when C. P. E. Bach was the conductor.

JOSEPH REICHA, born 1746 at Prague, uncle of the famous composer, Anton Reicha, was an excellent virtuoso on the violoncello, and was in the service of the Count Wallerstein. In 1787 he was appointed member of the famous private band of the Prince Elector at Bonn, where Beethoven was then engaged as tenor player. Reicha became soon afterwards conductor of the National Theatre at Bonn. In his thirty-fifth year gout deprived him almost entirely of the use of his limbs, and he need to dictate his compositions, consisting of a symphony concertante for violin and violoncello, as well as concertos and duos for his instrument, which have been published. Eitner mentions twelve concertos, one as Op. 2, one in D as Op. 3, and ten others without opus number. He does not state whether some of the latter are duplicates. Also three duos concertans for violin and violoncello. The author is in possession of the manuscript score of a concerto in A by Reicha, which shows good workmanship, melodious invention, and a remarkable technique, resembling that of Romberg, though not so fully developed in the passages.

E. VINCESLAUS PETRIK, born 1727 at Libachovice, in Bohemia, was a pupil of Kozsek, and afterwards studied under Capellmeister Potz. He was considered one of the best violoncellists of his time. In 1747 he entered the Church, was ordained as a priest, and obtained the post of chorus-master at the church of St. Benedict, Prague. It is related of him that he executed the violin compositions of Giardini, Zyke and other contemporaries on the violoncello. In that respect he did only the same as the other prominent violoncellists of that time, as the literature for their own instrument was very limited. Lindley used to play Corelli's violin sonatas in public as late as 1850. Petrik died at Prague about 1798; he left a number of church and chamber music compositions which were in high esteem. He was also a chief exponent of the violoncello compositions by Himmelbauer.

IGNAZ MALZAT, born about 1730 in Vienna, a virtuoso on the horn, wrote a concerto for the violoncello, mentioned in Träg's catalogue of music of 1799. It remained in manuscript, and probably exists still in the Salzburg library.

JOSEPH B. ZYKA, born about 1720, received his musical education at Prague, and was violoncellist in the famous private band of the Prince Elector of Saxony at Dresden from 1743 to 1764. Fétis's statement that he *was appointed* there in 1756 arises from the misunderstanding of Marpurg's note that the violoncellists of the Royal chapel at Dresden *in 1756* were: "Jos. Zyka, N. Hofmann, Joh. George Knechtel and Ant. Pincinetti, jun.," which does not mean that they were only then appointed. In 1766 he was appointed Royal chamber musician in Berlin, where he died at the beginning of last century. His compositions, consisting of a double concerto for two violoncellos, several concertos, solos and duets, remained in manuscript. His son:

FREDERICK ZYKA was born at Dresden. He became, under his father's tuition, also an excellent violoncellist. He went to Berlin in 1764, where he was appointed as a member of the Royal chapel, together with his father. It is noteworthy that six members of the Zyka family are to be found among the foremost chamber musicians of the Berlin court orchestra.

JOHANN HETTISCH (HETES), born 1748 at Liblin, in Bohemia, was a prominent virtuoso of his time. He received his first education at the Piarists (religious order) College at Schlan, and afterwards went to Prague for his musical education. In 1772 he is mentioned as the foremost virtuoso in Prague, but shortly after he received an appointment as government official at Lemberg, in which position Gerber found him in 1788. He died at Livon, in Polonia, in 1793, leaving several concertos and solos in manuscript. His playing was distinguished by beauty of tone. Dr. Burney, who knew him personally, speaks highly of him in his diary.

FILSL, an excellent violoncellist, organist, composer and great contrapuntist of the early part of the eighteenth century. He lived still in Prague after 1750 and died there, but the exact date of his decease is not known. Dlabacz, who speaks very highly of his compositions, relates that some of his masses, etc., are preserved in the church library (choir) of the Monastery of Strahov, near Prague, and that he left numerous concertos for the violoncello. Two of these concertos were in the musical library of Dlabacz about 1815.

JOSEPH CHRIST, born about the middle of the eighteenth century at Ponikla, in Bohemia, was a choirboy at St. Nicholas at Prague (Auf der Kleinseite). He lost his voice and took to the violoncello, which he studied without a master.

In 1786 he went to Riga, where he joined the private band of the Duke of Kurland, who was a great lover of music, and who ranked Christ among the greatest violoncellists of his time. In 1798 he revisited Prague in the company of the Duke who rewarded his services in a princely manner. About his later life nothing is known.

JOSEPH FIALA, born 1751, was the son of a schoolmaster in Sochowitz, and is one of the most interesting and romantic figures among all the musicians of his time. His birthplace formed part of the feudal possessions of the Countess Netolitzky, an arbitrary and tyrannical woman, who, like other sovereigns of her time, made use of the absolute ownership of her subjects to the fullest extent. Early signs of musical talent were carefully fostered by his father until the Countess took him to Prague, where she placed him under the celebrated oboe player, John Stiastny, father of the two great violoncellists, Jean and Bernard Stiastny. At the same time he studied the violoncello under Werner. At home, that is, in the Countess's house, he was treated as servant-boy, and put to wash up dishes in the kitchen, much in the same way as Lully in the palace of Louis XIV. This treatment exasperated the high-spirited youth, who, under the excellent tuition of his master, was ripening fast into the most perfect oboe virtuoso of his time. One day he made his escape, together with other musicians of the Countess, and placed himself under the protection of Count Hartiz, at Ratisbon. The Countess, nettled by his independent spirit, lured him back to Prague, where he was treated with every indignity. His life was made intolerable, and he escaped a second time. The Countess, on hearing of his flight, sent out a body of mounted and armed men, who overtook and recaptured poor Fiala, who was forthwith thrown into prison. The Countess then conceived the diabolical scheme of having his front teeth pulled out, that he might be permanently incapacitated from playing the oboe, and she gave orders to that effect to his gaoler. This man, however, had more human feeling than his high-born mistress. He took Fiala secretly into his house, and despatched a messenger to the Emperor to inform him of the poor artist's impending fate. The Emperor, who had heard Fiala on several occasions, and who was greatly impressed with his talent, ordered his immediate release and his absolute freedom from his bondage to the Countess. In 1777 he was a member of Prince Wallenstein's orchestra in Vienna, where the Elector, Max Joseph of Bavaria, heard him, and induced him to follow him to Mannheim. There he married Josepha Prochaska, the daughter of one of the court musicians. In the following year 1778, he accepted an engagement from the Bishop of Salzburg, when he became intimately acquainted with the Mozart family and Michael, the brother of Joseph Haydn.

His gentle and refined nature seems to have won him the friendship of all the distinguished people with whom he became acquainted. His friendship with W. A. Mozart was such that the latter arranged several concerts for him in Vienna, and C. F. Pohl tells us of various instances which testify to their friendly relations (Pohl, "Mozart and Haydn in London"). The Archbishop admired his oboe playing so much that it caused his ruin, as he made him play sometimes as many as ten or twelve concertos in one night. The consequent over-exertion caused the rupture of a blood-vessel, which obliged him to abandon the oboe for a time, and he could never again play that instrument for any length of time. He devoted himself now chiefly to the violoncello and the viol da gamba. The latter instrument he had taken up at the instigation of a prebendary of the Salzburg Cathedral, who presented him with a very fine specimen. At one of the concerts which Mozart arranged for him at Vienna he played the gamba as well as the oboe. Count Besborodkow, who heard him on that occasion, induced him to join his own private music and to go with him to Russia, where the Count resided. He did so after visiting Ratisbon, Gotha, Berlin and Warsaw, where he appeared in his new capacity as gambist and violoncellist. In Russia his fame spread rapidly, and Prince Orloff entrusted him with the formation of his private band, for which he rewarded him very liberally. His next step would have been into the imperial chamber music. But his health had received rude shocks, and his wife suffered from homesickness, which finally induced him to return to Prague, where he arrived with his wife and son, Franz, who was eight years old, in 1790. On March 16 he gave a concert in the Kleinseiter Theatre belonging to Count Thun. On that occasion he played the oboe as well as the gamba and the violoncello for the last time. At the Monastery of Strahov, near Prague, he was greatly beloved, and gave several so-called "Academies" (concert recitals) there during his sojourn in Prague. After a stay of about a year in his native town, he went with his family to Mannheim, and thence to Berlin. In 1792 he settled in Donaueschingen as violoncellist to Prince Fürstenberg, whose famous private band was at one time (about 1831-51) conducted by Kalliwoda, when C. Leopold Boehm was the solo violoncellist. Fiala remained in this position until his death, which occurred in 1816. His compositions, which were highly esteemed in their time, consist of a mass which was performed for the first time in 1804, and is his only choral work; several symphonies, and chamber music in various combinations. He wrote several concertos for the violoncello, which apparently remained in manuscript. A duet for flute or oboe and violoncello or bassoon has been republished by C. F. Schmidt in Heilbronn. It is of the conventional type of the time. A little sonata in three short movements for viol da gamba, violin or violoncello, of which the author of these lines has a copy, is not above the average composition of Vanhal, Gyrowetz, etc. His son, Franz, who wrote a biographical sketch of his father's eventful life, was an excellent violoncellist and court musician to the Grand Duke of Baden.

FATHER FRANCIS MENSI, born March 27, 1753, at Bistra, near Chrudim, the son of the bailiff of Count Hohenems. His father was of Italian birth. He showed early signs of musical talent with a predilection for the violoncello. His parents, who settled in Prague, placed him under Joseph Reicha for the study of that instrument, while Cajetan Vogel conducted his theoretical studies. He was also a good executant on the violin. In 1808 he was "pastor" at Pher, where he devoted all his leisure hours to music, writing a considerable amount of church music, symphonies and string quartets, which were highly praised, and are partly preserved in the church library of the Monastery of Strahov, near Prague. He produced many excellent pupils on the violin as well as on the violoncello. Among the latter were Johann Brodeczky, a clever violinist, who wrote, among other works, a number of violoncello solos. Czizek and Count Spork, whom Wasielewski mentions, were also violin pupils of Mensi.

WENZESLAUS CZIZEK lived towards the end of the eighteenth and beginning of the nineteenth century. He was a pupil of Mensi, and a clever executant.

WENZESLAUS HIMMELBAUER, whose biography appeared in page 182, was also a native of Bohemia.

JOHANN PATZELT, born about the middle of the eighteenth century, in Bohemia, was a virtuoso on the violoncello and on the piano, as well as a composer. He served in an Austrian artillery regiment, but quitted the service to devote himself entirely to music. After touring for several years, he settled in Vienna in 1788, where he died about 1818. His private history is for the greater part shrouded in mystery. He wrote variations, sonatas, solos and concertos. The latter remained in manuscript. A sonata for violoncello is in the library of the "Gesellschaft der Musikfreunde." in Vienna.

JACOB JOHANN RYBA, born at Przesstiez, in Bohemia, October 26, 1765, was an excellent violoncellist, as well as violinist and organist. In 1780 he entered the seminary of St. Wenzeslaus at Prague, and in 1788 he was appointed Rector of the College (Gymnasium) at Roczmittal. He was a prolific composer with a strongly marked nationality. He left forty-eight trios, seventy-two quartets, seven quintets, eighty-seven sonatas, one hundred and thirty sets of variations, and thirty-eight concertos for sundry instruments; also six operas, sixteen masses, twenty-four short masses, and other choral works. He died in 1815 at Roczmittal.

VINCENZ HAUSCHKA was born at Mies on January 21, 1766, and died at Berlin on September 21, 1840. His father, who was a schoolmaster, instructed him in the elements of music, and at the age of eight he became a choirboy of the Cathedral at Prague, where he received a good musical as well as general education. He remained there for six years, during which time he took up the study of the violoncello under the guidance of Joseph Christ, and theory under Seeger. His studies under Christ were but of a short duration, as that artist went to Riga in 1780. Hauschka pursued his study of the violoncello assiduously without a master, and his progress was such that he was engaged by Count Thun as a violoncellist when he was only sixteen years old. Two years later the Count died, and Hauschka started on a concert tour, visiting the various courts and principal towns of Germany. In 1792 he was in Vienna, where he was greatly admired as a virtuoso. As an accomplished gentleman, he won for himself the good graces of the Empress Maria Theresa, and in 1793 he received the appointment of a Councillor in the Exchequer's Office and Administrator of Domaines—a curious change from an artist's career, but not infrequent in those days, as may be seen in the case of Schenck, Hesse and several other great virtuosos of the seventeenth and eighteenth centuries, who were rewarded with high positions in government offices. From this time Hauschka did not appear as a performer in public, but his musical talents were greatly appreciated in court circles, where he frequently played with the members of the imperial family—as, for instance, at Persenberg, on the Danube, where, on one occasion, he took part in a quintet with the Emperor, Prince Metternich, Count Wrbna, Kutschera, and the composer Eybler. The Grand Duke of Tuscany, brother of the Emperor, turned over for them. In 1805 he took up the baryton, at the special request of the Empress Maria Theresa. That instrument was much favoured at the Austrian court, and Haydn wrote a considerable number of compositions for it, including the celebrated cantata with baryton accompaniment on the death of Frederick the Great *(see page 114)*. Eybler, who was mentioned above, also contributed to its literature as did also Weigl and Pichel.

PLATE XXXIV.

A MUSIC PARTY IN THE GARDENS OF KEW PALACE. FREDERIC LEWIS, PRINCE OF WALES, PLAYING THE VIOLONCELLO. FROM A PAINTING BY PHILIP MERCIER, 1733.

To face page 344.

Hauschka was by that time one of the leaders of musical life in Vienna, and he was one of the founders of the "Gesellschaft der Musikfreunde" (Society of Friends of Music), to which Brahms bequeathed part of his fortune. He assisted also in the foundation of the "Concert Spirituel" and the Conservatoire.

He composed for the violoncello: Three Sonatas, Op. 1; Three Sonatas, Op. 2 (Vienna, Riedl); five duos for baryton and violoncello, songs with violoncello *obbligato*, divertimenti with bass, and three concertos with orchestra, which remained in manuscript. He composed also notturnos for three voices, with accompaniment of mandolin, viola and violoncello, an interesting combination.

By far the most important among Czechian violoncellists, and even among all his contemporaries, was JEAN STIASTNY. His father, John Stiastny, who died when member of the Prague orchestra in 1788, was a celebrated oboe player, and, as such, the master of Joseph Fiala. How far he may be credited with the education of his sons is uncertain; but, as a violoncellist, Jean Stiastny owed a great deal to his elder brother:

BERNHARD WENZESLAUS STIASTNY, who was born at Prague in 1770, and who received his musical education chiefly from the celebrated organist, Seger (or Seegr), devoted himself eventually entirely to the study of the violoncello, and was appointed as principal violoncello at the Prague Opera. From all reports which the author of these lines has received from some old musicians, and especially from his late master, Johann Hoecke, in Cologne, Bernhard Stiastny did not attain any marked degree of technical ability, but was a conscientious and sound player, and good teacher. His published compositions all point in that direction, one of the most important being his "Méthode de Violoncelle," a tutor, in two parts, which contains many excellent points, although it is in parts somewhat prolix, while the advanced technique, especially the thumb positions, do not receive sufficient attention. It has been republished by Schott, in Mayence, in German and French. The latter has also published two books, each containing six easy solos. Berra, in Prague, published six instructive and progressive sonatas for two violoncellos; and Simrock, in Bonn, "Il maestro é lo scolare," eight imitations, and six pieces with fugues for two violoncellos.

JEAN STIASTNY was also born at Prague in 1774. He was instructed in the art of violoncello playing by his brother, Bernhard, for whom he always retained an affectionate admiration, although he surpassed him, by a long way, both as a virtuoso and as a composer. His six duos for two violoncellos, in two series (published by Schott), are dedicated to his brother, and they form one of the finest monuments of violoncello literature. They contain effects which must have been an absolute revelation in their time, and which are admirable in these days. His passage-work shows immense ingenuity, and, although modern violoncello technique has entirely broken away from the old passage-work of the Romberg and the Stiastny school, and struck out bolder lines on the basis of the Beethoven, Schubert and Schumann technique, the works of Stiastny will always form an indispensable item in the educational literature for the instrument. It is interesting to note his fine feeling nature, in the way in which he wrote some of the most difficult passages in these duets for the *second* violoncello, which he reserved for himself, ceding the first to his brother, thus giving him the place of honour without placing before him a task which would have surpassed his strength. About 1810, Jean Stiastny was solo violoncellist to the Grand Duke of Frankfurt, Prince Primate von Dalberg, according to the title of his Divertimento, Op. 3, which has afterwards been republished by Schott. In 1813, he was still living at Frankfurt. Baudiot went there in that year to hear him play, but returned without gaining his object, as Stiastny was too nervous to play before strangers.

Johannes Höke, a pupil of F. A. Kummer, and first teacher in Cologne of the writer of these lines, used to relate that he too, had heard from his master, and some of his elder colleagues, that the only way to hear Stiastny play was to obtain access to the house where he lived, and listen to his playing outside his room without his being aware of anybody's presence. This nervousness kept him away from the concert platform, although he appeared in public now and again.

Wasielewski states that in 1820 Stiastny was "Musik Direktor" of Nüremberg, and lived at Mannheim, but it is more likely that he went there about 1824-5, as the "Allgemeine Musikalische Zeitung" contains a letter of musical events from Nürnberg for the winter season, 1825-6, stating that: "Music Director Stiastny, *who, unfortunately, has gone to Mannheim*, played a concerto by Stowray" in that town. This was probably the work of an English composer, judging from the name. Certain it is that Stiastny was in England, where he made the acquaintance of Crosdill and Lindley, and other distinguished artists and amateurs. His Concertino, Op. 7, is dedicated to Lindley, while his trios, Duos Concertans, Op. 8, are dedicated to Crosdill, and Six Pièces Faciles, Op. 9, to Sir William Curtice. About the exact time and extent of his sojourn in England nothing appears to be known, nor are there any particulars of his latter life. His compositions for the violoncello are: Two Sonatas, with bass, Op. 2; Divertimento, with alto and bass, Op. 3; Twelve Short Pieces, Op. 4; Six Easy Pieces, Op. 5; Three Grand Duos, Op. 6; Concertino, Op. 7; Three "Duos Concertans," Op. 8; Six Easy Pieces, Op. 9; Andante and Variations, Op. 10; Six Solos, Op. 11; Rondo and Variations, Op. 12, with quartet accompaniment; and the above-mentioned six duets, dedicated to his brother, which bear no opus number. Most of these works have been republished.

JOSEPH VALENTIN DONT, the father of the celebrated violinist, Jacob Dont, who is famous by his studies, was born at Nieder-Georgenthal, in Bohemia, on April 15, 1776. He was sent to a school in Prague, and there he studied the violoncello under Stiastny (Bernhard ?). After the completion of his studies he was engaged by Count Breuner as violoncellist in the Count's quartet. He filled that post for about six years, when he became a member of the orchestra of the Kärntner Thor Theatre in Vienna in 1804. In 1828 he joined the orchestra of the "Burgtheater" in that town. He enjoyed a high reputation as quartet and orchestral player. His compositions are not numerous, and they remained for the greater part unpublished. Schilling states that he left a complete tutor, which his son intended to publish.

FRIEDRICH WRANITZKY, son of Anton Wranitzky, the composer and conductor of Prince Lobkowitz's private music (1794-1819), was known as a good violoncellist. No details regarding his career are obtainable.

JOSEPH THEODOR KROV (KROB, KROFF), was born in 1797 at Strasic. Krov was destined for the career of a lawyer. In 1821 he studied philosophy at the University of Prague, where he made the acquaintance of Count Clam-Gallas, with whom he lived on terms of friendship until the Count's death in 1822. At that time he pursued most assiduously the study of the violoncello under B. Hastuy, professor of that instrument at the Prague Conservatoire, and also the study of musical theory under Tomaczek. His endeavours to found a Czechian opera in 1823 remained fruitless. After completing his studies as a lawyer, he went on the stage as an actor and singer. In the latter capacity he made his debut in Budapest, after which he visited the principal towns of Austria and Germany. In 1831 he composed the famous "Hussit Hymn," which has been arranged by Liszt and also found its way into Balfe's "Bohemian Girl" and Dvorák's "Hussitska." Theo Schulz, in his interesting articles on Czechian violinists, says that it was composed at "Mentz" and published by Schott. As there is no such place as Mentz to be found in the popular geographical works, it is in all probability meant for Mayence (Mainz), the seat of the firm of R. Schott and Sons. The song, composed to the German words of the Polish poet Workinski, was suppressed by the government on account of its revolutionary character, and Krov fled first to Holland, and then to England. Piczek sang it as a national song in 1846, and Liszt, under the impression that it was an ancient song, arranged it as the "Hussit Hymn." As a matter of fact, it finishes with a few bars of the old hymn to Saint Venceslas. Krov composed also a set of six English songs. In his later years he lived at Nice, where he used to play Hasting's duets with his intimate friend, Leopold Jansa. Krov died at Draguignan in 1859.

KRENES, born 1787 in Vienna, was an excellent violoncellist and teacher of his instrument, who was afterwards appointed as a government official at Lemberg, where he continued as soloist and teacher of the violoncello up to the time of his death, which occurred in 1823. He left a number of compositions, which, for the greater part, were considered very difficult. C. Lipinski, was his most prominent pupil.

CARL LIPINSKI, born 1790 at Radzyú, who afterwards became a famous violinist, started his career as violoncello virtuoso. He studied that instrument under Krenes at Lemberg, and played Romberg's concertos in public with perfection.

JOSEPH SCHUBERT, born at Warnsdorf, instrumentalist and prolific composer, 1779-88, chamber musician of the Markgrave of Schwedt, died as chamber musician at Dresden in 1812. He wrote a concerto for violoncello.

CHAPTER XIX.

SUMMARY OF THE DEVELOPMENT OF THE VIOLONCELLO UP TO 1800.

THE rivalry which had existed for over a century and a half between the viols and the violin family terminated towards the middle of the eighteenth century by the total extinction of the former, leaving the violoncello as victor in possession of the field.

The viol da gamba or bass viol (French basse de viole) held its place as principal solo instrument and in the orchestra longer than any other member of the viol family. The reasons for this are manifold. In the first instance, it had the largest compass of any bowed instrument, combining both treble and bass in one single instrument, thus rendering both parts singly as well as combined, in chords, arpeggios and skipping passages, touching alternately upon melody and bass notes as well as intermediate parts, as described by Christopher Simpson in his instructions for "playing upon a ground" *(see page 47)*. This latter technique was essentially in the nature of the bass viol, and one of the features which, misapplied, helped to retard the progress of the violoncello, as we shall see presently.

Another reason for the predominance of the bass viol was

the beauty and volume of its tone. Although it was surpassed in the latter by the violoncello, it surpassed all other viols in both qualities, its only rival in these being the viol d'amour.

The quality of tone of the bass viol is of great beauty. It is silvery, very sweet, and though lacking the power of the violoncello it is carrying, and capable of being heard in every part of a large concert hall. The very refined quality of its tone was particularly sympathetic to the manners and tastes of the educated classes of the seventeenth and early eighteenth centuries. The bass strings are the weakest, with the result that in all gamba music the upper strings are used for all melody parts from which the middle and lower strings are almost entirely excluded.

The technique of the bass viol or viol da gamba had, moreover, reached a very high degree of perfection, while the violoncello was still essentially a bass instrument, and only in isolated cases does it appear as a solo instrument of a very primitive nature previous to the fourth decade of the eighteenth century.

It is not surprising under these circumstances to hear Thomas Mace speak disdainfully of "the scoulding violins," and to read Dr. Hubert Le Blanc's amusing "Defence of the Viol."

The one great mistake all these ardent devotees of the viol made was that they judged the members of the violin family from the *gambist's* point of view, and took it for granted that they should compete with the viols on their own ground. They never perceived that the newer instruments had an entirely separate mission to fulfil, which could not be achieved until their real nature and possibilities revealed themselves by degrees to those who approached them in an earnest and loving spirit.

That the first players of the violoncello should have turned to the bass viol as a model for fingering, bowing, and the style of their music, is but natural. Hence we find, here and there, attempts at fretting the neck of the violoncello, adding a fifth string tuned to D, like the first string of the gamba, and the tuning C, G, D, G, for the four-stringed violoncello. The fretting and various tunings soon disappeared, while the five-stringed violoncello was never in general use.

Of greater consequence for the technical development of the violoncello was the tenacity with which composers followed the lines of the viol da gamba music when writing for the newer instrument. Skipping passages, double stops and chords, as far as the latter were possible, intermixed with running scale passages, formed the groundwork, while repeated figures moving backwards and forwards across the strings in one position of the hand were almost unknown.

The elements of improvisation, as practised on the bass viol, particularly in England, showed their features likewise here and there in the early violoncello music.

The passages which were most effective on the bass viol were for the greater part hostile to the true nature of the violoncello, and their adaptation retarded the development of its technique, which only commenced to flow into its natural channel under Cervetto, Berteau and J. P. Duport, about the middle of the eighteenth century.

It is not surprising, therefore, to find that some musicians and musical amateurs still clung to the viol da gamba down to the latter part of the eighteenth century, when it found its last great representative in C. F. Abel.

But the great struggle between the viol and the violoncello commenced early in the eighteenth century, when a considerable number of viol da gambists (the brothers Saint-Sevin, called L'Abbé, Berteau, and others) exchanged their instrument for the violoncello, which was rapidly coming to the front. In 1740 Hubert Le Blanc, a doctor of law, published at Amsterdam his quaint little book, "Defense / de la Basse / de Viole / Contre les Entreprises du / Violon / Et les Prétentions du / Violoncel."/ In this he tells us: "Sultan Violon, un avorton,

PLATE XXXV.
ROBERT LINDLEY. FROM A MEZZOTINT.

un Pygmée, se met en tête d'en vouloir a la Monarchie universelle. Non content de l'Italie son partage, il se propose d'envahir les Etats voisins, et rendre à la Basse de Viole à son tour, ce qu'elle avait prêté aux Luths, Thuorbe et Guitarre, sans même excepter la Harpe du Roi David, qui étoient anéantis par le charme des Pièces du Père Marais . . . . "

> Sultan Violin, a freak, a Pigmy takes it into his head that he wants to be King of the Universe. Not content with Italy, his heritage, he proposes to invade the neighbouring countries, and to do to the Basse Viol in its turn, what that had done to the Lute, Theorbo and Guitar not excepted the Harp of King David which were annihilated by the charme of the Pieces of the Father Marais [*Marin Marais, see page 102*]. . . . . The two Acolytes of Sultan Violin are called Messire Harpsichord and Sir Violoncello. . . . . The Violoncello which hitherto found itself a miserable crab, penitential garment (?"haire") and poor Devil, whose condition bordered on starvation, no feasting, flatters itself now that it will be caressed in place of the Bass Viol, it builds up visions of happiness which make it weep with emotion.

One should imagine Dr. Le Blanc could never have been bilious again after this effusion of gall, but one must read it in the original to enjoy the comicality of this tempest in a teacup. But he cannot console himself.

"'A clever violinist at Dijon,' he tells us, 'spoke to me in a slighting manner of the viol as if it were in the case of the Milesians of whom it was said that "once upon a time they were a brave people." Placing the violoncello above the viol, he said that the violoncello did not try to usurp the treble part but was content in its sphere of a bass.'

"I answered him openly that it was a shameful restriction of an instrument if one could not play treble parts (melody) on it, as they form the soul of music. Violoncellists feel the importance of this to such an extent that they stubbornly sail against wind and waves on the endless sea of the trebles of sonatas.

"His opinion cannot be admitted if one hears the latest violoncellists, who have vanquished by hard work such immense difficulties that it makes one shudder to hear them prelude. One must admit they are most estimable, but not that their instrument is agreeable (amiable)."

This is very interesting as a contemporary description of the efforts which were made at the beginning of the eighteenth century to develop the technique of the violoncello. What would Le Blanc have said could he have heard Duport and Romberg only fifty years later?

There was still a lurking prejudice in favour of the viol, which was considered the instrument suitable for a gentleman of quality. This prejudice was very strong in England during the seventeenth century, as we have already remarked. Le Blanc says the viol combined "the qualities of the Greek lyre with still higher ones," and he gives a very good definition of its qualities by describing the tone as "half round, penetrating but not piercing. It should therefore not be played together with nor before the instruments of Cremona (violin, viola and violoncello)." In recompense the viol had its revenge on the harpsichord, although it is true that when it called the latter a "bunch of keys," the harpsichord retorted by calling the viol "Mrs. Teakettle"! Very explicit is Le Blanc's characterisation of the tone of the viol as of "female quality" as against the "male quality" of the violoncello.

This describes the difference between the two instruments better than anything else could, and it is applicable to other instruments of the present day, for instance, the flute and the oboe.

Le Blanc compares the viol with the bells of the Abbey of St. Germain, near Paris, which have a very sweet sound, and the violin with the bells of the clock over the Palace in Paris, which were very loud.

In Italy the viols were no longer used as soon as the violin came into practice at the beginning of the seventeenth century. In "Familiar Letters of Abraham Hill" (London, 1767), there is a letter dated "Lucca, October 1" (1657) containing the following passage:

> The instrumental music is much better than I expected. The organ and violin they are masters of, but the bass viol they have not at all in use, and to supply its place they have the bass violin with four strings, and use it as we do the bass viol.

From the memoirs of Sir Roger North (about 1700) we obtain the earliest information about the cultivation of the violoncello in England. This is what he tells us:

> There was a society of gentlemen of good esteem whom I shall not name, as some of them are still living, that used to meet often for consorts after Baptist's (Draghi, 1667-1706 ?) manner and performing exceeding well with bass violins (a cours instrument as it was then, which they used to hire), their friends and acquaintances were admitted, and by degrees, as the fame of their meeting spread, so many auditors came that their room was crowded, and to prevent that inconvenience, they took room in Fleet Street, and the Taverner pretended to make formall seats, and to take money, and then the society disbanded.

The taverner then engaged professionals, the meeting became fashionable and led to the erection of York Buildings in 1680.

In 1739 Dr. Burney ("History of Music," Volume IV, page 66), tells us that: The elder Cervetto is now first mentioned as just arrived, and this worthy professor, who remained in England till the time of his death, at above a hundred, with Abaco, Lanzetti, Pasqualini and Caporale, about this time brought the violoncello into favour, and made us nice judges of that instrument."

Mattheson testifies already to the important position which the violoncello had acquired in his " New eröffnete Orchester," which appeared in 1713: "Der hervorragende Violoncello, die Bassa Viola und Viola di Spala, sind kleine Bass-Geigen, in Vergleichung der gröszern, mit 5 auch wol 6 sayten, worauff man mit leichterer Arbeit als auff den groszen Maschinen allerhand geschwinde Sachen, Variationes und Mannieren machen kan."

(The pre-eminent Violoncello, Bassa Viola and the Bassa di Spala, are small Bass-Geigen in comparison with the larger ones, with five, sometimes six strings, on which one can execute quick things, variations and graces with less trouble than on the big machines; by which Mattheson means the double bass.)

It is not quite clear whether the "five, sometimes six strings," applies to the larger or smaller "bass-geigen," but five-stringed violoncellos existed down to Mattheson's time, although four-stringed violoncellos were in the majority even from the very beginning.

The Abbé Tardieu, of Tarrascon, owes his popularity in all the musical dictionaries to the fact that he was credited (among others by Gerber) with the invention of the five-stringed violoncello, the upper string of which was tuned a fourth higher than the A string, viz., D. This instrument was used down to the latter part of the eighteenth century *(see the description and illustration of the Rev. F. W. Galpin's five-stringed violoncello on pages 122-3)*. The fact is mentioned, among others, in an article, "The Rise and Progress of the Violoncello," from the "Quarterly Musical Magazine and Review" of 1824. The good Abbé in this, appears to have made his invention about a hundred years before his birth. But the article gives us a good idea of the estimation of the instrument at that period, mentioning among other things, the fact that the "violone," which is indicated as the accompanying instrument to many Italian violin sonatas, was not the double-bass, but the violoncello. The following are some extracts:

"The violoncello has been rising gradually *since the beginning of the last century* into estimation, and may now be said to enjoy an almost equal reputation with the violin as a concerto instrument, and as an accompaniment its merits as well as its character are far higher. . . . .

"It appears to have derived its present excellence in some measure from the alteration which was made in its mode of stringing in the beginning of 1600, by the Abbé Tardieu, of Tarrascon. . . . . But about the year 1725, the upper D string was taken off, as from the improved method of fingering it was perfectly useless. . . . .

"The violoncello was the violone of former times, for in the earlier editions of Corelli, particularly that of opera three, printed at Bologna in 1690, the bass part, which is not for the organ, is entitled violone, whereas in the latter editions, printed at Amsterdam by Estienne Roger, the same part is entitled violoncello, which is the proper name for the instrument, as it is half the size of the violone or double-bass. . . . .

"One of the greatest difficulties attending the study of the violoncello is the size of the instrument; so many different positions of the hand and fingers occur that the learner's attention is divided, and the worst habits thus insensibly formed. The constant shifting of the hand required in performing a piece of music, of even ordinary difficulty, renders the time as well as the proper tone of the performer most uncertain, unless he is particularly careful and laborious in his practice. If anyone wishes to play the violoncello well he must not too suddenly attempt to play difficult music—he must by dint of application and attention, obtain a good tone and a secure tune first, by a slow and steady practice of the scale, which it will be found absolutely necessary to continue even during a long period. A good tone is produced more by the pressure of the fingers than by the force of the bow."

Although, as we pointed out before, the influence of the bass viol upon the violoncello retarded its progress to some extent, it benefited it in more than one way, as they showed a close kinship in many points, for instance, the almost identical distance between tones and semitones on the finger-board. Then again it induced players who turned from the older to the newer instrument to adapt as much as possible of the double stopping and chord playing, which was highly developed on the bass viol, although very difficult on the violoncello.

THE TUNING.

The tuning, as we have shown, was subject to variations. Although Mersenne, in his "Harmonie Universelle" (1636-7), gives already the tuning in fifths: C, G, D, A, we find other tunings in use down to Bach who wrote one of his solo suites for a violoncello tuned: C, G, D, G. A similar tuning was employed by Galli, with B flat or B natural for the fourth string *(see page 141)*.

That under such circumstances a uniform system of fingering was impossible is evident, and also that before such a system had been established, florid passages and a rich figuration as we find it in the seventeenth century viol da gamba music could not be attempted. That Italy was making rapid strides in that direction is evident from the compositions of Gabrieli and Galli, which are so far the oldest monuments of violoncello literature, the date of their publication being 1689 and 1691 respectively.

Another important achievement of the Italian violoncellists was the introduction of

THE THUMB POSITION.

This is attributed to Francischello, and has its origin in the technique of the "trompetta marina," a long triangular monochord on which the notes were stopped by the thumb of the right hand. Applying this system to the violoncello it enabled the player to make a freer use of the higher positions. Unfortunately, none of Francischello's compositions are to be found, as it would be very interesting to see what use he made of this new method of fingering. None of his contemporaries exceed the "B" or "C" at most beyond the fourth position on the A string. Carlo Ferrari has been credited with the introduction of the thumb position in France, but as Corrette mentions it in his "Méthode" in 1741, the credit belongs apparently to J. B. Struck.

The signs by which it was indicated varied widely. Some used a ✗, others an O, but as the latter sign served likewise to indicate open strings and harmonics, it was eventually altered to ϙ as we know it still.

THE HOLDING OF THE BOW.

During the seventeenth and first half of the eighteenth century many violoncellists held the bow gamba fashion, i.e., with the hand *under* the nut as illustrated by Christopher Simpson *(see the "Division-Viol," page 48)*, one of the latest to follow this manner of holding was J. G. C. Schetky, who died in 1824, others held the bow with the hand *over* the stick but about an inch and a half in front of the nut. This holding is shown in the portrait of Francischello, and was practised by many violoncellists as late as the second half of the eighteenth century. Some placed the thumb *against* the narrow end of the nut which closes on to the stick, and the author's first master, who was a pupil of F. A. Kummer, still held his bow in this way. The modern holding of the bow appears, however, to have come into practice in the eighteenth century, and although it was not generally followed, it is clearly indicated among others in Robert Crome's tutor which appeared in 1765.

TUTORS.

The earliest instructions for playing any instrument of the violin family are given in the "Harmonie Universelle," by the Minorite Father Marin Mersenne, published in Paris 1636-7. He describes the various members of the violin family, enumerating five which were called: "Dessus, Taille, Cinquiesme, Haute Contre and Basse Contre." The basse contre, as well as the dessus, are illustrated together with their respective bows, and the compass of the open strings of all the members of the violin family. The portrait of Mersenne and title page of the above work appeared in the author's "The Romance of the Fiddle."

With regard to these he tells us that the haute-contre, taille and cinquiesme, although of different size had the same compass and that the twenty-four "violons du roy," called cinquième, what the ordinary musicians called haute-contre, and, in fact, that there was a rare confusion with regard to these instruments. What he calls "la basse" was our violoncello which is evident from the tuning which is given in the compass of the "concert" (the complete ensemble) as:

A second "basse à la façon de Lorraine" (corresponding to the double-bass) is mentioned as going down to E. We see from the illustration that the two lower strings were already covered with wire. Mersenne gives no intimation as to the fingering of this instrument, but it appears taken for granted that it was analogous to that of the "dessus" (our violin) for which the fingering is given, commencing with the first finger at the distance of a *full* tone from the open string, whereas on the viols it commenced with the first fret at a *semitone* distance from the open string. With regard to the bowing he says that the first beat of a bar commences with a *down* bow while the next note is taken with an up bow, this reverses the order of bowing on the bass viol. To illustrate the capabilities of the violins he gives a "Fantaisie à 5, composée par le Sieur Henry le Jeune." Part of this has been republished in modern notation in the author's "The Romance of the Fiddle."

Speculation has been rife as to who this Henry le Jeune was, but without success. Mersenne's work is, to our knowledge, the only work of the seventeenth century dealing with the technique of the violoncello or "basse du violon." The Italians who produced several instructive works on the violin have not given us any for the violoncello, and John Playford, in his "Skill of Musick," which appeared about the middle of that century, deals only with the "treble" violin.

The first work which throws any light upon the early technique of the violoncello is the "Méthode théorique et pratique, pour apprendre en peu de tems le Violoncelle .... composé par Michel Corrette, XXIV[e.] ouvrage. A Paris chez l'auteur,

Mᵉ· Boivin et le Sʳ· Le Clerc; a Lyon chez Mʳ· de Bretonne. Avec Privilège du Roy MDCCXLI."

We have not been able to examine this rare work, of which a unique copy is preserved in the Paris Conservatoire Library.

It commences with general instructions on the elements of music and then goes on to: (1) the manner of holding the violoncello; (2) the manner of holding the bow; (3) its use in up and down stroke; (4) tuning of the violoncello; (5) division of the finger-board in diatonic and chromatic series of notes; (6) fingering of the first and following positions; (7) the manner of returning from higher positions to the first position; (8) shakes and appoggiatura; (9) different bowings; (10) double stops and arpeggios; (11) thumb position. With a concluding chapter giving instructions for those who wish to exchange the viol da gamba for the violoncello, and instructions for the accompaniment of the voice or instrumental solos. Wasielewski, who has evidently examined the book, gives but a meagre description of it.

THE FINGERING.

This was still in its experimental stages. Violoncellists of the seventeenth and early eighteenth centuries evidently tried to follow the example of the contemporary violinists who had already advanced the technique of their instrument to a considerable degree of perfection. They appear at the same time to have overlooked the disparity with regard to the dimensions of the neck and the consequent difference in the distance between tones and semitones.

Corrette gives the fingering for the first position as "one, two, four," uniformly for all four strings without taking notice of the fact that in that case a full tone falls between the first and fourth fingers on the C and G string, whereas the

CORRETTE'S FINGERING.

semitone is compassed by the second and fourth finger. The fourth position is fingered "one, two, three," instead of one, two, four or one, three, four, respectively. For this latter position he appears to have generally used the thumb position, explaining that the fourth finger was too short to be used in the fourth position as it would necessitate limitations in the use of the left arm, owing to the short neck of the instrument.

Exceptionally—he says—the fourth finger might be used for the B flat and B natural on the A string and the corresponding notes on the other strings in the fourth position, *without changing the position of the thumb.*

Higher notes than these were not employed by him nor by Buononcini, whom he appears to have taken for his model.

The use of the fourth finger in the thumb positions has been avoided, not only by Corrette and his contemporaries, but even by many later masters down to the beginning of last century. This was due to a slanting position of the left hand which drew the fourth finger up whereas a position of the hand at almost a right angle to the strings brings that finger right over the string making its use comparatively easy, although it can never stop the notes with the same force as the other fingers.

The fingering given by Corrette was followed by many players even down to the latter part of the eighteenth century, although many adopted slightly different methods. Still more curious was Corrette's fingering of the chromatic scale:

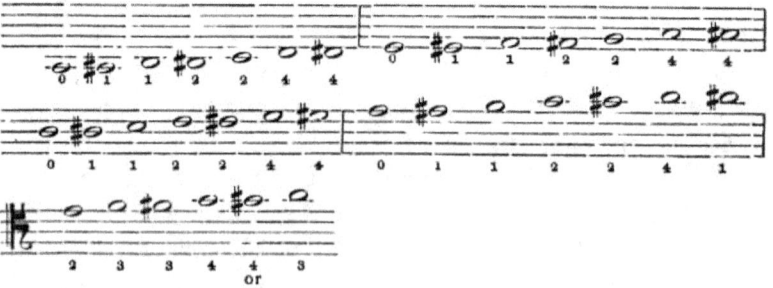

It is interesting to compare this with English publications of that period. The first is entitled: "The Gamut for the Violoncello, Printed by Henry Waylett at the Black Lyon in Exeter Change. Price 6d.," already referred to on page 318. It consists of a single sheet printed on one side only, and it was published between 1745 and 1746. After illustrating the tuning of the instrument the following scales are given:

* Evidently a misprint for "A natural."

Here we see the third finger used instead of the fourth on the two lower strings, while the fingering on the A string from the D upwards is absolutely impossible. On the other hand, he differentiates between the enharmonic notes in his chromatic scale except in the case of C sharp and D flat, which latter note does not appear.

The scales are followed by two lessons. We give an extract from the second which appears too exacting for beginner.

In the third bar from the end is an evident mistake; the first quaver should be a crotchet and the following triplet should be quavers.

As this sheet must have been published with a knowledge of the requirements of the time it does not impress one unfavourably with the ability of the average amateur for whose use it was destined.

Another very quaint publication is: "The Compleat Tutor for the Violoncello containing the best and easiest Instructions for Learners by Robt. Crome, already referred to on page 318 This work was published in 1765, and gives the same fingering for the chromatic scale as Corrette, but does not exceed :  which, in fact, he only uses on rare occasions. He still recommends the fretting the neck of the violoncello for the use of beginners, and to tune it in the following manner: "You must screw up the first string till it is in tune with the upper A in the bass of the harpsichord, or the upper A of the bassoon or an eighth below an A tuning fork; then screw up the second, till by putting the finger just below the seventh fret on the second string it has the same sound as the first string open, then if you strike the second open it will be D. The same method will do for the third and fourth string. But the best way of learning to tune is by ear, that is by solmisation. . . . ."

He explains this by means of the tune of the bells, a primitive, though certainly very practical, way. Amusing is his explanation of time *(see page 320)*.

His holding of the bow is "near the nut with the thumb and forefinger, and (the bow) supported with the other fingers near the end at a small distance from each other." We see thereby that he had relinquished the gamba fashion which was followed by many down to about the middle of the eighteenth century. He distinguishes "four principal kinds of using the bow": "*Bowing*, which is drawing the bow backward and forward for every note; *slurring*, which is by drawing the bow but once for two or any number of notes; *feathering the bow*, which is done like the slur, only it must be taken off the string after touching it; *the spring*, which last can't be explained but by demonstration." By the spring he means no doubt our spiccato.

Of the "feathering" he makes very early and frequent use in his examples.

The compass of the latter does not exceed: which is used only on rare occasions. The fourth position was still very awkward on account of the shortness of the neck which brought that position as high up as the fifth position on a modern instrument.

In the fingering he follows the system of Corrette, avoiding the use of the third finger in the first position entirely.

For the purpose of tuning he advises to "tie a piece of fiddle string on the neck under the strings" over "the seventh or last line which will make a frett, and will be a standard for tuning all the strings." He evidently did not care to rely too much on the "tuning by ear," in spite of his previous remarks on solmisation and the bells.

After a few meagre explanations about "graces" he gives a collection of pieces *(see page 320)*. Such collections formed the material for study in all the English tutors of the time, not only for the violoncello, but for all other instruments.

Similar but even more primitive tutors were those by Preston, published after 1778, Cahusac, between 1784-98 and Addison and Hodson, about 1800 *(see pages 321-2)*.

In the French tutors of the second half of the eighteenth century we see already a very considerable advance. Berteau had evidently used already the modern system of fingering in its essential parts, as both his pupils, Cupis and Tillière, employ it in their tutors. The former appeared about 1772, as the volumes of Clement's "Journal de Clavecin," advertised on the back of the title page, show the date 1762 to 1771. The title is "Méthode nouvelle et raisonnée pour apprendre jouer du Violoncelle .... avec un nombre de Leçons, Romances, Ariettes et Menuets variés, etc., par Mr. Cupis Le Jeune, Professeur du Violoncelle et Eleve du célèbre Bertaud. Prix 7 lbs., 4ˢ· [= four shillings]. Paris, Le Menu; London, Calkin and Budd, 118 Pall Mall." The compass does not exceed: and the thumb position is not even mentioned, although the demands upon the bow are very considerable. There are two pages of bowing exercises followed by thirty-five exercises, mostly with a second violoncello part containing staccato passages and even spring bow arpeggios!

It is interesting that he adopts the use of the tempered scale, as he explains that A sharp and B flat, D sharp and E flat, etc., are stopped in the same place.

Tillière, in his "Méthode pour le Violoncelle," dedicated to Mr. Rigaut, Physicien de la Marine, Paris, Bailleux; gives the thumb position a prominent place in his work, starting on

368 THE HISTORY OF THE VIOLONCELLO.

 and going up to , sounding an octave lower. He also gives a number of scales in that position commencing with the thumb in the *first* position; they are followed by arpeggios employing the *fourth finger* in the thumb position. In his exercises he has only one without the use of the thumb, four for double stopping and one for syncopation. The work is brought to a close by a "sonnata" for two violoncellos introducing cadenzas in the first allegro and the adagio. The finale requires a fair amount of technique especially in bowing.

PLATE XXXVI.

SEBASTIAN LEE (AGED FORTY-FIVE). FROM A PRINT KINDLY LENT BY
MR. CHARLES VOLKERT.

To face page 368.

CHAPTER XX.

THE PROGRESS OF THE VIOLONCELLO *(continued)*.

THE technique of the violoncello during its early stages owed much to the viol da gamba. We find in the earliest violoncello music, as, for instance, in the sonatas by Galli and ricercare by Gabrieli the same motives of figuration which we find in the gamba music in the seventeenth century, viz., the frequent skipping across strings intermixed with scale passages. Moreover, Gabrieli tunes the upper strings in fourths (D-G), in order to obtain chords with one or two open strings in a similar manner as they occur on the gamba. The varieties in bowing was far greater than that in figuration. Almost all the movements were based upon the repeated use of one particular figure. This continued right into the eighteenth century, when the Italian sonata di camera began to assert its paramount influence in instrumental music. From that time the violoncello began to adopt the technique of the violin for its model, as shown already in a primitive manner in the sonatas by Benedetto Marcello and in a higher degree in those of his followers. Very remarkable is the technique shown in the sonatas by Abaco. Here we find a very free use of the thumb position going right up to the higher registers of the instrument. In some instances, his movements become absolutely virtuoso pieces so, for instance, a movement from one of his sonatas called "La Zampogna" (the bagpipes) which makes a brilliant solo even at the present day, and in the author's arrangement, has become a very favourite piece in Mr. Boris Hambourg's repertoire.

CLEFS.

Another inheritance from the viol da gamba was the use of the various C clefs which are frequently employed by Abaco and even Boccherini employed them to a great extent. Haydn likewise used the alto clef still in his Concerto in D. Cramer's magazine, of November 8, 1783, contains a proposal for the simplification of clefs in violoncello music in which it says: "One has at last arrived at a stage where it has been found necessary to add to the troubles of the already overburdened violoncellist, the use of tenor, alto, treble, G and F clefs. . . . . It is very disagreeable that composers cannot come to an understanding about the octaves in which to use the G clef, and consequently compel the player to guess at the real meaning of the composer, and sometimes leave the question entirely undecided. Carlo Graziani, in his Sonata, Op. 2, makes use of the C clef on the second line, called by Rousseau 'taille clef.' Lully uses the same as 'base taille clef.' The writer of the article advocates the use of this clef for the violoncello, saying that it will save the use of any other but the F clef, commencing its use from .

"In some cases, of course, the use of more than one clef is

unavoidable; especially in arpeggio passages where the open C and G strings are used together with notes of the higher registers of the D and A string."

The simplification in the use of the various clefs was due to Boccherini and Bernhard Romberg, who reduced the C clefs to the use of the tenor clef only, and who introduced a rule that the G clef, when following the bass clef, had to be read an octave lower than its actual compass. But when following the tenor clef it resumed its usual position.

Through Boccherini the technique of the violoncello was advanced very considerably. It is due to him and Jean Louis Duport that the violoncello took its rank as a solo instrument by the side of the violin. Boccherini freed the passage-work from its archaic austerity. His figures are graceful and flowing, and employ the full compass of the violoncello as far as the highest positions.

The next, and even more important, step was made by Bernhard Romberg, who, although a distinct classicist as a composer, developed hitherto undreamed of bravura and virtuosity. His passage-work was distinctly new and extremely varied. Romberg's influence lasted beyond the middle of last century, and even now his concertos are indispensable to every student of the instrument. Another part of the inheritance of the violoncello from the gamba was

THE SOLO ACCOMPANIMENT OF THE RECITATIVE.

This was practised still in the early part of last century and required much skill and good musicianship, being to some extent a survival of the old style of improvisation. Baudiot tells us in his "Méthode": It happens sometimes that the singers remain on the stage silent, because they have forgotten their part or for some other reason; at other times they enter too late. In such cases, the accompanying violoncellist may play short preludes and embellishments according to his own fancy and taste. But he must be modest therein, and use his ornamentations at the proper time and with taste.

Robert Lindley had a great reputation as accompanist, but in England and Germany it was not practised after the middle of last century, while Wasielewski tells us that he heard it in Italy as late as 1873.

The method of the Paris Conservatoire by Baillot, Levasseur, Catel and Baudiot which appeared in 1804, gives more precise instructions:

"To accompany a recitative well one must have a perfect knowledge of harmony as well as of the violoncello. One must be well versed with figured basses, and able to execute them readily.

"He who can do that has reached the summit of his art, for this presupposes the necessary knowledge and good judgment.

"If the accompanying bass player (violoncellist) is not sure in resolving dissonances, if he does not indicate to the singer whether he has to make a full cadence or an interrupted cadence, if he does not know how to avoid consecutive fifths and octaves: he runs a risk to embarrass the singer, and in any case, he will produce a bad effect.

"As in good works the recitative runs along a well-defined course, and is ruled by the character of the rôle, the situation and the voice of the singer, it is necessary: (1) to adapt the gradation of tone according to the idea of the situation, the object of the accompaniment being to bring the voice into relief, and to enhance its beauty, not to spoil and cover it; (2) the chord must not be repeated except at a change of harmony; (3) the accompaniment must be quite simple without runs or florid ornamentations. A good accompanist always acts in the interest of the work itself, and if he fills out certain gaps with short interludes he must only sound the notes of the chord; (4) the chord should be played without arpeggio, generally in the following manner:

The French called this: "Le recitatif italien."

The "Allgemeine Musikzeitung," of 1809, in an article on the violoncello, says that at that time the "art of accompaniment" had greatly decreased as players did no longer study sufficient "thorough bass" (the contemporary name for "harmony").

EARLY VIOLONCELLO LITERATURE.

For a more extensive discussion of this subject we must refer the reader to the author's "The Literature of the Violoncello," which appeared in serial form in the columns of "The Strad," and which we hope to produce in book form later on. We must content ourselves in this place with a bird's-eye view thereof, as it would swell this volume to an inordinate length.

Until the middle of the seventeenth century the violoncello only served as a simple bass in the orchestra. In chamber music, where the bass viol held its sway, it was not admitted. During the second part it gradually crept in as a solo instrument in *obbligato* accompaniments of arias in some Italian operas. The first compositions for violoncello solo, which it has been our good fortune to discover, by the aid of the late Count Luigi Francesco Valdrighi, are the twelve ricercari e sonate (without basso continuo) by Domenico Gabrieli *(see the latter)*, bearing the date January 15, 1689, and the "Trattenimento musicale" by Domenico Galli, dated 1691.

Both works, although showing a distinct influence of the technique of the viol da gamba, prove that their composers began to recognise the true nature of the violoncello. Never exceeding the neck positions they move about freely within their compass, using now and again sequences of figures which are distinctly peculiar to the violoncello, and would be ineffective and almost impossible on the gamba. These compositions instil respect for the technique of their executants as some of them cannot be termed easy even at the present day. A concerto by Domenico della Bella, published in Venice in 1705, and the concertos by Leonardo Leo we have been unable to examine. The latter are in the library of the Naples Conservatoire, and many difficulties have been placed in the way of those that have tried to obtain access to the manuscripts. On the other hand, we owe to the courtesy of Mr. Alfred Wotquenne, of the Brussels Conservatoire, a copy of a concerto, composed probably between 1710-20, by Antonio Vivaldi, the great violinist who died at Venice in 1743.

As a composer of instrumental music he was considered one of the greatest masters of his time, and his greatest merit consisted in the formal development of the instrumental concerto. His importance in that respect may be gauged by the fact that J. S. Bach arranged no less than sixteen of his violin concertos for harpsichord, and three for the organ, besides a first movement from one of the former sixteen. Bach's Concerto in A minor, for four harpsichords, with accompaniment of string orchestra, which Forkel considered an original composition is, as we know now, an arrangement of one of Vivaldi's concertos for four violins. The technique of the violin had already been advanced to a considerable height by Corelli and Tartini, whereas the violoncello was still in its infancy, and it is therefore particularly interesting to see how it was treated as a solo instrument by so great a master.

Vivaldi's Concerto in D major, consists of three movements: (1) allegro, (2) affettuoso, (3) vivace. The accompanying orchestra consists of two violins, viola and cembalo (harpsichord). After a vigorous fugato opening the violoncello enters with a *motif* taken from the end of the first subject followed by a passage which shows the influence of the viol da gamba, while the second solo entry brings already an indigenous violoncello figure. The third entry of the violoncello begins with a joyful melody developed from the principal subject and ends with a very clever "bariolé" arpeggio passage, using the whole of the fourth position on the G and D strings with the open A string. This is a device which is far in advance of the works of violoncello composers of the early eighteenth century. The passage is accompanied by violins only while the other solo parts are accompanied by the harpsichord alone or with the addition of the violins, very sparingly used. The "Affettuoso," a fine expressive melody of only eight bars, finishes on the dominant, and is really only an introduction to the final vivace in 6-4 time, very primitive in its figuration, which is distinctly dominated by the influence of the technique of the viol da gamba. The compass of this concerto never exceeds the fourth position.

Nicolo Porpora wrote a sonata with bass and a Concerto, G major, with accompaniment of string orchestra. They belong in all probability to the period when Porpora was at the head of the Italian Opera in Lincoln's Inn Fields from 1729-36. Manuscript copies of both works are preserved in the British Museum. The concerto, which is by far the more important of the two, is a very fine composition in the Italian sonata style beginning with a very polyphonic adagio followed by a

376   THE HISTORY OF THE VIOLONCELLO.

very bright allegro in common time. After this comes an Adagio quasi Largo in 6-4 time with a tender and plaintive melody accompanied by a bass motif in quaver figures, leading to a spirited allegro in 3-8 time, finishing with a repeat of the first section "presto" as coda. Needless to say that it is well constructed, etc., when speaking of a work by such a master as Porpora. What concerns us more in this place is the nature of his passage work, particularly in his quick passages which were intended for technical display. Curious to say, they still are based upon the viol da gamba figures which we find in Vivaldi's concerto, and, in fact, are chiefly reducible to one figure only, which appears from the fourth bar of the solo part in the first allegro, and forms not only the basis of

Porpora Concerto. First Allegro.

the passage work of that, but also of the last movement. The manner in which it is used is very dexterous, with a free use of thumb position, "e" being the highest note used in the concerto.

The Sonata in F major is a sonata da chiesa, consisting of: adagio, allegro, adagio, allegro non presto. It is an effective little work well worth the notice of violoncellists. The solo passages, however, are again based upon the well-known viol da gamba figures, and in this respect it is even behind some of the compositions by Gabrieli and Galli, who employ already figures—though only now and again—which are essentially in the nature of the violoncello. A considerable advance is shown in the sonatas by Lanzetti, of whom one book appeared already in 1736 in Amsterdam (others in Paris, etc., see "The Literature of the Violoncello," by E. van der Straeten).

Although they do not exceed the compass of the Porpora concerto, they have entirely broken the fetters of the viol da gamba, and follow the lines of the violin technique.

THE STACCATO.

The passages are richly varied, "staccato" passages are used very freely. Lanzetti is said to have mastered the staccato with equal facility in the up bow and the down bow, and he is apparently the first who employed it in his compositions. Of Francischello, who was credited with a remarkable technique, we know, unfortunately, too little to judge of his actual achievements.

About 1740 Abaco was in London, and the considerable volume of his manuscript sonatas, now in the British Museum, shows him as a virtuoso who towered high above his contemporaries. Especially in the way of double stopping in all positions, he proceeds with a boldness that is astounding in a virtuoso of his time. A brilliant example of this is to be found in his charming piece, "La Zampogna" ("The Bagpipe"), which, in the author's arrangement, forms a most successful item in Mr. Boris Hambourg's repertoire, and taxes all the resources of a modern virtuoso.

As soon as the violoncello had freed itself from the influence of the bass viol, and followed the lines of the violin, its progress was very rapid. The reason for this is very simple, although people were misled by outward reasons to connect the violoncello more closely with the former instrument, and are apt to do so even now. Yet when we consider both in their proper light the great distance becomes apparent. The viols form a family *entirely* to themselves, and so do the violins. All they have in common is a *slight* resemblance in their outward shape and the fact that both possess arm and knee instruments representing the several voices or parts. In every other respect they differ. The quality of the tone differs entirely, as Dr. Hubert Le Blanc pertinently puts it: The tone of the viols is of a female quality, that of the Cremona instruments (violin family) is of a male quality. The fretting of the viols, the number of strings and manner of their tuning, leads to polyphone and chord playing, while it hampers the free movement of the left hand in running passages with frequent and rapid interchanges of positions.

The latter are the proper domain of the violin family, where the fingers of the left hand connect the notes between each two strings by a regular system of fingering, at least in the case of the violin and the viola, while on the violoncello the additional use of either an open string or the thumb is required for that purpose.

Luigi Boccherini was the first to lead the technique of the violoncello into more modern channels by the frequent use of harmonics, arpeggios and thumb passages up to the highest registers. Long staccato runs and whole passages in double stopping are of frequent occurrence, as well as passages which run across several strings in each one of the higher thumb positions. This latter feature of the violoncello technique was, of course, entirely taken from the violin, where a scale passage can be played across the four strings in every position, whereas on the violoncello they require the use of the thumb in all positions except the first. This latter technique was further developed by J. L. Duport, to whom falls, moreover, the credit of having introduced a standard system of fingering which in its essential parts is followed to the present day.

A still greater step in the development of the passage work on the above lines was made by Bernhard Romberg, whose concertos have consequently remained indispensable for the use of every student, although they are mostly antiquated from a musical point. Apart from their virtuoso passages they contain, however, material for the study of the "cantabile" (bel canto) that is almost unequalled in the whole literature of the violoncello. We need only to refer the reader to the beautiful slow movement of the Concerto No. 2, in D.

F. W. Rust, who lived before Romberg, wrote several concertos for violoncello, but only one, in F major, has survived in MS. It is very Mozartian in style, and the technique, as in the case of most of his works, is remarkably modern. It contains octave passages leading into the higher register, and his figuration is in many cases bolder and much more modern in character than Romberg's. It is regrettable that the work has not been made more accessible by publication, as the slow movement is a perfect gem, and the last movement a delightfully spirited rondo.

END OF PART I.

History of the Violoncello, the Viol da Gamba, their Precursors and Collateral Instruments

VOLUME 2

HISTORY OF THE VIOLONCELLO, THE VIOL DA GAMBA, THEIR PRECURSORS AND COLLATERAL INSTRUMENTS

WITH

BIOGRAPHIES OF ALL THE MOST EMINENT PLAYERS
OF EVERY COUNTRY

BY

EDMUND S. J. VAN DER STRAETEN

Author of " Technics of Violoncello Playing," " The Revival of the Viols," " Hints to Violoncellists," " The Viola," " The Romance of the Fiddle," etc.

THE RESULT OF THIRTY YEARS RESEARCH

Illustrated with Portraits, Musical Examples, Facsimile Letters,
Reproductions from Rare and Curious Paintings and Engravings

VOL. II.

LONDON: WILLIAM REEVES, 83 CHARING CROSS ROAD, W.C.
MCMXV

PART II.
THE VIOLONCELLO FROM 1800-1900.

CHAPTER XXI.

THE VIOLONCELLO IN GERMANY DURING THE NINETEENTH CENTURY.

IN 1800 the violoncello as a solo instrument had passed through the first century of its existence, and arrived at the age of manhood. Although a few compositions had been written before 1700, none were printed apparently before that year. The oldest monuments still in existence are probably the ricercari, by Domenico Gabrieli (1689), and the sonatas by Domenico Galli (dated 1691), which are described in Part I. Whether Buononcini or Scarlatti wrote anything before the year 1700 is uncertain; their principal activity falls within the eighteenth century.

In 1700 and the following years several concertos, sonatas and solos for the violoncello were published, so that date may be regarded, except for the solitary examples of Gabrieli and Galli, as marking the appearance of the violoncello as a solo instrument.

Up to the middle of the eighteenth century the progress was steady but comparatively slow. The sonatas by Buononcini, Marcello and Porpora show a distinct advance over the compositions by Gabrieli and Galli, although they remain within the same compass; yet their passages are more free and flowing, apart from the superior invention and construction. These pieces were written within a period of about thirty-five years. The sonatas by Cervetto and Abaco, again, show a distinct advance over the former. The passage work as well as the compass is extended. They commence also to break away from the old style by using arpeggios of a more advanced type, and by introducing the use of the thumb. Double stoppings in the thumb position are very frequent in the compositions of Abaco, which are both more interesting and more advanced than those by Cervetto. They really mark the first step which led from the Corelli school to the more modern of Philipp Emanuel Bach, Boccherini and Haydn, while the sonatas by Johann Sebastian Bach are the final and culminating point of the older schools—at least, as far as the instrumental technique is concerned. From the middle of the eighteenth century the technique of the instrument made rapid strides, which can be easily followed by comparing the still primitive works of Berteau with those of Duport, although even the former are advanced for their time.

Then comes the great Romberg, who completely revolutionised violoncello playing, and whose school reigned supreme in the violoncello world until the end of the eighteenth century, when Beethoven's influence altered again the whole technique of the instrument in a way which was so opposed to the style of Romberg that the latter declared his music to be foreign to the nature of the instrument, and in parts quite unplayable. The greatness of the composer has made it imperative for the executant to submit to his ideas, and the whole of our technique of the present day is based upon those lines; while all the fine passage work of Romberg has become obsolete, and no composer would dream of reviving it. That does not mean that it is not effective for the instrument, nor that the study of his works could be dispensed with. On the contrary, it remains one of the finest schools for study, although to follow in his style of composition is not advisable, no more than to follow Beethoven's example by writing passages which, at the time of their appearance, appear unplayable. Supreme genius will enforce their study. But the composer who is not on the same level will see his compositions absolutely neglected if he attempts to do the same thing, even though his work possess merit. At the commencement of the nineteenth century Romberg, Bohrer and Dotzauer represented the most advanced technique of their instrument, and it is therefore that the present chapter commences with their school.

JOHANN NICOLAUS PRELL, born November 6, 1773, at Hamburg, was a pupil of Bernhard Romberg. He was the last "Discantist" (soprano boy) of Carl Philipp Emanuel Bach. After finishing his studies under Romberg, he was engaged as principal violoncello at the theatre, and soon gained a high reputation as a soloist. He instituted regular chamber concerts, or "Quartet Academies," as they were then called, together with Andreas Romberg, the composer of Schiller's "Lay of the Bell." In 1842 he retired into private life, and died March 18, 1849. His son, August Christian, of whom we shall hear later on, followed in his father's footsteps.

JOHANN FRIEDRICH KELZ, born April 11, 1776, in Berlin. He received his early musical training from the "Stadtmusikus" (town-musician), Fuchs, with whom he studied until 1801, acquiring a fair knowledge of nearly every instrument in use. This general knowledge of instruments was one of the qualifications of the old town musicians, who were excellent practical musicians, although frequently very pedantic schoolmasters.

His predilection for the violoncello placed him under the special care of his uncle, Adolph Friedrich Metke, conductor and solo violoncellist to the Duke of Brunswick-Oels, at Oels, in Silesia. Metke directed his studies on the violoncello, and procured him an appointment in the ducal orchestra, to which he belonged from 1801 to 1805, when the Duke died. In the latter year he returned to Berlin, where he benefited by the advice of the elder Duport. In 1811, he was appointed as a royal chamber musician, and retired in 1857. Kelz was a most prolific composer, but of his two hundred and eighty, or more, works for the violoncello, none have survived, although some might still be used for educational purposes. He wrote a great number of variations on popular songs and airs, with the quaintest titles and texts—as, for instance: eight variations on "Die Milch ist Gesünder" ("The Milk is more wholesome"), or variations on "Die Würzburger Glöckli" ("The Bells of Würzburg"), etc. Most of his compositions, which comprised also twenty four-part fugues for strings, were published by Paez, in Berlin. (See the author's "Literature of the Violoncello" in the "Strad," Volume X, page 369.) As a teacher of the violoncello, Kelz enjoyed a high reputation. He died in Berlin, in January, 1862.

Born in the same year as Kelz, viz., 1776, was also W. A. J. ALBERT, an excellent amateur on the violoncello, and promoter and protector of the high-class concerts, who died as "Oberbergrath" (chief inspector of mines) to the court of Hanover, at Clausthal, in the Harz mountains, on July 4, 1846.

J. H. FACIUS is described as a good violoncellist, who lived in Vienna about 1810. Three duets for two violoncellos, Op. 1, were published there in 1799. Three sonatas with bass, Op. 2, in two books, were published by Artaria in 1802, and a Concerto in D minor, Op. 3, by Witzendorf.

CHRISTIAN URBAN, born October 16, 1778, at Elbing, was an excellent violoncellist and town musician at Elbing, then at Berlin, and after that musical director at Dantzig. He published lectures on musical theory and musical training, and composed an opera, "Der Goldene Widder," and music to Schiller's "Bride of Messina."

JOHANN NEPOMUK HÜTTNER (Wurzbach gives his name as Johann B. Hüttner) was born January 1, 1793, at Gratz, in Styria. After completing his studies under J. Zimmermann, he was appointed as principal violoncello at the Opera in Pesth. This position he held for two years, then going to Lemberg. He remained there but a short time when he started on a tour through Poland and Russia. This was in 1820. In 1822 he returned to Austria, and received an appointment as professor of the violoncello at the Conservatoire at Prague, and as solo violoncello of the Opera of that town. He combined a fine tone and technique with a great deal of feeling, and stood in very high esteem as a quartet player. As a teacher, Hüttner produced a number of excellent pupils, among the foremost being Franz Hegenbarth. Hüttner died March 1, 1839, and was succeeded at the Conservatoire by his pupil, Bühnert.

JOSEPH ALEXANDER, excellent violoncellist, who lived about 1800, as teacher of his instrument at Duisburg. Less renowned for his technique of the left hand than for the beauty and purity of his tone, he wrote several educational works, including a tutor, "Anweisung für das Violoncellspiel," published in 1801 by Breitkopf and Härtel; and an "Air avec XXXVI variations progressives pour le violoncell avec le doigté et différentes clefs, accomp. d'un violon et d'une basse," published in 1802. About his life, no further particulars are known. His brother, Leopold, died a few years ago (after 1905) at Düsseldorf, where he was principal violin under Schumann and Mendelssohn.

PHILIPP MORALT, born 1780, as twin brother to Jacob Moralt. They belonged to a family of excellent musicians who were all members of the Court Chapel at Munich. Philipp Moralt was one of the best violoncellists of his time, but his uneventful life passed quietly in the service of the Prince Elector. He died at Munich in 1829. Joseph Moralt, a younger member, was also in the Court Chapel at Munich. He made a successful debut as solo violoncellist at the Gewandhaus concert in Leipzig on January 21, 1847. Nothing else is known about this artist. Baptie ("Musicians of All Times") mentions a Joseph Moralt, born in Mannheim, August 5, 1775, who died in Munich, November 14, 1855. Although he states that he was a violinist, it appears probable that it was the above violoncellist.

JOSEPH BRAUN, a virtuoso on the violoncello and on the pianoforte, was born at Ratisbone in 1787, as the son of an organist. He showed great talent as a conductor, and was engaged in that capacity for a theatre in Philadelphia in 1826. His wife followed him soon after with an engagement as *prima donna* for the same institute. The brutality of the public of that town, who, by threats and even violence, tried to compel Braun to submit to their degraded taste, so disgusted him that he resolved to forsake that golden misery for less remunerative, but more honourable engagements in Germany. In 1828 he left Philadelphia, and gave a number of concerts in various American towns. In 1830 he was back in Germany. He wrote two operas and a number of vocal and instrumental compositions, including some good pieces for violoncello and pianoforte.

AUGUST FERDINAND CUBELIUS, born January, 1798, commenced his musical career as a flutist. At the same time he showed great talent for the violoncello, which eventually he chose as his principal instrument at the recommendation of the famous Capellmeister Zelter. In 1816 he was appointed as violoncellist in the Royal Chapel in Berlin. Further details are wanting.

KARL RIPFEL, born 1799 at Mannheim, appeared first in public as a prodigy on the pianoforte. The minister de Touche, of Baden, persuaded him to exchange the piano for the violoncello, and gave him his first instruction on that instrument.

He acquired an immense technique, which elicited the remark from Bernard Romberg that he considered him the greatest virtuoso on the violoncello. His technique was compared with that of Paganini. Unfortunately, he had the same failing as Jean Stiastny, to be extremely nervous, so that he withdrew from the concert platform at an early age. Ripfel was an original, and this was also apparent in his playing, which was described as bizarre. As an orchestral player, he appears to have excelled, and he was gifted with an uncommonly good memory, so that he could retain his part of whole operas. He was principal violoncello at the Frankfurt Theatre for forty-five years. His compositions are highly praised by his contemporaries, but his very retiring disposition prevented him from publishing any of his work. Jean Becker asked him once for some of his string trios, which he intended to produce in public, but met with a curt refusal. He died March 8, 1876, according to the inscription on his tombstone. The "Signale für die Musikalische Welt," of March 19, and Dr. Hugo Riemann, in his dictionary (probably from that paper), give February 6 as the date of his decease, but the inscription on the tombstone could hardly be wrong.

SIEGFRID WILHELM DEHN, born February 25, 1799, at Altona, the son of a wealthy banker. He studied the violoncello under Paul Winneberger in Hamburg and theory under the organist, Dröbs. The loss of his fortune decided him to choose music as a profession. Through Meyerbeer's recommendation he was appointed as librarian of the music department of the Royal Library at Berlin, which he set completely in order and added to very largely. Although an excellent violoncellist, he acquired a greater reputation as the author of theoretical works and teacher of counterpoint and composition. Among his pupils he numbered Glinka, Rubinstein, Kullak and H. Hofmann. He died in Berlin, April 12, 1858.

ADAM HERMANN, a German, born at Warsaw in 1800 (*see Polish Violoncellists*).

KARL DRECHSLER, born May 27, 1800, at Kamenz, in Saxony, started his musical career as member of a military band at Dresden. He devoted himself chiefly to the violoncello, and was appointed in the town orchestra as additional violoncellist. In 1820 he was engaged in the court orchestra, and the Duke of Dessau, at Frederic Schneider's request, allowed him, in 1824, the means to perfect himself under Dotzauer's tuition. In the following year he started on a prolonged tour, which brought him through Holland to England and Scotland. Everywhere he met with great success, and when he returned, in 1826, he received the title "Conzertmeister," with the life membership in the court orchestra. On June 13, 1835, he played a divertimento by Dotzauer, at the eighth "Elb Musical Festival." In a report which appeared in the "Allgemeine Musik Zeitung" about that performance, his tone and phrasing in the cantabile are praised as being exceptionally fine. Also his great agility of the left hand, but it says that the technique of the fingers was at the expense of his tone, although in the *highest* mastery they should both be equal, as only then *bravoura* could be looked upon as music (!).

He was an excellent orchestral player, and much sought after as principal violoncello at musical festivals. In 1871 he retired with a pension to Dresden, where he died in 1873. As a teacher he was very successful, and among his pupils we find some of the most prominent names of the violoncellists of the past century—as Lindner, Cossmann, Grützmacher, Espenhahn and others.

His son, Louis, born 1822, was also violoncellist *(see later on)*.

JOHANN FRIEDRICH WILHELM SCHLICK, born January 24, 1801, was the son of Johann Conrad Schlick and Regina Strinasacki. He acted as secretary to a country gentleman named

Lucas, who had a large estate near Grossglogau. He played the violoncello and the violin, and was appointed as a member of the Royal Chapel at Dresden in 1825.

Schlick was also a clever instrument maker, and received a gold medal at the Saxonian Industrial Exhibition of 1840 for some of his violins and violoncellos. He died April 24, 1874, at Dresden.

AUGUST THEODOR MÜLLER, born September 27, 1802, at Brunswick, founded, together with his brothers, Karl Friedrich (first violin), George (second violin), and Gustav (viola), the once world-famed Müller Quartet, of which he was the mainstay. They were sons of Ægidius Christoph Müller, who died in 1841 as court musician at Brunswick. Between 1831 and 1855 the Müller Quartet enjoyed a world-famed reputation, and they undertook numerous concert tours through Germany, France, Russia, the Netherlands and Denmark. In 1839 they undertook their second tour, when they appeared at the court of Dessau. F. Schneider, who heard them on that occasion, speaks of their playing in terms of highest praise. They went thence to Leipzig, Berlin and St. Petersburg.

FIG. 45.
A. THEODOR MÜLLER.

August Theodor Müller died at Brunswick, May 22, 1875. The quartet, however, was dissolved through the death of Gustav Müller in 1855, but was continued by the four sons of Karl Friedrich, William, the youngest, being the violoncellist. We shall speak of him later on.

FRANZ HINKEL, born 1804 at Altenburg. He was appointed as royal chamber musician at Berlin in 1835. In the following year he instituted chamber concerts with the assistance of Constantin Decker, and died at the early age of thirty-four in 1838. (Messrs. Trowell give the date as April 20.)

EDUARD BOCK, principal violoncello at the Berlin Opera and royal chamber musician at Berlin, was born at Strelitz about 1804, and died April 16, 1834. No further particulars.

AUGUST CHRISTIAN PRELL, the son of Johann Nicolaus Prell, born August 1, 1805, was trained by his father in the art of violoncello playing upon the basis of Romberg's school. The latter master then took him personally in hand, and he may be looked upon as the last of his pupils.

He inherited his master's classical style and nobility of phrasing. When only twelve years of age he played Romberg's Concerto in E minor in public. At the age of sixteen he was appointed as chamber musician at the court of Meiningen, and two years later, in 1824, he became principal violoncello at Hanover, where he remained until February 1, 1869, when he retired. He died at Hanau on September 3, 1885. His celebrated violoncello by Amati became the property of Friedrich Grützmacher.

FRIEDRICH WILHELM GRAENSER, or GRÄNSER, born November 5, 1805, at Dresden, was principal violoncello in the Leipzig (Gewandhaus) Orchestra from 1827 till 1856. His social talents and amiable personality secured him numerous friends among leading musicians. He died at Leipzig, January 1, 1859.

SEBASTIAN LEE, who was born at Hamburg, December 24, 1805, and was therefore only about four months younger than A. C. Prell, showed an early predilection for the violoncello, and his studies were placed under the guidance of the elder Prell. About 1830 he made his debut as a soloist in Hamburg, then at Leipzig, and afterwards he visited Cassel and Frankfurt, and eventually wended his way to Paris, where he arrived in April, 1832, and appeared with great success at the "Theatre Italien." In 1836 he appeared in London, and afterwards accepted an engagement as solo violoncellist at the Opera in Paris, where he remained from 1837 to 1868. After retiring from that position, he returned to his native town, where he devoted himself chiefly to composition. A great many of his works have been published, embracing almost every branch of violoncello composition, but only his studies have proved to be of lasting value, while his numerous divertimentos, fantasias, etc., are forgotten. His fine Etudes, Op. 57, forty studies, duets, and albums for beginners will be found very useful for students. The portrait on Plate XXXVI, which represents Lee at the age of forty-five years, is taken from a scarce print kindly lent by Mr. Charles Volkert, of Messrs. Schott and Co.

GUSTAV KNOOP was the third violoncellist of renown who was born in 1805. His birthplace was Göttingen. After finishing his studies on the violoncello, which he commenced at an early age, he joined the ducal chapel at Meiningen, where he remained until 1832. In 1833 he appeared with great success in London, where he played a concerto by Kummer at the Philharmonic Society on April 29. His playing was likened to that of Romberg, especially with regard to beauty of tone. It is related of him that he got married simply to become the possessor of a very fine violoncello, the property of his wife, whom he left soon after their marriage. In 1843 he went to the United States, and died December 25, 1849, in Philadelphia.

MORITZ GANZ, born at Mayence on September 13, 1806 (not 1804, as Wasielewski has it, who also gives the date of his decease wrongly as January 22), as the second of three musical brothers, was one of the foremost German violoncellists of the early nineteenth century. He received his first instructions from his father, and played the violoncello in public when he was only eleven years old. He pursued his studies afterwards under Jean Stiastny in Frankfurt, and on emanating from the school of that excellent master, he was appointed in the orchestra of the National Theatre at Mayence, which was conducted by his elder brother, Adolph. In 1826 he became principal violoncello in the Berlin Court Orchestra, and was so much admired that the king honoured him by conferring the title of "Conzertmeister" upon him. His playing testified to the most careful study of every technical detail, combined with great facility and elegance of style, without creating any deeper impression. Between 1833 and 1837, he undertook several concert tours, mostly in the company of his brother Leopold, who was also "Conzertmeister" in the Court Orchestra at Berlin. In 1835 they appeared together in Vienna, according to Hanslick, and in 1837, on May 1, they appeared in London at the fifth Philharmonic concert of that season, when Moritz played a concerto of his own composition, and, together with his brother, a duet by Ganz and Bohrer. He died January 23, 1868.

His compositions included two concertos, two concertinos and numerous solo pieces, well written for the instrument, but of no intrinsic merit. His "Characteristic Pieces," Op. 31, have been reprinted by Augener.

The most prominent of his pupils were Julius Rietz, Giese, Lotze and Klietz.

CARL LEOPOLD BOEHM, a very remarkable violoncello virtuoso, wrote a short biographical notice of his life at the request of Moritz Bermann for a "Universal Lexicon," which the latter was then compiling. The original manuscript of that notice, which has been copied in the works of Gassner, Gandy and Schilling, is at present (1914) in the possession of the author of these lines, and the following is an exact translation of the German text: "Carl Leopold Boehm, born in Vienna November 4, 1806. His father, Joseph Boehm, merchant and house owner in Vienna, Josephstadt No. 2, intended to bring him up for commercial life, but unexpected losses which he suffered through no fault of his own induced him to change his plans for the future of his son. At the advice of Francis Krommer, conductor of the imperial chamber music, C. L Boehm was destined for the musical profession, and entered the National Conservatoire in Vienna, where he joined the violoncello classes under Professors Joseph Merk and Salzmann. On the conclusion of his studies, C. L. Boehm received a certificate from the committee of the conservatoire (there were no prizes given at that time) on August 13, 1828, stating that he had just claims to the name of an excellent artist.

"He received an appointment at the theatre in the 'Josephstadt' under Director Häusler, and later on at the theatre 'An der Wien' under Director Carl, where he earned great applause by his solos in pantomime and ballet music. He played at many charity concerts in Vienna, Vienna-Neustadt, Baden v. W., and Pressburg, entered on March 1, 1831, upon his appointment for life in the chapel of the art-loving Prince Fürstenberg at Donaueschingen. During his annual holidays he undertook concert tours in Germany, Switzerland and a part of France, meeting everywhere with great success at musical festivals as well as at his own concerts. On several of these occasions he was elected an honorary member of important musical societies.

"His very effective solos and violoncello compositions have been published by Artaria, Mechetti, Witzendorf in Vienna, and Peters in Leipzig. When all the musicians who were not life members of the prince's chapel were dismissed in consequence of the revolution in Baden in 1848, and part of their number pensioned, the noble Prince Egon of Fürstenberg retained nine artists for his private chamber music under the direction of the famous J. W. Kalliwoda, and C. L. Boehm was one of these."

The above notice is signed by Boehm, and dated Donaueschingen, October 30, 1851. The dates given in Wasielewski are nearly all incorrect as far as Boehm is concerned, whose name is, moreover, spelled incorrectly. Boehm undertook his first concert tour at the age of eighteen, when he visited the principal towns of Austria-Hungary.

FIG. 46. REPRODUCTION OF THE FIRST PAGE OF AN ADAGIO AND RONDO-LETTO FOR VIOLONCELLO BY C. L. BOEHM. ORIGINAL IN THE POSSESSION OF THE AUTHOR.

His compositions are mostly antiquated. They comprise two concertinos, fantasias and airs with arrangements. A number of his manuscripts, including the second Concertino, Op. 18, and several fantasias, etc., are in the possession of the author. They testify to a very high degree of executive skill, combined with good musicianship, and some of them would be worth publishing for the use of students.

Interesting is a piano score which he made of a Concertante in D, for two violoncellos, by Dotzauer, as it is signed at the end "Strassburg, der 22 December, 1850, Boehm," and was in all probability written out for a performance in that town.

Another manuscript of his, "Fantaisie sur un Thême original pour le violoncelle avec accompagnement de l'Orchestre," is dated "Carlsruhe, April 16, 1855." On the title page he still describes himself as "Violoncelliste de S. A. S. le Prince de Fürstenberg." The score is written (as well as all the other manuscripts in the writer's possession) in a beautifully clear and artistic—one might even call it picturesque—hand. Our illustration, Fig. 46, gives a reproduction of the original MS. of an "Adagio and Rondoletto" in the author's possesion.

During the last years of his life Boehm was a great sufferer. After using the waters at Dürrheim he recovered so far that he could play difficult solos again. This improvement was not long maintained. His left side became paralysed, and he died October 2, 1859, at Donaueschingen.

KARL HENNING, born February 26, 1807, at Halberstadt, played several instruments, but was essentially violoncellist. In 1837 he was appointed Capellmeister at Zeitz, where he died about 1866. He wrote a considerable number of educational pieces for violoncello as well as for violin, including elementary tutors for both instruments. His son is a violinist and musicographer living in America.

PIERRE LEGRAND, of Munich, appeared in Vienna in 1807 without particular success (Hanslick, "Concertsaal").

CYPRIAN ROMBERG, son of Andreas Romberg, was born at Hamburg in 1807. He showed exceptional talent which augured a brilliant career. His uncle, Bernhard Romberg, instructed him in the art of violoncello playing. After the completion of his studies he undertook a prolonged concert tour through Germany, Austria-Hungary, and finally to Russia. There he was appointed as chamber musician to the court, which position he retained for some years. In 1835 he started on another tour through Germany, and played some of his own compositions at Dresden with great success. When he started on this tour, Dr. jur. Th. Töpken, of Bremen, gave him a letter of introduction to his friend, Robert Schumann, in Leipzig. The latter wrote to Töpken on February 6: "I have received your Cipriano. He has pleased me very much—not only for your sake—especially the compositions, wherein one recognises the good old stock (das alte tüchtige Blut). As a virtuoso, however, he will still have to study some time, say a year. I would even have dissuaded him from going to Paris, where I have given him letters to Panofka" (famous singing master, and contributor to Schumann's "Neue Zeitschrift für Musik"). "To share a famous name with an older (member of the family), like he, has its good and evil side, and the young Mozart, the sister of Sonntag (Henriette Sonntag, famous operatic soprano) find an easier entry but also a more difficult exit."

His second soirée at Leipzig took place on February 21, and the "Allgemeine Musik Zeitung" says that he played in Bernhard Romberg's style and that his technique was faultless, and adds that if he would, through the possession of an exquisite violoncello, study more the tone and less the difficulties, he would become a shining star. This is rather conflicting with Miltitz's notice from Prague, which latter deserves probably more credence.

In the same year he played at Prague in the Platteissaal his Concerto, Op. 1 (allegro, andante and rondo), an introduction and variations, and a fantasia entitled "Souvenir de la Suède." B. von Miltitz, who heard him on that occasion, says in his notice in the "Allgemeine Musik Zeitung" that his concertino pleased best, that his tone was good and that he played on a Guarneri violoncello. He married Miss Wallburga Rehsteiner, daughter of the prince's master of the horse in 1832, and his salary was fixed at seven hundred florins, besides a house, garden and the usual supplies of wood, etc. He writes in a letter from Strassburg that he had the honour of playing with Mlle. Theresa Milanollo, who wrote some very flattering lines in his album which he valued above all the praise that the press bestowed upon him (gewiss werthvoller als eine geschmiedete Zeitungs Lobhudelei). The latter years of his life he spent at Hamburg where he was drowned when bathing in the Elbe on October 14, 1865. He left several published compositions including the Concerto, Op. 1 (Peters), Fantasia, Op. 5 (Richauld), and Variations, Op. 21, on a theme by Schubert (Breitkopf and Härtel).

BERNHARD BREUER, born at Cologne in 1808, received his first instructions in violoncello playing as well as in musical theory from his grandfather, who was a director of music at that town. After finishing his studies at one of the Cologne colleges, he went to Berlin in 1828, where he placed himself under Maurice Ganz for the study of the violoncello, while Zelter, Bernhard Klein and A. W. Bach directed his theoretical studies. Returning to Cologne about 1830, he received an appointment in the orchestra of the Cologne theatre, but left that position in 1839, when he went to Paris in order to perfect himself in composition under Cherubini. Shortly afterwards he produced his opera, "Das Rosenmädchen" ("The Rose Maiden") which was performed in Paris and in Cologne, but failed on account of the feeble book.

In 1840 he returned to Cologne, and was appointed professor of the violoncello at the conservatoire. In the same year he married the daughter of the violoncellist Knecht, of Aix-la-Chapelle. He was the founder of an excellent quartet party which flourished for a number of years. In 1845 he purchased the music shop and publishing business of Eck and Co. In his later years he suffered from gout to such an extent that he had to relinquish the violoncello altogether.

Frederick William III bestowed the medal for art and science upon him for a Te Deum dedicated to the king. His violoncello compositions were popular in their time: they consist of a sonata with pianoforte, six duos and three grand duos for two violoncellos, three duos for violin and violoncello, and variations with orchestra. He composed also a number of chamber music works. The manuscript of a quintet for two violins, two violas and violoncello in E flat, Op. 62, is in the possession of the writer. It is a well conceived and well written work which resembles the style of Romberg, Ries, Fesca, etc. Breuer died at Aix-la-Chapelle October 16, 1877.

His younger brother, ADOLF BREUER, who survived him, was an excellent double bass player and teacher of his instrument at the conservatoire.

JOSEPH ADAM LEIBROCK was born at Brunswick, January 8, 1808. His father, a well-known author, had destined him for the Church. He received some elementary instructions in music from his father, and studied the violin under Maucourt. Very soon, however, he showed a predilection for the violoncello which he studied henceforth under the chamber musician Goedecke, making such rapid strides that his father became reconciled to his choice of music as a profession. At the age of eighteen he became a member of the Ducal Chapel.

He received an excellent liberal education acquiring the degree of doctor of philosophy, and a philosophical turn of mind always directed his judgment and imbued him with a desire to investigate his art also from a scientific point of view. He followed the theoretical courses of Zinkeisen, who tells us of the remarkable progress of his pupil. After the completion of his studies he travelled to enlarge his knowledge of the world, and in 1830 he accepted the post of conductor at the theatre at Ratisbon. Finding the material of that orchestra inadequate for the realisation of his artistic aims, he relinquished the post after one year, and returned to Brunswick. Here he devoted himself entirely to composition, study and teaching. His reputation as a very learned man and excellent teacher gathered a large number of pupils round him anxious to benefit by his instructions and advice.

He collected an excellent musical library. His compositions comprise: incidental music to Schiller's "Die Räuber," operas, overtures and violoncello pieces, including numerous arrangements which are still very popular. He wrote also a theoretical work, "Musikalische Akkordenlehre," in which he emphasises the importance of the subdominant in the logical construction of a period.

Besides this he wrote a history of the private music of the House of Brunswick, which appeared in the "Braunschweigische Magazin" for 1865-6. He died August 8, 1886, in Leipzig, where he resided during the last years of his life.

MORITZ HANEMANN, born February 28, 1808, at Löwenberg, received his early musical training from his father, who was an oboe player, and from the violoncellist Taschenberg at Breslau. In 1828 he went to Berlin to study the violoncello under Hausmann and theory under Türrschmidt, and was appointed royal chamber musician in 1830.

He was a teacher of the violoncello as well as of the piano and flute. He contributed nothing to the literature of the violoncello, but earned a great popularity by his contributions to musical papers, which sparkled with wit and spirit. In 1874 he was still a member of the royal chapel, though released from active service since 1870 on account of ill-health. He died at Berlin June 7, 1884.

JOSEPH MENTER, born January 19, 1808, at Teisbach, near Landshut, in Bavaria, according to Hanslick: Wasielewski mentions Daudenkofen and Riemann Deutenkofen as his birthplace. As I have not been able to discover either of these two latter names on the map, I am inclined to think that Hanslick, who knew Menter personally, is right. He began his musical career by studying the violin, but soon exchanged that instrument for the violoncello. His first master was Pierre Le Grand of Munich, after which he became a pupil of Philip Moralt. At the age of twenty-one he was appointed violoncellist in the court orchestra at Hohenzollern-Hechingen, and in 1833 he came to Munich to join the royal chapel, where he remained to his death, which occurred on April 18, 1856. In 1839 he made his debut in Vienna, and wherever he appeared he met with enthusiastic reception. His tone is described as combining great power and richness with velvety sweetness, and his technique was brilliant. He visited all the principal towns of Europe. As teacher of his instrument Menter stood in high repute, and the long list of excellent violoncellists which he produced includes: Hippolyt and Valentin Müller, Ferdinand Büchler, Joseph Werner and many more.

He has also written a number of compositions for his instrument, which are obsolete with the exception of some of his studies, which are still used at many music schools.

JULIUS GRIEBEL, born October 25, 1809, in Berlin, received his first instructions on the violoncello and the French horn from his father, who was a bassoon player in the royal chapel His principal instrument was originally the horn, which he played as a solo instrument until about 1823 when failing health compelled him to abandon it. He continued the study of the violoncello under Max Bohrer, and on January 1, 1827, he joined the royal orchestra, rising eventually to the post of solo violoncellist, which position he shared with Ganz. About 1835 he was a member of the Zimmermann Quartet, in which Lotze followed him in 1838. He was also violoncellist in the Ries Quartet, being highly esteemed as a chamber music player. Between 1835-41 he made several successful concert tours through Holland and Denmark. Wasielewski gives the year of his death as 1865. Mendel and Reissmann says he was pensioned in 1872 and decorated with a Prussian order.

JOHANN ANDREAS GRABAU, born October 19, 1809, received his training as a violoncellist for the greater part by Gustav Knoop, finishing his studies under F. A. Kummer at Dresden. After completing his studies he went to Leipzig where he acquired a great reputation as chamber music player. He was also a clever soloist and Kummer had imparted some of the power and beauty of his tone to him, but extreme nervousness made the career of the virtuoso distasteful to him. A notable event in his life was the first performance of Beethoven's triple concerto on March 25, 1836, when Mendelssohn played the pianoforte, Ferdinand David, violin, and Grabau, violoncello. On his marriage with a lady of means he retired from his professional duties but remained a member of the Gewandhaus Orchestra until the time of his death, which took place in August, 1884. Messrs. Garnet C. and J. Arnold Trowell ("Violoncellists Past and Present") give the year as 1886, but state no authority.

LUDWIG PAPE, born May 14, 1809, at Lübeck. He was for some time violoncellist at the Königstädter Theatre, in Berlin, and in 1846 he held the appointment of solo violoncellist and composer to the Duke of Oldenburg. Schilling says that in his later years he cultivated the violin more than the violoncello, which, however, appears more than doubtful. He was highly esteemed as a composer of orchestral and chamber works, his string quartet, Op. 6, and a quintet for two violins, viola and two violoncellos, being considered the finest he has written.

JOHANN BENJAMIN GROSS, born at Elbing, September 12, 1809. Showing an early predilection for the violoncello, he was sent to Berlin in his boyhood, and placed under Ferd. Hausmann. In 1824 he was appointed to the Royal Orchestra, of which he was a member until 1829. He was also a violoncellist at the Königstädter Theatre, to which he belonged until 1831. About that time he went to Leipzig, where he appeared repeatedly with great success at the Gewandhaus concerts. In the early part of 1833, he was principal violoncello at the theatre at Magdeburg. But later on in the same year he joined the string quartet of von Lipphardt at Dorpat, of which Ferdinand David was the leader. In 1835 he became solo violoncellist of the theatre at St. Petersburg. Two years later he started on a concert tour, visiting the towns of Bremen, Lübeck, Halberstadt, Nordhausen, Hildesheim (where his brother held the post of a musical director of the town), and the principal towns in South Germany, returning to St. Petersburg in 1838. He remained there until 1847, when he retired to Germany with a pension. Soon after the Grand Duke Michael recalled him for his private music, but he died of the cholera on September 1, 1848, leaving behind a considerable number of compositions for his instrument, including three concertos, Op. 14, Op. 31, and Op. 38, one concertino, a sonata with bass, one with piano, Op. 7, in B minor, an instruction book, elements of violoncello playing, Op. 36, a number of duets, including twenty-four elementary duets, Op. 42, divertimenti and solos, also two string quartets. The total number of his compositions is in excess of 120, and although they are not exactly inspirations, they are conceived in a serious and noble spirit, and show good musicianship.

FRIEDRICH GROSS is mentioned as an excellent virtuoso, who possessed a brilliant technique. He was for some time in Vienna about 1828, where he had great success in his rendering of Romberg's compositions.

CHARLES SCHUBERTH, born February 25, 1811, was the son of the celebrated oboe and clarinet virtuoso, Gottlob Schuberth, of Magdeburg, who went to Hamburg in 1833. His eldest brother, Julius, founded the celebrated firm of music publishers. Charles showed very early signs of musical talent, and received his first lessons on the violoncello at the age of five from Hesse, a town musician of Magdeburg. At the age of eleven he made his first appearance in public as a soloist. In 1825 his father sent him to Dotzauer at Dresden, who gave him his final training in the art of violoncello playing. His first appearance after his return to Magdeburg was at a concert given by Mme. Catalani, in 1828, where he met with great success. At the end of that year he started on a concert tour, which brought him to Copenhagen early in 1829, and he remained there for some time. On his return to Magdeburg he was appointed principal violoncello at the theatre. In 1833 he started again on tour with the financial assistance of his brother Julius, the publisher. He visited the Rhine, Belgium and Paris. In 1834 he went to Holland, and 1835 to London. Riemann says that there he was the successful rival of Knoop and Servais at a court concert. It seems strange that three great violoncellists should have appeared together at court, although Servais was in London that season, as he played at the Philharmonic Society on May 25, 1835. Towards the end of that year Schubert went to St. Petersburg, where he met with an enthusiastic reception, and was appointed conductor of the court orchestra, musical director of the university, and inspector of a school of music in connection with the theatre. He retained these positions until his death, which occurred on July 22, 1863, at Zürich, where he had gone to recruit his health. His playing was brilliant, but lacking in breadth and grandeur, and the same applies to his numerous compositions, which all the same reveal a rare amount of melodic invention, and which have been too severely judged by the austere "professor." They are most effectively written for the instrument, and therefore grateful compositions which will always find friends in amateur circles. His caprices with pianoforte are, moreover, excellent studies for advanced players. He wrote also two concertos, one sonata and a quintet with a violoncello *obbligato*, besides numerous chamber music works and solos with orchestra and pianoforte, mostly published by Schuberth and Co. Foremost among his pupils was Charles Davidoff, the greatest among the Russian violoncellists. His portrait, Fig. 47, is taken from a print by F. Schroeder.

FIG. 47. CHARLES SCHUBERTH.

KARL LUDWIG DOTZAUER, younger son of Justus Johann Friedrich Dotzauer, born December 7, 1811, at Dresden, began to study the violoncello under his father when he was only seven years old. At the age of nine he played a solo before the King of Saxony. Spohr heard him in 1829 and engaged him for the grand ducal chapel at Cassels. He was an excellent chamber music player and toured successfully with his elder brother, Justus B. F., who was a pianist.

L. ESPENHAHN, born at Sandersleben, between 1810-20, was for some time violoncellist in the court chapel at Dessau. In 1837 he made a successful debut as soloist in Berlin, which procured him an appointment as supernumerary (accessist) in the Royal Chapel. At the invitation of Prince Narishkin, he followed that nobleman to Russia as solo violoncellist in his private chapel. That chapel was dissolved after the death of Prince Narishkin, and Espenhahn returned to Berlin and re-entered the Royal Chapel. In 1852 he succeeded Griebel as violoncellist of the Zimmermann Quartet. He was also esteemed as a teacher, and continued in his varied occupation till the time of his death, which occurred in 1879.

JULIUS SCHAPLER, born August 21, 1812, at Graudenz. He studied the violoncello at Berlin under Bernhard Romberg and F. Hausmann, and made his debut at the Royal Opera in Berlin with great success, afterwards appearing at the Gewandhaus at Leipzig with equally good result. He then started touring as a soloist, but receiving an appointment as solo violoncellist to the Duke of Nassau, he settled at Wiesbaden and devoted a great deal of his time to composition, chiefly that of chamber music, in which he was very successful. Robert Schumann speaks of him as a composer of distinct talent, standing high above the average of his time. For his instrument he wrote very little, and apparently only one piece is published: "Mosaique sur les martyrs, with second violoncello or pianoforte." During the revolutionary year 1848, the Duke of Nassau dismissed his private music, and Schapler settled as teacher of music in Thorn. The latter part of his life he spent in retirement in Berlin. He was an excellent virtuoso, who combined beauty of tone with a well-developed technique.

CHARLES G. P. GRÄDENER, born January 14, 1812, at Rostock, violoncellist, composer and writer on musical subjects, studied at the universities of Halle and Göttingen, before he embraced the musical career. He lived for three years as solo violoncellist and member of a string quartet at Helsingfors. Afterwards he was successively musical director at the university of Kiel, founder of a vocal academy at Hamburg (1851), professor of singing and musical theory at the Vienna Conservatoire (1862-5), conductor of the Evangelical Choral Society, and finally professor at the conservatoire at Hamburg, where he died June 10, 1883. He composed a sonata for violoncello and pianoforte and various chamber music works which were highly spoken of by Schumann.

JULIUS RIETZ, born December 28, 1812, in Berlin, was the younger son of Johann Friedrich Rietz, a viola player and royal chamber musician. Schmidt and M. Ganz conducted his first studies of the violoncello, and after a comparatively short period, Bernhard Romberg became his master on that instrument, and his progress was such that he was engaged for the orchestra of the Königstädter Theatre at the early age of sixteen. His brother, Edouard, gave him his first instruction in the art of composition, and his first work was the incidental music to a play, "Lorbeerbaum and Bettelstab," for the above theatre. After the death of his brother in 1832, who was an intimate friend of Mendelssohn, the latter supervised his studies, and exercised a marked influence on his style, although he possessed sufficient individuality to imbue his works with a vitality which made them popular favourites, and secured them a lasting place in the concert rooms, at least of his own country. At the end of 1833, Mendelssohn, associated with Immermann, in order to raise the Düsseldorf Theatre to the highest possible standard of art, and for that purpose they secured the co-operation of Rietz as second capellmeister at the beginning of 1834. Here he made the acquaintance of Schumann, who speaks of him as an excellent violoncellist and a clever musician. Mendelssohn resigned the conductorship of the theatre towards the end of that year in favour of Rietz, and when the former left Düsseldorf definitely, and entered upon his duties as director of music at Leipzig, Rietz was appointed in the same capacity for Düsseldorf. The artistic atmosphere of that town, the merry and lively spirit of the Rhenish people, and the beauty of the country with all its romantic associations, could not fail to assert that influence which is patent in the works of Schumann and Mendelssohn, also upon the highly impressionable nature of Rietz, and it was during that period that he produced his best works. In 1847 he followed his friend Mendelssohn to Leipzig as conductor of the theatre, and was soon elected as director of the "Singakademie" (choral academy), and after Mendelssohn's death as director of the Gewandhaus Concerts. At these latter concerts he made his last appearances as a solo violoncellist, and took part in chamber concerts as late as 1849. After that time he abandoned solo playing altogether, and in 1854 also his position as conductor of the opera, devoting his whole energies to the Gewandhaus Concerts, and his duties at the conservatoire. In 1860 he received his nomination as successor to Reissiger at Dresden, and the artistic management of the conservatoire, after becoming Doctor of Philosophy on the occasion of the 450 years' jubilee of the University of Leipzig in 1859. After this he ceased altogether to play in public, but continued to take part in chamber music in private circles. 1874 he celebrated his forty years' jubilee as a conductor, and the King of Saxony nominated him on that occasion his "director general of music." In the same year he began the complete edition of Mendelssohn's works for Messrs. Breitkopf and Härtel. His retirement from public duties was fixed for October 1, 1877, but he died on September 12 of that year. He was beloved and esteemed by all who had the privilege of his acquaintance. Rietz wrote two concertos for his instrument, and a fantasia appassionata, which latter he played at the Gewandhaus on February 15, 1844, and Piatti played it at the Philharmonic Society on June 29, 1863. In the programme it says "first time of performance," but of course, that is correct only as far as London is concerned. His concerto in E, Op. 16, has been republished by Alwin Schroeder; it was a very meritorious undertaking as, though very Mendelssohnian, it is better music than many existing violoncello concertos, and, moreover,

FIG. 48. KARL SCHLESINGER.

makes such demands upon the executant that it is an excellent piece for study.

OTTOMAR VON RODA, born 1813 at Rudolstadt, received instruction on the violin from the chamber musician, Brömmel, when he was only a child, and the little virtuoso was soon appointed to the court orchestra. At the age of twelve years he exchanged the violin for the violoncello, which he studied under Knoop. After fulfilling an engagement in the Bethmann Orchestra at Magdeburg, he was appointed at the German Theatre in Copenhagen, and returned in 1836 to Rudolstadt, where he was engaged as a court musician. In 1837 he started on a concert tour with the violinist Brand, and they had great success with their duets for violin and violoncello. This tour came to a premature close by the death of Brand. Further particulars wanting.

ALEXANDER VON RODA, brother of the former, lived in Switzerland about 1840 as violoncello virtuoso and teacher of his instrument.

KARL SCHLESINGER, born August 19, 1813, in Vienna, commenced his remarkable career like von Roda, and many of his colleagues, as a violinist. After a few years he devoted himself entirely to the violoncello, and was engaged as solo violoncellist for the National Theatre at Budapest in 1838, and in 1846 he went to Vienna, where he held the same position at the Imperial Opera, and joined the famous Hellmesberger Quartet, which he left in 1855, when Borzaga, Cossmann, Roever and Popper followed him in succession. From November 18, 1858, to 1867, he was principal violoncello of the Imperial Chapel. In 1862 he was appointed teacher of his instrument at the Conservatoire, where Udel, Sulzer, Hummer and Hegyesi were among his pupils. His portrait is given here, Fig. 48.

HEINRICH AUGUST BOCK, born July 17, 1815, in Berlin, where he died August 27, 1837, is mentioned by Mendel and Reissmann as a clever violoncellist.

FERDINAND CHRISTIAN WILHELM PRAEGER, born January 1, 1815, died in London. He was a composer of symphonic works for orchestra as well as numerous pianoforte works. He came to London in 1834, and was correspondent of the "Neue Zeitschrift für Musik," edited by Schumann. He began his musical career as violoncellist, but exchanged it, at Hummel's advice, for the piano. He was one of the earliest champions of Wagner, and together with others caused the master's appointment as conductor of the Philharmonic in 1855. He published some pieces for violoncello with piano accompaniment. His father:

HEINRICH ALOYS PRAEGER, born December 23, 1783, died at Magdeburg, August 7, 1854, violinist (violoncellist?), guitar player and conductor, left several compositions for violoncello, of which the English Standard Edition has republished the following: twelve easy preludes, twelve adagios, twelve sacred melodies.

JOSEPH HUBER, born about 1816, in Vienna, studied at the Conservatoire of that town from 1835 till 1839. He appeared at the Conservatoire concerts of that town in 1836-7, and was for some time principal violoncello of the Opera at Budapest, composed some melodies for violoncello with pianoforte and also various operatic works.

BERNHARD ENGELMANN, born 1816, at Querfurt, studied the violoncello under Kummer in Dresden. In 1834 he returned for a short time to his native town on completing his course of studies, and in November of that year he went to Leipzig, where he enjoyed the reputation of an excellent virtuoso. Further particulars are missing.

JOSEPH, EDLER (baronet) VON PORTHEIM, born January 6, 1817, at Prague, excellent amateur violoncellist, a pupil of Hüttner, deserves to be remembered for his serious efforts to cultivate chamber music in his native town, where he took part also in the foundation of the Chamber Music Society in 1876, of which he was the president. He was still living in 1889. Forino, mistaking his title for his family name, describes him as Joseph Edler.

WILHELM LOTZE, born January 17, 1817, in Berlin, received his first instruction on the violoncello from the chamber musician, Töpfer, who died 1865, and finished his studies under

Ganz. In 1837 he became a member of the court orchestra, and was violoncellist of the Zimmermann Quartet from 1838 to 1852. In 1872 he retired with a pension.

FERDINAND BÜCHLER, born March 17, 1817, at Darmstadt, as the son of one of the chamber musicians of the Duke of Hesse. His first instructor on the violoncello was August Daniel Mangold, the excellent virtuoso at the court of Darmstadt, of whom we have spoken before *(page 234)*. After he had already attained a high standard of perfection, Büchler placed himself under Joseph Menter at Munich, and when the latter visited Vienna, during the winter season 1838-9, Büchler took his place in the chamber concerts of the Munich Quartet. After finishing his studies under Menter he returned to Darmstadt, resuming his place in the Ducal Chapel, where he was now appointed as principal violoncello. He contracted a complaint of the right arm, which caused him to give up his career of a soloist and restrict himself to chamber music and the orchestra. He retired in 1881 with a pension, after forty-six years' service.

Büchler's chief importance lies in the studies which he wrote for his instrument, and which are becoming deservedly more popular. They testify to the thorough knowledge which he had acquired of the technique of his instrument, combined with musical feeling, and possessing also a certain amount of melodic invention. He received his theoretical training from the celebrated Cantor Rinck in Darmstadt. His compositions do not extend, however, beyond studies, a few works for teaching purposes, viz., three sonatas of medium difficulty with accompaniment of a second violoncello, a number of arrangements of classical pieces, and two effective short pieces for four violoncellos.

JULIUS STAHLKNECHT was another distinguished violoncellist, who was born at Posen on the same day that Büchler first beheld the light of day, at Darmstadt, viz., on March 17,

1817. He went to Berlin, where he studied the violoncello under Drews and Friedrich Wranitzky. In 1838 he joined the Royal Chapel (Hofkapelle) in Berlin. With his brother, Adolph, a very good violinist, he undertook a prolonged concert tour, and on July 3, 1835, they appeared at Dresden with great success in a duet by Bohrer, and another of their own composition, with an introduction by Spohr ("Allgemeine Musik Zeitung," 1835, page 482). They were joined about 1844 by Charles Albert Löschhorn, with whom they gave chamber concerts in Berlin which enjoyed great popularity. After the retirement of Moritz Ganz (not "after the death of Leopold Ganz," as Wasielewski says) he followed the latter in his position and title as solo violoncellist and "Conzertmeister" of the Royal Orchestra. On his retirement in 1881, Louis Lübeck became his successor. He composed Two Concertos, Op. 14 and 15, a Divertissement, Op. 3, Three Pieces with Piano, Op. 5, fantasia on "Linda di Chamounix," Op. 8, Serenade Espagnole, Op. 9, Fantaisie Caprice, Op. 11, "Impromptu sur Norma," Op. 17, etc.

ANTON TRÄG, born 1818 at Schwechat, near Vienna, was the son of a Viennese composer, who taught him the elements of music before he was six years old. He studied the violoncello at the Vienna Conservatoire under Merk. February 28, 1845, he became professor of his instrument at the Prague Conservatoire. He resigned his position in 1850 (Wasielewski's statement that he remained for *ten* years is wrong), and returned to Vienna, where he died, July 7, 1860. He was an artist of high aims, devoted to the study of the classical masters, for which he found ample opportunity at the palace of the art-loving Prince Clam Gallas. Among his pupils Henry Röver takes a prominent position. Apparently he has not published any compositions for his instrument.

FRANZ XAVER HEGENBARTH, born May 10, 1818, at Gersdorf, in Bohemia, studied the violoncello under Hüttner at the Prague

Conservatoire from May 1, 1831, till May 16, 1837, at the expense of Prince Kinsky. In 1838 he was appointed solo violoncellist at the theatre at Gratz, and afterwards went to Linz in the same capacity, and in 1844 to Lemberg. From 1852 to 1865 he was professor of his instrument at the Mozarteum at Salzburg, and in the latter year he succeeded Moritz Wagner as professor of the Conservatoire at Prague, which he held still at the time of his death, December 20, 1887. His compositions, which, according to Wasielewski, included a violoncello tutor and various solos, remained in manuscript. He was highly esteemed by contemporary musicians, as is shown by the dedication of several important compositions by eminent composers, and at least two of his pupils, Wihan and Grünfeld, do him great credit as a teacher.

LOUIS LEE, the younger brother of Sebastian, was born at Hamburg in 1819. His masters' names are not mentioned, but probably his brother Sebastian and the elder Prell initiated him in the art of violoncello playing. He was also an excellent pianist who played whole orchestral scores from memory. At the age of twelve he appeared as soloist in Northern Germany and at Copenhagen. For some time he was violoncellist at the Hamburg Theatre, lived for some years in Paris and returned to Hamburg, where he arranged chamber music soirées with Hafner, and afterwards with Böie. Lee was principal violoncello of the Hamburg Philharmonic Society for many years and professor at the conservatoire until 1884. He appeared at all the principal towns of Europe with great success. His compositions are few, viz., a Sonata, Op. 9, Three Progressive Sonatinas, Op. 14, and Wasielewski mentions as especially good "Trois Pièces Gracieuses."

KARL GRIMM, born April 28, 1819, at Hildburghausen, was principal violoncello at the Court Theatre at Wiesbaden for about fifty years. He died at Freiburg in Silesia, on January 9, 1888. He is deservedly known by his many effectively-written compositions, including an adagio for two violoncellos and pianoforte, which may be characterised as of the lighter genre.

JEAN JACQUES OFFENBACH, born June 21, 1819, at Cologne, studied the violoncello from an early age, and went to Paris in 1842 to perfect himself under Vaslin. He did not attain sufficient facility of the bow to make his mark as an executant on the violoncello, and never rose beyond the position of an orchestral player at the Opera Comique. But during that time he turned his attention to the theatre itself, and in 1847 he became conductor at the Theatre Français, and soon after he commenced to produce his operettas which made his name known all over the world. He wrote some solos and a number of very useful and instructive duets for the violoncello. He died in Paris, October 5, 1880.

PLATE XXXVII.
BERNHARD COSSMANN.

To face page 417.

CHAPTER XXII.

GERMAN VIOLONCELLISTS FROM 1820-40.

WILHELM HENNING, born 1820 at Potsdam, was the son of the director of the Military Orphanage Music School. In 1844 he became a royal chamber musician and violoncellist in the orchestra of the Royal Opera in Berlin.

ROBERT EMIL BOCKMÜHL, born 1820, at Frankfurt-on-Main, where he died on November 3, 1881. He came from a musical family. His aunt, Frau F. Bockmühl, who was a great-aunt of the writer of these lines, was the solo soprano at the first Rhenish musical festival under Burgmüller. Bockmühl was very delicate in his youth, and spent a considerable time in the South of France for the benefit of his health. About 1850 he settled in Düsseldorf, and when Schumann composed his violoncello concerto he consulted Bockmühl with regard to the passages and other technical questions. He appeared rarely in public as a soloist, but, living in circumstances which placed him beyond the necessity of exercising his art for pecuniary considerations, he devoted himself chiefly to composition and a careful and systematic study of the technicalities of his instrument. Although a good musician, he lacked inspiration, and that is the reason which rendered his numerous compositions obsolete, except his "Etudes pour le Developpement du Mécanisme du Violoncelle," Op. 47, which were adopted for the elementary classes of the Brussels and Munich Conservatoires, and which are excellent studies, especially for the art of bowing *(see "Franchomme," letter to Bockmühl)*.

AUGUST LINDNER, born October 29, 1820, at Dessau, died in June, 1878. He combined great beauty of tone with an excellent technique of the left hand. His master on the violoncello was the elder Drechsler, who formed so many excellent virtuosos on that instrument, and Schneider instructed him in the intricacies of musical theory and form. That he benefited by the latter as well as by the former is evident from his compositions, some of which rank to this day among the standard works of violoncello literature. In 1837 he was appointed solo violoncello to the court of Hanover, and he remained in that town to the end of his life.

The most important of his works is the fine Concerto in E minor, Op. 34, with its brilliant tarantella as a finale. Other works are: Fantasia, Op. 3; "L'Infidèle Elegy," Op. 4; Ops. 9, 12, 16, 26, 28, 32 and 39 are arrangements and fantasias on operas, of which he wrote a great number, many appearing without an opus number. Nine "Salonstücke," Op. 18; "Chant d'Amour," Op. 21; Caprice, Op. 22; Concertstück, Op. 25; "Scènes Suisses," Op. 28; six "Phantasiestücke," Op. 38. He wrote also a new edition of L. Duport's "Essay on the Art of Fingering."

WILHELM LINDNER was an excellent violoncellist, who died as chamber musician to the Grand Duke of Baden on August 19, 1887.

FERDINAND BILSE, brother of the popular conductor, and founder of the Bilse Orchestra in Berlin, was born in Liegnitz about 1820. He was the solo violoncellist in his brother's celebrated orchestra, which appeared at the Paris Exhibition in

1867, and after visiting the principal towns of North Germany, settled in Berlin.

JOHANNES HOECKE, born near Flensburg, in Holstein, in 1820, was a horn player and violoncellist. In his younger years he visited England, taking part in a French horn quartet. Afterwards he relinquished the horn altogether and became principal violoncello at the Cologne Opera and member of the town orchestra during the latter half of the nineteenth century. He was a pupil of F. A. Kummer, and the first master of the writer of these lines. He died at Cologne on February 13, 1897, in his seventy-seventh year.

KARL BERGMANN, born at Ebersbach (Saxony) in 1821. He was a pupil of Zimmermann in Littau, and Hesse in Breslau, and became a clever violoncellist and pianist. In 1850 he went to the United States of America, where he joined the touring orchestra, "Germania," as violoncellist, and became its conductor a few months later. After the dissolution of that orchestra in 1854, he went to New York and became conductor of the Philharmonic Orchestra, together with Th. Eisfeld. Since 1862 he was the sole conductor of these concerts, and also of the male choir, "Arion." In 1870 he conducted a monster performance of Weber's opera, "Der Freischütz," with the assistance of that choir. He earned great merit for raising the standard and taste for music in the United States. His compositions consist of a few pieces for orchestra. He died August 10, 1876.

In 1822 appeared in Vienna a violoncellist, FUNKE, who played as soloist in some of the leading concerts, without, however, obtaining any marked success. No particulars about this artist appear to be obtainable. The same was the case with FERDINAND FRANZEL, who played in Vienna in 1825.

JOSEPH GIESE, born November, 1821, at Coblenz on the Rhine, studied the violoncello under M. Ganz in Berlin. After a prolonged tour through France and Switzerland, he settled at the Hague as professor of violoncello at the Royal Conservatoire and principal violoncello at the French Theatre. He enjoyed the reputation of an excellent teacher, and counted among his pupils many violoncellists of note, including his son Fritz (q.v.).

LOUIS DRECHSLER, born October 5, 1822, at Dessau, developed under his father's training into an excellent violoncellist. He devoted also his attention to the art of singing, which he studied in Italy and Paris. He settled in Edinburgh, where he lived as a highly respected violoncellist and teacher of music until the time of his death, which occurred on June 25, 1860.

LEOPOLD ALEXANDER ZELLNER, born September 23, 1823, at Agram, as son of the cathedral organist, commenced at an early age the study of the violoncello, organ, oboe and composition.

In 1868 he succeeded Sechter as professor of musical theory at the Vienna Conservatoire and secretary of the Society of the Friends of Music. In 1859-66 he instituted historical concerts which proved very successful. He was also lecturer and writer on musical subjects. He contributed various compositions to the literature of the violoncello, and died in Vienna, November 24, 1894.

SELMAR BAGGE, born June 30, 1823, in Coburg. In 1837 he became a pupil of Hüttner at the Prague Conservatoire, studying theory and composition under D. Weber in Prague and the famous Simon Sechter in Vienna. In 1853 he became professor of musical theory at the Vienna Conservatoire, but relinquished that post in 1855, embracing a literary career. When Messrs. Breitkopf and Härtel revived the "Allgemeine Musik Zeitung" in 1863, Bagge was appointed editor, and held that position until the paper was transferred to Rieter and Biedermann in 1866.

In 1868 he was appointed director of the Conservatoire at Basle, where he died, July 17, 1896.

He composed several works for chamber music, a symphony, songs, and wrote also a book on musical theory.

BERNHARD COSSMANN, born May 17, 1823, at Dessau, as the son of a Jewish merchant. His first master on the violoncello was Espenhahm at Dessau, and afterwards successively Karl Drechsler, and from 1837 to 1840, Theodor Müller, violoncellist of the celebrated Müller Quartet at Brunswick. He finished his studies under F. A. Kummer at Dresden. From 1840 to 1846 he was violoncellist at the Théatre Italien in Paris (not Grand Opera, as stated by some biographers), and during that period he paid occasional visits to London, Berlin, Leipzig and other important towns. In 1847 he was appointed by Mendelssohn as solo violoncellist for the Gewandhaus concerts at Leipzig, and pursued the study of composition under Moritz Hauptmann. In 1849 he started on a prolonged concert tour through England and Ireland, playing before Queen Victoria at Windsor Castle, in London, and at the Philharmonic Society at Dublin.

On his return from England he made a prolonged stay in Paris. During his Leipzig period he had made the acquaintance of Liszt, which ripened into friendship, and this brought Cossmann to Weimar in August, 1850, where Liszt was conducting the first rehearsals of "Lohengrin." Liszt induced him to remain as solo violoncellist to the Duke of Weimar and principal violoncello in the Weimar orchestra. In that position he remained for sixteen years, spending the summer at Baden-Baden as he had done already since 1843.

A feature of his activity in Weimar was his quartet playing, for which he became justly famous, Joachim, Laub, Singer and other great violinists being alternately leaders of his quartet. Ferdinand Laub's influence brought him to Moscow in 1866, where he was appointed as professor at the Imperial Conservatoire, Laub being professor of violin, and Nicholas Rubinstein (brother of Anton), the director, in whose memory Tchaïkovsky wrote his famous trio.

In 1870, Cossmann returned to Germany, settling at his beloved Baden-Baden, whence he undertook numerous concert tours in conjunction with Brahms, von Bülow, Pauline Lucca and other famous artists. The time between these tours he devoted chiefly to composition and the editing of important works for violoncello by various masters. In 1878 he was appointed professor at the Hoch Conservatorium at Frankfort-on-Main, which post he held until his death, which occurred in 1911. Of his compositions only his studies are still of practical value. As a virtuoso he ranks with the greatest masters of his instrument, and he has formed a great number of pupils taking a high rank among present-day violoncellists. His portrait appears on Plate XXXVII.

GEORG EDWARD GOLTERMANN, born August 19, 1824, at Hanover, was the son of an organist of that town, which possessed in August Christian Prell an excellent violoncellist, who instructed Goltermann in his art. In 1847 Goltermann went to Munich, where he pursued the study of the violoncello under Joseph Menter, while Ignatz Lachner introduced him to the mysteries of counterpoint and composition. He finished his studies in 1849, and in 1850 he commenced his career as a virtuoso, visiting the principal towns of Germany. In 1851 he produced his first symphony, which was performed with decided success at Leipzig. The following year saw the end of his virtuoso career, as he received an appointment as musical director at Würzburg. In 1853 he accepted the post of second conductor at the Frankfurt Theatre. In 1874 he became first conductor (Capellmeister), and he retained that position until his retirement a few years before his death, which occurred December 29, 1898. Though but small importance attaches to Goltermann's career as an executant on the violoncello, he takes a high rank among the composers for his instrument. His muse does not aspire to soar into higher spheres; she is a

FIG. 49. GEORG GOLTERMANN.

homely and comely dame with a pleasant countenance of strongly pronounced Mendelssohnian features, and also Mendelssohnian form. We must not quarrel with this, for she proves pleasant company, like one that entertains you with a merry chatter, eschewing all deep problems that would tax the brain.

The great advantage of his compositions, as far as the amateur is concerned, lies in the fact that they are written with an intimate knowledge of the resources of the violoncello, producing the greatest possible effect with a comparatively small demand upon the executive powers. This, combined with melodious flow, will maintain their popularity, especially among amateurs, for a long time to come. Of his seven concertos, the first in A minor, Op. 14, and the third, in B minor, Op. 51, occupy a place among the standard violoncello compositions. His two duos for violoncello and pianoforte, his romances, many of his numerous solo pieces, as well as his songs with violoncello *obbligato*, are pleasing and effective. A more extensive list of his compositions may be found in "The Literature of the Violoncello," by E. van der Straeten. The portrait is taken from a photograph presented by Goltermann to the author in 1894 *(see Fig. 49)*.

KARL HÜLLWECK, who wrote a number of effective solo pieces for violoncello, is mentioned by G. C. and T. A. Trowell as professor and chamber musician at Dresden. The year of his birth they give as 1824 appears to be erroneous, as the better-known violinist, Ferdinand Hüllweck, was born October 8, 1824. The author has not been able so far to find any more particulars about Charles Hüllweck, who is not now living.

JOH. AUG. JULIUS GOLTERMANN, born July 15 (Trowell gives July 25, but states no authority), 1825, at Hamburg. He studied under F. A. Kummer and emerged from that famous master's care as one of the foremost virtuosos, and was engaged for a time at the Hamburg Theatre. In 1850 he was appointed professor of violoncello at the Prague Conservatoire, where he remained until 1862, when he went to Stuttgart as solo violoncello in the royal chapel. A spinal trouble incapacitated him from playing—as Höke, his co-student under Kummer told the author—and he retired on a pension in 1870, and died April 5, 1876. He wrote a few solos for his instrument, including a Caprice on Slavonic Melodies, Op. 9.

Fig. 50 gives the reproduction of a letter of his, apparently addressed to Georg Goltermann, with a reference to the violoncellist, Bockmühl. We translate it as follows:

DEAR FRIEND,—All in haste I beg you will kindly forward the enclosed letter to the address, the "Herr Capellmeister" (conductor) will call upon you. I hope to have within this year still the pleasure to see you, as I shall be moving nearer Frankfort soon, and beg of you at the same time to have me booked for the concert season. I should be very pleased if Herr Cp. Steraup would bring me the orchestral parts of your concerto.

Hearty greetings to friend Mayer, Bockmühl,* and especially your amiable wife, from your

April 30, 1861.   JULIUS GOLTERMANN.

HEINRICH MOLLENHAUER, born September 10, 1825, at Erfurt in the Prussian province of Saxony, was instructed in pianoforte and violin playing when he was only four years old. Later on he studied the violoncello under Knoop at Meiningen. Together with his two brothers he appeared as a prodigy at a very early age, visiting the principal towns of Germany. In 1839 they started on their second tour, which brought them to Dessau, where they played at the court. F. Schneider, the celebrated composer, who was the director of the court chapel, complimented the boys very highly on their performance. The same tour brought them eventually to Leipzig, Berlin and St. Petersburg. In 1853 he belonged to the royal chapel at Stockholm, where he remained for three years, at the end of which he followed his younger brother, the violinist, Edward Mollenhauer, to the United States of America, where he toured suc-

---

* Emil Bockmühl *(see page 417)*.

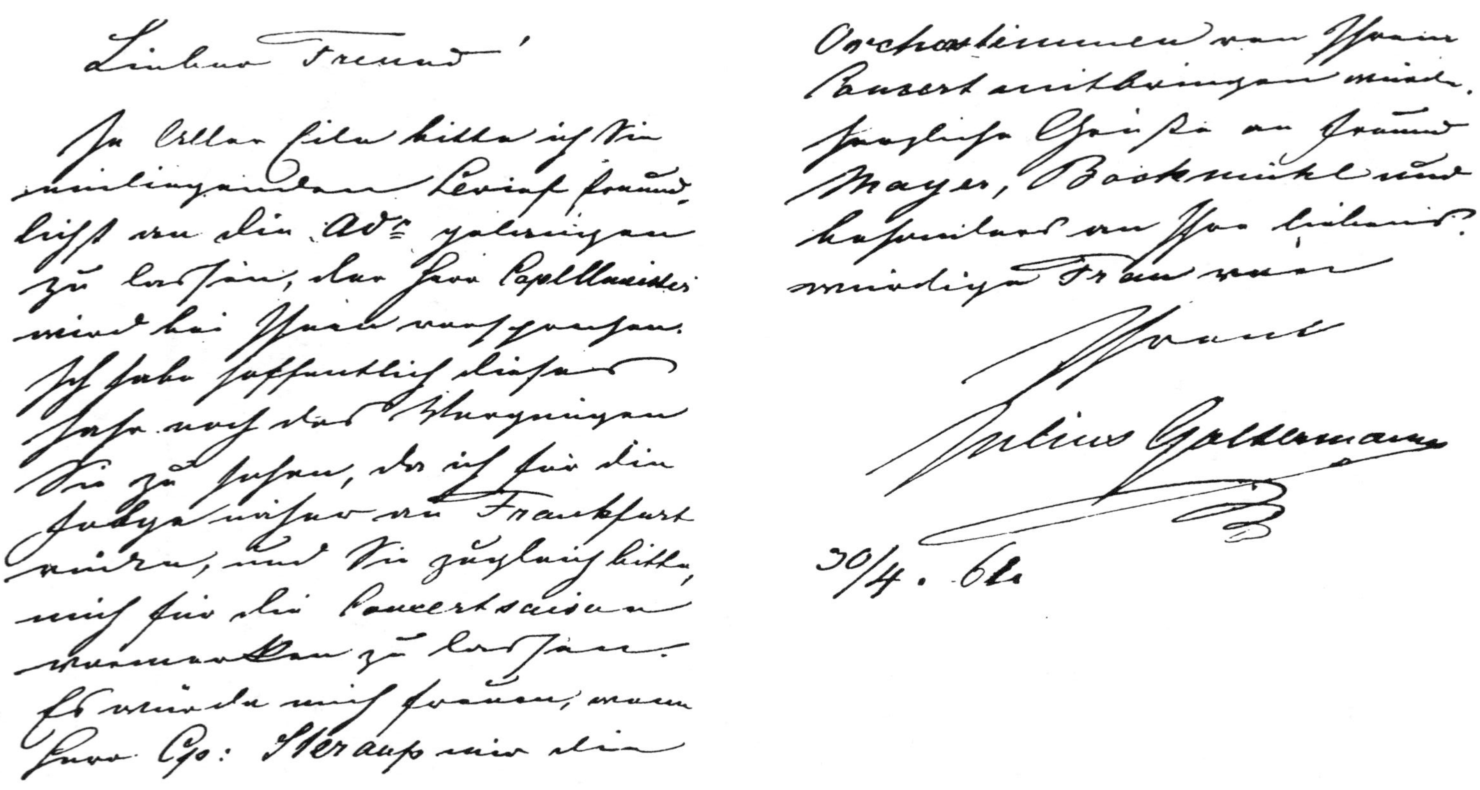

Lieber Freund!

In aller Eile bitte ich Sie
einliegenden Brief freund-
lichst an die Adr. gelangen
zu lassen, der Herr Capellmeister
wird bei Ihnen vorsprechen.
Ich habe hoffentlich dieses
Jahr noch das Vergnügen
Sie zu sehen, da ich für die
[illegible] in Frankfurt
reisen, und Sie zugleich bitte,
mich für die Concertsaison
vormerken zu lassen.
Es würde mich freuen, wenn
Herr Cp: Strauss mir die
Orchesterstimmen von Ihrem
Concert mitbringen würde.
Herzliche Grüsse an Freund
Mayer, Bockmühl und
besonders an Ihre liebens-
würdige Frau von
Ihrem
Julius Goltermann
30/4. 66

FIG. 50.

cessfully as a virtuoso. In 1867 he settled in Brooklyn, where he founded a school of music.

HENRY RÖVER, born in Vienna, May 27, 1827. He began his musical career as a violinist, but at the age of eighteen he exchanged the violin for the violoncello. Fétis considered him the foremost representative of his instrument about 1863. He was solo violoncellist at the Opera and teacher of his instrument at the Vienna Conservatoire until the time of his death. One of his most prominent pupils was Reinhold Hummer, who became his successor at the conservatoire. Röver died May 12, 1875. Among his compositions which are of the lighter genre a "Sérénade du Savoyarde" was very popular.

MAGNUS KLIETZ, born April 29, 1828, at Altenkirchen, on the Isle of Ruegen in the Baltic. He commenced his musical apprenticeship at the age of fourteen under the town musician, Abel, at Greifswalde. After studying the violin and sundry wood-wind instruments after the custom of the old town musicians (Stadtpfeifer) he chose the violoncello as his principal instrument. In 1848 he went to Berlin and continued his studies for one year under Moritz Ganz. At the end of that time he settled in Hamburg, where he succeeded Johann Aug. Julius Goltermann as principal violoncello at the theatre in 1850. He retained that position for seventeen years, after which time he joined the Philharmonic Orchestra and became one of the founders of the Hamburg Quartet Society (Quartettverein).

BAXMANN, a violoncellist living in Strassburg, founded a school of music in that town in 1824. Nothing else is known about him.

VALENTIN MÜLLER, born February 14, 1830, at Münster in Westphalia, commenced his study of the violoncello under Josef Menter at Munich, and went to Brussels in 1848 to continue with François Servais. He remained for several years in the Belgian capital, acting for some time as deputy teacher of violoncello at the Royal Conservatoire. In 1858 he succeeded Chevillard as violoncellist of the Maurin Quartet. In 1868 he went to Frankfurt as member of the quartet of the "Museums-Gesellschaft" and teacher of his instrument at the Hoch Conservatoire.

FRIEDRICH WILHELM LUDWIG GRÜTZMACHER, born March 1, 1832, at Dessau, received his first instruction in music from his father, who was a member of the ducal chapel. He chose the violoncello at an early age, and for the study of that instrument he became a pupil of Charles Drechsler, thus continuing the school of Dotzauer (Drechsler's master) at the very town from which it originated. Frederic Schneider instructed him at the same time in musical theory. In 1848 he went to Leipzig, joining one of the private orchestras to gain experience in orchestral playing. Through the influence of Ferdinand David, who recognised his talent, he was heard at the Euterpe concerts in February, 1849, playing some variations by Franchomme. Bernhard Cossmann had been engaged as soloist for the Gewandhaus and theatre orchestras, to assist Wittmann, the principal violoncello, who was not a great soloist. Cossmann left Leipzig in 1850, and Grützmacher was appointed as his successor for the theatre and Gewandhaus concerts as well as for the post of teacher at the Conservatoire. The brilliant technique of his left hand, which knew no difficulties, and his accomplished musicianship, placed him in the foremost rank of violoncellists of his time, and among them he acquired a dominant position.

His tone was by no means equal to the perfection of the technique of his left hand, and the author had it from several old musicians that his succession to F. A. Kummer in Dresden, whither Julius Rietz had summoned him in 1860, was not much appreciated by the Dresden amateurs, who were accustomed to the rich and powerful tone of Kummer. On May 6, 1867, he appeared at the fourth London Philharmonic concert, playing the violoncello concerto by Molique. During the following years he undertook numerous concert tours, visiting St.

Fig. 51.

Petersburg, Moscow, and all the principal towns of Europe. During this time he was the recipient of numerous marks of distinction and orders from various courts. The King of Saxony bestowed upon him the title of royal chamber virtuoso, and some time after that of a "Concertmeister." Not only as soloist did Grützmacher shine, but even more as chamber music player, his interpretation being always marked by breadth and dignity such as most of our readers were wont to admire in Joachim's playing. His greatest merit, however, lay in his ability to impart his art to his pupils, and this fact drew around him a very large number of promising young violoncellists, who, under his guidance, rose to prominent positions. Their list is too long to be included here, moreover, the master's name will be found in each individual biography. To give a superficial idea of the bevy of illustrious names in that list we mention: Leopold, Grützmacher, F. Hilpert, E. Hegar, R. Bellmann, W. Fitzenhagen, M. Kahnt, Bruno Wilfert, L. Krumbholz, W. Herlitz, etc. Grützmacher died after a long and distinguished career, on January 23, 1903, at Dresden. Fig. 51 gives his portrait, and an autograph reproduction from his Concerto No. 3, Op. 40, in Fig. 52.

As a composer and arranger of the works of older masters he was very prolific. They are for the greater part enumerated in the author's "Literature of the Violoncello." The majority of his original compositions are a negligible quantity of a professorial physiognomy. Exceptions are his studies, especially the "Technology of Violoncello Playing," Op. 38, although the second book is in many instances overladen with difficulties of a transcendental nature, which make their value somewhat problematic except for the virtuoso. The first book stands in no relation to these Paganini-like feats, and that is a book of great value to all students of moderately advanced technique. His daily studies likewise are very useful. Very meritorious was Grützmacher's activity as an editor of classical works which had been practically lost, especially such rare treasures as the concertos by Haydn, P. E. Bach, Boccherini, sonatas by Duport, Geminiani and others. Unfortunately he treated these masters with little reverence as re-

FIG. 52. FACSIMILE OF AN ALBUM LEAF FOR MR. WILLY VON MUMM IN GRÜTZMACHER'S HANDWRITING.

gards the text of their compositions, and in various cases he pieced together "sonatas" from about half-a-dozen original compositions and edited them as if they appeared in their original form. In the case of the six solo sonatas by Bach, he went so far as to edit a "Concert Edition," in which he crowds additional chords, passages and embellishments, distorting these great and fine works in the most unpardonable manner. Yet for all that, we must be thankful for the many works which he has rescued and made accessible. Where other editions exist we can easily compare them, and restore them to their original condition, which is unfortunately necessary in the case of almost all the works by older masters in this age of editing mania, which is chiefly to be laid to the door of the publishers, who, by deliberate falsification, seek to establish a new copyright for ancient compositions.

LUDWIG EBERT, born April 13, 1834, at Chateau Kladrau in Bohemia. His father was a Rentmeister (bailiff) of Prince Windischgrätz, and being very musical himself, he recognised the early signs of his son's musical talent. After giving him some elementary musical education at home he sent him to Prague in 1846, where he became a pupil of Träg at the Conservatoire. In 1850 Träg went to Vienna, and Ebert continued his studies under Jul. Goltermann until the autumn of 1852, when he was appointed violoncellist for the Opera at Temesvar. About Easter, 1854, he went to Oldenburg as principal violoncello in the ducal chapel, where he remained until 1874, and the Grand Duke honoured him with the title of Concertmeister.

In the latter year he went to Cologne as teacher at the "Rhenish School of Music" (Conservatoire) and principal violoncello in the Gürzenich Orchestra. He was also a member of the quartet of the professors of the Conservatoire, with Otto von Königslöw as leader and George Japha and Adolph Jensen as second violin and viola. They cultivated chiefly the works of the classical masters, while the Robert Heckmann Quartet, to which Ebert also belonged for a time, represented the modern school. When Brahms's Pianoforte Quartet in A was first performed at Cologne about 1878, Heckmann announced the work for production at one of his *matinées*. No sooner had Hiller (the director of the conservatoire and the chamber concerts of the professors) seen the announcement when he wrote to Heckmann asking him to withdraw the work, as he considered it as belonging to the *classical school* and therefore should receive its first performance by the professors of the Conservatoire. Heckmann explained that the demand was unreasonable, as he had all along championed the cause of Brahms, and thereupon he received a letter finishing with the words: "Should we happen to meet anywhere, I must request that you will no longer salute me."

This letter found its way into the "Cologne Gazette" to the greatest amusement of the public. Unfortunately for Hiller, this happened just a few days before carnival, and the humour of the Cologne people never misses an opportunity. During the three carnival days everybody wore a band round the hat with Hiller's bumptious request: "Ich bitte mich nicht mehr zu grüssen" ("I request that you will no longer salute me").

Heckmann produced the quartet first, and the performance met with an enthusiastic reception. The professors quartet followed suit, but more than in time did they lag behind in vigour and temperament.

From that time there was war between the Heckmannites and Hillerites, and Ebert, remaining with the conservatoire professors, left the Heckmann Quartet and was succeeded by R. Bellmann. Another memorable occasion on which Ebert played in the Heckmann Quartet was the first performance in Cologne of Verdi's string quartet. The performance took place at Heckmann's house, and was honoured by the presence of Verdi and Mme. Verdi. The quartet contains a scherzo (or minuet?) and trio, the latter consisting of a rather sugary but pleasing melody of the earlier Verdi type. At the end of the trio Verdi turned to Ebert, and addressing him in French, said: "Bravo! very well played, but I should like it a little softer and sweeter, would you mind playing it again." After the second time Verdi said: "But, my dear sir, I want it *much* sweeter, try once more, if you please." The writer of these lines, who was then a pupil of Ebert and second violoncello in Heckmann's chamber concerts, was present on the occasion. Ebert turned round to him and remarked: "Why does he not call in one of his countrymen with a barrel-organ?" and he played it again, this time "extra dry," to the disgust of Verdi.

It must be admitted that the emotional element was no weakness of Ebert's although he was a good solid player and a good teacher. He left Cologne on April 1, 1888, and went to Wiesbaden, where he lived as a private teacher for some years, afterwards removing to Coblenz, where he is still living. He wrote four pieces in form of a Sonata, Op. 3, and Three Characteristic Pieces, Op. 7, for violoncello and pianoforte.

FIG. 53. WILHELM MÜLLER.

WILHELM MÜLLER, born June 1, 1834, at Brunswick, was the son of Charles, the leader of the first "Müller Quartet." He received his first instructions on the violoncello from his uncle Theodor. Together with his three brothers he formed the second Müller Quartet, which was from about 1855 attached to the court of Meiningen. In 1866 they settled in Wiesbaden, until the leader, Charles Müller-Berghaus, was appointed as capellmeister (director of music) in Rostock, when the whole quartet removed to that town until Wilhelm was called to Berlin as solo violoncellist in the royal chapel and teacher at the Conservatoire (Hochschule), as successor of De Swert, in 1873. He retained that position until the time of his death, and formed a great number of notable violoncellists. His portrait appears in Fig. 53.

CHARLES LÜSTNER, born November 10, 1834, at Breslau, violoncellist and pianist, was appointed in the Kur-Orchestra at Wiesbaden, in 1872, and still active in 1899 in that position, and as teacher and contributor to Riemann's "Dictionary of Music" and other musical publications, also as teacher of the pianoforte.

About 1876 he left his position in Berlin and went to America. He died September, 1897, in New York.

HIPPOLYTE MÜLLER, born May 16, 1834, at Hildburghausen, received his first music lessons from his father. At the age of eleven he appeared in public as a prodigy on the violoncello, and soon after he was sent to Menter, under whose guidance he completed his studies. In 1854 Müller joined the royal chapel at Munich, and became at the same time teacher at the Royal Conservatoire. He died August 23, 1876.

LEOPOLD GRÜTZMACHER, born September 4, 1835, at Dessau, was a brother of Frederic Grützmacher. He received his first instruction on the violoncello from C. Drechsler, afterwards studying under his brother, while F. Schneider instructed him in musical theory. His first appointment was in the Gewandhaus Orchestra at Leipzig. After some time he became principal violoncello in the Grand-Ducal Chapel at Schwerin, then he went to Prague as principal violoncello at the "Landestheater." When the Müller Quartet left Meiningen he succeeded William Müller in the ducal chapel. In 1876 he was appointed first violoncello at Weimar, with the title of a chamber virtuoso. He died on February 26, 1900. During the eighties he was principal violoncello of the Bayreuth Theatre, where he was a general favourite on account of his amiable personality. He was overshadowed by his brother's fame, although he surpassed him in beauty of tone, while his finger technique left nothing to be desired. He was, moreover, an excellent teacher and sound musician. His two concertos and minor pieces for violoncello are well constructed and pleasing. He revised and edited a considerable number of classical works for his instrument.

MORITZ KAHNT, born April 27, 1836, at Löbnitz (near Leipzig). He commenced to learn to play the pianoforte and the violin at the age of seven, receiving instructions from his father, who also taught him several wind instruments. His favourite instrument eventually proved to be the violoncello, which he studied for three years at the Leipzig Conservatoire under Grützmacher. At the same time he studied the organ and musical theory. In 1855 he was appointed as principal violoncello in the municipal orchestra and teacher of his instrument at the conservatoire at Basle on its foundation in 1867. He died August 16, 1904.

BRUNO WILFERT, born July 26, 1836, at Schmalzgrube in Saxony. Like so many violoncellists he commenced by studying the violin, on which he received instructions from the town musician Schmidt at Kirchberg (Kreis Zwickau). He followed his master when the latter removed to Glauchan, and there he commenced his study of the violoncello. Twice a week he trotted to Zwickau with his violoncello under his arm, a fully three hours' walk, to take lessons from a pupil of F. A. Kummer, named Fr. Hermann. After a time he managed under difficulties to go to Leipzig, where he became a pupil of Grützmacher. By dint of application and studious work he obtained the post of first solo violoncello at the Landestheater in Prague in 1864. On the foundation of the Prague Chamber Music Society in 1876 he became violoncellist of the original string quartet.

He wrote a few solos and a notturno for four violoncellos.

JOSEPH DIEM, born 1836 at Kellmünz, near Meiningen, in Bavaria. As boy he was a herdsman with a passion for music. From his small savings he bought first a flute and then a fiddle on which he practised day and night. At the age of fifteen he joined a band of wandering musicians and played second violin at country fairs, etc. Reduced by poverty and destitution he was compelled to leave his comrades in Switzerland, where he would have perished had it not been for a Jewish landowner, by whose recommendation and influence he was enabled to visit the conservatoire at Munich, where he became a pupil of H. Müller. At the end of three years' study he played at Augsburg with so much success that a Nüremberg manufacturer presented him with a Guarneri violoncello. He then went to Weimar to perfect himself under Cossmann. Johann Christian Lobe drew the attention of the public to him in the "Gartenlaube" of 1870 (No. 14), in an article called "Ein Sauhirt" (a swineherd). In 1866 he was appointed professor of the violoncello at Moscow. Every year he toured in Germany, the Netherlands and England. In 1872 he went to America where he remained for a few years returning to Constance, in Switzerland, where he founded a school of music in 1889, and died on January 1, 1894.

JOSEPH WERNER was born June 25, 1837, at Würzburg, where his father was musical director of the theatre. He received his first musical training at the Fröhlich musical institute at that town. In 1852 he went to Munich, where he became a pupil of Joseph Menter at the conservatoire. After Menter's death in 1856, he continued his studies under Hippolyt Müller. About this time, at the age of nineteen, Werner was already appointed as violoncellist in the royal chapel. Wasielewski relates that he visited Dresden in 1867 to acquaint himself with Grützmacher's method of teaching. In that year he became a teacher of his instrument at the conservatoire and solo violoncello in the royal chapel, with the title of royal chamber musician, and afterwards he was elected professor at the Royal Academy of Music. Werner is not only an excellent soloist, but he is equally esteemed as chamber music player, and in that capacity he was for some time associated with Hans von Bülow. As pedagogue and composer his name is a household word in the musical world, and his merit has been acknowledged by the bestowal of high honours and orders from various countries. He has written a considerable number of compositions for his instrument, including a quartet and an elegy for four violoncellos. His most important works are his violoncello tutor (with a pianoforte part for the exercises) and his numerous studies, containing valuable material for the modern technique of violoncello playing. Werner is still active as teacher and composer.

KARL LÜBBE, born February 11, 1839, at Halberstadt. He commenced his musical career as member of a military band in Magdeburg, and thence went to Ballenstedt as member of the Duke of Bernburg's chapel. On the amalgamation of the Anhalt dukedoms he removed to Dessau, where his talents were recognised by the duke who sent him to Dresden to perfect himself under Grützmacher. He possessed great technical facilities, and was more virtuoso than musician, which inclined him to indulge in technical feats and extravaganzas. These formed also the essence of his compositions which remained unpublished. In 1871 Lübbe succeeded Carl Drechsler, on the latter's retirement, as principal violoncello in the ducal chapel at Dessau. He died in the best years of his manhood on January 7, 1888.

WILLIAM HERLITZ, born June 21, 1839, at Meuselwitz in the Duchy of Altenburg. He studied the violoncello under Friedrich Grützmacher, and became solo violoncellist in Bilse's orchestra in Berlin in 1858. In 1861 he went to Ballenstedt as violoncellist, with the title of concertmeister in the ducal chapel.

CHAPTER XXIII.

GERMAN VIOLONCELLISTS FROM 1840-50.

ALBERT RÜDEL, born February 29, 1840, at Wittstock (Ostpriegnitz), as the son of the town musician. He studied the violoncello under Stahlknecht in Berlin between 1859 and 1867. In the latter year, on June 1, he was appointed as royal chamber musician, and in 1880 as solo violoncellist in the royal chapel. In that capacity he had often to appear at the court concerts, where his playing was greatly appreciated by the Emperor William I, who frequently took occasion to address Rüdel, expressing his appreciation. Rüdel composed a number of solos for his instrument, including drawing-room pieces with pianoforte for the use of students.

THEODOR KRUMBHOLZ, born December 24, 1841, at Dietendorf in the duchy of Saxe-Gotha. He studied the violoncello under Friedrich Grützmacher in Leipzig, while Moritz Hauptmann instructed him in musical theory. On the conclusion of his studies he was appointed chamber musician in the court chapel at Meiningen. This position he exchanged after a short time for that of violoncellist in the Gewandhaus and theatre orchestra at Leipzig. When Davidoff left Leipzig about 1861 Krumbholz became his successor as principal violoncello in the Gewandhaus orchestra and teacher at the conservatoire. In 1864 he removed to Stuttgart as member of the royal chapel. Shortly afterwards he was appointed as royal chamber virtuoso and teacher at the conservatoire. He was also a member in Singer's quartet. This talented artist died at the early age of thirty-seven in 1878.

WILHELM KASIMIR FRIEDRICH HILPERT, born March 4, 1841, at Nüremberg. He studied at the Leipzig Conservatoire under Friedrich Grützmacher and received his first appointment in the court chapel at Carlsruhe. Later on he received an appointment at Zürich, where he met the celebrated violinist, Jean Becker.

In 1865 the latter received an engagement to lead ten concerts of the Chamber Music Society in Florence. He induced Hilpert to accompany him, and on arrival they found the Florence quartet combination in a state of dissolution, L. Chiostri the viola, and Isadelli the violoncellist, alone remaining. Becker induced E. Masi (violinist) and Chiostri to join him in a new quartet in which Hilpert was the violoncellist. A year's studious practice resulted in an ensemble of such perfection as had been quite unknown before, and when they started on their first concert tour as the Florentine Quartet, they took the world by storm. The balance and beauty of tone and the finesse of phrasing were such that they created a furore, and wherever they appeared the concert-rooms were filled to overcrowding. The author well remembers their debut in Cologne, where they appeared with the well-known impresario Ullmann early in the seventies of last century when they played the famous minuet by Boccherini which they had revived, and played in such a manner that it caused an absolute sensation. That dainty little piece might have remained in obscurity had it not been for the Florentine Quartet. Hilpert left the quartet in 1875 (when Hegyesi succeeded him) to fill the vacant post of solo violoncello at the opera. A year later he went to Meiningen as chamber virtuoso and solo violoncellist in the ducal chapel, which acquired fame by its concert tours under Bülow's direction in the years 1880-5. The Meiningen chapel was reduced when Bülow left it. Hilpert was appointed as solo violoncello in the royal chapel and professor at the conservatoire at Munich, where he died February 6, 1896.

OSCAR EBERLE, born June 5, 1841, at Krossen on the Oder, received his first violoncello lessons from his father who was the town musician of that place. At the age of fourteen he was already far enough advanced to accept an engagement in Bilse's orchestra, then in Liegnitz. When he left the orchestra at the age of nineteen he had already on several occasions played as soloist in the concerts of Bilse. He then went to Dresden where he studied for two years under Friedrich Grützmacher to perfect himself in his art. In 1867 he went to Rotterdam as teacher at the conservatoire and solo violoncellist of the "Matchappy tot bevordering van Toonkunst" (Society for the Promotion of Tonal Art) and of the opera. He retired from that position in 1886, being made an honorary member of the society as well as of the student's society, "Sempre Crescendo," at the University of Leyden.

JULIUS CABISIUS, born October 15, 1841, at the university town of Halle on the Saale, received his first music lessons from his father. From 1855 to 1861 he studied under Julius Goltermann at the Prague Conservatoire. He held successively appointments in the court chapels of Loewenberg and Meiningen. The latter appointment he exchanged for the position of principal violoncello in the royal chapel at Stuttgart, and was a member of the Bayreuth orchestra in the eighties.

He wrote a few solos for violoncello, the best known being "Souvenir de Loewenberg," Op. 2. He died at Stuttgart April 4, 1898.

EMIL HEGAR, born January 3, 1843, at Basle, was one of the

best of Friedrich Grützmacher's numerous pupils at the Leipzig Conservatoire. His rare talent procured him not only the position of violoncellist in the Gewandhaus Orchestra, but even that of a teacher at the conservatoire in 1866 when he was only twenty-three years old. The foremost of his many excellent pupils is Julius Klengel, also Heberlein and Rensburg were his pupils. Johann Svendsen dedicated his beautiful Concerto in D major to Hegar, which is unfortunately much neglected for the reason that it affords the soloist so little opportunity for technical display. A nervous complaint which affected the left hand, compelled him to abandon his favourite instrument. He devoted himself to the art of singing, of which he was a professor at the Conservatoire at Basle until 1907. Since then he lives at Basle as private teacher.

FERDINAND BÖCKMANN, born January 28, 1843, at Hamburg, where he studied the violoncello under Magnus Klietz and Seb. Lee, receiving his theoretical instruction at the hand of Ignaz Lachner. The influence of the court capellmeister Carl Krebs procured him an appointment as violoncellist in the court chapel at Dresden in 1861, where he studied the pianoforte and composition under A. Reichel. He perfected himself at the same time in the art of violoncello playing under Friederich August Kummer. He distinguished himself both as soloist and chamber music player, and appeared in both capacities successfully in many of the principal towns of Germany. Several German kings and princes showed their appreciation of his merit by the bestowal of high orders, and in 1891 he received the title of royal chamber virtuoso.

GEBHARD GRAF, born February 4, 1843, at Waal, near Buchloe, in Bavaria, went to Munich in 1857, where he studied for four years under Hippolyt Müller. After a prolonged concert tour through the north of Germany and part of Russia, he was, in 1886, appointed C. Schroeder's successor as solo violoncellist in the court chapel at Sondershausen, where he remained for six years. After that time he was for one year as first violoncellist in the Bilse orchestra, again as Schroeder's successor; then he was for some time a member of the grand ducal chapel at Strelitz. In 1874 he was appointed principal violoncello in the court chapel at Brunswick where he was still living about 1900, but owing to extreme nervousness he has practically retired from his active career.

ALBERT GOWA, also a native of Hamburg, was born on April 14, 1843. He commenced his study of the violoncello under Louis Lee in Hamburg, continuing at the Leipzig Conservatoire under Davidoff and Louis Lübeck. Later on he went to Dresden to finish his education under Friedrich Grützmacher. He appeared with great success in several German towns.

In 1867 he made his debut in London, and in 1868 he visited Copenhagen, meeting with equally good receptions in both towns. In the following year he was appointed solo violoncellist at the court of Prince Schaumburg Lippe at Bückeburg. There he remained until 1872 when he returned to Hamburg where he held the post of principal violoncellist in the Philharmonic Orchestra for twenty years. He was for some time violoncellist in Professor Leopold Auer's quartet, afterwards joining the quartet of capellmeister Karl Bargheer. Since 1875 he was a member of Florian Zajic's quartet. Equally distinguished as soloist and quartet player he has also shown himself an excellent teacher, numbering among his many pupils, Henry Warnke, the solo violoncellist of the Kaim Orchestra at Munich.

LOUIS NOEBE, born April 17, 1843, at Güstrow, as son of the organ builder, Carl Noebe. He studied the violoncello under Louis Lübeck at the Leipzig Conservatoire from 1862 till 1865, and at the same time he had Dr. O. Paul as teacher of counterpoint. On the conclusion of his studies he was for some time a member of the Gewandhaus Orchestra at Leipzig, and of the court chapel at Weimar. Afterwards he was engaged as solo violoncellist at Homburg and in the orchestra of the Museums Concerts at Frankfort-on-Main. Since 1883 he has been teacher of the violoncello and ensemble playing at the Raff Conservatoire at the above town. In 1876 he resigned his position as solo violoncellist at Homburg, and founded a studio for violin making and employing various patents for the improvement of the quality and power of tone in his instruments. A number of the leading virtuosos speak in very flattering terms of the excellent quality of instruments which they purchased from Mr. Noebe, to wit: Sarasate, Wilhelmj, De Swert, Auer, Popper, Cossmann, E. de Munck, Hubay, Singer and many more.

RICHARD BELLMANN, born June 8, 1844, at Freiberg in Saxony, was a pupil of Friederich August Kummer at Dresden, where he finished his studies under Friedrich Grützmacher. His theoretical education he received at the Dresden Conservatoire where he studied for three years. After absolving his studies at Dresden he went to Paris to acquaint himself with the French school, and to study Franchomme's compositions under that master's personal guidance. Shortly after he was appointed first solo violoncellist at the court of Schwerin, where he met with so much success that the grand duke honoured him by nominating him his chamber virtuoso. In 1878 Bellmann left Schwerin and settled in Bonn, following for some time the career of a virtuoso without binding himself to any permanent engagement, succeeding Ebert as violoncellist of Robert Heckmann's quartet in Cologne which acquired universal fame during its concert tours through Germany, Italy and England, where it came to a tragic end through Heckmann's sudden death at Glasgow in 1891. Bellmann died about 1900. He was a virtuoso in the best sense of the word. With a well-developed technique of the left hand he combined a tone of great power and beauty, absolute purity of intonation and a refined and elegant style. He was the possessor of a beautiful Maggini violoncello, formerly the property of Bernhard Romberg.

CHARLES UDEL, born February 6, 1844, at Warasdin in Croatia, as the son of the capellmeister of that town, who instructed him in music from his early childhood. In September, 1859, he was sent to Vienna, where he commenced to study violin playing under Charles Heissler. After one year's study he exchanged the violin for the violoncello and became a pupil of Schlesinger. In 1867 he was appointed second principal violoncellist at the Budapest opera, but in 1868 he returned to Vienna where he accepted an engagement in the orchestra of the New Opera in 1869. When Röver died in May, 1875, Udel succeeded him as teacher at the conservatoire, while Hilpert filled his place as solo violoncellist at the opera. Hilpert left in the following year and Udel became his successor. In 1877 he divided the professorship at the conservatoire with R. Hummer, who conducted the three upper classes while Udel took the three lower ones. After three years' activity at the conservatoire he received the official title of "professor." An affliction of the hand compelled him to relinquish his career as an executant, and to devote himself entirely to teaching.

FRANCIS BENNAT, born August 17, 1844, at Bregenz. At an early age he came to Munich, where he studied the violoncello under Hippolyte Müller at the conservatoire. At the end of his course at that school he went to Brussels to acquaint himself with the style of that school and perfect himself under Servais. After a series of successful concert tours he was in 1864 appointed as member of the royal chapel at Munich, some time later receiving the title of "chamber virtuoso." Since 1888 he has been violoncellist of the Walter Quartet, which combination undertakes annually an extended concert tour, and from 1901 he has also been violoncellist of the chamber music union Stavenhagen, von Kaulbach-Scotta.

He is one of the principal collaborators of the "Denkmäler der Tonkunst in Bayern" ("Monuments of Music in Bavaria"), where he published sonatas of Felice dall' Abaco, viol da gamba sonatas by Kühnel, etc.

EMIL BOERNGEN, born February 2, 1845, at Verden. His father was soon after appointed musical director at Emden, and there he began to instruct his son Emil, who was still a small boy, in the elements of music and instrumental playing. Later on he was sent to Hanover, where he studied the violoncello under the chamber virtuoso, Karl Matys. Finally he went to Friedrich Grützmacher at Dresden, with whom he studied for three years. In 1870 he was appointed first violoncellist at the theatre at Helsingfors, frequently appearing as soloist and quartet player. In 1872 he went to Strasburg as solo violoncellist at the theatre, and a few years later he went in the same capacity to the Mozarteum at Salzburg. In 1875 he was appointed teacher of the violoncello at the Würzburg Conservatoire, where he received the title of professor in recognition of his distinguished services. He died at Würzburg December 21, 1893.

DAVID POPPER, born June 18, 1846, at Prague, is one of the greatest masters of his instrument of all times. He studied the violoncello under Julius Goltermann as a pupil of the Prague Conservatoire. His first appointment he received as chamber virtuoso in the court chapel of the Prince of Hohenzollern at Löwenberg (where he was succeeded by Cabisius). In 1863 he commenced his concert tours and soon acquired fame as a great soloist as well as a highly-gifted composer of exquisite solo pieces for his instrument. At the musical festival at Carlsruhe in 1865 and in Vienna in 1867 he was received with enthusiasm, and in 1868 he was engaged as solo violoncellist for the Imperial Opera in Vienna. In 1872 he married the famous pianist, Sophie Menter, and in 1873 he relinquished his position and started, together with his wife, on a concert tour, which extended over several years, and during that time they visited all the principal towns of Europe with phenomenal success. His marriage was dissolved in 1886.

In 1891 he revisited England, and played one movement of his Concerto in C at the Crystal Palace on November 10. On the twenty-first of that month he made his only appearance at the Monday Popular Concerts at St. James's Hall, playing in Schubert's Quartet in D minor with Strauss as leader, and for his solo an adagio by Tartini and minuet of his own composition. On November 25 he gave an orchestral concert where he played his beautiful suite, "Im Walde," the requiem for three violoncellos (with Delsart and Howell), and Saint-Saëns's Concerto in A minor. He made several appearances at the concerts of the Philharmonic Society.

In 1896 he settled at Budapest as professor of the Royal Conservatoire. His compositions for the violoncello include three concertos, suites and numerous solos, all of which belong to the best and most effective standard literature for the instrument *(see "Violoncello Literature")*. His technical studies (forty studies in four books and one book of ten preparatory studies) are most important for the study of the most advanced modern technique. Popper died August 7, 1913, at Budapest. Only a few days before his death the honorary title of Hofrath was conferred upon him by the Emperor Francis Joseph. His portrait with a dedication to the author appears on Plate XXXVIII.

HERMANN JACOBOWSKY, born October 19, 1846, at Neustrelitz. His father, a clarinet player in the court orchestra, instructed him in pianoforte playing when he was in his early boyhood. At the age of sixteen he choose the musical career as his profession and went to Berlin, where he studied the violoncello under J. Griebel and musical theory under Richard Wuerst. In 1864 Jacobowsky was appointed solo violoncellist

PLATE XXXVIII.
DAVID POPPER.

in Liebig's Symphony Orchestra. At the same time he played as "accessist" (probationer) in the royal chapel, where he passed his examination in solo playing in 1868, and was promised a definite appointment whenever a vacancy should occur. In 1870 he went to Jaffy, as teacher of the violoncello at the conservatoire of that town. He had not long entered upon his new duties when the war broke out between France and Germany, and he served in the German army throughout that campaign. After his return he received the promised appointment as chamber musician in the royal chapel. He is not only an excellent soloist but distinguished himself likewise as chamber music player in the trio-soirées given in conjunction with H. Bischof and Waldemar Meyer. He has contributed many valuable works to the violoncello literature in the shape of solos, studies, etc.

KARL MATYS, born about the middle of the forties of last century, at Hanover, received his first instructions on the violoncello from his father. Afterwards he went to Brussels where he studied under François Servais. On his return to Hanover he was appointed chamber musician in the royal chapel. Towards the end of the sixties he received the title of a chamber virtuoso and succeeded Aug. Lindner as first solo violoncellist about 1878. In 1897 he retired on a pension, and died at Hanover during the latter part of 1908. About 1895 the German Emperor honoured him by bestowal of the Order of the Crown of Prussia. Matys composed some solos and a book of duets for two violoncellos.

FRIEDRICH MONHAUPT, born September 30, 1846, at Dannenberg (Hanover). At the age of ten he came to Hamburg, where he studied the violoncello under Serpentien and pianoforte and theory under G. Armbrust. In 1864 he was appointed violoncellist at the theatre of Altona. He retained this position but for a short time when he went to Trêves as violoncellist in the Municipal Orchestra. From April, 1871, to September, 1872, he studied again, this time under Friedrich Grützmacher at Dresden. At the end of that time he was appointed solo violoncellist in the court chapel at Sondershausen, which was then flourishing under the direction of court capellmeister Erdmannsdörffer. During that time Monhaupt distinguished himself as soloist, chamber music and orchestral player. On September 1, 1878, he was engaged as solo violoncellist at the court theatre at Cassels, where he celebrated his twenty-five years' jubilee as royal chamber virtuoso and member of the Cassel String Quartet (Hoppen, Keller, Kruse, Monhaupt), to which he still belongs (1909).

RICHARD VOLLRATH, born December 16, 1848, at Sonneberg in Thuringia, where his father was engaged as town musician. The latter instructed him, according to the requirements of his profession in the playing of various instruments. Of these the violoncello proved the most attractive, and he commenced the serious study of it under the chamber musician Roda at Rudolstadt. From 1865 to 1867 he studied under Friedrich Grützmacher at Dresden. After serving his prescribed term in the army at Coblenz Vollrath was appointed first violoncello in the Chur Orchestra at Ems, filling that position from 1871 to 1873. During the winter, 1873-4, he was engaged in the Mannsfeld Orchestra at Dresden, and during that period he renewed his studies with Grützmacher. On his return he fulfilled a two years' engagement as solo violoncellist at Wiesbaden, and since September, 1876, he is the principal violoncello in the Municipal Orchestra and teacher of his instrument at Schumacher's Conservatoire, Mayence.

KARL FRIEDRICH WILHELM FITZENHAGEN, born September 15, 1848, at Seesen, in the Duchy of Brunswick, where his father was musical director. At the age of five he received his first lessons on the pianoforte, three years later he commenced to play the violoncello and at the age of eleven he added the study of the violin, besides playing several wind instruments in order to assist his father in case of emergency, which not infrequently happened in that little orchestra. This gave him a great deal of experience which stood him in good stead in later years. The chamber musician Plock, of Brunswick, was the first master under whom he commenced his regular studies of the violoncello, while he still continued to play the violin and the pianoforte, and about this time he made his debut as a soloist on the former instrument. In 1862 he became a pupil of Theodor Müller, and from that time he devoted himself chiefly to the study of the violoncello. In 1865 he played a solo at the theatre for the approval of the Duke of Brunswick, who declared himself so well satisfied that he freed Fitzenhagen from military service. By the aid of high patronage he was also enabled to continue his studies under Grützmacher from May, 1867, till 1868, when he was engaged for the royal chapel at Dresden. From that time commenced also his career as a soloist. In 1869 he played at the meeting of musical artists at Leipzig and in the following year at the Beethoven Festival at Weimar. Liszt wished him to remain at that town but he preferred an appointment as professor at the Imperial Conservatoire at Moscow, whither he went in August, 1870. There commenced the most active and important part of his career. Besides solo and chamber music playing he devoted a great deal of his time to teaching and composing. Among his many talented pupils we mention Adamowsky. Over sixty opus numbers of violoncello compositions comprise four concertos, solos, studies, etc. *(see "Violoncello Literature")*. He was nominated concertmeister of the Imperial Russian Musical Society, and in 1884 he became director of the Moscow Musical and Orchestral Society. Of lasting importance for the present and future generations of violoncello players are Fitzenhagen's technical studies, with most systematic and excellent thumb position exercises, his charming little pieces in the first position and a few of his solos.

HUGO JÄGER, born May 17, 1848, at Warmbrunn, in Silesia, studied in Vienna under D. Popper, and afterwards finished his studies under Friedrich Grützmacher at Dresden. His first appointment was in the chapel of the Prince of Hohenzollern, memorable by the number of excellent artists who have at times belonged to it. Jäger, who succeeded Popper and Cabisius, remained in Löwenberg until the chapel was dissolved, when he was engaged as solo violoncellist successively at Ems, Altenburg, Brunswick and Pawlowsk, near St. Petersburg. In 1874 he became a member of the ducal chapel at Dessau, in which he advanced to the position of first solo violoncellist in 1880.

CARL SCHRÖDER, born December 18, 1848, at Ouedlinburg, studied the violoncello under Drechsler at Dessau. His progress was so rapid that he received an appointment in the court chapel at Sondershausen when he was only fourteen years old. His father, who was about that time musical director at Neuhaldensleben, near Magdeburg, had formed a family string quartet with three of his sons, in which he played the viola and Carl the violoncello. About 1866 Alwin Schröder took his father's part and the four brothers (Hermann, Francis, Alwin and Carl) toured as the Schröder Quartet during the years of 1871-2, establishing a considerable reputation as an ensemble as well as individually. At the end of 1872 the quartet was dissolved as Carl received an appointment as solo violoncellist in the court chapel at Brunswick, where he remained only for the space of one year when he was called to Leipzig in a similar capacity as well as teacher of violoncello at the conservatoire. In May, 1877, he played with marked success at the musical festival at Hanover. Being an excellent all-round musician he soon showed extraordinary talent for conducting, and in 1881 he was appointed court capellmeister at Sondershausen as successor to Erdmannsdörffer, where he founded a conservatoire which under his capable management soon developed into a flourishing establishment. This he sold to Ad. Schultze in 1886 when he went to Rotterdam as conductor of the German Opera. In 1887 he became court capellmeister in Berlin and in 1888 he conducted the opera, etc., at Hamburg as successor to Sucher. In 1890 he returned to Sondershausen as court capellmeister and director of the conservatoire, which, by that time, had been acquired by the Government. There he is still active in both capacities (in 1909). He wrote a considerable amount for his instrument, particularly editions of the works of older masters. In these the violoncello parts are very carefully revised, bowed and fingered, while the accompaniments often suffer from a way of doubling the solo part in the upper octave which has a disagreeable and inartistic effect. His violoncello school is an excellent work and so are his caprices which offer valuable material for very advanced students, and the ten "Spezial Studien" (studies of specialities) containing excellent studies for the bow (spiccato, staccato, detaché, etc.). Among his original compositions there are many deserving of notice, particularly the three "Concertstücke" for the use of students, which, apart from being useful from a technical point, contain also some charmingly melodious parts. Carl Schröder has also written several operas and "catechisms" of violoncello playing, violin playing and conducting.

RUDOLF HENING, born 1848 at Güstrow, as son of the musical director of that town. He studied the violoncello at the Leipzig Conservatoire from 1862 till 1864. In 1866 he toured as soloist in the northern United States of America and settled in the following year in New York. In 1868 he was engaged as professor of violoncello at the Philadelphia Conservatoire. Further details are missing.

FRANZ FISCHER, born July 20, 1849, at Munich, was a pupil of Hippolyte Müller at the conservatoire. In 1870 he was appointed solo violoncellist at the National Theatre at Budapest, where Hans Richter conducted. He held afterwards a similar post in Munich and played in the first "Nibelung's Ring" performances at Bayreuth in 1876. In 1877 he was appointed court capellmeister at Mannheim, and in 1879 he went to Munich in the same capacity, and he was considered one of the best opera conductors of his time. He is still living in Munich, having retired in 1911.

ADOLF HARTDEGEN, born November 17, 1849, at Cassel (Hesse). He studied from 1864 till 1869 under François Servais and Jules de Swert at the Brussels Conservatoire, which he left with the first prize for violoncello playing. Bosselet and Fétis were his masters in composition. He toured with great success in the United States of America, where he was for some time solo violoncellist in the celebrated Thomas Symphony Orchestra. Afterwards he toured in a similar capacity with the Boston Philharmonic Club and the New York Beethoven String Quartet. He has been decorated with several orders for art and science and honoured with the title of chamber virtuoso. At present he is living at Cassels, his native town. Hartdegen has published a number of compositions for his instrument.

CHAPTER XXIV.

GERMAN VIOLONCELLISTS FROM 1850 TO 1860.

JOSEPH SULZER, born February 11, 1850, at Vienna, was one of the best pupils of Schlesinger, with whom he studied at the Vienna Conservatoire until 1869. His first appointment was as solo violoncellist at the Italian Opera and teacher at the conservatoire at Bukarest, where he remained for four years. In 1875 he was engaged in the orchestra of the court theatre in Vienna. Overwork compelled him to relinquish that position after three years. After his recovery he devoted himself to renewed studies which he pursued assiduously with Popper's advice and assistance. In 1880 he was appointed solo violoncello at the Imperial Opera in Vienna, at the same time accepting concert engagements and pupils. From 1882 till 1885 he was violoncellist of the Hellmesberger Quartet.

Sulzer has published original compositions as well as arrangements and editions of older masters.

ANTON LANG, born November 10, 1850, at Carlsbad in Bohemia, commenced the study of the violin and the pianoforte when he was about ten years old. At the age of thirteen, however, he declared in favour of the violoncello, and two years later, in 1865, he became a pupil of Hegenbarth at the Prague Conservatoire. After concluding his studies he was engaged as solo violoncellist in various orchestras. In 1877 he was appointed solo violoncellist of the grand ducal chapel at Schwerin, where he received the title of chamber virtuoso. He is also a member of the Bayreuth Orchestra, and was, in 1909, still living at Schwerin.

MORITZ HETZEL, born September 12, 1850, at Stuttgart, he went to Brussels to study the violoncello under Joseph Servais, professor at the conservatoire, and afterwards finished his studies under Julius Stahlknecht in Berlin. He was appointed solo violoncellist at Mannheim.

He wrote some compositions for his instrument, including a Concerto, Op. 10, which is not very interesting.

ROBERT HAUSMANN, born August 13, 1852, at Rottleberode, in the Harz Mountains. He attended the "Gymnasium" (collegiate school) at Brunswick from 1861 to 1868, and during that time he was instructed in violoncello playing by Theodor Müller, the violoncellist of the elder Müller Quartet. On the foundation of the "Hochschule" in 1869 Hausmann entered as one of the first pupils for violoncello, and he proved to be the first pupil in more than one sense. He studied there under Wm. Müller until 1871. Joachim recognised his exceptional talent and induced him to accompany him to London where he introduced him to Piatti, who henceforth conducted his studies, and became so much attached to him that he invited him to his villa in Cadenabbia, where he spent the winter. During the years 1872-5 he fulfilled his first engagement in the quartet of Count Hochberg at Dresden, which was dissolved about the beginning of 1876 when Count Hochberg became "general intendant" (director in chief) of the royal theatres in Berlin. At that time Hausmann was elected second teacher of his instrument at the Hochschule, and on the death

JOSEPH JOACHIM.   ROBERT HAUSMANN

PLATE
THE BERLIN JO.

To face page 456.

EMMANUEL WIRTH.   KARL HALIR.

XXIX.
HIM QUARTET.

of Wm. Müller, Hausmann took his place and received the title of professor.

In 1877 he came to London where he played the D minor Concerto by Raff at the fifth concert of the Philharmonic Society on April 30. In 1878 Hausmann joined the Joachim Quartet and was associated with that famous organisation until the dissolution on the death of the great violinist in August, 1907. Hausmann appeared on many occasions at the old St. James's Hall in the capacity of soloist, as well as chamber music player, and he won golden opinions from his audiences. The *London* Joachim Quartet, the principal quartet of the Monday and Saturday Popular Concerts, was then an institution quite apart from the Berlin quartet, and Piatti was the principal

FIG. 54. AUTOGRAPH OF ROBERT HAUSMANN.

violoncellist. When Piatti retired to Cadenabbia during the latter years of last century that combination was dissolved, Strauss (viola) having died, and Louis Ries retired. From that time, viz., 1897 until 1907, Joachim always brought the members of his Berlin quartet with him during the season. After Joachim's death the remaining members chose Carl Halir for their leader, and continued their visits to London as the Joachim Quartet. Hausmann died suddenly whilst on a visit to Vienna on January 9, 1909. Robert Hausmann combined an excellent technique of the left hand with great facility of the bow. His tone was round and powerful, but not always free from a slight roughness. A highly-gifted musician and refined artist, he excelled in the performance of chamber music, and it is characteristic of him that the viol da gamba, perhaps the most intimate of all stringed instruments, fascinated him to such an extent that he devoted much time to the study of that instrument and played it with great mastery. Apart from his executive powers he was also one of the foremost teachers of his instrument, and many excellent violoncellists emanated from his school. To the literature of the violoncello he contributed chiefly carefully revised editions of classical studies. A portrait group of the Berlin Joachim Quartet with Hausmann appears on Plate XXXIX.

JOHANNES KLINGENBERG, born August 28, 1852, at Görlitz in Silesia, began to study the violoncello as a pupil of the "Gymnasium" (Latin college) of that town. In 1871 he went to Dresden and studied two years under Friedrich Grützmacher, while Gustav Merkel instructed him in musical theory and composition. His first engagement was at Homburg near Frankfort, afterwards he filled engagements in Hamburg and Wiesbaden, and in 1877 he was appointed to the membership of the ducal chapel at Brunswick, and a few years later he was honoured with the title of a ducal chamber musician. He was an enthusiastic devotee of the viol da gamba, and spent part of his holidays in searching the principal libraries of Germany for old manuscripts and books containing music for that instrument. In that way he brought together a very remarkable collection of compositions for the viol da gamba, which he was ever ready to place at the disposal of other votaries of the viol. Artist and enthusiast he was ever ready to assist those who were like himself trying to recover the musical treasures of the seventeenth and eighteenth centuries, and spread the knowledge thereof, as well as that of the viol da gamba. The author has to thank him for volumes of copies of rare gamba music which he presented to him, and other friends had to thank him for similar kindnesses. He was, in fact, indefatigable in his work, apart from his professional duties in the ducal chapel, and as editor of violoncello music for Litolff, the music publisher at Brunswick. This strenuous work weakened his eyesight, and he tried to recoup his strength by

FIG. 55. JOHANNES KLINGENBERG.

long walking tours in the mountains during his autumn holidays. In July, 1905, he went to Tyrols on his annual tour, and on July 25 he wrote to his sister from Langkofelhütte, near St. Cristina in the Grödner valley. On the evening of that day he was seen on the Rondella, where he spoke of his intention to descend the same evening to Campitello and proceed thence on foot to Trient. From that moment all trace of him is lost. The disappearance of his valise which he used to send on by post to his next halting-place points unmistakably to foul play. There is no doubt that he was murdered and robbed, and that the valise was claimed by the murderer on the post office reverse. That is the tragic end of an excellent artist and an amiable man, deeply deplored by his numerous friends. His autograph portrait is given in Fig. 55.

His most valuable addition to the literature of the violoncello is the "Dotzauer-Klingenberg" tutor, an amalgamation of Dotzauer's three tutors systematically arranged with the addition of some exercises by Duport. It is by far the most systematic and thorough tutor that has ever been written for the violoncello. Of his many arrangements of viol da gamba music by various composers none have been published.

JOSEPH SIEMANN, born January 30, 1852, at Münster in Westphalia, is a pupil of Friedrich Grützmacher, under whom he studied as pupil of the Dresden Conservatoire. In 1873 Duport, the conductor of the Nuremberg municipal theatre engaged him as principal violoncello. In 1874 he went to Basle, as solo violoncellist of the "Allgemeine Musikgesellschaft" (General Musical Society), and in 1880 he accepted a similar post for the "Concerts Classiques" in Paris, which were conducted by Saint-Saëns, Massenet, Godard, etc. During that time he acquainted himself with the technique of the French school by renewed studies under Professor Leon Jacquard. In 1881 he went to Nice as solo violoncellist of the Atheneum Concerts, and in 1883 he settled in Aix la Chapelle, where he is still living as an esteemed teacher of his instrument and an excellent chamber music player.

PHILIPP ROTH, born October 25, 1853, at Tarnowitz in Silesia, commenced the study of the violin at the age of eight, but exchanged that instrument for the violoncello when he was twelve years old. At his parental home he took part with his brothers in a family quartet, whereby he acquainted himself at an early age with the works of the classical masters, and obtained routine in chamber music playing. Later on he went to Berlin where he studied at the "Hochschule" the violoncello under Wm. Müller, and afterwards under Robert Hausmann, composition under Wilhelm Taubert and Woldemar Bargiel, attending also the quartet and orchestral classes under Joachim. After the conclusion of his studies he commenced touring as solo violoncellist, visiting the principal towns of Germany and Austria. He went on a prolonged tour through America and in 1885 also to Russia.

Roth has written a number of original compositions including some excellent solos, studies and a tutor with an appendix containing a guide through violoncello literature, which has appeared separately and experienced a second edition, revised and augmented by C. Hüllweck. This is a very useful book for amateurs, although it might to its advantage be considerably enlarged. Roth has also written a "waltz" for four violoncellos and a number of arrangements of compositions by various masters.

ERNST BEYER, born 1853, at Wittgendorf (Oberlausitz), was originally intended to become a horn player, but as he showed a decided preference for the violoncello he was sent to Dresden where he studied under the chamber musician, Jos. Büschel. Later on he continued for a time under Richard Vollrath at Mayence and finished his studies under Professor Carl Schröder at Leipzig. After playing in various concert and opera orchestras he accepted in 1880 an engagement for Long Back and Milwaukee, as teacher of the united conservatories. He is an excellent soloist and chamber music player and has done a great deal to popularise chamber music in the north-west of the United States of America.

BERNHARD THIEME, born June 11, 1854, at Altenburg, commenced his musical career as pupil of the town musician at Penig in Saxony. At the age of eighteen he returned to Altenburg, where he received some instructions in violoncello playing from the musical director Toller. He was engaged soon after in the Berlin Reichshallen Orchestra. He left that orchestra after a short time to accept the post as principal violoncello in Fliege's orchestra, playing during one summer season in St. Petersburg. On his return he was appointed in a similar capacity in the court chapel at Bückeburg, and after that he was engaged for two years at the court theatre of Hanover. During that time he studied again under the famous August Lindner. In 1879 he was appointed solo violoncellist in the Municipal Orchestra at Baden-Baden.

ALBERT HARTMANN, born October 13, 1854, at Lichtenau (Saxe-Weimar), was a pupil of Lorleberg at Hanover. He received his first engagement in the Langenbach Orchestra at Barmen (Rhine province), and in 1879 he was appointed as violoncellist in the Mannheim court orchestra. He is now in Nordhausen. He has composed various pieces for his instrument.

RICHARD SEITZ, born October 28, 1854, at Gera in Saxony, received his first instructions on the violoncello from the chamber musician W. Klieber, while court capellmeister Tschirsch instructed him in pianoforte playing and musical theory. He continued the study of the violoncello under chamber musician H. Tietz at Dresden, and then went to Leipzig, where he was a pupil of Julius Klengel. After various engagements as solo violoncellist in different orchestras he was, in 1890, appointed solo violoncellist in the royal chapel at Stuttgart with the title of chamber virtuoso. He is also professor of violoncello at the Stuttgart Conservatoire, and member of the Stuttgart Trio, with Professors Max Pauer and

E. Singer. In all these capacities he enjoys the highest reputation.

EDMUND SEBASTIAN JOSEPH VAN DER STRAETEN, born April 29, 1855, at Düsseldorf, commenced his musical studies in early boyhood, continuing under Hermann Kipper at the Jesuit Gymnasium at Cologne. At the age of twelve he commenced to study the violoncello under Johannes Hoecke, the principal violoncello of the Cologne Theatre, a pupil of Friederich August Kummer, and a thorough and conscientious teacher, though a little old-fashioned in some ways. At the age of eighteen, van der Straeten became a pupil of Ludwig Ebert, teacher of the violoncello at the conservatoire, and about 1875 he made his debut as soloist at the musical society which held its weekly orchestral concerts at the conservatoire. Shortly after he became also second violoncello in Robert Heckmann's chamber concerts. His father would not allow him to enter the profession, which he considered incompatible with the traditions of an ancient Rhenish noble family, and van der Straeten continued to pursue the study of music as amateur, while he followed various vocations which eventually brought him to London. His aversion to the commercial career, and his want of success therein, decided him at last to abandon all else and follow his true vocation. He renewed his studies of the violoncello under Gustav Libotton at the Guildhall School and afterwards under Louis Hegyesi, who proved one of his best and truest friends. At the same time he studied theory successively under Engelberth Humperdinck, Max Laistner, Alfred Richter and Louis B. Prout. After several successful appearances as soloist van der Straeten abandoned that career on account of great nervousness, and devoted himself chiefly to the cultivation of chamber music, instituting chamber concerts with the assistance of Professor Ebenezer Prout, Messrs. Algernon Ashton, Réné Ortmans, Alex. Kummer and others at the North-East London Institute, of which he became a teacher in 1888. He also instituted the society for the cultivation of modern chamber music, which for several seasons gave its concerts at Brinsmead's and Ibach's Rooms, producing for the first time in London the quartets by Benjamin Godard, clarinet trio by Vincent d'Indy, quartets by Raff and many other previously unknown works by modern composers as well as neglected works by older masters, as, for instance, the string quintet by Haydn. About this period van der Straeten played also on several occasions at the Cambridge University Musical Union, with Mr. Charles (now Sir Charles) Villiers Stanford and Mr. Richard Gompertz. Since 1891 he has made a special study of the viol da gamba, and with the assistance of his friend, the late Johannes Klingenberg, collected a considerable amount of literature for that instrument which he has played with great success at his lecture-concerts in London and the provinces. In 1909 he formed an ensemble of old instruments for the production of seventeenth and eighteenth century music, with the assistance of the Misses Chaplin, Miss Kate Chaplin, viol d'amour; Miss Mabel Chaplin, viol da gamba; Miss Nellie Chaplin, harpsichord; and his son, Ludwig, viol da gamba. With the latter and Mr. Norman Greiffenhagen, his pupil on the viol da gamba, he produced consorts by Christopher Simpson, John Jenkin and suites by Marin Marais for three viol da gambas at various London concerts. As composer for his instrument Mr. Van der Straeten has written a number of solos, a suite on English airs, Romance in F, two albums (Ashdown, Limited), and "Chant du Troubadour" (Laudy), being the only published pieces so far. He has also published a book on violoncello techniques, "The Revival of the Viols," "History of the Viol" and "History of Violoncello Literature" (only in serial form), all in the "Strad Library," the present "History of the Violoncello," "Hints to Violoncellists," and a number of essays on music and musicians.

HEINRICH GRÜNFELD, born April 21, 1855, at Prague, was a pupil of Hegenbarth at the Conservatoire of that town. In 1873 he was appointed solo violoncellist at the Opera Comique in Vienna, and in 1876 he went to Berlin as teacher of his instrument at Kullak's Conservatoire. From time to time he toured with his brother Alfred in Germany, Austria and Russia. He combines a brilliant technique with beauty of tone, and has also earned a great reputation as chamber music player. In the latter capacity he has been associated with X. Scharwenka, G. Holländer, E. Sauret, and at present (1909) he is violoncellist of the Florian Zajic Quartet. In 1886 he was honoured by the title of royal court violoncellist to the King of Prussia (the German Emperor).

REINHOLD HUMMER, born October 7, 1855, at Linz, on the Danube, commenced his musical career as a student of the violin in Vienna. After devoting six years to the study of that instrument he decided in favour of the violoncello, and studied first under Schlesinger and afterwards under H. Röver at the Vienna Conservatoire, which he left after obtaining the first prize. His first appointment he received on January 1, 1873, in the orchestra of the Imperial Opera. In 1877 he became a teacher at the Conservatoire, and in the following year also solo violoncellist in the royal chapel. In 1876 he played in the Bayreuth orchestra, when Wagner's "Ring of the Nibelung" was performed for the first time. For nine years he was violoncellist in the Hellmesberger Quartet, and in 1887 he joined the famous Rosé Quartet, to which he still belonged in 1898. His distinguished services were acknowledged by conferring the title professor and the Golden Cross of Merit with the Crown upon him. In 1903 he resigned his position in the royal chapel to devote himself exclusively to solo and quartet playing.

ALFRED GALLREIN, born October 15, 1855, at Magdeburg, studied the violoncello at the Hochschule in Berlin, where he gained a royal scholarship, and afterwards under Hugo Daubert in London. He was for three years teacher of his instrument at Uppingham, and was from 1909 till 1911 in a similar capacity at the Hampstead Conservatoire. Gallrein was also a member of the Richter Orchestra in London, and was heard to advantage as a soloist at his chamber concerts at Steinway Hall. He has written several solo pieces for violoncello as well as songs and pianoforte pieces. On account of an eye trouble he retired in 1911 to his native town.

ALWIN SCHRÖDER was born in 1855 at Neuhaldensleben, near Magdeburg, where his father was musical director, and every member of the family was a musician. At the age of seven he received lessons from his father on the pianoforte and from his brother Hermann on the violin. At the age of eleven he was able to take his father's place in the family string quartet as viola player, and toured with his brothers in that capacity until the quartet was dissolved in 1872, when Carl (the violoncellist) received an appointment in the court chapel at Brunswick.

About that time Alwin felt an inclination to acquaint himself with the technique of the violoncello, and commenced by practising the solo from Rossini's "William Tell" overture. He succeeded so well that when his brother Carl heard him he encouraged him to continue his studies. Soon after this he joined Liebig's orchestra in Berlin as viola player. When Liebig offered him a renewal of his contract in 1875, he accepted on condition that the engagement should be as violoncellist. Liebig treated the matter as a joke, but when Schröder insisted, he asked him to come to his house and play to him. Schröder went and played the concerto by August Lindner with such taste and skill that Liebig embraced him and gave him the post he desired. In 1876 he went to Hamburg as violoncellist in Laube's orchestra, and in 1880 to Leipzig, where he played as deputy for his brother Carl in the

Gewandhaus Orchestra. When the latter went to Sondershausen, Alwin was appointed principal violoncello, conjointly with Jul. Klengel, in the Gewandhaus and theatre orchestras, and teacher at the Conservatoire, and joined. Anno Hilf as member of his quartet. The Prince of Schwartzburg Sondershausen conferred the gold medal for art and science upon him. He toured with immense success in Germany and Russia, receiving the highest eulogies for the power and beauty of his tone and the brilliancy of his technique. About 1899 he went to Berlin, and soon after accepted an appointment as solo violoncellist in the Boston Symphony Orchestra and violoncellist in the Kneisel Quartet, which played at St. James's Hall in 1896 and 1897, proving itself one of the finest string quartets in the world. He is at present still active as soloist and teacher in America.

Alwin Schröder has written some very useful books of studies, an edition of Bach's solo sonatas, and two albums of classical pieces (Simrock).

His violoncello is one of the most perfect specimens of Nicolas Amati's work, valued at £1,200.

ALBERT PETERSEN, born October 23, 1856, at Lübeck, studied under Friedrich Grützmacher. He filled engagements as principal violoncellist in orchestras at Dresden, Kreuznach and Cassel. After that he toured in America, and on his return he accepted an engagement for Pawlowsk, near St. Petersburg. Since 1878 he was solo violoncellist and teacher at the Conservatoire at Magdeburg, with the title of "Conzertmeister."

EUGEN SANDOW, born in northern Germany, September 11, 1856, received instruction from his father in violin playing from his sixth to his eighth year. As two of his brothers were already violinists, he took up the study of the violoncello under the royal chamber musician, Adolph Rohne.

At the age of nine and a half years he made his debut on the concert platform, together with his brother, appearing successfully in Berlin and other German towns. On the opening of the Hochschule at Berlin, in 1869, he entered that institution as pupil of William Müller, and ten years later he succeeded his master as chamber musician and solo violoncellist in the royal chapel. He has toured with great success on the Continent, together with his wife, Mme. Adeline Sandow-Herms, an excellent concert singer. Sandow is also a distinguished chamber music player and member of the Gustav Hollander Quartet. As teacher of his instrument he has been for some time engaged at the Stern Conservatoire.

HEINRICH BAST, born July 29, 1856, at Germersheim, in the Palatinate of the Rhine. He studied under August Theodor Müller, of the elder Müller Quartet, at Brunswick. He was successively a member of the court orchestras of Munich and Mannheim, and solo violoncellist in Bilse's orchestra in Berlin. Between the years 1887-9 he toured in Switzerland, and in 1890 he was appointed as principal violoncello in the Philharmonic Orchestra and teacher at the Conservatoire at Hamburg. He is now a professor of the Royal Irish Academy of Music at Dublin. He contributed to the literature of the violoncello by writing studies and arrangements (albums). M. Esposito dedicated his sonata for violoncello and pianoforte, Op. 43, to Bast.

SIEGMUND BÜRGER, born February 8, 1856, in Vienna, received his first instruction in violoncello playing from J. Moser, a member of the Opera orchestra. He continued his studies afterwards under D. Popper, while Grädener and Nottebohm instructed him in theory and composition. In 1873, Bürger made his debut as soloist at an orchestral concert of the Vienna "Musikverein" (Musical Union). In 1874 he toured with Carlotta Patti and Theodor Ritter, and appeared at the Gewandhaus in Leipzig, and in Berlin with Sophie Menter. In 1875 he was engaged as solo violoncellist at Baden-Baden, and in 1880 he received an appointment in the same capacity for the court chapel at Munich, touring in the meantime with Adelina Patti, Henry Wieniawski, A. Grünfeld and others. In 1882 H. Richter (now Dr.), engaged him for the Richter Orchestra in London. In the following year he went to Paris to institute chamber concerts with Marsick and Breitner. In 1887 Bürger, together with Johannes Wolff and Lewita, toured in Denmark and Sweden as the Trio Parisien. On his return he was called to Budapest as teacher at the conservatoire, solo violoncellist at the Opera, and professor of the "Musikverein." Together with A. Grünfeld, he instituted popular quartet soirées. He published studies for virtuosos and arrangements for violoncello and pianoforte.

ARTHUR STENZ, born 1857, at Leipzig, studied at the Dresden Conservatoire under F. A. Kummer and Friedrich Grützmacher. On the completion of his studies, he became a member of the court chapel at Dresden, where he is still active. With Bachmann and Bärtich, he founded a trio combination which has met with great success.

He has been decorated with the Order of Albrecht, the Order of Franz Joseph and the Carola Medal in silver.

His compositions consist of various solo pieces for violoncello.

OSCAR BRÜCKNER, born January 2, 1857, at Erfurt. He studied the violoncello under Friedrich Grützmacher and theory under Felix Draseke at the Dresden Conservatoire.

After absolving his studies, he toured successfully in Germany, Russia, Poland and Holland. From 1882 to 1884 he was solo violoncellist at the Court Theatre, at Neustrelitz, which he left with the title of chamber virtuoso. Since 1886 he was solo violoncellist at the Court Theatre and teacher at the Conservatoire at Wiesbaden, where he was honoured in 1896 with the title of Concertmeister and (after 1903) professor, besides being decorated with several high orders. He combines an excellent technique of the left hand and the bow with a fine and powerful tone. Among his numerous compositions for violoncello are a concerto with orchestra, solos, studies and arrangements of considerable merit.

KARL EBNER, born November 6, 1857, at Bipperdorf (Bavaria), received his first violoncello lessons from a brother of Joseph Menter, continuing as a pupil of the Munich Conservatoire under Professor Jos. Werner. At the recommendation of Professor Franz Wüllner, who was court capellmeister at the time, he received an engagement for the court chapel at Carlsruhe. From 1875 till 1879 he was solo violoncellist, and played frequently at court concerts before the late Grand Duke. On October 1, 1879, he was appointed violoncellist in the court chapel at Munich, where he is still (1913), as royal chamber virtuoso. He is an excellent soloist as well as chamber music player, and has written a number of effective compositions for his instrument.

EMIL BLUME, born December 20, 1857, at Hanover, where his father was a member of the court orchestra. He studied the violoncello from 1871 till 1878 under the famous August Lindner. At the age of fifteen he became already a member of the royal orchestra. The German Emperor honoured him with the title of royal chamber musician and the Order of the Crown. As a soloist he is often heard in Hanover, as well as in other German towns. He is solo violoncellist of the Royal Theatre at Hanover, and toured with great success in Germany. For fifteen years he was also violoncellist of the Hänflein Quartet, and since the dissolution of that institution he belongs in the same capacity to the quartet of Professor Riller. As a teacher he is much in request. He has also composed a number of pieces for violoncello.

AUGUST DÖTSCH, born 1858, was one of the best pupils of Jules de Swert. He was fast making his way to the front rank of violoncellists when death overtook him, November 19, 1882, at Wiesbaden, at the early age of twenty-four.

FRITZ GIESE, born January 2, 1859, at the Hague. His father was the excellent German violoncellist, Joseph Giese, who instructed his son Fritz in the art of violoncello playing. Such was the talent of the son and the soundness of the father's teaching, that he made his debut at the Hague with Romberg's Concerto No. 2, in D, when he was only ten years old. Soon after this he was sent to Dresden, where he continued his studies under Grützmacher, finishing with a course under Léon Jacquard at Paris. After a successful tour through Scandinavia he was for one year solo violoncellist in the Park Orchestra at Amsterdam. At the end of that time he joined the Mendelssohn Quintet Club at Boston. He toured annually in North America as one of the most prominent members of that society, eventually settling as solo violoncellist at Boston.

JULIUS KLENGEL, born September 24, 1859, at Leipzig, is one of the greatest violoncellists of all times. He studied the violoncello as a private pupil of Emil Hegar, and composition under Jadassohn. In 1881 he was appointed teacher at the Conservatoire, and about the same time he became a member of the Gewandhaus Orchestra. Since 1876 he has toured all over Europe and established his reputation as a veritable Paganini on the violoncello. His technique of the left hand is probably unparalleled, as he plays most of Paganini's compositions on the violoncello with a facility that is quite marvellous. On the other hand, it must be admitted that his tone is inclined to be a trifle thin and wiry, a characteristic which he shares with the few violoncellists who, like Friedrich Grützmacher of old, and Földessy of late, also acquired that great command of the finger-board. Julius Klengel belongs to a family which for several generations has given excellent musicians to the world. One of his ancestors (not in direct line) was August Alexander Klengel, a famous theorist, organist and pianist, who, besides numerous compositions for various instruments, wrote forty-eight canons and fugues which offer valuable material for students. Klengel's father was a notable musical amateur and friend of Mendelssohn, and his brother Paul is well known as pianist, composer and writer on musical subjects. This musical atmosphere which surrounded him from his childhood has awakened his musical faculties to such a degree that nothing will escape his ear, be it in chamber music or the full orchestra. His knowledge of chamber music is so great that he knows by heart the parts of every instrument in all the standard compositions up to the present day. As a teacher he has an immense reputation. Including his chamber-music classes, he gives as many as fifty lessons a week, and still finds time for composing and a certain amount of daily practice on his instrument. He has contributed over fifty works to the literature of the violoncello, which include every branch and combination, including a concerto for two violoncellos and a theme and variations for four violoncellos. A set of variations which he wrote in his youth as forfeit for a lost "Phillipine," number among the most difficult works in violoncello literature, and Mrs. B. Henderson ("The Strad," Vol. XIX, page 409) tells us that Klengel attributes his claims to virtuosity rest on surmounting the technical difficulties of these variations. Certain it is that they roused his hearers at the old St. James's Hall to an enthusiastic ovation about the beginning of the nineties of last century. His expression and phrasing in the performance of classical works is unexceptionable, and as a quartet player he has few equals. He was the violoncellist of the Brodsky Quartet until Dr. Adolph Brodsky left Leipzig, and now is joined in another quartet by Messrs. Wollgandt, Wolsche and Hermann.

He has also composed a number of chamber music works. Klengel is the fortunate owner of a beautiful Amati violoncello, dated 1608.

HERMANN HEBERLEIN, born March 29, 1859, at Markneukirchen in Saxony, the town known for its numerous instrument makers. He studied at the Leipzig Conservatoire from 1873-7, where he had the advantage of being instructed in violoncello playing successively by Emil Hegar and C. Schröder, finishing his studies afterwards under Bernhard Cossmann. During 1877 he toured in South Germany, and at the end of that year he was appointed as solo violoncellist at the Municipal Theatre at Königsberg in Prussia. In 1883 he was appointed teacher at the conservatoire.

His contributions to the violoncello literature include a tutor, studies, three concertstücke, solos, etc.

VICTOR HERBERT, born February 1, 1859, at Dublin, is the grandson of Samuel Lover, the famous Irish novelist. He showed early signs of musical talent, and consequently his parents resolved to send him to Frankfort-on-Main, where he studied the violoncello under Cossmann at the Hoch Conservatoire. His first appointment as violoncellist was in the court chapel at Stuttgart, where he was much appreciated as a soloist. In 1886 he accepted an engagement for the Metropolitan

FIG. 56. VICTOR HERBERT.

Orchestra in New York. An accident to his arm caused him to abandon the career of a violoncellist and to devote himself entirely to composing and conducting. He went to Pittsburg, where he held an appointment as conductor until 1905. He has been most successful with his comic operas, which have made the round of the world. His Suite, Op. 3. for violoncello and pianoforte, is a favourite with all violoncellists who can master the technical difficulties. His two concertos and a number of solo pieces are most welcome contributions to the literature of the instrument. His portrait appears on Fig. 56. He died recently in America.

MAX EISENBERG, born October 11, 1859, at Brunswick, was a pupil of C. Schröder at the Leipzig Conservatoire from 1876-9. His first engagement was as solo violoncellist in the Laube Orchestra at Hamburg. With this orchestra he toured with great success as soloist in Russia and Poland. After filling engagements in a similar capacity in the Helsingfors Philharmonic Orchestra and the "Konzerthaus" in Berlin, he returned as solo violoncellist to Hamburg in 1888, where he rejoined the Laube Orchestra and became solo violoncellist at the theatre. In the latter capacity he took part in the first performances of Wagner's "Ring of the Nibelung" in London, under Mahler. In 1891 he was appointed principal violoncello of the Philharmonic and Fiedler concerts, and teacher at the Hamburg Conservatoire. He has published several compositions for his instrument.

JOSEF MELZER, born September 3, 1859, at Bürgstein, in Bohemia, received his musical education at the Prague Conservatoire, where Franz Hegenbarth was his teacher for the violoncello. After finishing his studies in 1876 he was appointed solo violoncellist at the German Theatre in Budapest. In the following year he held a similar post in the Kur-Orchestra at Baden-Baden. In 1878 he was appointed as solo violoncellist for the Breslau Orchestral Union, which post he holds still. He has been honoured with the title of Concertmeister, and as an excellent chamber music player he is a prominent member of the chamber music association of the Breslau Orchestral Union. As an excellent teacher of his instrument he is much in request.

CHAPTER XXV.

GERMAN VIOLONCELLISTS FROM 1860 TO 1870.

ALFRED STEINMANN, born June 5, 1860, as son of the royal chamber musician, Chr. Steinmann, at Hanover. He commenced his studies of the violoncello under August Chr. Prell, and afterwards for four years under the royal chamber musician, Karl Matys, at Hanover. After that he went to Wiesbaden to finish his studies under Jules de Swert, and then undertook several concert tours through Germany and a four months' tour through Russia. After his return he received an appointment as chamber musician in the orchestra of the Court Theatre at Hanover. He lives at present at that town as soloist, chamber music player and teacher. He conducts the Hanover Ladies' Choir, and in 1896 he founded a permanent trio with Georg Schumann and R. Sabla. The members are now Schmidt, Taegener and Steinmann.

HUGO DECHERT, born September 16, 1860, at Potschappel, Dresden. His first lessons on the violin and the violoncello he received from his father when he was a small boy, and after a time he continued the study of the latter instrument under H. Tietz at Dresden with so much success that he was appointed principal violoncello in the Belvedere Orchestra at the age of fourteen. Eighteen months later he started touring in Saxony, Silesia, Poland, etc., and eventually came to Berlin in 1877, where he visited the Hochschule from 1878-80, studying under William Müller, Hausmann (violoncello), Joachim, Succo and A. Dorn (chamber music, composition and pianoforte).

On the completion of his studies he toured again as solo violoncellist, soon after, in 1881, he was appointed as a member, and in 1894 solo violoncellist of the royal chapel. In 1898 he received the title of royal chamber virtuoso. He was one of the founders of the Halir Quartet—not to be confounded with the Joachim Quartet, of which Halir was leader after Joachim's death in 1907—and the Schumann-Halir-Dechert Trio. To all those institutions he still belongs. He combines a faultless technique with a powerful tone of noble quality, and he is equally esteemed as soloist, chamber musician and teacher. In the latter capacity he has trained many excellent pupils.

PAUL PRILL, born October 1, 1860, in Berlin, received his first music lessons on the violin and on the pianoforte from his father, a military bandmaster, who afterwards taught him also the cornet. He continued his pianoforte studies afterwards under W. Handwerg, while the chamber musician, W. Sturm, instructed him in musical theory. At the age of about thirteen he toured with his father and his brothers Emil and Karl, the celebrated violinist, in Germany, Sweden, Holland and Russia.

At the age of seventeen his wish to take up the violoncello was at last fulfilled, when the chamber musician, Mahneke, instructed him gratuitously for about nine months. His progress was so rapid that at the end of that time he obtained a scholarship for free tuition at the Hochschule, where he studied for four years under Hausmann. After another course of studies in composition under Waldemar Bargiel at the

"Meisterschule" (a kind of higher form of the Hochschule, for very advanced students) and continuing his violoncello studies under Hausmann, he was appointed solo violoncellist in the Berlin Symphony Orchestra and the Italian Opera. From September, 1882, until the end of April, 1885, he was solo violoncellist in Bilse's Orchestra. That career, however, did not satisfy his ambition. He wanted to become a conductor, and on the dissolution of Bilse's Orchestra he received his first appointment in that capacity at the Belle Alliance Theatre in Berlin, conducting also temporarily at the Wallner Theatre. As a position of that kind gave no promise to lead up to the higher and more artistic work, he decided to accept the post of solo violoncellist at the German Opera at Rotterdam. He played as soloist in many of the Dutch towns during that period, and eventually received the post as second conductor at the Rotterdam Opera.

KARL BACKHAUS, born October 15, 1860, at Leipzig, is a brother of the famous pianist. He studied under Grützmacher at Dresden from 1879 till 1883. He toured in Germany and Holland until 1885, when he was appointed as royal chamber musician at the Court Theatre at Wiesbaden, and teacher at the conservatoire of that town.

HUGO MARTINI, born 1861, at Schlotheim in Thuringia, studied the violoncello under Professor Rothe at Strasburg, continuing under Kufferath at Oldenburg. He received his first appointment in the Court Theatre at Oldenburg, and afterwards he was for some time a member of the Laube Orchestra at Hamburg. In 1886 he was appointed solo violoncellist at the Municipal Theatre at Riga, and soon after also as teacher at the conservatoire. He has the reputation of an excellent chamber music player.

ADOLPH KAPP, born July 13, 1861, at Weida in Thuringia. Like so many violoncellists, he commenced his musical career in his earliest boyhood as a violinist under the local town musician. After a few years he exchanged that instrument for the violoncello. In 1875 he studied at the Weimar Conservatoire, and on leaving that institute he joined the band of the Thirty-first Infantry regiment at Altona as solo violoncellist. After serving in that way his stipulated time in the army he was engaged by the royal director of music, Albert Parlow, to play at Hamburg during the winter and at Kreuznach during the summer. In 1888 Professor von Bernuth engaged him for the Philharmonic Orchestra, and afterwards he was appointed solo violoncellist in the Laube Orchestra (conductor, J. Laube), which played in Hamburg during the winter and in Pawlowsk, near St. Petersburg, during the summer. In 1892 he was engaged as solo violoncellist and chamber music player for the municipal orchestra at Baden-Baden, where he was still active in 1903.

OTTO KÖHLER was born December 21, 1861, at Neuhaldensleben (near Merseburg). In 1879 he joined the Grenadier Guards regiment at Dresden to have the opportunity of studying under Fr. Grützmacher. He remained there until 1882. In January, 1883, he was appointed violoncellist in the court chapel of the Duke of Coburg-Gotha. During the two years which he remained in that position he studied musical theory under court Capellmeister Langert. In 1885 he received an appointment as solo violoncellist at Neustrelitz.

EMIL SCHENCK, born at Rochester, U.S.A., at the beginning of the sixties of last century. In 1879 his father, a native of the Duchy of Baden, sent him to Dresden to study under Grützmacher. His eminent talent procured him an appointment in the royal chapel in 1880, while he was still Grützmacher's pupil. After absolving his studies, he returned to America, where he appeared with great success as a soloist, and was engaged in that capacity by Theodore Thomas for his orchestra.

As the restless life of a touring orchestra was not in harmony with his own inclinations, he resigned his position, and lived in New York as soloist and teacher, highly esteemed in both capacities.

FRIEDRICH KOCH, born July 3, 1862, at Berlin, belongs to a well-known artist's family. He commenced his musical studies at the age of eleven, but not before he was in his fourteenth year did he commence to play the violoncello. In 1879 he became a pupil at the Hochschule, studying the violoncello under Hausmann and theory and composition under Succo and Bargiel. In the summer of 1883 he passed his examination as a solo player and received his nomination as royal chamber musician. In 1886 he founded a string quartet with three of his colleagues, which acquired an honourable reputation in Berlin musical society. He composed also a few pieces for his instrument.

SIEGMUND GLASER, born February 9, 1862, at Rokycan in Bohemia, commenced his study of the violoncello at the Prague Conservatoire under Hegenbarth in 1876. After finishing his studies in 1882 he received an appointment as teacher at the Imperial Conservatoire at Charkov in Russia. In 1884 he had to relinquish his position to absolve his military duties. In 1886 he toured successfully in Austria and Germany. Afterwards he occupied for the space of three years the post of teacher of the violoncello at the Odessa Conservatoire, and at the end of that period he returned to Charkov, where he occupies his former position as teacher of the conservatoire and soloist in the symphony orchestra. A number of his compositions for violoncello, including a Concerto in A minor, Op. 8, are published by Jürgenson in Moscow.

FRITZ ESPENHAHN, born October 24, 1862, in Berlin, is a member of a distinguished family of musical artists, to which also belongs the chamber musician and violoncellist, L. Espenhahn. His father, a celebrated basso, was also a royal chamber musician, who gave him his first music lessons. He continued his studies under the chamber musicians, F. Manecke and Louis Lübeck, finishing with a course of studies at the Hochschule. His first engagement, lasting for three years, was in the Bilse Orchestra. In 1887 he received an appointment in the royal chapel in Berlin, and in 1890 he was made a royal chamber musician, and later on a chamber virtuoso. He is much in request as a teacher, and numbers among his pupils also Prince Frederic Charles of Prussia. Espenhahn is an excellent chamber music player and, as such, a member of the Dessau Quartet.

OTTO HUTSCHENREUTER, born April 24, 1862, at Königsee (Thuringia), commenced the study of the pianoforte at the age of five. In 1881 he took up the violoncello as a pupil of the Leipzig Conservatoire, under C. Schröder, continuing under Alwin Schröder and Professor J. Klengel. In 1883-4 he was a pupil of Louis Lübeck in Berlin. In the latter year he finished his studies under Klengel at the Leipzig Conservatoire, which he left, carrying off a prize. From 1885-92 he was engaged at Helsingfors as solo violoncellist of the Philharmonic Orchestra and teacher at the conservatoire. Returning to Berlin, he studied another year under Professor Hausmann and Joachim. In 1893-4 he was teacher at the Stern Conservatoire, and from 1895-8 solo violoncellist at Hamburg. After two successive engagements at the "Theater des Westens" in Berlin and again in Helsingfors, he accepted, in 1900, the post of director of the Schwantzer Conservatoire in Berlin. He is also one of the founders of the Berlin Association for Chamber Music. Hutschenreuter is an excellent teacher, and published a "Reform Violoncello School."

AUGUST BIELER, born at Hamburg, May 9, 1863, received his first lessons at the age of thirteen from Sebastian Lee. In January, 1879, he entered the Leipzig Conservatoire as pupil of C. Schröder. In 1881 he was appointed solo violoncellist in the court chapel and teacher at the conservatoire at Sondershausen, where he remained until 1890. In 1883 he received the title of chamber musician. On April 1, 1890, he went to Brunswick as solo violoncellist of the court chapel, and in 1898 Prince Albrecht honoured him with the title of chamber virtuoso. He is an excellent chamber musician as well as a soloist of distinction.

FREDERIC HESS, born 1863, at Mannheim, belongs to a well-known family of musicians. He received his first music lessons from his father. Choosing the violoncello as his favourite instrument, he went to Frankfort, where he studied under Cossmann at the Hoch Conservatoire. In 1885 he went to America, where for ten years he followed a successful career as soloist and teacher of his instrument. In 1895 he returned to Frankfort to conform with the wishes of his parents. He was appointed solo violoncellist at the Opera. As chamber music player he has also appeared successfully in many concerts.

GEORGE WÖRL, born March 3, 1863, at Franzensthal in Bohemia, where he received his first musical instruction from the choirmaster, A. Horner. At the age of fourteen he commenced the study of the violoncello under Franz Baudisch, of Prague, and after a time went to Dresden to finish his education under Friedrich Grützmacher. At the age of seventeen he made his debut as soloist at the Kursaal at Ischl. Since then he has held various appointments in Vienna, Zürich and Carlsbad, and since 1892 he has been first solo violoncellist in the court chapel and teacher of the conservatoire at Sondershausen, with the title of chamber virtuoso. He has published a number of original compositions as well as arrangements for the violoncello.

HUGO BECKER, born February 13, 1864, at Strasburg in Alsace. His father, Jean Becker, the founder and leader of the world-famed Florentine Quartet, instructed him at an early age in violin and pianoforte playing. At the age of nine the boy heard a violoncello solo played in a church, which made such an impression upon him that he decided in favour of that instrument, and commenced the study thereof under Kanut Kündinger, an excellent violoncellist at Mannheim, at the same time receiving theoretical instruction from his father. At the age of fifteen, the post of second violoncellist in the court orchestra was offered to him, which he accepted, but at the end of one year he went to Dresden, where he studied a few months under Grützmacher. On his return home, his father conducted his further studies by playing his exercises and concertos to him on the violin, which, apart from teaching him artistic phrasing, caused him to absorb many important items from the technique of that instrument. Together with his father, his sister and an elder brother, he went on tour in 1880 as member of the "Jean Becker Family Quartet." In the autumn of that year they appeared at Wesel on the Rhine, where the author attended their concert, and the young violoncellist played to him afterwards the A minor Concerto by Goltermann with a perfect command over the technical difficulties and in a very artistic style. The cultivation of chamber music had always found a prominent place in his parental home, and this circumstance remained not without influence upon his artistic and musical development. With his sister Jeanne, a highly gifted pianist who died at the early age of thirty-four, and his brother Hans, a violinist, he formed a permanent trio, touring with great success on the Continent and visiting London in 1882, where he came into contact with Piatti, who took great interest in the young artist, and exercised a decided influence upon his further artistic and technical development. Of importance in this respect was also his study of De Swert's concerto under the guidance of the violoncellist-composer. From 1884-6 Becker was solo violoncellist of the Opera at Frankfort, and joined also the Heermann Quartet, of which he is still a member. About 1895 he was appointed as first teacher of the violoncello and director of the chamber music classes at the Hoch Conservatoire.

In 1896 he received the title of Royal Prussian Professor in addition to the title of chamber virtuoso of the Grand Duke of Baden. In June, 1892, he made his debut at the London Philharmonic with the D minor Concerto by Raff.

After visiting all the principal towns of Europe, he went on an extensive tour through the United States of America in 1901, where he experienced a repetition of his phenomenal successes in the Old World. He is essentially a classical player in the same sense in which we apply that term to Joachim and Piatti. His style is noble and refined, carefully avoiding anything approaching vulgar trickery and cheap effect. His technique, both of the bow and the left hand, is equal to that of the greatest masters of the instrument, and he combines with it a fine and powerful tone. As an exponent of the works of the great classical masters he has but few equals. He has contributed already a considerable number of compositions to the literature of the violoncello, including concertos, suites, solos and a violoncello tutor.

RUDOLPH GLICKH, born February 28, 1864, in Vienna, as son of the common councillor, Dr. A. Glickh. His father had destined him for the career of a lawyer, and it was not until after the death of the former that he could devote himself entirely to music. He chose the violoncello for his principal instrument, which he studied under Hellmesberger, while F. Jaksch instructed him in composition. His first engagement was in Kretschmar's first symphony orchestra. After two years' service in that orchestra he toured for some time successfully as a soloist, and then accepted the post as professor at the church music school of the Votiv-Church in Vienna and teacher of the violoncello and musical theory at the music school of L. Liebing. He is now Capellmeister at the Votiv-Church and a well-known composer of church music, including a "Missa Solemnis" which has been performed in the court chapel on the occasion of the Emperor's jubilee, December 2,

1898. To dramatic art he has contributed an opera and an operetta, and to violoncello literature some excellent "Universal Studies," sonata with pianoforte in D, and solo pieces.

CÆSAR SCHWORMSTÄDT, born October 14, 1864, at Hamburg, commenced the study of the violoncello under A. Gowa, while Professor A. Krug instructed him in theory and composition. He continued his studies successively under Friedrich.Grützmacher, R. Hausmann, and finally under Professor H. Becker. From 1885-7 Schwormstädt was solo violoncellist at Crefeld and member of the Richard Barth Quartet. During that time he played on several occasions with Johannes Brahms. On the foundation of Bülow's orchestra in 1888, he was induced to return to Hamburg and join that body. In the quartets of Blaha and Schradieck he filled the part of the violoncellist, and since 1896 he has instituted successful chamber music soirées with the assistance of local and foreign artists (Professor Spengel, Kahn, Barth, Mühlfeld, Dessau and others). Apart from his activity as a soloist and chamber music player, he conducts at the Orchestral Union, several choirs, and he is director of a school of music.

OTTO LÜDEMANN, born September 7, 1864, at Berncastel on the Moselle, studied the violoncello at the Cologne Conservatoire under L. Ebert. In 1880 he went to Berlin, where he became a pupil of Hausmann at the Hochschule, and in 1884 he was appointed chamber musician in the royal chapel, where he advanced to the post of solo violoncellist in 1901. He has acquired a considerable reputation as teacher, and counts among his pupils the Prince Joachim Albert of Prussia. He has received the medal for arts and science with the crown and many marks of distinction from the German Empress and other high personages. Both as soloist and chamber musician he is held in high esteem.

CARL FUCHS, born June 3, 1865, at Offenbach near Frankfort, commenced the study of the violoncello at the early age of nine under Riedel, the first violoncellist of the Frankfort opera. In 1881 he entered the Hoch Conservatoire, where he became a pupil of Professor Cossmann. During that time he was a member of the Museums Orchestra. On the completion of his studies in 1885 he played the Schumann concerto as a farewell performance in the presence of Frau Clara Schumann, the composer's widow. After his military service he re-entered the Hoch Conservatoire in 1886, and during the summer of that year Davidoff came to Frankfort and heard him play. He was so impressed with his talent that he invited him to St. Petersburg, where he had the advantage of that great master's teaching. During his sojourn at St. Petersburg he was member of the Imperial Orchestra under Anton Rubinstein. In 1887 Fuchs visited Sir Charles Hallé in Manchester with a letter of introduction by Mme. Schumann, and was appointed principal violoncellist in the Hallé Orchestra, a position which he still occupies. He also joined the Schiever Quartet at Liverpool. On the foundation of the Royal Manchester College of Music by Sir Charles Hallé in 1893 he was invited to become professor of violoncello at that institution, where he is still active. In 1895 he toured in south Germany with Miss Magda Eisele, and on the occasion of his visit to Cassel he was appointed solo violoncellist to H.R.H. the Grand Duke of Hesse. In 1898 he was commanded to play before Queen Victoria at Windsor Castle.

Fuchs, who is an exceptionally fine chamber music player is violoncellist of the Brodsky Quartet at Manchester since its formation. He is also a clever pianist and teacher of that instrument.

He has toured frequently and with marked success in England, Germany, Holland and Italy. In 1906 he published his "Violoncello Method" in three volumes (Schott and Co.), which soon after experienced a second edition.

DR. HEINRICH PUDOR, born August 29, 1865, as son of court councillor, J. F. Pudor, the proprietor of the Dresden Conservatoire. He studied the violoncello under Friedrich Grützmacher, and received his first appointment in the Gewandhaus Orchestra at Leipzig. After taking his doctor of science degree at Heidelberg University he studied for some time in Paris to acquaint himself with the French school of violoncello playing. After visiting Italy and Austria he returned to Dresden to take over the management of his father's conservatoire. He published some essays of an extravagant nature which little accorded with the meaning of his name, and after selling the conservatoire to Prof. Eugen Krantz he came to England eventually settling in Edinburgh. He possesses a beautiful instrument by Camillo Camilli. To the violoncello literature he contributed some studies.

ADOLF THOMAS, born September 11, 1865, in Berlin, was a pupil of Prof. Robert Hausmann for violoncello, and of Dr. Joseph Joachim and Prof. H. de Ahna for chamber music at the Hochschule from 1881 till 1886. His first appointment was as solo violoncellist in the Berlin Symphony Orchestra and the "Oper des Westens" (opera of the West End). Afterwards he went to Christiania (Norway) where he was engaged at the National Theatre, and at present he is living at Eisenach as soloist, member of a chamber music combination and teacher of his instrument. He has composed several solo pieces for violoncello.

RUDOLPH EHRLICH, born January 17, 1866, at Prague, where he studied the violoncello under Hegenbarth. After touring for some time as a soloist he settled in Moscow as teacher of the conservatoire. In 1897 he joined the Moscow Trio (Schor-Kreïn, Ehrlich).

JULIUS HERNER, born June 27, 1866, at Hanover, studied the violoncello under Carl Schröder at Sondershausen. In 1887 he came to London and was for some time principal violoncello in the Crystal Palace Orchestra.

HEINRICH KRUSE, born April 16, 1866, at Arolsen. The son

of musical parents he received his early musical education at home. From 1880 till 1885 he studied at the Hoch Conservatoire, which he entered with the idea of becoming a violinist. Prof. Cossmann induced him to exchange that instrument for the violoncello, whereon he made rapid progress. After leaving the conservatoire he went to Switzerland, going to Russia in 1886 and a year later to Poland. After a short sojourn in Hamburg he was appointed as violoncellist at the Court Theatre at Cassels, appearing frequently as soloist at concerts of neighbouring towns. In 1897 he left Cassels and settled at Altona. He is member of the Hamburg Philharmonic Orchestra and of the Max Fiedler Orchestra, an esteemed chamber music player, teacher and solo violoncellist. He has written several pieces for his instrument which prove his talent as a composer.

MAX JÄHNIG, born June 1, 1866, at Dresden, where he studied under Friedrich Grützmacher, as a pupil of the conservatoire from 1881 till 1887. His first appointment was as solo violoncellist in the Kur orchestra at Carlsbad and afterwards he was engaged in a similar capacity in the Tonhalle Orchestra at Zurich, where he remained until 1892. In the latter year he competed for and obtained an appointment in the court chapel at Stuttgart, where he is now living as an esteemed soloist, chamber music player and teacher.

FRIEDRICH GRÜTZMACHER, born October 2, 1866, at Meiningen, is the son of the court concertmeister, Leopold Grützmacher, who instructed him in the art of violoncello and pianoforte playing. At the age of ten young Friedrich II made his debut as soloist at Weimar with great success. The summer holidays he spent with his famous uncle, Friedrich I, at Dresden, benefiting by his instruction during that time. Franz Liszt introduced him in Weimar with the words: "This youth will take care that the violoncellist dynasty of the Grützmachers will not die out." After touring for some time with great success and playing at the Wagner festivals at Bay-

JOSEPH LIDEL. FROM AN ENGRAVING IN THE POSSESSION OF MESSRS. WM. E. HILL AND SONS.

To face page 488.

reuth, he was in 1890 appointed solo violoncellist in the court chapel and teacher at the conservatoire at Sondershausen, going shortly after to Budapest as concertmeister at the opera and professor at the conservatoire. Since 1893 Grützmacher lives at Cologne in a similar capacity and has added to his fame of an excellent soloist that of a refined chamber music player by his connection with the Cologne Quartet, of which Willy Hess was leader until he left Cologne, when concertmeister Bram-Eldering took his place. Grützmacher has been honoured by the title of concertmeister as well as various orders.

EMIL LEICHSENRING, born March 13, 1867, at Klingenthal (Vogtland). He studied at the Leipzig Conservatoire under Professors Alwin Schröder and Julius Klengel. He has been a member of the Meiningen Court Orchestra, Bülow Orchestra at Hamburg and Bayreuth Festival Orchestra. In 1889 he toured with great success in Scandinavia and afterwards with the string quartet of the Meiningen court chapel in northern and middle Europe. At present he lives at Hamburg as soloist and teacher of his instrument.

KARL PIENING, born April 14, 1867, at Bielefeld, where his father was well known as organist and teacher of music. After some instructions from local musicians he went in 1884 to Sondershausen, where he entered the conservatoire as pupil of Professor C. Schröder. In 1886 he left Sondershausen for Berlin, where he continued his studies at the Hochschule under Hausmann until 1890, attending also the chamber music classes under Joachim and W. Bargiel. He is also indebted to Professor H. Becker for part of his artistic education. From 1890 till 1892 Piening was violoncellist of the newly-founded Glasgow Quartet. In 1893 he was solo violoncellist at Crefeld and in the following year he was appointed in a similar capacity for the ducal chapel at Meiningen. As chamber music player he had on several occasions the honour to be associated with Brahms. He is member of the Meiningen Quartet as well as a trio with the composer, Wm. Berger, and concertmeister Treichler. The Meiningen Quartet has made successful tours throughout the Continent and England, and Piening has been honoured by the grand duke for his many achievements, by conferring upon him the title of chamber virtuoso and the gold medal for science and art.

ERNST DÖRING, born May 25, 1867, at Oldenburg, showed early signs of musical talent with a strong predilection for the violoncello. He studied at the Leipzig Conservatoire under Klengel and other distinguished masters with such success that he was awarded the Schleinitz Prize. Jules de Swert was so much impressed with Döring's talent that he accepted him as a pupil, and the influence of that great violoncellist composer on his future development was most marked. His career as a soloist which followed was very successful from the beginning. In England he received the title professor. Together with his wife, Mme. Döring-Brauer, a clever pianist, he toured successfully in north and south America and the West Indies, and on their return they visited the principal towns of northern Europe and Russia. They are living at present at Coburg.

PAUL MICHAEL, born July 4, 1867, at Auerbach i. V., was intended for the career of a school teacher. After many hard struggles he obtained an entry into the Dresden Conservatoire, where he became a pupil of Friedrich Grützmacher in 1882. For his further education he is indebted to Professor Döring, Rischbieter and Alban Förster. In 1887 he was appointed as member of the Dresden Philharmonic Orchestra, under J. L. Nicodé. At the same time he appeared frequently and with success in the capacity of solo violoncellist. After a further course of study under concertmeister Georg Wille, he competed for a vacancy in the royal chapel and was appointed royal chamber musician. He is now much in request as a teacher, and has published a number of compositions which are of decided merit.

ALBRECHT LÖFFLER, born August 16, 1867, at Tilsit, studied the violoncello under Heinrich Grünfeld, the chamber musician, Charles Philipsen and Robert Hausmann. In 1894 he was violoncellist of the Krasselt Quartet, and is now in the same capacity a member of the Waldemar Meyer Quartet in Berlin.

EDUARD WELLENKAMP, born April 26, 1868, at Hamburg. He studied under Carl Schröder at the Sondershausen Conservatoire, 1884-7, and under Alwin Schröder at Leipzig, 1887-8. On the completion of his studies he became a member of the Bülow Orchestra, and afterwards of the Fiedler and the Philharmonic Orchestras at Hamburg. Wellenkamp is also an excellent chamber music player. He was for eight years violoncellist of the Koperzky Quartet, and for two years he was a member of Professor Barth's Quartet at Hamburg. Since 1902 he is organist at the church of St. Gertrud. He appeared as solo violoncellist successfully in Berlin and several towns of northern Germany. He has composed a sonata for violoncello and pianoforte and a number of successful vocal compositions.

FRITZ PHILIPP, born July 11, 1868, at Mayence, studied at the Leipzig Conservatoire under Professors Alwin Schröder and Julius Klengel. After completing his studies he toured with great success in Russia. Afterwards he was engaged as solo violoncellist in several symphony orchestras. During the summer of 1908 he toured very successfully in Switzerland, where, on the occasion of a concert at Wengen, Julius Klengel, who attended the concert, presented him with his portrait with a flattering dedication. Mr. Philipp is at present (1909) solo violoncellist at the Court Theatre at Mannheim.

FRIEDRICH BUXBAUM, born 1869, in Vienna, studied under Hellmesberger at the Vienna Conservatoire, which he absolved in 1887 after obtaining the first prize for seniors. For two years he toured with great success in Great Britain, after which he joined the Fitzner Quartet. About 1900 he joined the famous Rosé Quartet, of which he is still a member. He is also first solo violoncellist at the Imperial Opera and professor at the Imperial Academy for Music (K. K. Akademie für Musik und darstellende Kunst). Buxbaum has toured with unvarying success in Germany, Holland, France, England, Spain and Russia.

GEORG WILLE, born September 20, 1869, at Greiz (Reuss, older line), is the son of the well-known director of music, Gustav Wille. Commencing the study of the pianoforte and violin at an early age, he was sent to Leipzig in 1885, where he studied the violoncello under Julius Klengel at the conservatoire, while Dr. Wilhelm Rust, the famous cantor of St. Thomas, was his teacher for musical theory and composition. In 1889 he received already an appointment in the theatre and Gewandhaus orchestras, and in 1891 he succeeded Alwin Schröder as first solo violoncellist. In 1899 he became solo violoncellist at the Dresden Opera, receiving the title of court concertmeister in 1902 and that of professor in 1909. He has toured with great success, and is much admired for his excellent technique and tone. Wille takes a high rank among contemporary violoncellists. He is a member of the Petri Quartet in Dresden as well as the Anno Hilf Quartet in Leipzig. In 1914 he appeared with great success in London.

1870-80.

HEINRICH APPUNN, born January 20, 1870, is the son of the well-known acoustician, Anton Appunn, of Hanau o/M. He was a pupil of Professor Bernhard Cossmann at the Hoch Conservatoire at Frankfort. In 1896 he was appointed teacher at the Frankfort School of Music, and violoncellist of the Frankfort Quartet (Frankfurter Quartet Vereinigung). He lives at Hanau in an independent position of soloist, teacher and chamber music player. He has also published some pieces for his instrument.

WILLY DECKERT, born June 4, 1870, at Naumburg on the Saale. He commenced the study of the violoncello as a private pupil of Friedrich Grützmacher at Dresden. In 1894 he entered the Royal Conservatoire as a pupil of Professor Julius Klengel, with whom he studied for two years.

The Grand Duke of Luxemburg was a great admirer of his talent and gave him a brilliant certificate. Later on he re ceived the title of "conzertmeister."

He toured successfully in Norway and afterwards in Russia and Austria. For three years he was deputy capellmeister at the court of Luxemburg.

At present he is living at Berlin as teacher of the violoncello at several of the principal conservatoires, member of the Berlin Trio (of which he is one of the founders) and soloist in symphony and other concerts. He has composed songs without words for violoncello and published a number of arrangements. He is also engaged in literary pursuits in a most versatile manner, for he not only contributes to various musical periodicals but also to—comic papers.

HEINRICH WARNKE, born August 30, 1870, at Wesselburen, belongs to a family of well-known musicians. He received a thorough musical grounding in his parental home, and thus well prepared he studied the violoncello under A. Gowa at the Hamburg Conservatoire. He went afterwards to Leipzig, where he finished his studies at the conservatoire under Professor Julius Klengel. After filling positions as solo violoncellist in Baden-Baden and Homburg, he was appointed in the same capacity in the Kaim Orchestra at Munich, which was dissolved a few years ago. As soloist he has established a considerable reputation, and as chamber musician he has toured with Felix von Weingartner.

MAX WÜNSCHE, born January 12, 1871, at Warnsdorf. He studied at the Leipzig Conservatoire under Professor Julius Klengel, Professor Jadassohn being his master in composition and Ad. Ruthardt in pianoforte playing. He received the Schumann and Beethoven scholarships, and a prize (prämie) on leaving. Since then he has been a member of the Gewandhaus Orchestra, and teacher at the Royal Conservatoire.

CARL MÜLLER, born May 21, 1871, at Kreuznach on the Nahe, studied under Professor Hugo Becker at Frankfort from 1888 till 1894. He is an excellent soloist and chamber music player, and in the latter capacity he is co-founder of the Hoch String Quartet and deputy for his master, Professor H. Becker, in Professor Heermann's String Quartet. Since 1900 he has been solo violoncellist at the National Theatre at Mannheim and member of the Mannheim String Quartet. He has toured with marked success in Germany and Switzerland, and arranged numerous sonata soirées with court capellmeister Hermann Kutzschbach, Hedwig Reichmann and others.

RICHARD ELLINGER, born September 4, 1871, at Mittelhausen. He studied at the Leipzig Conservatoire under Professor Julius Klengel. After various engagements in important German orchestras he settled in Constantinople as solo violoncellist of the "Grands Concerts de l'Union Française" and member of the Constantinople String Quartet and the Centola Trio. These positions he still occupied at the beginning of 1909.

OTTO ETTELT, born November 1, 1871, at Klein-Corbetha (district of Merseburg), received his first music lessons from his father and the local "Cantor." In 1890 he entered the Leipzig Conservatoire as pupil of Alwin Schröder, continuing later on under Professor Julius Klengel until 1896. His masters in musical theory were Paul Homeyer and Wendling. He was the winner of two important prizes at the conservatoire. From 1896-8 he was member of the Gewandhaus Orchestra, and at the end of that period he was appointed solo violoncellist in the Municipal Orchestra at Bremen. In 1899 he obtained also the distinguished position of solo violoncellist and member of the string quartet of the Philharmonic Society of that town, where he holds likewise the reputation of an excellent teacher.

HERMANN HOPF, born 1871, at Weimar, received his training as a violoncellist from Leopold Grützmacher at the conservatoire of that town. After absolving his military duties at Mannheim, he was engaged successively as solo violoncellist at Baden, Vienna, St. Petersburg and Görlitz. Since 1896 he has been first solo violoncellist at the theatre at Königsberg in Prussia, and member of the Königsberg String Quartet. He has established a widespread reputation as a concert soloist, and for some time past he has also been a member of the Bayreuth Festival Orchestra. To the literature of his instrument he has contributed a number of solos with pianoforte.

LUDWIG LEBELL, born August 26, 1872. When he was only three years old his pianoforte playing attracted the attention of musical circles in Vienna. At the age of fifteen he took up the study of the violoncello, afterwards becoming a favourite pupil of David Popper at Budapest, with whom he studied for five years. In 1896 he made his debut at the Promenade Concerts at the Queen's Hall in London, and met with great success, which followed him throughout his concert tours, extending over the principal towns of England. He is an excellent teacher and has also composed a number of works for his instrument (besides other compositions), including a violoncello sonata (as yet unpublished) and Twenty Studies, Op. 13.

Lebell has also published revised editions of the studies by Kummer and Dotzauer.

HUGO SCHLEMÜLLER, born October 2, 1872, at Königsberg in Prussia, is the son of very musical parents, who settled in Leipzig in 1881. There he commenced the study of the violoncello while visiting the "Gymnasium." After leaving that school he studied simultaneously at the university and the conservatoire, where Alwin Schröder and Julius Klengel conducted his studies on the violoncello. After several engagements in important orchestras (Kaim Orchestra in Munich, Winderstein Orchestra in Leipzig, etc.), he was appointed teacher at the Gotha Conservatoire. He toured with great success in Germany and Russia, and was frequently heard to advantage in his own compositions. In 1898 he went to Frankfort for a renewed course of studies under Hugo Becker, and was eventually appointed teacher at the Hoch Conservatoire, which position he still holds. He is also the violoncellist in the quartet of the Popular Chamber Music Society in Frankfort, the Trio Association at Coburg and highly esteemed as a soloist. He has published two concertos and a number of solos for his instrument, and has become honourably known as an author on musical subjects.

OTTO BERGER, born 1873 at Machau in Bohemia, was a pupil of Hanns Wihan, and with Karel Hoffmann, one of the founders of the now famous Bohemian String Quartet, formed by pupils of the Prague Conservatoire. He was a very exceptionally talented violoncellist, but fell an early prey to that demon-fiend consumption, which laid him low in the prime of his youth. He died on June 30, 1897, at Machau, at the age of twenty-four. His late master, H. Wihan, filled the place in the quartet that was left vacant by the departure of his talented pupil.

CHRISTIAN BERTRAM, born January 20, 1873, at Heddesdorf, was a pupil of the late Louis Hegyesi at the Cologne Conservatoire. After the death of his first master he studied four more years under Professor Friedrich Grützmacher. In 1897 he was appointed solo violoncellist at the Elberfeld Opera, and thence he went for some time as deputy violoncellist to the Court Theatre at Carlsruhe. In 1899 he was engaged as solo violoncellist in the court orchestra at Bückeburg and member of the Sahla Quartet. In 1901 he was engaged at Pawlowsk, near St. Petersburg, where he was greatly admired as a soloist.

WALTER SCHILLING, born March 5, 1873, at Bad Elster. His early signs of musical talent were greatly encouraged by members of the well-known Hilf family. In spite of his own inclination, however, he complied with the wishes of his mother and entered a teacher's seminary to prepare himself for the career of school teacher. At the end of two years he left that institute and entered the Leipzig Conservatoire as pupil of Alwin Schröder, continuing afterwards under Julius Klengel. After various minor engagements, including one year in Winderstein's Orchestra at Leipzig, he was appointed solo violoncellist of the Society of Friends of Music at Lübeck. There he remained for two years until 1899, when he was called to Carlsruhe as member of the court orchestra and teacher at the conservatoire. Early in 1903 he competed for a vacancy of principal violoncello at the Dresden Opera, and succeeded so well that he was appointed as royal chamber musician. He is also violoncellist of the Lewinger Quartet, which enjoys the reputation of high excellence.

MAX SCHANZE, born in January, 1874, at Munich, where he studied the violoncello under Professor Jos. Werner, at first privately and afterwards as pupil of the Royal Conservatoire, where Jos. Rheinberger became his master in theory and composition. He left the Academy of Music in 1894, and after a short engagement in the Kaim Orchestra, he was appointed as teacher at the Royal Conservatoire at Würzburg. That position he filled for one year only, at the end of which he returned to Munich and rejoined the Kaim Orchestra. In 1897 he received an appointment as teacher for the conservatoire at Innsbruck, and in 1899 he accepted a similar post at the Zürich Conservatoire. Afterwards he held an appointment in the Philharmonic Orchestra at Hanover, and then he toured in the northern part of Europe with great success, and in 1902 he became teacher at the Breslau Conservatoire and member of the Conservatoire quartet. He tours occasionally as soloist with great success.

JOHANNES HEGAR, born June 30, 1874, at Zürich, is a son of the well-known composer and conductor, Dr. Fr. Hegar. He commenced the study of the pianoforte at the age of nine, and a year later he took up the violoncello. After acquiring his general education at a private school and at the "Gymnasium," he entered the conservatoire of which his father was the principal. There he studied the violoncello under Julius Hegar, pianoforte under Rob. Freund and theory under Kempter. In 1893 he went to Frankfort to study under Professor H. Becker at the Hoch Conservatoire. In 1897 he became violoncellist of the Frankfort Trio (C. Friedberg, A. Rebner, J Hegar) and also Becker's deputy in the Heermann Quartet. He toured with great success in Germany, France, Spain and Switzerland, and in 1899 he was appointed teacher of his instrument at the Hoch Conservatoire.

OTTO KRIST, born 1874, in Vienna, studied at the Vienna Conservatoire under Professor R. Hummer. In 1898 he joined the Duesberg Quartet, being succeeded by Natalie Duesberg, who appears as violoncellist in 1909.

HEINZ BEYER, born August 28, 1875, in Berlin, studied the violoncello as amateur until he was eighteen years old. In 1893 he decided to make the musical career his profession, and for that purpose he entered the Hochschule, where he became a pupil of R. Hausmann. Louis Lübeck, the well-known solo violoncellist of the Royal Chapel, exercised also a great influence on his technical and artistic development, and Professor Succo and Fr. Neumann conducted his theoretical studies.

In 1901 he was appointed member of the Royal Chapel in Berlin, but relinquished that position in the following year to form a permanent trio with Otto Hegner and the Russian violinist, Boris Sibor. He is now living in Berlin.

ERNST CAHNBLEY, born September 3, 1875, at Hamburg. His uncle, Ferdinand Cahnbley, instructed him in pianoforte and violin playing from his seventh year. In 1887 he went to Berlin to continue the study of the pianoforte under Professor E. Breslauer. In 1890, he returned to Hamburg, and gave his chief attention to the study of the violoncello, receiving instruction from Max Eisenberg, while Armbrust and Arnold Krug became his masters of theory and composition. After fulfilling successive engagements in the Laube Orchestra at Hamburg and the Kaim Orchestra at Munich, he held appointments as solo violoncellist at Hanover, Riga and St. Petersburg. Since 1900 he has been teacher of his instrument at the Dortmund Conservatoire, solo violoncellist in the Philharmonic Orchestra of that town and member of the conservatoire quartet. He published several compositions for violoncello.

KARL KLEIN, born September 27, 1878, at Aix-la-Chapelle, is the son of Benedict Klein, a violoncellist in the Municipal Orchestra of that town, who instructed him at an early age in the art of violoncello playing. He continued his studies for four years at the Hoch Conservatoire at Frankfort under Professor Bernhard Cossmann and Hugo Becker, which he left, receiving a diploma with honours. After a successful debut as soloist he was, in 1899, appointed solo violoncellist in the Municipal Orchestra at Düsseldorf, where he is also engaged as teacher at the conservatoire and member of the Conservatoire quartet and the Rhenish Trio for chamber music.

He toured successfully in Germany, Switzerland and Holland, and was honoured by flattering remarks from the Dutch Prince Consort, before whom he played by special command He has composed a concerto and a number of solos for violoncello, also a number of songs.

RUDOLF KRASSELT, born January 1, 1879, at Baden-Baden, commenced to play the pianoforte when he was five years old, and at the age of twelve he took up the violoncello under H. Warnke. He made his debut as soloist already in the following year, and took part in chamber music performances together with his father, brother and sister. From 1894-7 he studied under Professor Julius Klengel at the Leipzig Con servatoire. After a short engagement as soloist in the Kur-Orchestra at Baden-Baden and a similar one at the theatre at Rostock, he was appointed solo violoncellist in the Berlin Philharmonic Orchestra, often touring with that famous orchestra from 1898 till 1902. In the latter year he was engaged as solo violoncellist at the Opera in Vienna, but had to return to Berlin in the autumn of that year on account of his military service. He lived at Berlin in 1909 as solo violoncellist, devoting himself entirely to concert playing, wherein he excels by a well developed technique and sympathetic tone.

PAUL GRÜMMER, born February 26, 1879, at Gera (principality of Reuss, younger line). His father, Detlev Grümmer, a court musician, instructed him in violin playing until he was fourteen. In 1893 he commenced the study of the violoncello, his first masters being Friedrichs, a member of the court chapel, and Emil Böhme, violoncellist in the Municipal Orchestra. From 1894-8 he studied at the Leipzig Conservatoire under Professor Julius Klengel. During the latter part of that time he played as solo violoncellist at several seaside towns of the Baltic, and twice at the "Liszt Verein" at Leipzig. In 1900 he went to England as teacher of a school of music, but returned to Leipzig after eighteen months to resume his studies under Klengel, finishing with a course under H. Becker. On April 2, 1902, he made a successful debut as soloist in London, where he had the honour to appear before the King and Queen. After touring in England he went to Vienna, where he is (1914) member of the Wiener Konzerthaus Quartet.

FRANZ BORISCH, born March 16, 1879, at Kottbus in Prussia, studied at the Hochschule in Berlin under R. Hausmann. His first engagement was as solo violoncellist in the Berlin Philharmonic Orchestra, and in that capacity he appeared with success in various towns of northern Europe, including the principal towns of Russia. In 1901 he received the title of royal chamber musician, and settled in Berlin as teacher, soloist and member of a string quartet founded in 1897 in conjunction with his brothers. He is at present living in Berlin as member of the Royal Chapel.

ANNA BALLIO, although born in 1879 in Milan, should be enumerated among German violoncellists, as her family settled in Germany when she was in her infancy. She studied the violoncello at the Cologne Conservatoire under Professor Fr. Grützmacher. She combines a remarkably fine and powerful tone with an easy and elegant technique of the left hand, and combines the reputation of a brilliant soloist with that of an excellent chamber music player. In the latter capacity she has toured successfully with two of her sisters, with whom she formed a permanent trio. She lives at present at Heidelberg as soloist and teacher of her instrument.

ANTON WALTER, born April 3, 1883, at Carlsbad in Bohemia. He studied under Professor Ferdinand Hellmesberger at the Vienna Conservatoire from 1896 till 1901, gaining the silver medal of the Society of Friends of Music. Since then he is the violoncellist of the celebrated Fitzner Quartet. He has toured with great success in Austria, Germany, Holland, Denmark and the Orient, including Egypt.

ROSA BRACKENHAMMER studied under Jos. Werner at

Munich. She appeared as soloist at Copenhagen in March, 1896, when the press spoke very highly of her big and noble tone, combined with a brilliant technique. They state, moreover, that she possesses emotional qualities as well as musical intelligence of a high order. She has since been heard to great advantage in many Continental towns.

JOSEFINE DONAT, born in Vienna, a pupil of Ferdinand Weidunger (member of the Imperial Chapel) and afterwards of Professor Reinhold Hummer. She toured as a soloist in Sweden, Norway, Russia and Holland. In 1900 she settled in Vienna as soloist, teacher and quartet player.

ALFRED HEYN, born at Dresden during the first half of last century, was a pupil of Friedrich Grützmacher. He was for some time engaged in the orchestra of the German Opera at Rotterdam, and afterwards he became first violoncellist in the Grand Ducal Chapel at Darmstadt.

GOEDECKE, a violoncellist at Brunswick during the early part of last century, was the master of Joseph Leibrock.

EMIL HERBECK, a highly gifted pupil of Jos. Werner in Munich, is at present at St. Petersburg.

EDUARD ROSÉ, born in Vienna, studied from 1876-9 at the Imperial Conservatoire, and made his debut as solo violoncellist in 1881. In 1882 he joined the string quartet of his brother, Arnold Rosé. In 1884 he was appointed solo violoncellist at the Royal Opera at Budapest, where he remained for several years. Between 1890 and 1900 he was engaged by Nikisch for the Boston Symphony Orchestra, and during the summer time he played in the Bayreuth Festival Orchestra. In 1900 he went to Weimar, where he is engaged as solo violoncellist at the Court Theatre and teacher at the conservatoire with the title of "court concertmeister."

BRUNO STEINDEL, born at Zwickau as son of the director of music of that town. He studied the violoncello under Friedrich Grützmacher. He was for some time solo violoncellist at

Crefeld, and afterwards first solo violoncellist in the Berlin Philharmonic Orchestra, where he was often heard as soloist. In 1901 he was engaged in a similar capacity in the Thomas Orchestra at Chicago, U.S.A. Apart from being an excellent soloist, he is also highly esteemed as chamber music player. His son, Bruno, made a sensational appearance as solo pianist.

PHILIPP ABBAS, who appeared in London in 1904, is a young violoncellist possessing a very remarkable technique combined with a powerful tone of very fine quality. His playing showed, moreover, that he is possessed of excellent musicianship. He is at present teacher at the Brighton Conservatoire.

DR. J. SAKOM is mentioned in "The Strad" of February, 1910, as first solo violoncellist of the Society of Friends of Music at Hamburg, which has an excellent orchestra conducted by José Eibenschütz. He is also member of Professor Kwast's Trio.

RUDOLFINE EPSTEIN appeared about 1876 as violoncello virtuoso, together with her sister Eugenie (violinist). They were the daughters of Julius Epstein, a professor at the Vienna Conservatoire.

CHAPTER XXVI.

THE VIOLONCELLO IN ENGLAND FROM 1800 TO 1900.

FREDERICK NICHOLLS CROUCH, the son of F. W. Crouch *(see the latter)*, was born July 31, 1808, in Warren Street, Fitzroy Square, London. He commenced his musical studies at a very early age, and played in the band of the Royal Coburg Theatre when he was only nine years old. After touring for some time in York shire and Scotland, necessity compelled him to serve as a common seaman on smacks plying between London and Leith. Through the intervention of William Watts, the secretary of the Philharmonic Society, he obtained an engagement in the orchestra of Drury Lane Theatre. Developing a remarkably fine voice, he studied singing under William Hawes and joined the choirs of Westminster Abbey and St. Paul's Cathedral. In 1822 he entered the Royal Academy of Music, where he studied under Lindley, Crotch, Attwood, etc., after which he became a member of the Philharmonic Orchestra, the Ancient Concerts and the Royal Italian Opera. After that he travelled for a time for a firm of metal brokers, and invented the engraving process known as zincography. His engagement as commercial traveller he exchanged for one of musical supervisor of D'Almaine and Company.

About 1838 he gave an entertainment on the songs and legends of Ireland, and was for years known as the Irish lecturer. In 1838 he published a series of songs, "The Echoes of the Lakes," containing "Kathleen Mavourneen," which has secured his lasting fame. In 1849 he went to America, where he was engaged as conductor in various towns, but his roving element prompted him to join the army of the confederates, in which he served through the Civil War. His last years were spent in Baltimore, and he died August 19, 1896, at Portland, Maine. He wrote two operas and a considerable number of songs which were very popular in their time. For the violoncello he has apparently left no compositions.

SIR JAMES HOPE GRANT, born 1808, an excellent amateur violoncellist and musician, entered the army in 1826, and served in China, etc., retiring eventually with the rank of a general. He composed three sketches for violoncello and pianoforte, "The Sea and the Lake," notturno and "The Three Violoncello Makers." He died in 1875. His portrait, painted by his brother, Sir Francis Grant, P.R.A., is in the National Portrait Gallery, London. See "Life of General Hope Grant," by H. Knollys. London, 1894. Two volumes.

LOUIS HENRY LAVENU, born 1818, in London, studied at the Royal Academy under Cipriano Potter and Bochsa. He was for some time violoncellist at the Royal Opera. After founding and conducting for some time a music seller's business in company with N. Mori, he went to Sydney as conductor of the theatre of that town, where he died, August 1, 1859.

GEORGE CALKIN, born in London, August 10, 1829, the youngest son of James Calkin, organist of St. Mark's, Regent's Park. He was for many years a violoncellist in the Philharmonic Orchestra, Royal Italian Opera and at provincial festivals, including the Birmingham festival of 1846, when "Elijah" was produced. He was also a teacher of singing and a conductor, and wrote a number of compositions for the organ which enjoyed great popularity.

WALTER PETTIT, born March 14, 1835, studied the violoncello at the Royal Academy. He was principal violoncello in the Queen's band, at the Philharmonic Society, H.M. Theatre, etc. He died in London, December 11, 1882.

WILLIAM H. PETTIT, his son, is also a violoncellist of repute.

JOHN BOATWRIGHT, born 1838 in London, was for about forty years a member of the Philharmonic Orchestra. He was also for several years principal violoncello of the Royal Italian Opera, played at the King's coronation in Westminster Abbey, and all the principal provincial festivals. He was held in high esteem as a teacher, counting among his pupils many of the best English violoncellists of the present day, including Miss Mabel Chaplin. He died February 25, 1905.

CHARLES OULD, born July 19, 1835, at Romford, in Essex, was an excellent violoncellist who appeared as soloist in London and provincial concerts. He was on various occasions the violoncellist of the Monday Popular Quartet, member of the Queen's band and of the Gompertz String Quartet.

KATE OULD, daughter of the above, is a good quartet player, soloist and teacher in London.

FRANK D'ALQUEN, of German parentage, born 1839, in London, studied the violoncello under Piatti, and appeared as a soloist at his concerts in Brighton, where he settled as a teacher of music. He studied singing under Gaetano Nava and Visoni at Milan, and toured successfully as a basso. As a composer he is well known as the author of a number of songs and solo pieces for violoncello.

EDWARD HOWELL, born February 5, 1846, was a pupil of Alfredo Piatti, and held a prominent position among English violoncellists. He was musician-in-ordinary to the Queen, principal violoncello in the Queen's band, the Leeds festivals (from 1880) and the Three Choirs. He made his debut as a soloist at the Crystal Palace concerts with Goltermann's Third Concerto in B minor. When D. Popper produced his "Requiem" for three violoncellos at St. James's Hall in 1891, Howell took part in the performance with the composer and Jules Delsart. From 1872 he was member of the Covent Garden Theatre orchestra, and for some years solo violoncellist of the Royal Italian Opera. He was an excellent teacher, and as such he was appointed at the Royal Academy, Royal College of Music and the Guildhall School of Music. Mr. Herbert Walenn, who is now his successor at the Royal Academy, is the most eminent of his numerous pupils. Howell died January 30, 1898. He is the author of a "First Book for the Violoncello," also some solos published in the "English Standard Library."

WILLIAM EDWARD WHITEHOUSE, born in London, May 20, 1859, is the third son of the late Henry Whitehouse, who was a gentleman of the Chapel Royal and lay vicar of Westminster Abbey. W. E. Whitehouse, like many other violoncellists, commenced his musical career as a student of the violin under Adolphus Griesbach. His predilection for the violoncello asserted itself when he was thirteen years old, and in 1873 he became a pupil of Walter Pettit, first violoncellist of the Queen's band. After four years' study under that master, he entered the Royal Academy, where he became a pupil of Alfredo Piatti and Alessandro Pezze. After one year's study under these masters he gained already the Bonamy Dobree prize in 1878. In the following year he was awarded the bronze medal and in 1880 the silver medal. In 1882 followed his appointment as assistant professor at the Royal Academy, and a year later he obtained the professorship of that institution, which he still holds. In the same year he was elected Associate of the Royal Academy, and in 1884 he became a member of the Royal Society of Musicians, professor of Cambridge University in 1886, and professor of the

Royal College of Music in 1886, and of King's College in 1892. In 1895 he was elected Fellow of the Royal Academy of Music and a member of the Royal Court of Assistance of the Royal Society of Musicians. He frequently took part in the performances at the Saturday and Monday Popular Concerts, where his excellent ensemble playing was greatly admired. As a soloist he is held in high esteem throughout the United Kingdom as well as in Italy, where he toured as the violoncellist of the London Trio, with the violinist, Simonetti, and the pianist, Amina Goodwin. With the excellent violinist, Joseph Ludwig, he formed a string quartet which acquired great popularity. Also of the String Club, the Jacoby Quartet, the Subscription Concerts at Bath and others, he was, and in some cases still is the violoncellist. As a teacher of his instrument he has been most successful, and he counts among his pupils a greater number of eminent young violoncellists than any other teacher in London. We only mention the following, which will be dealt with later on: Paul Ludwig, Herbert Withers, Paterson Parker, Warwick Evans, Watton O'Donnel, Edward Mason, Ivor James, Purcell Jones, Felix Salmond, R. Grimson, Carrodus, T. Weist Hill, and the following ladies: Misses Kate Ould, van Hulst, Beatrice Evelyn, Beatrice Harrison and Adelina Leon.

Professor Whitehouse is the fortunate possessor of a magnificent instrument by Francesco Ruggeri.

VICTOR HERBERT, born at Reven Oaks in Ireland, February 1, 1859, is a grandson of the famous Irish novelist, Samuel Lover. Developing early signs of musical talent, he was sent to Frankfort-on-Main, where he entered the Hoch Conservatoire and studied the violoncello under Professor B. Cossmann. At the conclusion of his studies he was appointed as violoncellist in the Royal Chapel at Stuttgart, where his solo playing was greatly admired. Afterwards he lived for some time in Vienna, where his most popular work for the violoncello, the Suite, Op. 3, was produced in 1885. He married Fräulein Förster, soprano of the Dresden Opera. In 1886 he accepted an engagement as solo violoncellist for the Metropolitan Orchestra in New York. An accident to his arm brought his career of a virtuoso to a sudden conclusion, and he devoted himself henceforth to composing and conducting. Some of his comic operas, "The Fortune Teller," "The Wizard of the Nile," etc., have met with phenomenal success. Besides the above-mentioned suite, Victor Herbert composed two concertos and a few solo pieces for the violoncello. Victor Herbert died in America a few years ago.

WILLIAM CHARLES HANN, belonging to a well-known family of musicians, born in January, 1863, occupies a prominent position among English violoncellists of the present day. He studied at the Royal Academy of Music under Alfredo Piatti, gaining successively the bronze and silver medals, certificate and Associate R.A.M., as well as the Bonamy Dobree prize for which he afterwards acted as adjudicator on several occasions. At the early age of seventeen he entered the orchestra of the Royal Italian Opera, Covent Garden, under Guye, and was a member for seven years. He is at present a member of the Philharmonic and most of the leading metropolitan orchestras as well as the provincial festivals. He toured successfully on various occasions as a soloist with Edward Lloyd, Johannes Wolff, Watkin Mills and other well-known artists. Hann is a member of the King's band and much in request as a soloist.

W. NOËL JOHNSON, born May 22, 1863, at Repton, Derby. After passing through Emmanuel College, Cambridge, he entered the Royal Academy of Music in London, where he studied the violoncello under Professor W. E. Whitehouse, afterwards continuing his studies of that instrument at the Leipzig Conservatoire under Alwin Schröder, at the same time studying composition, etc., under Oscar Paul and Paul Klengel. In 1893 he settled in London as soloist, composer and teacher. He toured in the provinces as solo violoncellist with marked success, but has of late devoted himself chiefly to conducting and composing. A play, "The Tournement of Love," with his music, was produced in Paris at the Theatre d'Application, La Bodinière. Some of his pieces for the violoncello have met with great success, but it is particularly through his songs that he has acquired widespread popularity. A few years ago he accepted the post as musical conductor at the Criterion Theatre.

BERNARD REYNOLDS, born 1865, at Notting Hill, London, is the son of Thomas Reynolds, a well-known viola player, his uncle being the famous double-bass player, John Reynolds, chief representative of his instrument at the Saturday and Monday Popular Concerts. Bernard Reynolds studied the violoncello privately under the late William Buels, and he is now widely known both as soloist and chamber music player in the provinces as well as in London, where he belongs also to the principal orchestras. Of late he has been chiefly engaged in teaching in London and Cambridge. In 1904-5 Reynolds was a governor of the Royal Society of Musicians.

SYDNEY BROOKS, born September 23, 1866, at Birmingham, studied the violoncello at the Paris Conservatoire under Joseph Hollmann and Jules Delsart. After the conclusion of his studies he returned to England, where he toured successfully as a soloist in at least twenty concert tours, including two Harrison tours. He appeared as a soloist at one of Madame Patti's Albert Hall concerts, and also at the Crystal Palace and other important orchestral concerts. He is a teacher at the London Academy of Music and has published several solo pieces for his instrument.

HERBERT WALENN, born in London, June 25, 1870. He belongs to a numerous family of artists and musicians, and studied the violoncello at first under Edward Howell at the

Royal Academy and Royal College of Music in London. Afterwards he went to Frankfort-on-Main, where he completed his studies under Professor Hugo Becker. He made rapid progress and soon appeared with great success as a soloist of a very high rank at Frankfort, Berlin, Mayence, etc. In London and throughout the British Isles he is well and honourably known as an eminent soloist and exceptionally fine chamber music player. In the latter capacity he appeared already at the Saturday concerts, St. James's Hall; then he was for four years violoncellist of the Kruse Quartet, and at present he has a quartet of his own of which his brother Gerald Walenn is the leader. They appear frequently in London as well as in the provinces, and are always sure of a welcome for their interesting and unconventional programmes and their refined, well-balanced ensemble. For some years past Herbert Walenn has been professor of the Royal Academy of Music, of which he is also a Fellow and Associate He has received many more marks of distinction which he is too modest to enumerate. As a teacher of his instrument he holds a very high reputation, and among his many talented pupils he counts young Cherniavsky, who appeared as a prodigy, together with his brother and sister, in the Cherniavsky Trio, a few years ago. This young Polish boy is promising to become a violoncellist of the first rank.

THOMAS JACKSON, born June 13, 1870, at Leeds, received his first instruction on the violoncello in his native town, afterwards going to Berlin, where he entered the "Hochschule für Musik," studying the violoncello under Professor Hausmann and ensemble playing under Joachim and Professor Kruse. After four years' study in Berlin, he went to Leipzig, where he became a pupil of Julius Klengel at the conservatoire. On the completion of his studies he became the violoncellist of the "Leipziger Novitäten Quartett-Verein," a quartet party which was artistically highly successful, but was dissolved after three years, owing to financial difficulties. Jackson then settled at Freiburg i/B. as teacher at the conservatoire and violoncellist of the "Süddeutsche Streich Quartett" (South German String Quartet).

JAMES RICHARDSON, born at Manchester, April 22, 1871, commenced his studies of the violoncello under a pupil of Lindley, with whom he remained for four years, continuing for nine more years under the guidance of Carl Fuchs. In 1899 he entered the orchestra of the Manchester Philharmonic, becoming principal violoncellist about 1906. Since 1900 he has been principal professor of violoncello at the Manchester School of Music, where pupils come to him from all parts of the United Kingdom. As a soloist he is chiefly known in the northern and midland counties. In Manchester he gives annual violoncello recitals since 1900, where he produces a great number of new or unfamiliar compositions for his instrument, including some of his own compositions, which comprise solos, two quartets for violoncellos and a series of solos in progressive order. He is also a successful lecturer on violoncello matters (history, literature, etc.), and he has done a great deal to popularise his instrument in his part of the country.

WILLIAM HENRY SQUIRE, born August 8, 1871, at Ross, Herefordshire, received his first instructions in music from his father, a gifted amateur violinist. He made his first public appearance at Kingsbridge, south Devon, as a prodigy, when he was only seven years old. In 1883 he gained a scholarship at the Royal College of Music which was extended for a second period of three years, and studied the violoncello under Edward Howell, receiving casual advice also from Alfredo Piatti. Dr. Hubert Parry (now Sir Hubert) instructed him in the art of composition. Squire made his debut as a soloist at the Albeniz concerts, St. James's Hall, February 12, 1891. His success on that occasion was followed by numerous public appearances at various concerts, where he has

ARNAUD DANCLA. FROM AN ENGRAVING IN THE POSSESSION OF
MESSRS. WM. E. HILL AND SONS.

To face page 512.

always met with enthusiastic receptions. In 1894 he was violoncellist of the British chamber music concerts at Queen's Hall, and on April 20, 1895, he made his debut at the Crystal Palace concerts with Saint-Saëns's Concerto in A minor, and in the same year he was appointed principal violoncello at the Royal Italian Opera, Covent Garden. He was elected an Associate of the Royal College of Music in 1889. Squire has not only distinguished himself as a violoncellist but also as a conductor and composer. He is the author of two operettas, orchestral and chamber music pieces, numerous songs, etc. For the violoncello he has composed a concerto, performed at the Royal College of Music concerts, twelve easy exercises, and a large number of solo pieces, which for the greater part have become very popular.

Squire is the owner of a fine Bergonzi violoncello formerly the property of Gustave Libotton.

PAUL LUDWIG, son of the well-known violinist, Joseph Ludwig, was born at Bonn on the Rhine, August 11, 1872. His father removed to London, where he studied first under Hugo Daubert and afterwards under Edward Howell and W. E Whitehouse at the Royal College of Music, and Alfredo Piatti He gained a scholarship at the Royal College, and became an associate of that institution on leaving. For five years he was engaged at the Saturday and Monday Popular Concerts, St. James's Hall, and distinguished himself as an excellent soloist and chamber music player. He has appeared at many of the principal London and provincial concerts with great success, and is one of the examiners of the Associated Board of the Royal Academy and Royal College of Music. In May, 1908, he was presented with a beautiful Stradivarius violoncello by his numerous friends and pupils.

ARTHUR BROADLEY, born 1872, at Bradford, was originally destined for the Civil Service. He studied the violoncello under one David Lee, and was appointed teacher at the

Brighton School of Music in 1905. He wrote some books on violoncello playing which appeared in "The Strad Library," London.

BEATRICE EVELINE, born October 3, 1877, at Llanbedr, Breconshire, South Wales, was the holder of the John Thomas Welsh scholarship at the Royal Academy of Music and an open scholarship at the Royal College of Music, which enabled her to study under Professor Whitehouse. She had already distinguished herself at the national eisteddfods of Wales, where she obtained a prize when only nine years old, defeating nine male competitors. At the end of her studies she gained the Schoefield prize for string players at the Royal College. In April, 1908, she made a very successful debut at the Queen's Hall ballad concerts, and since then has toured in Italy, on the Riviera and in Wales.

EDWARD MASON, born June 24, 1878, at Coventry, studied under Edward Howell and Professor Whitehouse at the Royal College of Music in London, gaining several exhibitions and eventually becoming an associate of that institution. He is a teacher of the violoncello and violin at Eton College and member of the Grimson String Quartet. He has lately devoted himself chiefly to conducting, and in that capacity has appeared successfully at the head of the New Symphony Orchestra and his own choir.

PERCY SUCH, born June 27, 1878, in London, is the son of Edwin Charles Such, conductor and composer, and brother of the well-known violinist, Henry Such. Percy Such studied at the "Hochschule" in Berlin, where he studied the violoncello under Robert Hausmann and ensemble playing under Joseph Joachim. After concluding his studies he toured very successfully as soloist in Germany, Austria, Holland and Great Britain. He frequently took his master's place in the Joachim Quartet in England, and also at the Beethoven Festival at Bonn on the Rhine. During the last two seasons of the Saturday and Monday Popular Concerts he was engaged as violoncellist in the famous quartet of that institution. He has been heard to great advantage at many important London and provincial concerts. His compositions for the violoncello consist of various arrangements and studies.

ROBERT PURCELL JONES, born December 14, 1879, at Ruabon, North Wales, commenced his musical studies as a violinist, when he was a pupil at a school in Dolgelley. The headmaster induced him to take up the violoncello with a view of assisting the weakest part of his school orchestra, and allowed him the special privilege to practise during some of the school hours. After thirteen months' work in this way he gained, in 1894, an open scholarship at the Royal College of Music, London, where he studied under Edward Howell and Professor Whitehouse. In 1896 he was presented with the Morley scholarship for four years' more study at the same institution. At the end of that time he became an associate of the Royal College. During the autumn season of 1909 and the first performances of Wagner's "Ring" he was principal violoncellist at the Royal Opera, Covent Garden. He is also a gifted chamber music player and as such belongs to the Molto String Quartet.

C. DARBISHIRE JONES, born in the eighties of last century, at Dartmoor. When he was only two years old his family went to Brazil, where he commenced to play the guitar, showing distinct musical talent. When the family returned to England some years later his father suggested that he should learn to play the violoncello, and he was consequently placed under Herr von Gelder at Bath. His progress was so rapid that it was decided to send him to Frankfort-on-Main, where he studied for four years and a half under Hugo Becker. During that time he met with a cycling accident and broke his left arm, which resulted in a long illness and serious interruption to the study of his instrument. During this time he devoted himself zealously to the study of composition under Ivan Knorr. On his recovery he resumed his study of the violoncello for some time under H. Becker, who by that time had become not only his teacher but also his friend. On the conclusion of his studies at Frankfort he went to Budapest, where he obtained some lessons from David Popper. He speaks with great enthusiasm of his sojourn in that beautiful town, where he gained the friendship of Hubay, Földesy, Szigeti, von Vecsey and Dohnányi, whose sonata he played subsequently with the composer in Berlin. Returning afterwards to England, his remarkable technique, elegant and refined rendering, and a round and beautiful tone, soon attracted the attention of the musical public. He has since appeared in many concerts in London and the provinces with marked success.

He acquired from the widow of Victor Herbert the latter's beautiful Nicholas Amati violoncello, which is said to be the only specimen by that maker now in existence.

HERBERT WITHERS, born March 6, 1880, in Abbey Road, St. John's Wood, London, showed early signs of musical talent which were carefully fostered in a musical family circle. H. J. Trust was his first master on the violoncello, and after several years of careful training at his experienced hands he entered the Royal Academy of Music, where he continued his studies under Professor Whitehouse, while Fred. Corder instructed him in musical theory. In 1899 he went to Frankfort-on-Main, where he became a pupil of Hugo Becker. Already in 1897 he made his debut at St. James's Hall in London, in Beethoven's Sonata in A and a sonata by Locatelli. In 1899 he gave a concert with the pianist, Herbert Fryer, at the Salle Bechstein in Berlin, where they met with an enthusiastic reception for their rendering of Brahms's Sonata in F. Shortly after he played H. Becker's violoncello concerto at the Crystal Palace, and since then he has been frequently heard at the Queen's

Hall and many provincial concerts. He married the pianist, Margaret Elzie, and in company with her and Madame Louise Sobrino he started in the autumn of 1908 on a concert tour round the world, meeting with such success that he had to return to Japan before the end of the tour. In 1910 he was still touring in America, at present (1914) he resides again in London. Withers plays on a fine Francesco Ruggerius, dated 1679.

GERTRUDE ESS, born about the middle of the eighties of last century, is the daughter of the conductor of the Garrison Band, Newcastle-on-Tyne. She studied the violoncello under Alessandro Pezze, and made her debut at the Steinway Hall, London, in 1903, when the "Musical Times" (April number) spoke in the most flattering terms of her playing, and her subsequent appearances at the Queen's Hall and other important concerts have borne out that verdict. Miss Ess possesses the technique of a virtuoso of the highest order, combined with a powerful tone of fine quality rarely to be met with in the case of lady violoncellists. Apart from this she displays gifts of a higher order in her refined and thoughtful readings of classical and modern works, and her artistic quartet playing. She possesses also the merit of familiarising her audiences with new works by contemporary composers, as in the case of Algernon Ashton's fine Sonata, Op. 128, in B flat, a work which presents immense difficulties to both violoncellist and pianist. She played it with the composer at the small Queen's Hall in 1908, and met with an enthusiastic reception. She was also the first to play Charles Schuberth's "Concerto Dramatique," which forms a parallel to Paganini's concertos for the violin. Miss Ess has toured with great success in the provinces, and in 1906 she joined the Henley Quartet, which appeared successfully in London as well as in provincial towns. She died about 1910.

ADELINA LEON, born 1885 in London, commenced her studies

under B. Patterson Parker and Paul Ludwig, gaining a three years' scholarship, open to the world, at the Royal College of Music, she became a pupil of Professor W. E. Whitehouse. At the end of that time she was made an associate of the Royal College, and finally went to Paris, where she finished her studies under Pablo Casals. Miss Leon has since appeared at numerous London and provincial concerts, where she has always met with great success, and she has a brilliant career as a soloist before her.

M. A. BEATRICE HARRISON, born December 9, 1892, at Roorkee, N.W.P. India, studied the violoncello under Professor Whitehouse at the Royal College for a period of four years. At the early age of ten she gained the gold medal in the senior examination of the Associated Board of the Royal Academy and Royal College of Music, London, obtaining the full number of marks among four thousand competitors, mostly adults.

At the age of fourteen, on May 29, 1907, she gave a most successful concert with Mr. Henry J. Wood's orchestra at the Queen's Hall, London. Shortly after she entered the Hochschule für Musik in Berlin, where she studied under Professor Hugo Becker. Miss Harrison was the first violoncellist to win the coveted Mendelssohn prize at the Hochschule. Her debut at the Bechstein Hall, Berlin, in the autumn of 1910 was so successful that it was followed by an orchestral concert at the Sing Akademie, with the assistance of the Philharmonic Orchestra, conducted by Professor H. Becker. The success was so great that it was followed by engagements from all parts of Europe, and since then Miss Harrison has been touring mostly in company of her sister May, the talented violinist. During the past season (1913) the great pianist, Eugen D'Albert, paid her the compliment to join her in a sonata recital at Bechstein Hall, and in the autumn she will visit America. Miss Harrison plays on a fine Petrus Guarnerius violoncello, from the famous collection of the late Baron

Knoop, which was presented to her by an American lady admirer.

HANS DRESSEL, the son of a German violinist, born in London (?), has toured successfully in England, Northern Europe and America. He published a "Method for the Violoncello." About 1906 he was appointed director of Upper Canada College, Toronto, but resigned that position owing to a breakdown in consequence of typhoid fever. In 1907 he founded an ensemble club at Spokane, Washington, which is in a flourishing condition.

AMY FLOOD-PORTER, one of the most talented young English lady violoncellists, has appeared with great success as a soloist at a number of London and provincial concerts. She is also an accomplished chamber music player, and as such took part in a fine performance of Schubert's pianoforte quintet at a meeting of the Tonal Art Club, London, in 1906. She is now (1913) touring in Mr. Burt's musical sketch.

ROSA CROW gave a recital at Bournemouth in December, 1909, where she played the Boëllmann variations, and was declared "a violoncellist of undoubted talent with a charming refined style."

DORA PETHERICK, born in Croydon, as the daughter of a painter, who, besides, is an authority on old instruments. She forms part with her sisters in the Petherick Quartet, and has gained the reputation of a good soloist and chamber music player. On January 15, 1910, she produced the first movement of a new violoncello sonata by Guido Papini with much success at the Mozart Society, founded by the pianist-composer, J. H. Bonawitz.

JEAN MARCEL made a successful debut at the Queen's Hall Promenade Concerts on August 12, 1908.

MABEL CHAPLIN, born in London, commenced the study of the violoncello as a private pupil of John Boatwright, continuing under Alessandro Pezze at the London Academy of

Music, where she gained certificates as well as the bronze and silver medals, and a scholarship. Afterwards entering the Brussels Conservatoire, she became a pupil of Edw. Jacobs, and there she gained, besides a scholarship, the second prize, first prize with distinction, and the first prize for solfège. Returning to England, she formed a permanent trio with her talented sisters, Nellie (pianoforte), and Kate (violin). They have appeared in London with great success on numerous occasions, and toured likewise in all the principal provincial towns. In Berlin they made their debut in 1910 and met with a most cordial reception. Miss Mabel Chaplin has been a professor of the London Academy for some time past. Latterly she has also taken up the viol da gamba, which she has studied with the author, becoming in a very short time an excellent player on that difficult instrument.

MURIEL HANDLEY studied the violoncello under Chevalier Ernest de Munck at the Guildhall School of Music, London, and afterwards under Professor Robert Hausmann in Berlin. She has appeared in London and toured all over the United Kingdom with great success, and is one of the best English lady violoncellists. She possesses a very fine instrument by one of the lesser known Ruggeri brothers, dated 1717, upon which Piatti made his reputation in England, and only parted with it when Captain Oliver presented him with his famous Strad.

MAY MUKLE, belonging to a well-known family of musicians, was born in London, and entered the Royal Academy of Music at the age of thirteen as a pupil of Signor Pezze. In her progress she carried off all the prizes, medals and certificates available for violoncello players, including the Bonamy Dobree prize, finally being elected an A.R.A.M., an honour not usually conferred on students at the early age of seventeen. She has since appeared in London and also in Paris with remarkable success. Apart from various tours in Eng-

PLATE XL.

AUGUSTE FRANCHOMME. PENCIL DRAWING FROM AN ORIGINAL PORTRAIT
BY LUDWIG VAN DER STRAETEN.

To face page 520.

land, she visited Australia in 1903 in the company of the great English tenor, Edward Lloyd, and in 1905 she joined a concert party which gave forty-two concerts in South Africa in the remarkably short space of seven weeks. In January, 1908, she went on a concert tour to America with Maud Powell, the distinguished violinist, when she met with a somewhat serious accident. Going out with Mr. G. Turner, the husband of Maud Powell, to see the New Year's crowd in Broadway, New York, she was knocked down by a gang of young ruffians, sustaining severe bruises and cuts. She had to be taken to the Rooseveldt Hospital, where a bad wound was attended to. Fortunately, she recovered in time for her concert which was advertised for the following Saturday, and met with an enthusiastic reception. Of late she has devoted much time to the study of chamber music, and joined the Norah Clench Quartet, which has been well received by the musical public. Miss Mukle was presented with a superb Montagnana violoncello. Although this is an instrument of very large dimensions Miss Mukle commands it with perfect ease, producing therefrom a powerful tone of a very beautiful quality.

WILLIAM W. C. BUELS, member of a family of musicians, was principal of the Kensington School of Music. He wrote a catechism of the rudiments of music, and was much in request as a teacher, counting among his pupils Mr. Bernard Reynolds. He died in London, December 6, 1890.

CHARLES HOBY, born in London, studied the violoncello, organ and pianoforte at the Royal College of Music. He went to India as military bandmaster, and returning to England became organist at the Royal Military Asylum, Chelsea. To the "Orchestral Times," afterwards the "British Musician," he contributed some papers on the violoncello. In 1891 he went to South Africa with Daniel Godfrey, junior, as a pianist, and settled in Natal as bandmaster of the Royal Rifles. An orchestral suite of his, "Scenes from Childhood," was produced at Durban in 1896.

LEO STERN, born at Brighton, April 5, 1862, studied chemistry and obtained a situation at a chemical factory, practising the violoncello after business hours till late at night. Being attacked by an inflammation of the lungs, he undertook a sea voyage, and on his return he took up the violoncello seriously, studying for two years under Piatti. Then he went to Leipzig for another year, studying under Klengel and Davidoff. On his return he toured with Patti, Nikita and Albani. Dvorák entrusted him with the first performance of his violoncello concerto at the Philharmonic Concert in March, 1896, when he conducted in person, and afterwards Stern played it at Prague, Leipzig and Berlin by the express wish of the composer. He played on several occasions before Queen Victoria, who showed her appreciation by presenting him with a diamond pin with V.R.I. surmounted by the imperial crown. Prince Henry of Battenberg became a pupil of his, and he was greatly patronised by royalty. He was presented with a magnificent Stradivarius violoncello, which he naturally cherished and played on all occasions. He married the violinist, Nettie Carpenter, but the union proved an unhappy one and was dissolved some time after. Leo Stern wrote a number of solo pieces for violoncello, mostly published by André and Cocks and Co. He died at the early age of forty-two, September 10, 1904.

FLORENCE HEMMINGS, the talented violoncellist of the Skinner Quartet, studied in London under Daubert. Unfortunately we are without further data.

A. H. EARNSHAW, who has of recent years frequently and successfully appeared as soloist, was appointed sub-professor of violoncello at the Royal Academy of Music, London, in 1896.

C. WARWICK EVANS, who studied under Professor Whitehouse at the Royal Academy of Music, has gained a considerable reputation as soloist among the younger generation of English violoncellists.

B. PATTERSON PARKER has gained a considerable reputation as soloist and chamber music player. He is the violoncellist of the Hans Wessely Quartet, and a successful teacher. Among his most prominent pupils appears Miss Adelina Leon.

The following occupy also a prominent position among English violoncellists of the present day: ARTHUR BROADLEY, author of "Hints to 'Cello Students," CHARLES A. CRABBE, violoncellist in the Reeves Quartet, J. E. HAMBLETON, WALTER HATTON (played Tchaïkovsky's "Roccoco Variations" at Southport in 1907), J. A. LLOYD, R. V. TABB, H. T. TRUST, C. TWELVETREES, TENNISON WERGE, and the following pupils of Professor Whitehouse: A. L. CARRODUS, J. F. CARRODUS, R. GRIMSON and FELIX SALMOND, son of the well known singer, Norman Salmond, who has lately entered the front rank of the younger solo violoncellists.

CHAPTER XXVII.

FRANCE.

AT the commencement of the nineteenth century France had acquired a very high standard in the art of violoncello playing as well as in violin playing, and vied with Germany for the first place in that art, which down to the latter part of the eighteenth century had belonged to Italy.

The chief characteristics of the German and French schools had by that time developed in a marked degree. The deep thinking, deep feeling, massive and powerful Teutonic mind expressed itself in its music, and the rendering of that music required a technique of a like nature. The consequence was a great technique of the left hand and a powerful tone capable of expressing the full scale of human feeling, from towering dramatic passion to the sweetest tenderness of love.

The French musical art corresponded in every way with the grace and elegance of the court of Louis XV and Louis XVI. The free abandon to the workings of the heart and mind was repressed by conventional rules, and the result was great elegance, perfect polish and daintiness. There could be no titanic greatness like that of Bach and Handel, but there was the pleasing grace of a Rameau, a Boccherini and a Viotti, for the latter, though born Italian, was more French in character. The result was a wonderful technique of the bow, particularly in all the lighter graces, viz., staccato, spiccato, sautillé, etc., not without considerable facility of the left hand, though that never came up to the standard of a Romberg. Each of the two countries was so proud of its own achievements that it looked down upon those of its neighbour. The writer well remembers how German violoncellists during the seventies of last century used to speak of "flighty tricks" when they referred to French bowing, while the French musicians scorned the German's clumsy roughness. Since then both have learned better, to their mutual advantage. The Frenchman studies the emotional depths of Beethoven, Schumann and Brahms, while the German is keenly alive to the advantages of the elegance, lightness and smoothness of the French technique of the bow, which, as applied to the violoncello, had been developed in a marked degree by Duport and Boccherini and was to be still further advanced by Franchomme and the Belgian school with Servais at its head. Let us see then who the artists were who led on to the astounding heights of modern technique.

PIÈRRE (PETER) BAUMANN, born at Lille the "29th Brumaire of the year IV" of the French Revolution (November 19, 1796), was appointed professor of violoncello at the Lille Conservatoire in 1832, and occupied that post until the time of his death in 1872. He was an artist of remarkable talent and the master of Auguste Franchomme.

GEORGE FRANÇOIS HAINL, born November 19, 1807, at Issoire (Puy-de-Dome), entered the Paris Conservatoire as pupil of Norblin on April 22, 1829, and received the first prize in 1830. During the first decade of his musical career he toured all over Europe with great success, and in 1840 accepted the post of conductor at the theatre of Lyons. On the decease of Girard, Habeneck's successor, in 1863, he was appointed conductor of the Grand Opera at Paris, and in the following year also of the conservatoire concerts. He died of congestion of the brain, June 2, 1873. Besides three operas and a book, "De la Musique à Lyons depuis 1713 jusqu'an 1852," he wrote several solos for violoncello.

ALEXANDER TILMANT, born 1808, at Valencienne, was one of the founders of the conservatoire concerts. He was a violoncellist at these concerts as well as at the Theatre Italien, where his brother was second conductor before he became principal conductor at the Opéra Comique. Alexander Tilmant died in Paris, June 13, 1880.

AUGUSTE FRANCHOMME, born April 10, 1808, at Lille, is one of the greatest masters of the violoncello. He commenced the study of the violoncello at the Lille Conservatoire under a mediocre master named Maes. In 1821 he gained the first prize, and continued at the same institute under Pièrre Baumann, a remarkable musician, who may be looked upon as his real and principal master. In 1825 he entered the Paris Conservatoire, where he studied successively under Levasseur and Norblin. His progress was so rapid that he gained the first prize after the first year of his studies at the conservatoire. He combined a full and sympathetic tone with a great command of the fingerboard. His soulful and refined playing, especially in slow movements, never failed to rouse his audience to a pitch of enthusiasm. He was the intimate friend of Chopin, whose influence may be clearly traced in his compositions, which are for some part of a high merit. He collaborated even with Chopin in the grand duo concertant on themes of "Robert le Diable," and Chopin's Sonata, Op. 65, dedicated to Franchomme, and his Introduction and Polonaise are in a large measure due to his admiration for Franchomme's playing. Already in the first year of his studentship at the conservatoire Franchomme held an appointment at the "Ambigue-Comique" Theatre. In 1827 he was engaged for the Grand Opera, but after one year he exchanged that post for one as solo violoncello at the Theatre Italien. After a few years he left that also and devoted himself entirely to solo and chamber music playing, and to teaching. On the foundation of the conservatoire concerts in 1828, Franchomme became a member of that institution, and solo violoncello of the Royal Chapel (Chapelle Royale). He was appointed second professor of his instrument at the Royal Conservatoire, where, on January 1, 1846, he succeeded Norblin as first professor, and he held that position to the time of his death. Franchomme formed a permanent string quartet with the famous violinist, Delphin Alard, and also chamber music soirées in conjunction with the latter and the pianist, Charles (afterwards Sir Charles) Hallé.

As professor of violoncello at the conservatoire he trained many excellent pupils, including A. Vidal, L. A. Jaquard, J. F. Barbot and Louis Hegyesi, the master of the writer of these lines.

Franchomme acquired L. Duport's famous Strad from the son of the latter. After Franchomme's death it was purchased by Messrs. Hill and Sons.

Franchomme's portrait, drawn by Ludwig van der Straeten, the author's son, from a small photograph, appears on Plate XL, and the following interesting letter addressed to the author's relative, R. E. Bockmühl *(see page 417)*, refers to Franchomme's arrangements for the violoncello of Beethoven and Mozart violin sonatas. We translate from the French original as follows. The music illustrations and autograph are in facsimile:

PARIS, *December 4, 1866.*

My dear and obliging Mr. Bockmühl,

I hasten to tell you as soon as possible how much I am touched, and grateful for all the trouble you have *again* given yourself on my behalf, I wish it might be in my power to render you some important service in return. Please believe me I should seize the opportunity with the greatest eagerness. In the meantime receive my sincerest thanks.

I shall write immediately to Mr. André, and send him the detailed note which he asks of me, that is to say the engraved index of the sonatas.

I have made no alterations in the piano part of these sonatas. I only indicate certain passages which (with the violoncello) must be played an octave lower or an octave higher. In Mozart there will be nothing but this to add in the *existing* plates.

As regards Beethoven there are in the sonata

often consecutive sharp sixths with the violin which it is impossible to play on the violoncello, for instance:

I think this ought to go as follows:

The sonata arranged like this becomes quite playable and even effective at the same time. Mr. André would have nothing to re-engrave in these works which he has [possess] no doubt. He need only make these small and very easy changes.

I cannot send them to him just yet as the title are not ready, but it will not be long before they will be.

When shall I have the pleasure to make your personal acquaintance and to tell you by word of mouth how great my affection is for you?

How deeply do I regret that your son did not find it possible to become a Frenchman. I hope that our exhibition will bring you hither! Awaiting this great pleasure, believe me, my dear Mr. Bockmühl, with my affectionate sentiments,

Your devoted

Aug^{te} Franchomme

Franchomme died January 21, 1884. He wrote a considerable number of solos with orchestra and pianoforte, a very fine Concerto in C and the famous Twelve Caprices, Op. 7, which form part of the standard literature of the violoncello.

FELIX BATTANCHON, born April 9, 1814, in Paris, where he studied the violoncello under Vaslin and Norblin at the conservatoire. He acquired a brilliant technique and met with great success as a virtuoso on his instrument. In 1840 he became a member of the orchestra of the Grand Opera. Between 1846-7 he endeavoured to resuscitate the baryton *(see Part I, page 112)*, but he was unable to awaken more than a passing interest in its favour. Battanchou died in July, 1893. He published a considerable number of compositions for violoncello, which are for the greater part of an ephemeral character. Still of importance are some of his fine studies, which are not only very useful for technical purposes but also musically interesting. His two trios for three violoncellos will also remain welcome to amateurs, on account of the scarcity of works for that combination. His Fantasia, Op. 22, on Beethoven's serenade-trio, was a favourite solo about the middle (1850-70) of last century.

HIPPOLYTE PROSPER SELIGMANN, born July 28, 1817 (of German descent) in Paris. He entered the conservatoire on December 2, 1829, as a pupil of Norblin, Halévy being his master in composition. In 1834 he obtained the second, and in 1836 the first prize. About the middle of 1838 he left the conservatoire and soon after began touring in the South of France, Italy, Spain, Belgium and Germany. He combined a remarkably fine tone with a brilliant technique of the left hand. He was the fortunate owner of a very fine Niccolo Amati of a large pattern.

His compositions, fairly numerous, are of the well-known drawing-room type of the period.

LOUIS ANTOINE VIDAL, born July 10, 1820, at Rouen, studied the violoncello under Auguste Franchomme. He devoted himself afterwards chiefly to literary work, the most important being "Les Instruments a Archet," which contains much valuable information and splendid portraits and illustrations engraved by Fréderic Hillemacher. Other interesting works of his are "La Chapelle St. Julien des Ménétriers" and "La Lutherie et les Luthiers." He died January 1, 1891, in Paris.

ARNAUD DANCLA, brother of Charles Dancla, the famous violinist, born January 1, 1820, at Bagnères de Bigorre (Haute Pyrenées), was a pupil of Norblin at the Paris Conservatoire. He was awarded the second prize in 1839, and in 1840 he left that institute after gaining the first prize. He shone particularly in quartet playing. As a composer for his instrument he published a tutor, "Le Violoncelliste Moderne," studies, two books of duets and some solos. He died at his birthplace, Bagnères de Bigorre, in February, 1862.

CHARLES JOSEPH LEBOUC, born December 22, 1822, at Besançon He entered the Paris Conservatoire in 1840, where he studied the violoncello, according to Wasielewski, at first under Vaslin, then under Norblin. According to Mendel,

Franchomme was his master, but this can only refer to some finishing studies of a later period, as Lebouc left the conservatoire about the end of 1843, while Franchomme only became teacher of that institute in 1846. In 1842 Lebouc received the first prize for violoncello playing, and in the following year the first and second prize for composition, which he studied under Halévy. From 1844-8 he was voloncellist at the Grand Opera. He made his debut at the concerts of the conservatoire in 1842, and from 1856-60 he was the secretary of that institution. He founded the "Soirées de Musique Classique," which flourished under his management. He was a very fine chamber music player as well as an excellent soloist. His compositions for violoncello consist of a tutor, "Methode Complète et Pratique de Violoncelle," and a number of solo pieces with pianoforte accompaniment.

JULES GALLAY, born at St. Quentin in 1822, was, according to Forino, a distinguished amateur violoncellist and collector of instruments, who wrote on the art of violin making.

LISA B. CHRISTIANI, born December 24, 1827, in Paris, was one of the first lady violoncellists. She played little solos with a rather small tone but in a graceful and elegant manner. On a successful tour through northern Europe she gave a concert at Leipzig on October 18, 1845, when Mendelssohn honoured her by accompanying her solos. He was evidently impressed by the young artist, who combined with her sympathetic playing an imposing appearance of considerable personal charm, and he expressed his admiration by writing a "Song Without Words" for her, which was published as Op. 109, No. 38 of the posthumous works, with the remark: "Composed in 1845 and dedicated to Mlle. Lisa Christiani." The King of Denmark conferred the title of chamber virtuoso upon her. In 1853 she toured in Russia, and her triumphal successes led her as far as Tobolsk in Siberia, where she was attacked by the cholera and died within a few days, at the

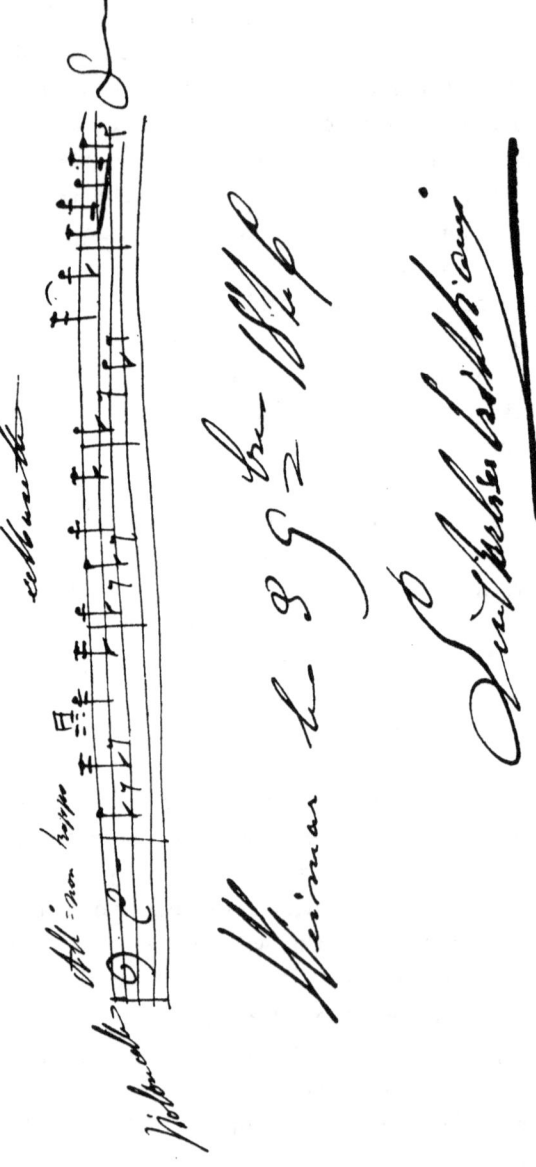

Fig. 57. Facsimile of an Album Leaf by Lisa B. Christiani, giving the Opening Bars of Offenbach's Musette.

early age of twenty-six. Her portrait appears on Plate XLI, and is reproduced from a print in the possession of Messrs. W. E. Hill and Sons. For a facsimile of an album leaf by Lisa Christiani, *see Fig. 57.*

LEON JEAN JACQUARD, born November 3, 1826, in Paris, spent his earlier years at Pont le Voy near Blois, where he received his first instruction in violoncello playing from Hus-Desforges, who had retired to this quiet little place, after an adventurous career, as teacher at a local school of music. Hus-Desforges died early in 1838, and Jacquard continued his studies under a violoncellist named Levacq until he entered the Paris Conservatoire, where he became a pupil of Norblin. His progress was such that he gained the second prize in 1842 and the first prize in 1844. Highly esteemed as soloist and orchestral player in the conservatoire concerts, he shone equally in chamber music. In 1855 he joined Armingaud, Mas and Ed. Lalo (the celebrated composer, who played the viola) in the formation of a string quartet, which, by the addition of wind instruments, developed afterwards into the Société Classique. In 1877 he succeeded Chevillard as teacher of his instrument at the conservatoire. He died March 27, 1886, leaving a few compositions for violoncello.

ALFRED SAUVAGET, born 1830, is mentioned by Forino as a pupil of Franchomme at the Paris Conservatoire, and afterwards teacher at the Conservatoire of Toulouse.

AUGUSTE TOLBECQUE, born March 30, 1830, in Paris, is the son of a celebrated violinist (pupil of Rud. Kreutzer). He entered the conservatoire at the early age of eleven as pupil of Vaslin. In 1849 he obtained the first prize. From 1858-65 he lived as soloist and teacher at Niort (Deux-Sèvres), and from that date until 1871 he was teacher at the Marseilles Conservatoire. Towards the latter part of last century he returned to Paris as violoncellist of the conservatoire concerts. Saint-Saëns, Godard and other eminent composers, have honoured him by the dedication of compositions for violoncello, and he himself has written some effective studies and solos for his instrument. In 1890 he published a literary work on the violin, "Quelques considerations sur la Lutherie," and later, 1896, his "Souvenirs d'un Musicien en Provence." He was also an executant on the viol da gamba and possessed a fine specimen by Francis Baker, in St. Paul's Churchyard, dated 1696, whilst at one time he owned a considerable collection of ancient musical instruments, which are now in the Brussels Conservatoire.

LOUIS AUGUSTE JACQUARD, born December 26, 1832, at Pont le Voy, was a pupil of Franchomme at the Paris Conservatoire, where he distinguished himself by carrying off the second prize in 1850 and the first in 1852. He was appointed violoncellist of the conservatoire concerts.

JULES LASSERRE, born July 29, 1838, at Tarbes, studied the violoncello under Franchomme at the Paris Conservatoire from 1852-5, when he gained the first prize. After that he toured successfully in France and Spain. In 1869 he settled in London as principal violoncello in Costa's orchestra and that of the Musical Union. Later on he was for some time solo violoncellist of the Scotch Orchestra in Glasgow. He returned to Paris, where he died.

Saint-Saëns dedicated his Sonata, Op. 32, to him, and Lasserre left a number of solos of his own composition.

HYPPOLITE FRANÇOIS RABAUD, born June 29, 1839, at Lalelles d'Ande. He studied at the Paris Conservatoire under Franchomme, where he obtained the first prize. Afterwards he was solo violoncello at the Opera and the conservatoire concerts, and professor of his instrument at the conservatoire. He was an excellent and conscientious teacher who trained a great number of the prominent French violoncellists of the present day. He published a tutor and a number of solos for his instrument.

JEAN FRANÇOIS BAREOT, born at Toulouse in 1847, studied the violoncello at the Paris Conservatoire, and afterwards settled at his native town as soloist and teacher of his instrument.

JULES DELSART, born 1844, at Valencienne. He received his first instruction in violoncello playing at the conservatoire of his native town, and afterwards at the Paris Conservatoire, where he gained the first prize in 1866 and succeeded Franchomme—his former master—on his death in 1884. He held that position until the time of his death, which occurred July 3, 1900, and during that period he trained many excellent young violoncellists, including Paul Bazelaire, Henri Casadesus, Marguerite Baude. About the latter part of the eighties Delsart began to direct his attention to the study of the viol da gamba, of which he became very fond in a short time. In 1889 he played some old music with Diémer, who was a virtuoso on the harpsichord. They were joined after a time by two more enthusiasts, L. van Waefelghem, who played the viol d'amour, and L. Grillet, a viellist (hurdy-gurdy player), who had received through his father and grandfather the traditions of the celebrated old French school of viellists. These four artists formed the Sociétée des Instruments Anciens, which travelled all over Europe with phenomenal success *(see Part I, page 119)*. Delsart who as violoncellist, was one of the foremost artists of France, possessed a faultless technique, an elegant bow and sympathetic though not very powerful tone. He was heard in London on several occasions, one being the first performance of Popper's Requiem for three violoncellos, in which he took part with the composer and Edward Howell. His contributions to violoncello literature consist chiefly of arrangements and editions of classical and modern compositions, including the Violin Sonata in A by César Franck.

JEAN FRANÇOIS GASTON BARBOT, excellent violoncellist and pianist, born 1847, at Toulouse.

EMILE DIENNE, born 1843, at Cambrai, studied under Fr. Servais at the Brussels Conservatoire, which he left in 1863, when he settled in Lille as teacher of music and principal violoncello in the municipal orchestra.

ALBERT BOUBÉE, born at Naples in 1850, originally destined for a mercantile career, and as he showed an aversion for this, his parents intended him to become a school teacher. His love for music eventually asserted itself triumphantly, and he studied the violoncello under Gaëtano Ciaudelli. Afterwards he received also advice and encouragement from Servais and Piatti. He toured successfully in Scandinavia, and filled passing engagements at Spa and Scarborough. His principal field of activity is London, where he settled in 1867, and became well known under the name of B. Albert, as soloist, chamber music player and teacher of his instrument. He has also established a great reputation as singing master. He has written a number of solos and a useful book of exercises, "La Gymnastique du Violoncelliste."

JULIUS LEOPOLD LOEB, born May 13, 1852, at Strassburg in Alsace, studied at the Paris Conservatoire under Chevillard, where he gained the first prize, and eventually succeeded J. F. Rabaud as teacher. He is solo violoncello at the Opera and the conservatoire concerts, and member of the Marsick Quartet.

ALBERT SAUTREUIL, born at Havre, in 1858, received the first instructions in violoncello playing from his father. Afterwards he entered the Paris Conservatoire, where he studied under Franchomme. He was appointed violoncellist in the Pasdeloup Orchestra and at the Opera Comique. He founded, together with other musicians, a society for the performance of classical and modern music at Havre.

PLATE XLI.
LISA B. CHRISTIANI.

ERNEST GILLET was born September 13, 1856, in Paris, where he entered Niedermeyer's school of music at the age of twelve. In 1871 he became a pupil of Auguste Franchomme at the Paris Conservatoire, where he gained the first prize in 1874. He was for some time solo violoncellist of the Grand Opera, and afterwards went to London, where he resided until the commencement of this century as soloist, member of various orchestras and teacher. About the beginning of this century he returned to France. He has written a number of drawing-room pieces, some of which attained great popularity ("Loin du Bal"), and also a number of arrangements, including some melodious and clever pieces by the late G. Contin (Count Giuseppe Contin de Castel Szeprio).

JEAN TOLBECQUE, born at Niort, October 7, 1857, a son of Auguste Tolbecque, is mentioned by Riemann as a talented violoncellist. He took the first violoncello prize at the Paris Conservatoire in 1873.

JULES RÉNÉ PETIEAU, born 1869, gained the first prize for violoncello playing in 1889. He is mentioned by Forino as professor of the Rouen Conservatoire and principal violoncello at the theatre of that town.

HORACE BRITT, born in the seventies, in Paris, is member of a very musical family. His brother Roger is an excellent viola player, who at an early age was solo viola in Colonne's orchestra, and his sister, Mme. Merk-Britt, is a distinguished harpist. Horace Britt studied the violoncello at the Paris Conservatoire under Delsart, and gained the first prize. In 1896 he played at the Ostend Kursaal, where, according to the "Musical Courier," he made a favourable impression, and on July 15 he made a successful debut at the Sallé Pleyel with an interesting programme, including the first Saint-Saëns concerto, "Chants Russes" from Lalo's concerto, and a manuscript "Concertstück" by J. Calaerts.

ALBERT HUSSO, born (according to Forino) at Douay, in 1874 ( ) studied at the Paris Conservatoire under Chevillard and Jacquard. He was appointed teacher of the National School of Music at Douay in 1888, and died there in 1899. The dates given above would make Husso a *teacher* at the age of fourteen, which is evidently erroneous.

THÉODORE VERGUET, born May 27, 1881, at Villefranche (Saône-Rhône), studied at the Paris Conservatoire under Professor Loeb and Joseph Hollman. He left that institution with the "first accessit." and also obtained the prize for violoncello at the Lyons Conservatoire. He is at present professor at the National School of Music and solo violoncellist at the Grand Theatre at Tours.

MARCEL RINGEISEN, born December 14, 1885, at Dyon (Côte d'Or), studied at the Paris Conservatoire under Professor Loeb. On July 16, 1906, he obtained the first prize at that institute, and he is now professor of violoncello at the Conservatoire of Toulouse and solo violoncellist at the concert society of that town.

PAUL BAZELAIRE, born 1886, studied the violoncello under Delsart at the Paris Conservatoire, where he obtained the first prize in 1897. He has appeared with great success in some of the principal towns of northern Europe, and is still living at Paris. He is also a good pianist.

ANDREAS HEKKING, nephew and pupil of Charles J. Hekking, teacher of the Conservatoire at Bordeaux, is now living as violoncellist of that town, of which he is a native.

Among French violoncellists of the present day we have still to mention: PROFESSOR A. BARETTI, MARIE (MARGUERITE?) BAUDE, born at Lille studied at the Paris Conservatoire under Jules Delsart, gaining the first prize, she ranks among the foremost lady violoncellists; MARCEL CASADESUS, pupil of Jules Delsart at the Paris Conservatoire, also excellent gambist, and member of the Société des Instruments Anciens *(see Part I, page 119)*; MLLE. CLÉMENT; DACHAMBEAU; DESCORTE; PIERRE DESTOMBE; LOUIS HASSELMANS; R. LAFARGE; MLLE. LARONDE; A. MERCADIER; SCHIDENHELM (mentioned by Forino); F. TOUCHE.

CHAPTER XXVIII.

THE VIOLONCELLO IN BELGIUM FROM THE END OF THE SEVEN-
TEENTH CENTURY TO 1900.

WILLIAM DEFESCH (DE FESCH), born in the Netherlands about the end of the seventeenth century, was an excellent musician, noted in his time as violoncellist, violinist, organist, choirmaster and composer. He was organist of Antwerp Cathedral, and there succeeded Alfonso d'Eve as master of the chapel in 1725, but owing to ill-treatment of some of the choirboys, he was dismissed in 1731. He went to London, where he produced his oratorio, "Judith," in 1733, and another one, "Joseph," in 1745, which met with a fair amount of success. He composed also a mass for voices and orchestra, and solos and concertos for various instruments, including Six Solos for Violoncello, Op. 8, published at Amsterdam. Burney characterises his compositions as dry and uninteresting, but he was like most amateurs of his day, so saturated with the prevailing operatic style of the Italians, that anything like a healthy melody bearing the character of national songs did not appeal to him. As a matter of fact, Defesch has written most delightful music, as may be seen from A. Moffat's edition of some of his violoncello sonatas, etc. Defesch died in London about 1758 (Grégoir mentions 1760 as the year). The accompanying portrait (Plate XLII), is from an engraving dated 1751 by F. Morellon le Cave after a painting by A. Soldi.

Fétis, in his biographical notice of d'Eve, says that in 1719 he composed a mass for two choirs with orchestra, in which appears a "violoncello *obbligato*." This is undoubtedly one of the first instances of such a part.

PETER WILLIAM WINKIS, born in 1735 at Liège, was engaged as violoncellist in the court chapel at Cassels, where we find him, in 1782 (according to Cramer's "Magazine," Volume I, January 22), together with Thorwart, who left before 1783. Winkis remained until some time after the dissolution of the chapel in 1787. About 1788 he was, according to Gerber, a member of the chapel of the Queen of Prussia, and had the reputation of possessing great skill in the accompaniment of the recitative from a figured bass. That art, which required taste and musicianship, was obviated by the writing out and scoring of these accompaniments.

JOSEPH MÜNTZBERGER, born 1769, at Brussels, of German parentage, was the son of Wenceslas Müntzberger, a chamber musician of Prince Charles of Lorraine, Governor of the Netherlands. At the age of six he played, according to Fétis, a concerto before the Prince on a large viola which he held violoncello fashion. Fétis adds that the Prince was so struck with the boy's talent that he placed him under Van Maldere, the famous violinist, to be further educated. This statement, however, is based on some erroneous tradition, as Van Maldere died the year before Müntzberger was born. At the age of fourteen he went to Paris, where he studied without a master solely by the aid of Tillière's tutor, until he could play the most difficult pieces of that time. In 1790 he received an appointment at the Théatre Lyrique et Comique, which he exchanged soon after for a similar appointment at the Théatre

Feydeau (not Favart, as in Fétis), as appears from the title page of his violoncello tutor. Later on he succeeded Cardon as principal violoncello at that theatre. He was also a member of the Imperial Chapel of Napoleon, and afterwards of the Royal Chapel. As a soloist he appeared frequently in public, especially at the concerts of the "Rue de Clery," which were in great favour at the beginning of last century. He retired in 1830 on a pension, and died January, 1844.

Müntzberger was a prolific composer for his instrument; he published five concertos, a "Symphonie Concertante," duets, trios, sonatas, fantasias, variations, studies, and a "Nouvelle Methode pour le Violoncelle," mentioned above. The latter, which appeared before 1800, still contains the use of the alto and treble C clefs which were employed by Haydn, Boccherini, etc., but fell into desuetude from the commencement of last century.

HENRY FEMY, the younger, born at Gand about 1787, studied in 1807 under Baudiot at the Paris Conservatoire. On April 5, 1807, he played with distinction a concerto by his master at the conservatoire concerts. In 1808 he played again at the concerts, this time a concerto by J. De Lamarre *(see page 292)*, and in the same year he gained the first prize in Baudiot's class. He travelled successfully in France, Italy and England, and is also the composer of a number of pieces and duets for his instrument.

LOUIS DECORTIS, born at Liège, November 15, 1793, as the son of a violoncellist of some merit. His father gave him the first instructions in violoncello playing, and about 1824 sent him to Paris, where he studied at the conservatoire successively under Hus-Desforges, Benazet and Norblin. On May 1, 1827, he was elected professor at the Liège Conservatoire, where, on his retirement, he was succeeded by Léon Massart. He died at Liège in 1871.

ADRIEN FRANÇOIS SERVAIS, born June 6, 1807, at Hal, near

Brussels. His father, the organist of Hal, instructed him in the art of violin playing and the elements of music. The Marquis de Sayre, who resided in the neighbourhood of Hal, heard the boy play, and was so struck with his talent that he

FIG. 58. A. F. SERVAIS.

sent him to Brussels to study under Van der Planken, the leader of the Brussels Opera. One day he heard Platel, and the playing of that remarkable artist made such an impression upon his youthful mind that he resolved to devote himself to the study of the violoncello. He entered the conservatoire and became a pupil of Platel, making such rapid strides that he gained the first prize at the end of his first year at that institute. Platel appointed him as his assistant at the conservatoire, and at the same time he joined the orchestra of the Opera. He remained in that position for three years, only to find that nobody is a prophet in his own country. Not before his debut in Paris did he meet with great and decided success. In 1834 he appeared for the first time, and met with an enthusiastic reception. Instead of flattering his vanity, these successes awakened in him still higher artistic aspirations, and on his return to Brussels he entered upon a period of renewed study. In 1836 he revisited Paris, where he renewed his former success. In the following year he visited Holland, in 1839 he went to St. Petersburg, and in 1840 he returned to Hal and thence he revisited Brussels and Antwerp, where he was now at last recognised as the great artist the world had seen in him from the very outset of his career. In 1841 he toured again in eastern Europe, Vienna, Prague, Warsaw, and thence to Russia, meeting with the greatest enthusiasm. In 1842 he was married in St. Petersburg. In the following year he toured in Holland, and in 1844 he revisited Germany, where, among many eminent artists, he was greatly admired by Mendelssohn, who played Beethoven's Trio in B flat, Op. 7, with David and Servais at the latter's concert at Leipzig, and also conducted the orchestra at his concert in Berlin on January 19 of that year. In 1847 he was in Paris again, and afterwards toured in Scandinavia. In 1848 the King of Belgium nominated him his solo violoncellist and teacher at the Brussels Conservatoire, and from that time he devoted himself chiefly to the duties of his office and to composition. In 1866 he was induced to revisit Russia, extending his tour right into Siberia. The exertions of that tour appear to have been the cause of his death, which took place on November 25, 1866, at his native town of Hal, where he had

PLATE XLII.
WILLIAM DEFESCH.

gone for rest and recovery. As a virtuoso Servais had not his equal during his lifetime. From a contemporary writer we hear that: "Under his big and powerful hand the violoncello vibrated as easily as a 'kit' (pochette). His staccato in single notes, thirds and octaves up to the highest registers, showed a crispness and surety of intonation that was quite phenomenal." Another says: "His music is the embodiment of virtuosity, and as such can never serve as a model for the student to work upon like that of Duport, Romberg, Dotzauer, Kummer, etc. The works of the latter masters, studied systematically, will assist in the acquisition of a light and supple, yet powerful bow, whereas the fountain spray of Servais's fireworks will only incite to imitation, which at the best will but produce a copy, and generally a weak one." This was the general idea of violoncello teachers during the seventies and eighties of last century, but we have since learned that with the far higher standard of the technique of our present day, no more valuable and very little more attractive material for the study of very advanced pupils can be found. The writer has it from many artists who recollect Servais's playing well and from some who studied under him that he combined with a powerful tone of the finest quality, a brilliant execution of unfailing accuracy, and a most subtle and delicate phrasing. Moreover, he was an excellent musician, and apart from his own and Charles Schuberth's virtuoso pieces, he played a good many compositions by the classical masters. Servais's appearance denotes an epoch in violoncello playing, as he opened entirely new roads. Especially with regard to the passage work he was distinctly original, and if some of his effects savoured a little of the musical acrobat, they are in a minority against many elegant and beautiful figures and passages. Among his numerous compositions are three concertos, sixteen fantasias, a number of duos with piano or violin, partly in collaboration with Grégoire, Léonard and Vieuxtemps, and six excellent caprices. Among his numerous pupils we mention: Meerens, De Swert, Fischer and Bekker. Servais played on a Stradivari violoncello of the large pattern, called "basso di chiesa," in Italy. These instruments were also used in processions, and frequently had a little hole in the centre of the back through which a hook attached to a strap (bandolier) was passed, to enable the player to carry it suspended from the shoulders. Servais's violoncello belonged formerly to Raoul, the French violoncellist, who was also the owner of the famous Duiffoprugcar gamba with the plan of Paris (*see Part I, page 15*).

PIERRE ALEXANDRE FRANÇOIS CHEVILLARD, born January 15, 1811, at Antwerp, received his first music lessons in his parental home. He went to Paris at an early age and entered the famous conservatoire on March 15, 1820, where he studied under Norblin until 1827, when he carried off the first prize for violoncello playing. He received an appointment as solo violoncellist at the Théâtre Gymnase, where he remained until 1831, continuing his theoretical studies under Fétis. During that time he undertook several very successful concert tours. In 1829 he made his debut at the Théâtre Royale at Brussels with an "Air Varié" by Merk, when his brilliant technique and refinement of style were generally commented upon. In 1831 he became solo violoncellist of the Italian Opera in Paris, and in 1859 he succeeded Vaslin as professor at the conservatoire. Chevillard was not only an excellent virtuoso but also an artist filled with the highest ideals. He was one of the few in his time who recognised the greatness of the later quartets of Beethoven, which caused him to found, in 1835, a string quartet called Société des derniers Quatuors de Beethoven. In 1839 they gave *matinées* at the Salon Petzold with Alard as leader, but Chevillard's zeal and intelligence could not compensate for the want of these qualities in some of his colleagues, and it was not until 1849 that he found in Maurin,

Vignier and Sabbatier, kindred spirits who proved themselves equal to the task. Their clear and intelligent rendering soon awakened a better understanding of those monumental compositions in their listeners, and they emerged from private performances by taking the Salle Pleyel, where all the more serious amateurs rallied round them. Vignier had by that time been replaced by Mas. In 1855-6 they travelled in Germany, visiting Cologne, Frankfort, Darmstadt, Berlin, Hanover, etc., where they did much to popularise those latter Beethoven quartets, which were very little known at that time among the great master's own countrymen. In 1868 Chevillard retired from that combination and Ernest De Munck took his place. Chevillard died on December 18, 1877, in Paris.

A humorous account of him by Louis Roux appeared in the "Salon" of 1868, under the title "Joli croquis a la gaguine de Chevillard." He composed a concerto, a number of solos and a "Méthode Complète de Violoncelle, contenant la théorie de l'instrument, gammes, leçons progressives, études, airs variés et leçons pour chacune des positions."

JOACHIM BOISSEAUX, born at Namur about 1812, went to Paris at an early age, and studied the violoncello under Romberg and Norblin. He was appointed solo violoncellist at the Paris Opera, and his eminent talent gained for him the friendship of Baillot, the great violinist. On December 24, 1845, he played at a concert at Namur, where he met with great success. In 1860 he was appointed teacher of violoncello at the Luxemburg Conservatoire. He died at the latter town.

CONSTANT NOËL ADOLPHE WAROT, born November 28, 1812, at Antwerp, commenced at an early age the study of violin playing, but exchanged the violin afterwards for the violoncello. He was appointed teacher at the Brussels Conservatoire in 1852, and trained many excellent pupils. A "Méthode pour Violoncelle" of his was used at that institute, and besides this he composed some duets for two violoncellos and an "Air Varié" with pianoforte. Warot died at Brussels, April 10, 1875.

JULES DENEFRE, born 1814, at Chimay, in the Belgian province of Hainault, entered the Brussels Conservatoire in 1833 —the same year as Warot—and studied the violoncello successively under Platel and De Munck, Fétis being his master in musical theory. After leaving the conservatoire he was for some time principal violoncello at the Brussels Opera, and later on also a teacher of violoncello at the Mons School of Music, and conductor of the Société des Concerts at Mons. In 1841 he founded the choral society "Roland de Lattre" (Orlandus de Lassus), of which he was also the conductor.

Three operas of his composition were performed at Mons; besides these he wrote a number of cantatas, a requiem and minor choral works, but apparently nothing for the violoncello. He died August 19, 1877.

FRANÇOIS DE MUNCK, born October 6, 1815, at Brussels. His father was a teacher of music and bandmaster (chef d'orchestre de la Grande Harmonie in 1824), who instructed him in the elements of music, etc., and sent him at the age of ten to the conservatoire, where he became a pupil of Platel. In 1828 he played at a public concert at the old school of music, and in 1834 he left the conservatoire with the first prize. In 1835 he was appointed Platel's substitute at that institute. He combined a brilliant technique and elegance of style with breadth and nobility of tone. In 1842 he produced at the Société Philharmonique at Brussels a fine concerto by Ch. Hanssens with great success.

Failing health prevented him from fulfilling the arduous duties of his professorship, and in 1845 he obtained leave to travel. In company with a lady vocalist, he toured in Germany, and in 1848 he relinquished definitely his position at the conservatoire, where he was succeeded by Servais. De

Munck then accepted an engagement as principal violoncello at Her Majesty's Theatre in London. The continued decline of his health, however, compelled him to renounce that position also, and he returned to Brussels early in 1853, and died there on February 28, 1854. He published a fantasia on Russian airs as Op. 1. His portrait appears on Plate XLIII. His son Ernest is now living as an eminent violoncellist in London *(see page 553).*

J. B. VAN VOLXEM, born November 30, 1817, at Uccles (Brussels). He studied under Platel at the Brussels Conservatoire, which he entered in 1833, and left eventually with the second prize for violoncello playing as well as for composition. He was afterwards engaged as chorus master at the Brussels Opera and devoted himself henceforth to choir training, in which capacity he established a great reputation in his native country.

PIÈRRE DE MOL, born November 7, 1825, at Brussels, studied the violoncello and composition at the Royal Conservatoire. In 1855 he obtained the Prix de Rome for his cantata, "Les Premiers Martyres," another cantata, "Hercula," was also performed with success, but neither was published. De Mol was appointed teacher of violoncello at the conservatoire and solo violoncello at the theatre at Besançon.

CHARLES DETRY, born at Brussels about the second decade of last century, was an excellent violoncellist who appeared in Paris as a soloist in 1846. He played a concerto and "Souvenir de Spa" at a *soirée musicale* by Mr. Coche with great success. His daughter:

ELISA DETRY, was also an excellent violoncellist, who made her debut at the musical society, Diligentia, at the Hague on January 10, 1866, and afterwards in Paris, meeting with great success on both occasions. She married a Mr. Doutrelon, of Paris, and retired from public life.

J. LEJEUNE, born at Namur about 1820, gained the first prize for violoncello playing at the Brussels Conservatoire in 1845.

550   THE HISTORY OF THE VIOLONCELLO.

He was appointed solo violoncellist at the theatre at Bordeaux, and for twenty years he was professor at the Société de Sainte

Fig. 59. William Paque.

Cécile of that town. His pupil, Mirekki, obtained the laureate ship of the Paris Conservatoire.

WILLIAM (GUILLEAUME) PAQUE was born at Brussels, July 25, 1825. At the age of ten he entered the conservatoire, which he left in 1841 after gaining the first prize. His first appointment was at the Opera (Théâtre de la Monnaie), which he left a few years later with the intention of settling in Paris. In 1845 he accepted an offer of the directorship of the conservatoire at Barcelona and solo violoncellist at the Italian Opera of that town. In 1849 he played before the Queen of Spain, and in 1850 he toured in the south of France, thence going to England, where he remained, settling in London. He was solo violoncello at the Royal Opera, Covent Garden, member of the Queen's band and teacher at the London Academy of Music, where he obtained a high reputation as a pedagogue. Paque died March 3, 1876. He composed about thirty works for violoncello, including the well-known quartet for four violoncellos, "Souvenir de Curis." His portrait appears in Fig. 59.

CHARLES MONTIGNY, born January 30, 1827, at Brussels, was for some time solo violoncellist to the Duke of Saxe-Coburg. In 1848 he was solo violoncello in E. Stumpf's orchestra at Amsterdam, where he played the solo part in Gregoir's symphony, "Les Croisades." Afterwards he was professor at the Imperial Conservatoire at St. Petersburg. He died at Brussels, February 1, 1866.

LÉON PANGAERT D'OPDORP, an accomplished violoncellist, who wrote a Concerto in E minor, Op. 3, for violoncello and pianoforte (Schott).

HENRI POSSOZ, born 1827 at Hal, studied the violoncello and composition at the Brussels Conservatoire, where he obtained the laureateship in 1844. He was appointed solo violoncellist at the Théâtre Royale and professor at the school of music. Possoz was an excellent all-round musician, and as such he was chosen as director of the Cercle Artistique, conductor of the German Liedertafel and several other choral societies. In 1854 he settled at Antwerp, where he gave chamber concerts with Voué and Stephanie. In 1882 he became professor of the École Normale de l'État at Antwerp, and solo violoncellist in the municipal orchestra.

CHARLES HERREYNS, born at Antwerp in 1828, was a pupil of François Servais and H. Simon. For a period of twenty years he filled the post of solo violoncellist at the Antwerp theatre and in the concert orchestra of that town. On February 17, 1857, a festival play or cantata in praise of the Netherlandish poet and dramatist, "Tollens" (Tollens Verheerlijkt), was performed with great success. Like his colleague, Van Volxem, he had the cultivation of choral singing at heart, which always received, and still receives great attention in Belgium, and he became conductor of several choral societies, writing a number of compositions for chorus of male voices. He composed also a number of solos, etc., for violoncello, and died at Antwerp, January 28, 1884.

ISIDORE JEAN GASPAR DE SWERT, born January 6, 1830, at Louvain, was an elder brother of the famous Jules De Swert *(see page 553)*. He studied under François De Munck, obtained the first prize at the Brussels Conservatoire in 1846, and was appointed teacher of the violoncello at the school of music, and solo violoncello at the theatre of Bruges in 1850. In 1856 he succeeded Warot in the same capacity at the Brussels Opera (Théâtre de la Monnaie), and afterwards he was appointed as teacher at the Royal Conservatoire at Brussels and the Louvain Conservatoire. For a number of years he was a member of the Rhenish Festival Orchestra. He died at Brussels in September, 1896.

LAMOURY, born 1837 at Brussels, shared the first prize of the conservatoire with E. De Munck in 1855.

CHARLES MEERENS, born at Bruges, December 26, 1831, was the son of a flautist who settled at Antwerp in 1845. He received his first lessons on the violoncello from Joseph Bessems and continued under Dumont at Gand. Returning to Bruges, he founded an amateur musical society Les Francs

PLATE XLIII.

François De Munck. From a Portrait in the Possession of Henry Francis Brown, Esq.

To face page 552.

Amis, and managed a music shop established by his father. In 1855 he went to Brussels to renew his studies of the violoncello under Servais. He established a considerable reputation as acoustician and author on various musical subjects.

PIERRE JOSEPH ERNEST DE MUNCK, born December 21, 1840, at Brussels, is the younger of two sons of François De Munck *(see page 548)*. Studying under his father's guidance, he appeared in public as a prodigy on the violoncello at the early age of eight. Two years later he made a successful debut in London. In 1854 he became a pupil of Fr. Servais at the Brussels Conservatoire, and in the following year he shared the first prize with Lamoury. After this he travelled as soloist with Jullien's orchestra in Great Britain. In 1864 he played an unpublished duo for violin and violoncello by Vieuxtemps with his brother Camille at Saint-Saëns's concert in Paris. From 1868-70 he was violoncellist of the Maurin Quartet. At the Pasdeloup concert he played the ninth concerto by Romberg with such success that the Société des Concerts de Paris awarded to him the grand commemorative medal. In 1871 he went to Weimar as solo violoncello of the grand ducal chapel, and became very friendly with Liszt. An attack of paralysis of the left hand in October, 1874, compelled him to relinquish a tour in Germany. He returned to Brussels, where he was completely cured, so that he was able to tour with Rubinstein in Russia in 1876. In 1879 he married Carlotta Patti, and they toured together in California, Australia, etc., arriving 1881 in Batavia, where they gave a number of very successful concerts. In 1882 De Munck played Saint-Saëns's Concerto in A minor at the last "Concert Populaire," meeting with a sensational reception. During the latter part of last century he became professor at the Guildhall School of Music, London, which he resigned about 1912.

JULES DE SWERT, born August 16, 1843, at Louvain. His father, choirmaster at the cathedral and a well-known singing master, gave him the first instructions in violoncello playing, and produced him as his pupil at public concerts. Servais, who heard the boy on one of these occasions, was struck with his talent and induced him to enter the conservatoire, where he became Fr. Servais's pupil. At the age of fourteen he was "laureate" of the conservatoire. He then went to Paris, where he was greatly admired, especially by Rossini, who said that "if he only preserved his mecanisme pure and simple he would be one of the greatest violoncellists of the age."

After a period of successful touring in Scandinavia and a visit to the court at Hanover, he was, in 1869, appointed as concertmeister at Cologne, but soon after settled at Düsseldorf, where, in conjunction with Madame Schumann and Professor Leopold von Auer, he gave trio soirées where the works of classical and modern masters were performed in a manner that has rarely been equalled. In 1868 De Swert went to Weimar as solo violoncellist of the ducal chapel, but already in the following year he was induced to go to Berlin as royal concertmeister, solo violoncellist of the royal chapel and teacher at the Hochschule. In 1873 he relinquished that position, and after a tour through Russia and a visit to Italy (Milan) he took up his residence at Sonnenberg, near Wiesbaden, where he devoted himself chiefly to composition. In 1876 he went to Bayreuth, where, at the request of Wagner, he undertook the formation of the orchestra in which he was the solo violoncellist. In 1878 his first opera, "Die Albigenser," was produced at Wiesbaden, Frankfort, Hamburg, etc., and met with a favourable reception. In 1881 he went to Leipzig, where he wrote his second opera, "Graf Hammerstein," which had its *première* at Mayence in 1884. In 1888 he went to Ostend as director of the local conservatoire and teacher of the conservatoire of Gand and Bruges. He died at Ostend, February 24, 1891.

De Swert is one of the most remarkable personalities in

the history of violoncello playing. He was of short stature and square-built; very broad-chested and muscular. In appearance he was very much like a sailor, and in his ways and manners still more. His tone was superb, powerful yet full of sweetness, and technical difficulties were unknown to him. He was an excellent musician, who never lowered his art to mere firework displays. The writer remembers well his playing of the Sixth Solo Sonata by Bach, which was such that the impression of that performance, early in the seventies of last century, never faded. The violin concertos by Beethoven and Mendelssohn, arranged by himself, had both their place in his repertoire, while the compositions of Servais and Charles Schuberth were included as virtuoso pieces.

Among the many honours and distinctions which were showered upon him was the title of solo violoncellist to the Emperor of Austria. Apart from the above-mentioned operas he composed a symphony, "Nordseefahrt," and a number of compositions for the violoncello which are often distinguished by their melodious invention and interesting harmonic treatment. His concertos and many of his minor pieces are deserving of notice. He has also written a tutor which, however, is rather primitive.

ADOLPHE FISCHER, born November 22, 1847 (1850 according to Wasielewski), of German origin. He received his first instructions in music from his father, a well-known conductor of choral societies. Later on he entered the Brussels Conservatoire, where he studied under Servais and gained the first prize at the age of sixteen. In 1868 he went to Paris, and visited thence the principal towns of Germany, where he met with great success. Failing health compelled him to abandon the violoncello for the latter part of his life, and retiring to Belgium, he died near Brussels in 1891. He has written a considerable number of solo pieces for the violoncello which belong to the so-called *salon* music. They are effectively written for the instrument, and some have become very popular, particularly his "Tarantelle" and "Czardas." He has also published a number of clever transcriptions.

JEAN PREUVENEERS, born March 26, 1865, at Brussels, studied the violoncello under Watelle (government inspector of music in the Belgian schools) and Joseph Servais, at the Brussels Conservatoire, where Jos. Dupont instructed him in harmony and composition. He received his first engagement at the conservatoire concerts and the Concerts Populaires at Brussels. Later on he became a member of the Lamoureux Orchestra in Paris, and thence he went to London, where he was appointed as violoncellist in the Queen's Hall Orchestra. Under Gottlieb he played at the court concerts at Sandringham and Windsor. He was until recently principal violoncellist in the New Symphony Orchestra and member of the John Saunders Quartet in London. He has toured in England as violoncellist of the Harrison chamber concerts. He possesses a Jean Baptiste Vuillaume violoncello which by some is considered the finest specimen of that maker.

EDOUARD JACOBS, born 1851, at Hal, was a choirboy at the age of fourteen. When Claes, the double-bass player, a cousin of Servais, died, Jacobs was offered the place on condition that he studied that instrument for one year at the Brussels Conservatoire. He did so, and received the first prize at the end of the year. At the age of twenty he took up the violoncello and was awarded the first prize in the class of Gustave Libotton. After that he received some finishing lessons by Joseph Servais. He was appointed member of the Ducal Chapel at Saxe-Weimar under Ed. Lassen. Returning to Brussels, he became solo violoncello at the Théâtre de la Monnaie. In 1879 he was appointed second professor of violoncello at the conservatoire. In 1878 he toured in Germany and France, etc., and played the Vieuxtemps concerto at the "Intrumentalverein" at Aix-la-Chapelle with great success. In

1885, after the death of Joseph Servais, he succeeded his former master as first professor at the conservatoire. He instituted chamber concerts at the Palais des Beaux Arts with Hermann, Coëlho and van Hamme. Jacobs has toured with immense success in France, Belgium, Germany and Holland, and since 1892 he is engaged every year for the season at Pawlowsk, near St. Petersburg. He is an excellent soloist, possessing a powerful tone of great beauty. Moreover, he is a very fine chamber music player and an incomparable executant on the viol da gamba, and as such he appeared recently with great success at the Queen's Hall.

FRANÇOIS ARNOUTS, born May 10, 1857, at Antwerp, studied about 1876 at the Brussels Conservatoire under Joseph Servais, and gained the first prize. In 1878 he was appointed teacher at the Conservatoire of Port Louis, Isle of Mauritius, where he died on September 2, 1882.

ALFONS JUSLEGERS, born January 1, 1869, at Bruges, studied under Rappé, De Swert, and finally under Ed. Jacobs at the Brussels Conservatoire. He was in 1903 teacher at the conservatoire at Douai.

CHARLES VAN ISTERDAEL, born 1873, at Mons, studied at the Brussels Conservatoire under Ed. Jacobs, and gained the first prize. He was appointed teacher at the Mons Conservatoire and afterwards solo violoncellist at the Hague Opera. Since 1903 he is also teacher at the conservatoire of that town.

JEAN GÉRARDY, born December 6, 1878, at Liège, as the son of Dieudonné Gérardy, a teacher of the pianoforte at the conservatoire of that town. At the early age of five he commenced the study of the violoncello under Richard Bellmann. Eighteen months later he obtained already the second prize at the conservatoire, and in 1889 he received the gold medal by unanimous consent of the jury. In the previous year he had already appeared in various Belgian towns as a soloist, and even taken part in a trio with Ignaz Paderewski and Eugene

Ysaye at a charity concert (at Anstrudel ?) says Mr. B. Windust and Messrs. G. C. and T. A. Trowell. While Bellmann was on tour—that last tour of the Heckmann Quartet whicn ended fatally with the death of its founder—Massau conducted Gérardy's studies at the conservatoire. In December, 1890, he made his debut in London in the company of eminent artists, and was received with enthusiasm. The fame of the twelve-year-old boy spread like wildfire, it was difficult to obtain admittance at his subsequent recitals, and he was commanded by Queen Victoria to play before the court at Windsor. In the following year, at the early age of thirteen, he played at a concert of the Philharmonic Orchestra under Hans Richter in Vienna. After that he went to Dresden, where he studied for some time under Friedrich Grützmacher, and then began a long period of touring which extended all over the civilised world. Mr. Heymann tells us in a letter to "The Strad" from San Francisco, how he dined with Gérardy, the lion of the day, at the principal hotel, which a few days later, was a smouldering heap of ruins. On February 26, 1903, Gérardy made his reappearance in London, no longer the little prodigy in knickerbockers but now one of the greatest violoncellists the world possesses. With a powerful singing tone Gérardy possesses to the fullest the agility, grace and elegance of the French style of bowing, with the deep thoughtfulness, breadth and dignity of reading which he inherited from Bellmann, Grützmacher and the German school.

There is no need to speak of the technique of the left hand, for that is a matter of course with all modern virtuosos. Be it said to his praise that he is in every respect an artist of the highest order who looks for the best and noblest in art, and although he has an open eye to the finest productions, he eschews anything trivial or merely calculated for outward show or technical display.

His instrument, which he acquired from Mr. George Hart in London, is a Stradivari dated 1710.

GABRIELLE PLATTEAU was a native of Belgium. She studied at the Brussels Conservatoire under Fr. Servais (unless we are greatly mistaken.) In 1873 she made a very successful debut at the Crystal Palace, London, and in that or the following year the writer heard her at the Gürzenich at Cologne. She played Servais's "Souvenir de Spa" and some smaller solos with a facile and brilliant technique. Her tone was always beautiful but not very powerful, which could only be expected from a young lady scarce out of her teens. She was of prepossessing appearance and had before her a brilliant career which was unfortunately cut short by her untimely death, which took place on March 9, 1875, at Ixelles, a suburb of Brussels.

DAMBOIS is mentioned in "The Strad" of April, 1907, as taking part at the Scola Musica at Brussels, on March 11, in a performance of chamber music compositions by M. Jongen, with the composer Chaumont, violin, and Engelbrot, viola. The music and performance is noticed in very eulogistic terms. It is worth notice that M. Jongen is also the composer of a violoncello concerto.

GUSTAVE LIBOTTON, a Belgian by birth, studied at the Brussels Conservatoire under François Servais. In 1864 he appeared with Strauss at St. Petersburg, where he met with great success. In 1869 he was appointed junior professor at the Brussels Conservatoire and solo violoncellist at the Théâtre de la Monnaie. In 1880 he became professor at the Guildhall School of Music, where he was highly esteemed as teacher. He died in London.

CHAPTER XXIX.

THE VIOLONCELLO IN HOLLAND FROM THE END OF THE EIGHTEENTH CENTURY TO 1900.

JEAN ARNOLD DAMMEN (DAHMEN) born at the Hague in 1760, belonged to a numerous family of Dutch musicians. He was an excellent violoncellist who settled in London towards the end of the eighteenth century. In 1794 he was principal violoncello at Drury Lane Theatre, and in 1796-7 he toured in South Germany. He composed a number of solos (sonatas) and duets for his instrument, besides string trios and quartets. His son, born in London, appears among the English violoncellists.

PETER BATTA, born August 8, 1795, at Maastricht, was for some time teacher of the violoncello and solfèges at the conservatoire at Brussels, where he died, November 20, 1876. The name of his teacher is not recorded. The most prominent among his pupils was his son, Alexander *(see below)*.

ANDREW TEN CATE, born 1796, at Amsterdam, was originally intended to become a merchant, but his predilection for music, and the violoncello in particular, decided him at the age of fourteen to devote himself

Facsimile Autograph (Much Reduced) by A. Batta of an Album Leaf for the Wife of Ad. Henselt. It is taken from His "Etudes Characteristiques."

entirely to the study of that art. Jean Georg Bertelman was his teacher for the violoncello. He became chiefly known as a composer of three operas and vocal songs for single voices and choir of male voices. For the violoncello he wrote a few violoncello concertos. He died July 27, 1858.

JACQUES FRANCO MENDES, born at Amsterdam in 1816 (Mendel says 1812), descended from a family of Portuguese Jews. He showed early signs of musical talent, and commenced to study the violoncello under Präger, while Bertelman instructed him in musical theory. In 1829 he went to Vienna, where Merk became his master. Mendes, who had so far studied music as an amateur, decided at that period to choose music for his profession. In 1831 he toured with his brother, a talented violinist visiting Paris and London. In the latter town he made a successful debut at a concert given by Johann Nepomuk Hummel. On his return the King of Holland bestowed upon him the title of chamber violoncellist. In 1833 the brothers Franco Mendes gave successful concerts in Frankfort, Leipzig and Dresden, and in the following year Jacques was nominated first solo violoncellist to the King of Holland. In 1836 the two brothers revisited Paris where they remained for a longer period. In 1841 the violinist died, and his loss fell so heavily upon the brother that he renounced touring for several years, merely playing in the orchestra of the subscription concerts at Amsterdam, and in a few concerts of his own. In 1845 he took part in the grand festival at Bonn on the occasion of the unveiling of the Beethoven memorial. The "Allgemeine Musik Zeitung," in its report of the festival, says that his solos on that occasion were of a very superficial nature, ill suited for the occasion, and he failed to make any impression upon his audience. In 1860 (according to Wasielewski—Torino says 1861) he took up his permanent residence in Paris.

Franco Mendes wrote a considerable number of solos, a

duet for two violoncellos, fantasias, caprices, etc. An Adagio, Op. 48, retained its popularity for a long time. He left also a number of chamber music works, including two quintets and several quartets.

One of his most talented pupils was Charles Ernest Appy *(see following page)*.

ALEXANDER BATTA, born July 9, 1816, at Maastricht, received his first instructions in violin playing from his father, Peter Batta *(see above)*. When the latter became teacher at the Brussels Conservatoire, Alexander had an opportunity to hear the famous Platel, whose playing impressed him to such an extent that he decided to choose the violoncello for his instrument. His father consented, and he became Platel's pupil at the conservatoire, making such rapid progress that he divided the first prize with De Munck in 1834. In the following year he went to Paris where the tenor Rubini was at the zenith of his fame. Batta admired him so much that he adopted him as his model for style and delivery. Rubini shared the fault of many "virtuoso" singers, of inartistic exaggeration in *pianos* and *fortes* as well as in the "rubato" for the sake of startling and cheap effects. Batta copied his faults as well as his admirable qualities, adding an affected and coquettish mannerism which pleased the Parisians, and particularly the society ladies, making him the lion of the day. Batta possessed a magnificent Stradivari violoncello which he acquired from a French dealer in 1838 for the then considerable sum of 7,300 francs. He had several offers of various sums up to about ten times that amount, but he always refused to part with his treasure until 1895, when he sold it to Mr. E. Hill, of London, for £3,200. Though in his eightieth year, the parting from his beloved instrument caused him a feeling of intense regret, and he would not leave it before he had reverently kissed the instrument after it was placed in the train which was to take Mr. Hill with his newly acquired treasure to

England. Batta wrote a considerable amount of compositions for violoncello which is for the greater part entirely antiquated. Some of his studies, however, are very excellent, and will prove both useful and interesting. He died in Paris.

LOUIS VAN DER WULP, born April 19, 1824, at the Hague, studied at the Royal Conservatoire of that town. He was a very talented violoncellist and composer of some very effective cantatas for children. For some time he was director of music at Gouda, where he died at the early age of twenty-six in 1850.

CHARLES ERNEST APPY was born October 25, 1834, at the Hague, of French parentage. His father was a viola player in the royal chapel, but removed to Amsterdam, where the son commenced the study of the pianoforte under Richard Hol. At the age of fifteen he began to study the violoncello, his first master being Charles Montigny, and later on, Merlen, the first violoncellist in the Amsterdam Orchestra. He finished his studies under Franco Mendes, who was also his master in composition. He received his first appointment at Zaandam in 1851 as violoncellist of the concert orchestra, and appeared frequently as soloist in many towns of Holland. In 1854 he accompanied Joseph Gungl to Scotland as solo violoncellist of his orchestra, and remained there for six months. In 1856 we find him again at Amsterdam as member of the Park Orchestra and the society "Felix Meritis." In 1857 he played for six months at the Crystal Palace in London, returning in the winter of that year to Amsterdam as violoncellist in the St. Cäcilia Orchestra, and in 1862 he joined the Franz Coenen string quartet with which he was connected for nine years, during that time he played together with many great artists of the day like Mme. Schumann, Alfred Jaëll, Ernst Lübeck and others. In 1864 he was appointed teacher at the "Maatschappij tot Bevordering van Tonkunst," where he remained until 1883, with the exception of six months in 1871 when he went to New York as solo violoncellist of the Thomas Orchestra.

During that period Daniel de Lange took over his duties in Amsterdam. On his return from America Appy settled for a time at Haarlem as teacher of the violoncello and pianoforte, but removed again to Amsterdam in 1882 when he founded a prosperous school of music.

He wrote a number of fantasias, etc., on Italian operas and a few solos, his Nocturne, Op. 2, being both melodious and pleasing.

LOUIS LÜBECK, born February 14, 1838, at the Hague, is the son of Joh. H. Lübeck, the director of music at that town, and personal friend of Schumann. He received his first instructions in pianoforte playing, etc., from his father, but it was not before he was in his seventeenth year that he decided upon making music his profession, choosing the violoncello as his instrument. In 1857 he went to Paris where he studied under Léon Jacquard for two years, at the end of which time he toured successfully in France and Holland, and taking up his residence at Colmar. From that town he joined Mme. Schumann and Julius Stockhausen in concerts on various occasions. In 1866 he was appointed principal violoncellist in the Gewandhaus Orchestra and teacher at the conservatoire. Ferdinand von Hiller, who knew him well during that period, told the writer that he was an artist in every sense of the word. His technique, style and tone were alike beautiful, but an unconquerable bohemianism spoilt his career for many years after. In 1868 he left Leipzig for Frankfort-on-Main, where he was engaged at the conservatoire, but shortly after he left that position again and toured through Germany, Holland and England. In 1871 he was solo violoncellist in the court chapel at Carlsruhe, which he also left after about two years. In 1873 he went to Berlin and thence to St. Petersburg. On his return he was for one year a member of the court chapel at Sondershausen, and then left for North America where he toured for some years. In 1881 he returned to Berlin and was appointed solo violoncello of the royal chapel as successor of Julius Stahlknecht.

He wrote two concertos for violoncello (only one being published) and a number of minor solo pieces and transcriptions.

R. P. BEKKER, born May 23, 1839, at Winschoten, studied at the Brussels Conservatoire under François Servais from 1852 until 1855, when he obtained the first prize for violoncello playing.

He settled in Utrecht and received the title of solo violoncellist to the King of Holland in 1861. Bekker died in 1875, highly esteemed as a soloist and as a teacher.

EMILE DUNKLER, born about 1840 at the Hague, where his father (a Belgian from Namur) was bandmaster of the Dutch Grenadiers. No particulars about his earlier career are at hand. He lived the greater part of his life in Paris, where he established the reputation of a violoncellist possessing elegance of style combined with sweetness of tone, although his technical equipments did not permit of his being ranked with the virtuosos of the time. He is best known by a number of brilliant and effective, though superficial, compositions for violoncello which have been published by Fromant in Paris, in an edition revised by Jules Delsart.

DANIEL DE LANGE, born July 11, 1841, at Rotterdam, studied the violoncello under Simon Ganz and François Servais, and composition under Verhulst and Damcke. After completing his studies he toured with his brother, Samuel de Lange, a pianist, organist and composer. They visited Austria, and Daniel was appointed teacher of the violoncello at the conservatoire at Lemberg, where he remained for three years. In 1863 he went to Paris where he studied the pianoforte under Mme. Dubois, and also the organ. He was for some time organist of the evangelical church at Montrouge, the "free congregation," and conductor of the German "Liedertafel." In 1870 he returned to Amsterdam as teacher of the school of music (afterwards "conservatoire"), became secretary of the "Maatschappij tot bevordering van Tonkunst," deputy conductor of the Amstel male choir (for Coenen), and conductor of several other male choirs at Leyden and Amsterdam, with whom he toured in Germany and England, producing with sensational success, old Netherlandish *a capella* music. In 1895 he was appointed director of the Amsterdam Conservatoire. He is also musical critic and reporter of the "Niews van den Daag." He has written many important vocal and orchestral works, including a concerto for violoncello.

ANTON OUDSHOORN, born about 1840 at Leyden, studied at Brussels under François Servais. He held appointments at Colmar and Strasburg and toured with great success. He was not only an excellent violoncellist but likewise a good musician, who composed a number of solos, etc., for violoncello.

JACQUES RENSBURG, born May 22, 1846, at Rotterdam, commenced the study of the violoncello under Giese and continued under Daniel de Lange and Emil Hegar. Originally destined for the mercantile career, he did not obtain his father's permission to enter the musical profession until 1867. About the middle of the latter year he went to Cologne for a course of finishing lessons from the highly gifted violoncellist, Alexander Schmitt, whom he found, however, in such an advanced stage of consumption that his wish to benefit by his advice and teaching was not fulfilled. He was, however, engaged as Schmitt's deputy for the Gürzenich Orchestra and as teacher at the conservatoire. In both capacities he met with general approbation, and on April 1, 1868, he received both appointments definitely, as Schmitt had died meanwhile. Rensburg toured successfully as soloist visiting many towns of northern Germany and making his debut at the Gewandhaus Concerts at Leipzig in 1872. A nervous complaint compelled him to relinquish the musical career and in the autumn,

1874, he returned to Rotterdam. In 1880 he settled in Bonn, where he took over a business, and died there about the end of last century. His only published composition is a concertstück (Breitkopf and Härtel).

CHARLES G. HEKKING, born towards the middle of last century, at the Hague, was an excellent violoncellist who toured successfully in Holland, Germany and England. In 1860 he was appointed solo violoncellist at the theatre and teacher at the conservatoire, Bordeaux, where his nephew and pupil, ANDREAS HEKKING, is also living as violoncellist. The brothers Trowell mention his brother Gerard as an excellent violinist.

GERRARD HEKKING, a violoncellist of note, is now living at Amsterdam. He is successor of J. Mossel as solo violoncellist in the Concertgebouw Orchestra.

AUGUSTE VAN BIENE, born about 1850 at Rotterdam, studied at Brussels under François Servais, came to London in 1867, and was for some time in Sir Michael Costa's orchestra. He toured afterwards with the Harrison Orchestra, and was best known as the author of a play called "The Broken Melody," in which he appeared as actor, impersonating a Russian amateur violoncellist who plays various popular melodies in the course of the piece. These melodies he played also on London music-hall stages. He died at Brighton in 1913.

JOSEPH HOLLMANN, born October 16, 1852, at Maestricht, showed great musical talent from his early youth. His strong inclination for the musical career eventually conquered his father's objections, and he began to study the violoncello under Keller, a local teacher, making such rapid progress that after the one year's study he became a "pensionnaire du Roi." This was the name given to young musicians who were educated at the expense of King William III. He was sent to Brussels where he studied the violoncello under François Servais, and theory and composition under Bosselet and Fétis.

In 1870 he left the Brussels Conservatoire with the first prize for violoncello as well as for solfège and harmony. For the next four years he continued his studies at the Paris Conservatoire, under Léon Jacquard and Savart, the latter being his master for musical theory. At the conclusion he was engaged by the impresarios, Strakosch and Ullmann, for tours in Scandinavia, Germany and Russia. Since then he has travelled all over Europe with phenomenal success. His concerts at Bechstein Hall, where he appeared a few years ago, together with Saint-Saëns, will still be fresh in the memory of London concertgoers. He has been the recipient of numerous orders and marks of distinction from many courts of Europe. Queen Victoria, with whom he was a great favourite, presented him with a magnificent diamond ring, and King Edward VII (then Prince of Wales) presented him with a pin bearing his initials set in diamonds and surmounted by the crown. Hollmann's playing is distinguished by an extraordinarily powerful tone and faultless technique. Saint-Saëns is so great an admirer of Hollmann's art that he wrote his second violoncello concerto for him, which he produced at the "Singakademie" in Berlin in 1903, where it met with great success, although in England it failed to make any great impression. He was also the first to play Bruch's beautiful "Kol Nidrei"—which still holds its place as a favourite in violoncellists' repertoires—with orchestra in England. Hollmann has largely contributed to the literature of his instrument by two concertos and a considerable number of effective solo pieces. His concerts at Bechstein Hall, together with Camille Saint-Saëns, are still fresh within the memory of music-lovers.

ANTOON ALPHONS JOHANNES BOUMAN, born October 18, 1855, at S'Hertogenbosch. He received his first musical training from his father and his late brother Johannes. Afterwards he went to Rotterdam where he studied the violoncello under Oscar Eberle and composition under Woldemar Bargiel.

He became one of the so-called "pensionnaires du Roi,' and was thereby enabled to continue his studies successively under Lindner in Hanover, Grützmacher in Dresden, Jos. Servais in Brussels and Jacquard in Paris. After touring successfully for some time he was appointed solo violoncellist at Pau in France. About 1878 he came to London, and played at the Promenade Concerts at Covent Garden and at the Alexandra Palace. In 1881 he was appointed solo violoncellist in the municipal orchestra and teacher at the school of music at Utrecht; in 1890 he went to Berlin as solo violoncellist of the Philharmonic Orchestra and Hans von Bülow's concerts. About the beginning of this century Bouman returned to Holland as teacher at the Royal Conservatoire at the Hague and the Rotterdam Conservatoire. He toured successfully in all the principal towns of middle and northern Europe and appeared frequently at the court concerts at the Hague by command of King William III, who showed his appreciation by presenting him with a valuable instrument. Bouman composed four concertos and a number of solo pieces for violoncello.

ANTON HEKKING, born September 7, 1856, at the Hague, received his first instructions on the violoncello from Fritz Giese at the conservatoire of that town. At the early age of sixteen he became already solo violoncellist in the municipal orchestra at Utrecht but left that position eighteen months later to perfect himself under the famous masters Chevillard and Jacquard at the Paris Conservatoire, where he gained the first prize. He toured for some time with the famous pianist, Annette Essipoff, and then accepted an engagement as solo violoncellist in the Bilse Orchestra in Berlin. On the foundation of the Berlin Philharmonic Orchestra he was engaged in a similar capacity under particularly favourable conditions. In 1882 he toured with Ysaye for fifteen months all over Europe. On a visit to the Hague the king decorated him in person with the order of the Golden Lion of Nassau. 1884 to 1888 he was re-engaged for the Berlin Philharmonic Orchestra and again from 1898 to 1902. Between 1888 and 1898 he travelled in North America and filled engagements of longer periods as soloist in Boston and New York. In 1902 he founded popular trio soirées in Berlin, together with Arthur Schnabel (pianoforte) and Alfred Wittenberg (violin). Hekking has also established the reputation of being one of the foremost teachers of the present day.

JAN MULDER, born September 19, 1861, at Amsterdam. He studied at first under Ernest Appy at his native town and afterwards in London under Joseph Hollmann. His masters in composition were Franz Coenen and L. Emil Bach.

He settled in London about 1889, and played for two seasons in Sir Augustus Manns's orchestra in Scotland. As a soloist he has appeared successfully in London and many English provincial towns. Latterly he has devoted himself chiefly to the cultivation of chamber music. For the same purpose he founded some years ago the "King Cole Club," which is now in a flourishing condition.

The following are mentioned by Forino without further particulars: G. VOLMAR, born 1859, at the Hague is now living in Sydney, Australia. S. DE GROEN, born 1862, at Rotterdam. D. HAAGMANS, born 1866, at Rotterdam. L. MERLOO, born 1863, at the Hague. H. VAN DEN VELDE, born 1863, at Zutten. J. HOFSTEDE, born 1870, at Rotterdam. H. OUSHOORN (Oudshoorn ?), born 1874, at Rotterdam. WM. HEUKERSTH, born 1877, at Amsterdam. F. KWAST, born 1883, at Rotterdam. DART WIERTZ, born at the Hague, studied at the conservatoire of that town and is now solo violoncellist of the classical concerts at Groningen.

JAN VAN UNEN, born January 20, 1862, at Zwolle, commenced his musical studies at the conservatoire of his native town, continuing and finishing his study of the violoncello under Henri Bosmans at Amsterdam. He received his first engagement as second violoncellist at the "Paleis for Volksvlijt.' In 1900 he became solo violoncellist of the Orchestral Union at Arnheim, which position he still occupies. He is equally esteemed as soloist, chamber musician and teacher.

THOMAS C. DE MAARÉ, born January 14, 1863, studied under Oscar Eberle. At the age of twenty-two he was appointed second solo violoncellist of the Amsterdam Orchestral Union, and later on first solo violoncello at the French Opera at Amsterdam, which post he still occupies.

JOSEPH SALMON was born April 5, 1864, at the Hague, where he commenced the study of the violoncello. In 1880 he went to Paris where he became a pupil of Franchomme at the conservatoire. In 1883 he gained the first prize, and received an appointment as solo violoncellist in Pasdeloup's Orchestra. From 1886 to 1895 he was engaged in the same capacity for the Lamoureux Concerts. He toured successfully throughout northern Europe, is a member of the Hayot Quartet since 1894, and has shared the immense successes of that combination in the various capitals of Europe. He gives also chamber music soirées at the Salle Pleyel in Paris, together with the pianist, Chevillard. Since 1896 Salmon has no fixed engagement, but lives in Paris as concert soloist and teacher. He plays a Bergonzi violoncello, dated 1733, which Mr. Windust (in "The Strad," May, 1909) rather suspects to be a Gofriller, but declares it all the same an instrument of perfect shape, varnish, and what is most valuable of all, exquisite beauty of tone.

JOHAN SNOER, born June 28, 1868, at Amsterdam, received his first instructions in violoncello playing from Alexander Pohle, a pupil of Friedrich Grützmacher. After the death of Pohle he studied under Fr. Giese and Henry Bosmans. He studied also the harp under Schnecker. After playing for some time in the Park Orchestra he was appointed violoncellist and harpist at the Park Theatre, and since 1885 first solo violoncellist and harpist at the Amsterdam Orchestral Union.

JOHANNES SMITH, born January 27, 1869, at Arnheim, commenced his study of the violoncello at the age of nine, and shortly afterwards received regular instruction from Alfred Hayn at Aix-la-Chapelle, and later on from Ernest Appy at Amsterdam. In 1883 he went to Dresden, where he became a pupil of Friedrich Grützmacher, studying composition under Felix Draeseke. In 1887 he made his debut as a soloist at Dresden and met with great success. Then commenced a time of travel, visiting the principal towns of northern Europe in the company of Hermine Spies, Rosa Papier and Nikita. In 1890 he was appointed solo violoncellist of the Philharmonic Society at Bremen, where he joined the Heckmann Quartet in 1891, and afterwards the Halir Quartet. In 1895 Smith became solo violoncellist and chamber virtuoso in the court chapel at Bückeburg, and member of the Sahla Quartet. Since 1899 he is teacher at the Royal Conservatoire at Dresden. He has published several solo pieces, etc., for violoncello.

G. HENRI HAAGMANS, born December 26, 1870, at Rotterdam, commenced to study the violin and the pianoforte at an early age. In 1887 he chose the violoncello for his instrument, and this he studied under Carl Schröder, who was then conductor of the Rotterdam Opera. Later on he continued his studies for a time under Paul Prill and Oscar Eberle, after which he went to Leipzig, where he became a pupil of J. Klengel. In 1891 he held an appointment at Majorenhof, near Riga, and thence he went to Berlin for a finishing course of studies under R. Hausmann. This was followed by a period of concert tours, at the end of which he went to America as solo violoncello of the New York Philharmonic Club. In that capacity he appeared as soloist in the principal towns of the United States, where he met with great success. Afterwards returning to Holland he was appointed teacher at the school of the "Maatschappij tot Bevordering van Toonkunst" at Dordrecht, and conductor of choral societies in Kinderdyk and Breda. Haagmans is an excellent chamber music player as well as a brilliant soloist.

ISAAC MOSSEL, born April 22, 1870, at Rotterdam, is one of the foremost Dutch violoncellists of the present time. From his fifth to his eighth year his father instructed him in violin playing. At the age of eight he commenced the study of the violoncello under Louis Köhler. In the following year he became Oscar Eberle's pupil and finished his education in 1884 under that excellent master. In 1886 Mossel toured with great success in Switzerland and Germany. He was appointed solo violoncellist at the "Konzerthaus" in Berlin, and in the following year also of the Berlin Philharmonic Orchestra. In 1887 he accompanied Charles Davidoff, at that master's request, on his last tours through Germany and Holland. In 1888 he was appointed solo violoncellist at the Concertgebouw at Amsterdam, teacher at the conservatoire and at the school of the "Maatschappij tot bevordering van Toonkunst," as well as member of the conservatoire quartet. Many successful concert tours have established his reputation as an excellent soloist also in England, Germany, France and Belgium. Among many honourable distinctions he received the title of "Officier de l'Instruction Publique" from the French government. A few years ago Mossel relinquished his position at the Concertgebouw, where he was succeeded by Gerard Hekking. He divides his time now exclusively between his duties as professor of the conservatoires of Amsterdam and Rotterdam and concert-playing as a virtuoso. He possesses a beautiful Nicolas Amati which he uses alternately with a fine Alex. Gagliano. Mossel, who is an excellent musician as well as virtuoso, is also an ardent votary of the viol da gamba which he plays with great perfection.

JACQUES VAN LIER, born April 24, 1875, at the Hague,

appeared already as a soloist at the early age of nine. He received his first violoncello lessons from Hartog, a member of the royal opera at the Hague. Afterwards he became a pupil of Giese at the Royal Conservatoire of that town, and finally he studied for four years under Oscar Eberle at the Rotterdam Conservatoire where he gained three first prizes and a special prize of honour. In 1891 he was appointed as solo violoncellist at the Paleis for Volksvlijt at Amsterdam. In 1892 he went to Basle, where he was engaged in a similar capacity until 1895. The following year was devoted to touring throughout the principal towns of Europe, and in 1897 he went to Berlin as solo violoncellist of the Philharmonic Orchestra, which position he resigned in 1899. In that year he became principal professor of violoncello at the Klindworth-Scharwenka Conservatoire, and founded the Dutch Trio with Conraad V. Bos and Jos. van Veen, which has established a high reputation on its numerous tours. Van Lier combines a rich and beautiful tone with great technical mastery. He has published important works of study and forty transcriptions for violoncello.

KATO VAN DER HOEVEN, born September 20, 1879, at Amsterdam, commenced the study of the violin at an early age. After she had made already considerable progress she exchanged that instrument for the violoncello, which she studied under I. Mossel, taking a finishing course from Anton Hekking. On the completion of her studies she toured successfully in Holland and then accepted an engagement for the Concertgebouw Orchestra in Amsterdam. Since then she has visited many German towns (Berlin, Cologne, etc.), meeting everywhere with great success.

WILLEM DURIEUX, born 1880 at the Hague, studied at the conservatoire of his native town, under Joseph Giese. In 1898 he went to Berlin where he finished his studies under Anton Hekking. In 1902 he gave a very successful concert in Berlin.

At present he lives at the Hague, highly esteemed as soloist and chamber music player. He has published a number of solos, etc., for his instrument.

DANIEL VAN GOENS, born in Holland during the latter part of last century, studied the violoncello under Léon Jacquard at the Paris Conservatoire. He was a young artist of remarkable talent, who unfortunately fell an early victim to consumption. Even his short career lays a claim to lasting fame by his fine compositions for his instrument, including two concertos and a considerable number of melodious and brilliant solo pieces, of which an elegy and a scherzo have become standard pieces of violoncello literature. The second concerto, Op. 30, in D minor, was produced by Mr. Jacques Renard at the Queen's Hall Promenade Concerts in 1904. During the latter part of his life van Goens lived at Nice.

CHAPTER XXX.

THE VIOLONCELLO IN SWITZERLAND DURING THE NINETEENTH CENTURY.

ADOLPHE REHBERG, born February 16, 1868, at Morges, is the son of a teacher of music from whom he received his first instruction. In 1884 he entered the Leipzig Conservatoire, where he studied the violoncello under Alwin Schröder. In 1887 he gained the Helbig prize at that institute, and shortly after toured for some time as soloist. In 1888 he became a teacher of his instrument at the Lausanne Conservatoire, and in the following year he exchanged that position for a similar one at the more important conservatoire at Geneva. In 1897 he was elected an officer of the French Academy, and in 1908 officer of Public Instruction by the French Government. In 1900 he joined the celebrated Marteau Quartet, to which he belonged until 1905, when it was dissolved by Marteau's appointment as Joachim's successor at the Hochschule in Berlin. Rehberg enjoys the reputation of an excellent soloist and chamber music player, and as such he is at present violoncellist of the Berlin Quartet. His concert tours extend over Switzerland, France, Germany and Austria. The latter country he visited during the winter, 1909, when he played the Beethoven sonatas with Risler.

EMIL BRAUN, born September 18, 1870, at Lenzburg (Switzerland), studied at the Leipzig Conservatoire under Alwin Schröder and Professor Julius Klengel from 1889 till 1893. He left the conservatoire after gaining the Helbig prize, and was appointed teacher for the violoncello and ensemble playing at the conservatoire at Basle, acting also as teacher of his instrument for the towns of Mülhausen and Colmar in the Alsace. He has toured successfully in Switzerland and the Alsace, where he is often heard as soloist at the principal concerts; also the principal German towns, Berlin, Leipzig, Munich, Cassel, etc., know him as an excellent solo violoncellist. He is also an executant on the viol da gamba, which he has played in public at the concerts of the Historical Museum at Basle and many other occasions.

ELSA RUEGGER was born December 6, 1881, as the daughter of a high government official, who was also Mayor of Lucerne. As well as her two elder sisters, she showed a marked love and talent for music from her earliest youth, and this circumstance induced her mother to remove with her daughters to Brussels to give them every opportunity to develop their talents. All three entered the Brussels Conservatoire. Wally as pianist, Charlotte as violinist and little Elsa as violoncellist, studying under Edward Jacobs, Anna Campawsky and other eminent masters. At the age of fourteen (Gamba, in his interview in "The Strad," says "eleven"), while still a student at the conservatoire, she made her debut at a charity concert, and a leading Brussels paper spoke of her "perfect finish, fine technique and absence of all crudities peculiar to youthful prodigies." When she had finished her studies she played two movements from a concerto by Rubinstein at the conservatoire *concours* (competition), and this occasion proved a veritable triumph for her. She carried off the first prize with highest honours in 1895. Soon after this she toured in company of her two sisters through Switzerland and in October of the same year she made her debut in Berlin, earning the highest praise from an enthusiastic press. After this she visited Cologne, Munich, Aix, Metz, Strasburg, Ostend, Bruges, Antwerp, Brussels, Paris and St. Petersburg. In October, 1897, Mlle. Ruegger made her debut at the London Promenade Concerts, where she met with an enthusiastic reception. In 1899 she paid a second visit to Berlin, giving a concert with the assistance of the Philharmonic Orchestra, and soon after she appeared by command before the German Emperor and Empress at the Schloss in Berlin. In the autumn of that year she accepted an engagement for an extensive tour in America, meeting with such success that she returned in 1902. Since then she has travelled all over the civilised world, revisiting England and America several times and winning golden opinions from the most critical audiences.

CHAPTER XXXI.

THE VIOLONCELLO IN ITALY FROM THE EIGHTEENTH CENTURY TO 1900.

PIETRO CASELLA was the head of a long dynasty of violoncellists and founder of the Turin School. He is said to have been born in 1762 at Genoa, and died in 1844. In 1831 he became member of the court chapel with a salary of 1,500 lire per annum. He took part in the first performance of Mercadante's opera, "The Regent." Among his pupils were his sons, Cesare Giovacchino and Carlo Casella. There is a good deal of uncertainty as to the history of some of the members of this distinguished family.

FILIPPO RAIMONDI, born about 1785, was principal violoncellist in the orchestra at Rome. He died about the middle of last century, and was succeeded by Costaggini, with whom he shared his post for some time.

MARIANNA RAIMONDI, daughter of Filippo, born at Rome at the beginning of the nineteenth century, was also a member of the orchestra, where she held the post as solo accompanist for the recitatives which were accompanied by the violoncello and harpsichord. She took part in the first performance of Verdi's "Gerusalemme" in 1859, and was spoken of as a distinguished executant.

GIUSEPPE CANTINELLI, born at Leghorn about 1790, was principal violoncello at the Apollo Theatre at Rome, where he enjoyed the reputation of an excellent violoncellist. He died about 1850.

GIUSEPPE STURIONI was principal violoncellist at the Scala Theatre at Milan from 1809 to 1819, and professor of the first (highest) class for violoncello playing at the Milan Conservatoire, to which he was appointed on its foundation in 1808.

VINCENZO MERIGHI, born at Parma, December 7, 1795, was professor at the Milan Conservatoire from 1826 to 1849, and as such the teacher of Alfredo Piatti. Merighi, who is looked upon as head of the Lombardian school of violoncello playing, numbered among his pupils, besides Piatti, Alexander Pezze, Guglielmo Quarenghi and Leonardo Moja.

The MARQUIS PIETRO LAUREATI, born at Grottamara in 1802, who died in February, 1874 (Schmidl gives the year as 1876), was an amateur violoncellist of extraordinary ability. He was a pupil of Giovanni Vitali at Ascoli, and after touring for some time he came to London where he was first violoncello at the opera for twenty years. He possessed a magnificent Nicolas Amati violoncello.

CARLO CURTI, born at Bologna, November 4, 1807, commenced his musical studies on the violin as a pupil of Rolla, but afterwards took up the violoncello under the guidance of Parisini. In 1853 he was elected teacher at the Parma School of Music. He combined a round and powerful tone with a great deal of expression. He retired in 1872 on account of failing health and died soon after. Some of his compositions for violoncello were published by Ricordi.

CARLO PARISINI, born 1809 at Bologna, was an excellent violoncellist and teacher of his instrument at the conservatoire of that town from 1831 till 1871. He died in 1884.

LOVERI. There were three highly gifted violoncellists of that name. Carlo and Piedro were teachers at the Naples

Conservatoire; Carlo, during the early part of last century; Piedro from 1835 to 1861. Vincenzo Loveri, who likewise resided at Naples, enjoyed also the reputation of an excellent violoncellist.

MICHELE LOMBARDI, born about 1817, was teacher of the violoncello at the conservatoire of St. Pietro a Majella at Naples, together with Labocetta, as successor to Ciaudelli, between the years 1866-97. He is said to have studied with Lutgardo Pecoraro at Aversa and afterwards with Ziffirini, of whom nothing is known. Lombardi died in 1897.

The records of the court chapel of Turin mention the following violoncellists as members in 1814:

PAOLO CANAVASSO, with a salary of six hundred lire per annum. He was in all probability a son or relative of A. Canavasso mentioned in Part I.

ANTONIO LAVARIA, who received four hundred and eighty lire, and AGOSTINO LEA, with three hundred lire.

LUIGI VENZANO, born 1815, was the first teacher of the violoncello at the conservatoire of Genoa from 1855 till 1874 and Pietro Casella is supposed to have been his master. He was principal violoncello at the theatre Carlo Felice. His opera, "La notte degli schiaffi," was performed at Genoa in 1873. He died in 1878.

GAËTANO CIAUDELLI, a celebrated Neapolitan violoncellist, was teacher at the conservatoire of St. Pietro a Majella from 1844 till 1865. He was a pupil of Fenzi and was highly esteemed as a teacher, counting among his pupils such well known names as Braga, Labocetta, Ferd. Forino and Giarritiello.

ANTONIO PANZETTA was contemporary of Ciaudelli, being teacher at the same institute (St. Pietro a Majella at Naples) from 1843 till 1873, when he died.

LEONARDO MOJA was born at Milan in April, 1811. He studied the violoncello under Merighi. In 1843 he was appointed by King Charles Albert as member of the royal chapel at Turin. He died on February 5, 1888, leaving several compositions for his instrument. Moja was held in high esteem both as artist and man.

CESARE A. DE CASELLA, born 1819 at Lisbon, was a son of Pietro Casella *(see page 579)*. There has been a deal of confusion with regard to the history of this distinguished family of musicians, and historians have either ignored them like Wasielewski, or their notes have been very meagre and hazy, as in the case of Forino and others. The following details were obtained from Count Luigi Francesco Valdrighi, who received them from the wife of Carlo Casella. Cesare, as well as his two brothers, Giovacchino and Carlo, studied the violoncello under their father Pietro. Cesare developed into a remarkable virtuoso, and was for a number of years engaged at the court of Madrid, where he was made a chevalier of the Royal Order of Charles III of Spain. About 1868 he revisited Italy and was greatly admired at Rome for his playing of concert pieces by Servais and Piatti. He wrote a number of compositions for his instrument which are mostly of the *salon* genre. His six "Grandes Etudes," Op. 33, are very melodious and excellent studies. He died at Lisbon in 1886.

ALFREDO PIATTI, born January 8, 1822, at Bergamo, is one of the "grand masters" of his instrument. His father, a violinist, instructed him at an early age in violin playing, but the boy soon evinced a predilection for the violoncello on which he received his first training from his granduncle Zanetti. In 1832 he was sent to Milan, where he continued his studies under Merighi, and in 1837 he made his first appearance as a soloist. It is worth mentioning that Giuseppe Rovelli, the master of Merighi, who was born 1753 at Bergamo and died 1806 at Parma, was distantly related to Piatti. In April, 1838, he gave a concert at the Scala Theatre, the results of which enabled him to embark on a prolonged concert tour extending over the principal towns of Europe. In 1839 he appeared with phenomenal success in Vienna and on his return he gave concerts at Padua and Milan. In 1843 he appeared in Munich at a concert given by Franz Liszt. In the following year he visited Frankfort-on-Main, Berlin, Breslau, Dresden, Paris, and thence he came to London, where he made his debut on June 24, 1844, at the seventh Philharmonic Concert (the Philharmonic concerts were held until 1868, at the Hanover Square Rooms) playing a concerto by F. A. Kummer, on a fine Amati violoncello, presented to him by Liszt. Mendelssohn, who conducted the concert and played also Beethoven's pianoforte concerto in G, was so much impressed by Piatti's playing that he composed a violoncello concerto with the avowed object of dedicating it to Piatti. The MS. was lost in transit and Mendelssohn never attempted to write it again. Piatti, who knew the MS., told the writer that the work did not come up to the violin concerto by a long way. In 1845 Piatti made his first appearance at St. Petersburg, and in the following year he was offered the post of teacher at the Milan Conservatoire, which he refused, returning to London, where henceforth he took up his permanent residence, touring a great deal and spending most of the winter months at Caddenabbia on the Lake of Como. In 1884 the Naples Conservatoire tried to secure his services as teacher, but there also he refused. In 1857 the Popular Concerts were instituted at St. James's Hall in Regent Street, which was pulled down in 1904 and a restaurant built on its site. These concerts were entirely devoted to chamber music and Joachim, Straus, Zerbini and Piatti formed a quartet which was permanently engaged for the Popular Concerts. Mr. Louis Ries joined this combination afterwards as second violinist, while Straus took over the viola. For nobility of style, beauty of tone and perfection of ensemble that combination has never been surpassed. Mr. Louis Ries, the last surviving member, died in 1913.

In 1858 Piatti revisited Vienna, and it is interesting to read what the famous critic, Professor Robert Hanslick, has to say about him on that occasion. We cull a few sentences from his lengthy article, which summarise his opinion: "His tone," he says, "is of rare beauty, sympathetic, round and full. Perhaps for the first time one missed that humming, grumbling accessory sound of the deeper strings from which the playing of even the very greatest of violoncellists was never quite free. But Piatti refrains from attacking his instrument with too strong a hand, and so his playing lends itself the better to alternations of tone-colour, to deeper shading, in fact . . . . His playing, which for beauty of tone, is incomparable, is also as fully developed in the direction of virtuosity as in that of refinement and perfection of style. . . . . The method of the virtuoso, pure and simple, is never allowed by Piatti to stand in the way when it is necessary to perform a simple cantilena; and in the latter case, for instance, when playing Schubert's 'Litanei,' there is a complete absence of that horrible sentimentality which is so often found among violoncellists. When rendering an adagio, too, that perpetual vibrato, which with many passes for feeling, is quite absent in the case of Piatti. To judge by the compositions of Piatti that we have been able to hear, we are bound to say he possesses no extraordinary talent for composition, yet in the treatment of form he exhibits both refined taste and complete understanding" (from an article by "Gamba" in "The Strad").

Hanslick's appreciation will be upheld by all who heard the great master. A very remarkable fact is that his beauty of tone, perfect intonation and agility of the left hand held out to the last. At one of the last Popular Concerts at which he appeared in 1897-8, the writer heard him play his own arrangement of a violin sonata by Haydn with a nobility of style which was quite monumental. It was free from all sentimentality, as Hanslick justly remarked, but had a tender deli-

PLATE XLIV.

ALFREDO PIATTI.

By permission of Messrs W. and D. Downey, 61 Ebury Street, London, S.W.

cacy and graceful ease which was delightful and for ever memorable. His second solo on that occasion was a tarantella of his own composition in which he proved himself still in full possession of all the cunning of his left hand and his bow with an astounding mastery.

This appears even more wonderful when taking into account that some years previous his right arm was broken in a carriage accident, which prevented him for a whole season from taking part in the Saturday and Monday Popular Concerts, from which he was rarely absent during a period of thirty-eight years, viz., 1859-97. At the end of 1897 he retired to his villa at Caddenabbia, on the Lake of Como, and died on Friday, July 18, 1901, at his villa, "delle Crocette," at Bergamo, his native place, where he stayed with his sister. He was very reserved, in fact, unapproachable to all who sought his company or tried to engage him merely from curiosity, personal vanity or any outward motive. To those in whom he recognised seriousness of purpose and the desire to advance themselves in their art, he proved a true and kind friend, and the writer remembers gratefully the large amount of valuable assistance he received from that great master when compiling his "Technics of Violoncello Playing," and the patience with which he discussed difficult technical points. In all circles of society, both in England and Italy, who enjoyed the privilege of his acquaintance and intercourse he was a great favourite. As a pastime he enjoyed nothing better than a game of whist, in which he was a past master of the old and steady school, never missing a point that could be secured by finesse and judicious play, but he abhorred all innovations in the shape of American "leads," etc.

It was on a visit to Dublin in 1844 that Piatti first saw the Stradivari violoncello which afterwards became his favourite instrument. It had been brought from Spain to Ireland by a wine merchant and sold at a low price. Piatti saw it in the possession of a violoncellist named Piggot, who would not part with it even if Piatti had not been too poor to pay even its moderate value. Piggot died, and the instrument, after passing through several hands, was eventually bought for £350 by General Oliver, an intimate friend of Piatti, who refused an offer of £1,000 from Vuillaume for it. One day the General, who had several valuable instruments, asked Piatti which he considered the best, and when the latter unhesitatingly pointed to the Strad, the General said: "Take it home, keep it, and enjoy playing on it." Piatti hesitated to accept so generous an offer, but the next day it was sent to his house with a note from the General, asking its acceptance, in the kindest terms. After the master's death it was bought for four thousand pounds by Mr. Robert Mendelssohn, a nephew of the great composer, and excellent amateur violoncellist.

His compositions for the violoncello are for the greater part doomed to oblivion, except the very fine caprices for violoncello solo, which will remain standard studies. Piatti's portrait appears on Plate XLIV.

LUTGARDO PECORARO was teacher of the violoncello at the "Reclusarios" at Naples and Aversa, and at the blind school of St. Joseph and Lucia. He died very young, on August 1, 1838.

DOMENICO LABOCETTA, born May 9, 1823, was a pupil of Ciaudelli. Gifted with a fine voice, he appeared as operatic tenor on the principal stages of Europe and America, but eventually devoted himself exclusively to the study of his beloved violoncello. In 1877 he succeeded Giaritielli as teacher at the Conservatoire of St. Pietro a Majella at Naples, where he died August 6, 1896. He was also principal violoncello in the St. Carlo Orchestra, and composed a good deal for his instrument, but his compositions are of a very superficial nature.

GIOVACCHINO CASELLA, son and pupil of Pietro, born 1826,

at Genoa, was principal violoncello at the Teatro Regio at Turin, where he was still active in 1896.

GUGLIELMO QUARENGHI, born October 22, 1826, at Casalmaggiore, studied under Merighi at Milan from 1839 till 1842. On the completion of his studies he was appointed principal violoncello at the Scala Theatre, and in 1851 he became a teacher of his instrument at the Milan Conservatoire. In 1879 he succeeded Boucheron as "maestro di capella" at the cathedral, and died February 3, 1882.

Apart from a number of solo pieces, he wrote an important tutor and six caprices for violoncello. Cristoforo Merighi, his master's son, was one of his numerous pupils.

CRISTOFORO MERIGHI, a pupil of Quarenghi, about whom we possess no exact dates, was for some time teacher at the music school of Bergamo while actually residing at Milan. He was held in high esteem as a clever violoncellist by Piatti.

GIUSEPPE DISEGNI, born July 5, 1828, at Leghorn, succeeded Venzano as principal violoncello at the Carlo Felice Theatre at Genoa.

GAËTANO BRAGA, born June 9, 1829, at Giulianova. He was originally destined for the church. When his love for music was asserting itself as supreme, his parents wished him to become a singer, but he decided in favour of the violoncello. His master on that instrument was Ciaudelli, while he studied composition under Mercadante. After finishing his studies in 1852 he toured through northern Italy and Austria. In Vienna he joined Mayseder's Quartet, to which he belonged for a short period. In 1855 he went to Paris, where he was in great favour as a soloist. He returned to Italy, where F. and L. Forino still played with him at a concert given at Rome about the beginning of this century, but L. Forino, who mentions the fact in his book, "Il Violoncello," says that he could not form an opinion about his playing as he was too advanced in years. Apparently he is still living at Florence. He wrote a number of operatic and other compositions for the theatre, and for the violoncello he wrote a concerto and a number of solos, as also the famous "Serenata" for voice, with violin or violoncello *obbligato*, still greatly in favour with the numerous lovers of sentimental superficialities. Braga published also an edition of Dotzauer's studies.

JEFTE SBOLCI, born September 5, 1833, at Florence, was an excellent violoncellist, quartet player and conductor. He was professor of the Royal Institute of Music, and founder of the orchestra of that society. He is also the founder of the school of violoncello playing of that town, which possessed no violoncellist of distinction before him. He died December 7, 1895.

CARLO CASELLA, born at Turin, 1834, was a son and pupil of Pietro Casella. He was teacher at the "Liceo Musicale" from 1868 till 1895, and principal violoncello at the Royal Theatre at Turin. A spinal complaint compelled him to retire in 1895, and he died in August, 1896. His son Alfred, who was then eleven years old, showed remarkable talent as a pianist.

ALESSANDRO PEZZE, born 1835 at Milan, received his first musical training from his father, a clever amateur. In 1846 he entered the Milan Conservatoire, where he studied the violoncello under Merighi. After being appointed principal violoncellist at the Scala Theatre he was, in 1857, engaged by Lumley as principal violoncello for Her Majesty's Theatre in London. This position he retained until the theatre was destroyed by fire in 1867. He belonged to the Philharmonic Orchestra and was for some years principal violoncellist at the Royal Opera, Covent Garden. He also filled the post as second violoncello at the Popular Concerts, Piatti being the first violoncellist.

As teacher at the London Academy of Music, where he is still active, he formed many excellent pupils, one of the foremost was Miss Gertrude Ess.

PIETRO COSTAGGINI, who died in 1869, was a pupil of the double-bass player, Carracini, with whom he played together in the Municipal Orchestra at Rome, sharing the principal part with Cantinelli. Paganini, on his visit to Rome, amused himself by playing chamber music with Costaggini.

SALVATORE TREMENTINI was, about 1847, principal violoncello in the Municipal Orchestra at Rome. He died there in March, 1904, over seventy years old, and must therefore have been born about 1832-3.

ALLESSANDRO RUSPANTINI is mentioned by Forino as a pupil of Cantinelli and contemporary of Trementini, F. Raimondi, etc. A violoncellist over seventy years old, who, in 1905, lived in retirement at Rome.

GIOVANNI CORSI, a contemporary of the former, was a pupil of Costaggini, and lived as violoncellist at Rome.

PIETRO RACHELLE wrote a tutor for the violoncello which was published by Ricordi in 1837. Nothing is known about him except that he was teacher of the violoncello at Parma and violoncellist in the ducal chapel.

FERDINANDO FORINO, born at Naples in 1837, studied under Ciaudelli at the Conservatoire of St. Pietro a Majella, and joined the violinist, Ramacciotti, in 1863, in the foundation of chamber concerts at a concert room in the Via del Vantaggio at Rome. In 1867 he became principal violoncello at the Apollo Theatre, and in 1870, on the foundation of the "Liceo Musicale," he was appointed professor of violoncello at that institute, where he was succeeded by his son in 1901. He is still living at Rome. Among his numerous compositions for the violoncello are a complete and well-graduated tutor, a number of fantasias on operas, and a tarantella.

GENNARO GIARITIELLO, born in 1838, was a co-student of F. Forino under Ciaudelli, and a highly-gifted violoncellist. He succeeded Panzetta as teacher at the Conservatoire of St. Pietro a Majella at Naples in 1873, but died suddenly in 1876.

ANDREAS GUARNERI, born August 22, 1840, at Pieve d'Olmi (Cremona), a pupil of Quarenghi, succeeded Venzano as teacher at the Musical Institute of Genoa in 1875, where he remained until 1882. He died as conductor of the municipal band of Milan, September 19, 1899. He composed an opera but apparently no published compositions for violoncello.

FRANCESCO SERATO, born September 17, 1843, at Castelfranco, succeeded Parisini as teacher of the violoncello at the Conservatoire of Bologna in 1871. He was originally a violinist, and acquired the art of violoncello playing by attentively studying the movements, etc., of various noted violoncellists. He attained a great elegance of bowing, combined with a remarkable technique of the left hand. As a teacher he is held in great esteem, and numbers many excellent violoncellists among his pupils. He is still active as teacher and as violoncellist of the Bolognese Quartet, led by Sarti.

DOMENICO TESCARI, born July 21, 1848, at Vicenzo, was a pupil of Serato at the Bologna Conservatoire and was appointed as teacher of the violoncello at the Instituto Musicale at Genoa in 1882, but relinquished his position in 1894, and lives now in America. He composed among other things a "Miserere" for chorus and orchestra.

CESARE CASELLA, born April 2, 1848, at Malaga, apparently a son of C. A. de Casella (according to Forino—Valdrighi says he was born 1849 at Oporto), is a distinguished violoncellist apparently still living in Paris. Attacked by a severe malady, he was for a long time in a convalescent home, but eventually recovered, and in 1896 we find his name mentioned as taking part in Lalo's pianoforte trio with Philipp and Herwegh at a concert of the "Société des Petites Auditions" in Paris.

Piatti told an amusing episode concerning Cesare Casella: at a fashionable *salon* the vain and conceited violoncellist, Nathan, played a solo which met with a very favourable reception, and which he declared to be of his composition. Casella, who was present on the occasion, recognised the piece as one of his own. He taxed the impostor with his effrontery, whereupon Nathan excused himself by saying he thought the piece was by an old master who died long ago.

JAC. BARAGLI, born 1852, studied at the Rome Conservatoire. For about twelve years he was teacher at the Conservatoire at Padua, and for about ten years after that he was in a similar position at Palermo.

ELIGIO CREMONINI, born 1854, near Bologna, studied under Barbi and afterwards under Serato at the Bologna Conservatoire. He was for many years professor at the Modena Conservatoire, where he counted among his pupils the celebrated music historian, Count Luigi Francesco Valdrighi.

About 1900 he was appointed professor at the Liceo Rossini at Pesaro, where he is still living. He has composed several solos for his instrument.

LEANDRO CARINI, born towards the middle of last century, was a pupil of C. Curti. He was appointed teacher of his instrument at Parma, where he formed a considerable number of excellent pupils, of whom Forino enumerates the following: Luigi Provesi, Italo Stocchi, Ulderico Giraud, Feruccio Pezzani, Guido Rocchi, Umberto Candiolo, Claudio Ferrari, Pietro Zilioli, Cesare Castelli, Giulio Valdemi, Mario Rognoni, Serafino Massé, Guglielmo Verojo, Alberto Franceschini, Arturo Preti, Alberto Dardani, Giuseppe Cacciali, Francesco Carnaglia and Gino Fornaroli.

EUGENIO CUCCOLI, born 1861, was a pupil of Serato at the Bologna Conservatoire. He died at the early age of thirty-five on March 2, 1896.

ARTURO CUCCOLI, brother of Eugenio, was born in 1869. Like his brother, he studied under Serato at the Bologna Conservatoire. After completing his studies he had several engagements as principal violoncello in various important orchestras.

For six years from about 1894 he was member of the Heller Quartet in Trieste, and with the Nachtigal Trio of Warsaw he toured successfully in Russia and Austria. Since 1901 he is teacher of his instrument at the Padua Conservatoire, and is held in high esteem as teacher, soloist and chamber musician.

LUIGI STEFANO GIARDA, born near Pavia, in 1868. He studied at the Milan Conservatoire under Magrini, and obtained the first prize on leaving in 1888. For some time he was teacher of violoncello at the Padua Conservatoire and principal violoncello successively at the Scala Theatre at Milan, the Royal Theatre at Turin, and the Fenice Theatre at Venice. He succeeded Labocetta as professor at the Naples Conservatoire in 1897, and remained sole professor when the two violoncello classes were amalgamated in 1898. He has toured successfully in Italy, and distinguished himself also as an opera composer.

The "Musical News," January, 1896, said: "Signor Giarda from Padova, an excellent violoncellist, excited lately in Florence the same enthusiasm he had raised last year by his beautiful tone and full command of his instrument, for which qualities he can have very few competitors. He has also shown himself at his best as a composer by a suite for string quartet, cleverly written and effective."

F. RONCHINI, born at Fano, October 23, 1865, commenced his studies under Pettinari as a violinist, but went afterwards to Serato at the Bologna Conservatoire. He was appointed teacher of his instrument at the Institute of Reggio Emilia. He made a successful concert tour through Europe in the company of the singer, Etelka G. Giardini. After some engagements as solo violoncellist in various orchestras he went to Paris, where he devoted himself chiefly to composition.

PIETRO MARINELLI, born at Bergamo in 1877, studied under Magrini at the Milan Conservatoire. After travelling abroad and holding engagements in various orchestras, he was ap-

VIOL DA GAMBA BY BARAK NORMAN (1688-1740) WITH ORIGINAL INLAID FINGER-BOARD AND TAILPIECE, BELONGING TO MR. HENRY SAINT-GEORGE, LONDON. See page 52.

pointed teacher of the Frescobaldi Institute at Ferrara. Piatti showed a decided predilection for this violoncellist. About the following we possess but very few dates, they are therefore added in alphabetical order:

CESARE BEDETTI, studied under Ferdinando Forino at Rome. He was violoncellist of the Gulli Quintet, which toured in Europe with great success. He is now teacher of the Co-operative School of Music at Rome.

LUIGI BROGLIO, a pupil of Magrini, is teacher at Florence Conservatoire.

LUIGI CERASOLI, who died about the beginning of this century, was teacher of violoncello at the "Instituto Morlacchi" at Perugia.

EGISTO DINI, a pupil of Sbolci, who had a fine tone and sure technique, was teacher at the "Liceo Benedetto Marcello" at Venice (founded by Count Giuseppe Contin de Castel Szeprio, an excellent violinist and composer). Dini died in 1903.

GIUSEPPE FIORAVANZO, from 1832 till 1835 principal violoncello in the Venice Orchestra.

LUIGI FORINO, professor at the Rome Conservatoire, studied under his father, Ferdinando Forino, professor at the Naples Conservatoire until 1901, when his son Luigi succeeded him in that position. The latter is the author of a very well-compiled book on the violoncello, its technique, literature, history and players.

TANCREDI FORNEROS was held by Giovanni Bolzoni, director of the Turin Conservatoire, to be a violoncellist of distinct merit.

FERDINANDO FRASNEDI, a pupil of Serato at the Bologna Conservatoire, was for some time principal in the Rome Orchestra. He succeeded Dini in 1903 as teacher at the "Liceo Benedetto Marcello."

SAMUELE GROSSI, one of the numerous pupils of Serato at

the Bologna Conservatoire, is professor at the Turin Conservatoire since 1895.

GIUSEPPE MAGRINI, professor at the Milan Conservatoire, was a pupil of Labocetta at the Naples Conservatoire. He is not only an excellent executant but also an eminent teacher, who counts many violoncellists of merit among his numerous pupils.

PROSPERO MONTECCHI, studied under Serato at the Bologna Conservatoire until 1882. In 1887 he went to Rennes in the Bretagne as teacher at the conservatoire. He appeared with success in many French towns as well as in Manchester and Oxford. About 1905 the French Government honoured him by electing him an Officer of the French Academy.

GAETANO MORELLI was a pupil of Ferdinando Forino at the Rome Conservatoire. He was violoncellist of the quintet of Queen Margareta of Italy, of which Sgambati was the pianist. He has for some years taken up his residence in London.

HORAZIO PACHELLI, who died about 1905 at the early age of twenty-five, was for some time a member of the famous quintet of Queen Margareta, which is under the direction of Sgambati, and first violoncellist of the Orchestra Massima at Rome.

ANGELO PERACCHIO, born August 10, 1876, at Turin, studied at his native town under Professor Casella. After gaining the Diploma of Honour for violoncello, harmony and composition, he was appointed at the Royal Theatre at Turin. He exchanged that position for the post of solo violoncellist at the Theatre Bellecourt at Lyons, and appeared as soloist with marked success in Paris and other important French towns. Afterwards he went to Nantes, and he is at present first professor of violoncello and ensemble playing at the Conservatoire of St. Etienne, with the title of an Officer of the French Academy.

He has written several arrangements of pieces for violoncello.

MARIO PEZZOTTA was a pupil of Magrini at the Milan Conservatoire after a course of preliminary studies under C.

Merighi at Bergamo, where he is now engaged as teacher of the conservatoire.

OTTAVIO DE PICCOLELLIS, son of the Marquis Giovanni de Piccolellis, best known by his work on ancient and modern instrument makers, is a very clever amateur violoncellist, who studied under Sbolci and Servais. He is the fortunate owner of a fine collection of valuable instruments, and conductor of the orchestral society, "Cherubini," at Florence, where he lives.

SILVIO RISPOLI, another distinguished amateur violoncellist possessing a very remarkable collection of old violoncellos, is still living in Naples.

PAOLO ROTONDO, a distinguished amateur violoncellist, who died about the beginning of this century at Naples, and published a few compositions for violoncello. He had a magnificent collection of instruments, including violoncellos by Bergonzi, Gagliano, Grancino, Gofriller, Tecchler, etc., and an equally fine collection of bows by Tourte, Peccatte, Voirin, Vuillaume, etc., which was dispersed after his death; L. Forino securing a fine Tecchler, and other violoncellos being secured by de Piccolellis of Florence, Filippio and Rispoli of Naples. Martucci dedicated his fine violoncello sonata to Rotondo.

ENRICO SCOGNAMILLA, a clever Neapolitan violoncellist, was for some time in Buenos Ayres where Forino heard him. His present whereabouts are unknown.

FRANCESCO TASCA, who composed a number of solos and duets for violoncello, lived at Milan and Parma during the first half of the nineteenth century.

ENRICO TIGNANI was for several years teacher at the Liceo Rossini at Pesaro. He died at the age of thirty-eight somewhere about 1904, after he had been elected professor of the Florence Conservatoire.

PIETRO TONASSI (Tonazzi), was violoncellist and conductor at Venice between 1827-41. Some of his compositions for violoncello were published by Ricordi.

ISIDORO TRUFFI, a pupil of Vincenzo Merighi, was with Quarenghi together principal violoncellist at the Scala Theatre and teacher at the Conservatoire at Milan. The latter post he occupied until 1884. The favourite violoncello of Truffi came into the possession of Ferdinando Forino and belongs now to his son Luigi.

CHAPTER XXXII.

THE VIOLONCELLO IN SPAIN AND PORTUGAL.

IN spite of numerous inquiries we have failed to obtain any direct information about Spanish violoncellists, although from that country comes one of the foremost violoncellists of the present day.

PABLO DE CASALS was born in 1878 in a small town near Barcelona, where his father was an organist. Showing early signs of musical talent, he began to play the flute, violin and several other instruments until his predilection for the violoncello became manifest. At the age of thirteen he was sent to Barcelona, where he studied that instrument under José Garcia. After two years' study he carried off the first prize. Count Morphy, who heard him on that occasion, presented him to Queen Christina, and they decided to give him assistance in completing his studies. For two years these were carried on in Madrid, and at the end of that time his patrons sent him to Brussels, where the late principal of the Conservatoire, the celebrated Gevaert, advised him to go to Paris. His august patrons took umbrage at what they considered a disregard of their wishes, and young Casals was thrown back upon his own resources. He returned to Barcelona, where he obtained the recently vacant professorship for violoncello at the conservatoire. Shortly afterwards a reconciliation with Count Morphy took place, and the latter sent him to Lamoureux in Paris with a letter of recommendation. Lamoureux was ill at the time, and told him that he was not disposed to hear newcomers, but the manner and personality of Casals struck him so much that he told him to come again the next day. Mrs. B. Henderson, in "The Strad" (in an interview with Casals) tells us that the next day Lamoureux appeared even more indisposed, and remained writing at his desk while Casals played, apparently paying no attention to him. When Casals had finished, however, he rose from his seat, and crossing the room with great difficulty, he offered him an engagement for the next concert. As this only left him two days to prepare, Casals was on the point of refusing, but quickly collected himself and took the opportunity. His success was so great that he was re-engaged for the next concert, and henceforward he became the rage in Paris. Not content with his fame as a violoncellist, he appeared also as conductor, and conducted the Lamoureux orchestra on several occasions, introducing several important works by modern composers. He has set himself the task to encourage the latter, especially with regard to compositions for the violoncello. The English and Dutch composers he has singled out as most promising for the future.

Casals is a virtuoso of the highest order, who does not waste his great talent on trashy tricks to dazzle the eyes of the multitude. His performances of Bach's solo sonatas are not only delightful to the serious listener, but an object lesson to all young violoncellists. His playing is full of poetical emotion, yet always dignified, like that of his great countryman, Pablo de Sarasate.

He met with phenomenal success on his tours, which have extended all over Europe and America. In North America he toured with great success in 1904, and in March, 1905, he made his debut at the London Philharmonic Society with Saint-Saëns's A minor Concerto, playing on a fine Gagliano violoncello which was presented to him by the Queen of Spain. Since then we have heard him on several occasions, also in company with the pianist, Harold Bauer, with whom he gave a number of concerts in Paris. He married Guillermina Suggia, who studied under him in Paris. Gabriel Fauré wrote a double concerto for the young violoncellist couple, which they performed together in public. Casals has of late years been regularly before the London public, and his trio concerts with Kreisler or J. Thibaut as violinist and Bauer as pianist are fresh in all music-lovers' memories.

PORTUGAL.

Of this country we only know of two violoncellists of note:

GUILLERMINA SUGGIA, of whom Julius Klengel wrote in a letter to a friend: "I am myself the greatest admirer of her phenomenal talent . . . . such eminent executive powers, combined with so wonderful a musical temperament, is only to be found in the elect circle of artists." This version was fully borne out by her appearance at the Curtius Concert Club on January 21, 1905, when she gave a brilliant rendering of Dvořák's Concerto, Op. 104, and Piatti's "Tarantella," as well as Svendsen's "Romance" and Victor Herbert's "Serenade" (from suite). Not only was her technique remarkable, but her tone was of a masculine power seldom heard from a lady violoncellist. She has since studied under P. Casals, whom she married a few years ago, and has appeared in public in double concertos with her husband.

CARLOS DE MELLO, a distinguished amateur violoncellist, who has been engaged also for many years in researches concerning the history and literature of the violoncello. He was engaged for some time as lecturer on scientific subjects at the Carnegie Institute. In South America he had the misfortune of losing the whole of his valuable collection of violoncello music, including rare old works and numerous portraits of violoncellists, together with notes for an intended history of the violoncello. A most regrettable catastrophe to all lovers and players of that instrument. He is at present living again at Lisbon, collecting fresh material and always ready to assist those who are interested in the study of the history or literature of his beloved instrument.

CHAPTER XXXIII.

CZECHIAN VIOLONCELLISTS FROM 1800 TO 1900.

FRANZ DE BOCH, born February 14, 1808, at Poterstein, studied the violoncello at the Prague Conservatoire. In 1853 he settled in Stuttgart, where he was appointed a member of the court chapel, and in 1856 teacher of the conservatoire.

JAROMIR HRIMALY, brother of Johann, the celebrated violinist, was a violoncellist of merit. He settled at Amsterdam, where he was engaged at the Paleis voor Volksvlijt.

KASIMIR PRINCE LUBOMIRSKI, born February 13, 1813, at Czerniejow, studied the violoncello under Dotzauer. He published some fifty vocal and instrumental pieces of the lighter genre. In 1860 he lived at Równo, in Volhynia, as curator of a Latin college founded by his father, the famous patron of Beethoven.

FRANZ NERUDA, born December 3, 1843, at Brünn in Austria, travelled as solo violoncellist at an early age with his father and his sister Wilma, afterwards Lady Hallé. From 1864 till 1867 he was member of the royal chapel at Copenhagen, and in 1868 he founded the Chamber Music Society at that town. Since 1892 he is Gade's successor as conductor of the

Musikverein at Copenhagen and likewise of the Musical Union at Stockholm. He has composed a concerto and a number of solo pieces for the violoncello, as well as orchestral and choral works, chamber music, etc. In 1894 he was honoured by the title of "professor." Neruda is still (1913) active at Copenhagen.

ALOIS NERUDA is mentioned by Theo. Schulz as another brother of Lady Hallé, who was for many years violoncellist at the National Theatre at Prague and about 1892 solo violoncellist at the Imperial Opera in Vienna. Further particulars are wanting.

ALOIS KAREL studied at the Prague Conservatoire under Professor Yanatka. He finished his studies in 1859 and went to Russia, where about 1895 he was still living as a highly esteemed violoncellist (Theo. Schulz).

HANUS VYHAN (Wihan), born June 5, 1855, whose parents were at first opposed to his choice of a musical career but finally consented, studied the violoncello under Hegenbarth at the Prague Conservatoire from 1868 to 1873, finishing his studies under Charles Davidoff. Towards the end of 1873 he was appointed teacher of his instrument at the Mozarteum at Salzburg, and thence went to Berlin as solo violoncellist of Bilse's Orchestra, and from 1877 until 1880 he was chamber virtuoso in the court chapel at Sondershausen. In the latter year he became solo violoncellist in the Court Orchestra at Munich and member of the private quartet of Ludwig II. In 1888 he left Munich on his appointment as professor of the Prague Conservatoire. In 1894 he succeeded his pupil, Otto Berger *(see the latter)* as violoncellist of the famous Bohemian Quartet, which has become universally known for its perfect ensemble and poetic rendering, especially of the works of the Czechian composers. Dvorák dedicated his violoncello concerto to Wihan

ANTHONY CINK, born June 21, 1863, at Pribram, studied the

violoncello for six years at the Prague Conservatoire, under Franz Xaver Hegenbart. On leaving that institution in 1882 he was appointed professor of his instrument at the Cracow Conservatoire, and after serving his term in the army he went to Elberfeld (Rhine province) as solo violoncellist in the Municipal Orchestra. At the same time he was teacher of his instrument at Rauchenecker's school of music at that town. In 1891 he was appointed as professor at the school of the Warsaw Musical Union, and he also joined the Herman Quartet at that town. Cink has toured successfully in Austria, Germany and Russia, where he played before Nicholas II and the Tsarina.

J. KOVARIK, violoncellist of the famous Dannreuther Quartet, which tours in the United States of America, is also a Czech to judge by his name, but we have no further particulars concerning him.

OTTO BERGER, born 1873 at Machau, studied the violoncello under Wihan at the Prague Conservatoire. He founded with his co-students, Hofmann, Nedbal and Suk, the famous Bohemian String Quartet, which commenced touring with phenomenal success in 1892. In 1894 his failing health compelled him to leave the quartet, his place being taken by his late master, Wihan. Berger retired to his native place, Machau, as teacher of his instrument, and died there on June 30, 1897. All that heard him lament the early death of one who promised to become one of the foremost players of the violoncello. Theo. Schulz gives (in "Strings," 1895-6) a few names of Czechian violoncellists, about whom we possess no further particulars. They are:

THEOBALD KRETSCHMANN, contemporary violoncellist, conductor at the Salvator Votary Cathedral and leader of the Czechian Song Club in Vienna. His violoncello compositions (published by Rorich) are described as standard violoncello compositions.

ALOIS MUZIKANT (in Russia called Belagucelabre Aclouzre), an exceedingly brilliant violoncellist, who studied at the Prague Conservatoire. He was about 1895 principal violoncellist at the Imperial Opera and professor at the conservatoire at Odessa, where his extraordinary talent is greatly admired.

EM. NEPOMUCKY (Ney-pom-ooct-skee), another pupil from the Prague Conservatoire, who was in 1895 professor of violoncello at Upsala in Sweden.

HASTUY, about 1821 teacher of Krob, and composer of duets, and YANATKA, teacher of Karel before 1859, are both mentioned by Schulz as teachers of the violoncello at the Prague Conservatoire. No further details respecting them are to hand.

JULIUS JUNEK, born at Brandeis on the Elbe in 1873 was for six years a pupil of Professor H. Wihan at the Prague Conservatoire, where he studied composition under Anton Dvorák. On leaving the conservatoire in 1895 he became Berger's deputy in the Bohemian String Quartet during the illness of that remarkable artist. On his appointment as solo violoncellist at the Landestheater at Agram, he was succeeded in the former position by his late master, Wihan. Afterwards he was for three years professor of violoncello at the conservatoire at Laibach. From 1900 to 1906 he occupied the position of solo violoncellist at the Royal Theatre at Prague, where he was afterwards appointed teacher at the conservatoire and joined the Prague Trio. He is at present as imperial chamber musician, a member of the Imperial Opera Orchestra in Vienna, where he founded a string quartet in conjunction with the celebrated violinist, Ondricek. Junek has toured with great success as a soloist in Austria, and composed a number of solos for his instruments besides some songs.

WILHELM JERAL, born October 2, 1861, studied the violoncello under Hegenbarth at the Prague Conservatoire between 1873-9. Besides the violoncello he studied the pianoforte, and composition, for which he showed remarkable talent. His

Concerto, Op. 10, and some of his solos rank among the best modern works for the violoncello. The former was selected as a test piece for the Bonamy-Dobree violoncello prize at the Royal Academy, London, a few years ago. In 1880 he was appointed solo violoncellist at the Landestheater and teacher at the Styrian Musical Union at Graz, appearing frequently with marked success as soloist at important concerts. In 1888 he went to Rotterdam as solo violoncellist of the German Opera, where he occupied later on the post of conductor. He toured with great success in Germany, Austria and Holland. In 1896 he settled in Vienna where he was in 1899 engaged as solo violoncellist of the Imperial Opera, which post he still occupies. In 1901 he joined the Prill Quartet in Vienna, proving himself an excellent chamber music player.

JANTSY, the master of a *zingaro* band in the Hungarian County (Komitat) of Pressburg, was an excellent violoncellist in the earlier part of last century. His son, who was likewise a *zingaro* bandmaster, was a famous violinist, but he never could read music as he did not know the notes.

CHAPTER XXXIV.

THE VIOLONCELLO IN HUNGARY FROM 1800 TO 1900.

FERY KLETZER, born about 1830 in Hungary. He toured all over Europe in the sixties of last century and acquired a certain amount of popularity. Although he possessed distinct talent his playing did not attain a high artistic standard. Goltermann's Concerto in B minor, Op. 51, is dedicated to Fery Kletzer.

LOUIS HEGYESI, born November 3, 1853, at Arpàs in Hungary, belonged to an artistic Jewish family named Spitzer, of which "Hegyesi" is a Magyarisation. His brother is the genre painter, Spitzer, of Munich, who was very popular about the latter part of last century. Showing early signs of musical talent Hegyesi, at the age of eight years, was sent to Vienna where he commenced the study of the violoncello under Denis, and afterwards he continued under Schlesinger as a pupil of the Imperial Conservatoire. In 1865 he went to Paris where he studied under Franchomme, and held several appointments until the outbreak of the Franco-German War, when he returned to Vienna where he was engaged in the orchestra of the Imperial Opera. In 1875 he took Hilpert's place as violoncellist in the Florentine Quartet, which stood then in the zenith of its fame, but was dissolved soon after through differences between Jean Becker, the leader, and Chiostri, the viola player, who was of a quarrelsome nature. Hegyesi then commenced touring as a virtuoso and met with great success. He possessed a faultless technique, and his style was very refined and full of classical dignity, though sometimes slightly inclining to the sweetly sentimental which at that time was greatly in favour with the the musical public. His tone was exceedingly beautiful, of a sweet and singing quality, but not very strong. About the middle of the eighties he toured with the celebrated pianist, Benno Schönberger, when they visited the principal towns in Austria and Hungary. In 1886-7 he gave concerts in London, where he was well received. During that time the author became his pupil and fast friend, and followed him to Cologne where Hegyesi was appointed professor at the Rhenish Conservatoire as successor to L. Ebert. He made his debut as professor at the Gürzenich concerts in autumn 1878 with the Volkmann concerto. He played on that occasion on a Giov. Grancino of large size and opaque colour, which proved to be of insufficient power for so large a hall. The author, who was smitten with the beautiful quality of its tone, bought it, but had to abandon it for the same reason, and he sold it to Messrs. Hill and Sons, in part exchange for the beautiful and very powerful light yellow Grancino which he still uses. Hegyesi acquired soon after an exquisite Francesco Ruggerius. In 1888 he married a lady from Berlin, but soon after, his health, which had not been strong for years, gradually began to fail and he died February 27, 1894. He composed a few solos and "New Rhythmical Scale and Chord Studies for the Technical Development of the Fingers and the Bow," which is the most complete and valuable work of its kind.

AUREL VON CZERWENKA, born December 31, 1860, at Karánsebes in the county (Komitat) of Szörenyi. He commenced his studies at the "Steiermärkische Musikverein" (musical society of Styria) at Graz. In 1882 he entered the Dresden Conservatoire and continued afterwards as a private pupil of Friedrich Grützmacher. After a concert tour through Germany he was engaged as violoncellist in the celebrated Mannsfeld Orchestra. Later on he started again on prolonged concert tours in Germany, eventually settling in Graz, where he is now living as solo violoncellist at the Landestheater and professor at the Styrian Musical Union. Czerwenka is not only an eminent soloist, but also one of the finest chamber music players of the present time.

ADOLF SCHIFFER, born August 14, 1873, at Apatim, he studied at the Royal Academy, Budapest, under David Popper. On the completion of his studies he received the artist's diploma, and was appointed professor of violoncello at that institute by the side of his former master. He is also an excellent chamber music player and violoncellist of the Budapest String Quartet (Kemény, Mambriny, Szerémi, Schiffer).

DESZÖ KORDY, born at Arad in 1881, began his musical studies under his father, a violinist and conductor, at the age of six. In 1893 the family came over to London, and Deszö entered the Royal Academy of Music, where he studied the violoncello under Chevalier Ernest de Munck. In 1896 he won the Bonamy-Dobree prize and the certificate of merit in 1897. At the conclusion of his studies he was appointed as violoncellist in the orchestra of the Royal Opera Covent Garden, being then only seventeen years of age, and the youngest member of that famous institution. Afterwards he went to Brussels, where he studied for some time under Professor E. Jacobs. He possesses a fine technique of the left hand, combined with an excellent style of bowing and a powerful tone of fine quality; moreover, he is a thorough musician of a very artistic temperament. At Brussels he made his debut with E. de Munck's difficult "Concerto Dramatique," and "La

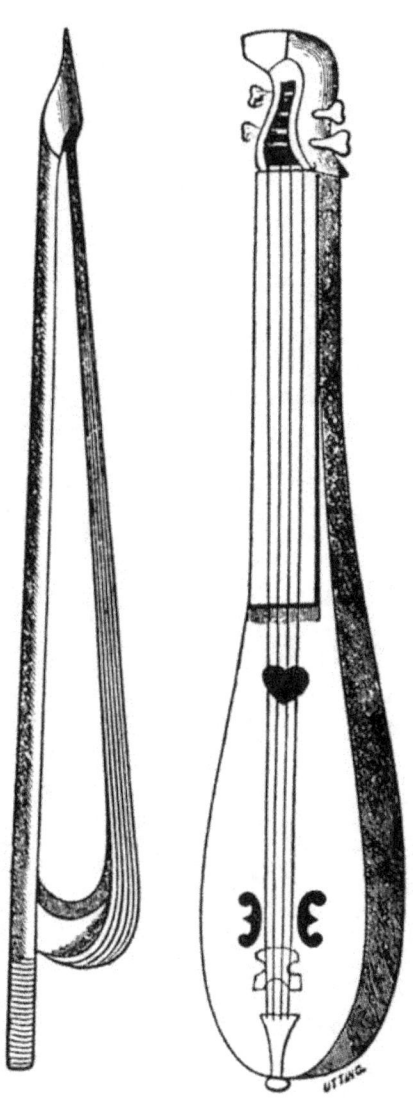

POCHETTE OR DANCING MASTER'S FIDDLE. FROM MERSENNE'S
"HARMONIE UNIVERSELLE." See page 4.

Federation Artistique" in a notice of the concert speaks of him as "Le Jean Gerardy Hongrois." He was a favourite at the house of Mrs. Lewis-Hill, the munificent art patroness in London, where he often played with Schönberger, Johannes Wolf and other celebrated artists. On her death that lady left him a legacy of five hundred pounds.

Kordy has toured with great success in Great Britain, France, Belgium and Hungary, and is at present still travelling as a soloist. He has composed a number of effective solos and arrangements published by Schott and Co.

ARNOLD FÖLDESY was born at Budapest in September, 1882. Showing early signs of musical talent, his father, a member of the Royal Hungarian Opera Orchestra, intended him to become a violinist. The boy, however, showed a decided preference for the violoncello, on the ground that he would not practice standing! His progress on the violoncello was so rapid that he made his first public appearance at Budapest when he was only seven years old, and took his audience by storm. In consequence he received many engagements, including one to play at a concert conducted by Arthur Nikisch. In 1891 he studied for a short time under David Popper, and then he went to Frankfort-on-Main, where he became a pupil of Professor Hugo Becker. At Frankfort he applied himself seriously to his work for two and a half years, at the end of which he went to Berlin, where he finished his studies under Robert Hausmann, making his public debut in the Prussian capital with the Philharmonic Orchestra, and achieving great success. After this he toured all over Europe. He made his first appearance in England in 1902, when he was received with enthusiasm.

Földesy has since been heard in London on many occasions, each subsequent appearance confirming the first impression.

His technique is phenomenal and his tone is good; in fact, he is a veritable Paganini on the violoncello, though in breadth of style and thoughtfulness he cannot yet compare with our best masters of the instrument.

There are several Hungarian violoncellists of distinction, about whom we have so far failed to obtain particulars. They are: VON SEBESTHAL at Graz; N. C. ZUPANCIC at Oedenburg; W. FIEDLER, teacher at the conservatoire at Szeged; A. RIEGELE and K. SKRIPECZ at Pressburg; W. RIESER, teacher at the conservatoire at Temesvar; DR. B. GARZO and E. MARKO, violoncellists of two different permanent quartets at Kecskemét.

CHAPTER XXXV.

POLISH VIOLONCELLISTS OF THE NINETEENTH CENTURY.

ADAM HERMANN, born in 1800, of German parents, at Warsaw. He was a successful teacher at the Imperial Conservatoire and solo violoncellist of the Imperial Opera of that town. Among his many pupils were his son Adam *(see later on)*, Komorowski, Thalgrün, Moniuszko and Kontski.

SAMUEL KOSSOWSKI, born 1805 in Galicia, was an entirely self-taught violoncellist, who nevertheless acquired a high degree of virtuosity. According to Wasielewski, he appeared with great success at Vienna, Berlin, Warsaw, Kieff, etc., during the years 1842-52, and died at Kobryn in the Government of Grodno in *1851!* According to this, he was not only autodidact but also a sort of phantom violoncellist, who appeared as concert-giver during the year after his death.

JOSEPH SZABLINSKI, born June 8, 1809, at Warsaw, was for over forty years principal violoncellist at the Imperial Theatre of his native town. He combined virtuosity and beauty of tone with high artistic qualities, and excelled particularly as quartet player.

STANISLAUS SZCZEPANOWSKI, born 1814, at Krakow, was a

virtuoso on the violoncello and the guitar. He toured successfully in his double capacity in France and England during the year 1839. His wife and children remained in the latter country, where his son is still living as teacher of the violin at Trinity College. Stanislaus Szczepanowski made a successful debut at Berlin in 1843. He died about 1875.

MORITZ KARASOWSKI, born September 22, 1823, at Warsaw, studied the violoncello and pianoforte under Valentin Kratzer, director of music of that town. In 1851 (Wasielewski gives the date as 1852) he became a member of the theatre orchestra at Warsaw. In 1858 and 1860 he visited Berlin, Vienna, Dresden, Munich, Cologne and Paris for the sake of further study, and in 1864 he was appointed chamber musician in the Royal chapel at Dresden. He published a few effective solos for violoncello and pianoforte, and some songs. As a music historian he acquired a world-wide reputation by his "Life of Chopin," which, like his "History of Polish Opera," lives of Haydn and Mozart, Chopin's youth, etc., was originally published in Polish. The first German translation was published in 1877, and the third enlarged edition appeared in 1881.* Karasowski died at Dresden, April 20, 1892.

IGNACE KOMOROWSKI, born February 24, 1824, at Warsaw, was a pupil of Adam Hermann. After completing his studies he was appointed at the theatre of his native town. He acquired great popularity by his poetical and charming Polish songs, and died October 14, 1857.

ADAM HERMANN, son of the above-mentioned Adam Hermann, born 1836 at Warsaw, changed his name to Hermanowski. He received his first instruction from his father. In 1852 he entered the Brussels Conservatoire as pupil of Servais. In

---

* The second English edition was issued in 1906. "Frederic Chopin, His Life and Letters," by Moritz Karasowski. Translated by Emily Hill. Two volumes. (William Reeves.)

1854 he left that institute with the first prize, and returned to Warsaw, whence he toured successfully in Poland and Russia. In 1888 he was still living in retirement at Warsaw.

JOHANN KARLOWICZ, born May 28, 1836, in Lithuania, commenced the study of the violoncello under Julius Lyko at Wilna, continuing under Göbella at Moscow, Sebastian Lee at Hamburg, and finally, in 1859-60, under Servais at Brussels. He was for several years teacher at the Warsaw Conservatoire. In his native country he enjoyed the reputation of one of the greatest linguists of his time.

SIGISMUND KONTSKI is mentioned by Wasielewski as a pupil of the elder Hermann, who settled in St. Petersburg. He appears to have been a relation of the celebrated four brothers Kontski.

STANISLAUS THALGRÜN, born August 16, 1843, of German origin, at Warsaw. After completing his studies, he was appointed principal violoncellist at the theatre of his native town.

BOLESLAF MONIUSZKO, born October 25, 1845, son of the Polish composer, Stanislaus Moniuszko, was violoncellist of the Warsaw Theatre in 1888.

JOSEPH ADAMOWSKI, born 1862, in Warsaw, commenced his studies at the conservatoire of his native town, continuing under Fitzenhagen at Moscow from 1877 to 1883. He left that institute with a diploma and the large silver medal. After touring in Poland and Galicia, he was appointed teacher at the Krakow Conservatoire, which position he held until 1887. After nearly two years of touring he went to America in 1889, where he was engaged for the Boston Symphony Orchestra, and joined the string quartet founded by his brother, the violinist, F. Adamowski, in conjunction with his brother and his wife, the pianist Antoinette Adamowski-Szumowska, the Adamowski Trio, which has gained renown in America. Since 1902 he is teacher at the New England Conservatory of Music in Boston, where he is also in great request as a private teacher.

CHAPTER XXXVI.

THE VIOLONCELLO IN RUSSIA FROM 1700 TO 1900.

IN Russia, as in all Slavonic countries, music presents an essential feature of the national life, entering into all phases of the existence of its people. All their joys and sorrows, longings of the heart and exuberance of spirit find spontaneous expression in their national songs and dances. Rhythm and elementary form are always clearly defined in these healthy productions, the direct children of Nature, which bear all the elementary features of music as a fine art, as a child bears those of a grown-up person. Civilisation is of very recent date among Russians. They were a wild race of Asiatic warriors until they came into closer contact with vanquished Western neighbours.

Not before the reign of Peter the Great did they become acquainted with the social and artistic life of Western Europe.

In 1720 the Duke Carl Ulrich of Holstein-Gottorp took refuge at the court of Peter the Great, whose daughter he afterwards married. He brought with him his small private band, consisting of excellent musicians, including the brothers Hübner, of whom one was conductor, the other principal violinist of this little orchestra. The instruments represented therein were: several violins, viol d'amour, viola, one violoncello (bassette), one double-bass (large bass violin), two oboes, two flutes, two horns, two trumpets and kettledrums.

They played chiefly compositions by German and Italian masters of their time (Telemann, Keiser, Heinichen, Schulz, Fuchs, Corelli, Tartini, Porpora, etc.), which so delighted the Czar and his nobles that they were commanded to appear regularly at court, and formed the nucleus of the imperial court chapel. Peter's successor, Peter II, was so enthusiastic a lover of music that he took up the study of the violoncello under Riedel *(see page 179)*, a Silesian, who was a member of the court chapel and fencing-master to the Czar. The Tsarina Anna enlarged the court chapel by the addition of several prominent artists which were sent to her by August II of Poland, who selected them from his large court orchestra. Among these were the Italian violoncellist, Gasparo, and later on Giuseppe dall'Oglio from Padua arrived likewise via Dresden. Dall'Oglio was succeeded in 1763 by his compatriot:

CICIO POLLIARI. These became the teachers of the Russians in the art of violoncello playing, with the result that we find the name of CHORCHEWSKI as that of one of the violoncellists in the Imperial Chapel about 1770. The instrument gradually became a great favourite among the Russian aristocracy, and during the first half of the nineteenth century we find the names of PRINCE TRUBETZKOI, BARON STROGANOW and

COUNT MATHIEU JÜRGEWITCH WIELHORSKI among the eminent violoncellists of their time. The latter was of Polish origin, his family having settled in Russia after the first partition* of Poland in 1772. He was born in Vol-

---

* Wasielewski says: "After the *third* partition." That is evidently wrong as that took place eight years after the birth of M. Wielhorski, viz., in 1795.

hynia, October 19, 1787, and showing early musical talent, he studied first the pianoforte, and afterwards also musical theory and the violoncello. Romberg became his master for the latter instrument, on which Wielhorski excelled. The high esteem in which he was held by his contemporaries is shown in the many works dedicated to him, among others, the famous "Morceau de Concert," by Servais, and the "Duo Brilliant," for violin and violoncello with orchestra, Op. 39, by H. Vieuxtemps.

Wielhorski was director of the Imperial Musical Society at St. Petersburg. He died in 1863, leaving his extensive and important library to the St. Petersburg Conservatoire and his Stradivari violoncello to Charles Davidoff. His brother:

COUNT MICHAEL WIELHORSKI, born 1788, was violinist and a gifted composer, who wrote two songs with violoncello *obbligato*, which were sung by Mantius in 1835 and described in the "Allgemeine Musikzeitung" as "full of feeling, and original." Schumann, who visited the brothers Wielhorski in Moscow in 1844, says of Michael: "He is the most talented ("genialste"—possessing most genius) amateur I have ever met." He composed also variations for violoncello, a string quartet, etc. The youngest brother:

COUNT JOSEPH WIELHORSKI, was also a talented violoncellist as well as pianist and composer.

Wasielewski describes Joseph and Michael erroneously as *nephews* of Mathieu Wielhorski.

NICOLAS DE WLADIMIROFF, to whom Servais dedicated his Fantasia, Op. 8, was another distinguished amateur violoncellist belonging to the aristocracy of St. Petersburg about the middle of last century.

ARVED POORTEN, born at Riga in 1835, was one of the foremost Russian violoncellists, who was particularly esteemed as a teacher, and formed a great number of excellent pupils. He was himself a pupil of F. A. Kummer, and afterwards visited the Brussels Conservatoire. After touring in Belgium, Hol-

NICOLAUS ZYGMANTOWSKI. FROM AN ENGRAVED PORTRAIT BY
C. SATZEN.

To face page 616.

land, Germany and Russia, he was appointed a member of the Imperial Chapel and teacher at the Conservatoire of St. Petersburg. He published "Six Morceaux Caracteristiques" for violoncello.

He died at Riga June 1, 1901.

CHARLES DAVIDOFF, born March 15, 1838, at the little town of Goldingen in Kurland, is the first Russian violoncellist who ranks with the great masters of his instrument. In 1840 his parents removed to Moscow, where Charles began his musical studies at a very early age, and soon developed a decided predilection for the violoncello. At the age of twelve he became a pupil of H. Schmidt, who was then principal violoncellist at the Moscow Theatre. At the beginning he studied the violoncello only as amateur, visiting first the Gymnasium (grammar school), and from 1854-8 the Moscow University as a student of mathematics. After studying the violoncello for some time under Charles Schuberth at St. Petersburg, he went to Leipzig, where he devoted himself chiefly to the study of composition under Moritz Hauptmann. His progress was so remarkable that he intended to choose that art as the principal aim of his life. His love for the violoncello, however, gained the upper hand. On December 15, 1859, he produced his first violoncello concerto, Op. 5, at one of the Gewandhaus Concerts at Leipzig with such phenomenal success that this occasion finally decided his career, and ranked him at once with the greatest violoncellists of his time. Although his technique was equalled by few, and surpassed by none, he never evinced the ambition to shine as a virtuoso but rather strove to develop the means of poetical expression of his instrument in an ingenious and thoughtful manner. In this sense he treated also the virtuoso side of his art by the invention of novel and brilliant passages which were always subservient to the poetical idea of his compositions, and not a mere technical display of fireworks strung together by threadbare themes which in other virtuoso pieces merely serve as an apology for the former.

He was one of the first masters to study the nature of his instrument, and to bring out its intrinsic beauties in their proper light, instead of trying to find out how many gymnastics are possible, which after a deal of weary practice give no better effect than played on a second-rate violin.

Davidoff came to the just conclusion that the two lower strings can only be used effectively within one octave from the open strings, except for harmonics which, of course, allow but a limited use. Neither produces the D string a beautiful tone throughout its compass. This leaves only the A string on which to roam about at will. With regard to his concertos, he says: "To produce well sounding virtuoso passages I considered it necessary to remain chiefly on two strings, D and A, if not on one, the A string only." (See Wassili Hutor, "Carl Davidoff und seine Art das Violoncell zu behandeln.")

In this sense he altered also the fingering in many passages of Romberg's concertos. Romberg was very partial to passages in thumb positions, running right across the strings, thus employing the higher register of the G and even C string; which passages never sound quite satisfactorily, although in the case of these concertos they are often conceived in such a manner that it is impossible to employ any other but Romberg's fingering.

With regard to the technique of the bow, Davidoff laid down important rules as the result of a searching analysis of all that had been achieved by previous masters, comparing it with the bowing used by the greatest violinists of his time. In this he stood not alone as the influence of the violin technique upon the violoncello is clearly traceable in older masters, and Vaslin, professor of the Paris Conservatoire, acknowledges his indebtedness to the great violinist, Baillot, in his "L'art du Violoncelle."

Davidoff used to advise his pupils to "go and listen attentively and observantly to the best violinists, as it was to them he owed all he had learned." Jokingly, he added: "I should be glad to listen also to a good violoncellist sometimes, but, alas—there are none!"

This is, of course, an absurd statement, at a time when Servais, Franchomme, De Swert and Kummer were in the zenith of their glory.

Davidoff's playing was distinguished by absolute purity of intonation. His tone was always beautiful, rich and full, even in the most rapid and difficult passages which he played with such ease and perfection that the listener would never be made aware of their difficulty. His style was dignified and full of reserve, except when a climax was reached which required the fullest expression. At such moments Davidoff would show great emotional power, with all the resources at his command to give it the fullest expression. All cheap sentimentality which tries to win the applause of the multitude was alien to his nature, he detested it. A short time after his debut in Leipzig Grützmacher resigned his position in 1860 and went to Dresden. His post was offered to Davidoff, who accepted it but resigned it again after a short period, in order to travel. He visited Holland, returning through northern Germany to Russia, where he toured for some time, and was appointed imperial solo violoncellist to the Tsar and of the Imperial Musical Union. In 1862 he became professor of violoncello at the Petersburg Conservatoire. In the following years he visited Germany, Belgium and England. In 1871 he was director of the music section at the great Polytechnic Exhibition at Moscow. In 1874 he appeared as soloist at the Paris Conservatoire concerts. In 1876 he was appointed director of the St. Petersburg Conservatoire and the Imperial Musical

Union. He resigned these positions in 1887 and toured again in 1888.

During this tour he played among other compositions, Kousnetzoff's "Berceuse" and the "Cantabile" by Cesar Cui. His portrait appears in the accompanying Fig. 60.

Davidoff was a great admirer of Schumann's Concerto in A

FIG. 60. CHARLES DAVIDOFF.

minor, which he did his utmost to popularise by playing it frequently in public, and by preparing a carefully fingered and bowed edition (published by Hugo Poh'e in Hamburg). He induced also his favourite pupil, Alexander Werzbilowicz, to make his first debut with this concerto, which he considered as thoroughly in the nature of the instrument, showing off its beauties in a manner that stands out from anything that has ever been written for the violoncello, in spite of the somewhat heavy and lengthy finale.

As a composer Davidoff stands above the virtuoso-composer. He has contributed successfully to almost every branch of his art, and although he was not endowed with marked originality, he had a distinct melodious vein which showed a fine poetical nature. His style is based upon the German romantic school with a strong admixture of the Slavonic element. This is particularly noticeable in his pianoforte quintet, a work of intrinsic merit, containing many exquisite beauties. His numerous solos for the violoncello are too well known to require detailed comment here. His "Am Springbrunnen" is one of the most popular solos in the whole literature of the violoncello.

His "Waltzer" (from the four pieces published by Peters) is another exquisite and brilliant piece. His concertos form part of the repertoire of all well-known virtuosos. For a detailed account of his compositions see E. van der Straeten, "The Literature of the Violoncello." Davidoff died on February 26, 1889, at Moscow, a brilliant star, extinguished too soon. His death was mourned by many young musicians, who received scholarships, and even the means of sustenance, through his instrumentality. As director of the St. Petersburg Conservatoire he increased the number of scholarships at that institution to a considerable extent.

Davidoff possessed one of the finest Stradivari violoncellos, which was presented to him by Count Mathieu Wielhorski. It was sold after his death to a French amateur for 80,000 francs.

ALEXANDER WIERZBILOWICZ, born January 8, 1850, at St. Petersburg, stands foremost among Russian violoncellists of the present time. He studied at the Imperial Conservatoire of St. Petersburg under Charles Davidoff, where his exceptional

622 THE HISTORY OF THE VIOLONCELLO.

talent was recognised by the bestowal of the gold medal. He received his first appointment as solo violoncellist of the Imperial Opera, and toured with great success in Russia and Europe. The Czar honoured him by nominating him his solo

S. KORGUEFF.   E. KRÜGER.   A. WERZBILOWITSCH.   L. VON AUER.

FIG. 61. THE ST. PETERSBURG QUARTET.

violoncellist. At present he is professor for his instrument at the Imperial Conservatoire and violoncellist of the St. Petersburg Quartet. His portrait appears in a group of the Petersburg Quartet, of which Professor Leopold von Auer is the leader.

ALFRED VON GLEHN, born January 6, 1858, at Reval, studied at the Imperial Conservatoire at St. Petersburg under Charles Davidoff, obtaining the grand medal and a diploma.

He received his first appointment in the orchestra of the Imperial Opera at St. Petersburg, afterwards going to Berlin as solo violoncellist of the Philharmonic Orchestra. His successful concert tours brought him to Moscow, Kiev, Charkov, Voronesh, Reval, Riga, Berlin, Leipzig, Dresden, London, Paris, New York and many other important towns. Returning from his Berlin engagement, he was appointed professor of violoncello at Charkov, and at present he holds a similar position at the Moscow Conservatoire.

He has published a number of arrangements of pieces by Russian composers. Like the late Dr. Alfred Stelzner he holds the opinion that the string quartet should consist of four instruments of different compass, instead of having two violins of equal tuning. For this reason he constructed a new instrument which he calls the "Tenorgeige" (tenor violin). It is tuned exactly like Dr. Stelzner's "violotta," viz., thus holding the middle between the viola and the violoncello. In the orchestra it is intended to enforce the tone of the violoncellos in their higher register.

ANATOLE BRANDOUKOFF, born 1859 at Moscow, studied the violoncello under Fitzenhagen at the Moscow Conservatoire from September, 1870, until May, 1878. He left that institute after gaining the gold medal and a diploma of honour, starting on a tour in Switzerland where he met with particularly great success at Bern and Geneva. In 1879 he visited Paris, and thence went on a tour through the French provinces. In 1887-8 he appeared with great success in Moscow and St. Petersburg. In 1890 he settled in Paris where he is highly esteemed as soloist and quartet player. Early in the nineties he revisited London, where his refined playing and excellent tone were greatly appreciated. Tchaïkovsky admired his playing so much that he wrote his "Pezzo Capriccioso" for him. Brandoukoff has published a violoncello concerto and a number of solo pieces for his instrument.

PETER DANIELTSCHENKO, born 1860 at Kiev, entered in 1873 the Moscow Conservatoire, where he studied the violoncello under Fitzenhagen until 1880. After gaining the small gold medal with a diploma of merit and a special prize for composition he left that institute and was appointed professor of the violoncello at the Imperial Conservatoire at Charkov, which position he occupied for one year, during which he toured also with great success in southern Russia. In 1881 he made a brilliant debut at the Moscow Exhibition as the result of which he was appointed member of the Moscow Imperial Chapel and teacher at the Philharmonic Institute (school of music). He resigned that position in 1887 in order to tour as soloist in France, Switzerland and southern Russia.

IWAN SARADSCHEV, born 1863 at Tiflis in the Caucasus, studied the violoncello under Fitzenhagen at the Moscow Conservatoire from 1879 till 1886. He gained the large silver medal with diploma, and was appointed director of the Imperial Conservatoire at Tambov. This position he exchanged in 1887 for the professorship at the Imperial Conservatoire of Tiflis.

GEORG TALENT, born 1863 at St. Petersburg, commenced the study of the violoncello when he was already twenty-one years old. After leaving the polytechnic at Riga he went to St. Petersburg, where he entered the Imperial Conservatoire, studying the violoncello under Davidoff and composition under Rubinstein. He then went to Tiflis as soloist and teacher at the conservatoire, where he remained for some years. Afterwards he went to Dresden to resume his studies under Friedrich Grützmacher. He has appeared in many towns with brilliant success as soloist, and he is at present solo violoncellist at the Municipal Theatre at Breslau in Silesia.

KARL VON SKARZYNSKI, born January 6, 1873, at Libawa on the Baltic. He commenced his musical studies as a violinist and flute player, but on leaving the college (gymnasium) he decided in favour of the violoncello. He entered the Warsaw Conservatoire, which he left with a diploma in 1896. Thence he went to Leipzig where he entered the conservatoire, and studied under Professor Klengel until 1899. After touring for some time successfully in Germany, Austria and Russia he was offered the professorship for his instrument at the Krakow Conservatoire, which position he still occupies. He has published a number of compositions for his instrument.

JEAN SCHWILLER, born 1885 in Russia, studied under Julius Klengel at Leipzig and afterwards under Hugo Becker at Frankfurt and Massau at Verviers. He combines temperament and musicianship with a remarkable technique and fine tone, and has toured successfully on the Continent, as well as in England and America. In 1907 he took part in the first performance in London of a new violoncello sonata by Bruno Muggelini, at one of that pianist-composer's concerts. He appeared in the same year (1907) at the Promenade Concerts where he played Lalo's Concerto in D.

MISCHEL CHERNIAVSKY, born November 2, 1894, is a pupil of Herbert Walenn, who considers him a remarkable genius. "His talent is heaven-born," says Mr. Walenn, "and he should prove a second Gerardy!" He appeared in London a few years ago as a prodigy, together with a sister and brother in the Cherniavsky Trio, when the three children created quite a sensation. They visited South Africa in 1908 and in the following year they toured in German South-West Africa, East Africa, Egypt, Australia, New Zealand and Tasmania. Wherever they appeared they met with phenomenal success. In 1910 they toured in America, and since then have given several concerts in London again.

LOUIS ALBRECHT is mentioned as one of Davidoff's best

pupils. He wrote an elegy for violoncello published by Rahter in Leipzig.

DR. SERGE BARJANSKY, a native of Odessa, who made a successful debut in London in June, 1909, is at present living in Hamburg, where he has established a high reputation as soloist and chamber music player. In 1912 he appeared with success at a concert of the London Symphony Orchestra. He is the possessor of a very fine Stradivari violoncello which was illustrated in "The Strad" (November, 1909).

ALEXANDER KOUSNETZOV, of whose life and career we possess unfortunately but few particulars, was a pupil of Davidoff. Of his career as a violoncellist we know equally little except that he took part in the first performance of Tchaïkovsky's sextet at the Hotel Rossiya at St. Petersburg in 1890. It was then played to a small circle of friends, including Glazounov, Liadov and Laroche. His name in Rosa Newmarch's "Life of Tchaïkovsky," appears as Kousnietzov. He is a gifted composer and has contributed to the literature of his instrument a delightful quartet for violoncellos which shows strongly the influence of Tchaïkovsky, also a very poetic berceuse for the same combination, and several effective solo pieces.

Among the Russian composers for the violoncello we have to mention CESAR CUI, whose "Cantabile" figured with Kousnetzov's "Berceuse" (arranged by the composer for violoncello solo with pianoforte) as one of the favourite solo pieces in Davidoff's repertoire. There are also several other solo pieces by this composer.

BORIS HAMBOURG, born 1884, at Voronez in South Russia, belongs to a family of eminent musicians. His father, Michael Hambourg, from whom he received his first musical training in pianoforte playing, was likewise the teacher of his brothers, Mark Hambourg, the famous pianist, and Jan Hambourg, an excellent violinist. He showed an early predilection for the violoncello, which he studied for some time under

Herbert Walenn and afterwards for a period of five years under Professor Hugo Becker. In 1901 Joachim heard him at a pupils' concert at the Hoch Conservatoire in Frankfort-on-Main, and predicted a brilliant future for him. In 1902 he made his debut at the Tchaïkovsky festival at Pyrmont, where he took his master's place, who was prevented through sudden illness. He played Tchaïkovsky's "Roccoco Variations" and obtained a great success. After a number of successful concerts in Germany, he visited Australia and New Zealand in 1903 in company with his brother Mark. During this tour he played one hundred different pieces in sixty-five concerts. Meanwhile he had come to the conclusion, like Vaslin and others before him, that much was to be learned in the art of bowing from a great violinist, and in 1904 he went to Ysaye's country house at Godine in the Ardennes and studied with him for some time. This led him to the reversal of many accepted theories, especially with regard to the use of the point and upper part of the bow, and the attack of accented notes in the up bow, which is much sharper and incisive than in the down bow. That theory had, by the by, already found expression in the author's "The Technics of Violoncello Playing." The result of Hambourg's studies were great elegance and freedom in bowing, combined with great agility of the left hand. On his return he gave a series of historical recitals at the Æolian Hall, London, where he brought forward a number of works by older masters, specially arranged for him by the author, including a fine concerto by Porpora, andante from a concerto by F. W. Rust, pieces by Abaco, Gabrieli, as well as the adagio from the author's "Suite on English Airs." Since then Hambourg has toured all over Europe and America with constant success, which also attended his appearance in London during the season 1913. He has settled with his father and brother Jan in Toronto since 1911.

LENNART VON ZWEYGBERG, born at Jyvaskyla (Finland),

visited the University of Helsingfors, where, besides the study of philosophy, he devoted himself to the violoncello under G. Schnéevoigt at the orchestral school, Jan Sibelius being his master for theory and composition. From 1898 to 1899 he studied under Professor C. Schröder at the Sondershausen Conservatoire, and afterwards he acquainted himself with the Belgian school, studying for some time under Ed. Jacobs at Brussels. After filling various engagements in Finland and Russia, where he distinguished himself as soloist, he received a scholarship from the Finnish government which enabled him to finish his studies under Ed. Jacobs at Brussels. In 1902 he was appointed teacher at the conservatoire at Krefeld (Rhine province), solo violoncellist of the Municipal Orchestra and member of the Krefeld String Quartet. In all three capacities he is held in high esteem. In December, 1911, he played with success Brahms's Sonata in F in London with the pianist, Johann Wysman.

CHAPTER XXXVII.

AMERICAN AND NEW ZEALAND VIOLONCELLISTS

LUCY MÜLLER-CAMPBELL, born at Lexington, Kentucky, U.S.A., showed very early signs of musical talent. After studying the violin and the pianoforte for some years she took up the violoncello when she was in her tenth year. The family had meanwhile removed to Berlin where the violoncellist Koch became her first master. Afterwards she entered the Hochschule, where she studied under Professor Robert Hausmann. After touring for some time as a soloist she went to Vienna, where she joined the Soldat-Röger Ladies' Quartet, which with the Shinner Quartet, takes the foremost rank among ladies' quartets. They have toured with great success all over the Continent, and at their regular concerts in Vienna they were on several occasions joined by the Joachim quartet. In 1900 they played at the Beethoven Festival at Bonn. In November, 1900, Miss Campbell married the imperial notary, Dr. Guido Müller, since when she has retired from her public professional career.

ANTON HEGNER, a violoncellist at New York, who was for some time a member of the Damrosch Orchestra, accompanied Mme. Patti on her last American tour. Apparently he is of

German or Swiss origin—related to Otto Hegner, the pianist. He has composed a violoncello concerto and a number of solos for that instrument said to be of distinct merit.

FRANZ LISTEMANN, born December 17, 1873, in New York, studied between 1887-90 at the Boston Conservatoire, under Fries and Giese. Afterwards he went to Leipzig, where he studied under Professor Julius Klengel, and he finished his studies at Berlin under Professor Robert Hausmann, with whom he remained from 1893 till 1895. His first appointment he received as principal violoncellist in the Pittsburg Orchestra, but resigned after one year, and settled in New York, where he is now living as soloist, chamber music player and teacher of the violoncello.

America has no doubt since produced a number of excellent young violoncellists, but of these we possess so far no particulars.

The youngest continent as regards modern civilisation has so far produced but few violoncellists, one of whom is occupying a prominent position as a virtuoso and talented composer.

ARNOLD TROWELL was born June 25, 1887, at Wellington, New Zealand, and commenced the study of music, together with his twin brother, Garnet, under his father's guidance, the former on the violoncello, the latter on the violin.

Jean Gerardy, who heard Arnold on his visit to Australia, was so much impressed by his latent talent that he gave him some lessons, and on leaving recommended him to go to Europe for his further studies. He went to Frankfort-on-Main, where he became a pupil of Hugo Becker, continuing his studies later on at the Brussels Conservatoire, where he took lessons in composition from Paul Gilson. At the age of seventeen he gained the first prize for violoncello playing at that institute, and soon afterwards made his European debut in the Belgian capital.

In 1907 he gave a number of very successful recitals in London, and since then he has toured extensively throughout Great Britain with many of the foremost artists of the time.

In 1912-3 he gave a number of recitals in London, producing some almost forgotten works by Galliard, De Fesch, Caporale, Veracini and other old masters. He also gave some fine renderings of the solo suites by J. S. Bach, including the sixth Suite in D, which has been undeservedly neglected by violoncellists. To the literature of his instrument he has already contributed very extensively, including two concertos. The first, in D minor, Op. 33, he played at one of the Liverpool symphony concerts in March, 1909, and at the Crystal Palace, London, in July, 1911. The second Concerto in B minor was heard for the first time at a Free Trade Hall concert at Manchester, in December, 1910. Apart from his compositions for violoncello, mostly published by Schott and Co., Trowell has written a symphony (G minor, Op. 39), and a symphonic poem, which have both been performed with success; also a String Quartet, Op. 44, a pianoforte trio, a violin concerto, as well as a number of pieces for violin, pianoforte, and songs. Trowell's remarkable technique places him in a line with the greatest virtuosos of the present time.

CHAPTER XXXVIII.

THE VIOLONCELLO IN SCANDINAVIA FROM 1800 TO 1900.

THOUGH the Scandinavians are a distinctly musical nation noted for their beautiful folk-songs and national dances, the latter being chiefly cultivated by the Norwegian fiddlers, yet their study of music as a fine art is of comparatively recent date. Copenhagen was the first town to produce some musicians of note during the eighteenth century, but not before the commencement of last century do we meet with the names of Scandinavian violoncellists who became known beyond the limits of their native country. CLOOS, a Swedish violoncellist, was member of the royal chapel at Stockholm in November, 1783. The first Scandinavian violoncellist of importance was:

CHRISTIAN LAURENTZ KELLERMAN, born January 27, 1815, at Randers in Jütland. He was destined for a mercantile career, but his love for music supervened, and at the age of fifteen he went with some relatives to Vienna. His grandfather, an enthusiastic amateur violoncellist, had expressed a wish that one of his grandchildren should take up the study of that instrument. This induced his father to buy him a violoncello. Christian showed so much talent that in his thirteenth year he made his debut as a soloist, and in the same year he was admitted to the Imperial Conservatoire, where he studied the

FIG. 62. CHRISTIAN LAURENTZ KELLERMAN.

violoncello under Joseph Merk from 1830 till 1835. At the conclusion of his studies he filled the post of first violoncellist at various theatres in Vienna, afterwards touring with great success in Austria and Hungary. In 1837 he visited St. Petersburg, where he met Ole Bull, with whom he toured for several years in Germany and northern Europe. "The Illustrated London News," of May 30, 1848, says: "Herr Kellerman arrived in London last month and first appeared at Mr. Blewett's morning concert, where his performance was received with great enthusiasm. He has since played at several other concerts with equal success." In 1847 he was appointed solo violoncellist at Copenhagen, where he remained for a number of years. In 1862 he toured again in northern Germany, visiting Stettin, Danzig, Königsberg and other important towns. In 1864 he toured with Carlotta Patti, Ferd. Laub and Jaëll in the Netherlands and Germany, but in February of that year he was attacked by an apoplectic stroke at Mayence, which prematurely ended a brilliant career. He returned to Copenhagen, where he died December 3, 1866. He left a few compositions for the violoncello which have not proved of lasting value, and are now entirely obsolete. His portrait appears in Fig. 62.

F. RAUCH succeeded him as solo violoncellist in the royal chapel at Copenhagen, but we possess no further details, except that he was the master of Rüdinger *(see later on)*.

WULF FRIES, born in or about 1825, went to America and was appointed principal violoncellist in the Boston Symphony Orchestra soon after its foundation. He was also for twenty-three years a member of the Mendelssohn Quintet Club at that town, where he died at the age of seventy-seven in 1902.

KANUT KÜNDINGER, born November 11, 1830, studied under Jos. Menter at Munich. In 1849 he became a member of the Royal Court Orchestra at that town. He is held in high esteem as soloist and teacher of his instrument. Among his many pupils he counts Professor Hugo Becker.

FRITZ ALBERT CHRISTIAN RÜDINGER, born 1838 at Copenhagen. He studied the violoncello under F. Rauch, and was appointed member of the royal chapel at Copenhagen in 1864.

In 1866 he went to Dresden, where he studied for some time under Friedrich Grützmacher, and returned to his native town as royal chamber musician. In 1874 he became first violoncellist in the court orchestra and professor at the Royal Conservatoire. He is also an excellent chamber musician.

SIEGFRIED NEBELONG, born 1859 at Christiania, in Norway, commenced his study of the violoncello at Copenhagen, afterwards going to Dresden, where he became a pupil of Friedrich Grützmacher. He is (1909) a royal chamber musician and violoncellist at the Royal Opera at Dresden. He has toured with great success in Germany and Scandinavia, and has been decorated by the King of Saxony with the Order of Albrecht.

OSSIAN FOHSTRöM, born November 21, 1873, at Helsingfors in Finland, where he commenced his studies of the violoncello. In 1893 he went to Brussels, where he entered the Royal Conservatoire as a pupil of Ed. Jacobs. In 1894 he gained the second prize, and in the following year the first prize for violoncello playing. Afterwards he toured successfully in Finland and Russia, extending his tours even to Siberia.

GEORG SCHNÉEVOIGT, born November 8, 1872, at Wiborg in Finland, where his father was conductor of the Orchestral Union. He commenced his studies at the orchestral school of the Philharmonic Society in Helsingfors, continuing under Carl Schröder at the conservatoire at Sondershausen, afterwards he studied for some time under Julius Klengel and finished his studies under Ed. Jacobs at Brussels. In 1892 he was appointed solo violoncellist of a concert orchestra at Moscow, and in the following year he joined the Laube Orchestra at Hamburg. In 1895 he was appointed solo violoncellist of the Philharmonic Orchestra at Helsingfors, and in the following year he became a professor at the conservatoire and the orchestral school of that town. He tours every year in the company of his wife, an excellent Finnish pianist, visiting the principal towns of Scandinavia, Russia, Germany and England. In 1898 he gave his first concerts at Berlin with the Philharmonic Orchestra and met with great success. The press was unanimous in praising his brilliant technique and his full and sympathetic tone. Schnéevoigt is not only an eminent violoncello virtuoso, he excels also as conductor. In 1901 he was engaged as conductor of the Exhibition Concerts at Riga, meeting with such success that he was permanently engaged for the summer concerts of that town.

A few years ago (about 1910) he made a successful appearance in London.

AGGA FRITSCHE is a talented young Danish violoncellist, born at Copenhagen, who studied under Albert Rüdinger, afterwards going to Leipzig, where she entered the conservatoire as a pupil of Professor Julius Klengel. After touring successfully in Scandinavia, Russia and Germany she settled in Copenhagen.

GASTON BORCH is a contemporary violoncellist, composer (pupil of Massenet) and conductor of the Philharmonic Society at Christiania.

Of the following violoncellists we possess no further particulars: E. OULIE, professor at the conservatoire at Christiana (1913); A. ANDERSÉN, professor at the Royal Academy of Music, Stockholm; R. CLAËSSON and CARL LINCKE, both soloists at Stockholm.

CHAPTER XXXIX.

VARIOUS FORMS OF THE VIOLONCELLO.

THE model which served for the various members of the violin family has never altered since it first made its appearance about the middle of the sixteenth century, except for slight modifications, especially in the shape of the *ff*'s and the scroll, which characterise the workmanship of various makers, but do not deviate from the essential points which distinguish the violins from the viols. Nevertheless, the progressive instinct of human nature has now and again impelled an attempt at alterations in the model and the stringing of the violoncello which generally proved ephemeral.

THE VIOLONCELLO WITH FIVE STRINGS

has already been dealt with in the first chapter of Part I.

THE VIOLONCELLO PORTATILE

by Johann Wilde, a viol d'amour virtuoso and native of Bavaria, who died in 1770 *(see page 255)*, resembled an oblong box, two feet long and nine inches wide. The neck with the finger-board was detachable, and could be placed inside this box together with the bridge and tail-pin.

J. A. Hiller, speaking about the instrument in his "Wöchentliche Nachrichten" (weekly news) says that it could be fixed up in a few minutes, and equalled in power of tone any violoncello three times its size. He does not say anything about the quality of that tone!

THE HARMONICELLO

was an invention of Joh. Carl Bischoff *(see page 183)*, and made its appearance towards the end of the eighteenth century. It had five strings and ten metal strings which ran underneath but over another finger-board so that they could be played separately. We are not informed how this was made possible. In 1797 he played the harmonicello in Hamburg with such success that enthusiastic stanzas in praise of him and his invention appeared in the papers. The latest innovation is one by the late Dr. Alfred Stelzner, of Dresden, who reformed the model of the violin family, adding two new members, viz., the violotta and the cellone.

Seeing that violin making had so far proceeded entirely on

empirical lines, he resolved to ensure the acoustic properties by scientific analysis and mathematical calculation. The first thing of importance appeared to him that the centring points of sound waves inside the body of the instrument should become concentric, otherwise there would always be a friction between waves meeting in adjoining points which would cause a certain amount of jarring. In order to obviate this it was necessary to alter the curves of the outline from circular sections to lines constructed from the ellipse and parabola; as from the latter *only* is it possible to find the centring points of reflecting sound waves. Stelzner also considered the combination of the string quartet as unsatisfactory, two treble instruments being used against one tenor and one bass. He adopted the viola therefore as "alto," and added a new tenor instrument which he called "violotta" and which is tuned:

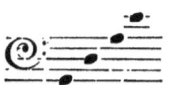 or an octave lower as the violin. In order to gain a lower bass for chamber music, for which he considered the contrabass as too heavy, he added also another bass instrument called

THE CELLONE.

This is a large violoncello about an inch higher in the body and tuned like the violotta, but an octave lower, thus taking the lower G of the three stringed contrabass. From our personal experience this string is too heavy for the size of the instrument and the tone is rather muffled while the upper strings are fairly bright. Personally we should prefer a good three-stringed contrabass to the cellone.

As for Stelzner's violoncellos the case is different. One of his instruments in the writer's possession has steadily improved, and it combines power of tone with a beautiful resonant quality and great brilliancy. The harmonics are particularly clear and strong. We give an illustration of the model of

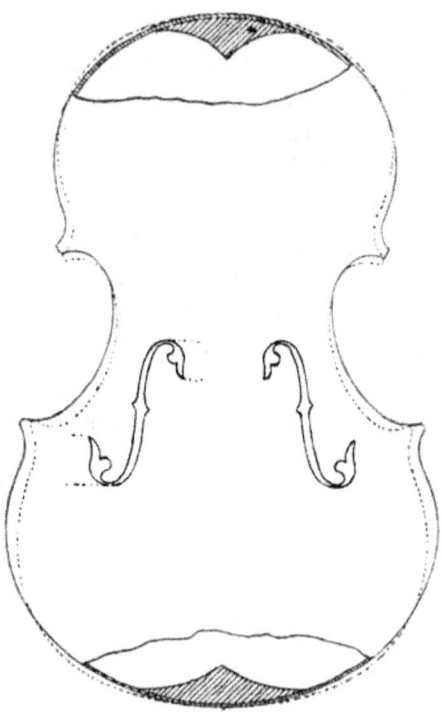

FIG. 63. SHOWING THE MODEL INVENTED BY DR. STELZNER FOR HIS GROUP OF STRINGED INSTRUMENTS. THE DOTTED LINES SHOW THE OUTLINE OF THE ORTHODOX VIOLIN FAMILY.

his instruments, and draw the reader's attention to the shape of the soundholes which are so designed that they form at both ends a larger vibrating tongue which strengthens the tone emanating from the body of the instrument.

CHAPTER XL.

CONCLUSION.

AT the beginning of the nineteenth century the violoncello had already acquired a great amount of popularity, although it was not taken up by amateur players to the extent to which we find it used during the second half of last century.

The position it held about 1800 was no less due to the technical achievements of J. L. Duport, Romberg, Bohrer and Dotzauer, than to the compositions by Boccherini which had considerably developed the virtuoso side of the instrument, and thus enlarged the scope of its general usefulness not only as a solo instrument but also in chamber music and the orchestra. Haydn had already entrusted it with important passages in his quartets and likewise in his choral and orchestral works. Under Mozart it rose to greater importance still as may be easily seen from the so-called violoncello quartets where the violoncello has many important solo or rather leading passages. Beethoven went still farther and many of his violoncello parts were considered almost unplayable even by the great Romberg *(see his biography)*. This had, of course, the effect of stirring the ambition of genuine artists among violoncellists to overcome these difficulties, and preparing the road for a modern technique which dispensed with the old-fashioned symmetrical figures which were often repeated *ad nauseam*. Broader passages of a more dramatic nature brought out the inherent beauties of the instrument in greater radiance. Not that the repeated symmetrical figure should be entirely condemned for it has a great effect when used in the right manner and in the right place as, for instance, the famous passages in the overtures to "Coriolanus" and the "Freischütz."

Mendelssohn was particularly fond of the violoncello and his works abound with most effective passages and melodies for the instrument which gave a further impetus to the executant. Schumann's works were destined to advance the technique of the violoncello even more, as his treatment of the instrument is very bold and original, and the execution of his passages require the skill of a virtuoso.

An essential quality for the adequate rendering of the German classics is a powerful tone of great breadth and roundness, and the consequence is that we find this more developed in German violoncellists of that time than the lighter and more elegant bowing of the French school. There was unfortunately another element, the bitter feeling dating from the Napoleonic wars, which prevented the recognition and adoption by either French or German of all modern achievements coming from the other side.

The German violoncellists treated the elegant spiccato, staccato and other bowings of the French in many cases as flimsy, while the French considered the greater power and solidity of the German bowing as clumsy and heavy.

This has in more recent times fortunately given way to a better insight into the true nature of art. The result has been a rapid improvement in the technique of the instrument all round. An improvement which is still steadily increasing. We cannot agree with those who opine that modern technique has reached a point where further development is unthinkable. Art stands never still, it must either progress or recede. It may recede for a time, as has been the case at intervals, but history teaches us that such periods only denote a momentary lull followed by renewed and energetic progress. If we recount the names who had the greatest share in furthering the art of violoncello playing during the first half of the nineteenth century, we must give the first places to Romberg, Dotzauer, Kummer, Franchomme and Servais.

After these came Davidoff, who freed the technique of the system of playing certain passages in fixed thumb positions across the lower strings where they lose both power and brilliancy. He taught us to avoid the lower strings in their higher register by changing the position of the hand, moving up and down freely and boldly on the upper strings.

Some of the latest violoncellists have turned their attention again to the art of the best living violinists, as some of their predecessors have done before, for instance, Vaslin, who stated that he owed his art of bowing entirely to Baillot.

Mr. Boris Hambourg studied for some time under Ysaye, adopting many features which hitherto were considered quite unsuitable to violoncello bowing. A very important item is the liberal use of the upper part of the bow, and the use of the point in up-bow for crisp and sharp attacks instead of the down-bow at the nut, which was the rule hitherto in such cases. The result is most satisfactory, as the upper part of the bow does not weight the string, and allows a much freer vibration. The writer has already advocated a freer use of the upper part of the bow in his "Technics of Violoncello Playing." The power of the stroke will, by dint of practice, become equally strong in the upper and lower part of the bow.

Unfortunately, modern composers in writing passages for concertos or solo pieces, lose sight of the fact that although the actual tone-power of the violoncello is very considerable, the slower vibrations of the notes in the middle compass of the instrument are easily covered by the more rapid vibrations of notes from higher instruments, except from such of an entirely contrasting character and a soft quality, like the flute. In the orchestra, where a number of violoncellos appear in combination, the sound-waves issuing from one will increase those issuing from another in a reciprocal manner, with the result that the volume of tone increases to such an extent that the violoncellos are able to stand out even from a *fortissimo* of the other instruments, as we know from several instances in Wagner's operas, especially in "Parsifal." In the case of a solo violoncello, however, the low compass of its notes, especially of the middle register, will be easily overshadowed by the use of too many accompanying instruments. The older masters kept this fact in mind when orchestrating violoncello solos, but some of our greatest masters of modern times have failed in this respect, as, for instance, Dvorák in his otherwise beautiful concerto. Here the arpeggio passages which should show off the instrument and the art of the player, become at times absolutely inaudible. On the other hand, the epic and dramatic grandeur of the violoncello have been brought to the fore by the best modern composers, who have not wasted their energy in writing yards of meaningless florid passages which become most tedious to the listener.

We cannot enter into details respecting modern composers and their works for the violoncello, as our space will not permit thereof, but must again refer our reader who wishes to know more about this subject to the author's "The Literature of the Violoncello," which appeared in the "Strad," and which in itself will fill a considerable volume when it appears as a book in revised form at some future date. In conclusion, let it be said that the present-day student of the violoncello is in a much happier position than the student of former times. To the latter the average master would present everything in a mysterious shroud, telling him that only the heaven-born talent could acquire this, that, or the other, which for him, the unhappy student, it would be almost useless to try. This was particularly the case with staccato bowing, which very few teachers had mastered themselves. The great violoncellists of modern times, such as Franchomme, Servais, Grützmacher, Popper and many more of the present day, have thrown open the gates of the temple of our art, and, given a natural aptitude which forms a primary condition, there is nothing therein that cannot be acquired by every student who will apply himself with intelligence and persistent zeal to his studies. The perusal of this book, apart from introducing the violoncellist to the past masters of his art, will tell him what the qualities were that appeared and appear most valued, and how they presented themselves singly or combined in various individuals.

Titles published by Travis & Emery Music Bookshop:

Bathe, William: A Briefe Introduction to the Skill of Song
Bax, Arnold: Symphony #5, Arranged for Piano for Four Hands by Walter Emery
Burney, Charles: An Account of the Musical Performances in Westminster-Abbey
Burney, Charles: The Present State of Music in France and Italy
Burney, Charles: The Present State of Music in Germany, The Netherlands ...
Crimp, Bryan: Dear Mr. Rosenthal ... Dear Mr. Gaisberg ...
Crimp, Bryan: Solo: The Biography of Solomon
Frescobaldi, Girolamo: D'Arie Musicali per Cantarsi. Primo Libro & Secondo Libro.
Geminiani, Francesco: The Art of Playing the Violin.
Hawkins, John: A General History of the Science and Practice of Music (5 vols.)
Herbert-Caesari, Edgar: The Science and Sensations of Vocal Tone
Herbert-Caesari, Edgar: Vocal Truth
Hopkins and Rimboult: The Organ. Its History and Construction.
Isaacs, Lewis: Hänsel and Gretel. A Guide to Humperdinck's Opera.
Isaacs, Lewis: Königskinder (Royal Children) A Guide to Humperdinck's Opera.
Lascelles (née Catley), Anne: The Life of Miss Anne Catley.
Mainwaring, John: Memoirs of the Life of the Late George Frederic Handel
Malcolm, Alexander: A Treaty of Music: Speculative, Practical and Historical
Mellers, Wilfrid: Angels of the Night: Popular Female Singers of Our Time
Mellers, Wilfrid: Bach and the Dance of God
Mellers, Wilfrid: Beethoven and the Voice of God
Mellers, Wilfrid: Caliban Reborn - Renewal in Twentieth Century Music
Mellers, Wilfrid: François Couperin and the French Classical Tradition
Mellers, Wilfrid: Harmonious Meeting
Mellers, Wilfrid: Le Jardin Retrouvé, The Music of Frederic Mompou
Mellers, Wilfrid: Music and Society, England and the European Tradition
Mellers, Wilfrid: Music in a New Found Land: ... ... American Music
Mellers, Wilfrid: Romanticism and the Twentieth Century (from 1800)
Mellers, Wilfrid: The Masks of Orpheus: ...... the Story of European Music.
Mellers, Wilfrid: The Sonata Principle (from c. 1750)
Mellers, Wilfrid: Vaughan Williams and the Vision of Albion
Playford, John: An Introduction to the Skill of Musick.
Purcell, Henry et al: Harmonia Sacra ... The First Book, [1726]
Purcell, Henry et al: Harmonia Sacra ... Book II [1726]
Quantz, Johann: Versuch einer Anweisung die Flöte traversiere zu spielen.
Rastall, Richard: The Notation of Western Music.
Rimbault, Edward: The Pianoforte, Its Origins, Progress, and Construction.
Rubinstein, Anton : Guide to the proper use of the Pianoforte Pedals.
Simpson, Christopher: A Compendium of Practical Musick in Five Parts
Spohr, Louis: Grand Violin School
Tans'ur, William: A New Musical Grammar; or The Harmonical Spectator
Van der Straeten, Edmund: History of the Violoncello, The Viol da Gamba ...
Van der Straeten, Edmund: History of the Violin, Its Ancestors... Vol.1.
Van der Straeten, Edmund: History of the Violin, Its Ancestors... Vol.2.

Travis & Emery Music Bookshop
17 Cecil Court, London, WC2N 4EZ, United Kingdom.
Tel. (+44) 20 7240 2129

© Travis & Emery 2009

APPENDIX

Containing Additional Information, Biographies and some Errata.

Page 12. KERLINO. A well preserved viol by this maker dated 1452, forms part of the Donaldson collection.

Pages 15-6. THE SEVEN-STRINGED VIOL. The earliest known illustration of a seven-stringed viol occurs in a book by Carmine Augurelli, 1491, a reproduction of which appears in E. Heron-Allen's "De Fidiculis Bibliographia."

Page 16. Introduction of metal covered strings. The time of their first use appears uncertain. The statement on page 16 requires modification, as Prätorius bass viol, from the "Organographia," 1620, Fig. 10, page 21, evidently shows two covered strings. See also footnote on page 102.

Page 24. THE BARYTON. The number of Haydn's compositions for that instrument was 175 : six duets for two barytons; twelve sonatas for baryton and violoncello; twelve divertimenti for two barytons and bass; 125 divertimenti for baryton, viola and violoncello; seventeen cassations in several parts; three concertos for baryton with two violins and bass. In addition, he composed several divertimenti for pianoforte with accompaniment of violins and baryton, and the cantata on the death of Frederick the Great (1786).

Page 24. SCHLOSS EISEN. The date of its destruction by fire should be 1779, not 1774.

Page 25. ANTON LIDL. Kinsky gives his christian name as Andreas, and says that he was in the service of Prince Esterhazy at Eisenstadt from 1769 to 1774. He died in London before 1789, see also page 113. By accident the biography of A. Lidl has here been connected with that of the violoncellist, JOSEPH LIEDEL, who gave the concerts mentioned with Regondi in Vienna in 1841. They appeared also in London, where they repeated their previous successes.

Page 25. LYRA TEDESCHA. G. Kinsky, in his catalogue of the Wm. Heyer Museum, proves that the name applied to the vielle or hurdy-gurdy, and not to the baryton.

Page 26. ARPEGGIONE. A rare specimen in splendid preservation with original, though damaged, label—[Joannes] Georgius Staufer [fecit Viennae anno] 1824—is in the Wm. Heyer Museum. Description and illustration in G. Kinsky's catalogue. Vincenz Schuster, who wrote a tutor for this instrument, published by Diabelli in Vienna, was the first to play F. Schubert's sonata composed in November, 1824, in public. Another virtuoso on the arpeggione was H. A. Birnbach, see pages 238-9.

Page 26. THE LYRA may be looked upon as the direct precursor of the violin, as Kinsky points out by comparison of the interesting specimen by Ventura Linarolo in the Heyer Museum with other existing specimens, drawings and illustrations, and the remarkable fact that its strings over the fingerboard were tuned exactly like those of the violin, except for the addition of a fifth string between G and D, tuned an octave higher than the fourth string of the violin (see G. Kinsky's catalogue of the Wm. Heyer Museum, Volume II, page 385 ff.).

Pages 26 *and* 33. ALFONSO FERRABOSCO, the elder, was according to Maugars, the greatest *lyra* player of his time, as well as viol da gambist. He returned to Italy in his later years, and died at Turin in 1588.

Pages 27-8, *also pages* 115-6. VIOLA POMPOSA AND VIOLONCELLO PICCOLO. In the course of last autumn the author had an opportunity to examine the instruments in the Heyer Museum, they prove beyond doubt that the viola pomposa *could* be played and no doubt *was* played like the violin. Also that the violoncello piccolo must not be confounded with the viola pomposa, but was in fact nothing more or less than a half-size violoncello. Several specimens of the violoncello piccolo are to be found in the Heyer Museum.

Another interesting fact which Dr. Kinsky has brought to light is that the sixth of the solo suites for violoncello which Bach wrote for the violoncellist and viol da gambist, Christian Ferdinand Abel (father of Carl Friedrich Abel) during his sojourn at Cöthen, was intended for a five-stringed violoncello and not for the viola pomposa as stated by A. Dörffel and Ph. Spitta. The latter instrument was only constructed after Bach had removed to Leipzig. The suite is, of course, well adapted for the viola pomposa and that has caused the error as well as the statement by some historians that the viola pomposa be tuned like the violoncello,

APPENDIX. 649

whereas in reality it is an octave higher like the viola. Christ. Gius. Lidarti wrote a sonata for viola pomposa which is in the library of the Gesellschaft der Musikfreunde in Vienna.

Page 32. LEONARDO VINCI. The autograph is that of the opera composer, born 1690 at Strongoli, therefore of a later generation than the famous painter.

Page 35. ALFONSO FERRABOSCO, the younger. Dr. Kinsky gives the date of his birth as 1570. In 1626 he was appointed as "composer of music to the king" with forty pounds per annum. In 1628 he was dead as on March 15 Thos. Tompkins was appointed in the place of Alfonso Ferrabosco, deceased.

Page 35. ALPHONSO FERRABOSCO, junior, son of the younger Ferrabosco, was appointed March 28, 1628, to the king's band with fifty pounds per annum, which his father received before him as teacher of the king when Prince of Wales, and Henry Ferrabosco (his brother ?) was appointed "composer of the king's music" with forty pounds and an additional forty pounds as musician in ordinary. Both were still in the king's band in 1641 and dead in 1661, see page 36. The confusion of these two younger Alfonsos has lead to many errors including Riemann's statement of Alfonso the younger's death, which is probably correct with regard to the third Alfonso.

Page 44. THEODORUS STEFKINS (STEFFKEN). The Steffken family were evidently of German (Netherlandish) origin as the name indicates. Chr. Huygens, in a letter to Mersenne, dated November 26, 1646, says: "On dit que le merveilleux Stepchen en est (de la Musique de l'Electeur de Brandenbourg), qu'il fait plus des miracles sur la viole de gambe, qu'homme qui fut jamais, qu'autre en faict encore d'avantage sur la viole garnie derrière la manche et ailleurs de chordes d'airain." ("It is said that the wonderful Stepchen is there (in the music of the Elector of Brandenburg) doing more wonders on the viol da gamba than any man that ever was, besides he does still more on the viol fitted at the back of the neck with metal strings.") This refers probably to the viola bastarda invented by D. Farrant at the beginning of the century. The baryton which *might* be thus indicated was apparently not known before the latter part of the seventeenth century.

Page 52. THOMAS BRITTON. A full account of his music club, as well as several fine portraits of him by Woolaston, may be found in E. van der Straeten's "The Romance of the Fiddle."

Page 53. ANN FORD. There is an interesting and entertaining account of that lady's romantic career in Miss Olga Racster's "Chats on Violoncellos." Sarah Ottey mentioned in the author's

"The Romance of the Fiddle," was a viol da gamba player who appeared in London between 1720-2, for more details see Olga Racster, "Chats on Violoncellos." Ann Ford gave concerts where she performed on the bass viol, lute, musical glasses, harmonica, guitar and sang hymns of her own composition. One of these took place in 1761, "at the Large Room, late Cock's Auction Room over the great China shop near Spring Gardens."

Page 53. Samuel Pepys, in his diary, speaks of a MRS. JAGGARD (1661) who played the bass viol "so well as I did not think any woman in England could, and but few men." Mrs. Pepys and her maid Mercer were also taught to play the "vyall" as Pepys calls it.

Page 57. HOLBORN was apparently a bass viol player of distinction. There were two brothers of this name, Anthony and William. The former was a gentleman of the Royal Chapel, who published "The Cittharone Schoole" in 1597, to which are added three-part Neapolitan airs by William Holborne. The British Museum possesses also some lute pieces by Anthony Holborn in MS.

Page 63. A. KÜHNEL. The illustration showing title page is on Plate VII, the page from the book on Plate VIII.

Page 85. CHRISTIAN FERDINAND ABEL. Was both gambist and violoncellist in J. S. Bach's orchestra at Cöthen. Bach wrote his six suites for violoncello for Abel. See above note on viola pomposa.

Page 90. J. S. Bach's gamba *obbligato* from "St. John" passion music. The illustration mentioned in footnote appears on Plate XIIA.

Page 98. TALLEMAUT DES REAUX read "TALLEMANT."

Page 110. MADAME "ADÉLAIDE" DE FRANCE. It should be MME. "HENRIETTE." The error arose from a reproduction, sent to the author, on which the former name appeared in print.

Page 114. THE BARYTON. Georg Kinsky in his catalogue of the Heyer Museum gives, besides the composers mentioned here: Aloys Tomasini, Twenty-four Divertimenti per violino, baryton and violoncello ("Gesellschaft der Musikfreunde," Vienna); Johann Georg Krause, IX Partien auf die Viola Paradon, dedicated to the Duke Christian Ulrich of Württemberg (Royal Library, Dresden); an anonymous collection of one hundred and one pieces, about 1700 (Cassels); Joseph Burgksteiner, Twenty-four Divertimenti for baryton, viola and bass; Neumann, Twenty-four Divertimenti per il Pariton, col viola e basso (MS.), (the latter two works belong to Konzertmeister G. Gutsche, Berlin); Anton Kraft, Niemecz and Ferdinand Paër likewise composed music for the baryton. Felix Battanchon (see page 529) tried unsuccessfully to revive the baryton about 1846-7.

APPENDIX.

Page 116. A concert for old instruments was given at the "Ancient Concerts," Hanover Square Rooms, April 16, 1845, before Queen Victoria and the Prince Consort (see "Illustrated London News," April 19, 1845, and Olga Racster's "Chats on Violoncellos"), when HATTON played on the beautiful Tielke gamba, now in the South Kensington Museum.

Pages 116-20. THE REVIVAL OF THE VIOL DA GAMBA. Auguste Tolbecque was an enthusiastic executant on the gamba, and possessed a fine instrument by Francis Baker, in St. Paul's Churchyard, 1696 (Thomas Britton's?).

Page 118. JEAN MARIE RAUOL read "RAOUL."

Pages 126 *and* 347. SIR WILLIAM CURTIS, amateur violoncellist and owner of the famous Andreas Amati violoncello, was the same as Sir William Curtice to whom J. Stiastny's Op. 9 is dedicated. The name is mis-spelled in the dedication.

Page 138. GALLI's "TRATTENIMENTO." Miss Racster says: "The title page . . . . furnishes us with the information that this work is the earliest known attempt at a method for the violoncello." The author's copy of the work has no text whatever although it is *supposed* to be complete. Should Miss Racster's assumption arise from an enallage of trattenimento with "trattamento"?

Pages 157 *and* 163. For TORINO read "FORINO."

Page 160. CAPORALE. In 1745 Caporale was engaged at Ranelagh Gardens, Vauxhall. Six Sonatas, Op. 1, appeared, together with six sonatas by Galliard, who published them in 1746 as "Twelve solos dedicated to the Prince of Wales," and mentioning the recent death of Caporale in the preface. One of these sonatas has lately been republished with a pianoforte accompaniment by Alfred Moffat.

Page 164. Cramer, in his magazine of the year 1783, says that the "HOFKAMMERRATH" (privy councillor) VON MASTIAUX at Bonn never missed an opportunity to hear ABACO play. Von Mastiaux was an enthusiastic amateur, who possessed a fine violoncello by Paul Aletze.

Page 164. For THAYER read "THALER."

Page 169. For FRANCESCA ZAPPA read "FRANCESCO ZAPPA."

Pages 170 *and* 581. GAËTANO CHIANDELLI, mentioned by Mendel and Reissmann, and Ciaudelli mentioned by Forino are evidently identical, and the latter's information correct. He does not speak, however, of his having been a pupil of Paganini as the former say, who are generally correct in their statements.

Page 171. For TORCALE (in notice of Chiabrano) read "FORCADE."

Page 177. CHRISTIAN FERDINAND ABEL (see page 85) should be mentioned among the early German violoncellists as well as gambists.

Page 197, *line* 11. For *last century* read "eighteenth century."

Pages 202-3. For ABBÉ VOLGER read "ABBÉ VOGLER."
Page 204. For SCHULZ'S read "SCHULZE'S."
Page 208. H. B. PREYSING and J. D. SCHEIDLER. The latter married the former's daughter (see page 195).
Page 234. AUGUST DANIEL MANGOLD composed a duet for violin and violoncello, published by Schott, and destined for performance with his brother, also a piece for viol d'amour, the MS. of which is in the British Museum.
Page 240. For HENSCHKEL (article DOTZAUER) read "HEUSCHKEL."
Page 247. ROSE, the cousin of Voigt, was Johann Heinrich Victor Rose (see page 193).
Page 247. SCHWENCKE'S serenade was performed by command of the Emperor William II, who admired the piece and requested to hear it at the Imperial Palace in Berlin by pupils of the Hochschule. The violoncellist, ALFR. GALLREIN, who took part in the performance, gave an account of it to the author.
Page 252. AGOSTINO POLI was the master of Zumsteeg about 1780.
Page 258. For SALMON read "SALOMON."
Page 260. STRUCK came to Paris at the beginning of the eighteenth century, not *last* century as in eighth line from end of page.
Page 280, *line* 10. For F. SERVAIS read "J. SERVAIS."
Page 290. For LEVASSEUR, JEAN PIERRE read "PIERRE FRANCOIS."
Page 292, *line* 1. For VILEL read "VIDAL."
Page 311. BENJAMIN HALLET. The programme of a concert given in January, 1752, at the Castle Tavern in Paternoster Row, enumerates "an epilogue spoken by Master Hallet in the character of Cupid." The author's "The Romance of the Fiddle," page 137. Further references in Olga Racster's "Chats on Violoncellos," chat the sixth.
Page 325. CH. F. ELEY was a good English violoncellist about the beginning of the nineteenth century and prolific composer for his instrument.
Page 386. J. H. FACIUS (according to Cramer's "Magazin" of 1783, page 394) was the son of the Russian agent at the Electoral court of Bonn. His two elder brothers were amateur flute players.
Page 387. PHILIPP MORALT's teacher was Anton Schwarz, the master of M. Bohrer (see page 244).
Page 388. JOSEPH MORALT was the eldest of four brothers, famed in Munich for their rendering of Haydn's quartets.
Pages 401, 403 *and* 407. F. HANSMANN, not "HAUSMANN," was teacher of Hanemann.
Page 464. E. VAN DER STRAETEN has also written a handbook on "Musical Form," "How to Play Violin Solos," "How to Play Violoncello Solos" (all published by William Reeves, London).

APPENDIX. 653

Page 473. VICTOR HERBERT. By accident a later notice of his career was printed on page 508.

Page 533. A. TOLBECQUE was appointed professor of his instrument and organist. In 1856 (*not* 1858 as in text) he went to Niort. In Paris he belonged for many years to the Morin Quartet. He lives at present in retirement at Niort. Tolbecque was also a maker of violins and violoncellos, and repairer of ancient instruments.

Page 535. For HENRI CASADESUS read "MARCEL."

Page 535, erroneously also page 536. BARBOT. The Christian name is given by C. Liégeois and E. Noguet as Jean Pierre Gaston, and the date of his birth as June 3, 1846. He studied at the Paris Conservatoire under Franchomme and received the first prize at the age of seventeen. He served in the "Garde Mobile" during the Franco-German War, toured in Holland and Belgium during 1872, settled as teacher of his instrument at Carcasson, and died November 5, 1905

Page 536. For J. F. RABAUD read "H. F. RABAUD." He died April 20, 1900.

Page 537. JEAN TOLBECQUE was a pupil of César Franck for composition and obtained a certificate (1er. accessit) for organ playing at the Paris Conservatoire.

Page 569. ANTON HEKKING. His first teacher was *Joseph* not "Fritz" Giese.

Page 579. PIETRO CASELLA, according to Count Valdrighi's information given to the author (obtained from Signora Carlo Casella) was born in 1791. The date given by Forino as 1762 is taken from Dassori's "Opere e Operisti" (Genoa, 1903) and appears to refer to Pietro's father, also violoncellist, who was the composer of seven operas. Forino admits that he is uncertain about the identity, but the birth dates of the sons seems to confirm Valdrighi.

Page 637. VARIOUS FORMS OF THE VIOLONCELLO. Apart from the five-stringed violoncello there are exceptional cases even of three-stringed and six-stringed instruments.

A three-stringed violoncello in the Wm. Heyer Museum at Cologne, attributed to Bartolomeo Obici, of Verona, belonging to the second half of the seventeenth century, shows the close relation between the violoncello of that period and the contra-bass. The varnish is reddish-brown, the corners not very pronounced, and the scroll is very heavy. Total length, 1.24½ metre; length of body, 0.71½ metre (the normal length is about 0.75 metre).

The six-stringed violoncello was, as Dr. G. Kinsky suggests, probably tuned like the viol da gamba, viz., D, G, c, e, a, d¹. He states that the famous Servais Strad was a notable specimen of this kind, which was altered, of course, for the purpose of modern use.

Another curious form is the "Violoncello da spalla," by Lorenzo Arcangioli, Florence, 1825. A monstrosity made for the use of violinists or viola players, with the left upper bout projecting outward while the right one is cut back to enable the player to hold it like a violin. The violoncello piccolo, which was simply a half-size instrument, mentioned above (appendix to pages 27-8).

It remains still to mention that there are several kinds of "mute" or "skeleton" violoncellos made for the convenience of practising in places where the sound of an ordinary instrument might be objected to. They generally consist of an open framework fitted with an ordinary neck, fingerboard, bridge and tailpiece, with various modifications of outline, etc., and are obtainable from almost every instrument maker.

MODERN FRENCH VIOLONCELLISTS.

C. Liégeois and E. Nogué ("Le Violoncelle," Paris, Constallat) mention the following:

CROS SAINT-ANGE, born at Castres, September 11, 1855, commenced his studies at the Toulouse Conservatoire, where he received a special prize at the age of nine. After continuing for some time under Tolbecque at Marseilles, he finished his studies at the Paris Conservatoire under Franchomme, where he obtained the first prize in 1870. Between 1872-5 he appeared on sundry occasions at the popular concerts at St. James's Hall, Crystal Palace, Oxford, and before Her Majesty at Windsor Palace. After the death of Franchomme he joined the Alard Quartet and also the Nadaud Quartet. In 1900 he succeeded Delsart as professor at the Paris Conservatoire, where he enjoys a high reputation as teacher. Among his best pupils are: Benedetti, Mas, Vaugeois, Laggé, Adèle Clement, Mlle. Soyer, Lopès and Marcel Casadesus.

RAYMOND FRANCOIS MARTHE, born at Tarbes, March 15, 1858, pupil of F. Servais and Franchomme, member of the Paris Opera orchestra and Conservatoire concerts till 1889, since then travelling and teaching.

GEORGES PAPIN, born in Paris, November 26, 1860, a pupil of Franchomme, received the first prize at the Conservatoire in 1881. He founded with Nadaud the quartet known under the latter name. In 1901-9 he was solo violoncello at the Opera. He followed Delsart as viol da gambist in the Société des Instruments Anciens. Since 1905 solo violoncello of the Conservatoire concerts. Papin is a prolific and successful composer for violoncello.

RENÉ SCHIDENHELM, born at Strasburg after the war, 1870-1. He studied under Franchomme and Delsart at the Paris Conservatoire, obtaining the first prize at the age of nineteen. After Delsart's decease he took over his class at the Conservatoire until the appointment of Cros Saint-Ange. He is at present professor at the Conservatoire Femina-Musica.

LOUIS FEUILLARD, born at Dijon, June 20, 1872, studied at the local conservatoire till 1889, when he became a pupil of Delsart at the Paris Conservatoire, obtaining the first prize in 1894. He founded a quartet with Vuillaume which travelled all over Great Britain. He is a distinguished teacher and several of his pupils have gained a laureateship at the conservatoire. He has published an adaptation of the Sevcik method for the violoncello (Bosworth and Co.).

FRANCIS TOUCHE (see page 539), born February 25, 1872, at Toulouse, studied first at provincial conservatoires and afterwards at the Paris Conservatoire under Rabaud. He is now conductor of the Concerts Rouge.

LOUIS FOURNIER, born July 8, 1877, at Marseilles, obtained in 1901 the first prize at the Paris Conservatoire, where he studied under Delsart. He is a member of the Parent Quartet, which gives numerous concerts at the Schola Cantorum, at the Salon d'Automne, etc. Fournier is considered an artist in the highest sense of the word.

JEAN BEDETTI, born December 25, 1883, at Lyons, where his father was teacher of violoncello at the local conservatoire. There Jean commenced his studies, continuing under Loeb at the Paris Conservatoire, where in 1902 he obtained the first prize. He has toured with considerable success and is now solo violoncellist at the Colonne concerts.

ADÈLE CLEMENT, born February 2, 1884, at Saint-Gengoux-le-National, commenced her studies under Gust. Girod, principal violoncello at the Opera Comique in Paris, continuing at the conservatoire under Cros Saint-Ange, and obtaining the first prize with distinction in 1902. She gave several concerts at the Salle Erard, an orchestral concert with the Chevillard Orchestra in Paris, and the Blüthner Orchestra in Berlin. After extensive and highly successful tours in Europe she founded a touring trio with Mlle. Baillet, piano, and Mlle. Talluel, violin.

MARGUERITE CAPONSACHI, born March 5, 1884, at Bordeaux, the daughter of an Italian father and Spanish mother. At the age of twelve she received some desultory lessons from provincial teachers, which were followed by self-study, while she was travelling with a little band of her father. In 1903 she joined Professor Loeb's class at the Paris Conservatoire and carried off the first prize after only eight months. She has toured all over Europe. Madame Caponsachi-Zeisler is considered one of the foremost lady violoncellists of the time.

PAUL BAZELAIRE (see page 538), apart from his fame as violoncellist, has since established the reputation of a gifted composer, whose compositions include choral, orchestral and chamber music works. He is also solo violoncellist and second conductor of the Concerts Secchiari.

UMBERTO BEDETTI, born November 28, 1886, at Leghorn. He studied under Cros Saint-Ange at the Paris Conservatoire from 1903 till 1906, when he gained the first prize. After touring in France with Mme. Roger-Miclos and the singer Bataille, he became solo violoncellist at the Concerts Hasselmans, and is at present in a similar capacity at Monte Carlo.

CLAUDE FIÉVET received two first prizes at the Lille Conservatoire in 1886. In 1888 he was appointed professor of violoncello at the National School of Music at Valenciennes. He has written a tutor and pieces for violoncello and pianoforte, also an opera, "Le Magicien," which was performed at Milan in January, 1908.

ALFRED SAUVAGET, born *about* 1830 (see page 533), died in 1908.

PIERRE SAMAZEUILH, born July 7, 1883, at Bordeaux, received the first prize at the age of sixteen at the conservatoire of that town, where he studied under Lasserre and André Hekking. He continued his studies under Anton Hekking at Berlin. He toured in Germany, Spain and France. In Tours he appeared with the Bataille Quartet, at Bordeaux with Ysaye and Pugno. He is now living at Toulon.

LOUIS ROSOOR, born September, 1883, at Tourcoing, was a pupil of Dienne at Lille, where he obtained the first prize, gaining a similar distinction at the Paris Conservatoire where he studied under Loeb. He was solo violoncello at the Concerts Hasselmans, and joined the Marsick Quartet in a successful tour through Egypt. Since 1909 he is successor of A. Hekking at the Bordeaux Conservatoire.

ADDITION TO BELGIAN VIOLONCELLISTS.

JULES CIRIADÈS, born September 10, 1855, at Namur, studied at the local school of music under Jacquet. In 1871 he received the first prize for violin playing, and in 1873 for violoncello. In 1881 he became professor at the Conservatoire of Charleroi, and in 1884 at that of Namur. He has the reputation of an excellent teacher.

CORNÉLIS LIÉGEOIS, born March 25, 1860, at Namur, where he commenced to study the violoncello under Jacquet, continuing under Isidore De Swert and Joseph Servais at the Brussels Conservatoire. In 1879 he received the first prize for violoncello and chamber music playing. In 1882 he joined the Bilse Orchestra at Berlin, where he remained for several years as solo violoncello. In 1885 he made a successful debut at the Concerts Lamoureux in Paris, where he played Bruch's "Kol Nidrei" for the first time in that town, which made a great impression. Since then he has toured as soloist, and produced several important works for the first time, including the quartet by César Franck (April 10, 1890). He is living as naturalised Frenchman at Paris, where he has a school for violoncello playing visited by numerous pupils. Liégeois has published an important tutor in three volumes, duets and instructive pieces for his instrument and a history of the violoncello in conjunction with E. Nogué.

GEORGES LIÉGEOIS, brother of Cornélis Liégeois, born 1862 at Namur, studied the violoncello under Joseph Servais at the Brussels Conservatoire, obtaining the first prize in 1881. He also obtained first prizes for harmony and for the clarinet. At present he is professor of violoncello at Brussels.

RAOUL PREUMONT, born February 13, 1868, studied under E. Jacobs at the Brussels Conservatoire, obtaining the first prize at the age of nineteen. After touring in France, Holland and Scandinavia, he settled at Mons, where he holds the post of professor of violoncello at the school of music.

JULES MARNEFF, born May 16, 1874, where he studied the violoncello under Ciriadès, continuing at the Conservatoires of Brussels and Paris.

At the latter he gained the first prize and the Georges Haim prize in 1894. He received an appointment in the Colonne Orchestra, which he left after five years, when he joined the Lamoureux Orchestra as solo violoncello. After touring for some time he became naturalised in France to qualify him for an appointment at the Opera in 1910. Marneff is violoncellist of the Firmin Touche Quartet and co-founder of the Double Quintet of Paris (wind and strings).

ALPHONSE JNSLEGERS. The name is erroneously spelt "JUSLEGERS" on page 557.

JEAN BONNIN, a pupil of E. Jacobs, received the first prize at the Brussels Conservatoire. He is at present solo violoncello of the classical concerts at Marseilles, and much esteemed as a soloist and teacher.

JACQUES GAILLARD, born April 4, 1875, at Ensival, near Verviers, at which latter town he commenced to study the violoncello, continuing at the Brussels Conservatoire, where he obtained the first prize. After some engagements in Paris he became professor of "solfège" at the Geneva Conservatoire. From 1896 till 1900 he was professor at the Mons Conservatoire. During that time he founded with Schörg, a Bavarian violinist, the Brussels Quartet, which toured all over Europe and America with great success. In March, 1908, they appeared in London, where they met with a very cordial reception. An article on the quartet with portrait of its members appeared in the April number of "The Strad." Gaillard is at present professor at the Liège Conservatoire.

—— GODENNE, a talented pupil of E. Jacobs, is professor of violoncello at the Anvers Conservatoire.

PRINCE PIERRE DE CARAMAN CHIMAY, residing at Brussels, is an excellent amateur violoncellist and possessor of the famous Servais Strad.

HUNGARY.

GLASER, a pupil of J. Goltermann, professor at the Musical Institute of Karkoff, in Russia, and KERBECK, principal violoncello at the Imperial Theatre of St. Petersburg, are mentioned by Liégeois and Nogué.

SPAIN.

Liégeois and Nogué mention the following violoncellists:

CASTELLANO, late professor at the Madrid Conservatoire.

BENAVENT, late principal violoncello at the Spanish Opera Comique.

ALEXANDER RUIZ DE TÉJADA, living at Madrid, and LOUIS AMATO, violoncellist at the Paris Opera, both obtained the first prize at the Madrid Conservatoire.

MANUEL CALVO and JOSÉ-GONZALES SERNA are violoncellists at the Opera at Madrid.

LUIZ SARMIENTO lived for some time in Paris, afterwards moving to Buenos Ayres, where he died.

ALFRED LARROCHA, professor of violoncello at the school of music at St. Sebastian.

LUIZ VILLA, excellent quartet player at the Madrid Opera.

RICHARD ARNILLAS, professor at the Bilbao Conservatoire.

JOAN RUIZ-CASAUX, touring at present (1913) in Portugal.

ANICET PALMA and DOMINICO TALTAVUL are known as good violoncellists.

VITTORIO DE MIRECKI commenced the study of the violoncello at Bordeaux, where he joined the Society Sainte-Cécile, received the first prize, and finished his studies under Franchomme at the Paris Conservatoire, where he gained the first prize in 1868. He has done much to popularise his instrument in Spain, and is still active as professor of the Madrid Conservatoire. He toured in Germany, France and England, gave concerts in Spain, together with Sarasate, Planté and Rubinstein, and was appointed professor at the Madrid Conservatoire in 1874. He is Officer of the Royal Order of Charles III of Spain and Knight of the Legion of Honour.

AGOSTINO RUBIO, who settled in London a number of years ago, is well known to the British public as an excellent soloist, possessing a brilliant technique of both left hand and bow combined with a fine tone. He has a remarkable technique of the pizzicato, which he employs in solos of his own composition as an accompaniment to a sustained melody, treating it much like a guitar or mandolin, and changing from accompaniment to melody with extraordinary rapidity. Together with Messrs. Fernandos Arbos (violin) and Carlos Sobrino (pianoforte), he has frequently appeared at the Spanish court. Rubio is living in London at the present time (1914).

The small number of Spanish violoncellists is explained by Liégeois and Nogué by the fact that the violoncello was never popular in Spain, and that it is not more than forty years ago that it has been cultivated to any extent.

PORTUGAL.

Except MADAME GUILLERMINA SUGGIA-CASALS, this country has not produced any great virtuosos on the violoncello. The following information about Portuguese violoncellists has been obtained from Liégeois and Nogué:

CÉSAR DE CASELLA, the elder (see page 582) came to Portugal in 1849.

Liégeois and Nogué state that the younger César was composer of the works mentioned on page 582. As the name on the title page is, however, given as Cesare A. de Casella and as the elder César was Chevalier of the Royal Order of Charles III, the present author's statement appears more probable, and is confirmed, moreover, by a statement made by the wife of Carlo Casella to Count Valdrighi. The younger Cesare, who became a naturalised Frenchman, has unfortunately been confined to a nursing home for some years past.

The names of Portuguese violoncellists are:

JOSÉ-JOACHIM DE SILVA (1750-1820).

JOSÉ DA SILVA REIS, violoncellist and contrapuntist, died 1779.

JOÂO JORDANI (1793-1860), violoncellist-composer and professor at the Lisbon Conservatoire.

JOSÉ NARCISO DA CUNHA E SILVA (1825-92). More remarkable as contra-bass player.

IGNACIO-MIGUEL HIRCH lived during first part of nineteenth century.

GUILHERME-ANTONIO COSSOUL (1828-80). Professor of violoncello since 1861, and afterwards director of Lisbon Conservatoire, also composer and conductor. Gave concerts at Lisbon, Paris and London.

ANTONIO-MARIA ARREYO, died 1893.

EUGENIO SAUVINET (1833-83). Distinguished amateur, pupil of Servais and Franchomme.

JOSÉ-AUGUSTO SERGIO DA SILVA (1838-90). Talented musician.

DOMINGOS CYRIACO DE CARDOSO (1846-1900). Violoncellist-composer and good chamber music player.

FREDERIC DO NASCIMENTO (second half of nineteenth century). Professor of violoncello at the National Institute of Music at Rio de Janeiro. Some of his compositions have become known also in England.

EDUARDO-OSCAR WAGNER (1852-99). Professor at Lisbon Conservatoire and good quartet player.

LORENÇO DALHUNTY (1858-77). Toured in Portugal and Spain.

JOÂO EVANGELISTA DA CUNHA E SILVA. Professor at the Lisbon Conservatoire at the present time.

JULIO AUGUSTO SERGIO DA SILVA (1865-1902).

JOÂO CARLOS D'OLIVEIRA PASSOS.

CARLOS QUILLEZ, born 1873. Spanish violoncellist residing in Portugal.

PROFESSOR LUIZ FIGUÈRAS made a successful debut at Bechstein Hall in November, 1911. We do not know whether he belongs to the Spanish or Portuguese violoncellists.

RUSSIA.

GABRIEL KELLERT, born 1891 of Russian parents at Chicago, commenced to play the violoncello at the age of six and toured in the United States at the age of ten. He completed his studies in Berlin, Vienna, Paris and Brussels, settled at Paris and tours with his brothers, Michael (piano) and Raphael (violin) with great success on the Continent.

SCANDINAVIA.

Within the last few years Messrs. —— BRAMSEN and —— SANDBY have appeared with great success as soloists in London. The latter

660   THE HISTORY OF THE VIOLONCELLO.

appeared at Bechstein Hall about two years ago, when he played some variations written for him by Percy Grainger, with the composer.

WILHELM POPPER, a brother of David Popper, a violoncellist of whom we possess no further particulars, has written a number of solo pieces of distinct merit for his instrument.

ENGLISH VIOL DA GAMBA PLAYERS.

ANNE OF CLEVE consoled herself in her retirement frequently by playing on a six-stringed viol.

VARIOUS FORMS OF THE VIOLONCELLO.

A violoncello d'amore or small violoncello with sympathetic strings, was in the possession of Count Luigi Francesco Valdrighi at Modena. Signor Eligio Cremonini had known the instrument before the dispersal of the count's collection.

SEVENTEENTH CENTURY SERENADERS, FROM A DUTCH WOODCUT.

INDEX.

A.

Abaco, Evariste Felice d'all, 164, 447.
———, Giuseppe Clemens Ferdinand, Barone d'all, 153, 160, 265, 309-10, 316, 355, 377, 384.
———, Giuseppe Clemens Ferdinand, Barone d'all, "La Zampogna," 370, 378.
———, Giuseppe Clemens Ferdinand, Barone d'all, sonatas, etc., 164 ff, 369.
Abbas, Philipp, 503.
Abbé, Brothers (see L'abbé), 110, 157.
Abel, Carl Friedrich, 53, 85 ff.
———, Carl Friedrich, Abel's concerts, 198, 298, 312, 314-5, 352, 648.
———, Carl Friedrich, Bach-Abel Concerts, 86, 89, 131.
———, Carl Friedrich, Hannover Square Concerts, 86.
———, Carl Friedrich, Professional Concerts, 86.
———, Christian Ferdinand, 85, 648, 650-1.
———, Clamor Heinrich, 83.
———, Cousin of C. F., 329.
———, Leopold August, 88.
———, town musician, 427.
Abingdon, Lord, 161, 171, 277, 313, 315.
Academies, Concerts called, 385.
Accro, 31.
Acero of Saluzzo, 12.
Adamowski, F., 451, 613.
———, Joseph, 613.
Adamowski-Szumowska, Antoinette, 613.
Adams, David, 52, 73.
———, Thomas, publisher, 40.
———, violoncellist at Riga, 208.
Addison and Hodson, 367.
———, John, 322.
Adélaide, Mme. (see also Appendix, page 650), 110.
Adó, Pietro, 206.
Affabili, singer, 184.
Agazzi, Gaetano, sonatas, 159.
Agricola, Martin, advice for tuning the "geige" in "Musica instrumentalis," 8, 18.
———, ridicules tablature, 20.
Agus, Eude, 303.
———, Henry, 303.
Ahle, Johann Georg, 83.
Ahna, H. de, 487.
Aimon, Esprit, 284.
———, Pamphile Leop. François, 284.
Alard, D., 546.
Albani, Mme., 522.
Albert, B. (see Boubée, Albert), 536.
———, W. A. J., 386.
Alberti, Alexander, 193, 252.
Alborea, Franz, 206, 208.
Albrecht, Louis, 625.
Alcock, Dr. John, 49.
Aletze, Paul, 651.
Alexander, Jos., 387.
———, Leopold, 387.
Alexandra, Queen of England, 501.
Aliani, Francesco, 168.
Alipandri, Bernardo, 168.
———, Gerhard, 168.
"Allgemeine Musikalische Zeitung," 293, 347.

"Allgemeine Musikzeitung," 190, 247, 256, 373, 390, 398, 414, 420, 561, 616.
Almanach, Musikalische-für Deutschland ab. Francischello, 155.
Alto clef, Use of, 370.
Amadio, Pippo, 166.
Amalia, Princess of Prussia, 84, 193.
Amati, 130.
——, Andreas, 14, 30, 126, 258.
——, Andreas, violoncello, 651.
——, Nicolas, 227.
——, Nicolas, Alwyn Schröder's, 467.
——, Nicolas, Darbishire Jones's, 516.
——, Nicolas, Marquis Laureati's, 580.
——, Nicolas, Mossel's, 573.
——, Nicolas, Seligman's, 530.
—— violoncello, Prell's, acquired by Grützmacher, 392.
—— violoncello presented to Piatti by Liszt, 583.
Amato, Louis, 657.
Amelia Sophia Eleonora, Princess of England, 317.
Amicourt, Catherine d', 103.
Amstel Male Choir, 566.
Andersén, A., 636.
André, Anton, 232.
——, the father, 105.
Andries, Jean, 118.
Anfossi, 324.
Angoulême, Duke of, 267.
Angurelli, Carmine, 647.
Anhalt Bernburg, Prince of, 193.
—— Dessau, Prince of, 193, 199.
—— Köthen, Prince of, 28.
Anna, Tzarina, 615.
Annales de la litterature et des Arts, 288.
Anne, Princess of England, 316.
Antheaume, 261.
Antient Concerts, 327.
Antoniotti, Giorgio, 33, 159.
Antony, Franz Jos., 200.
——, Jos., 200.
Appun, Anton, 492.
——, Heinrich, 492.
Appy, Charles Ernest, 562-4, 570, 572.
Aquila, Marco d', 9.
Arbos, Fernandos, 658.
Arcangioli, Lorenzo, 653.
Ariosti, Attilio, 146.
Armbrust, G., theorist, 449, 499.

Arne, Dr., "Comus," 153.
Arnillas, Richard, 658.
Arnold, violoncellist, 240.
——, Joh. Gottfr., 233.
Arnouts, François, 557.
Arpeggione, Schubert sonata for, 239.
——, specimen in Heyer Museum, 239.
——, The, 26, 115, 648.
——, Tuning of, 238.
Arreyo, Antonio-Maria, 659.
Ashley, Charles Jane, 327.
——, John, conductor, 328.
Ashton, Algernon, 463, 517.
Attwood, 504.
——, C., 329.
Aubert, D. F. E., composer of Lamarre's violoncello concertos, 292.
——, Pierre François Olivier, 289.
Auberti, 289.
Auer, Leopold von, 445, 554, 622.
August II of Poland, 615.
Augusta, Empress of Germany, 578.
Augustus, King of Poland, 162.
Austria, Emperor of, 77, 344.
——, Emperor of, conducts at piano, 198.
Avandonno, Antonio Pietro, 161.
Ayres to sing or play for lute or viol, 39.
Azaïs, Pierre-Hyacinthe, 285.

B.

Bach, A. W., 399.
——, Carl Ph. Em., 91, 180, 337, 384-5, 430.
——, J. C., 86, 180, 191, 524.
——, J. S., 22, 27-8, 80, 85-6, 90, 115, 240, 384, 648.
——, J. S., arrangement of Vivaldi concertos, 374.
——, J. S., gamba obbligato St. John's Passion, 650.
——, J. S., gamba obbligatos, 117-8.
——, J. S., gamba solos and obbligatos, 90.
——, J. S., Grützmacher's concert edition of suites, 432.
——, J. S., orchestra in Cöthen, 650.
——, J. S., performance of Sixth Brandenburg Concerto, 119.

Bach, J. S., solo sonatas, 75, 598.
——, J. S., viola pomposa from his orchestra, 116.
—— ——, L. Emil, 570.
Bachmann, 469.
Backhaus, Karl, 478.
Bacon, Francis, "Natural History," 23, 45.
Baden, Grand Duke of, 342, 470, 484.
Bagge, Baron, 222, 276.
——, Selmar, 420.
Baillet, Mlle., 655.
Bailleux, publisher, 272, 285, 311.
Baillot, 290, 298, 547, 619, 643.
—— and Vaslin, 306.
——, Levasseur, Catel and Baudiot tutor, 338, 372.
—— Quartet, 305.
——, recitative accompaniment, 372.
Baker, Francis, 651.
—— of Oxford, Britton's viol by, 52.
Balbi, Lorenzo, his sonatas, 158.
Balfe, M., "Hussit Hymn" in "Bohemian Girl," 348.
Ballenstedt Ducal Chapel, 439.
——, Prince of, 199.
"Ballet comique de la Royne," 127.
Ballio, Anna, 501.
Baltazarini, 127.
——, Balet comique, 258.
—— introduces violoncello in France, 258.
Baltzar, Thomas, the incomparable Lubicer, 51.
Baptie, D., "Musicians of All Times," 388.
Baptist (Draghi?), 355.
Baptiste, 209.
Baptistin, 261.
—— (Battistin), (see Struck, J. B.).
Baragli, Jac., 591.
Barbi, violoncellist, 591.
Barbot, Jean Francois (Pierre Gaston), 527, 535-6, 653.
Bardi, Count, 32.
Baretti, A., 538.
——, Antonio, 170.
——, Giuseppe, 171.
——, Luca, 170.
Bargiel, Woldemar, 461, 477, 480, 489, 568.
Barjansky, Dr. Serge, 626.
Barni, Camillo, 169.
Baroni, Leonora, 33, 99.
Barre, Pièrre de la, 104.
Barrière, apparent use of thumb, 262.
——, Jean, 261-2.
Barron, Master, 314.
Barrow, Dr., 50.
Barth, R., 485.
Barthelemon, 88.
Bärtich, 469.
Bartolozzi, 87, 315.
Baryton, 23, 42, 60, 111 ff., 344, 650.
——, Battanchon's attempted revival, 529.
——, famous players, 24-5.
——, Haydn's compositions for, 24, 647-9.
Basevi, Giacobo (see Cervetto), 151 ff.
Bass, Double, 129.
—— viol d'amore, 23.
—— viol (gamba), 263.
—— viol in England, 20, 35 footnote, 39.
—— violin, The, mentioned by Abraham Hill and Sir Roger North, 355 (see also basse du violon).
Bassa viola, 355-6.
Bassani, Horatio (Horatio of Parma), 31.
Basse à la façon de Lorraine, 361.
—— contre, 360.
—— de viole, 35 footnote, 258.
—— du violon, 361 (see also bass violin).
—— viol, 41.
Bassetel, 130.
Bassgeig, Kleine, 130.
Basso di camera, 258.
Bassoon, The, 365.
Bast, Heinrich, 468.
Bataille, singer, 655.
Bathyani, Cardinal Prince, 113.
Batta, Alexander, 302, 560, 562.
——, Peter, 560, 562.
Battanchon, Felix, 529, 650.
Battenberg, Prince Henry of, violoncellist, 522.
Baude, Marguerite, 535.
——, Marie (Marguerite?), 538.
Baudiot, 281, 290-1, 304, 306, 346, 542.
——, Charles Nicolas, 298 ff.
——, curious holding of bow, 300.
—— on solo accompaniment, 371.

Baudisch, Franz, violoncello, 482.
Bauer, Harold, 599.
Bauersachs, Christian Friedrich, 231.
Baumann, Katherine, actress, wife of P. Ritter, 203.
―――, Pièrre, 525-6.
Baumgarten, 315.
Baumgartner, Johann Baptist, 181.
Bavaria, Elector of, 198.
―――, Elector of, at Munich, 387.
―――, King of, 245.
Bavarian Palatinate, Elector of the, 316.
Baxmann, 427.
Bayreuth, Markgrave of, 205.
Bazelaire, Paul, 535, 538, 655.
Beauharnais, Hortense, 287.
Beaujoyeux (Baltazarini), 127.
Beaulieu, Charles de, 127.
Beck, Philipp, 83.
Becker, Dietrich, 83.
―――, Hans, 483.
―――, Hugo, 482 ff., 485, 489, 494, 496, 498-9, 511, 515-6, 518, 609, 625, 627, 630, 634.
―――, Jean, 389, 441, 482, 607.
―――, Jeanne, 483.
Bedetti, Cesare, 593.
―――, Jean, 655.
―――, Umberto, 655.
Beer, 330.
Beethoven, 213, 224, 243, 317, 330, 337, 346, 384-5, 525, 601, 641.
―――― Festival at Weimar, 451.
―――― Festival, Bonn, 629.
―――, septet, 325.
Beethoven's Triple Concerto, first performance, 403.
Bekker, R. P., 546, 565.
Bel canto, 379.
Belgium, King of, 544.
Bella, Domenico della, compositions, 165.
―――, Domenico della, concerto, 374.
Bellermann, Constantin, 81.
Belleval, violoncellist, 284.
Bellier, 109.
Bellini, Gentile, 9.
Bellmann, R., 430, 433, 445, 557-8.
Bellonò, Monsignor, Bishop of Carpi, 176.
Benavent, 657.
Bénazet, Bernard, 303, 542.
Benda, Franz, 80, 88, 155, 334.
Benedetti, 654.
Benecke, 231, 329.

Beneke, Friedrich Ernst, 231.
―――, Philipp Friedrich, 231.
Bennat, Francis (Franz), 446.
Bentheim, Steinfurt, court of, 205.
Berger, Friedrich, 198.
―――, Karl Gottlieb, 198.
―――, Otto, 496, 602-4.
Bergmann, Karl, 419.
Bergonzi, Carlo, 31.
―――, Carlo, violoncello, Squire's, 513.
―――, Salmon's suspected Gofriller, 571.
Beriot, Charles de, 299.
Berlin court chapel, 75.
―――― royal chapel, 499.
"Berliner Musikzeitung," 219.
―――― Musikzeitung" on Lindley, 326.
Berlioz, Hector, 116, 290.
Berman, Moritz, 394.
Bernburg, Duke of, 438.
Bernuth, Professor von, 479.
Bertau (Berteau), 272.
Bertaud (see Berteau), 266.
Berteau (Bertaud), 266-7.
―――, founder of French school, 262.
―――, holding of bow, 269, 271.
―――, Martin, 110, 124, 263-5, 273, 285, 352, 367, 384.
―――― uses thumb position, 262.
Bertelman, Jean Georg, theorist, 561.
―――, Jean Georg, violoncellist, 561.
Berti, Marc Antonio, 25, 112.
Bertoja, Two brothers, 169.
Bertolloti (see Gasparo da Salo), 30.
Bertram, Christian, 496-7.
Bertuzzi, Alessandro, 172.
Besborodkow, Count, 341.
Bessems, Joseph, violoncellist, 552.
Bethmann Orchestra, 213.
Betterton, 261.
Beyer, Ernst, 461.
―――, Heinz, 498.
Bideau (Bidaux), Dominique, 283.
―――, E. A., 284.
Bieler, August, 481.
Biene, August van, 566.
Bignon, publisher, 285.
Bilse, Ferdinand, 418.
Binfield, Thomas, 331.
Bird, William, 37 (see also Byrd).
Birkenstock, 80.

INDEX. 665

Birnbach, H. A., arpeggione virtuoso, 237-8, 648.
Bischof, H., 449.
Bischoff, Johann Carl, 638.
———, Johann Carl, "Harmonicello," 183.
———, Johann Georg, 183.
Bishop, John, translator of Duport's essay on fingering, 282.
Blainville, Charles Henri de, 264.
———, Charles Henri de, the third mode, 264.
Bland, J., publisher, 323.
Blow, Dr., 49.
Blume, Emil, 470.
Boatwright, John, 506, 519.
Boccherini, Luigi, 172-6, 255, 328, 378, 384, 430, 525, 542, 641.
———, Luigi, advances technique of violoncello, 371.
———, Luigi, characterisation of his music, 291.
———, Luigi, minuet, revived by Florentine Quartet, 441.
———, Luigi, simplification of clefs, 371.
———, Luigi, use of alto clef, 370.
Boch, Franz de, 601.
Bochsa, R., 280, 505.
Bock, Eduard, 391.
———, Heinrich August, 411.
Böckmann, Ferdinand, 443.
Bockmühl, Frau F., 417.
———, Robert Emil, 417, 425, 527.
Bode, Joh. Joachim, 183.
Boehm, Carl Leopold, 342, 394 ff.
———, Carl Leopold, MS. facsimile of adagio and rondoletto, 396.
———, Joseph, 394.
Boerngen, Emil, 447.
Böhme, Emil, violoncellist, 500.
Bohrer, Anton, violinist, 244-5.
——— brothers, 245.
———, four brothers, 244.
———, Franz, 244.
———, Max, 226, 244-5, 251, 254, 326, 385, 402, 641, 652.
———, Max, Duet by Ganz and, 394.
———, Max, Romberg's judgment of, 244.
———, Peter, 244.
Böie, 415.
Boismortier, 179.
Boisseaux, Joachim, 547.
Boivin, Madame, publisher, 109, 264, 268, 362.

Bolander, A., 205.
Bolles, John, 46.
———, Robert, 46.
———, Sir Robert, 50.
Bonamy Dobree prize, 507, 509, 520, 605, 608.
Bonawitz, J. H., 519.
Bonn, Elector, 252.
Bonnin, Jean, 657.
Bononcini *(see Buononcini)*, 268.
Borchgreving, 57.
Borde, De La, 265.
Borgh, Gaston, 636.
Borisch, Franz, 501.
Borzaga, 411.
———, Aegid, 207.
Bosmans, Henry, 571.
Bosselet, theorist, 454, 567.
Bossler, "Musikalische Correspondenz" ("Musical Correspondence"), 223.
Bostoni, Giovanni (Struck?), 158.
Bothof, Johann, junior, 197.
Boubée, Albert, 536.
Boucheron, 587.
Bouman, Antoon Alphons, 568.
———, Johannes, 568.
Bow, Baudiot's curious holding of, 300.
———, First application of the, 3.
———, Holding of, gamba fashion, 269.
———, Holding of, gamba fashion relinquished, 366.
———, Holding of, in Addison and Hodson's "Tutor," 322.
———, Holding of the, 359-60.
———, illustration in Tillière's "Methode," 273.
Bowing acquired from violinists *(see Vaslin, Davidoff, Boris Hambourg)*.
———, Crome's indications for, 320.
———, Crome's method of, 366.
———, Mersenne's instructions for, 361.
Boyer, publisher, 267.
Brackenhammer, Rosa, 501.
Brade, William, 42, 57.
Braga, Gaëtano, 581, 587.
Brahms, Johannes, 345, 422, 485, 525.
Brahms's Piano Quartet in A, first Cologne performance, 433.
Bramsen, 659.
Brand, violinist, 411.
Brandenburg-Culmbach, Frederic, Markgraf of, 89.

Brandenburg, Elector of, 147, 649.
———, Louisa Dorothea Sophia, Princess of, 147.
Brandoukoff, Anatole, 623.
Brandum, Walter, 213.
Braun, Emil, 577.
———, Johann, Daniel, 231.
———, Joseph, 246, 388.
"Braunschweigische Magazin," 401.
Breitner, 469.
Bremner, R., publisher, 172, 191, 276.
Brensio, Girolamo Hieronimus Brensius, 29.
Breslau, Bishop of, 193.
Breslauer, E., 499.
Bretonne, M. de, publisher, 268, 362.
Breuer, Adolf, contrabassist, 400.
———, Bernhard, 399.
Breuner, Count, 348.
Bréval, Jean Baptiste, 295-8, 303.
Brewer, Thomas, 41.
Bridges, Rev. A. H., 126.
Brissac, Marshal de, 127.
Britt, Horace, 537.
———, Madame Merk-, 537.
———, Roger, 537.
Britton, Thomas, 51, 649, 651.
Broadley, Arthur, 513, 523.
Broché, Marcus, Five-stringed violoncello by, 122.
Brodeczki, Johann, 343.
Brodlet, violoncellist, 331.
Brodsky, Dr. Adolf, 472.
Broglio, Luigi, 593.
Brömmel, violinist, 213, 410.
Brooks, Sydney, 510.
———, violoncellist, 326, 331.
Brouwer, Catharina, singer, wife of J. D. Braun, 232.
Brown, F. H., 298.
Brückner, Oscar, 469-70.
Brunswick court chapel, 444, 452, 466, 482.
——— ducal chapel, 458.
———, Duke of, 451.
———, Hereditary Prince of, 267.
——— Oels, Duke of, 385.
Brussels Conservatoire, Tolbecque collection, 534.
———, Museum of Conservatoire, 55.
Büchler, Ferdinand, 402, 413.
Buchner, P. F., 84.

Bückeburg court chapel, 462, 497, 572.
Buddhist monks still using the ravanastron, 1.
Buels, William W. C., 510, 521.
Bülow, H. von, 422, 438.
Buononcini, Angelo Maria, 148.
———, Antonio, 148.
———, Giovanni, 133, 147-51, 160, 208, 262, 269, 363, 383.
———, Giovanni, arrival in London, 149.
———, Giovanni, compositions, 148.
———, Giovanni, "David and Goliath," oratorio, 149.
———, Giovanni, Dean Swift's stanza, 151.
———, Giovanni, "Dido Abandoned in Vienna," 149.
———, Giovanni, first visit to Vienna, 149.
———, Giovanni Maria (father), 148.
———, Giovanni, "Mucio Scaevola," sonata for two violoncellos, 150.
———, Giovanni, return to Rome; second sojourn at Vienna, 149.
———, Giovanni, return to Vienna; his visit to Portugal, 151.
———, Giovanni, rivalry with Handel, 150.
———, Giovanni, the competition madrigal Lotti's work, 151.
———, Giovanni, the opera, "Camilla,". Antonio's work, 149.
———, Giovanni Battista, 121.
Bürger, Siegmund, 468.
Burgkmair, Hans, 5.
Burgksteiner, Joseph, 650.
Burgmüller, 417.
Buri, Oberstwachtmeister von, 190-2.
Burney, Dr., 37-8, 40, 43, 86, 89, 153, 160-1, 163-4, 166, 176, 192, 308, 310-1, 315, 339, 355, 540.
———, Miss, 314, 336.
Busch, 205.
Büschel, Jos., violoncellist, 461.
Busseto, Giovanni, 12, 29.
Butler, Henry, 42.
Buxbaum, Friedrich, 491-2.
Buxtehude, Dietrich, 57.
———, Friedrich, 84.
Byrd, William, 39 *(see also Bird)*.

INDEX.

C.

Cabisius, Julius, 442, 447.
Cacciali, Giuseppe, 591.
"Caecilia," periodical, 235.
Cahnbley, Ernst, 499.
———, Ferdinand, 499.
Cahusac, 367.
Caix d'Hervelois, Louis de, 106-7, 258.
——— d'Hervelois, three daughters, 110.
Caldara, 184.
———, "Euristes," 198.
Calkin and Budd, 266, 367.
———, George, 505.
Calmus, Martin, 195.
Calvo, Manuel, 657.
Camillo Camilli, violoncello, 487.
Campawsky, Anna, violoncellist, 577.
Campion, Dr. Thomas, 45, 49.
Canavasso, Alessandro, the elder, 163, 264, 581.
———, Paolo, 581.
Candiolo, Umberto, 591.
Cannabich, 202.
Cantabile, Study of, 379.
Cantinelli, Giuseppe, 580, 589.
Caponsachi, Marguerite, 655.
Caporale, Andrea, 153, 160 ff., 309, 355, 651.
———, compositions, 160.
———, death, 161.
Cappa, Gioffredo, 12.
Capperan, 171.
Caraman Chimay, Prince de, 657.
Carbonelli's concert, 166.
Cardon, F., 284.
———, Pierre, 284, 542.
Cardoso, Domingos Cyriaco de, 659.
Carini, Leandro, 591.
Carl, director, 395.
——— Theodor, Prince Palatine, 114, 232.
Carlsruhe, court, 497.
——— court orchestra, 470.
Carnaglia, Francesco, 591.
Caroline Elizabeth, Princess of England, 317.
Carpenter, Nettie, 522.
Carraci, Count, 145.
Carracini, contrabassist, 589.
Carrodus, 503.
———, A. L., 523.
———, J. F., 523.
Carwarden, John, 47.
Casadesus, 107.

Casadesus, Henry (should be *Marcel*), 535.
———, Marcel, 119, 538, 653-4.
Casals, Pablo, 518, 597-9.
Casella, Alfred, 119, 588.
———, Carlo, 579, 588.
———, Cesare, 579, 590-1.
———, Cesare A. de, 582, 590, 658.
———, Cesare de, the elder, 658.
———, Cesare, the younger, 658.
———, Giovacchino, 579, 586.
———, Pietro, 579, 581-2, 586, 588, 653.
———, Signora Carlo, 582, 653, 658.
Cassell, Landgrave of, 62.
Castellano, 657.
Castelli, Cesare, 591.
Castle Tavern (concerts), 652.
Catalani, Madame, 299, 405.
Catch Club, The, 167.
Catel, 290, 298.
Catherine de Medici, 127-8.
Cattanaro (Cattenaro), 12, 31.
Cattaneo, 147.
Cave, F. Morellon le, 541.
Celli, Edouard, 119
Cellini, Benvenuto, 29.
———, Giovanni, 29.
Cellone, The, 639-40.
Cerasoli, Luigi, 593.
Cermak, Joh., 333.
Cerreto, Scipio, 31.
Cervetto, Jacopo Bassevi, 151 ff., 160, 164, 265, 277, 309, 313-5, 324, 327, 329, 336, 352, 355, 384.
———, Jacopo, rebuked by Garrick; his son; his fortune; compositions, 154.
———, Jacopo, the elder, Burney's account of, appears at Hickford's room; solo violoncello at Drury Lane; his nickname Nosey, 153.
———, James, 88, 171, 277, 324, 327, 329, 336, 352, 384.
———, James, biography, 314 ff.
———, James, Burney and Cramer's characterisation of his playing, 315.
———, James, plays own concerto, 315.
Chabran (Chiabrano), 313, 315.
Chamber music, Berlin Association for, 487.
Chanot, luthier, 318.
Chapel Royal, His Majesty's, 300.
Chaplin, Kate, 464, 520.
———, Mabel, 119, 464, 506, 519.

Chaplin, Nellie, 464, 520.
Charles I, 23, 34, 36, 43-5, 49, 51, 307.
—— II, 51, 53, 308.
—— III, of Spain, 173.
—— IV, of Spain, 173, 279.
—— IX, of France, Amati's instruments for, 126.
——, Prince (Brussels), 197.
—— VI of Germany, 198.
Charlotte, Queen of England, 313.
—— Sophia, Princess (afterwards Queen of England), 85.
Chartres, Duke of, 107.
Cherniavsky, Mischel, 511, 625.
Cherubini, 299, 399.
Chest of viols, 38.
Chetara (Assyrian), 4.
Chévardière, 276.
Chevillard, pianist, 571.
——, Pierre Alexandre François, 428, 536, 538, 546, 569.
Chiabrano, Gaetano (Chabran), 171, 261, 651.
Childe, William, 36.
Chimay, Prince de, 301.
Chiostri, L., 441, 607.
Chitarra col arco, 238.
Chiterna, by Tielke, 55.
Choisnin, French court musician, 97.
Chopin, Frederic, 526.
——, Frederic, Karasowski's life of, 612.
Chorchewski, 615.
Chrestien (Chrétien), Charles Antoine, 282.
Chrétien, Gilles Louis, 282.
——, Gilles Louis, portrait painter, 283.
Christ, Joseph, 339, 344.
Christian Ulrich, Duke of Württemberg, 650.
Christiani, Lisa B., 531 ff.
Christina, Queen of Spain, 597.
Christopf (Christoph?), Johann Theodor, publisher, 60.
Chromatic scale, Corrette's fingering, 363.
Ciaudelli (Chiandelli), Gaëtano, 170, 536, 581, 586-7, 589, 651.
Ciciliano, 12.
Cink, Anthony, 602.
Cinquième (viol), 131.
Cipriani, 86-7, 315.
Ciriadès, Jules, 656.
Cirri, Giovanni Baptista, 167.
Cithara, also fidicula, 4-5.
Claes, contrabassist, 556.

Claësson, R., 636.
Clagget, Charles, patent fingerboard, 321.
——, Walter, 312.
Clagget's attic consort, 312.
Clam-Gallas, Count, 348.
——-Gallas, Prince, 414.
Clavicembalo, 30.
Clefs, alto, taille, base taille, 370.
——, C clefs used in Müntzberger's tutor, 542.
——, confusion of, 254.
——, F clef, 370.
——, simplification of, 371.
——, use of various in violoncello music, 370.
Clegg, violinist, 160.
Clemens X, Pope, 138.
Clément, Adèle, 539, 654-5.
Clementi, Muzio, 292.
Clément's "Journal de Clavecin," 266, 367.
Cleve, Anne of, 660.
Clochette, first known piece for violin family, 127.
——, music of, 128.
Cloos, Swedish violoncellist, 209, 632.
Coburg-Gotha court chapel, 479.
Coche, Mr., 549.
Coëlho, 557.
Coenen, Franz, 563, 570.
Colasse, director of opera, 103.
Colbran, Mlle., 279.
Coleman, Dr. Charles, 39.
Collins, George, 327.
Cologne, Elector of, 107, 164.
——, Prince Elector, at Bonn, 337.
Colonna, 148.
Comyn, George de, 35.
——, Innocence de, 35.
Concerts, Ancient, 199, 313, 322, 324, 328, 330-1, 504, 651.
——, Athenæum, Nice, 460.
——, ballad, Queen's Hall, 514.
——, Blewett's morning, 634.
——, British chamber music, 513.
——, called "academies," 385.
——, Cambridge University Musical Union, 464.
——, Castle, 159-60, 652.
——, classical, Groningen, 570.
—— Classiques, Paris, 460.
——, Colonne, 655.
——, Conservatoire (Paris), 526, 533-4.
——, Crystal Palace, 448, 507.

INDEX. 669

Concerts, Curtius Concert Club, 599.
———, Diligentia, Hague, 549.
———, E. van der Straeten's lecture, 464.
———, Exhibition, Riga, 636.
———, Gewandhaus, Leipzig, 211, 247, 617.
———, Hasselmans, 655-6.
———, Heckmann chamber, 463.
———, Historical Museum, Basle, 577.
———, Instrumental Verein, Aix-la-Chapelle, 556.
———, ladies', 313.
———, Lamoureux, 656.
———, modern chamber music, society for the cultivation of, 464.
———, Museum, Frankfort, 445.
———, Musikverein, Vienna, 468.
———, New Musical Fund, 328.
———, Pasdeloup, 553.
———, "Petites Auditions, Société des," 590.
———, Philharmonic, London, 324-5, 330-1, 428, 448, 457, 583, 599.
———, Philharmonic Orchestra, Hamburg, 444.
———, Philharmonique, Société, Brussels, 548.
——— Populaires, Brussels, 556.
———, Populaires, Paris, 553.
———, Popular, London, Saturday and Monday, 331, 448, 457, 510-1, 513, 515, 583-5, 588.
———, Professional, 277, 313, 315, 326, 329, 335.
———, Promenade, London, 495, 569, 578.
———, Quinzaine de Pâques, de la, 273.
———, Rue de Cléry, 225, 286, 301, 542.
———, Salomon, 323, 328.
———, Secchiari, 655.
———, Singakademie, Berlin, 568.
———, Société des, Mons, 548.
——— Spirituel, Paris, 163, 165, 171, 222-3, 261, 263-5, 267, 273, 276, 282, 286, 295.
——— Spirituel, Vienna, 345.
———, Union Française, Grands Concerts de l', 494.
Concialini, 180.
Conservatoire, Paris, 290, 298.
———, Vienna, 345.
Consorts for viols, 38.
Conti, composer, 198.

Conti, Prince, 271, 273.
———, Prince, dedication of J. P. Duport's sonatas, 276.
Contin, Count Giuseppe de Castel Szeprio, 537, 593.
Cooper, John (see Coperario).
Copenhagen, Royal Chapel, 634.
Coperario, Giovanni (John Cooper), 37, 44, 51, 53, 97.
Corder, Frederic, 516.
Corelli, 72, 79, 155, 176, 326, 357, 375, 384, 615.
———, A., calls the violoncello "violone" in earlier sonatas, 130.
———, "Concerti Grossi," 55.
———, first performance of Corelli sonata by Lindley and Dragonetti, 325.
———, "Folies d'Espagne," 297.
———, other performances by the same, 325.
———, sonatas, 338.
———, sonatas performed by Lindley and Howell, 326.
———, sonatas played by Lindley and Dragonetti, 324.
Corkine, William, 39.
Corna, 12.
Cornelis, Mrs., 86.
Corner blocks, introduction of, 5.
——— viols with only upper or lower corner blocks, 5.
Cornette, Victor, 306.
Corrette (Corette), Michel, 121, 262, 267 ff., 270, 272, 318, 359, 366.
———, Michel, "Methode Théorique," 268, 361 ff.
Corsi, Giovanni, 589.
Cossmann, B., 390, 411, 421-2, 428, 437, 445, 473, 482, 486, 488, 492, 499, 508.
Cossoul, Guilherme Antonio, 659.
Costaggini, Pietro, 579, 589.
Couperin, Louis, 109.
Court chapel, Elizabeth, private band of Queen, 129.
———, Mannheim, 468.
——— Orchestra, Munich, 468-70.
Cousser, conductor, 159.
Coutagne, Dr. Henry, 13, 288.
Crabbe, Charles A., 523.
Cramer, Joh. Baptist, 88, 326.
———, "Musical Magazine" ("Musikalische Nachrichten"), 85, 205, 211, 252, 254, 277, 315, 370, 541, 652.
———, Wm., 202, 326.

Crammer, Joh., 206.
Crawford, manager Covent Garden, 310.
Crawforde, Wm., 37, 39.
Cremonini, Eligio, 591, 660.
Crewe, Bishop of Durham, 307.
Cristelli, Caspar, 181-2, 198.
Crome, Robert, 271, 360.
———, Robert, "The Compleat Tutor," 365.
Cromwell, Oliver, 49.
———, Oliver, Elizabeth's minister, 39.
Cros Saint-Ange, 654-5.
Crosdill, John, 88, 171, 198, 277-8, 312 ff., 315, 317, 323, 335, 347.
Crotch, 504.
Crouch, F. W., 326, 329-30.
———, Frederick Nicholls, 504.
Crow, Rosa, 519.
Crwth played with a bow, 3.
———, The, 2.
Cubelius, August Ferdinand, 253, 388.
Cuccoli, Arturo, 591-2.
———, Eugenio, 591.
Cudmore, Richard, 328-9.
Cudworth, Dr., 50.
Cui, Cesar, 626.
Cumberland, Duke of, 317.
Cummings, W. H., 87.
Cunha e Silva, João Evangelista da, 659.
——— e Silva, José Narciso da, 659.
Cupis, François, violinist, 265.
———, Jean Baptiste, Le Jeune, 264 ff., 289-90, 295, 367.
———, L'Ainé, 265.
———, "Méthode Nouvelle," 367.
———, nephew, 265.
Curti, Carlo, 580, 591.
Curtis, Sir William, Andreas Amati violoncello, 126.
———, Sir William (Curtice), 347, 651.
Czerwenka, Aurel von, 607.
Czizek, Wenceslaus, 343.

D.

Dachambeau, 539.
D'Albert, Eugen, 518.
Dalhunty, Lorenço, 659.
Dall'Oglio, Domenico, 161.
———, Giuseppe, 161, 615.
D'Alquen, Frank, 506.
Dambois, violoncellist, 559.

D'Ambreville, violinist, 142.
Damcke, theorist, 565.
Dammen (Damen, Dahmen), Joh. Arnold (Andreas), 94, 328, 560.
———, junior, 95, 328.
Dance, Geo., engraver, 313.
——— movements in suite, 66-8.
Dancla, Arnaud, 530.
———, Charles, 530.
Danican, Nicolas, 109.
Danieltschenko, Peter, 624.
Danyel (Daniel), John, 40, 45.
Danzi, Franz, 197, 200, 203, 217-8.
———, Ignaz, 219.
———, Innocenz, 197, 202.
Dardani, Alberto, 591.
Dardelli, Pietro, viol maker, 12, 29.
Dardinelli, Baccio, design on Duiffoprugcar gamba, 17.
Darmstadt, Grand Ducal Chapel, 502.
Dassori, "Opere," etc., 653.
Daubert, Hugo, 466, 513.
Daverne (Davesne), 171, 261.
David, Ferdinand, 403-4, 428, 544.
Davidoff, Charles, 406, 440, 444, 486, 522, 573, 602, 616 ff., 621, 623-6, 643.
———, Charles, characterisation of playing, 617, 619.
———, crossing of strings in upper registers avoided, 618.
———, his compositions, 620-1.
——— imitates violinists, 619.
———, on bowing, 618.
——— on Schumann concerto, 620.
Dechert, Hugo, 476-7.
Decker, Constantin, 392.
Deckert, Willy, 493.
Decortis, Louis, 542.
Deering, 49.
Defesch, William, 540-1.
Degen, Joh. Phil., 182, 205.
Dehn, Siegfrid Wilh., 389.
De Lange, Daniel, 564-6.
———, Samuel, 565.
Delfino, Alessandro, 172.
Deller, composer, 194.
Delsart, Jules, 119, 448, 507, 510, 535, 537-8, 565, 654.
De Machy, 109.
De Mol, Pièrre, 549.
De Munck, Camille, 553.
———, François, 302, 548-9, 552-3, 562.
———, Pièrre Joseph Ernest, 445, 520, 546, 549, 552-3, 608.
Denefre, Jules, 548.

INDEX.   671

Denis, violoncellist, 606.
"Denkmäler der Tonkunst in Bayern," 62, 447.
——— Deutscher Tonkunst," 57.
Denmark, King of, 531.
Descorte, 539.
Desmarest, Henri, 106.
Dessau, 485.
——— Court Chapel, 452.
———, Duke of, 390.
Dessus de violon, 128, 131, 360-1.
Destombe, Pièrre, 539.
De Swert, Isidore Jean Gaspar, 552, 656.
———, Jules, 150, 161, 435, 445, 454, 470, 476, 483, 490, 545, 552 ff., 619.
———, Jules, characterisation of his playing, 555, 557.
Détry, Charles, 549.
———, Elisa, 549.
Deutokam, 94.
"Deutsch Herren" Order (German Knights), 223.
Devilliers, Maurice, 119.
Dieffenbruger, Caspar, 13.
Diem, Joseph, 437.
Diémer, Louis, 119, 535.
Dienne, Emile, 536, 656.
Dietelmaier, Michael, 81.
Diminution, The art of, introduced in England by Ferrabosco, 20.
Dini, Egisto, 593.
Disegni, Giuseppe, 587.
"Division-Viol," by Chr. Simpson, 22, 46, 359.
Dlabacz, 183, 339.
Doebbrecht, Joh. Elisabeth, 78.
Dohna, Count, 215.
Dohnányi, 516.
Dolmetsch, Arnold, 119.
———, Helène, 119.
Domergue, Claude, 285.
Donaldson collection, 55.
Donat, Josefine, 502.
Donau Eschingen, Prince of, 216.
Dont, Jac., 348.
———, Jos. Valentine, 347.
Dontrelon, Mr., 549.
D'Opdorp, Leon Pangaert, 551.
Dörffel, A., 648.
Döring-Brauer, Mme., 490.
———, Ernest, 490.
Dorn, A., 477.
Dötsch, August, 470.
Dotzauer, Joh. Justus Friedr., 240 ff., 247-9, 254, 385, 390, 397, 405-6, 428, 545, 601, 640, 642.
———, Justus B. F., 243, 406.

Dotzauer, Karl Ludwig, 243, 406.
Dowland, John, 39.
Dragonetti, 324, 326.
Dräseke, Felix, 469, 572.
Drechsler, Karl, 241, 390, 418, 421, 428, 435, 438.
———, Louis, 390, 420.
Drenger, Karl Fr., 206.
Dresden Royal Chapel, 490, 612.
Dressel, Hans, 519.
Drews, violoncellist, 414.
Du Buisson, 109.
Dubois, Mme., 565.
Dubourg, Mathew, 52.
Duesberg, Natalie, 498.
Duiffoprugcar, Gasparo, 13-6, 54-5, 102.
——— gamba with plan of Paris, 118, 546.
———, his device, 17.
Dulcimer in Notker's MS., 3.
Dumoncheau, Chs. François, 295.
———, Chs. Joseph, 295.
———, Silvain, 295.
Dumont, violoncellist, 552.
Dun, junior, 171, 261.
———, senior, 171, 261.
Dunkler, Emile, 565.
Dupont, Jos., theorist, 556.
Duport, 215, 217, 230, 232, 301, 354, 525, 545.
———, conductor, 460.
———, Jean Louis, 212, 223, 236, 243, 263, 269, 276 ff., 286, 290, 292, 300, 314-5, 371, 379, 384, 418, 430, 641.
———, J. L., compositions, 280.
———, J. L., concerto played by Ritter, 202.
———, J. L., duets with Crosdill, 278.
———, J. L., goes to Berlin, 278.
———, J. L., his son a violoncellist, 282, 284.
———, J. L., member of Marie Louise's chamber music, 279.
———, J. L., Napoleon and D.'s Strad, 279.
———, J. L., personality, 281.
———, J. L., plays Viotti's violin part, 277.
———, J. L., professor at Ecole Royale de Musique, 279.
———, J. L., steadiness of hand, 281.
———, J. L., Strad, 280.
———, J. L., Viotti of the violoncello, 278.
———, J. L., visits London, 277.

Duport, J. L., Voltaire's appreciation, 278.
———, J. L., works played by Jäger, 194.
———, Jean Pièrre (l'ainé), 168, 219, 231, 264, 273 ff., 285, 287, 313-4, 352, 386.
———, J.P., characterisation of his playing ("Mercure de France"), 273.
———, J. P., goes to Berlin, 276.
———, J. P., the pseudo, 275.
———, J. P., visits Francischello, 274.
Dürer, Albrecht, 17.
Durieux, Willem, 574.
Dusseck Piano Quartet, 325.
Dvorák, A., 348, 522, 602, 604.

E.

Earnshaw, A. H., 522.
Eberle, Oscar, 442, 568, 571-4.
Ebert, Ludwig, 432 ff., 445, 463, 485, 607.
Ebner, 84.
———, Karl, 470.
Eder, Karl Kaspar, 198.
Edouard, 171, 261.
Edward VII, 501, 568.
Ehrlich, Rudolph, 487.
Eibenschütz, José, 503.
Eiffert, Philipp Peter, 215.
Einstein, Dr. Alfred, "Zur Deutschen Literatur der Viola da Gamba," 11, 42, 53, 63, 66, 82, 84.
Eisele, Magda, 486.
Eisen, Schloss, 647.
Eisenberg, Max, 474, 499.
Eisert, Johannes, 234.
———, Johannes E., 234.
Eisfeld, Th., 419.
Eitner, Robert, "Quellenlexikon," 61, 72, 77, 159, 168, 172 176, 191, 194, 196, 210, 279, 294, 296, 311-2, 337.
Eley, Ch. F., 325, 652.
"Elijah," Production of, 505.
Elizabeth, Queen, 35.
Ellinger, Richard, 494.
Elner, Dr. Joh. Dan., 187.
Elzie, Margaret, 517.
Endeler, capellmeister, 190.
Engelmann, Bernhard, 412.
Epstein, Eugenie, 503.
———, Julius, 503.
———, Rudolfine, 503.
Erdmansdörffer, capellmeister, 450, 452.

Erdödy, Count, 243.
Erlebach, Phil. Hch., 83.
Ernst, von, 186.
Espenhahn, Fritz, 480-1.
———, L., 390, 407, 421, 480.
Esposito, M., 468.
Ess, Gertrude, 517, 588.
Essipoff, Annette, 569.
Est (Este, East), Michael, 40.
———, John, 40.
———, Thos., 40-1.
Este, Duke of, 171.
———, House of, 138.
Estense, Museo, 133.
Esterhazy, Prince, 113-4, 169, 188, 236, 253.
———, Prince, baryton player, 24.
———, Prince Nicolaus, 213.
Ettelt, Otto, 494.
Evans, C. Warwick, 508, 522-3.
Eve, Alfonso d', 540-1.
Eveline (Evelyn), Beatrice, 508, 514.
Evelyn's "Diary," 18, 51.
Exeter, Earl of, 313.
Eybler, 114, 344.
Eylenstein, Georg Christoph, 177.
Eysel, Johann Philipp, "Musicus autodidactus," 177-8.

F.

Faber, John, engraver, 310.
Facius, J. H., 386, 652.
Falco, 329.
Farabosco (see Ferrabosco), 31.
Fargett, James, 329.
Farinelli's ground, 297.
Farrant, Daniel, 23, 46, 649.
Felden, Magnus, 115.
Fémy, Henry, 542.
Fendt, father, 235.
Fenzi, 581.
Ferdinand VII of Spain, 225.
Ferrabosco, 97, 100.
———, Alfonso, 20, 23, 33, 35, 37, 45, 648.
———, Alfonso, junior (III), 648.
———, Alfonso, son (II), 33, 35, 37, 45, 648.
———, Henry, 649.
Ferrari, Anton, 164, 170, 230.
———, Carlo, 359.
———, Carlo, sonatas, 163.
———, Claudio, 591.
———, Domenico, violinist, 163.
Fesca, 400.
Fétis, 156, 169, 268, 283, 289, 293, 298, 303, 338, 427, 454, 541-2, 546, 548,, 567.

Fétis, "Antoine Stradivarius," 3, 12.
Feuillard, Louis, 654.
Fiala, Franz, 341-2.
———, Joseph, 333, 339, 345.
Fiddle, derivation of name, 4.
———, The, new model'd, by Robert Crome, 319.
Fidel, derivation of name, 4.
Fidicula, 4.
Fidula, derivation of name, 4.
Fiedel (vedel), 3.
———, Viol forms of the, 5.
Fiedler, W., 610.
Fiévet, Claude, 655.
Fifth string on violoncello abandoned, 255.
Figella, derivation of name, 4.
Figueras, Luiz, 659.
Figured bass, Execution of, in solo accompaniment, 373.
Filippio, 595.
Filsl, violoncellist, 339.
Filz, Anton, 188, 190, 197, 202.
Finck (Fink), Ignatius, 182, 198.
Finger, Gottfried, 83.
Fingerboard, lines for frets, 319.
———, New, invented by Clagget, 321.
———, Short, on bass viol, 259.
———, The movable, 256.
Fingering, Corrette's, 362 ff.
——— in Waylett's "The Gamut," 364.
———. R. Crome's, 366.
Fioravanzo, Giuseppe, 593.
Fiore, Angelo Maria, 159.
Fischer, Adolphe, 545, 555.
———, Franz, 453.
Fitzenhagen, Karl Friedrich Wilhelm, 430, 450-1, 613, 623-4.
Fitzwilliam, Messire (Earl), Duport sonatas dedicated to, 276.
———, Viscount, 313.
Fleischer, David, publisher, 60.
Fleischmann, Joh. Georg, 252.
Fleming, violoncellist, 243.
Flemming, Marshal, 64.
Flood-Porter, Amy, 519.
Fohström, Ossian, 635.
Földesy, Arnold, 471, 516, 609-10.
"Folies d'Espagne," Corelli's, 297.
Fontaine, Charles de la, 104.
Fontana, Giovanni Battista, 130.
Fontego, Ganassi del, tuning of viols, 19.
Fontico, Autentico del, 29.
Forcade, 171, 261.
——— (Torcade), 651.

Ford, Ann, 53, 649-50.
———, Thomas, 40.
Forino, 531, 537-9, 561, 651, 653.
———, Ferdinando, 581, 587, 589, 593-4, 596.
———, L., 157, 163, 412, 570, 582, 587, 589-91, 593, 595-6.
——— (Torino), 651.
Forkel, 169, 253, 374.
Fornaroli, Gino, 591.
Forneros, Tancredi, 593.
Forquerai (Forqueray), 22, 76-7, 258.
———, Antoine (le père), 107-8.
———, Jean Baptiste, 108-9.
———, Jean Baptiste Antoine, 108.
Förster, Alban, 490.
———, Fräulein, 509.
———, Kaspar, 84.
Forster, William, 210.
———, William, violoncello painted with royal coat of arms, 317.
Fournes, G. J., 220.
Fournier, Louis, 655.
Fraenzl, violinist, 200, 202.
France, Mme. Adelaïde, 650.
———. Mme. Henriette, 650.
Franceschini, Alberto, 591.
Franchomme, Auguste, 280, 418, 428, 445, 525 ff., 530-1, 533-4, 536-7, 571, 606, 643, 645, 653-4, 658-9.
———, Auguste, autograph music (facsimile), 528.
———, Auguste, facsimile of signature, 529.
Francis, Emperor of Austria, baryton player, 24.
——— I, King of France, 13, 17, 96, 288.
——— II, Duke of Modena, 138.
——— II, of Austria, 232.
——— Joseph, Emperor, 448.
Francischello, 154 ff., 262-3, 269, 274, 359-60.
——— in Vienna; in Genoa, 155.
——— meets Duport; thumb position attributed to; compositions, 156.
Franck, César, 653.
Franco-Mendes, Jacques, 561, 563.
Francs Amis, Les, amateur society, Bruges, 552.
Frank, Melchior, 56.
Frankfurt, Grand Duke of, 346.
Franz, Karl, 25, 112.
Franzel, Ferdinand, 419.
Frasi, Signora, 310.

Frasnedi, Ferdinando, 593.
Fratinelli, Marco, 33.
Frederic Charles, Prince of Prussia, violoncellist, 481.
——— II, of Prussia, 179.
——— Lewis, Prince of Wales, 316.
———, Prince of Hesse (afterwards King of Sweden), 62.
——— the Great, 80, 89, 344.
——— William, Elector of Brandenburg, 75.
——— William II, of Prussia, 78, 89, 168, 173, 202, 231-2, 276, 400.
Frei, Corna, 31.
———, Hans, of Bologna, 17-8.
Freistädtler, choirmaster at Salzburg, 230.
French royal chapel, 298-300.
Freschi, 130.
Frets, 10.
Fretting of neck, 365.
Freund, Rob., 498.
Frey, Hans, 17, 54.
———, John (son of Hans), 54.
Friedel, Sebastian Ludwig, 25, 114, 232.
———, Sebastian Ludwig, his Tielke baryton, 232.
Friedrichs, violoncellist, 500.
Fries, Wulf, 630, 634.
Fritsche, Agga, 636.
Fritscher, Eleonore Sophie Maria, 184.
Froebel, 245.
Fryer, Herbert, 516.
Fuchs, Carl, 485-6, 512.
——— (Fux?), 615.
———, stadtmusikus, 385.
Fuellsack, Zacharias, 57.
Fuetsch, Joachim Joseph, 164, 170, 230.
Funk, David, 59.
Funke, violoncellist, 419.
Fürst, Johannes, 218.
Fürstenau (Dresdener Hofmusik), 77.
Fürstenberg, Prince Egon of, 342, 395, 397.
Fux (Fuchs), Johann Joseph, 92, 615.
Fythele, derivation of name, 4.

G.

Gabrieli, Domenico, 133, 358, 369, 374, 377, 383.
———, Domenico, "Balletti, gighe," etc., Op. 1, 137, 148, 150.
Gabrieli, Domenico, "Canone a due Violoncelli," 135.
———, Domenico, "Ricercari," 133.
———, Domenico, specimen of Ricercare, 136.
Gade, Niels W., 601.
Gadgi, Giuseppe, 169.
Gagliano, gamba with modelled back, 34.
Gaillard, Jacques, 657.
Gainsborough, 87.
Galeotti, Stefano, 167-8.
Galilei, Galileo, 32.
———, Michael Angelo, 32.
———, Neapolitans first makers of violoncello, 124.
———, Vincenzo, 32.
Gallay, Jules, 531.
Galli, Domenico, 137, 358, 369, 374, 377, 383, 651.
———, Domenico, "Trattenimento," 138 ff., 148, 150.
———, Domenico, Violoncello by, 138.
Galliard, 651.
Galliardo, Mark Anthony, 35.
———, Paul de, 35.
Gallrein, Alfred, 465, 652.
Galpin, Rev. F. W., 122-3, 356.
Gamba d'amore, 46.
——— (see also viol da gamba), 258.
———, Viola da (see viola da gamba).
Gandy, 394.
Ganneaux-Sabatier, Mme., 303.
Gänsbacher, Joh. Bapt., 235.
Ganz, Adolph, 394.
———, Leopold, 394, 414.
———, Moritz, 245, 393, 399, 402, 408, 413-4, 419, 427.
———, Simon, 565.
Garcia, José, violoncellist, 597.
Gardiner, W., etcher, 88.
Garnier, 109.
Garrick, 153.
——— and Cervetto, 154.
Garzo, Dr. B., 610.
Gasparino, Quirino, 166.
———, wife of Cupis, 265.
Gasparo, violoncellist, 615.
Gassner, "Lexikon," 394.
Gatti, Luigi, 230.
———, Teobaldo, 33.
Gauss, 212.
Gavotte following gigue, 68.
——— starting on first beat of the bar, 128 footnote.

INDEX. 675

Gebel, Kapellmeister, 93.
Geer, Count de, 230.
Geige, The German, 2.
——, Tuning of grosse, 8.
——, Virdung's grosse, 5-6.
Gelder, Von, violoncellist, 515.
Gelsthorp, Edward, 47.
Geminiani, 154-5, 430.
George Frederic August, Prince of Wales (afterwards George IV), concerts at Carlton Place, 317.
—— IV, 314.
Gérardy, Dieudonné, 557.
——, Jean, 557, 630.
Gerber, 55, 146, 166-7, 194, 196, 199, 211, 216, 219, 253, 309, 356, 541.
——, about Mara, 336.
——, Ernst Ludwig, 189.
——, "Tonkünstler-Lexikon," 121.
Gerle, Conrad, 54.
——, Hans, "Musica Teutsch," 10, 18.
——, Hans (son of Conrad), 54.
——, Hans, tuning of grosse geige, 18.
——, Hans (younger brother of Hans), 54.
"Germany's Lament on the Death of Frederic the Great," song with baryton accompaniment, 113-4.
Gervaise, Claude, 96.
Gevaert, F. A., 118, 597.
Ghys, "Air de Louis XIII," 127.
Gianoti, 261.
Giarda, Luigi Stefano, 592.
Giardini, Etelka G., 592.
——, Felice de, 314-5, 337.
——, Felice de, opera, "Enea and Lavinia," 168.
Giaritiello, Gennaro, 581, 586, 589.
Gibbons, Orlando, 39, 49.
Giese, Fritz, 420, 471, 571, 630.
——, Fritz (should be *Joseph*), 569.
——, Joseph, 394, 419, 471, 566, 574.
——, Joseph (not Fritz), 653.
Gigue or German geige, 2, 4.
Giles, Nathaniel, 39, 45.
Gillet, Ernest, 537.
Gilson, Paul, 630.
Giordani, Tommaso, 167.
Giorgi, singer, 88.
Girard, 526.
Giraud, François Joseph, 286.
—— Ulderico, 591.

Girod, G., 655.
Glaser, Siegmund, 480, 657.
Glazounov, A., 626.
Glee Club, The, 327.
Glehn, Alfred von, 623.
Gleichmann, violinist, 240.
Glettinger, Johann, 75.
Glickh, Dr. A., 484.
——, Rudolf, 484.
Glinka, pupil of Dehn, 389.
Gloucester, Duke of, 317.
Gluck, 291.
Göbella, violoncellist, 613.
Godard, B., 333, 460.
Godenne, 657.
Godfrey, Daniel, junior, 521.
Goedecke, violoncellist, 212, 400, 502.
Goens, Daniel van, 575.
Goeser, kettle-drummer, 185.
Goethe, Wolfgang v., 29, 217, 245.
Goltermann, Georg Edward, 422 ff., 425.
——, Georg Edward, character of his compositions, 423-4.
——, Joh. Aug. Julius, 424, 432, 442, 447.
——, Julius, letter, 426-7.
Gompertz, Richard, 464.
Gordon, 310-1.
Gorz, Count, 193.
Gosling, Sub-dean, his round on the viol, 53.
Gotha, Charles Augustus of, 211.
Gottlieb, Caj., 207.
Goupillier, 106.
Gow, Donald, 331.
——, Niel, violinist, 331.
Gowa, Albert, 444, 485, 493.
Grabau, Johann Andreas, 403.
Grädener, Charles C. P., 407-8, 468.
Graenser, Friedrich Wilhelm, 392.
Graf, Gebhard, 443.
Grainger, Percy, 659.
Grammont, Duke of, 306.
Grancino, 130.
——, Ciciliano, 12, 31.
Granges, Claude de, 308.
Granier, 97.
Grant, Sir Francis, P.R.A., 505.
——, Sir James Hope, 505.
Grassalkowitz, Prince, 213.
Graul, Marcus Heinrich, 192-3.
Graun, Carl Heinrich, 80, 198.
——, Johann Gottlieb, 85.
Graupner, 79.
Graziani, Carlo, 168, 255, 370.
Grégoire, composer, 545.

Grégoire, musiciens Belges, 541.
Greiffenhagen, Norman, 464.
Grep, B., 57.
Gretsch, 196.
Griebel, Julius, 402, 407, 448.
Griesbach, Adolphus, 507.
———, George, 199.
———, Heinrich, 198, 314, 328.
———, oboist, 317.
Griffin, 330.
——— Piano Quartet, 325.
Grillet, Laurent, 119, 535.
———, Laurent, "Les Ancêtres du Violon," 16, 27, 96, 101, 104, 107, 109.
Grimm, Karl, 415-6.
Grimson, R., 508, 523.
Groen, S. de, 570.
Gross, Friedrich, 404.
———, Heinrich, 230.
———, Johann Benjamin, 403.
Grosse geige, Gerle's tuning of, 18.
Grossi, Samuele, 593.
Grove, Sir George, dictionary, 2.
Grümmer, Detlev, 500.
———. Paul, 500.
Grünewald, 79.
Grünfeld, A., 465, 469.
———, Heinrich, 415, 465, 491.
Grützmacher, Friedrich, junior, 488, 497, 501.
———, Friedrich Wilhelm Ludwig, 174, 215, 280, 390, 392, 428 ff., 435-6, 438-45, 447, 450-2, 458, 460, 467, 469, 471, 479, 482-3, 485, 487-8, 490, 493, 502, 558, 569, 571-2, 608, 619, 624, 635, 644.
———, Friedrich W. L., compositions, 430.
———, Leopold, 430, 435, 488, 495.
Guarneri, Andreas, 590.
——— violoncello, C. Romberg's, 398.
Guarnerius, Joseph, 227.
———, Petrus, Beatrice Harrison's, 518.
Guéméné, Prince de, 277.
Guérin brothers, 297.
———, Emmanuel (Guérin aîné), 302.
———, Emmanuel, his brother a violinist, 281, 303.
"Gugel, Die," dance tune, 11.
Guitar d'amour, 238.
———-fiddle, 4.
———, Spanish, 4.
Gungl, Joseph, 563.
Gunn, John, 323.

Günther, Prince of Sondershausen, 179.
Gutsche, G., Konzertmeister, 650.
Gyrowetz, 328, 342.

H.

Haagmans, D., 570.
———, G. Henri, 572.
Habeneck, 305, 526.
Habram, 171, 261.
Hacquart (Hakart), Carolo, 94.
Hafeneder, J., 230.
Hafner, 415.
Haid, Jacob, Francischello's portrait after Martin Meiten, 156.
Haillot, 283
Hainl, George François, 525.
Halévy, 530-1.
Halir, Carl, 457, 477.
Hallé, Lady (see also Norman, Wilma), 601-2.
———, Sir Charles, 486, 527.
Hallet, Benjamin, 311, 652.
Hambleton, J. E., 523.
Hambourg, Boris, 137, 165, 370, 378, 626 ff.
———, Boris, takes Ysaye as model in bowing, 627.
———, Jan, 626-7.
———, Mark, 626-7.
———, Michael, 626-7, 643.
Hamme, Van, 557.
Hammer, Franz Xaver, 89.
Hanbury, Charles, 327.
Hancock, violoncellist, 331.
Handel commemoration, 313.
———, G. F., 52, 90, 147, 316, 524.
———, gamba sonata played by Delsaert, 119.
———, "Resurrection," 90.
———, solo for Caporale, 160.
———, Sonata V played by Lindley and Dragonetti, 324.
Handley, Muriel, 520.
Handwerg, W., 477.
Hanemann, Moritz, 401.
Hanisch, organist, 243.
Hann, William Charles, 509.
Hanover Square Rooms, 328-9.
Hanslick, Robert, 225, 394, 401.
———, Robert, about Piatti, 584.
Hansmann, Ferdinand (not Hausmann, as printed), 219, 401, 403, 407, 652.
———, O. F. G., 220.
Hanssens, Charles, violoncello concerto, 548.

INDEX.

Hardeck, Johann Karl, Count von, 198.
Hardt, Johann Daniel, 81.
Hardy, violoncello preceptor, 322.
Harmonicello, 183, 638.
Harmonicon, 255.
Harp, 3.
Harrison, M. A. Beatrice, 508, 518.
Hart, George, 29, 55.
Hartdegen, Adolf, 454.
Hartinger, Joseph, 207.
Hartmann, Albert, 462.
Hartog, violoncellist, 574.
Hartwich, C., 180.
Hasse, Nicolas, 82, 85.
Hasselmans, Louis, 539.
Hasting's duets, 349.
Hastuy, B., 348, 604.
Hatot, 109.
Hatton plays gamba, 651.
———, Walter, 523.
Hauer, Gregor, 197.
Hauptmann, Moritz, 421, 617.
Hauschka, Vincenz, 343 ff.
Häusler, director, 395.
———, Ernst, 216.
Hausmann, F. (see Hansmann).
———, Georg (born Hanover, 1813, died 1860), 327.
———, Robert, 120, 456 ff., 461, 477-8, 480-1, 485, 487, 489, 491, 498, 501, 511, 514, 520, 572, 609, 629-30.
Haute contre (viola), 128, 360.
Hawes, William, 504.
Hawkins, Sir J., "History of Music," 36, 49, 159, 310.
Haydn, Joseph, 91, 114-5, 173, 188, 204, 213-4, 224, 254, 290, 296, 299, 331, 340, 344, 384, 542, 612, 641.
———, Joseph, benefit concert, 328.
———, Joseph, compositions for baryton, 24-5, 647.
———, Joseph, concerto, edited by Grützmacher, 430.
———, Joseph, concerto played by Cervetto, 315.
———, Joseph, "Creation" in Paris, 286.
———, Joseph, quartet, 325.
———, Joseph, "Qui Tollis" with obbligato played by Lindley, 325.
———, Joseph, twelve concerts, 329.
———, Joseph, use of alto clef, 370.
———, Michael, 197, 230, 340.
Hayn, Alfred, violoncellist, 572.
Hayne (Heine), Gottlob, 177.

Hebden, John, 192, 310.
Hebenstreit, Pantaleon, 77, 79.
Heberlein, Hermann, 443, 472-3.
Heckmann, Robert, 433, 445.
Hegar, Dr. F., 498.
———, Emil, 430, 442-3, 471, 473, 566.
———, Johannes, 498.
———, Julius, violoncellist, 498.
Hegenbarth, Franz Xaver, 387, 414, 456, 465, 474, 480, 487, 602-4.
Hegner, Anton, 629.
——— —, Otto, 630.
Hegyesi, Louis, 411, 441, 463, 496, 527, 606-7.
Heilig, Magister, 200.
Heinichen, 78, 615.
Heissler, Charles, 446.
Hekking, Andreas, 538, 567, 656.
———, Anton, 569, 574, 653, 656.
———, Charles G., 538, 567.
———, Gerard, 567, 573.
Heller, 252.
Hellmesberger, Ferdinand, 484, 491-2, 501.
Helwig, Joh. Friedrich, 75.
Hemmerlein, Anton, 185.
———, Eva Ursula, 184.
———, Franz Anton, 184.
———, Johann, 185.
———, Johann Nicolaus, 184.
———, Karl Ignaz, 187.
———, Thomas, 187.
Hemmings, Florence, 522.
Henderson, Mrs. B., 472, 598.
Hening, Rudolf, 453.
Henning, Karl, 397.
———, Wilhelm, 417.
Henry aux Vièles, 11.
——— II of France, 128.
——— le Jeune, le Sieur, "Fantaisie à cinq," 100, 361.
——— L'Escot, 11.
———, Prince of Prussia, 335.
———, Prince of Wales, 36, 45, 53.
——— VIII, 34.
——— VIII, Italian viol players in band of, 20.
Herbeck, Emil, 502.
Herberstein, Sigmund, Count, 198.
Herbert, Victor, 473, 508, 516, 653.
Herbig, 220.
Herlitz, William (Wilhelm), 430, 439.
Hermann, 557.
———, Adam, junior, 612.
———, Adam, senior, 390, 611-2.
———, F., pupil of F. A. Kummer, 436.
Hermanowski, A., 612-3.

Herner, Julius, 487.
Heron-Allen, Edward, 126.
——— (Claudius?), 312.
Herreyns, Charles, 552.
Hertel, John Christian, 78 ff.
Hervelois, Louis de Caix d', 22.
———, Louis de Caix d', "Le Papillon," 119.
Hess, Frederic, 482.
Hesse-Cassel, Charles, Landgrave of, 94, 231.
———-Cassel, Court of, 205.
———-Cassel, Frederic, hereditary Prince of, 147.
———, Christian Ludwig, 78.
———, Ernst Christian, 76, 79, 168, 344.
———, Grand Duke of, 413, 486.
———-Philippsthal, Prince of, 212.
——— (town musician), 405.
Hessner, trumpeter and violoncellist, 240.
Hettisch (Hetes), Johann, 338.
Hetzel, Moritz, 456.
Heukersth, Wm., 570.
Heuschkel (Henschkel), 652.
———, pianist, 240.
Heyer, Wilhelm, Museum, 176, 239, 648, 653.
Heymann, "Strad" letter, 558.
Heyn, Alfred, 502.
Hickford's Rooms, 168.
Hildebrand, Christian, 57.
Hill, Abraham, on the use of the "bass violin" in Italy, 355.
———, Emily, 612 footnote.
———, T. Weist, 508.
———, W. E. and Sons, 72, 176, 316, 533.
———, W. E. and Sons, Antonio Stradivari, 280-1.
Hillemacher, Frederic, 264, 305, 530.
Hiller, Ferdinand, 433, 564.
———, Joh. Adam, "Mus. Nachrichten," 80, 130, 155, 220, 255, 264, 638.
Hilpert, Wilhelm Kasimir Friedr., 430, 441-2, 446, 606.
Himmelbauer, Wenzel (Wenceslaus), 182, 196, 338, 343.
Hindle, Johann, 247.
Hindmarsh, 328.
Hingston, John, 49, 51.
———, Peter (nephew), 49.
Hinkel, Franz, 391.
Hipkins, "Musical Instruments," 55.
Hirch, Ignacio-Miguel, 659.

Hoby, Charles, 521.
Hochschule, Berlin, 456.
Hock, Anton, 179, 337.
Höcke, J. (see Hoecke).
Hodson, Geo. Alex., 322.
Hoecke, Johannes, 251, 345, 347, 419, 425, 463.
Hoeckner, Karl Wm., 209, 248.
Hoeven, Kato van der, 574.
Höffelmayer, Maria Jos. Ant., 252.
Höffler, Conrad, "Primitiæ Chelicæ," 74, 107.
Hoffmann, Johann Christian, 27-8, 116.
——— (Hofman), Karel, 496, 603.
Hofmann, Hch., Dehn's pupil, 389.
———, Joh. Nic., 206.
———, N., 197, 338.
Hofstede, J., 570.
Hohenems, Count, 342.
Hohenlohe, Prince, 223.
Hohenzollern-Hechingen, court orchestra, 402.
Hol, Richard, 563.
Holborn, 57.
———, Anthony, 650.
———, William, 650.
Holding of bow gamba fashion relinquished, 366.
Holland, King of, 287, 561, 565.
Holländer, G., 465.
Hollmann, Joseph, 510, 538, 567-8, 570.
Holmes, violinist, 325.
Holstein-Gottorp, Duke Carl Ulrich of, 614.
Holzbauer, 200-1.
Homeyer, Paul, 495.
Honeyman, ventriloquist, 52.
Hopf, Hermann, 495.
Hoppen, violinist, 450.
Hopper, Simon, 308.
Horatio de Parma, 31, 100.
Hotmann (Hotteman, Hautmann), 59, 100.
Houtem, Ignaz van, 223.
Howell, double bass, 325.
———, Edward, 326, 448, 506-7, 510, 512-5, 535.
Hrimalz, Jaromir, 601.
Hubay, Jenö, 445, 516.
Huber, Franz Xaver, 253.
———, Joseph, 412.
Hübner, brothers, 614.
Hudson, George and Richard, 308.
Huefnagel, Franz, 92.
———, Jos., 92.
Hüllweck, Ferdinand, 424.

INDEX.

Hüllweck, Karl, 424.
Hulst, Miss van, violoncellist, 508.
Hume, Tobias, 39-40.
Hummel, Joh. Nepomuk, 237, 411, 561.
———, publisher, 193.
Hummer, Reinhold, 411, 427, 446, 465, 498, 502.
Humperdinck, E., 463.
Hurdy-gurdy, 648.
Hurel, 109.
Hus-Desforges, Pierre Louis, his roving career, 294, 533, 542.
Hussit Hymn, The, by Krov, 348.
Husso, Albert, 538.
Hutor, Wassili, "Carl Davidoff," 618.
Hutschenreuter, Otto, 481.
Hüttner, 412, 414, 420.
———, Joh. Nepomuk, 387.
Huygens, Chr., 649.

I.

"Illustrated London News," 634.
Imbault and Frères, publishers, 210, 273, 302.
Immler, 214.
Imperial Chapel of Paris (Napoleon), 542.
——— Library, Berlin, 311.
——— Orchestra, Petersburg, 486.
Improvisation chiefly practised on viol da gamba, 20.
"In Nomine," The, 36-7.
Inslegers, Alfons (erroneously spelled "Juslegers"), 557, 657.
Instruments Anciens, Société des, 535.
Isadelli, violoncellist, 441.
Isterdael, Charles van, 557.
Itier, Gaston, 109.
———, Léonard, 109.
———, Nicolas, 109.
Ives, Simon, 41.

J.

Jacchini, Giuseppe, 166.
Jacksch, F., theorist, 484.
Jackson, Thomas, 511.
Jacobowsky, Hermann, 448.
Jacobs, Edouard, 107, 118-9, 520, 556-7, 577, 608, 628, 635, 656-7.
Jacquard, Leon Jean, 460, 471, 533, 538, 564, 568-9, 575.
———, Louis Auguste, 527, 534.
Jacquet, violoncellist, 656.
Jadassohn, 471, 494.

Jaëll, Alfred, 563, 634.
Jäger (Jaeger), 239.
———, Ernst, 195.
———, Hugo, 452.
———, Joh. Zachar. Leonhardt, 193-5.
Jaggard, Mrs., bass viol player, 650.
Jähnig, Max, 488.
James I of England, 97.
———, Ivor, 508.
———, Prince of Wales, afterwards James II, 138-9.
Janet and Cotelle, 280, 302.
Janiczeck, violinist, 239.
Jansa, Leopold, 349.
Janson, Jean Bapt. Aimée Joseph, 267, 293-4, 298.
———, pupil of Berteau, 264.
———, Louis Auguste Joseph, 293.
Jantsy, 605.
Japha, Georg, 432.
Jarnovick, violinist, 294.
Jay, Britton's viol by, 52.
Jenkins, John, 37-8, 42, 47.
———, Thomas, painter, 311.
Jensen, Gustav, 432.
Jeral, Wilhelm, 604-5.
Joachim Albert, Prince of Prussia, violoncellist, 485.
———, Joseph, 421, 456, 461, 477, 481, 484, 487, 489, 511, 514, 576, 583, 627.
Joachim's playing, 430.
Joannini del Violoncello, 169.
Johann Adolph, Duke of Jülich, Cleve, Berg, 74.
——— Wilhelm, Elector Palatine, 72.
"John come Kiss Me now" (see Gambists), 297.
Johnson, Bartholomew, 309.
———, W. Noel, 509.
Jolivet, publisher, 271.
Jomelli, 194, 197.
Jones, C. Darbishire, 515.
———, Robert Purcell, 508, 515.
Jonson, Ben, 45.
———, Ben, "St. Bartholomew Fair," 129.
Jordani, João, 659.
Joseph II of Austria, 113.
"Journal de Paris," 1787, 303.
Judenkünig, description of holding the grosse geigen, 8.
———, Hans, frontispiece from "Ain schone künstliche Unterweisung," 7.
Junek, Julius, 604.

680 THE HISTORY OF THE VIOLONCELLO.

Junker, Ludwig, court chaplain of Prince Hohenlohe, 223.
Juslegers (see Inslegers).
Jutien, Nicolas, 283.

K.

Kahn, Robert, 485.
Kahnt, Moritz, 430, 436.
Kaim Orchestra, 444.
Kalkbrenner, 329.
———, piano quintet, 325.
Kalliwoda, J. W., 342, 395.
Kapp, Adolph, 478.
Karasowski, Moritz, 612.
Karauscheck (Karaseck), 195-6, 253.
Karel, Alois, 602, 604.
Karlowicz, Johann, 613.
"Kathleen Mavourneen," composed by Crouch, 505.
Kaufmann, David, publisher of M. Franck's "Intradas," 56.
———, Joh., 201.
———, organist, 79.
Kaulbach-Scotta, von, 446.
Keiser, 615.
Keller, violinist, 450.
———, violoncellist, 567.
Kellermann, Christian Laurentz, 632 ff.
Kellert, Gabriel, 659.
Kelly, Lord, 89.
Kelz, Joh. Friedr., 385.
———, Matthias, 82-3.
Kempter, pianist, 498.
Kerlino, Giovanni, 10, 12, 647.
Kerll, I. K., 84.
Kerpen, Friedr. Hugo, Baron von, 201.
Kethara, Assyrian, 4.
Kindermann, J. E., 82.
King Cole Club, 570.
King's band, 509.
Kinsky, Count, 163.
———, Dr. Georg, 176, 648-50, 653.
———, Prince, 415.
Kipper, Hermann, 463.
Kircher, Athanasius, "Musurgia," 23.
Kit, The, 4.
Kittel, composer, 240.
Kleeberg, 220.
Klein, Benedict, violoncellist, 499.
———, Bernhard, 399.
———, Karl, 499.
Klengel, August Alexander, 471.
———, Julius, 443, 462, 467, 471-2,
481, 489-95, 497, 500-1, 511, 522, 572, 577, 625, 630, 635-6.
Klengel, Paul, 472, 509.
Kletzer, Fery, 606.
Klieber, Wm., violoncellist, 462.
Klietz, Magnus, 394, 427, 443.
Klingenberg, Johannes, 75, 120, 243, 280, 458 ff., 464.
Knecht, violoncellist, 399.
Knechtel, Joh. Georg, 197, 338.
Knollys, H., 505.
Knoop, Gustav, 212-3, 393, 403, 405, 411, 425.
Knorr, Ivan, 516.
Koch, Friedrich, 480, 629.
Köcher, Paul, 334.
Koechl, list of violoncellists in Vienna Court Chapel, 205.
Koehler, composer, 198.
Kohl, Johann, 54.
Köhler, Louis, violoncellist, 572.
———, Otto, 479.
Komarek, Jos. Ant., 334.
Komorowski, Ignace, 612..
Königslow, Otto von, 432.
Kontski, Sigismund, 613.
Kordy, Deszö, 608-9.
Kossowski, Samuel, 611.
Kotzebue, 204.
Kousnetzov, Alexander, 626.
Kovarik, J., 603.
Kozsek (Kozecz), 110, 337.
———, master of Berteau, 263.
Kraft, 253.
———, Anton, 213 ff., 236, 650.
———, Concerto, Op. 5, 331.
———, Frederic, 237-8.
———, Nicolaus, 236 ff.
Krantz, Prof. Eugen, 487.
Krasselt, Rudolf, 500.
Kratzer, Valentin, 612.
Kraus, Anton, 188.
Krause, Johann Georg, 650.
Krebs, Carl, 443.
Kreisler, F., 599.
Kremberg, Jacob, 83.
Krenes, 349.
Kress, Paul, 52, 73.
Kretschmann, Theobald, 603.
Kreutzer, 303.
———, Rudolph, 533.
Krieger, 83.
Kriegk, J. J., 212, 240.
Kriehuber, painter, 245.
Krist, Otto, 498.
Krommer, Francis, 395.
Krov (Krob, Kroff), Jos. Theodor, 348.
Krug, Arnold, 485, 499.

INDEX. 681

Krumbholz, Theodor (not L.), 430, 440-1.
Kruse, Heinrich, 487-8.
———, viola, 450.
———, violin, 511.
Kufferath, violoncellist, 478.
Kuhnau, 79.
Kühnel, August, 22, 52, 60, 68, 72, 119, 447, 650.
———, August, as baryton player, 25, 114.
———, August, serenata, 71.
———, August II, 64.
———, Johann Michael, 64.
Kullack, Dehn's pupil, 389.
Kummer, Alexander, violinist, 251, 463.
———, Ernst, 251.
———, Ferdinand Wilhelm, 251.
———, Friedrich August, 241, 248 ff., 254, 347, 360, 393, 403, 412, 421, 424-5, 428, 436, 443, 445, 463, 469, 545, 616, 619, 642.
———, Max, 251.
Kündinger, Kanut, 483, 634.
Kunstmann, Joh. Gottfr., 238.
Kunzen, J. A., 184.
Kurland, Duke of, 215, 220, 339.
Kutschera, 344.
Kutzschbach, Hermann, 494.
Kwast, F., 570.
Kythara, 2.
———, Etymological deduction of the word violino and fiddle from, 4.
———, musician playing kythara in Notker's MS., 3.

L.

L'Abbé, ainé *(see Abbé)*, 171, 260-1.
———, brothers, 352.
———, Cadet, younger, 171, 260-1.
———, fils, 261.
———, younger, visit to London, 261.
Labocetta, Domenico, 581, 586, 592, 594.
Laborde, B. de, "Essay sur la Musique," 12, 121.
Lacey, Rophino, 161.
La Chevardière, publisher of Boccherini, 172.
Lachner, Ignatz, 422, 443.
Ladies' Choir (Frauen-Chor), Hanover, 476.
Lafarge, R., 539.
Lafont, 299.
Laggé, 654.

Lahoussaye, 277.
Lamarre, Jacques Michel Hurel de, 291 ff., 301, 326.
———, a young Rode, 292.
———, concertos written in his name by Aubert, 292.
———, Jean François, 293.
Lamoureux, 598.
Lamoury, 552-3.
Lancilotto of Modena, 30.
Lanfranco, "Scintilla musice," 19
Lang, Anton, 455.
———, composer, 198.
Langert, capellmeister, 479.
Lanier (Lanière), Nicholas, 45, 308.
Lanzetti, Salvatore, compositions, 153, 160, 166-7, 309, 355.
———, master of staccato, 377.
———, sonatas, 377.
Laroche, 626.
Laronde, Mlle., 539.
Laroon, Captain Marcellus, 309.
———, the painter, 309.
Larrocha, Alfred, 658.
Lassabathie, "Histoire du Conservatoire," 303.
Lassen, Eduard, 556.
Lasserre, Jules, 534, 656.
Laub, Ferd., 421-2, 634.
Laureati, Marquis Pietro, 580.
Laval Montmorency, Prince, 212.
Lavaria, Antonio, 581.
Lavenu, Louis Henry, 505.
Lawes, Henry, 41, 45.
———, Wm., 41, 45.
Lea, Agostino, 581.
Lebell, Ludwig, 495.
Le Blanc, Dr. Hubert, 108, 131.
———, Dr. Hubert, characterisation of viol da gamba tone, 378.
———, Dr. Hubert, "Defense de la Basse de Viole," 351-4.
Lebouc, Charles Joseph, 530.
Le Brun, 202.
Leclair, 109.
Leclerc, le Sieur, publisher, 109, 268, 362.
Le Couvreur, 109.
Lee, David, violoncellist, 513.
———, Louis, 415, 444.
———, Sebastian, 392, 415, 443, 613.
Leero viol *(see Lyra Viol)*.
Legrand, Pierre, 397, 402.
Leibrock, Jos. Adam, 400, 502.
Leichsenring, Emil, 489.
Leighton, Wm., 36.
"Leipziger Musikalische Zeitung," 203.

Lejeune, J., 549.
Le Menu, publisher, 266, 367.
Le More, 109.
Lemoyne, 105.
Leo, Leonardo, 374.
———, Leonardo, his concertos, 158.
Leon, Adelina, 508, 517-8, 523.
Léonard, 545.
Le Pin, 283.
Lessing, G. E., 183.
"Lesson" from Waylett's "The Gamut," 365.
Lestang, Marquise de, 283.
L'Estrange, family in Norfolk, 37, 43.
———, Sir Roger, 51, 307.
———, Sir Roger, Cromwell's fiddler, 49.
Lesueur, J. F., 267.
Levacq, violoncellist, 533.
Levasseur, Jean Henry, 290, 298, 302, 304-6, 526.
———, Pierre François (erroneously Jean Pierre), 284, 290, 652.
Lewis-Hill, Mrs., 609.
Lewita, 469.
Leykam, Christ. Franz Ambros, Baron von, 235.
Liadov, A., 626.
Libotton, Gustav, 463, 556, 559.
Lichnowski, Prince, 214.
Lichtenstein, Prince, 155.
Lidarti, Cristiano Giuseppe, 176, 648.
Lidl, Anton, "Andreas," 25, 113, 647.
Liebing, L., 484.
Liedel, Joseph, 647.
Liégeois, C., and E. Nogué, 653-4, 657-8.
———, Cornélis, 656.
———, Georges, 656.
Lier, Jacques von, 573.
Linarolo, Ventura, 30, 648.
Lincke, Carl, 636.
———, Jos., 243.
Lindley, Robert, 225, 314, 324 ff., 327-8, 330, 338, 347, 504, 512.
———, Robert, as solo accompanist, 372.
———, Robert, plays in his own string trio at Philharmonic, 325.
———, William, 325-6.
Lindner, August, 390, 418, 449, 462, 470, 569.
———, Wilhelm, 418.
Lipinski, Carl, 349.

Lirone perfetto, 25.
Listemann, Franz, 630.
Liszt, Franz, 421, 451, 488, 553, 583.
———, Krov's Hussit Hymn, 348-9.
——— Verein, Leipzig, 500.
Literature of the violoncello by Straeten, E. van der (see Straeten).
——— of the violoncello, Guide to the, by Philipp Roth, 461.
Lloyd, Edward, 509, 521.
———, J. A., 523.
Lobe, Joh. Christ., 437.
Lobkowitz, Prince, 236, 238, 348.
Lochner, Karl, 201.
Locke, Matthew, 47.
Loeb, Julius Leopold, 536, 538, 655-6.
Löffler, Albrecht, 491.
Lolli, 211.
———, Antonio, 169.
———, Filippo, 169.
Lombardi, Michele, 581.
"London Gazette," The, 1685, Kühnel's advertisement, 62.
Longman, Clementi and Co., 171.
Lopes, 654.
Loret's "Muze Historique," 101.
Lorleberg, Richard, 462.
Lorraine, Duc de, 106.
———, Prince Charles of, 541.
Löschhorn, Chs. Albert, 414.
Lose, violoncellist, 243.
Lotti, Antonio, 78.
Lotze, Wilhelm, 394, 412.
Louis Ferdinand, Prince of Prussia, 292.
——— XIII, 101.
——— XIII, Air de, 127.
——— XIV, 106-8, 157-8, 340.
——— XV, 163, 524.
——— XVI, 524.
Lover, Samuel, 473, 508.
Loveri, Carlo, 580.
———, Piedro, 580.
———, Vincenzo, 581.
Löwe, J. J., 84.
Löwenberg, Prince of Hohenzollern, court chapel, 442, 447, 452.
Lubbe, 215.
Lübbe, Karl, 438.
Lübeck, Ernst, 563.
———, Joh. H., 564.
———, Louis, 414, 444, 481, 498, 564.
Lubomirski, Kasimir, Prince, 601.
Lucas, Chs., 326.
Lucca, Pauline, 422.
Lüdemann, Otto, 485.

INDEX. 683

Ludwig, Paul, 508, 513, 518.
Lugo, Father Maria Filippo da, 176.
Luiz, Infante Don, 172.
Lully, Baptiste, 147, 157, 255, 340.
———, basse taille clef, 370.
Lupo, Ambrose, 35.
———, Horatio, 35.
———, Joseph, 35.
———, Pietro, 35, 129.
———, Teophil (son of Thomas), 35.
———, Thomas, 37, 45.
———, Thomas (1640?), 37.
———, Thomas (son of Joseph), 35.
———, Thomas (son of Pietro), 35.
———, Thomas (son of Teophil?), 35.
Luscinius, Ottomar, 18.
Lüstner, Charles, 435.
Lute, The, 9, 20.
Lütgendorff, 55.
Luxemburg, Grand Duke of, 493.
Lyko, Julius, violoncellist, 613.
Lyon, 325.
Lyra d'amore (viol), 23, 46.
——— tedesca, 25, 115, 648.
———, The, 25, 648.
——— viol, 22, 38, 43-4, 111, 259.
——— viol, Ayres by Corkine for, 39.
——— viol, leero viol, 39.
——— viol, lessons by Ferrabosco, 36.
——— viol, lyra ways, 41.
——— viol, Tuning of (Fig. 20), 38.
Lyre, 2.
———, King David playing the, 3.

M.

Maaré, Thomas C. de, 571.
Mace, Thomas, 36, 38, 50, 351.
Maes, violoncellist, 526.
Maggini, 130.
Magrini, Giuseppe, 592, 594.
Mahillon, V. and J., 28.
———, Victor, 24, 124.
Mahler, Gustave, 474.
Mahon, violoncellist, 329.
Malade, Antoinette Sophie, 295.
Malagotti, Jos., 206.
Maldere, Van, 197, 541.
Malterre, Eberhard, 197.
———, L., 197.
Malzat, Ignaz, 183, 338.
Mandycewski, E. v., 24.
Manecke, F., 481.

Manfredini, Filippo, 172.
Mangold, A. D., 234, 413, 652.
———, Carl Amand, 234.
———, Wilhelm, 234.
Mannheim Court Orchestra, 462.
Mantius, singer, 616.
Mantua, Isabella of, 10.
Mara, Ignatius, 179, 193, 199, 334.
———, J. B., 220, 313, 333-7.
———, Mme., 314, 328.
Marais, Marin, 22, 31, 72, 76-7, 101-4, 258.
———, Marin, "Folies d'Espagne," 297.
———, Marin, gamba by Acero, 12, 16.
———, Marin (Père Marais), 353.
———, Roland, 104.
Marcel, Jean, 519.
Marcello, Benedetto, 369, 383.
———, Benedetto, sonatas, 159.
Marchand, Margarethe, 218.
Marcus, Johannes, 30.
Marella, violinist, 167.
Margaret of France, 97.
Maria Anna, Archduchess, 198.
——— Theresa, Empress, 344.
———-Theresia, Archduchess, 198.
Mariani, 30.
Marie Antoinette of France, 277.
Marinelli, Pietro, 592.
Marko, E., 610.
Marneff, Jules, 656.
Marpurg, 108, 110, 261, 338.
——— ("Beiträge"), 155.
———, Duport visits Francischello, 274.
Marschalk, Baron von, 184.
Marschall, Joh. Ant., 181, 198.
Marsick, M., 469.
Marteau, Hy., 576.
Marthe, Raymond François, 654.
Martin, François, 306.
———, Pierre, 104.
Martinelli, 197.
Martini, Hugo, 477.
Martucci, G., 595.
Marx, Joseph M., 246.
———, Pauline, dramatic singer, 246.
Mary, Queen of England, 35.
Mas, violin, 547.
———, violoncellist, 654.
Masi, E., 441.
Mason, Edward, 508, 514.
Massart, Léon, 542.
Massau, violoncellist, 558.
Masse, Jean Baptiste, 263.
Massé, Serafino, 591.

Massenet, 460, 636.
Mastiaux, Hofkammerrath von, 651.
"Matchappy tot bevordering van Toonkunst," 442.
Matern, A. W. F., 230.
Mattheson, J., 72, 355-6.
Matthison, poet, 217, 290.
Matys, Karl, 447, 449, 476.
Maucourt, violinist, 400.
Maugars (Maugard), André, 33, 52, 97 ff., 105.
——— (Maugard), André, "Reponse fait a un curieux," 31.
Maugey, Mlle., 109.
Maurice, Duke of Saxe Zeitz, 61.
Maurin, violinist, 546.
Max Emmanuel, Elector, 61.
——— Joseph, Elector of Bavaria, 340.
Maximilian, Emperor, Procession of, 5.
———, Franz, Elector, 223.
——— Joseph, Prince Elector of Bavaria, 89.
Mayence, Elector of, 211.
Maynard, John, 41.
Mayseder, 237.
Mazzinghi, 329.
McArdell, James, engraver, 311.
McDonald, Flora, 332.
———, John, Lieut.-Colonel, 332.
———, Malcolm, 331.
Medeck, 253.
Medici, Lorenzo di, 30.
———, Pietro di, 30.
Meerens, Charles, 545, 552.
Meglin (Megelin), Hch., 209, 211.
Meinberger, capellmeister, 217.
Meiningen court chapel, 442, 489.
Meissner, chamber musician, 234.
Melchior, 57.
Mell, Davis, 308.
Mello, Carlos de, 600.
Melzer, Joseph, 474-5.
Mendel-Reissmann, 63, 121, 226-7, 243, 262, 311-2, 403, 411, 531, 651.
Mendelssohn, Felix, 387, 403, 408-10, 421, 472, 531, 544, 583, 642.
———, Robert, 586.
Menel, violoncellist, 328.
Mensi, Father Francis, 342.
Menter, Joseph, 401 ff., 413, 422, 427, 435, 437, 470, 634.
———, Sophie, 447, 468.
Mercadante, 587.
Mercadier, A., 539.
Mercer, Pepys's maid, 650.

Mercier, Philipp (F.), painter, 310, 316.
"Mercure de France," 264, 271, 273, 283.
Merighi, Cristoforo, 587, 595.
———, Vincenzo, 580-2, 587-8.
Merk, Joseph, 207, 237, 243, 395, 414, 561, 633.
Merkel, Gustav, 458.
Merlen, violoncellist, 563.
Merloo, L., 570.
Mersenne, Marin, 52, 97, 100, 358, 360-1, 649.
———, Marin, chapter on viols, 259.
———, Marin, description of violin, 259.
———, Marin, "Harmonie Universelle," 131, 259.
———, Marin, instructions for bowing, 361.
———, the fifth string on violins, 260.
———, tuning of violoncello, 361.
Metke, Adolph Friedr., 385.
Metternich, Prince, 344.
Meyer, Waldemar, 449.
Meyerbeer, 235, 389.
———, viol d'amour *obbligato* in "Huguenots," 117.
Michael, Grand Duke, 404.
——— Paul, 490.
Mico, 39.
"Microcosme Musical," Tricklir's, 211.
Milanollo, Theresa, 399.
Miller, bassoon, 160.
Mills, Watkin, 509.
Miltitz, B. von, 398.
Mingheein del Viulunzel, 130, 133.
Mirecki (Mirekki), Vittorio de, 550, 658.
Modena, Duchess of, 133.
———, Francesco II, Duke of, 143, 148.
Moffat, Alfred, 168, 263, 297, 540, 651.
Moja, Leonardo, 580-1.
Mollenhauer, Edward, 425.
———, Heinrich, 425.
Monhaupt, Friedrich, 449.
Moniuszko, Boleslaf, 613.
——— Stanislaus, 613.
Mons, Thos., 57.
Montecchi, Prospero, 594.
Monti Chiaro, 30.
Montigny, Charles, 551, 563.
Moralt, Jacob, 387.
———, Joseph, 387-8, 652.

INDEX. 685

Moralt, Philipp, 219, 244, 387, 402, 652.
Morella, Morglato, 30.
Morelli, Gaëtano, 594.
Mori, N., 505.
Moria, 165.
Morphy, Count, 597-8.
Morrel, 205.
Moscow Imperial Chapel, 624.
Mosel, Ignaz Franz, Edler von, 233.
Moser, J., 468.
Mossel, Isaac, 567, 573-4.
Mozart family, 340.
——. Leopold, 91, 111, 164, 181, 197, 230, 271.
——, Miss and Master, 167.
—— Society, 519.
——. W. A., 168, 202, 214, 291, 341, 398, 612, 641.
——, W. A., string quintet, 325.
——, W. A., string trio, 325.
——, W. A., theme of fugue from "Magic Flute" in Schenck's suite, 69.
Mozarteum, 415.
Muggelini, Bruno, 625.
Mühlfeld, Rich. (clarinet), 485.
Mukle, May, 520.
Mulder, Jan, 570.
Mulgrave, Lord, 309.
Müller, A. Theodor, 391, 421, 434, 451, 456, 468.
——, Aegidius Christoph, 391.
——-Berghaus, Charles, 435.
——-Campbell, Lucy, 629.
——, Carl, 494.
——, Conrad, 54.
——, Conrad, viol maker, 18.
——, Dr. Guido, 629.
——, Friedrich, 246.
——, gambist at Warsaw, 93.
——, Georg, 391.
——, Gust., 391.
——, Hippolyt, 402, 435, 437, 443, 446, 453.
——. Karl Friedr., 391.
——, Valentin, 402, 427.
——, violoncello, 328.
——, Wilhelm, 391, 434-6, 456-7, 461, 468, 477.
Munich Court Orchestra, 602, 634.
Münster, Bishop of, 211.
Müntzberger, Joseph, 541-2.
——, Wenceslas, 541-2.
"Musical Courier," Philharmonic programmes, 325.
" —— Magazine," 286.
" —— News," 592.

Musical Society, Imperial Russian, 451.
Musicians, Royal Society of, 328, 331-2, 510.
——, Royal Society of, Crosdill's bequest, 314.
"Musick's Monument," Thomas Mace, 50.
"Musikalische Europa, Das," 293.
" —— Nachrichten" (Dall' Oglio), 161.
"Musikfreunde, Gesellschaft der," 176, 345, 420, 648, 650.
" ——, Gesellschaft der," Haydn's baryton compositions, 24.
Musikverein, Budapest, 469.
"Musikzeitung Allgemeine," 164-5.
Muzikant, Alois, 604.

N.

Nadermann, 280.
Naples, King of, 115.
——, King of, player of lyra tedesca, 25.
Napoleon, 176, 203, 225, 287.
Narishkin, Prince, 407.
Nascimento Fredericdo, 659.
Nassau, Duke of, 407.
Nathan, violoncellist, 590.
Nathaniel, Dr., Lord Crewe, 51.
National Portrait Gallery, 316.
Nattier, 110.
Nava, Gaetano, 506.
Neate, Charles, 330.
Nebelong, Siegfrid, 635.
Nedbal, 603.
Nemours, Duchess of, 101.
Nepomucky, Em., 604.
Neruda, Alois, 602.
——, Franz, 334, 601-2.
——, Joh. Chrysostomus, 334.
——. Joh. Georg, 333.
——, Wilma, Mme. Norman (see also Hallé, Lady), 334, 601.
Netolitzky, Countess, 339.
"Neue Zeitschrift für Musik," 227, 398, 411.
Neumann, baryton composer, 650.
——, Fr., theorist, 499.
Neumark, Georg, 58.
Newmarch, Rosa, 626.
Newton, Isaac, 50.
Nicholas II, Czar, 603.
Nicodé, L., 490.
Nicolai, J. M., 83.
Nicolini, accompanied by Francischello, 154-5.
"Niebelungen Lied," 3-4.

Niemecz, 650.
"Niews van den Daag," 566.
Nikisch, Arthur, 502, 609.
Nikita, 522, 572.
Nochez, 164, 265.
Noebe, Carl, 444.
———, Louis, 444.
Nogué, E., 656.
Norblin, Emile, de la Gourdaine, 305.
———, Louis Pièrre Martin, de la Gourdaine, 291, 299-300, 303 ff., 525-7, 529-30, 533, 542, 546-7.
Norcome (Norcum), Daniel, 41.
Norman, Barak, Britton's viol by, 52.
North, Francis, Lord Guildford, 51, 307.
———, Roger, 43-4.
———, Sir Roger, 51.
———, Sir Roger, about "bass violins," 307, 355.
Notker, Labeo, 3.
Nottebohm, 468.
Nub (Georg ?), 84.

O.

NOTE.—Orchestra. Court chapels and court orchestras, see under names of respective courts.

Obici, Bartoloméo, 653.
O'Donnel, Watton, 508.
Offenbach, Jean Jacques, 46.
Oglio, Giuseppe dall' *(see Da'l' Oglio)*, 161.
Oldenburg, Duke of, 403.
Olivari, Anna, 142.
Oliveira Passos, João Carlos d', 659.
Oliver, General, 586.
Omerti, ancient Hindoo instrument, 2.
Orange, Prince of, 80.
Orchestra, Allgemeine Musikgesellschaft, Basle, 460.
———, Amsterdam Orchestral Union, 572.
———, Berlin Philharmonic, 500-1, 503, 518, 569-70, 573-4, 578, 623, 636.
———, Berlin Symphony, 487.
———, Bethmann, Magdeburg, 213, 411.
———, Bilse, Berlin, 439, 442, 444, 468, 478, 569, 602, 656.
———, Blüthner, 655.
———, Boston Philharmonic Club, 454.
———, Boston Symphony, 467, 502, 613, 634.
Orchestra, Bülow's, Meiningen, 442, 485, 489, 491.
———, Cherubini Societa, 595.
———, Colonne, 537, 657.
———, Concertgebouw, Amsterdam, 573-4.
———, Costa, Sir Michael, London, 534, 567.
———, Crystal Palace, 563.
———, Damrosch, 629.
———, Dortmund Philharmonic, 499.
———, Dresden Philharmonic, 490.
———, Felix Meritis, Amsterdam, 563.
———, Fiedler, Max, Hamburg, 474, 488, 491.
———, Fliege's, 462.
———, Friends of Music, Society of, Hamburg, 503.
———, Friends of Music, Society of, Lübeck, 497.
———, Gewandhaus, 403-4, 407, 409, 421, 428, 443, 467-8, 471, 487, 492, 494-5, 564, 566.
———, Gürzenich, Cologne, 566.
———, Hallé, Manchester, 486.
———, Hamburg Orchestral Union, 485.
———, Hamburg Philharmonic, 488, 491.
———, Harrison, 567.
———, Helsingfors Philharmonic, 474, 481.
———, Jullien's, 553.
———, Kaim, Munich, 444, 493, 496-9.
———, Konzerthaus, Berlin, 474.
———, Kretschmar's First Symphony, 484.
———, Kur, Baden-Baden, 474, 500.
———, Kur, Carlsbad, 488.
———, Lamoureux, 556, 571, 598, 657.
———, Langenbach, Barmen, 462.
———, Laube, Hamburg, 466, 474, 478-9, 499, 635.
———, Leeds Festival, 506.
———, Liebich's Symphony, 449.
———, Liebig's, Berlin, 466.
———, London, Royal Italian Opera, Covent Garden, 504-7, 509, 515.
———, London Symphony, 626.
———, Manchester Philharmonic, 512.
———, Mannsfeld, 608.
———, Manns's, Sir Augustus, Scottish, 570.

INDEX. 687

Orchestra, Massima, Rome, 594.
———, Meiningen Court, 489.
———, Metropolitan, New York, 474.
———, Moscow Musical and Orchestral Society, 451.
———, Museum's, Frankfort, 486.
———, Musical Society (Musikalische Gesellschaft), Cologne, 463.
———, Musical Union, Stockholm, 602.
———, Musikverein, Copenhagen, 602.
———, New Symphony, London, 514, 556.
———, Paleis vor Volksvlijt, 571, 574.
———, Park, Amsterdam, 471, 563, 571.
———, Pasdeloup, 536, 571.
———, Philharmonic, Bremen, 572.
———, Philharmonic, Christiana, 636.
———, Philharmonic, Hamburg, 468, 474, 479.
———, Philharmonic, Hanover, 498.
———, Philharmonic, Helsingfors, 635.
———, Philharmonic, London, 588.
———, Philharmonic, Vienna, 557.
———, Pittsburg, 630.
———, Queen's Hall, 556.
———, Reichshallen, Berlin, 462.
———, Rhenish Festival, 552.
———, Richter, London, 466.
———, Scotch, Glasgow, 534.
———, St. Cäcilia, Amsterdam, 563.
———, St. Carlo, 586.
———, Stumpf's, E., Amsterdam, 551.
———, Subscription Concerts, Amsterdam, 561.
———, Thomas, Chicago, 503.
———, Thomas Symphony, New York, 454, 479, 563.
———, Three Choir's Festival, 506.
———, Tonhalle, Zürich, 488.
———, Winderstein, Leipzig, 496-7.
———, Wood's, Henry J. (Queen's Hall), 518.
Orchestral Union, Amsterdam, 571.
——— Union, Arnheim, 571.
——— Union, Breslau, 475.
——— Union, Wiborg, 635.
Organ, 141.
Organs with wooden pipes by Cellini, 30.

Oriana, Triumphs of, 41.
Orleans, Duke of, 106-7, 157, 260.
Orloff, Prince, 341.
Orsler, Franz, 251.
———, Joseph, 206-7, 252.
Ortiz, Girolamo, biographical notice of Abaco, 165.
Ortmans, Réné, 463.
Ostein, Count, 155.
Oswald, teacher of Hallet, 311.
———, violoncellist, 243.
Ottey, Sarah, 649.
Oudshoorn, Anton, 566.
Ould, Charles, 506.
———, Kate, 506, 508.
Oulie, E., 636.
Oushoorn, H., 570.

P.

Pace, D. Nicolo, 141.
Pacini, C., 285.
Paderewski, Ignaz, 557.
Paër, Ferdinand, 650.
Paganini, 170-1, 389, 589, 651.
———, "Carneval de Venice," 297.
Pages of the Royal Music, Institute of the, 292.
Palatine, Prince, 203.
Palma, Anicet, 658.
Panfili, Cardinal, 133.
Pannier, Paul, 65, 120.
Panofka, 398.
Panseron, Auguste, 306.
Panzetta, Antonio, 581, 589.
Pape, Ludwig, 403.
Papier, Rosa, 572.
Papin, Georges, 654.
Paque, William (Guilleaume), 550.
Paraguin, 252.
Parasisti, 164.
Paris, Chapelle Royale, 527.
——— Museum, Duiffoprugcar violin, 17.
Parisini, Carlo, 580, 590.
Parker, B. Patterson, 508, 518, 523.
Parlow, Albert, 479.
Parma, Farnese, Duke of, 142, 168.
Parry, Dr. Hubert, 512.
———, harpist, 315.
Partegiotti, Rosina, "Sister Illuminata," 144-5.
Partl, viola pomposa, 27.
Pasquali, the younger, 161.
Pasqualini, 153, 160-1, 164, 166, 309, 355.
Patti, Adelina, 469, 522, 629.
——— Carlotta, 468, 553, 634.

Patzelt, Johann, 343.
Pauer, Max, 462.
Paul, Dr. O., 444, 509.
Paulsen, Carl Friedrich Ferdinand, 252.
——, Friedrich, 252.
Paxton, Stephen, 311.
——, William, 310-1.
Pecoraro, Lutgardo, 581, 586.
Peile, John, 331.
Pembroke, Eliza, Countess of, 88.
Pepys, Mrs., 650.
——, Samuel, 51, 650.
Peracchio, Angelo, 594.
Percivall, violoncellist, 325, 331.
Pergen, Baptist, Count von, 198.
Perroni, Carlo, 208.
——, Giovanni, 206, 208.
Perrotti, Jean Augustin, 170.
Pertoja, 253.
Pestalozzi, 245.
Peter II, Czar, violoncellist, 179, 615.
—— the Great, 614-5.
Petersburg, Imperial Chapel, 617.
Petersen, Albert, 83, 467.
Peterzik, Emeric, 183.
Petherick, Dora, 519.
Petiau, Jules Réné, 537.
Petrides, 325.
Petrik, E. Vinceslaus, 334, 337.
Pettinari, violinist, 592.
Pettit, Walter, 506-7.
——, William H., 506.
Pezzani, Feruccio, 591.
Pezze, Alessandro, 507, 517, 519-20, 580, 588.
Pezzota, Mario, 594.
Pfister, "Regierungsadvokat," 188.
Philharmonic Society, London, 326-9, 412, 504-6, 509, 522.
Philidor, Pièrre Danican, 109.
Philipp, Fritz, 491.
—— V of Spain, 106.
Philippe, Don, Ferrari in orchestra of, 163.
Philipsen, Charles, 491.
Phillips, 329.
Piantanida, Francesco de, 172.
Piarelli, violoncellist, 169.
Piatti, Alfredo, 47, 147, 167, 174, 251, 456, 483-4, 506-7, 509, 512-3, 522, 536, 580, 582 ff., 587-8, 590, 593.
Piccolellis, Marquis Giovanni, 595.
——, Ottavio de, 595.
Pichl, Wenzel, 114, 344.
Piczek, 349.
Piening, Karl, 489-90.

Piggot, violoncellist, 586.
Pincinetti, Antonio, junior, 197, 338.
Pisendel, Johann Georg, 27, 116.
Pius V, Pope, 126.
Planken, Van der, 543.
Plantade, Charles Henry, 287.
Planté, 658.
Platel, Nicolas Joseph, 300, 543-4, 548-9, 562.
——, Nicolas Joseph, adventures and travels, 301.
——, Nicolas Joseph, appointed at Brussels Conservatoire, 301.
——, Nicolas Joseph, becomes founder of the Belgian school, 302.
——, Nicolas Joseph, his happy disposition, 302.
Platen, Count, 235.
Platteau, Gabrielle, 559.
Playford, John, "Musick's Handmaid," 43.
——, John, "Musick's Recreation," 41, 43, 46.
——, John, Purcell's round on the viol, 53.
——, John, "Skill of Musick," 49, 361.
Pleyel, Ignace, 240, 292, 299, 326.
——, publisher, 287.
Plock, violoncellist, 451.
Pochette, or dancing master's fiddle, 4.
Pohl, C. F., 341.
—— (about Abaco), 164.
—— (about Lanzetti), 166.
——, Mozart and Haydn in London, 310.
Pohle, Alexander, 571.
Poli, Agostino, 216, 252, 652.
Polliari, Cicio, 162, 615.
Poorten, Arved, 616-7.
Popper, D., 411, 447-8, 452, 455, 468, 495, 507, 516, 608-9, 645, 659.
——, D., compositions, 448.
——, Wilhelm, 659.
Porpora, N., 383, 615.
——. N., sonata and concerto, 375-7.
——, N., specimens from concerto, 376.
Porretti, 170.
Portheim, Jos. Edler von, 412.
Possen, Lauxmin, 54.
Possoz, Henri, 551.
Potter, Cipriano, 325, 330, 505.
Potz, capellmeister, 337.
Powell, Maud, 521.

INDEX.

Praeger, Ferd. Christ. Wilhelm, 411.
———, Heinrich Aloys, 412.
Prætorius, Michael, "Syntagma Musicum," 20, 25, 102, 111, 126, 130-1, 647.
———, reproduction of gambas, 21.
Präger, violoncellist, 561.
Prarelli, 283.
Precursors of the violoncello, The, 1.
Preisler, V. D., painter, 82.
Prell, Aug. Christ., 385, 392, 422, 476.
———, Johann Nicolaus, 385, 415.
Preston, 367.
Preti, Arturo, 591.
Preumont, Raoul, 656.
Preuveneers, Jean, 556.
Preysing, Charles, 208.
———, Frederic, 208.
———, H. B., 208, 652.
———, Sophie Elisabeth, 195.
Prill, Emil, 477.
———, Karl, 477.
———, Paul, 572.
Prince Consort, Dutch, 500.
Pronath, 253.
Prout, Ebenezer, 463.
———, Louis B., 463.
Provesi, Luigi, 591.
Prussia, Crown Prince, 219.
———, King of, 252.
———, Queen of, 541.
Pückl, Fred. Leopold, 206.
———, Georg, 208.
———, Paul, 208.
——— (Pickhl, Bickl) family, 208.
———, Virgil, 208.
———, Wm. Christ., 208.
Pudor, Dr. Heinrich, 486.
———, J. F., 486.
Pugno, Raoul, 656.
Purcell, Henry, 53.

Q.

Quantz, 107, 155, 198.
Quarenghi, Guglielmo, 580, 587, 590.
"Quarterly Musical Magazine and Review," 1824, 356.
Quartet, Adamowski, 613.
———, Alard, 527, 654.
———, Amsterdam Conservatoire, 573.
———, Armingaud, Mas, Lalo, Jacquard, 533.
———, Auer, Leopold, 444.
———, Baillot, 305.
———, Bargheer, Karl, 444.
———, Barth, Richard, 485, 491.
———, Barthelemon's, 328.
———, Bataille, 656.
———, Becker, Jean, family, 483.

Quartet, Berlin, 576.
———, Blaha, 485.
———, Bohemian, 496, 602-4.
———, Bolognese, 590.
———, Borisch, 501.
———, Bremen Philharmonic, 495.
———, Breslau Conservatoire, 498.
———, Brodsky, 472.
———, Brussels, 657.
———, Budapest String, 608.
———, Cassel String, 450.
———, Clench, Norah, 521.
———, Cologne Conservatoire, 432, 489.
———, Constantinople String, 494.
———, Dannreuther, 603.
———, Derniers, quatuors de Beethoven, Sociétée des, 546.
———, Dessau, 481.
———, Duesberg, 498.
———, Firmin Touche, 657.
———, Fitzner, 492, 501.
———, Florentine, 441, 482, 606.
———, Frankfort, Popular Chamber Music Society, 496.
———, FrankfurterVereinigung, 493.
———, Glasgow, 489.
———, Gompertz, Richard, 506.
———, Grimson String, 514.
———, Halir, 477, 572.
———, Hamburg Society, 427.
———, Hänflein, 470.
———, Hayot, 571.
———, Heckmann, 433, 445, 558, 572.
———, Heermann, 483, 494, 498.
———, Heller, Trieste, 592.
———, Hellmesberger, 411, 455, 465.
———, Henley, 517.
———, Herman, Warsaw, 603.
———, Hilf, Anno, 467, 492.
———, Hoch String, 494.
———, Hochberg, Count, 456.
———, Holländer, Gustav, 468.
———, Jacoby, 508.
———, Joachim, 120, 456, 477, 629.
———, Joachim, London, 457, 514.
———, Kneisel, Boston, 467.
———, Königsberg String, 495.
———, Konzerthaus, Vienna, 501.
———, Koperzky, 491.
———, Krasselt, 491.
———, Krefeld String, 628.
———, Kruse, 511.
———, "Leipziger Novitäten Quartett-Verein," 511.
———, Lewinger, 497.
———, Lipphardt, von, 404.
———, Ludwig II, 602.
———, Ludwig, Joseph, 508.
———, Mannheim String, 494.

45

Quartet, Marsick, 536, 656.
———, Marteau, 576.
———, Maurin, 428, 553.
———, Mayseder's, 587.
———, Meiningen Court Chapel, 489-90.
———, Meyer, Waldemar, 491.
———, Molto String, 515.
———, Morin, 653.
———, Müller (elder), 391, 434, 456.
———, Müller (second), 435.
———, Munich, 413.
———, "Museum's Gesellschaft," Frankfort, 428.
———, Nadaud, 654.
———, New York String, 454.
———, Ondricek-Junek, 604.
———, Petersburg, St., 622.
———, Petherick, 519.
———, Petri, 492.
———, Popular Concerts, Saturday and Monday, 506, 508, 583.
———, Prill, 605.
———, Reeves, 523.
———, Ries, 402.
———, Riller, 470.
———, Rosé, 465, 492. 502.
———, Sahla, 497, 572.
———, Salomon's, 329.
———, Saunders, John, 556.
———, Schiever, 486.
———, Schradieck, 485.
———, Schröder, 452.
———, Skinner (read Shinner), 522, 629.
———, Singer, 441.
———, Soldat-Röger, 629.
———, "Süddeutsche Streich Quartett," 512.
———, Walenn, 511.
———, Walter, 446.
———, Wessely, Hans, 523.
———, Wollgandt, Wolsche, Hermann and Klengel, 472.
———, Zajic, Florian, 444, 465.
———, Zimmermann, 402, 407, 413.
Queen's band (England), 506-7, 551.
Quillez, Carlos, 659.
Quinte (violin), 128, 131.
Quintet Club, Mendelssohn, Boston, 471, 634.
———, Gulli, 593.
———, Queen Margareta's, 594.

R.

Raaff, tenor, 202.
Rabaud, Hyppolite François (erroneously J. F.), 534, 536, 653, 655.
Rachelle, Pietro, 589.
Racster, Olga, 145, 649-52.

Radauer, violoncellist, 197.
Radziwill, Prince Anton, 230, 304.
Raimondi, Filippo, 579.
———, Marianna, 579.
Rajola, Anton, 206.
Ramacciotti, 589.
Ramcke, Katherina, wife of B. Romberg, 225.
Rameau, J. P., 109, 525.
Ramm, oboe, 202.
Randall, W. and J. Abell, successors of Walsh, 160.
Ranelagh Gardens, Vauxhall, 651.
——— Rotunda, 329.
Rantzau, Count, 284.
Raoul (Rauol), Jean Marie, 118, 287, 546, 651.
Raphael, viol from sketch for Apollo statue, 5.
Rappé, violoncellist, 557.
Rasch, Michael, 209.
Rasoumowski, Count, 243.
Rauch, F., 634.
Rauppe, Johann Georg, 217.
Ravanastron, its origin and present use, 1.
———, its tone described by Stoeving, 2.
Ravenscroft, Thomas, 37, 39.
Rebab, The, 2.
Rebec, The, 2, 4.
———, The, musician playing, in Labeo Notker's MS., 3.
"Recitatif italien, Le," 373.
Reeve, 325.
Regondi, Giulio, 647-8.
Rehberg, Adolphe, 576.
Rehsteiner, Walburga, 398.
Reicha, 233.
———, Anton, 337.
———, Joseph, 337, 342.
Reichardt, 314.
Reichel, A., 443.
Reichmann, Hedwig, 494.
Reinagle, 329.
———, Hugh, 323.
———, Joseph, 322.
Reinhold, Theodor Christlieb, 180.
Reissiger, 409.
Rensburg, J., 443, 566.
Reuter, violinist, 220.
Revival of the Viols, The, by E. van der Straeten, 47, 72, 111, 118.
Revue Musicale, 288.
Rey, Jean Baptist, 285, 287.
———, Louis Charles Joseph, 285.
Reyer (Rey), composer, 287.
Reynolds, Bernard, 510, 521.
———, John, 510.
———, Thomas, 510.

INDEX. 691

Rheinberger, Joseph, 497.
Rhiemann (Riemann), Jacob, 89.
Ricercari by Domenico Gabrieli, 133.
———, meaning of word, 133.
Rich, Sir Charles, 331.
Richardson, James, 512.
Richel, publisher, 82.
Richelieu, Cardinal, 98.
Richer, singer, 284, 300.
———, son of André, 262.
Richter, A., 463.
———. Hans, 454, 469, 558.
Ricordi, "Gazetta Milano," 172.
Ried, Dorothea von, 89.
Riedel, 179, 486, 615.
Riegele, A., 610.
Riemann, Dr. Hugo, 36, 305, 334, 389, 401, 405, 435, 537, 649.
Riepel, Joseph, 182, 185.
Ries, Ferdinand, 225, 317, 400.
———, Ferd., piano quintet, 325.
———, Ferd., sextet, 325.
———, Ferd., string quartet, 325.
———, Louis, 457, 583.
Rieser, W., 610.
Rietz, Eduard, 408.
———, Johann Friedrich, 408.
———, Julius, 394, 408 ff., 428.
Rigaud, painter, 104.
Rigaut, Physicien de la Marine, 272, 367.
Rigel, 280.
Rimbault, 87.
Rinck, Cantor, 413.
Ringeisen, Marcel, 538.
Ripfel, Karl, 388.
Rischbieter, 490.
Risler, pianist, 576.
Rispoli, Silvio, 595.
Ritter, Georg, 201.
———, Peter, 114, 201 ff., 232.
———, Theodor, 468.
———, Wenzel, 202.
Robinson, Thomas, 42.
Rocchi, Guido, 591.
Rochefort, Jean Baptist, 286.
Roczmittal, College at, 343.
Roda, A. von, 213, 411.
———, Ottomar von, 213, 410-1, 450.
Rode, 292, 329.
Roellig, Johann Georg, 179-80.
Roger, Estienne, Amsterdam, publisher, 64-5, 94, 130, 357.
————Miclos, Mme., 655.
Rognoni, Mario, 591.
Rohne, Adolph, violoncellist, 467.
Rolla, A., 580.
Rolle, Christian Ernst, 180.
Romance of the Fiddle, The, E. van der Straeten, 360-1.

Romano, Allessandro, 33.
Romberg, 325, 330, 400.
———, Andreas, 221-5, 227, 385, 397.
———, Angelika, 221.
———, Anton, 220-2, 237.
———, Anton, son of Bernhard, 221.
———, Balthasar, Theresa, 221.
———, Bernhard Heinrich, 195, 220 ff., 251, 254, 303, 326, 330, 337, 346, 349, 354, 379, 384-5, 389, 392-3, 397, 408, 545, 547, 616, 618, 641-2.
———, Bernhard, adagio by Pippo Amadio, 166.
———, Bernhard, advances technique of violoncello, 371.
———. Bernhard, characterisation of his playing, 223-4, 226.
———, Bernhard, compositions, 227.
———, Bernhard, his view of violoncello makers, 227.
———, Bernhard, professor at Paris Conservatoire, 225.
———, Bernhard, remarks on Beethoven's quartets, 229, 232, 234, 237, 240, 244, 247.
———, Bernhard, remarks on "staccato," 228.
———, Bernhard, remarks on tempo, 228.
———, Bernhard, simplification of clefs, 371.
———, Bernhard, tours and travels, 225-6.
———, Cyprian, 221, 397 ff.
———— family, 211.
———, Gerhard Heinrich, 221-2.
———, Heinrich, 221.
———, Karl (Charles), 221, 226.
Römisch, 212.
Ronchetti, David, 169.
Ronchini, F., 592.
Rosé, Eduard, 502.
Rose, Johann Heinrich Viktor, 193, 199, 246-7, 652.
Rosoor, Louis, 656.
Rossini, 279, 554.
Roth, Philipp, 321, 460.
Rothe, professor violoncello, 478.
Rotondo, Paolo, 595.
Röttig, Christ., 206.
Rousseau, Frédéric, 286.
———, Jean, 102, 255.
———, Jean, taille clef, 370.
———, Jean, "Traité de la Viole," 16, 105 ff.
———. Jean Jacques, 264.
Rousselot, Scipion, 300.
Roux, Louis, 547.
Rovelli, Giuseppe, 169, 582.
———, Guido, 168.

Röver (Roever), Henry, 411, 414, 427, 465.
Rowe, 42.
———, Walter, 42.
Royal Chapel, Dresden, 477, 479.
——— Chapel, Paris, 542.
——— Chapel, Vienna, 465.
——— Pages, Institute of, 300.
——— Society of Musicians, 507-8.
Rubini, 159, 562.
Rubinstein, A., 422, 486, 553, 624, 658.
———, A., Dehn's pupil, 389.
———, Nicholas, 422.
Rubio, Agostino, 658.
Rüdel, Albert, 440.
Rudhardt, A., pianist, 494.
Rüdinger, Fritz Albert Christ., 634-6.
Ruegger, Charlotte, 577.
———, Elsa, 577-8.
———, Wally, 577.
Ruger, Vincenzo, detto il per, 31, 34.
Ruggeri, 130.
———, Francesco, Whitehouse's, 508.
Ruggerius, Francesco, Withers's, 517.
Rühlmann, "Geschichte der Bogeninstrumente," 16 footnote, 26.
Ruiz-Casaux, Joan, 658.
Ruppert, J. H., 28.
Ruspantini, Allessandro, 589.
Rust, Dr. Wilhelm, 492.
———, F. W., 379.
Rutland, Duke of, 313.
Rüttinger, organist, 240.
Ryba, Jacob Johann, 343.

S.

Sabbatier, viola player, 547.
Sacchini, 86.
Saeger, 209.
Sainprae, Jacques, 112.
Saint Gall, famous library, 3.
———-George, George, 119.
———-George, Henry, 119.
———-Saëns, 460, 533-4, 553, 568.
———-Sévin, brothers, 352. ·
———-Sévin, Jos. Barnabé de, 261.
———-Sévin, master of Barrière, 261.
———-Sévin, Philippe Pièrre de, 110, 260-1.
———-Sévin, Pierre de, 110, 260-1.
Sainte-Colombe, 16, 101-4, 106, 110.
Sakom, Dr. J., 503.
Salentin, 171, 261.
Salis, 217, 290.
Salle Chantereine, 279.
Sallentin, Alexandre, 110.
Salmon, 328.
———, Jacques *(see Salomon)*, 258.
———, Joseph, 571.

Salmond, Felix, 508, 523.
———, Norman, 523.
Salo, Gasparo da, 12, 14, 30, 125, 258.
Salomo, 104.
Salomon, Jacques (erroneously Salmon), 127, 258, 652.
———, J. P., 323, 328-9.
Salzburg, Prince Bishop of, 181, 230, 340.
Salzmann, 395.
Samazeuilh, Pièrre, 656.
San Martini, oboe, 160.
Sancet, art critic, 139.
Sandby, Hermann, 659.
Sandonati, 170.
Sandow, Eugen, 467.
———-Herms, Adeline, 468.
Sandys and Forster, 192.
Santo, Samuel Benjamin, 234.
Saradschev, Iwan, 624.
Sarao, Joachimo, 93.
Sarasate, Pablo de, 445, 658.
Sardinia, King of, 166.
Sarmiento, Luiz, 657.
Sarti, violinist, 590.
Saubley, 171, 261.
Saunders, Wm., bass violin, 307.
Sauret, Émile, 465.
Sautreuil, Albert, 536.
Sauvaget, Alfred, 533, 656.
Sauvinet, Eugenio, 659.
Savart, theorist, 568.
Saxe-Coburg, Duke of, 551.
———-Weimar, Ducal Chapel, 556.
Saxony, Duke of, 75.
———, King of, 406, 409, 635.
———, Prince Elector of, 78, 283, 338.
Sayre, Marquis de, 543.
Sbolci, Jefte, 588, 593, 595.
Scarlatti, Allessandro, 147, 154, 383.
———, Allessandro, eulogy of Francischello, 155.
Scevioni, 170.
Schachtner, Andreas, 182, 198.
Schafrath, Christoph, 84.
Schale, Christian Friedrich, 179-80.
Schall, 205.
Schanze, Max, 497-8.
Schapler, Julius, 407.
Scharwenka, Xav., 465.
Schaumburg-Lippe, Prince of, 444.
Scheidler, Dav., 208.
———, Joh. Dav., 195, 652.
Scheiffelhut, Jac., 76, 83.
Schenck, Emil, 479-80.
———, Johann, 22, 64, 66-73, 107, 344.
———, "Scherzi Musicali," 66, 71, 75.
———, " Sonata di chiesa," 70-1.
———, thematic relationship in sixth suite, "L'Echo du Danube," 70.

INDEX. 693

Schenck, Peter, 72.
Scherer, Seb. A., 84.
Scherff, Balthasar, music printer, 56.
Schetky, Christoph (Joh. Georg), 189-90, 322, 359.
———, Ludmilla, 190.
Schick, E., violinist, 211.
Schidenhelm, René, 539, 654.
Schiffer, Adolf, 608.
Schiller, Fr., 216.
———, "Bride of Messina," 236, 386.
———, "Die Räuber," 401.
———, "Lay of the Bell," 385.
Schilling, "Musik Geschichte," 163, 170, 189, 216, 230, 235-6, 238, 283, 293, 295, 314, 348, 394, 403.
———, Walter, 497.
Schindler, Joh. Christ. Teophil, 232.
Schindlöcker, Philipp, 196, 207.
———, Wolfgang, 196.
Schlegel, Mich., court drummer, 185.
Schlemüller, Hugo, 496.
Schlesinger, Karl, 207, 411, 446, 455, 465, 606.
———, Kathleen, "Instruments of the Orchestra and Precursors of the Violin Family," 4.
Schlick, 240.
———, Joh. Fried. Wilh., 212, 390.
———, Johann Konrad, 187, 195, 211 ff., 390.
Schmeling (Schmähling), Gert. Elisabeth, wife of Mara, 314, 335-6.
Schmelzer, J. H., 84.
Schmid (father), 253.
———, Sebastian, 253.
Schmidbauer, Franz Anton, 93.
———, Karl, 92.
Schmidl, 580.
Schmidt, H., 408, 617.
Schmitt, Alexander, 566.
Schmitz, 253.
Schnabel, Arthur, 570.
———, composer, 239.
Schnautz, Ant., 206.
———, Franz Peter, 206.
Schnecker, harpist, 571.
Schnéevoigt, Georg, 628. 635-6.
———, Mme., pianist, 635.
Schneider, Friedr., 390-1, 418, 425, 428, 435.
Schoenaich, Count, Prince Karolath, 240.
Schönberger, Benno, 607, 609.
Schönborn, Phil. Franz von, Bishop of Würzburg, 82.
Schönebeck, Karl Siegmund, 214.
Schola cantorum, 655.
Scholl, A., 83.

Scholz, Caspar Gottlieb, 217.
Schörg, violinist, 657.
Schorn, Joseph, 182, 198.
Schröder, Alwin, 410, 452, 466-7, 481, 489, 491-2, 494-5, 497, 509, 577.
———, Brothers Hermann, Francis, Alwin and Carl, 452.
———, Carl, 167, 234, 240, 245, 280, 295, 299, 316, 443-4, 452-3, 461, 466, 473-4, 481, 487, 489, 491, 572, 576, 628, 635.
———, compositions, 453.
———, director of Hamburg Theatre, 224.
———, F., engraver, 406.
———, Hermann, 466.
Schroedel, Friedr. Ludw., 199.
Schubart, C. F. Daniel, 182, 193-4.
Schubert, Franz, 250, 346.
———. Franz, arpeggione sonata, 239, 648.
———, Franz, violinist, 248.
———, Jos., 349.
Schuberth, Charles, 241, 404 ff., 617.
———, Gottlob, 404.
———, Julius, 404.
Schultze, Ad., 453.
Schulz, 615.
———, Jac., 57.
———, Theo., 333, 348, 602-4.
Schulze, W., 201, 204, 652.
Schumann, Clara, 486, 554, 563-4.
———. Robert, 346, 387, 398, 407-9, 411, 525, 564, 616, 642.
Schuppanzigh, 213-4, 243.
Schuster, Vincenz, 26, 239, 648.
Schütz, Heinrich, 56.
Schütze, Gabriel, 81.
Schwachhofer, 212.
Schwartzburg Sondershausen, Prince of, 467.
Schwarz, Anton, 219, 244, 652.
Schwedler, Joh. Christian, 179.
Schwedt, Markgrave of, 349.
Schweinitz, Count, 235.
Schwencke, Joh. Friedr., 247, 652.
Schwerin court chapel, 445, 456.
Schwickert, Almanach, 206, 212, 251-2.
Schwiller, Jean, 625.
Schwormstädt, Cæsar, 485.
Scognamilla, Enrico, 595.
Scotto, Sebastian, 30.
Sczczepanowski, Stanislaus, 611-2.
Sebesthal, von, 610.
Sechter, Simon, 420.
Seeger (Seger, Seegr), 344-5.
Seeman, 194.
Seitz, Richard, 462.
Seligmann, Hippolyte Prosper, 530.

694 THE HISTORY OF THE VIOLONCELLO.

Sellenger's ground *(see Gambists)*, 297.
Sempre Crescendo, Leyden student's musical society, 442.
Serato, Francesco, 590-4.
Serna, José-Gonzales, 657.
Serpentien, violoncellist, 449.
Servais, 446, 525, 595.
———, Adrien François, 280, 302, 326, 405, 427, 449, 454, 536, 542 ff., 548, 553-6, 559, 565-7, 612-3, 616, 619, 642, 646, 654, 659.
———, characterisation of his playing, 545.
———. J. (not F.), 652.
———, Jos., 280, 456, 556-7, 569, 656.
———, Strad, 653.
Sforza, Ludovico, 32.
Sherrington, 328, 330.
Shram, Christopher, 326-8.
Sibelius, Jan, 628.
Sieber, publisher, 272.
"Siècle de Louis XV," 282.
Siegmann, J. C., 205.
Siemann, Jos., 460.
"Signale für die Musik. Welt," 389.
Silva, José Joachim de, 659.
———, Julio Augusto Sergio da, 659.
———, Reis, José da, 659.
———, Sergio da, 659.
Simon, H., 552.
———, Hofmusikus, 114.
———, Ludwig, 219.
Simonetti, 79.
Simpson, Christopher, 38, 46, 50, 71, 350.
———, Christopher, "The Division-Viol," 22, 359.
———, J., publisher, 150, 160-1.
———, Thomas, 46.
Singer, E., 421, 445, 463.
Siprutini, 312.
Sirmen, Magdalena, 277.
Skarżyński, Karl von, 625.
Skripecz, K., 610.
Smith-Burges, Mrs., 313.
———, Johannes, 572.
———, John, 329-30.
Snoer, Johan, 571.
Sobrino, Carlos, 658.
———, Louisa, 517.
Société Académique des Enfants d'Apollon, 277.
——— Classique, 533.
——— des Concerts, Paris, 553.
——— des Instruments Anciens, 119, 539, 654.
——— Olympique, 276.
Society for the performance of classical and modern music at Havre, 536.
Soirées de musique classique, 531.
Soldi, A., 541.
Solié, Jean Pièrre, 286.
Solo accompaniment, The, of recitative, 371.
———, Execution of figured bass in, 373.
Solomon's (Salomon's) concerts, 323.
Somers, Lady, 313.
Somerset, Duke of, 23.
Somis, 171.
Sommer, Joh., 57
Sonata di camera, 66-7, 369.
——— di chiesa by J. Schenck, 70-1.
Sondershausen court chapel, 450, 452, 489, 564, 602.
——— Günther, Prince of, 80.
———, Princes of, 190.
Sonnata, Tillière's, for two violoncellos, 368.
Sonntag, Henriette, 398.
Sor, concertante for Spanish guitar, 325.
——— String Trio, 325.
Sorette, 267.
Soundhole, Crescent or C-shaped, 6.
———, Various shapes of, 5.
Soyer, Mlle., 654.
Spain, Queen of, 551, 599.
Speer, Georg, 179.
Spengel, Professor, 485.
Spenser, Edmund, 129.
Sperati, 324.
Spies, Hermine, 572.
Spitta, Ph., 648.
Spitzer, Genre, painter, 606.
Spohr, 228-9, 241, 406.
Spork, Count, 343.
Spotorno, Agostino, 171.
Squire, William Henry, 512.
Staccato, The, 377.
Stahlknecht, Adolf, violinist, 414.
———, Julius, 413, 440, 456, 565.
Stainer, Jacobus, 115.
Stamitz, Anton Thaddaeus, 200.
———, J. C., 202, 326.
Stanford, Sir Charles Villiers, 464.
Stanislaus, King of Poland, 82.
Staudigl, 324.
Staufer, J. G., 26, 115, 238, 648.
Stavenhagen, pianist, 446.
Steffani, Agostino, 61.
Stefkins, Christian, 44.
———, Frederik, 44.
——— (Steiffkin, Stepkin, Steffken, Stepchen), Theodorus, 44, 649.
Steindel, Bruno, 502-3.
Steinmann, Alfred, 476.

INDEX.

Steinmann, Chr., 476.
Stelzner, Dr. Alfred, 623, 638.
Stenz, Arthur, 469.
Stephanie, 551.
Stern, Leo, 522.
Stiastny, Bernard Wenzeslaus, 340, 345 ff., 348.
———, brothers, 333.
———, Jean (John), 340, 345-6 ff., 389, 394, 651.
Stocchi, Italo, 591.
Stockhausen, Julius, 564.
Stockholm Royal Chapel, 632.
Stoeving, Paul, "The Story of the Violin," 2.
Stolberg, Prince Charles Christian of, 186.
Stölzl, 79.
Storioni, 12, 31.
Stowray, violoncello concerto, 347.
Stracciapane the minstrel, 143.
"Strad," The (periodical), 472, 598, 626, 644.
Stradivari, 130.
———, Antonio, Hill's book on, 280.
———, Hieronimus, 191.
——— violoncello, Batta's, 562.
——— violoncello, Duport's, 527.
——— violoncello, Gérardy's, 559.
——— violoncello, Mathieu Wielhorski-Davidoff's, 616.
——— violoncello, Piatti's, 585-6.
——— violoncello, Servais's, 546.
Stradivarius, 227.
Straeten, Edmund Sebastian Joseph van der, 337, 463 ff.
———, E. van der, arrangement of ricercare by Gabrieli played by B. Hambourg, 137.
———, E. van der, concerts of ancient music, revival of Marais's suites for three gambas, 119.
———, E. van der, "First Album for Violoncello," 90.
———, E. van der, Piatti's assistance in "Technics of Violoncello Playing," 585.
———, E. van der, "The Literature of the Violoncello," 229, 377, 386, 424, 430, 448, 451, 620, 644.
———, E. van der, "The Revival of the Viols," 8, 19, 26, 31, 47, 114.
———, E. van der, "The Romance of the Fiddle," 319, 360-1, 649, 652.
———, E. van der, "The Technics of Violoncello Playing," 627, 643.
———, Ludwig van der, 464, 527.
Strahov, Monastery of, 341-2.
Strakosch, 568.

Stratton and Brown, "Dictionary of English Musicians," 311-3.
Straube, instrument maker, 114.
Strauss, 583.
———, Ludw., viola, 457.
Strelitz Ducal Chapel, 444.
Strinasacchi, Regina, 211, 390.
Strings, Introduction of metal covered, 16, 647.
———, Periodical, 603.
———, Sympathetic, 23.
Stroganow, Baron, 615.
Struck, Joh. Bapt., 157 ff., 260, 262, 359, 652.
———, Joh. Bapt., introduces violoncello into France, called Baptistin, 157-8.
Strunck, Joh. Ad., 84.
———, Nic. Adam, 84.
Sturioni, Giuseppe, 580.
Sturm, W., theorist, 477.
Stuttgart Court Chapel, 473, 488
——— Royal Chapel, 462, 508.
Succo, theorist, 477, 480, 499.
Such, Edwin Chs., 514.
———, Henry, 514.
———, Percy, 514.
Sucher, Capellmeister, 453.
Sudlow, Edw., 327.
———, Wm., 327.
Suggia-Casals, Guillermina, 599, 658.
Suite, Italian, 66.
Suk, 603.
Sullivan, A., "The Mikado," 242.
Sulzer, Joseph, 411, 455.
Svendsen, Joh., 443.
Szablinski, Joseph, 611.
Szigeti, 516.

T.

Tabb, R. V., 523.
Tablature, 20.
Tacchinardi, Nicola, 170.
———-Persiani, 170.
Taille, 360.
——— (viola), 128.
Taillefer, Marquis de, 212.
Talent, Georg, 624.
Tallemant des Reaux, 98, 650.
Talluel, Mlle., 655.
Taltavul, Dominico, 658.
Tanken, Bruno L., publisher, 82.
Tardieu, Abbé, 121-2, 260, 268, 356-7.
Tartini, 130, 163, 176, 203, 375, 615.
———, letter to Maddalena Sirmen, 277.
Tasca, Francesco, 595.
Taschenberg, violoncellist, 401.
Tauber, August, 253.
Taubert, Wilhelm, 461.

Tchaïkovsky, 422, 623.
——— Festival, Pyrmont, 627.
——— sextet, first performance, 626.
Tchorchewski (Chorchewski), 162.
Téjada, Alexander Ruiz de, 657.
Telemann, Georg Phil., 79-80, 91, 615.
Ten Cate, Andrew, 560.
Tenorgeige, 623.
Tescari, Domenico, 590.
Testagrossa, Gio. Angelo, lutenist, 10.
Testator il Vecchio, 30.
Thaler (Thayer), Maria, 119, 651.
Thalgrün, Stanislaus, 613.
Theatre des Victoires, 225.
Theobalde, 159.
Thibaut, J., 599.
Thicknesse, Hon. P., 53.
———, Mrs. (see Ann Ford), 53.
Thieme, Bernhard, 462.
Thoinin, E., 99.
Thomas, Adolf, 487.
Thompson and Son, 312.
———, C. and S., 318.
———, Robert, 308.
Thorwart, 205, 541.
Three Choirs Festival, 313.
Thuilleries, Court of the, 286.
Thumb, Position of, 363.
——— position, Origin of, 262.
——— position, The, 359.
Thun, Count, 341, 344.
Thurn and Taxis, Count, 232.
——— and Taxis, Prince of, 195-6.
——— and Taxis, private band, 253.
Tieffenbrucker, Kaspar, 13, 54.
Tielke, Joachim, 54-5, 72, 114.
———, Joachim, baryton in Kensington Museum, 24.
———, Joachim, description of gamba, 55.
———, Joachim, Gamba by, 651.
Tietz, H., violoncellist, 462, 476.
Tignani, Enrico, 595.
Tillet, Titon de, 102, 104.
Tillière, Jos. Bonaventure, 264, 271 ff., 289, 367.
———, fourth position called thumb position, 272.
———, "Methode pour Violoncelle," 311, 367, 541.
———, "Sonnata" for two violoncellos, 368.
Tilmant, Alexandre, 526.
Time, Rob. Crome on, 320.
Tinti, Salvatore, 171.
Toeschi, 202.
Tolbecque, Aug., 533, 537, 651, 653-4.
———, Jean, 537, 653.
Toller, music director and violoncellist, 462.
Tomaczek, 348.
Tomasini, Aloys, 650.
Tompkins, Thos., 649.
Tonassi (Tonazzi), Pietro, 595.
Tone quality of the violoncello, 643.
Tonelli, Antonio de Pietri, called, 141-5, 192-3, 269.
——— founds free school of music, 144.
——— plays in market-place, 143.
——— walks to Denmark and back, 143.
Töpfer, violoncellist, 412.
Töpken, Dr., junior, Th., 398.
Torelli, 116.
Touche, de, Minister of Baden, 388.
———, Francis (François), 539, 655.
Träg, Anton, 414, 432.
Träg's catalogue, 338.
Treble violin, The, 361.
Trementini, Salvatore, 589.
Tricklir, Jean, 209-10, 283.
Triemer, Sebald, 178.
Trio, Adamowski, 613.
——— Association, Gotha, 496.
———, Ballio, Sisters, 501.
———, Berger, Wm., Treichler, Piening, 490.
———, Berlin, 493.
———, Centola, 494.
———, Cherniawsky, 511, 625.
———, Dutch, Berlin, 574.
———, Frankfort (Friedberg, Rebner, Hegar), 498.
———, Hegner, Otto, B. Sibor, H. Beyer, 499.
———, Kwast's, Professor, 503.
———, London (Amina Goodwin, Simonetti, Whitehouse), 508.
———, Moscow (Schor, Krein, Ehrlich), 487.
———, Nachtigall, Warsaw, 592.
———, Parisien (Lewita, Wolff, Bürger), 469.
———, Prague, 604.
———, Rhenish, Düsseldorf, 499.
———, Schnabel, Wittenberg, Hekking, popular soirées, Berlin, 570.
———, Schumann, G., Halir, Dechert, 477.
———, Schumann, Georg, R. Sabla, A. Steinmann, 476.
———, Schumann, Mme., Auer, Jules de Swert, 554.
Trompetta marina, 262, 359.
Troubadours, Provençale, The guitar fiddle of the, 5.
Trowell, A., 327, 630-1.
———, G. C. and T. A., 312, 330-1, 392, 403, 424, 558, 567.

Trowell, Garnet, 630.
Trubetzkoi, Prince, 615.
Truchsess, Count, 215.
Truffi, Isidoro, 596.
Truska, Simon, 93.
Trust, H. T., violoncellist, 516, 523.
Tschirsch, Capellmeister, 462.
Tuilleries, concerts under Napoleon, 279.
Tuning, Crome's method of, 365-6.
—— of grosse geige, 8.
—— of seven-stringed viol da gamba, 15.
—— of the violoncello, 358.
Turner, G., 521.
Türrschmidt, theorist, 401.
Tuscany, Grand Duke of, 344.
Tutors, Corrette's, 363.
——, Cupis's, Tillière's, 367.
——, Preston's, Cahusac's, Addison and Hodson's, 367.
——, Rob. Crome, "The Compleat Tutor," 365.
——, "The Gamut," printed by Hy. Waylett, 364.
Twelvetrees, C. 523.

U.

Uber, Alexander, 239.
Udel, Charles, 411, 446.
Uhlenfeld, Count, 155.
Uhlmann, 187.
Ullmann, J., impresario, 441, 568.
Ulrich, Edward, 248.
Unen, Jan van, 570.
Urban, Christian, 235, 386.
Uriot, 209.
Utrecht Psalter, illustrating the origin of the viol, 4-5.

V.

Vaccari, 330.
Valdemi, Giulio, 591.
Valdrighi, Count Luigi Francesco, 12, 29-30, 125, 133, 138-9, 145, 148, 151, 156, 158, 163, 374, 582, 590-1, 653, 658, 660.
Vandini, Antonio, 163.
Vanhal, 342.
Vanucci, Abbate, 172.
Vanvaelbeck, Ludwig. violmaker, 11.
Vaslin, 416, 529-30, 533, 546, 618-9, 627, 643.
——, "L'art du Violoncelle," 305.
——, "le Baillotin," 306.
Vaugeois, 654.
Vecsey, F. von, 516.
Velde, H. van den, 570.
Veneziano, Agostino, 17.
Venice, Albert de, 35.

Venice, Francis de, 35.
Venier, publisher of Boccherini, 172.
Venzano, Luigi, 581, 590.
Verdi with Mme. Verdi attends Heckmann's performance of his string quartet, 434.
Verdi's "Gerusalemme," first performance, 579.
Verguet, Theodore, 538.
Verhulst, 565.
Vernon, Lord, 313.
Verojo, Guglielmo, 591.
Victoria, Queen, 421, 486, 522, 558, 568.
Vidal, Antoine, 54, 109, 125, 159, 167, 172, 225, 265, 272, 292, 305, 527, 530.
——, A., on R. Lindley, 326.
—— (not Videl), 652.
Vielle, 648.
——, derivation of name, 4.
Vieuxtemps, Henry, 545, 616.
Vignier, violinist, 547.
Vihuela de arco, 4.
Villa, Luiz, 658.
Vincent, manager Covent Garden, 310.
Vinci, Leonardo da, 31-2, 96, 648.
Viol, Bass, 120, 307-8.
——, Bass (see Bass Viol).
——, bass, tenor, treble, 319.
——, bass viol d'amour (see Bass Viol).
——, Consort of, 307.
—— da gamba, 9 ff., 111, 130, 239, 298, 341, 350, 374, 376-7, 458, 464, 520, 535, 654.
—— da gamba, attempted revival by Raoul, 288.
—— da gamba by Duiffoprugcar, 288.
—— da gamba by Francis Baker, 534.
—— da gamba by Vinc. Ruger with modelled back, 34.
—— da gamba, Duets for one, 40.
—— da gamba in "consort," 38.
—— da gamba in England, 34.
—— da gamba in Germany, 54.
—— da gamba neglected in Italy, 23.
—— da gamba (see also Bass Viol and Basse de Viole).
—— da gamba superseded lute in accompanying the voices, 20.
—— da gamba, The, in Italy, 29.
—— da gamba, The revival of the, 116 ff., 651.
—— da gamba, Tone quality of, 351, 378.

46

Viol da gamba too weak as bass in modern orchestra, 22.
—— da gamba with seven strings, by Duiffoprugcar, 15.
—— da gambist (Casadesus), 539.
—— da gambist (E. Braun), 577.
—— da gambist (J. Mossel), 573.
—— da gambist (Jacobs), 557.
—— d'amour, 119-20, 615, 652.
—— d'amour, concertos by P. Köcher, 334.
—— d'amour, Hector Berlioz advocates reintroduction of the, 116.
—— d'amour played by Tonelli, 141.
——, Division (see Division-Viol), 38.
——, Double-bass, 38.
——, Earliest seven-stringed, 647.
—— fitted with metal strings at the back of the neck, 649.
——, Lyra (see Lyra Viol).
——, lyra viol d'amour (see Lyra Viol).
—— makers, First, 11.
—— makers, German, during fifteenth and sixteenth centuries, 17.
—— players, English, French and German, 20.
—— players, Italian, in band of Henry VIII. 20.
——, possible use in modern orchestra, 118.
——, Tenor, 38.
Viola bastarda, 25, 111, 649.
—— da Spalla, 355-6.
——, derivation of name, 4.
—— pomposa, 26, 115, 648, 650.
Viole, derivation of name, 4.
——, Dessus de, 264.
——, French name for the troubadour viùl, 6.
Violin family in existence about 1550, 127.
—— family, Members of the, according to Mersenne, 360.
—— introduced in England, 129.
—— sonata, Appearance of, 130.
Violino, derivation of name, 4.
Violoncello, 22, 117.
—— accompaniment, Decline of solo, 256.
—— accompaniment, Dvorák's concerto as instance, 644.
—— accompaniment, Orchestral, 644.
——, Birthplace of, 132.
——, bow, Holding of, 359.
—— bowing, Crome's method of, 366.
—— clefs, Use of various, 370.

Violoncello, Compass of, in Gabrieli's Ricercari, 134.
——, Compass of, in Gabrieli's Ricercari, chords used in same, 134.
—— d'amore, 660.
—— Denomination of, bass violin, 129, 355.
——, denomination, called "Basse" in ballet comique, 128.
——, Early music for, written on lines of viol music, 352.
—— fingerboard, Bevelling of, under C string condemned, 256.
—— fingering, Corrette's, 362 ff.
—— fingering in Waylett's "The Gamut," etc., 364.
——, forms of, Various, Dr. Stelzner's model, 639-40.
——, forms of, Various, five-stringed, 122, 637.
——, forms of, Various, five-stringed, used by Gabrieli, 134.
——, forms of, Various, harmonicello, 638.
——, forms of, Various, standard shape reached, 256.
——, forms of, Various, violoncello piccolo, 116, 648.
——, forms of, Various, violoncello portatile, 638.
——, forms of, Various, violoncino, 130.
——, fretting of neck, 365.
——, gamba technique, indebtedness to, 369.
——, Joannini del, 169.
——, Makers of first, 125.
——, overbalance of accompaniment, 644.
—— players chiefly Italians at beginning of eighteenth century, 308.
——, Playing of, by gentlemen considered effeminate, 309.
——, Position of the, in Germany at the end of the eighteenth century, 254.
——, power of tone in a number of violoncellos, 643-4.
——, solo instrument, first use of in France, 260.
——, solo instrument, first use of in Italy, 133.
—— staccato, 377.
——, Style of playing, difference between German and French school, 642.
——, Technical development of, 350, 640.
——, thumb position, 359.

INDEX. 699

Violoncello, tone quality of its various registers, 643.
——— tone, Wagner's "Parsifal" as an instance, 644.
——— tuning, 122.
——— tuning, Crome's method of, 365-6.
——— tuning, Mersenne's, 361.
——— tunings, various, 358.
——— tunings, various, used by Galli, 141.
——— tutors, 360.
——— tutors, "A New and Complete Tutor," Preston and Sons, 321.
——— tutors, Addison and Hodson's "Standard Tutor," 322.
——— tutors, first English tutor by Henry Waylett, 318.
——— tutors, Hardy's "Violoncello Preceptor," 322.
——— tutors, "New Instructions for the," Cahusac and Sons, 322.
——— tutors, on time, 320.
——— tutors, "The Complete Tutor," by Robert Crome, 318.
———, Various forms of, five-stringed, three-stringed and six-stringed, violoncello da Spalla, 653.
———, various forms of, violoncello d'amore, 660.
Violone, 119.
———, double-bass viol, 38.
———, the word used for the violoncello, 356-7.
Violons du roy, 360.
Violotta, 623, 639.
Viols, Chest of, 38.
Violuntzen (Prætorius), 130.
Viotti, J. B., 228, 277-8, 292, 525.
Viùl, troubadour name for the viol, 6.
Viulunzel, 130.
Virdung, Sebastian, 18.
———, Sebastian, grosse geige, 6.
———, Sebastian, "Musica getuscht," 6.
Virgil, Michael, 219.
Virgili, 219.
Virtuosität, Article on, 256.
Visoni, 506.
Vitali, Giovanni, 580.
Vivaldi, Antonio, 116.
———, Antonio, concerto, 374-6.
Voczitka (Woczitka), Franz Xaver, 184-5.
Vogel, Cajetan, 342.
Vogelsang, W. L., 73.
Vogler, Abbé (Volger), 200, 202-3, 218, 652.
Voigt, 241, 652.
———, Johann Georg Hermann, 246.

Voigt, Karl Ludwig, 247.
Volkert, Charles, 393.
Vollbach, Fritz, 176.
Vollrath, Richard, 450, 461.
Volmar, G., 570.
Voltaire, 278.
Volxem, J. B. van, 549.
Voué, 551.
Vuillaume, 14, 118, 288.
——— makes gamba for Raoul, 288.
Vyhan (Wihan), Hanus, 602.

W.

Wach, Carl Gottfried Wilhelm, 199.
Waefelghem, L. van, 119, 535.
Wagner, 220, 290.
———, Eduardo Oscar, 659.
———, Moritz, professor of violoncello, 415.
Waldhausen, Joseph, 253.
Walenn, Gerald, 511.
———, Herbert, 507, 510-1, 625, 627.
Wales, Prince of (afterwards George IV), 313.
Wallenstein, Prince, 200, 340.
Wallerstein, Count, 337.
Walsh, publisher, 160.
Walter, Anton, 501.
Walthew, R., Cervetto sonata, 316.
Ward (Edward?), 44.
———, John, 37, 39.
Warnke, Heinrich, 444, 493, 500.
Warot, Constant Noël Adolphe, 547-8, 552.
Wartensee, Schnyder von, 245.
Wasielewski, 43, 133, 170, 220, 226-7, 230, 265, 267, 271, 281, 283, 285, 289, 295, 305, 309-12, 323, 343, 347, 372, 396, 401-2, 414-5, 438, 530, 555, 561, 582, 611-2, 615-6.
Watelle, violoncellist, 556.
Waterhouse, violoncellist, 327, 331.
Waterson, Simon, publisher, 42.
Watts, William, 325, 330, 504.
Waylett, Henry, publisher of "The Gamut for the Violoncello," 364.
Waziers, Louis de, 17.
Weber, Aloysia, 202.
———, C. M. von, 204, 235, 239, 243, 248.
———, D., contrapuntist, 420.
Weber's "Freischütz," monster performance, 419.
Webster, Maurice, 44.
Weichsel, 325.
Weidinger, Ferd., violoncellist, 502.
Weigl, Franz Jos., 114, 188, 207, 344.
Weimar Court Chapel, 445.
———, Duke of, 421.
Weingartner, Felix von, 494.

Weinlig, Cantor, 235.
Wellenkamp, Eduard, 491.
Wendling, 202, 495.
———, Dorothea, 202.
Werge, Tennyson, 523.
Werner, Joseph, 402, 437-8, 470, 497, 501-2.
———, Joseph, his studies, 438.
——— (of Prague), 213, 340.
Wertheimer, Charles, 87.
Werther, The sufferings of, 290.
Westenholz, Carl Aug., 184.
White, William, 37, 39.
Whitehouse, Henry, 507.
———, W.E.,507,509,513-6,518,522-3.
Wiedemann, flute, 160.
Wielhorski, Count Joseph, 616.
———, Count Matthieu, 615-6.
———, Count Michael, 616.
Wielhorsky, 237.
"Wiener Zeitschrift," 226.
Wieniawski, Henry, 469.
Wiertz, Dart, 570.
Wierzbilowicz, Alexander, 620-1.
Wihan, H. (see also Vyhan), 415, 496, 603-4.
Wilde, Johann, 255, 638.
Wilfert, Bruno, 430, 436.
Wilhelm Ernst, Duke of Saxe-Weimar, 62.
Wilhelmj, August, 14, 445.
Wille, Georg, 490, 492.
———, Gustav, 492.
William, Elector Palatine, 55.
——— I, German Emperor, 440, 470.
——— II, Emperor, 578, 652.
——— III of Holland, 569.
——— III of Holland, "Les Pensionnaire du Roi," 567.
Willmann-Galvani beloved of Beethoven, 233.
———, Marie-Huber, pupil of Mozart, 233.
———, Maximilian, 233, 253, 325.
Wilmotte, M., 55.
Wilson, Dr., 39.
Windischgrätz, Prince, 432.
Windust, B., 558, 571.
Winkis, Peter William, 205, 541.
Winneberger, Paul Anton, 199, 389.
Wit, Paul de, 27, 34, 116, 118.
Withers, Herbert, 508, 516.
Wittenberg, Alfred, 570.
Wittgenstein Berleberg, Prince, 196.
Wittmann, principal violoncello of Gewandhaus concerts, 428.
Wladimiroff, Nicolas de, 616.
"Wöchentliche Nachrichten," 255-6, 638.
Woczitka (see Voczitka), 185.

Woelfl, 329.
Woeriot, Pierre, portrait of Duiffoprugcar, 13.
Wolff, Johann Wolfgang, 179.
———, Johannes, 469, 509, 609.
Wood, Anthony A., 307.
Woolaston, painter, 649.
Workinski, poet, 349.
Wörl, Georg, 482.
Wotquenne, Alfred, 374.
Wranitzky, Friedrich, 348, 414.
———, sons of, 237.
Wrbna, Count, 344.
Wuerst, Richard, 448.
Wüllner, Franz, 470.
Wulp, Louis van der, 563.
Wünsche, Max, 494.
Württemberg, Karl Eugen, Duke of, 82.
———, King of, 197, 237, 245.
Wurzbach, "Dictionary of Musicians," 237, 387.
Wysman, Johann, 628.

X.
Ximenes, 329.

Y.
Yanatka, Prof., violoncellist, 602, 604.
Yates's composers' concert, 311.
York, Beatrice, Duchess of, known as "Mary," 138.
——— Buildings, 355.
Young, Anna, pianist, wife of Gunn, 324.
———, the two Young's concerts, 51.
Ysaye, Eugène, 558, 569, 627, 656.

Z.
Zachæus (Zachov), Peter, 82.
Zamuri, Pietro, 30.
Zandonati, Luigi, 230.
Zanetti, 582.
Zanetto, Peregrino, 30.
Zappa, Francesco, 169, 651.
Zarlino, 32.
Zelenka, 180.
Zellner, Leopold Alexander, 420.
Zelter, 248, 253, 399.
Zerbini, 583.
Zerotin, Count, 113.
Ziegler, Johann Christoph, 82.
Ziffirini, 581.
Zilioli, Pietro, 591.
Zimmermann, J., 387, 419.
Zinkeisen, contrapuntist, 400.
Zumsteeg, J. R., 216, 652.
Zupanic, N. C., 610.
Zweygberg, Lennart von, 627.
Zyka, Frederic, 338.
———, Joseph B., 197, 338.
Zyke, 337.

www.ingramcontent.com/pod-product-compliance
Lightning Source LLC
Chambersburg PA
CBHW070356230426
43665CB00012B/1140